Geometry Formulas

Square

Perimeter: $P = 4s$

Area: $A = s^2$

Rectangular Solid

Volume: $V = LW$

Surface area: A

Rectangle

Perimeter: $P = 2L + 2W$

Area: $A = LW$

Cube

Volume: $V = e^3$

Surface area: $S = 6e^2$

Triangle

Perimeter: $P = a + b + c$

Area: $A = \dfrac{1}{2}bh$

Right Circular Cylinder

Volume: $V = \pi r^2 h$

Surface area: $S = 2\pi rh + 2\pi r^2$

(Includes both circular bases)

Parallelogram

Perimeter: $P = 2a + 2b$

Area: $A = bh$

Cone

Volume: $V = \dfrac{1}{3}\pi r^2 h$

Surface area: $S = \pi r\sqrt{r^2 + h^2} + \pi r^2$

(Includes circular base)

Trapezoid

Perimeter: $P = a + b + c + B$

Area: $A = \dfrac{1}{2}h(b + B)$

Right Pyramid

Volume: $V = \dfrac{1}{3}Bh$

B = area of the base

Circle

Diameter: $d = 2r$

Circumference: $C = 2\pi r = \pi d$

Area: $A = \pi r^2$

Sphere

Volume: $V = \dfrac{4}{3}\pi r^3$

Surface area: $S = 4\pi r^2$

Introductory Algebra

Lial
Hornsby
McGinnis

Taken from:
Introductory Algebra, Eighth Edition
by Margaret L. Lial, John Hornsby, and Terry McGinnis

Custom Publishing

New York   Boston   San Francisco
London   Toronto   Sydney   Tokyo   Singapore   Madrid
Mexico City   Munich   Paris   Cape Town   Hong Kong   Montreal

Taken from:

Introductory Algebra, Eighth Edition
by Margaret L. Lial, John Hornsby, and Terry McGinnis
Copyright © 2006 by Pearson Education, Inc.
Published by Addison Wesley
Boston, Massachusetts 02116

This special edition published in cooperation with Pearson Custom Publishing.

Printed in the United States of America

10 9 8 7 6 5 4 3 2

2009360913

LR

**Pearson
Custom Publishing**
is a division of

www.pearsonhighered.com   ISBN 10: 0-558-31491-0
ISBN 13: 978-0-558-31491-0

Contents

Index of Applications

v

Videotape and CD Index

Index of Focus on Real-Data Applications

Preface

The eighth edition of *Introductory Algebra* continues our ongoing commitment to provide the best possible text and supplements package to help teachers and students succeed. To that end, we have tried to address the diverse needs of today's students through an attractive design, updated figures and graphs, helpful features, careful explanations of topics, and a comprehensive package of supplements and study aids. We have taken special care to respond to the suggestions of users and reviewers and have added new examples and exercises based on their feedback. Students who have never studied algebra—as well as those who require further review of basic algebraic concepts before taking additional courses in mathematics, business, science, nursing, or other fields—will benefit from the text's student-oriented approach.

This text is part of a series that also includes the following books:

- *Essential Mathematics*, Second Edition, by Lial and Salzman
- *Basic College Mathematics*, Seventh Edition, by Lial, Salzman, and Hestwood
- *Prealgebra*, Third Edition, by Lial and Hestwood
- *Intermediate Algebra*, Eighth Edition, by Lial, Hornsby, and McGinnis
- *Introductory and Intermediate Algebra*, Third Edition, by Lial, Hornsby, and McGinnis.

HALLMARK FEATURES

We believe students and teachers will welcome the following helpful features.

Chapter Openers New and updated chapter openers feature real-world applications of mathematics that are relevant to students and tied to specific material within the chapters. Examples of topics include the Olympics, credit card debt, and movie revenues. (See pp. 107, 193, and 273—Chapters 2, 3, and 4.)

Real-Life Applications We are always on the lookout for interesting data to use in real-life applications. As a result, we have included new or updated examples and exercises from fields such as business, pop culture, sports, the life sciences, and technology that show the relevance of algebra to daily life. (See pp. 142, 208, and 308.) A comprehensive Index of Applications appears at the beginning of the text. (See pp. v–vii.)

Figures and Photos Today's students are more visually oriented than ever. Thus, we have made a concerted effort to include mathematical figures, diagrams, tables, and graphs whenever possible. (See pp. 196, 246, and 316.) Many of the graphs use a style similar to that seen by students in today's print and electronic media. Photos have been incorporated to enhance applications in examples and exercises. (See pp. 134, 328, and 455.)

Emphasis on Problem Solving Introduced in Chapter 2, our six-step problem-solving method is integrated throughout the text. The six steps, *Read, Assign a Variable, Write an Equation, Solve, State the Answer*, and *Check*, are emphasized in boldface type and repeated in examples and exercises to reinforce the problem-solving process for students. (See pp. 133, 301, and 445.) New **PROBLEM-SOLVING HINT** boxes provide students with helpful problem-solving tips and strategies. (See pp. 133, 135, and 529.)

Also new to this edition of the text is Appendix A Strategies for Problem Solving. (See pp. 687–700.) This appendix provides examples of additional problem-solving techniques, such as working backward, using trial and error, and looking for patterns. A wide variety of applications are included.

▶ *Learning Objectives* Each section begins with clearly stated, numbered objectives, and the included material is directly keyed to these objectives so that students know exactly what is covered in each section. (See pp. 31, 133, and 341.)

▶ *Cautions and Notes* One of the most popular features of previous editions, **CAUTION** and **NOTE** boxes warn students about common errors and emphasize important ideas throughout the exposition. (See pp. 235, 367, and 498.) The text design makes them easy to spot: Cautions are highlighted in bright yellow and Notes are highlighted in purple.

▶ *Calculator Tips* These optional tips, marked with calculator icons, offer basic information and instruction for students using calculators in the course. (See pp. 26, 160, and 387.) An Introduction to Calculators is included at the beginning of the text. (See pp. xxi–xxv.)

▶ *Margin Problems* Margin problems, with answers immediately available at the bottom of the page, are found in every section of the text. (See pp. 69, 303, and 481.) This popular feature allows students to immediately practice the material covered in the examples in preparation for the exercise sets.

▶ *Ample and Varied Exercise Sets* The text contains a wealth of exercises to provide students with opportunities to practice, apply, connect, and extend the algebraic skills they are learning. Numerous illustrations, tables, graphs, and photos have been added to the exercise sets to help students visualize the problems they are solving. Problem types include writing, estimation, and calculator exercises as well as applications and multiple-choice, matching, true/false, and fill-in-the-blank problems. In the *Annotated Instructor's Edition* of the text, writing exercises are marked with   icons so that teachers may assign these problems at their discretion. Exercises suitable for calculator work are marked in both the student and teacher editions with calculator icons   (See pp. 377, 455, and 479.)

▶ *Relating Concepts Exercises* These sets of exercises help students tie together topics and develop problem-solving skills as they compare and contrast ideas, identify and describe patterns, and extend concepts to new situations. (See pp. 266, 298, and 362.) These exercises make great collaborative activities for pairs or small groups of students.

▶ *Summary Exercises* Based on user feedback, every chapter now includes at least one set of in-chapter summary exercises. These special exercise sets provide students with the all-important *mixed* review problems they need to master topics. Summaries of solution methods or additional examples are often included. (See pp. 247, 299, and 525.)

▶ *Study Skills Component* A desk-light icon at key points in the text directs students to a separate *Study Skills Workbook* containing activities correlated directly to the text. (See pp. 24, 189, and 423.) This unique workbook explains *how* the brain actually learns, so students understand *why* the study tips presented will help them succeed in the course. Students are introduced to the workbook in the To the Student section at the beginning of the text.

▶ *Focus on Real-Data Applications* These one-page activities present a relevant and in-depth look at how mathematics is used in the real world. Designed to help teachers answer the often-asked question, "When will I ever use this stuff?," these activities ask students to read and interpret data from newspaper articles, the Internet, and other familiar, real sources. (See pp. 140, 278, 410, and 486.) The activities are well-suited to collaborative work and can also be completed by individuals or used for open-ended class discussions. A comprehensive Index of Focus on Real-Data Applications appears at the beginning of the text. (See pp. ix and x.) Teaching notes and extensions for the activities are provided in the *Printed Test Bank and Instructor's Resource Guide*.

▶ *Test Your Word Power* To help students understand and master mathematical vocabulary, this feature can be found in each chapter summary. Key terms from the chapter are presented along with four possible definitions in a multiple-choice format. Answers and examples illustrating each term are provided. (See pp. 258, 319, and 391.)

▶ *Ample Opportunity for Review* Each chapter concludes with a Chapter Summary that features Key Terms with definitions and helpful graphics, New Symbols, Test Your Word Power, and a Quick Review of each section's content with additional examples. A comprehensive set of Chapter Review Exercises, keyed to individual sections, is included, as are Mixed Review Exercises and a Chapter Test. Beginning with Chapter 2, each chapter concludes with a set of Cumulative Review Exercises that cover material going back to Chapters R and 1. (See pp. 257, 391, and 457.)

▶ *Diagnostic Pretest* A diagnostic pretest is included on p. xxix and covers material from the entire book, much like a sample final exam. This pretest can be used to facilitate student placement in the correct chapter according to skill level.

WHAT IS NEW IN THIS EDITION?

You will find many places in the text where we have polished individual presentations and added or updated examples, exercises, and applications based on reviewer feedback. Specific content changes you may notice include the following:

- Section 2.1 on solving linear equations in one variable includes twice as many examples as in the previous edition. Linear equations with no solution or infinitely many solutions, formerly covered in this section, have been moved to Section 2.3.

- Section 3.4 includes new exposition, an example, and exercises on graphing linear equations using slope and *y*-intercept.

- Systems of linear equations and inequalities are presented in Chapter 4, earlier than in the previous edition.

- All new sets of summary exercises appear in Chapters 1–5 and 8.

- Appendix A Strategies for Problem Solving and Appendix C Mean, Median, and Mode are new to this edition.

WHAT SUPPLEMENTS ARE AVAILABLE?

For a comprehensive list of the supplements and study aids that accompany *Introductory Algebra*, Eighth Edition, see pages xv and xvi.

ACKNOWLEDGMENTS

Previous editions of this text were published after thousands of hours of work, not only by the authors, but also by reviewers, teachers, students, answer checkers, and editors. To these individuals and all those who have worked in some way on this text over the years, we are most grateful for your contributions. We could not have done it without you. We especially wish to thank the following reviewers whose valuable contributions have helped to refine this edition of this text.

Randall Allbritton, *Daytona Beach Community College*
Jannette Avery, *Monroe Community College*
Linda Beattie, *Western New Mexico University*
Jean Bolyard, *Fairmont State College*
Tim C. Caldwell, *Meridian Community College*
Russell Campbell, *Fairmont State College*
Bill Dunn, *Las Positas College*
Lucy Edwards, *Las Positas College*
J. Lloyd Harris, *Gulf Coast Community College*
Edith Hays, *Texas Woman's University*

Karen Heavin, *Morehead State University*

Christine Heinecke Lehmann, *Purdue University—North Central*

Terry Haynes, *Eastern Oklahoma State College*

Elizabeth Heston, *Monroe Community College*

Harriet Kiser, *Floyd College*

Valerie Lazzara, *Palm Beach Community College*

Valerie H. Maley, *Cape Fear Community College*

Susan McClory, *San Jose State University*

Pam Miller, *Phoenix College*

Jeffrey Mills, *Ohio State University*

Linda J. Murphy, *Northern Essex Community College*

Celia Nippert, *Western Oklahoma State College*

Elizabeth Olgilvie, *Horry-Georgetown Technical College*

Larry Pontaski, *Pueblo Community College*

Diann Robinson, *Ivy Tech State College—Lafayette*

Rachael Schettenhelm, *Southern Connecticut State University*

Lee Ann Spahr, *Durham Technical Community College*

Carol Stewart, *Fairmont State College*

Cora S. West, *Florida Community College at Jacksonville*

Johanna Windmueller, *Seminole Community College*

Gabriel Yimesghen, *Community College of Philadelphia*

Over the years, we have come to rely on an extensive team of experienced professionals. Our sincere thanks go to these dedicated individuals at Addison-Wesley, who worked long and hard to make this revision a success: Greg Tobin, Maureen O'Connor, Jay Jenkins, Lauren Morse, Marcia Emerson, Sharon Smith, Sara Anderson, Tracy Rabinowitz, Ron Hampton, and Dennis Schaefer.

Thanks are due Gina Linko, Phyllis Crittenden, and Elm Street Publishing Services for their excellent production work. Barb Brown provided invaluable assistance updating the real data used in applications throughout the text. Abby Tanenbaum and Paul Lorczak did an outstanding job accuracy checking page proofs. Special thanks to Bernice Eisen who prepared the Index and Becky Troutman who compiled the Index of Applications.

As an author team, we are committed to the goal stated earlier in this Preface—to provide the best possible text and supplements package to help teachers and students succeed. We are most grateful to all those over the years who have aspired to this goal with us. As we continue to work toward it, we would welcome any comments or suggestions you might have via e-mail to math@awl.com.

Margaret L. Lial
John Hornsby
Terry McGinnis

Student Supplements	**Teacher Supplements**

Student's Solutions Manual
- By Jeffery A. Cole, *Anoka-Ramsey Community College*
- Provides detailed solutions to the odd-numbered, section-level exercises and to all margin, Relating Concepts, Summary, Chapter Review, Chapter Test, and Cumulative Review Exercises
  ISBN: 0-321-28580-8

Study Skills Workbook
- By Diana Hestwood and Linda Russell
- Provides activities that teach students how to use the textbook effectively, plan their homework, take notes, make mind maps and study cards, manage study time, and prepare for and take tests
- A desk-light icon at key points directs students to correlated activities in the workbook
  ISBN: 0-321-28581-6

Spanish Study Guide
- Homework exercises from the text have been translated into Spanish to assist nonnative speakers of English.

Videotape Series
- Features an engaging team of lecturers
- Provides comprehensive coverage of each section and topic in the text
  ISBN: 0-321-28582-4

Digital Video Tutor
- Complete set of digitized videos on CD-ROM for student use at home or on campus
- Ideal for distance learning or supplemental instruction
  ISBN: 0-321-28584-0

New! Additional Skill & Drill Manual
- Provides additional practice and test preparation for students
  ISBN: 0-321-33167-2

Addison-Wesley Math Tutor Center
- Staffed by qualified mathematics instructors
- Provides tutoring on examples and odd-numbered exercises from the textbook through a registration number with a new textbook or purchased separately
- Accessible via toll-free telephone, toll-free fax, e-mail or the Internet at www.aw-bc/tutorcenter

MathXL® Tutorials on CD—*Optional*
- Provides algorithmically generated practice exercises that correlate at the objective level to the content of the text
- Includes an example and a guided solution to accompany every exercise and video clips for selected exercises
- Recognizes student errors and provides feedback; Generates printed summaries of students' progress
- **For purchase only on an annual basis.**
  ISBN: 0-321-28579-4

Annotated Instructor's Edition
- Provides answers to all text exercises in color next to the corresponding problems
- Includes icons to identify writing and calculator exercises
  ISBN: 0-321-28585-9

Lesson Plans
- This booklet provides a section-by-section resource for teaching from the text.

Instructor's Solutions Manual
- By Jeffery A. Cole, *Anoka-Ramsey Community College*
- Provides complete solutions to all even-numbered, section-level exercises
  ISBN: 0-321-28577-8

Answer Book
- By Jeffery A. Cole, *Anoka-Ramsey Community College*
- Provides answers to all the exercises in the text
  ISBN: 0-321-28576-X

Adjunct Support Manual
- Includes resources designed to help both new and adjunct faculty with course preparation and classroom management
- Offers helpful teaching tips correlated to the sections of the text
  ISBN: 0-321-28586-7

Printed Test Bank and Instructor's Resource Guide
- By James J. Ball, *Indiana State University*
- Contains two diagnostic pretests, six free-response and two multiple-choice test forms per chapter, and two final exams
- Includes teaching suggestions for every chapter, additional practice exercises for each objective in every section, a correlation guide from the seventh to the eighth edition, phonetic spellings for all key terms in the text, and teaching notes and extensions for the Focus on Real-Data Applications in the text
  ISBN: 0-321-28575-1

TestGen
- Enables instructors to build, edit, print, and administer tests
- Features a computerized bank of questions developed to cover all text objectives
- Available on a dual-platform Windows/Macintosh CD-ROM
  ISBN: 0-321-28578-6

InterAct Math Tutorial Web site: <u>www.interactmath.com</u> Get practice and tutorial help online! This interactive tutorial web site provides algorithmically generated practice exercises that correlate directly to the exercises in the textbook. Students can retry an exercise multiple times with new values each time for unlimited practice and mastery. Every exercise is accompanied by an interactive guided solution that provides helpful feedback for an incorrect answer. Students can also view a worked-out sample problem that steps them through an exercise similar to the one they're working on.

MathXL **MathXL®—*Optional*** MathXL is a powerful online homework, tutorial, and assessment system that accompanies your Addison-Wesley textbook in mathematics or statistics. With MathXL, instructors can create, edit, and assign online homework and tests using algorithmically generated exercises correlated at the objective level to the textbook. All student work is tracked in MathXL's online gradebook. Students can take chapter tests in MathXL and receive personalized study plans based on their test results. The study plan diagnoses weaknesses and links students directly to tutorial exercises for the objectives they need to study and retest. Students can also access supplemental video clips and animations directly from selected exercises. **MathXL is available for purchase only on an annual basis**. For more information, visit our web site at <u>www.mathxl.com</u>, or contact your Addison-Wesley sales representative for more information.

Feature
Walk-Through

Chapter Openers Chapter openers feature real-world applications of mathematics that are relevant to students and tied to specific material within the chapters.

Systems of Linear Equations and Inequalities

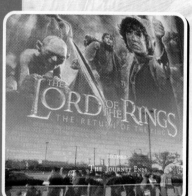

Although Americans continued their fascination with Hollywood and the movies in 2003, movie attendance and revenues dipped for the first time since 1991. Nonetheless, some 1.52 billion tickets were sold and revenues exceeded $9 billion for the second year in a row. The top box office draws of the year—*The Lord of the Rings: The Return of the King* and *Finding Nemo*—attracted scores of adults and children wishing to get away from it all for a few hours. (*Source:* Exhibitor Relations Co., Nielsen EDI.)

In Exercise 13 of Section 4.4, we use a *system of linear equations* to find out how much money these top films earned.

Section 3.2 Graphing Linear Equations in Two Variables **221**

37. Use the results of Exercises 35(b) and 36(b) to determine the target heart rate zone for age 30.

38. Should the graphs of the target heart rate zone in the **Section 3.1** exercises be used to estimate the target heart rate zone for ages below 20 or above 80? Why or why not?

39. Per capita consumption of coffee increased for the years 1995 through 2000 as shown in the graph. If $x = 0$ represents 1995, $x = 1$ represents 1996, and so on, per capita consumption y in gallons can be modeled by the linear equation
$$y = 1.13x + 20.67.$$

COFFEE CONSUMPTION

Source: U.S. Department of Agriculture.

(a) Use the equation to approximate consumption in 1995, 1996, and 1998 to the nearest tenth.

40. Sporting goods sales y (in billions of dollars) from 1995 through 2000 are modeled by the linear equation
$$y = 3.606x + 41.86,$$
where $x = 5$ corresponds to 1995, $x = 6$ corresponds to 1996, and so on.

SPORTING GOODS SALES

Source: U.S. Bureau of the Census.

(a) Use the equation to approximate sporting goods sales in 1995, 1997, and 2000. Round your answers to the nearest billion dollars.

Figures and Photos Today's students are more visually oriented than ever. Thus, a concerted effort has been made to include mathematical figures, diagrams, tables, and graphs whenever possible. Many of the graphs use a style similar to that seen by students in today's print and electronic media. Photos have been incorporated to enhance applications in examples and exercises.

Relating Concepts These sets of exercises help students tie together topics and develop problem-solving skills as they compare and contrast ideas, identify and describe patterns, and extend concepts to new situations. These exercises make great collaborative activities for pairs or small groups of students.

---

298 Chapter 4 Systems of Linear Equations and Inequalities

RELATING CONCEPTS (EXERCISES 41–46) For Individual or Group Work

Attending the movies is one of America's favorite forms of entertainment. The graph shows movie attendance from 1991 to 1999. In 1991, attendance was 1141 million, as represented by the point P(1991, 1141). In 1999, attendance was 1465 million, as represented by the point Q(1999, 1465). We can find an equation of line segment PQ using a system of equations, and then we can use the equation to approximate the attendance in any of the years between 1991 and 1999. Work Exercises 41–46 in order.

MOVIE BOX OFFICE ATTENDANCE/ ADMISSIONS

Source: Motion Picture Association of America.

41. The line segment has an equation that can be written in the form $y = ax + b$. Using the coordinates of point P with $x = 1991$ and $y = 1141$, write an equation in the variables a and b.

42. Using the coordinates of point Q with $x = 1999$ and $y = 1465$, write a second equation in the variables a and b.

43. Write the system of equations formed from the two equations in Exercises 41 and 42, and solve the system using the elimination method.

44. What is the equation of the segment PQ?

45. Let $x = 1998$ in the equation of Exercise 44, and solve for y. How does the result compare with the actual figure of 1481 million?

46. The data points for the years 1991 through 1999 do not lie in a perfectly straight line. Explain the pitfalls of relying too heavily on using the equation in Exercise 44 to predict attendance.

Focus on *Real-Data Applications*

The Magic Number in Sports

The climax of any sports season is the play-offs. Baseball fans eagerly debate predictions of which team will win the pennant for their division. The *magic number* for each first-place team is often used to predict the division winner. The **magic number** is the combined number of wins by the first-place team and losses by the second-place team that would clinch the title for the first-place team.

For Group Discussion

To calculate the magic number, consider the following conditions.

The number of wins for the first-place team (W_1) plus the magic number (M) is one more than the sum of the number of wins to date (W_2) and the number of games remaining in the season (N_2) for the second-place team.

American League

East Division

	W	L	Pct.	GB
New York	94	58	.618	—
Boston	89	63	.586	5
Toronto	79	73	.520	15
Baltimore	68	83	.450	25½
Tampa Bay	60	92	.395	34

Central Division

	W	L	Pct.	GB
Minnesota	84	69	.549	—
Chicago	80	72	.526	3½
Kansas City	79	73	.520	4½
Cleveland	66	88	.429	18½
Detroit	38	114	.250	45½

West Division

	W	L	Pct.	GB
Oakland	92	61	.601	—
Seattle	87	66	.569	5
Anaheim	72	81	.471	20
Texas	68	85	.444	24

Source: USA Today.

1. First, use the variable definitions to write an equation involving the magic number. Second, solve the equation for the magic number. Write the formula for the magic number.

2. The American League standings with about 10 games left in the 2003 baseball season are shown at the left. There were 162 regulation games in the 2003 season. Find the magic number for each team. The number of games remaining in the season for the second-place team is calculated as
$$N_2 = 162 - (W_2 + L_2).$$

   (a) AL East: New York vs Boston

   Magic No. _____

   (b) AL Central: Minnesota vs Chicago

   Magic No. _____

   (c) AL West: Oakland vs Seattle

   Magic No. _____

[*Note:* For the National League in the 2003 season, Atlanta and San Francisco were runaway winners of the Eastern and Western Divisions, respectively. Chicago, Houston, and St. Louis were locked in a dead heat for the Central Division lead, which was eventually won by Chicago.]

140

Focus on Real-Data Applications These one-page activities found throughout the text present even more relevant and in-depth looks at how mathematics is used in the real world. Designed to help instructors answer the often-asked question, "When will I ever use this stuff?," these activities ask students to read and interpret data from newspaper articles, the Internet, and other familiar, real sources. The activities are well suited to collaborative work and can also be completed by individuals or used for open-ended class discussions.

Calculator Tip Using a calculator to perform the arithmetic in Example 5 reduces the possibility of errors.

▶◀◀ Work Problem 5 at the Side.

OBJECTIVE 4 Find percentages and percents. Percents are ratios where the second number is always 100. For example, 50% represents the ratio of 50 to 100, 27% represents the ratio of 27 to 100, and so on. We can use the techniques for solving proportions to solve percent problems. Recall from **Section R.2** that the decimal point is moved two places to the left to change a percent to a decimal number. For example, 75% can be written as the decimal .75.

Calculator Tip Many calculators have a percent key that does this automatically.

We can solve a percent problem by writing it as the proportion

$$\frac{amount}{base} = \frac{percent}{100} \quad \text{or} \quad \frac{a}{b} = \frac{p}{100}.$$

The amount, or **percentage**, is compared to the **base** (the whole amount). Since *percent* means *per 100*, we compare the numerical value of the percent to 100. Thus, we write 50% as

$$\frac{p}{100} = \frac{50}{100}. \quad p = 50$$

Calculator Tips These optional tips, marked with calculator icons, offer basic information and instruction for students using calculators in the course.

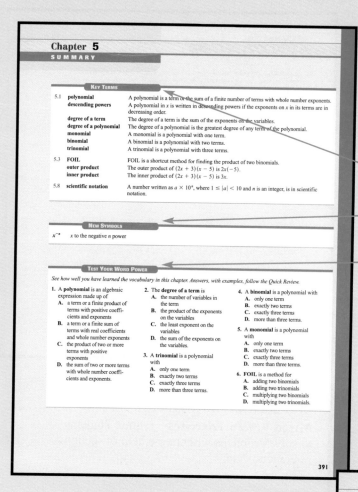

Chapter 5
SUMMARY

KEY TERMS

5.1 **polynomial** — A polynomial is a term or the sum of a finite number of terms with whole number exponents.
descending powers — A polynomial in x is written in descending powers if the exponents on x in its terms are in decreasing order.
degree of a term — The degree of a term is the sum of the exponents on the variables.
degree of a polynomial — The degree of a polynomial is the greatest degree of any term of the polynomial.
monomial — A monomial is a polynomial with one term.
binomial — A binomial is a polynomial with two terms.
trinomial — A trinomial is a polynomial with three terms.

5.3 **FOIL** — FOIL is a shortcut method for finding the product of two binomials.
outer product — The outer product of $(2x + 3)(x - 5)$ is $2x(-5)$.
inner product — The inner product of $(2x + 3)(x - 5)$ is $3x$.

5.8 **scientific notation** — A number written as $a \times 10^n$, where $1 \le |a| < 10$ and n is an integer, is in scientific notation.

NEW SYMBOLS

x^{-n} x to the negative n power

TEST YOUR WORD POWER

See how well you have learned the vocabulary in this chapter. Answers, with examples, follow the Quick Review.

1. A **polynomial** is an algebraic expression made up of
   A. a term or a finite product of terms with positive coefficients and exponents
   B. a term or a finite sum of terms with real coefficients and whole number exponents
   C. the product of two or more terms with positive exponents
   D. the sum of two or more terms with whole number coefficients and exponents.

2. The **degree of a term** is
   A. the number of variables in the term
   B. the product of the exponents on the variables
   C. the least exponent on the variables
   D. the sum of the exponents on the variables.

3. A **trinomial** is a polynomial with
   A. only one term
   B. exactly two terms
   C. exactly three terms
   D. more than three terms.

4. A **binomial** is a polynomial with
   A. only one term
   B. exactly two terms
   C. exactly three terms
   D. more than three terms.

5. A **monomial** is a polynomial with
   A. only one term
   B. exactly two terms
   C. exactly three terms
   D. more than three terms.

6. **FOIL** is a method for
   A. adding two binomials
   B. adding two trinomials
   C. multiplying two binomials
   D. multiplying two trinomials.

391

End-of-Chapter Material   One of the most admired features of the Lial textbooks is the extensive and well-thought-out end-of-chapter material. At the end of each chapter, students will find a Summary that includes the following:

Key Terms   are listed, defined, and referenced back to the appropriate section number.

New Symbols   are listed for easy reference and study.

Test Your Word Power   helps students understand and master mathematical vocabulary. Students are quizzed on Key Terms from the chapter in a multiple-choice format. Answers and examples illustrating each term are provided.

A Chapter Test   helps students practice for the real thing.

Chapter 5   Test   **399**

Chapter 5
TEST

Perform the indicated operations.

1. $(5t^4 - 3t^2 + 7t + 3) - (t^4 - t^3 + 3t^2 + 8t + 3)$ 1. _____

2. $(2y^2 - 8y + 8) + (-3y^2 + 2y + 3) - (y^2 + 3y - 6)$ 2. _____

3. Subtract.   3. _____
$$9t^3 - 4t^2 + 2t + 2$$
$$9t^3 + 8t^2 - 3t - 6$$

Simplify, and write each answer with only positive exponents.

4. $(-2)^3(-2)^2$ 4. _____

5. $\left(\dfrac{6}{m^2}\right)^3$, $m \ne 0$ 5. _____

6. $3x^2(-9x^3 + 6x^2 - 2x + 1)$ 6. _____

7. $(2r - 3)(r^2 + 2r - 5)$ 7. _____

8. $(t - 8)(t + 3)$ 8. _____

---

392   Chapter 5   Exponents and Polynomials

QUICK REVIEW

Concepts	Examples
5.1 Adding and Subtracting Polynomials **Addition** Add like terms.	Add. $\begin{aligned}2x^2 + 5x - 3\\ 5x^2 - 2x + 7\\ \hline 7x^2 + 3x + 4\end{aligned}$
Subtraction Change the signs of the terms in the second polynomial and add to the first polynomial.	Subtract. $(2x^2 + 5x - 3) - (5x^2 - 2x + 7)$ $= (2x^2 + 5x - 3) + (-5x^2 + 2x - 7)$ $= -3x^2 + 7x - 10$
5.2 The Product Rule and Power Rules for Exponents For any integers m and n: **Product rule** $a^m \cdot a^n = a^{m+n}$ **Power rules** (a) $(a^m)^n = a^{mn}$ (b) $(ab)^m = a^m b^m$ (c) $\left(\dfrac{a}{b}\right)^m = \dfrac{a^m}{b^m}$ $(b \ne 0)$.	$2^4 \cdot 2^5 = 2^9$ $(3^2)^4 = 3^8$ $(6a)^5 = 6^5 a^5$ $\left(\dfrac{2}{3}\right)^3 = \dfrac{2^3}{3^3}$
5.3 Multiplying Polynomials Multiply each term of the first polynomial by each term of the second polynomial. Then add like terms.	Multiply. $\begin{aligned}3x^3 - 4x^2 + 2x - 7\\ 4x + 3\\ \hline 9x^3 - 12x^2 + 6x - 21\\ 12x^4 - 16x^3 + 8x^2 - 28x\end{aligned}$

Quick Review   sections give students not only the main concepts from the chapter (referenced back to the appropriate section), but also an adjacent example of each concept.

Review Exercises are keyed to the appropriate sections so that students can refer to examples of that type of problem if they need help.

Chapter 5
REVIEW EXERCISES

[5.1] *Combine terms where possible in each polynomial. Write the answer in descending powers of the variable. Give the degree of the answer. Identify the polynomial as a monomial, binomial, trinomial, or none of these.*

1. $9m^2 + 11m^2 + 2m^2$

2. $-4p + p^3 - p^2 + 8p + 2$

3. $12a^5 - 9a^4 + 8a^3 + 2a^2 - a + 3$

4. $-7y^5 - 8y^4 - y^5 + y^4 + 9y$

Add or subtract as indicated.

5. Add.
$$-2a^3 + 5a^2$$
$$-3a^3 - a^2$$

6. Add.
$$4r^3 - 8r^2 + 6r$$
$$-2r^3 + 5r^2 + 3r$$

7. Subtract.
$$6y^2 - 8y + 2$$
$$-5y^2 + 2y - 7$$

8. Subtract.
$$-12k^4 - 8k^2 + 7k - 5$$
$$k^4 + 7k^2 + 11k + 1$$

9. $(2m^3 - 8m^2 + 4) + (8m^3 + 2m^2 - 7)$

10. $(-5y^2 + 3y + 11) + (4y^2 - 7y + 15)$

11. $(6p^2 - p - 8) - (-4p^2 + 2p + 3)$

12. $(12r^4 - 7r^3 + 2r^2) - (5r^4 - 3r^3 + 2r^2 + 1)$

[5.2] *Use the product rule or power rules to simplify each expression. Write the answer in exponential form.*

13. $4^3 \cdot 4^8$

14. $(-5)^6(-5)^5$

15. $(-8x^4)(9x^3)$

16. $(2x^2)(5x^3)(x^9)$

17. $(19x)^5$

18. $(-4y)^7$

19. $5(pt)^4$

20. $\left(\dfrac{7}{5}\right)^6$

---

85. There are 13 red balls and 39 black balls in a box. Mix them up and draw 13 out one at a time without returning any ball. The probability that the 13 drawings each will produce a red ball is 1.6×10^{-12}. Write the number given in scientific notation without exponents. (*Source:* Warren Weaver, *Lady Luck*, Doubleday & Company, 1963.)

86. According to Campbell, Mitchell, and Reece in *Biology Concepts and Connections* (Benjamin Cummings, 1994, p. 230), "The amount of DNA in a human cell is about 1000 times greater than the DNA in *E. coli*. Does this mean humans have 1000 times as many genes as the 2000 in *E. coli*? The answer is probably no; the human genome is thought to carry between 50,000 and 100,000 genes, which code for various proteins (as well as for tRNA and rRNA)."
Write each number from this quote using scientific notation.

(a) 1000   (b) 2000

(c) 50,000   (d) 100,000

MIXED REVIEW EXERCISES

Perform the indicated operations. Write with positive exponents. Assume that no denominators are equal to 0.

87. $19^0 - 3^0$

88. $(3p)^4(3p^{-7})$

89. 7^{-2}

90. $(-7 + 2k)^2$

91. $\dfrac{2y^3 + 17y^2 + 37y + 7}{2y + 7}$

92. $\left(\dfrac{6r^2s}{5}\right)^4$

93. $-m^5(8m^2 + 10m + 6)$

94. $\left(\dfrac{1}{2}\right)^{-5}$

95. $(25x^2y^3 - 8xy^2 + 15x^3y) \div (5x)$

96. $(6r^{-2})^{-1}$

97. $(2x + y)^3$

98. $2^{-1} + 4^{-1}$

99. $(a + 2)(a^2 - 4a + 1)$

100. $(5y^3 - 8y^2 + 7) - (-3y^3 + y^2 + 2)$

101. $(2r + 5)(5r - 2)$

102. $(12a + 1)(12a - 1)$

103. Find a polynomial that represents the area of the rectangle shown.

$2x - 3$
$x + 2$

104. If the side of a square has a measure represented by $5x^4 + 2x^2$, what polynomial represents its area?

$5x^4 + 2x^2$

Mixed Review Exercises require students to solve problems without the help of section references.

Cumulative Review Exercises
CHAPTERS R–5

Work each problem.

1. $\dfrac{2}{3} + \dfrac{1}{8}$

2. $\dfrac{7}{4} - \dfrac{9}{5}$

3. $8.32 - 4.6$

4. 7.21×8.6

5. A retailer has $34,000 invested in her business. She finds that last year she earned 5.4% on this investment. How much did she earn?

Find the value of each expression if $x = -2$ and $y = 4$.

6. $\dfrac{4x - 2y}{x + y}$

7. $x^3 - 4xy$

Perform the indicated operations.

8. $\dfrac{(-13 + 15) - (3 + 2)}{6 - 12}$

9. $-7 - 3[2 + (5 - 8)]$

Decide what property justifies each statement.

10. $(9 + 2) + 3 = 9 + (2 + 3)$

11. $-7 + 7 = 0$

12. $6(4 + 2) = 6(4) + 6(2)$

Solve each equation.

13. $2x - 7x + 8x = 30$

14. $2 - 3(t - 5) = 4 + t$

15. $2(5h + 1) = 10h + 4$

16. $d = rt$ for r

17. $\dfrac{x}{5} = \dfrac{x - 2}{7}$

18. $\dfrac{1}{3}p - \dfrac{1}{6}p = -2$

19. $.05x + .15(50 - x) = 5.50$

20. $4 - (3x + 12) = (2x - 9) - (5x - 1)$

Solve each problem.

21. A 1-oz mouse takes about 16 times as many breaths as does a 3-ton elephant. (*Source: Dinosaurs, Spitfires, and Sea Dragons,*

22. If a number is subtracted from 8 and this difference is tripled, the result is three times the number. Find this number, and you will

Cumulative Review Exercises gather various types of exercises from preceding chapters to help students remember and retain what they are learning throughout the course.

An Introduction to Calculators

There is little doubt that the appearance of handheld calculators three decades ago and the later development of scientific and graphing calculators have changed the methods of learning and studying mathematics forever. For example, computations with tables of logarithms and slide rules made up an important part of mathematics courses prior to 1970. Today, with the widespread availability of calculators, these topics are studied only for their historical significance.

Calculators come in a large array of different types, sizes, and prices. *For the course for which this textbook is intended, the most appropriate type is the scientific calculator,* which costs $10–$20.

In this introduction, we explain some of the features of scientific and graphing calculators. However, remember that calculators vary among manufacturers and models, and that while the methods explained here apply to many of them, they may not apply to your specific calculator. *This introduction is only a guide and is not intended to take the place of your owner's manual.* Always refer to the manual whenever you need an explanation of how to perform a particular operation.

SCIENTIFIC CALCULATORS

Scientific calculators are capable of much more than the typical four-function calculator that you might use for balancing your checkbook. Most scientific calculators use *algebraic logic*. (Models sold by Texas Instruments, Sharp, Casio, and Radio Shack, for example, use algebraic logic.) A notable exception is Hewlett-Packard, a company whose calculators use *Reverse Polish Notation* (RPN). In this introduction, we explain the use of calculators with algebraic logic.

Arithmetic Operations To perform an operation of arithmetic, simply enter the first number, press the operation key (+, −, ×, or ÷), enter the second number, and then press the = key. For example, to add 4 and 3, use the following keystrokes.

Change Sign Key The key marked +/− allows you to change the sign of a display. This is particularly useful when you wish to enter a negative number. For example, to enter −3, use the following keystrokes.

Memory Key Scientific calculators can hold a number in memory for later use. The label of the memory key varies among models; two of these are M and STO. The M+ and M− keys allow you to add to or subtract from the value currently in memory. The memory recall key, labeled MR, RM, or RCL, allows you to retrieve the value stored in memory.

Suppose that you wish to store the number 5 in memory. Enter 5, then press the key for memory. You can then perform other calculations. When you need to retrieve the 5, press the key for memory recall.

If a calculator has a constant memory feature, the value in memory will be retained even after the power is turned off. Some advanced calculators have more than one memory. It is best to read the owner's manual for your model to see exactly how memory is activated.

Clearing/Clear Entry Keys The Ⓒ or Ⓒᴱ key allows you to clear the display or clear the last entry entered into the display. In some models, pressing the Ⓒ key once will clear the last entry, while pressing it twice will clear the entire operation in progress.

Second Function Key This key, usually marked (2nd), is used in conjunction with another key to activate a function that is printed *above* an operation key (and not on the key itself). For example, suppose you wish to find the square of a number, and the squaring function (explained in more detail later) is printed above another key. You would need to press (2nd) before the desired squaring function can be activated.

Square Root Key Pressing (√) or (√x̄) will give the square root (or an approximation of the square root) of the number in the display. On some scientific calculators, the square root key is pressed *before* entering the number, while other calculators use the opposite order. Experiment with your calculator to see which method it uses. For example, to find the square root of 36, use the following keystrokes.

The square root of 2 is an example of an irrational number (**Chapter 8**). The calculator will give an approximation of its value, since the decimal for $\sqrt{2}$ never terminates and never repeats. The number of digits shown will vary among models. To find an approximation for $\sqrt{2}$, use the following keystrokes.

 An approximation for $\sqrt{2}$

Squaring Key The (x²) key allows you to square the entry in the display. For example, to square 35.7, use the following keystrokes.

The squaring key and the square root key are often found on the same key, with one of them being a second function (that is, activated by the second function key previously described).

Reciprocal Key The key marked (1/x) is the reciprocal key. (When two numbers have a product of 1, they are called *reciprocals*. See **Chapter R.**) Suppose that you wish to find the reciprocal of 5. Use the following keystrokes.

Inverse Key Some calculators have an inverse key, marked (INV). Inverse operations are operations that "undo" each other. For example, the operations of squaring and taking the square root are inverse operations. The use of the (INV) key varies among different models of calculators, so read your owner's manual carefully.

Exponential Key The key marked (xʸ) or (yˣ) allows you to raise a number to a power. For example, if you wish to raise 4 to the fifth power (that is, find 4^5, as explained in **Chapter 1**), use the following keystrokes.

Root Key Some calculators have this key specifically marked (ˣ√x̄) or (ʸ√x̄); with others, the operation of taking roots is accomplished by using the inverse key in conjunction with the exponential key. Suppose, for example, your calculator is of the latter type and you wish to find the fifth root of 1024. Use the following keystrokes.

Notice how this "undoes" the operation explained in the exponential key discussion.

Pi Key   The number π is an important number in mathematics. It occurs, for example, in the area and circumference formulas for a circle. By pressing the π key, you can display the first few digits of π. (Because π is irrational, the display shows only an approximation.) One popular model gives the following display when the π key is pressed.

$$\boxed{3.1415927}$$ An approximation for π

Methods of Display   When decimal approximations are shown on scientific calculators, they are either *truncated* or *rounded*. To see how a particular model is programmed, evaluate 1/18 as an example. If the display shows .0555555 (last digit 5), it truncates the display. If it shows .0555556 (last digit 6), it rounds the display.

When very large or very small numbers are obtained as answers, scientific calculators often express these numbers in scientific notation (**Chapter 5**). For example, if you multiply 6,265,804 by 8,980,591, the display might look like this:

$$\boxed{5.6270623\ 13}$$

The 13 at the far right means that the number on the left is multiplied by 10^{13}. This means that the decimal point must be moved 13 places to the right if the answer is to be expressed in its usual form. Even then, the value obtained will only be an approximation: 56,270,623,000,000.

GRAPHING CALCULATORS

While you are not expected to have a graphing calculator to study from this book, we include the following as background information and reference should your course or future courses require the use of graphing calculators.

Basic Features

In addition to the typical keys found on scientific calculators, graphing calculators have keys that can be used to create graphs, make tables, analyze data, and change settings. One of the major differences between graphing and scientific calculators is that a graphing calculator has a larger viewing screen with graphing capabilities. The screens below illustrate the graphs of $Y = X$ and $Y = X^2$.

If you look closely at the screens, you will see that the graphs appear to be jagged rather than smooth, as they should be. The reason for this is that graphing calculators have much lower resolution than computer screens. Because of this, graphs generated by graphing calculators must be interpreted carefully.

Editing Input

The screen of a graphing calculator can display several lines of text at a time. This feature allows you to view both previous and current expressions. If an incorrect expression is entered, an error message is displayed. The erroneous expression can be viewed and corrected by using various editing keys, much like a word-processing program. You do not need to enter the entire expression again.

Many graphing calculators can also recall past expressions for editing or updating. The screen on the left below shows how two expressions are evaluated. The final line is entered incorrectly, and the resulting error message is shown in the screen on the right.

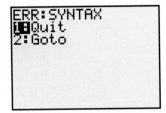

Order of Operations

Arithmetic operations on graphing calculators are usually entered as they are written in mathematical expressions. For example, to evaluate $\sqrt{36}$, you would first press the square root key, and then enter 36. See the screen on the left below. The order of operations on a graphing calculator is also important, and current models assist the user by inserting parentheses when typical errors might occur. The open parenthesis that follows the square root symbol is automatically entered by the calculator so that an expression such as $\sqrt{2 \times 8}$ will not be calculated incorrectly as $\sqrt{2} \times 8$. Compare the two entries and their results in the screen on the right.

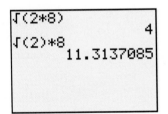

Viewing Windows

The viewing window for a graphing calculator is similar to the viewfinder in a camera. A camera usually cannot take a photograph of an entire view of a scene. The camera must be centered on some object and can capture only a portion of the available scenery. A camera with a zoom lens can photograph different views of the same scene by zooming in and out.

Graphing calculators have similar capabilities. The xy-coordinate plane is infinite. The calculator screen can only show a finite, rectangular region in the plane, and it must be specified before the graph can be drawn. This is done by setting both minimum and maximum values for the x- and y-axes. The scale (distance between tick marks) is usually specified as well. Determining an appropriate viewing window for a graph can be a challenge, and sometimes it will take a few attempts before a satisfactory window is found.

The screen on the left shows a standard viewing window, and the graph of $Y = 2X + 1$ is shown on the right. Using a different window would give a different view of the line.

Locating Points on a Graph: Tracing and Tables

Graphing calculators allow you to trace along the graph of an equation and display the co-ordinates of points on the graph. See the screen on the left below, which indicates that the point (2, 5) lies on the graph of Y = 2X + 1. Tables for equations can also be displayed. The screen on the right shows a partial table for this same equation. Note the middle of the screen, which indicates that when X = 2, Y = 5.

Additional Features

There are many features of graphing calculators that go far beyond the scope of this book. These calculators can be programmed, much like computers. Many of them can solve equations at the stroke of a key, analyze statistical data, and perform symbolic algebraic manipulations. Calculators also provide the opportunity to ask "What if . . . ?" more easily. Values in algebraic expressions can be altered and conjectures tested quickly.

Final Comments

Despite the power of today's calculators, they cannot replace human thought. ***In the entire problem-solving process, your brain is the most important component.*** Calculators are only tools and, like any tool, they must be used appropriately in order to enhance our ability to understand mathematics. Mathematical insight may often be the quickest and easiest way to solve a problem; a calculator may neither be needed nor appropriate. By applying mathematical concepts, you can make the decision whether or not to use a calculator.

To the Student: Success in Algebra

There are two main reasons students have difficulty with mathematics:

- Students start in a course for which they do not have the necessary background knowledge.

- Students don't know how to study mathematics effectively.

Your teacher can help you decide whether this is the right course for you. We can give you some study tips.

Studying mathematics *is* different from studying subjects like English and history. ***The key to success is regular practice.*** This should not be surprising. After all, can you learn to play the piano or ski well without a lot of regular practice? The same is true for learning mathematics. Working problems nearly every day is the key to becoming successful. Here is a list of things that will help you succeed in studying algebra.

1. **Attend class regularly.** Pay attention in class and take careful notes. In particular, note the problems your teacher works on the board and copy the complete solutions. Keep these notes separate from your homework.

2. **Ask questions.** Don't hesitate to ask questions in class. Other students may have the same questions but be reluctant to ask them, and everyone will benefit from the answers.

3. **Read your text carefully.** Many students go directly to the exercise sets without taking time to read the text and examples. Reading the *complete* section and working the margin problems will pay off when you tackle the homework problems.

4. **Reread your class notes.** Before starting your homework, rework the problems your teacher did in class. This will reinforce what you have learned. Teachers often hear the comment, "*I understand it perfectly when you do it, but I get stuck when I try to work the problem myself.*"

5. **Practice by working problems.** Do your homework only *after* reading the text and reviewing your class notes. Check your work against the answer section or the *Student's Solutions Manual.* If you make an error and are unable to determine what went wrong, mark that problem and ask your instructor about it. Then work more problems of the same type to reinforce what you have learned.

6. **Work neatly.** Write symbols neatly. Skip lines between steps. Write large enough so that others can read your work. Use pencil. Make sure that problems are clearly separated from each other.

7. **Review the material.** After completing each section, look over the text again. Decide on the main objectives, and don't be content until you feel that you have mastered them. (In this book, objectives are clearly stated both at the beginning and within each section.) Write a summary of the section or make an outline for future reference.

8. **Prepare for tests.** The chapter summaries in the text are an excellent way for you to review key terms, new symbols, and important concepts from the chapter. After working through the chapter review exercises, use the chapter test as a practice test. Work the problems under test conditions, without looking at the text or answers until you are finished. Time yourself. When you have finished, check your answers against the answer section and rework any that you missed.

9. **Learn from your mistakes.** Keep all graded assignments, quizzes, and tests that are returned to you. Be sure to correct any errors on them and use them to study for future tests and the final exam.

10. **Be diligent and don't give up.** The authors of this text can tell you that they did not always understand a topic the first time they saw it. Don't worry if you also find this to be true. As you read more about a topic and work through the problems, you will gain understanding; the thrill of finally "getting it" is a great feeling. Listen to the words of the late Jim Valvano: *Never give up!*

NOTE

Reading a list of study tips is a good start, but you may need some help actually *applying* the tips to your work in this mathematics course.

Watch for this icon as you work in this textbook, particularly in the first few chapters. It will direct you to one of 12 activities in the *Study Skills Workbook* that comes with this text. Each activity helps you to actually *use* a study skills technique. These techniques will greatly improve your chances for success in this course.

- Find out *how your brain learns new material*. Then use that information to set up effective ways to learn mathematics.

- Find out *why short-term memory is so short* and what you can do to help your brain remember new material weeks and months later.

- Find out *what happens when you "blank out" on a test* and simple ways to prevent it from happening.

All the activities in the *Study Skills Workbook* are practical ways to enjoy and succeed at mathematics. Whether you need help with note taking, managing homework, taking tests, or preparing for a final exam, you'll find specific, clearly explained ideas that really work because they're based on research about how the brain learns and remembers.

Diagnostic Pretest

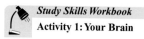

Study Skills Workbook
Activity 1: Your Brain

[Chapter R]

1. Find the quotient and write it in lowest terms.
$$\frac{42}{5} \div \frac{7}{15}$$

2. Find the sum and write it in lowest terms.
$$6\frac{7}{8} + 3\frac{2}{3}$$

3. Subtract $38 - 9.678$.

4. **(a)** Convert .99% to a decimal.
(b) Convert 4.72 to a percent.

[Chapter 1]

5. Select the lesser number from this pair: $|-35|, \ -|35|$.

Perform the indicated operations.

6. $(-3)(-8) - 4(-2)^3$

7. $\dfrac{-6 + |-11 + 5|}{4^2 - (-9)}$

8. Evaluate $\dfrac{6r - 2s^2}{-3t}$ if $r = -5$, $s = -3$, and $t = 4$.

[Chapter 2]

9. Solve and check $-8(x - 3) + 12x = 15 - (2x + 3)$.

10. The two largest cities in the United States are New York and Los Angeles. In 2002, the population of New York was 4,285,335 greater than the population of Los Angeles, and there were a total of 11,883,297 people living in these two cities. Find the population of each city, using these population figures. (*Source: World Almanac and Book of Facts,* 2004.)

11. Find the measure of each marked angle.

$(3x + 22)°$ $\qquad$ $(11x - 10)°$

1. _____

2. _____

3. _____

4. (a) _____

   (b) _____

5. _____

6. _____

7. _____

8. _____

9. _____

10. _____

11. _____

12. —+——+——+——+——+——+——+——→

12. Solve $-4x + 8 \geq -12$, and graph the solutions.

[Chapter 3]

13. *x*-intercept: _____

    y-intercept: _____

13. Graph $2x - 5y = 10$. Give the *x*- and *y*-intercepts.

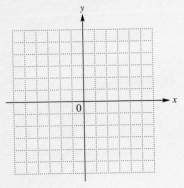

14. _____

14. Find the slope of the line through $(-2, 5)$ and $(1, -7)$.

15. _____

15. Write an equation in slope-intercept form for the line through $(-5, 6)$ and $(1, 0)$.

16.

16. Graph $2x + y > 4$.

[Chapter 4]

Solve each system of equations.

17. _____

17. $3x + y = 9$
    $x - y = -1$

18. _____

18. $-4x + 7y = 3$
    $12x - 21y = 9$

19. _____

19. Write a system of equations and use it to solve the problem.

Marla and Rick left from the same place at the same time and traveled in opposite directions. Marla drove 8 mph faster than Rick. After 2 hr, they were 228 mi apart. Find Marla's and Rick's speeds.

20.

20. Graph the solution of the system of inequalities.

$$3x - 5y < 15$$
$$y \geq -2x$$

[Chapter 5]

21. Subtract $(4m^3 - 5m^2 + m - 8) - (6m^3 - 5m^2 + 10m - 3)$.

21. _____

22. Multiply $(7z + 3w)^2$.

22. _____

23. Evaluate the expression $5^{-1} + 2^{-1} - 3^0$.

23. _____

24. (a) Write 445,000,000 in scientific notation.

    (b) Write 2.34×10^{-4} without exponents.

24. (a) _____

    (b) _____

[Chapter 6]

25. Factor $3x^2 + 2x - 8$.

25. _____

26. Factor $16n^2 - 49$.

26. _____

27. Solve $t^2 - 2t = 15$.

27. _____

28. The length of the cover of a road atlas is 4 in. more than the width. The area is 165 in.^{2}. Find the dimensions of the cover.

28. _____

[Chapter 7]

29. Write $\dfrac{x^2 + x - 20}{x^2 - 16}$ in lowest terms.

29. _____

30. Divide. Write your answer in lowest terms.

$$\frac{2r + 1}{r - 4} \div \frac{6r^2 + 3r}{4 - r}$$

30. _____

31. Subtract. Write your answer in lowest terms.

$$\frac{z^2}{z - 3} - \frac{z}{z + 3}$$

31. _____

32. Simplify.

$$\frac{\dfrac{1}{y} + \dfrac{1}{y + 2}}{\dfrac{1}{y} - \dfrac{1}{y + 2}}$$

32. _____

[Chapter 8]

Simplify when possible.

33. $4\sqrt{300} - 8\sqrt{75}$

34. $(\sqrt{5} - \sqrt{7})^2$

35. Rationalize the denominator.

$$\frac{4\sqrt{5}}{\sqrt{2}}$$

36. Solve $\sqrt{3r} + 6 = 15$.

[Chapter 9]

37. Solve $(x - 3)^2 = 20$.

38. Solve $2r^2 + 3r - 1 = 0$.

39. Sketch the graph of $y = -x^2 + 5$. Identify the vertex.

40. Decide whether the relation

$$\{(-2, 4), (-1, 1), (0, 0), (1, 1), (2, 4)\}$$

represents a function. Give the domain and range.

33. _____

34. _____

35. _____

36. _____

37. _____

38. _____

39. vertex: _____

40. _____

domain: _____

range: _____

Prealgebra Review

R.1 Fractions

The numbers used most often in everyday life are the **whole numbers,**

$$0, 1, 2, 3, 4, 5, \ldots$$

and **fractions,** such as

$$\frac{1}{3}, \quad \frac{5}{4}, \quad \text{and} \quad \frac{11}{12}.$$

The parts of a fraction are named as follows.

$$\text{Fraction bar} \longrightarrow \frac{4 \quad \longleftarrow \text{Numerator}}{7 \quad \longleftarrow \text{Denominator}}$$

OBJECTIVES

1. Identify prime numbers.
2. Write numbers in prime factored form.
3. Write fractions in lowest terms.
4. Multiply and divide fractions.
5. Add and subtract fractions.

 Study Skills Workbook
Activity 2: Your Textbook

If the numerator of a fraction is smaller than the denominator, we call it a **proper fraction.** A proper fraction has a value less than 1. If the numerator is greater than or equal to the denominator, the fraction is an **improper fraction.** An improper fraction that has a value greater than 1 is often written as a **mixed number.** For example,

$$\frac{12}{5} \quad \text{may be written as} \quad 2\frac{2}{5}.$$
$$\uparrow \qquad\qquad\qquad\qquad \uparrow$$
$$\text{Improper fraction} \qquad\qquad \text{Mixed number}$$

OBJECTIVE 1 Identify prime numbers.   In work with fractions, we will need to write the numerators and denominators as products. A **product** is the answer to a multiplication problem. When 12 is written as the product $2 \cdot 6$, for example, 2 and 6 are called **factors** of 12. Other factors of 12 are 1, 3, 4, and 12. A whole number is **prime** if it has exactly two different factors (itself and 1). The first dozen primes are listed here.

> 2, 3, 5, 7, 11, 13, 17, 19, 23, 29, 31, 37   Prime numbers

A whole number greater than 1 that is not prime is called a **composite number.** Some examples follow.

> 4, 6, 8, 9, 10, 12   Composite numbers

The number 1 is neither prime nor composite.

1

① Tell whether each number is *prime* or *composite*.

(a) 12

(b) 13

(c) 27

(d) 59

(e) 1806

EXAMPLE 1 Distinguishing between Prime and Composite Numbers

Decide whether each number is *prime* or *composite*.

(a) 33
33 has factors of 3 and 11 as well as 1 and 33, so it is composite.

(b) 43
Since there are no numbers other than 1 and 43 itself that divide *evenly* into 43, the number 43 is prime.

(c) 9832
9832 can be divided by 2, giving 2 · 4916, so it is composite.

▶▶ **Work Problem 1 at the Side.**

OBJECTIVE 2 Write numbers in prime factored form. To factor a number means to write it as the product of two or more numbers. Factoring is the reverse of multiplying two numbers to get the product.

Multiplication   Factoring
$6 \cdot 3 = 18$ $18 = 6 \cdot 3$
↑ ↑   ↑   ↑   ↑   ↑
Factors Product   Product Factors

In algebra, a dot · is used instead of the $\times$ symbol to indicate multiplication because $\times$ may be confused with the letter *x*. A composite number written using factors that are all prime numbers is in **prime factored form.**

---

② Write each number in prime factored form.

(a) 70

(b) 72

(c) 693

(d) 97

EXAMPLE 2 Writing Numbers in Prime Factored Form

Write each number in prime factored form.

(a) 35
Factor 35 as the product of the prime factors 5 and 7, or as $35 = 5 \cdot 7$.

(b) 24
We use a factor tree, as shown below. The prime factors are circled.

Divide by the smallest prime, 2, to get $\qquad$ $24 = 2 \cdot 12.$

Now divide 12 by 2 to find factors of 12. $\qquad$ $24 = 2 \cdot 2 \cdot 6$

Since 6 can be factored as $2 \cdot 3, \quad 24 = 2 \cdot 2 \cdot 2 \cdot 3,$ where all factors are prime. $\qquad$ $24 = 2 \cdot 2 \cdot 2 \cdot 3$

▶▶ **Work Problem 2 at the Side.**

OBJECTIVE 3 Write fractions in lowest terms. A fraction is in **lowest terms** when the numerator and denominator have no factors in common (other than 1). The following properties are useful.

Properties of 1

Any nonzero number divided by itself is equal to 1; for example, $\frac{3}{3} = 1$.

Any number multiplied by 1 remains the same; for example, $7 \cdot 1 = 7$.

ANSWERS
1. (a) composite   (b) prime   (c) composite
   (d) prime   (e) composite
2. (a) $2 \cdot 5 \cdot 7$ (b) $2 \cdot 2 \cdot 2 \cdot 3 \cdot 3$
   (c) $3 \cdot 3 \cdot 7 \cdot 11$ (d) 97 is prime.

Writing a Fraction in Lowest Terms

Step 1 Write the numerator and denominator in prime factored form.

Step 2 Replace each pair of factors common to the numerator and denominator with 1.

Step 3 Multiply the remaining factors in the numerator and in the denominator.

(This procedure is sometimes called "simplifying the fraction.")

EXAMPLE 3 Writing Fractions in Lowest Terms

Write each fraction in lowest terms.

(a) $\dfrac{10}{15} = \dfrac{2 \cdot 5}{3 \cdot 5} = \dfrac{2}{3} \cdot \dfrac{5}{5} = \dfrac{2}{3} \cdot 1 = \dfrac{2}{3}$

Since 5 is a common factor of 10 and 15, we use the first property of 1 to replace $\frac{5}{5}$ with 1.

(b) $\dfrac{15}{45} = \dfrac{3 \cdot 5}{3 \cdot 3 \cdot 5} = \dfrac{1 \cdot 3 \cdot 5}{3 \cdot 3 \cdot 5} = \dfrac{1}{3} \cdot \dfrac{3}{3} \cdot \dfrac{5}{5} = \dfrac{1}{3} \cdot 1 \cdot 1 = \dfrac{1}{3}$

Multiplying by 1 in the numerator does not change the value of the numerator and makes it possible to rewrite the expression as the product of three fractions in the next step.

(c) $\dfrac{150}{200}$

It is not always necessary to factor into *prime* factors in Step 1. Here, if you see that 50 is a common factor of the numerator and the denominator, factor as follows:

$$\frac{150}{200} = \frac{3 \cdot 50}{4 \cdot 50} = \frac{3}{4} \cdot 1 = \frac{3}{4}.$$

NOTE

When writing a fraction in lowest terms, look for the largest common factor in the numerator and the denominator. If none is obvious, factor the numerator and the denominator into prime factors. *Any* common factor can be used and the fraction can be simplified in stages.

For example, $\dfrac{150}{200} = \dfrac{15 \cdot 10}{20 \cdot 10} = \dfrac{3 \cdot 5 \cdot 10}{4 \cdot 5 \cdot 10} = \dfrac{3}{4}.$

Work Problem 3 at the Side. ▶▶▶

OBJECTIVE 4 Multiply and divide fractions.

Multiplying Fractions

To multiply two fractions, multiply the numerators to get the numerator of the product, and multiply the denominators to get the denominator of the product. The product must be written in lowest terms.

---

3 Write each fraction in lowest terms.

(a) $\dfrac{8}{14}$

(b) $\dfrac{35}{42}$

(c) $\dfrac{120}{72}$

4 Find each product, and write it in lowest terms.

(a) $\dfrac{5}{8} \cdot \dfrac{2}{10}$

(b) $\dfrac{1}{10} \cdot \dfrac{12}{5}$

(c) $\dfrac{7}{9} \cdot \dfrac{12}{14}$

(d) $3\dfrac{1}{3} \cdot 1\dfrac{3}{4}$

EXAMPLE 4 Multiplying Fractions

Find each product, and write it in lowest terms.

(a) $\dfrac{3}{8} \cdot \dfrac{4}{9} = \dfrac{3 \cdot 4}{8 \cdot 9}$ Multiply numerators.
Multiply denominators.

$= \dfrac{3 \cdot 4}{2 \cdot 4 \cdot 3 \cdot 3}$ Factor.

$= \dfrac{1}{2 \cdot 3} = \dfrac{1}{6}$ Write in lowest terms.

(b) $2\dfrac{1}{3} \cdot 5\dfrac{1}{2} = \dfrac{7}{3} \cdot \dfrac{11}{2}$ Write as improper fractions.

$= \dfrac{77}{6}$ or $12\dfrac{5}{6}$ Multiply numerators and denominators; write as a mixed number.

◀◀◀ Work Problem 4 at the Side.

Two fractions are **reciprocals** of each other if their product is 1. For example, $\frac{3}{4}$ and $\frac{4}{3}$ are reciprocals because

$$\dfrac{3}{4} \cdot \dfrac{4}{3} = 1.$$

The numbers $\frac{7}{11}$ and $\frac{11}{7}$ are reciprocals also. Other examples are $\frac{1}{5}$ and 5, $\frac{4}{9}$ and $\frac{9}{4}$, and 16 and $\frac{1}{16}$.

Because division is the opposite or inverse of multiplication, we use reciprocals to divide fractions.

Dividing Fractions

To divide two fractions, multiply the first fraction by the reciprocal of the second. The result, called the **quotient,** must be written in lowest terms.

The reason this method works will be explained in **Section 1.6.** However, as an example, we know that $20 \div 10 = 2$, and $20 \cdot \frac{1}{10} = 2$.

EXAMPLE 5 Dividing Fractions

Find each quotient, and write it in lowest terms.

(a) $\dfrac{3}{4} \div \dfrac{8}{5} = \dfrac{3}{4} \cdot \dfrac{5}{8} = \dfrac{3 \cdot 5}{4 \cdot 8} = \dfrac{15}{32}$

Multiply by the reciprocal of the second fraction.

(b) $\dfrac{3}{4} \div \dfrac{5}{8} = \dfrac{3}{4} \cdot \dfrac{8}{5} = \dfrac{3 \cdot 8}{4 \cdot 5} = \dfrac{3 \cdot 4 \cdot 2}{4 \cdot 5} = \dfrac{6}{5}$ or $1\dfrac{1}{5}$

(c) $\dfrac{5}{8} \div 10 = \dfrac{5}{8} \div \dfrac{10}{1} = \dfrac{5}{8} \cdot \dfrac{1}{10} = \dfrac{5 \cdot 1}{8 \cdot 10} = \dfrac{5 \cdot 1}{8 \cdot 2 \cdot 5} = \dfrac{1}{16}$

Write 10 as $\frac{10}{1}$.

Continued on Next Page

(d) $1\dfrac{2}{3} \div 4\dfrac{1}{2} = \dfrac{5}{3} \div \dfrac{9}{2}$ Write as improper fractions.

$\qquad\qquad = \dfrac{5}{3} \cdot \dfrac{2}{9}$ Multiply by the reciprocal of the second fraction.

$\qquad\qquad = \dfrac{10}{27}$ Multiply numerators and denominators.

5 Find each quotient, and write it in lowest terms.

(a) $\dfrac{3}{10} \div \dfrac{2}{7}$

(b) $\dfrac{3}{4} \div \dfrac{7}{16}$

(c) $\dfrac{4}{3} \div 6$

(d) $3\dfrac{1}{4} \div 1\dfrac{2}{5}$

CAUTION
Notice that *only* the second fraction (the divisor) is replaced by its reciprocal in the multiplication.

Work Problem 5 at the Side. ▶▶▶

OBJECTIVE 5 Add and subtract fractions.   The result of adding two numbers is called the **sum** of the numbers. For example, since $2 + 3 = 5$, the sum of 2 and 3 is 5.

Adding Fractions
To find the sum of two fractions with the *same* denominator, add their numerators and keep the *same* denominator.

EXAMPLE 6 Adding Fractions with the Same Denominator

Add. Write sums in lowest terms.

(a) $\dfrac{3}{7} + \dfrac{2}{7} = \dfrac{3 + 2}{7} = \dfrac{5}{7}$ Add numerators; denominator does not change.

(b) $\dfrac{2}{10} + \dfrac{3}{10} = \dfrac{2 + 3}{10} = \dfrac{5}{10} = \dfrac{1}{2}$ Write in lowest terms.

Work Problem 6 at the Side. ▶▶▶

6 Add. Write sums in lowest terms.

(a) $\dfrac{3}{5} + \dfrac{4}{5}$

(b) $\dfrac{5}{14} + \dfrac{3}{14}$

If the fractions to be added do not have the same denominator, the procedure above can still be used, but only *after* the fractions are rewritten with a common denominator. For example, to rewrite $\frac{3}{4}$ as a fraction with a denominator of 32,

$$\dfrac{3}{4} = \dfrac{?}{32},$$

we must find the number that can be multiplied by 4 to give 32. Since $4 \cdot 8 = 32$, we use the number 8. By the second property of 1, we can multiply the numerator and the denominator by 8.

$$\dfrac{3}{4} = \dfrac{3}{4} \cdot 1 = \dfrac{3}{4} \cdot \dfrac{8}{8} = \dfrac{3 \cdot 8}{4 \cdot 8} = \dfrac{24}{32}$$

ANSWERS

5. (a) $\dfrac{21}{20}$ or $1\dfrac{1}{20}$ **(b)** $\dfrac{12}{7}$ or $1\dfrac{5}{7}$
  (c) $\dfrac{2}{9}$ **(d)** $\dfrac{65}{28}$ or $2\dfrac{9}{28}$

6. (a) $\dfrac{7}{5}$ or $1\dfrac{2}{5}$ **(b)** $\dfrac{4}{7}$

7 Add. Write sums in lowest terms.

(a) $\dfrac{7}{30} + \dfrac{2}{45}$

(b) $\dfrac{17}{10} + \dfrac{8}{27}$

(c) $2\dfrac{1}{8} + 1\dfrac{2}{3}$

(d) $132\dfrac{4}{5} + 28\dfrac{3}{4}$

Finding the Least Common Denominator (LCD)

Step 1 Factor all denominators to prime factored form.

Step 2 The LCD is the product of every (different) factor that appears in any of the factored denominators. If a factor is repeated, use the largest number of repeats as factors of the LCD.

Step 3 Write each fraction with the LCD as the denominator, using the second property of 1.

EXAMPLE 7 **Adding Fractions with Different Denominators**

Add. Write sums in lowest terms.

(a) $\dfrac{4}{15} + \dfrac{5}{9}$

Step 1 To find the LCD, factor the denominators to prime factored form.

$$15 = 5 \cdot 3 \quad \text{and} \quad 9 = 3 \cdot 3$$

3 is a factor of both denominators.

Step 2 $$\text{LCD} = 5 \cdot 3 \cdot 3 = 45$$

In this example, the LCD needs one factor of 5 and two factors of 3 because the second denominator has two factors of 3.

Step 3 Now we can use the second property of 1 to write each fraction with 45 as the denominator.

$$\frac{4}{15} = \frac{4}{15} \cdot \frac{3}{3} = \frac{12}{45} \quad \text{and} \quad \frac{5}{9} = \frac{5}{9} \cdot \frac{5}{5} = \frac{25}{45}$$

Now add the two equivalent fractions to get the required sum.

$$\frac{4}{15} + \frac{5}{9} = \frac{12}{45} + \frac{25}{45} = \frac{37}{45}$$

(b) $3\dfrac{1}{2} + 2\dfrac{3}{4} = \dfrac{7}{2} + \dfrac{11}{4}$ Change to improper fractions.

$\qquad = \dfrac{14}{4} + \dfrac{11}{4}$ Get a common denominator.

$\qquad = \dfrac{25}{4}$ or $6\dfrac{1}{4}$ Add; write as a mixed number.

(c) $45\dfrac{2}{3} + 73\dfrac{1}{2}$

We use a vertical method here.

$$45\frac{2}{3} = 45\frac{4}{6}$$
$$+\ 73\frac{1}{2} = 73\frac{3}{6}$$

Add the whole numbers and the fractions separately.

$$118\frac{7}{6} = 118 + \left(1 + \frac{1}{6}\right) = 119\frac{1}{6}$$

Work Problem 7 at the Side.

ANSWERS

7. **(a)** $\dfrac{5}{18}$ **(b)** $\dfrac{539}{270}$ or $1\dfrac{269}{270}$

(c) $\dfrac{91}{24}$ or $3\dfrac{19}{24}$ **(d)** $161\dfrac{11}{20}$

The **difference** between two numbers is found by subtracting the numbers. For example, $9 - 5 = 4$, so the difference between 9 and 5 is 4. We find the difference between two fractions as follows.

> ### Subtracting Fractions
>
> To find the difference between two fractions with the *same* denominator, subtract their numerators and keep the *same* denominator.
>
> If the fractions have *different* denominators, write them with a common denominator first.

EXAMPLE 8 Subtracting Fractions

Subtract. Write differences in lowest terms.

(a) $\dfrac{15}{8} - \dfrac{3}{8} = \dfrac{15 - 3}{8}$ Subtract numerators; denominator does not change.

$= \dfrac{12}{8} = \dfrac{3}{2}$ Lowest terms

(b) $\dfrac{15}{16} - \dfrac{4}{9}$

Since $16 = 2 \cdot 2 \cdot 2 \cdot 2$ and $9 = 3 \cdot 3$ have no common factors, the LCD is $16 \cdot 9 = 144$.

$\dfrac{15}{16} - \dfrac{4}{9} = \dfrac{15 \cdot 9}{16 \cdot 9} - \dfrac{4 \cdot 16}{9 \cdot 16}$ Get a common denominator.

$= \dfrac{135}{144} - \dfrac{64}{144}$

$= \dfrac{71}{144}$ Subtract numerators; keep the same denominator.

(c) $2\dfrac{1}{2} - 1\dfrac{3}{4} = \dfrac{5}{2} - \dfrac{7}{4}$ Write as improper fractions.

$= \dfrac{10}{4} - \dfrac{7}{4}$ Get a common denominator.

$= \dfrac{3}{4}$ Subtract.

Alternatively, we could use a vertical method.

$$2\dfrac{1}{2} = 2\dfrac{2}{4} = 1\dfrac{6}{4}$$
$$-1\dfrac{3}{4} = 1\dfrac{3}{4} = 1\dfrac{3}{4}$$
$$\overline{\phantom{-1\dfrac{3}{4} = 1\dfrac{3}{4} = 1}\dfrac{3}{4}}$$

Work Problem 8 at the Side. ❱❱❱

We often see mixed numbers used in applications of mathematics, as shown in Examples 9 and 10 on the next page.

8 Subtract.

(a) $\dfrac{9}{11} - \dfrac{3}{11}$

(b) $\dfrac{13}{15} - \dfrac{5}{6}$

(c) $2\dfrac{3}{8} - 1\dfrac{1}{2}$

(d) $50\dfrac{1}{4} - 32\dfrac{2}{3}$

ANSWERS

8. **(a)** $\dfrac{6}{11}$ **(b)** $\dfrac{1}{30}$ **(c)** $\dfrac{7}{8}$ **(d)** $17\dfrac{7}{12}$

9 Solve the problem.

To make a three-piece outfit from the same fabric, Wei Jen needs $1\frac{1}{4}$ yd for the blouse, $1\frac{2}{3}$ yd for the skirt, and $2\frac{1}{2}$ yd for the jacket. How much fabric does she need?

EXAMPLE 9 Solving an Applied Problem Requiring Addition of Fractions

The diagram in Figure 1 appears in the book *Woodworker's 39 Sure-Fire Projects*. It is a view of a bookcase/desk. Add the fractions in the diagram to find the height of the bookcase/desk to the top of the writing surface.

We must add the following measures (" means inches):

$$\frac{3}{4}, \quad 4\frac{1}{2}, \quad 9\frac{1}{2}, \quad \frac{3}{4}, \quad 9\frac{1}{2}, \quad \frac{3}{4}, \quad 4\frac{1}{2}.$$

We begin by changing $4\frac{1}{2}$ to $4\frac{2}{4}$ and $9\frac{1}{2}$ to $9\frac{2}{4}$, since the common denominator is 4. Then we use the method of Example 7(c).

$$\frac{3}{4} \rightarrow \frac{3}{4}$$
$$4\frac{1}{2} = 4\frac{2}{4}$$
$$9\frac{1}{2} = 9\frac{2}{4}$$
$$\frac{3}{4} \rightarrow \frac{3}{4}$$
$$9\frac{1}{2} = 9\frac{2}{4}$$
$$\frac{3}{4} \rightarrow \frac{3}{4}$$
$$+ 4\frac{1}{2} = 4\frac{2}{4}$$
$$\overline{\qquad 26\frac{17}{4}}$$

Figure 1

Since $\frac{17}{4} = 4\frac{1}{4}$, $26\frac{17}{4} = 26 + 4\frac{1}{4} = 30\frac{1}{4}$. The height is $30\frac{1}{4}$ in.

Work Problem 9 at the Side.

10 Solve the problem.

A gallon of paint covers 500 ft². (ft² means square feet.) To paint his house, Tram needs enough paint to cover 4200 ft². How many gallons of paint should he buy?

EXAMPLE 10 Solving an Applied Problem Requiring Division of Fractions

An upholsterer needs $2\frac{1}{4}$ yd of fabric to cover a chair. How many chairs can be covered with $23\frac{2}{3}$ yd of fabric?

To better understand the problem, we replace the fractions with whole numbers. Suppose each chair requires 2 yd, and we have 24 yd of fabric. Dividing 24 by 2 gives the number of chairs (12) that can be covered. To solve the original problem, we must divide $23\frac{2}{3}$ by $2\frac{1}{4}$.

$$23\frac{2}{3} \div 2\frac{1}{4} = \frac{71}{3} \div \frac{9}{4}$$

$$= \frac{71}{3} \cdot \frac{4}{9}$$

$$= \frac{284}{27} \quad \text{or} \quad 10\frac{14}{27}$$

Thus, 10 chairs can be covered with some fabric left over.

Work Problem 10 at the Side.

Answers

9. $5\frac{5}{12}$ yd

10. $8\frac{2}{5}$ gal are needed, so he must buy 9 gal.

R.1 Exercises

FOR EXTRA HELP   Addison-Wesley Math Tutor Center   MathXL   Digital Video Tutor CD 1 Videotape 1   Student's Solutions Manual   MyMathLab   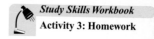 Interactmath.com

Study Skills Workbook
Activity 3: Homework

Decide whether each statement is true *or* false. *If it is* false, *say why.*

1. In the fraction $\frac{3}{7}$, 3 is the numerator and 7 is the denominator.

2. The mixed number equivalent of $\frac{41}{5}$ is $8\frac{1}{5}$.

3. The fraction $\frac{17}{51}$ is in lowest terms.

4. The reciprocal of $\frac{8}{2}$ is $\frac{4}{1}$.

5. The product of 8 and 2 is 10.

6. The difference between 12 and 2 is 6.

Identify each number as prime, composite, *or* neither. *See Example 1.*

7. 19

8. 99

9. 52

10. 61

11. 2468

12. 3125

13. 1

14. 83

Write each number in prime factored form. See Example 2.

15. 30

16. 40

17. 252

18. 168

19. 124

20. 165

21. 29

22. 31

Write each fraction in lowest terms. See Example 3.

23. $\frac{8}{16}$

24. $\frac{4}{12}$

25. $\frac{15}{18}$

26. $\frac{16}{20}$

27. $\frac{15}{75}$

28. $\frac{24}{64}$

29. $\frac{144}{120}$

30. $\frac{132}{77}$

31. For the fractions $\frac{p}{q}$ and $\frac{r}{s}$, which can serve as a common denominator?

    A. $q \cdot s$

    B. $q + s$

    C. $p \cdot r$

    D. $p + r$

32. Which is the correct way to write $\frac{16}{24}$ in lowest terms?

    A. $\dfrac{16}{24} = \dfrac{8 + 8}{8 + 16} = \dfrac{8}{16} = \dfrac{1}{2}$

    B. $\dfrac{16}{24} = \dfrac{4 \cdot 4}{4 \cdot 6} = \dfrac{4}{6}$

    C. $\dfrac{16}{24} = \dfrac{8 \cdot 2}{8 \cdot 3} = \dfrac{2}{3}$

    D. $\dfrac{16}{24} = \dfrac{14 + 2}{21 + 3} = \dfrac{2}{3} + \dfrac{2}{3} = \dfrac{4}{3}$

Find each product or quotient, and write it in lowest terms. See Examples 4 and 5.

33. $\dfrac{4}{5} \cdot \dfrac{6}{7}$

34. $\dfrac{5}{9} \cdot \dfrac{10}{7}$

35. $\dfrac{1}{10} \cdot \dfrac{12}{5}$

36. $\dfrac{6}{11} \cdot \dfrac{2}{3}$

37. $\dfrac{15}{4} \cdot \dfrac{8}{25}$

38. $\dfrac{4}{7} \cdot \dfrac{21}{8}$

39. $2\dfrac{2}{3} \cdot 5\dfrac{4}{5}$

40. $3\dfrac{3}{5} \cdot 7\dfrac{1}{6}$

41. $\dfrac{5}{4} \div \dfrac{3}{8}$

42. $\dfrac{7}{6} \div \dfrac{9}{10}$

43. $\dfrac{32}{5} \div \dfrac{8}{15}$

44. $\dfrac{24}{7} \div \dfrac{6}{21}$

45. $\dfrac{3}{4} \div 12$

46. $\dfrac{2}{5} \div 30$

47. $2\dfrac{5}{8} \div 1\dfrac{15}{32}$

48. $2\dfrac{3}{10} \div 7\dfrac{4}{5}$

49. In your own words, explain how to divide two fractions.

50. In your own words, explain how to add two fractions that have different denominators.

Find each sum or difference, and write it in lowest terms. See Examples 6–8.

51. $\dfrac{7}{12} + \dfrac{1}{12}$

52. $\dfrac{3}{16} + \dfrac{5}{16}$

53. $\dfrac{5}{9} + \dfrac{1}{3}$

54. $\dfrac{4}{15} + \dfrac{1}{5}$

55. $3\dfrac{1}{8} + \dfrac{1}{4}$

56. $5\dfrac{3}{4} + \dfrac{2}{3}$

57. $\dfrac{7}{12} - \dfrac{1}{9}$

58. $\dfrac{11}{16} - \dfrac{1}{12}$

59. $6\dfrac{1}{4} - 5\dfrac{1}{3}$

60. $8\dfrac{4}{5} - 7\dfrac{4}{9}$

61. $\dfrac{5}{3} + \dfrac{1}{6} - \dfrac{1}{2}$

62. $\dfrac{7}{15} + \dfrac{1}{6} - \dfrac{1}{10}$

Use the chart, which appears on a package of Quaker Quick Grits, to answer the questions in Exercises 63 and 64.

63. How many cups of water would be needed for eight microwave servings?

64. How many teaspoons of salt would be needed for five stove top servings? (*Hint:* 5 is halfway between 4 and 6.)

	Microwave		**Stove Top**		
Servings	1	1	1	4	6
Water	$\dfrac{3}{4}$ cup	1 cup	3 cups		4 cups
Grits	3 Tbsp	3 Tbsp	$\dfrac{3}{4}$ cup		1 cup
Salt (optional)	Dash	Dash	$\dfrac{1}{4}$ tsp		$\dfrac{1}{2}$ tsp

Solve each applied problem. See Examples 9 and 10.

65. A motel owner has decided to expand his business by buying a piece of property next to the motel. The property has an irregular shape, with five sides as shown in the figure. Find the total distance around the piece of property. This is called the **perimeter** of the figure.

196    $76\dfrac{5}{8}$

$98\dfrac{3}{4}$ $100\dfrac{7}{8}$

$146\dfrac{1}{2}$

Measurements in feet

66. A triangle has sides of lengths $5\dfrac{1}{4}$ ft, $7\dfrac{1}{2}$ ft, and $10\dfrac{1}{8}$ ft . Find the perimeter of the triangle. See Exercise 65.

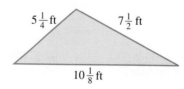

$5\dfrac{1}{4}$ ft $7\dfrac{1}{2}$ ft

$10\dfrac{1}{8}$ ft

67. A hardware store sells a 40-piece socket wrench set. The measure of the largest socket is $\frac{3}{4}$ in., while the measure of the smallest socket is $\frac{3}{16}$ in. What is the difference between these measures?

68. Two sockets in a socket wrench set have measures of $\frac{9}{16}$ in. and $\frac{3}{8}$ in. What is the difference between these two measures?

69. Under existing standards, most of the holes in Swiss cheese must have diameters between $\frac{11}{16}$ and $\frac{13}{16}$ in. To accommodate new high-speed slicing machines, the USDA wants to reduce the minimum size to $\frac{3}{8}$ in. How much smaller is $\frac{3}{8}$ in. than $\frac{11}{16}$ in.? (*Source:* U.S. Department of Agriculture.)

70. Tex's favorite recipe for barbecue sauce calls for $2\frac{1}{3}$ cups of tomato sauce. The recipe makes enough barbecue sauce to serve 7 people. How much tomato sauce is needed for 1 serving?

71. It takes $2\frac{3}{8}$ yd of fabric to make a costume for a school play. How much fabric would be needed for 7 costumes?

72. A cake recipe calls for $1\frac{3}{4}$ cups of sugar. A caterer has $15\frac{1}{2}$ cups of sugar on hand. How many cakes can he make?

More than 8 million immigrants were admitted to the United States between 1990 and 1998. The pie chart gives the fractional number from each region of birth for these immigrants. Use the chart to answer the following questions.

73. What fractional part of the immigrants were from other regions?

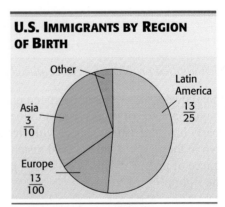

U.S. IMMIGRANTS BY REGION OF BIRTH

Source: U.S. Bureau of the Census.

74. What fractional part of the immigrants were from Latin America or Asia?

75. How many (in millions) were from Europe?

76. How many more immigrants were from Latin America than all of the other regions combined?

R.2 Decimals and Percents

Fractions are one way to represent parts of a whole. Another way is with a **decimal fraction** or **decimal,** a number written with a decimal point, such as 9.4. Each digit in a decimal number has a place value, as shown below.

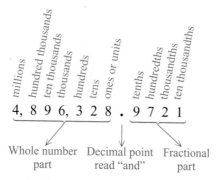

Each successive place value is ten times larger than the place value to its right and is one-tenth as large as the place value to its left.

Prices are often written as decimals. The price $14.75 means 14 dollars and 75 cents, or 14 dollars and $\frac{75}{100}$ of a dollar.

OBJECTIVE 1 Write decimals as fractions. Place value is used to write a decimal number as a fraction. For example, since the last digit (that is, the digit farthest to the right) of .67 is in the *hundredths* place,

$$.67 = \frac{67}{100}.$$

Similarly, $.9 = \frac{9}{10}$ and $.25 = \frac{25}{100}$. Digits to the left of the decimal point indicate whole numbers, so 12.342 is the sum of 12 and .342, and

$$12.342 = 12 + .342 = 12 + \frac{342}{1000} = \frac{12,000}{1000} + \frac{342}{1000} = \frac{12,342}{1000}.$$

These examples suggest the following rule.

Converting a Decimal to a Fraction

Read the name using the correct place value. Write it in fraction form just as you read it. The denominator will be a **power of 10,** a number like 10, 100, 1000, and so on.

For example, we read .16 as "sixteen hundredths" and write it in fraction form as $\frac{16}{100}$. The same thing is accomplished by counting the number of digits to the right of the decimal point, then writing the given number without a decimal point over a denominator of 1 followed by that number of zeros.

EXAMPLE 1 Writing Decimals as Fractions

Write each decimal as a fraction. Do not write in lowest terms.

(a) .95

We read .95 as 95 hundredths, so the fraction form is $\frac{95}{100}$. Using the shortcut method, since there are two places to the right of the decimal point, there will be two zeros in the denominator.

Continued on Next Page

1 Write each decimal as a fraction. Do not write in lowest terms.

(a) .8

(b) .431

(c) 20.58

2 Add or subtract as indicated.

(a)   68.9
      42.72
   + 8.973

(b)   32.5
    − 21.72

(c) 42.83 + 71 + 3.074

(d) 351.8 − 2.706

$$.95 = \frac{95}{100}$$

2 places   2 zeros

(b) $.056 = \dfrac{56}{1000}$

3 places 3 zeros

(c) $4.2095 = 4 + .2095 = 4 + \dfrac{2095}{10,000} = \dfrac{42,095}{10,000}$

4 places   4 zeros

◀◀◀ **Work Problem 1 at the Side.**

OBJECTIVE 2 Add and subtract decimals.

EXAMPLE 2 Adding and Subtracting Decimals

Add or subtract as indicated.

(a) 6.92 + 14.8 + 3.217

Place the digits of the numbers in columns, with decimal points lined up so that tenths are in one column, hundredths in another column, and so on.

$$\begin{array}{r} 6.92 \\ 14.8 \\ +\ \ 3.217 \\ \hline 24.937 \end{array}$$ Decimal points lined up

A good way to avoid errors is to attach zeros to make all the numbers the same length.

$$\begin{array}{r} 6.92 \\ 14.8 \\ +\ \ 3.217 \end{array} \quad \text{becomes} \quad \begin{array}{r} 6.920 \\ 14.800 \\ +\ \ 3.217 \\ \hline 24.937 \end{array}$$ Attach zeros.

(b) 47.6 − 32.509

Write the numbers in columns, attaching zeros to 47.6.

$$\begin{array}{r} 47.6 \\ -\ 32.509 \end{array} \quad \text{becomes} \quad \begin{array}{r} 47.600 \\ -\ 32.509 \\ \hline 15.091 \end{array}$$

(c) 3 − .253

A whole number is assumed to have the decimal point at the right of the number. Write 3 as 3.000; then subtract.

$$\begin{array}{r} 3.000 \\ -\ \ .253 \\ \hline 2.747 \end{array}$$

◀◀◀ **Work Problem 2 at the Side.**

OBJECTIVE 3 Multiply and divide decimals. We multiply decimals by slightly modifying multiplication of whole numbers. We will sometimes use the times symbol, ×, instead of a dot, to avoid confusion with the decimal point.

Multiplying Decimals

Ignore the decimal points and multiply as if the numbers were whole numbers. Then add together the number of **decimal places** (digits to the *right* of the decimal point) in each number being multiplied. Place the decimal point in the answer that many digits from the right.

EXAMPLE 3 **Multiplying Decimals**

Multiply.

(a) 29.3 × 4.52

Multiply as if the numbers were whole numbers.

```
      29.3    1 decimal place in first number
   ×  4.52    2 decimal places in second number
      586     1 + 2 = 3
     1465
     1172
   132.436    3 decimal places in answer
```

(b) 7.003 × 55.8

```
     7.003    3 decimal places
   ×  55.8    1 decimal place
     56024    3 + 1 = 4
     35015
     35015
   390.7674   4 decimal places
```

(c) 31.42 × 65

```
     31.42    2 decimal places
   ×    65    0 decimal places
     15710    2 + 0 = 2
     18852
   2042.30    2 decimal places
```

The final 0 here can be dropped and the result can be expressed as 2042.3.

Work Problem 3 at the Side.

To divide decimals, convert the divisor to a whole number.

Dividing Decimals

Change the **divisor** (the number you are dividing *by*) into a whole number by moving the decimal point as many places as necessary to the right. Move the decimal point in the **dividend** (the number you are dividing *into*) to the right by the same number of places. Move the decimal point straight up and then divide as with whole numbers.

```
                    5  ← Quotient
   Divisor → 25)125
                  ↑
               Dividend
```

3 Multiply.

(a) 2.13 × .05

(b) 9.32 × 1.4

(c) 300.2 × .052

(d) 42,001 × .012

4 Divide.

(a) $14.9\overline{)451.47}$

(b) $.37\overline{)5.476}$

(c) $375.1 \div 3.001$

EXAMPLE 4 Dividing Decimals

Divide.

(a) $233.45 \div 11.5$

Write the problem as follows.

$$11.5\overline{)233.45}$$

To change 11.5 into a whole number, move the decimal point one place to the right. Move the decimal point in 233.45 the same number of places to the right, to get 2334.5.

$$11.5.\overline{)233.4.5} \qquad \text{Move one decimal place to the right.}$$

To see why this works, write the division in fraction form and multiply by $\frac{10}{10}$ or 1.

$$\frac{233.45}{11.5} \cdot \frac{10}{10} = \frac{2334.5}{115}$$

The result is the same as when we moved the decimal point one place to the right in the divisor and the dividend.

Move the decimal point straight up and divide as with whole numbers.

$$\begin{array}{r} 20.3 \\ 115\overline{)2334.5} \\ \underline{230} \\ 345 \\ \underline{345} \\ 0 \end{array} \qquad \text{Move the decimal point straight up.}$$

In the second step of the division, 115 does not divide into 34, so we used zero as a placeholder in the quotient.

(b) $73.85\overline{)1852.882}$ (Round the answer to two decimal places.)

Move the decimal point two places to the right in 73.85, to get 7385. Do the same thing with 1852.882, to get 185288.2.

$$73.85.\overline{)1852.88.2}$$

Move the decimal point straight up and divide as with whole numbers.

$$\begin{array}{r} 25.089 \\ 7385\overline{)185288.200} \\ \underline{14770} \\ 37588 \\ \underline{36925} \\ 66320 \\ \underline{59080} \\ 72400 \\ \underline{66465} \\ 5935 \end{array}$$

We carried out the division to three decimal places so that we could round to two decimal places, obtaining the quotient 25.09.

Work Problem 4 at the Side.

A shortcut can be used when multiplying or dividing by powers of 10.

Multiplying or Dividing by Powers of 10

To *multiply* by a power of 10, *move the decimal point to the right* as many places as the number of zeros.

To *divide* by a power of 10, *move the decimal point to the left* as many places as the number of zeros.

In both cases, insert 0s as placeholders if necessary.

EXAMPLE 5 **Multiplying and Dividing by Powers of 10**

Multiply or divide as indicated.

(a) $48.731 \times 100 = 48.73.1 = 4873.1$

We moved the decimal point two places to the right because 100 has two zeros.

(b) $48.7 \div 1000 = .048.7 = .0487$

We moved the decimal point three places to the left because 1000 has three zeros. We needed to insert a zero in front of the 4 to do this.

Work Problem 5 at the Side. ▶▶▶

To avoid misplacing the decimal point, check your work by estimating the answer. *To get a quick estimate, round the numbers so that only the first digit is not zero,* using the rule for rounding. For more accurate estimates, the numbers could be rounded to the first two or even three nonzero digits.

Rule for Rounding

If the digit to become 0 or be dropped is 5 or more, round up by adding 1 to the final digit to be kept.

If the digit to become 0 or be dropped is 4 or less, do not round up.

For example, to estimate the answer to Example 2(a), round

$$6.92 \text{ to } 7, \quad 14.8 \text{ to } 10, \quad \text{and} \quad 3.217 \text{ to } 3.$$

5 or more   4 or less   4 or less

Since $7 + 10 + 3 = 20$, the answer of 24.937 is reasonable. In Example 4(a), round 233.45 to 200 and 11.5 to 10. Since $200 \div 10 = 20$, the answer of 20.3 is reasonable.

OBJECTIVE 4 Write fractions as decimals.

Writing a Fraction as a Decimal

Because a fraction bar indicates division, write a fraction as a decimal by dividing the denominator into the numerator.

---

5 Multiply or divide as indicated.

(a) 294.72×10

(b) 19.5×1000

(c) $4.793 \div 100$

(d) $960.1 \div 10$

ANSWERS
5. (a) 2947.2   **(b)** 19,500   **(c)** .04793
   (d) 96.01

6 Convert to decimals. For repeating decimals, write the answer two ways: using the bar notation and rounding to the nearest thousandth.

(a) $\dfrac{2}{9}$

(b) $\dfrac{17}{20}$

(c) $\dfrac{1}{11}$

EXAMPLE 6   Writing Fractions as Decimals

Write each fraction as a decimal.

(a) $\dfrac{19}{8}$

$$
\begin{array}{r}
2.375 \\
8\overline{)19.000} \\
16 \\
\hline
30 \\
24 \\
\hline
60 \\
56 \\
\hline
40 \\
40 \\
\hline
0
\end{array}
$$

$\dfrac{19}{8} = 2.375$

(b) $\dfrac{2}{3}$

$$
\begin{array}{r}
.6666\ldots \\
3\overline{)2.0000\ldots} \\
18 \\
\hline
20 \\
18 \\
\hline
20 \\
18 \\
\hline
20 \\
18 \\
\hline
20
\end{array}
$$

The remainder in the division in part (b) is never 0. Because 2 is always left after the subtraction, this quotient is a **repeating decimal.** A convenient notation for a repeating decimal is a bar over the digit (or digits) that repeats. For instance, we can write .6666 . . . as $.\overline{6}$. We often round repeating decimals to as many places as needed. Rounding to the *nearest thousandth,*

$$\frac{2}{3} = .667. \qquad \text{An approximation}$$

CAUTION
When rounding, be careful to distinguish between *thousandths* and *thousands* or between *hundredths* and *hundreds,* and so on.

Work Problem 6 at the Side.

OBJECTIVE 5 Convert percents to decimals and decimals to percents.   An important application of decimals is in work with percents. The word **percent** means "per one hundred." Percent is written with the sign %. One percent means "one per one hundred" or "one one-hundredth."

$$1\% = .01 \quad \text{or} \quad 1\% = \frac{1}{100}$$

EXAMPLE 7   Converting Percents and Decimals

(a) Write 73% as a decimal.
Since 1% = .01,
$$73\% = 73 \cdot 1\% = 73 \times .01 = .73.$$

Also, 73% can be written as a decimal using the fraction form $1\% = \frac{1}{100}$.

$$73\% = 73 \cdot 1\% = 73 \cdot \left(\frac{1}{100}\right) = \frac{73}{100} = .73$$

(b) Write 125% as a decimal.
$$125\% = 125 \cdot 1\% = 125 \times .01 = 1.25$$

Continued on Next Page

(c) Write $3\frac{1}{2}\%$ as a decimal.
First write the fractional part as a decimal.

$$3\frac{1}{2}\% = (3 + .5)\% = 3.5\%$$

Now change the percent to decimal form.

$$3.5\% = 3.5 \times .01 = .035 \qquad 1\% = .01$$

(d) Write .32 as a percent.
Since .32 means 32 hundredths, write .32 as $32 \times .01$. Finally, replace .01 with 1%.

$$.32 = 32 \times .01 = 32 \times 1\% = 32\%$$

(e) Write 2.63 as a percent.

$$2.63 = 263 \times .01 = 263 \times 1\% = 263\%$$

NOTE
A quick way to change from a percent to a decimal is to move the decimal point two places to the left. To change from a decimal to a percent, move the decimal point two places to the right.

Divide by 100;
Move 2 places left.

Decimal   Percent

Multiply by 100;
Move 2 places right.

EXAMPLE 8 **Converting Percents and Decimals by Moving the Decimal Point**

Convert each percent to a decimal and each decimal to a percent.

(a) $45\% = .45$

(b) $250\% = 2.50$

(c) $.57 = 57\%$

(d) $1.5 = 1.50 = 150\%$

(e) $.327 = 32.7\%$

> **Work Problem 7 at the Side.** ▶▶▶

⌨ **Calculator Tip** In this book, we do not use 0 in the ones place for decimal fractions between 0 and 1. Many calculators (and other books) will show 0.45 instead of just .45 to emphasize that there is a 0 in the ones place. Graphing calculators do *not* show 0 in the ones place. Either way is correct.

7 Convert as indicated.

(a) 23% to a decimal

(b) 310% to a decimal

(c) .71 to a percent

(d) 1.32 to a percent

(e) .685 to a percent

ANSWERS
7. **(a)** .23 **(b)** 3.10 **(c)** 71%
      (d) 132% **(e)** 68.5%

Real-Data Applications

Decimalization of Stock Prices

When the New York Stock Exchange (NYSE) was founded in 1792, Thomas Jefferson suggested that stock prices be based on a decimal system. Instead, stock prices were based on the Spanish *eight-reales* coin, or the Spanish milled dollar, which was a commonly used and legal currency in the United States until 1857.

The NYSE decision to base stock prices on an archaic coin resulted in the practice of representing a **price per share** as a mixed number with fractional parts of $\frac{1}{2}, \frac{1}{4}, \frac{1}{8}$, or $\frac{1}{16}$. After two centuries, the Securities Exchange Commission (SEC) and the NYSE proposed a change in stock pricing to a decimal system consistent with that used by foreign stock exchanges. If they had only listened to Thomas Jefferson!

On August 28, 2000, the U.S. stock markets began the 8-month process of decimalization, which was completed by April 9, 2001. The pilot program included seven stocks on the New York Stock Exchange and six stocks on the American Stock Exchange.

One of the primary issues had been whether to price stocks in one-cent increments or five-cent increments. Under the fraction-based pricing scheme, there were only 16 price changes per $1.00. At five-cent increments, there were 20 price changes per $1.00 compared to 100 price changes per dollar for one-cent increments. Trading in smaller increments increased competition because it lowered the spread between "bid" and "ask" prices—the difference between what a buyer is willing to pay for a security and what the seller is offering for a security.

Assume that stocks are priced in five-cent increments and that on April 9, 2001, you owned 50 shares of Allied Technology, priced at $65\frac{7}{16}$ or $65.4375 per share, resulting in an equity value of

$$\$65.4375 \times 50 = \$3271.875.$$

With decimalization, the price per share must be adjusted to the nearest nickel less than the original price, or $65.40. Since the equity is unchanged, the new number of shares would be

$$\$3271.875 \div \$65.40 = 50.02866972,$$

which is reported to the nearest thousandth as 50.029 shares. For a one-cent incremental scheme, the adjusted price would have been $65.43 and the adjusted number of shares 50.006.

For Group Discussion

For each stock given, calculate the equity, the adjusted price per share, and the number of shares (to the nearest thousandth).

| | Before Decimalization | | | After Decimalization | |
Stock	Number of Shares	Price per Share	Equity	Price per Share	Number of Shares
1. Aeroflex (five-cent pricing)	50	$61\frac{7}{8}$	_____	_____	_____
2. Philadelphia Suburban (one-cent pricing)	100	$23\frac{1}{16}$	_____	_____	_____

R.2 Exercises

1. In the decimal 367.9412, name the digit that has each place value.

   (a) tens   **(b)** tenths   **(c)** thousandths

   (d) ones or units   **(e)** hundredths

2. Write a numeral that has 5 in the thousands place, 0 in the tenths place, and 4 in the ten thousandths place.

3. For the decimal number 46.249, round to the place value indicated.

   (a) hundredths   **(b)** tenths

   (c) ones or units   **(d)** tens

4. Round each decimal to the nearest thousandth.

   (a) $.\overline{8}$ **(b)** $.\overline{5}$

   (c) .9762   **(d)** .8642

5. For the sum $35.89 + 24.1$, which is the best estimate?

   A. 40   **B.** 50   **C.** 60   **D.** 70

6. For the difference $119.83 - 52.4$, which is the best estimate?

   A. 40   **B.** 50   **C.** 60   **D.** 70

7. For the product 84.9×98.3, which is the best estimate?

   A. 7000   **B.** 8000   **C.** 80,000   **D.** 70,000

8. For the quotient $9845.3 \div 97.2$, which is the best estimate?

   A. 10   **B.** 1000   **C.** 100   **D.** 10,000

Write each decimal as a fraction. Do not write in lowest terms. See Example 1.

9. .4   **10.** .6   **11.** .64   **12.** .82

13. .138   **14.** .104   **15.** 3.805   **16.** 5.166

Add or subtract as indicated. Make sure that your answer is reasonable by estimating first. Give your estimate, and then give the exact answer. See Example 2.

17. $25.32 + 109.2 + 8.574$

18. $90.527 + 32.43 + 589.83 + 399.327$

19. $28.73 - 3.12$ **20.** $46.88 - 13.45$ **21.** $43.5 - 28.17$ **22.** $345.1 - 56.31$

23. $32.56 + 47.356 + 1.8$

24. $75.22 + 123.96 + 3.897$

25. $18 - 2.789$

26. $29 - 8.582$

Multiply or divide as indicated. Make sure that your answer is reasonable by estimating first. Give your estimate, and then give the exact answer. See Examples 3–5.

27. $.2 \times .03$ **28.** $.07 \times .004$ **29.** 12.8×9.1 **30.** $34.04 \times .56$

31. $57.2 \div 8$ **32.** $73.36 \div 14$ **33.** $19.967 \div 9.74$ **34.** $44.4788 \div 5.27$

35. 57.116×100

36. $.094 \times 1000$

37. $1.62 \div 10$

38. $24.03 \div 100$

39. Explain in your own words how to add or subtract decimals.

40. Explain in your own words how to **(a)** multiply decimals and **(b)** divide decimals.

Write each fraction as a decimal. For repeating decimals, write the answer two ways: using the bar notation and rounding to the nearest thousandth. See Example 6.

41. $\dfrac{1}{8}$

42. $\dfrac{7}{8}$

43. $\dfrac{1}{4}$

44. $\dfrac{3}{4}$

45. $\dfrac{5}{9}$

46. $\dfrac{8}{9}$

47. $\dfrac{1}{6}$

48. $\dfrac{5}{6}$

49. In your own words, explain how to convert a decimal to a percent.

50. In your own words, explain how to convert a percent to a decimal.

Convert each percent to a decimal. See Examples 7(a)–(c), 8(a), and 8(b).

51. 54%

52. 39%

53. 117%

54. 189%

55. 2.4%

56. 3.1%

57. $6\dfrac{1}{4}\%$

58. $5\dfrac{1}{2}\%$

59. .8%

60. .9%

Convert each decimal to a percent. See Examples 7(d), 7(e), and 8(c)–(e).

61. .75

62. .83

63. .004

64. .005

65. 1.28

66. 2.35

67. .3

68. .6

One method of converting a fraction to a percent is to first convert the fraction to a decimal, as shown in Example 6, and then convert the decimal to a percent, as shown in Examples 7 and 8. Convert each fraction to a percent in this way.

69. $\dfrac{3}{4}$

70. $\dfrac{1}{4}$

71. $\dfrac{5}{6}$

72. $\dfrac{11}{16}$

73. Brand new tires have a tread of about $\dfrac{10}{32}$ in. By law, if 80% of the tread is worn off, the tire needs to be replaced.

   (a) What fraction of an inch of tread (in $\dfrac{1}{32}$ of an inch) indicates that a new tire is needed?

   (b) How much tread wear (in $\dfrac{1}{32}$ of an inch) remains (according to the legal limit) if the tread depth is $\dfrac{4}{32}$?

The Real
Number System

A report in June 2003 indicated that of the 844,000 eateries in the United States, the number serving fast food was 177,000. Total sales of fast food that year were projected to be $120.9 billion. Despite these numbers, a recent trend indicates that consumers are opting for more healthy food, as indicated by McDonald's first-ever quarterly loss for the last three months of 2002. During that year, its domestic sales decreased 1.5%. (*Source:* "McDonald's losses reflect nation's changing tastes," *USA Today*, Jan. 24, 2003; USDA, National Restaurant Association Center for Science in the Public Interest, "Fast Food Nation" by Felix Schlosser.)

Increases and decreases can be represented by positive and negative numbers. In this chapter we examine such numbers. In Exercises 77 and 78 of Section 1.5, we consider increases and decreases in sales in the fast food industry.

1.1 Exponents, Order of Operations, and Inequality

OBJECTIVES

1 Use exponents.

2 Use the order of operations guidelines.

3 Use more than one grouping symbol.

4 Know the meanings of ≠, <, >, ≤, and ≥.

5 Translate word statements to symbols.

6 Write a statement that changes the direction of an inequality symbol.

 Study Skills Workbook
Activity 2: Your Textbook

1 Find the value of each exponential expression.

(a) 6^2

(b) 3^5

(c) $\left(\dfrac{3}{4}\right)^2$

(d) $\left(\dfrac{1}{2}\right)^4$

(e) $(.4)^3$

In preparation for the study of algebra, we begin by introducing some basic ideas and vocabulary that we will be using throughout the course.

OBJECTIVE 1 **Use exponents.** In algebra, we use a raised dot for multiplication as shown in **Chapter R,** where we factored a number as the product of its prime factors. For example, 81 is written in prime factored form as

$$81 = 3 \cdot 3 \cdot 3 \cdot 3,$$

where the factor 3 appears four times. Repeated factors are written in an abbreviated form by using an *exponent.* The prime factored form of 81 is written with an exponent as

$$\underbrace{3 \cdot 3 \cdot 3 \cdot 3}_{\text{4 factors of 3}} = 3^4.$$

Exponent ↘ Base ↗

The number 4 is the **exponent** and 3 is the **base** in the **exponential expression** 3^4. The exponent always follows the base. Exponents are also called **powers.** We read 3^4 as "3 to the fourth power" or simply "3 to the fourth."

EXAMPLE 1 Finding Values of Exponential Expressions

Find the value of each exponential expression.

(a) $5^2 = \underbrace{5 \cdot 5}_{} = 25$

5 is used as a factor 2 times.

Read 5^2 as "5 to the second power" or, more commonly, "5 squared."

(b) $6^3 = \underbrace{6 \cdot 6 \cdot 6}_{} = 216$

6 is used as a factor 3 times.

Read 6^3 as "6 to the third power" or, more commonly, "6 cubed."

(c) $2^5 = 2 \cdot 2 \cdot 2 \cdot 2 \cdot 2 = 32$ 2 is used as a factor 5 times.

Read 2^5 as "2 to the fifth power."

(d) $7^4 = 7 \cdot 7 \cdot 7 \cdot 7 = 2401$ 7 is used as a factor 4 times.

Read 7^4 as "7 to the fourth power."

(e) $\left(\dfrac{2}{3}\right)^3 = \dfrac{2}{3} \cdot \dfrac{2}{3} \cdot \dfrac{2}{3} = \dfrac{8}{27}$ $\frac{2}{3}$ is used as a factor 3 times.

◀◀◀ **Work Problem 1 at the Side.**

CAUTION
Squaring, or raising a number to the second power, is *not* the same as doubling the number. For example,

$$3^2 \quad \textbf{means} \quad 3 \cdot 3, \quad not \quad 2 \cdot 3.$$

Thus $3^2 = 9$, not 6. Similarly, cubing, or raising a number to the third power, does *not* mean tripling the number.

OBJECTIVE 2 **Use the order of operations guidelines.** Many problems involve more than one operation. To indicate the order in which the operations should be performed, we often use *grouping symbols*. If no grouping symbols are used, we apply the order of operations discussed below.

Consider the expression $5 + 2 \cdot 3$. To show that the multiplication should be performed before the addition, parentheses can be used to write

$$5 + (2 \cdot 3) = 5 + 6 = 11.$$

If addition is to be performed first, the parentheses should group $5 + 2$ as follows.

$$(5 + 2) \cdot 3 = 7 \cdot 3 = 21$$

Other grouping symbols used in more complicated expressions are brackets $[\ \ ]$, braces $\{\ \ \}$, and fraction bars. (For example, in $\frac{8 - 2}{3}$, the expression $8 - 2$ is considered to be grouped in the numerator.)

To work problems with more than one operation, use the following **order of operations.** This order is used by most calculators and computers.

Order of Operations

If grouping symbols are present, simplify within them, innermost first (and above and below fraction bars separately), in the following order.

Step 1   Apply all **exponents.**

Step 2   Do any **multiplications** or **divisions** in the order in which they occur, working from left to right.

Step 3   Do any **additions** or **subtractions** in the order in which they occur, working from left to right.

If no grouping symbols are present, start with Step 1.

A dot has been used to show multiplication; another way to show multiplication is with parentheses. For example, $3(7)$ means $3 \cdot 7$ or 21. Also, $3(4 + 5)$ means 3 times the sum of 4 and 5. By the order of operations, the sum in parentheses must be found first, then the product.

EXAMPLE 2 **Using the Order of Operations**

Find the value of each expression.

(a) $4 \cdot 5 - 6$

Using the order of operations given in the box, first multiply 4 and 5, then subtract 6 from the product.

$$4 \cdot 5 - 6 = 20 - 6 \quad \text{Multiply.}$$
$$= 14 \quad \text{Subtract.}$$

(b) $9(6 + 11)$

Work first inside the parentheses.

$$9(6 + 11) = 9(17) \quad \text{Add inside parentheses.}$$
$$= 153 \quad \text{Multiply.}$$

Continued on Next Page

2 Find the value of each expression.

(a) $7 + 3 \cdot 8$

(b) $2 \cdot 9 + 7 \cdot 3$

(c) $7 \cdot 6 - 3(8 + 1)$

(d) $2 + 3^2 - 5$

3 Find the value of each expression.

(a) $9[(4 + 8) - 3]$

(b) $\dfrac{2(7 + 8) + 2}{3 \cdot 5 + 1}$

(c) $6 \cdot 8 + 5 \cdot 2$

Perform any multiplications from left to right, then add.

$$6 \cdot 8 + 5 \cdot 2 = 48 + 10 \qquad \text{Multiply.}$$
$$= 58 \qquad \text{Add.}$$

(d) $2(5 + 6) + 7 \cdot 3 = 2(11) + 7 \cdot 3 \qquad$ Add inside parentheses.
$$= 22 + 21 \qquad \text{Multiply.}$$
$$= 43 \qquad \text{Add.}$$

(e) $9 + 2^3 - 5$

Following the order of operations, calculate 2^3 first.

$$9 + 2^3 - 5 = 9 + 8 - 5 \qquad \text{Use the exponent.}$$
$$= 12 \qquad \text{Add, then subtract.}$$

Work Problem 2 at the Side.

OBJECTIVE 3 Use more than one grouping symbol. An expression with double parentheses, such as the expression $2(8 + 3(6 + 5))$, can be confusing. We avoid confusion by using square brackets, [ ], in place of one pair of parentheses.

EXAMPLE 3 Using Brackets and Fraction Bars as Grouping Symbols

Find the value of each expression.

(a) $2[8 + 3(6 + 5)]$

Begin inside the parentheses. Then follow the order of operations.

$$2[8 + 3(6 + 5)] = 2[8 + 3(11)] \qquad \text{Add.}$$
$$= 2[8 + 33] \qquad \text{Multiply.}$$
$$= 2[41] \qquad \text{Add.}$$
$$= 82 \qquad \text{Multiply.}$$

(b) $\dfrac{4(5 + 3) + 3}{2(3) - 1}$

Simplify the numerator and denominator separately.

$$\frac{4(5 + 3) + 3}{2(3) - 1} = \frac{4(8) + 3}{2(3) - 1} \qquad \text{Add inside parentheses.}$$
$$= \frac{32 + 3}{6 - 1} \qquad \text{Multiply.}$$
$$= \frac{35}{5} \qquad \text{Add and subtract.}$$
$$= 7 \qquad \text{Divide.}$$

Work Problem 3 at the Side.

Calculator Tip Calculators follow the order of operations given in this section. Try some of the examples to see that your calculator gives the same answers. Be sure to use the parentheses keys to insert parentheses where they are needed. To work Example 3(b) with a calculator, you must put parentheses around the numerator and the denominator.

OBJECTIVE 4 Know the meanings of ≠, <, >, ≤, and ≥.   So far we have used only the symbols of arithmetic, such as $+$, $-$, $\cdot$, and $\div$ and the equality symbol $=$. The equality symbol with a slash through it means "is *not* equal to." For example,

$$7 \neq 8$$

indicates that 7 is not equal to 8.

  If two numbers are not equal, then one of the numbers must be less than the other. The symbol $<$ represents "is less than," so "7 is less than 8" is written as

$$7 < 8.$$

Also, we write "6 is less than 9" as $6 < 9$.

  The symbol $>$ means "is greater than." We write "8 is greater than 2" as

$$8 > 2.$$

The statement "17 is greater than 11" becomes $17 > 11$.

  Keep the meanings of the symbols $<$ and $>$ clear by remembering that ***the symbol always points to the lesser number.***

$$\text{Lesser number} \rightarrow 8 < 15$$

$$15 > 8 \leftarrow \text{Lesser number}$$

Work Problem 4 at the Side.

  Two other symbols, $\leq$ and $\geq$, also represent the idea of inequality. The symbol $\leq$ means "is less than or equal to," so

$$5 \leq 9$$

means "5 is less than or equal to 9." ***If either the $<$ part or the $=$ part is true, then the inequality $\leq$ is true.*** The statement $5 \leq 9$ is true because $5 < 9$ is true. Also, $8 \leq 8$ is true because $8 = 8$ is true. But $13 \leq 9$ is not true because neither $13 < 9$ nor $13 = 9$ is true.

  The symbol $\geq$ means "is greater than or equal to," so

$$9 \geq 5$$

is true because $9 > 5$ is true.

EXAMPLE 4 Using the Symbols ≤ and ≥

Tell whether each statement is *true* or *false*.

(a) $15 \leq 20$ The statement $15 \leq 20$ is true because $15 < 20$.

(b) $12 \geq 12$ Since $12 = 12$, this statement is true.

(c) $\dfrac{6}{15} \geq \dfrac{2}{3}$

  To compare fractions, write them with a common denominator. Here, 15 is a common denominator and $\frac{2}{3} = \frac{10}{15}$. Now decide whether $\frac{6}{15} \geq \frac{10}{15}$ is true or false. Both statements $\frac{6}{15} > \frac{10}{15}$ and $\frac{6}{15} = \frac{10}{15}$ are false; therefore, $\frac{6}{15} \geq \frac{2}{3}$ is false.

Work Problem 5 at the Side.

OBJECTIVE 5 Translate word statements to symbols.   Word phrases or statements often must be converted to symbols in algebra. The next example illustrates this.

---

4 Write each statement in words, then decide whether it is *true* or *false*.

(a) $7 < 5$

(b) $12 > 6$

(c) $4 \neq 10$

(d) $28 \neq 4 \cdot 7$

5 Tell whether each statement is *true* or *false*.

(a) $30 \leq 40$

(b) $25 \geq 10$

(c) $40 \leq 10$

(d) $21 \leq 21$

(e) $3 \geq 3$

6 Write in symbols.

(a) Nine is equal to eleven minus two.

(b) Seventeen is less than thirty.

(c) Eight is not equal to ten.

(d) Fourteen is greater than twelve.

(e) Thirty is less than or equal to fifty.

(f) Two is greater than or equal to two.

7 Write each statement with the inequality symbol reversed.

(a) $8 < 10$

(b) $3 > 1$

(c) $9 \leq 15$

(d) $6 \geq 2$

EXAMPLE 5 Converting Words to Symbols

Write each word statement in symbols.

(a) Twelve **is equal to** ten **plus** two. $12 = 10 + 2$

(b) Nine **is less than** ten. $9 < 10$
Compare this with 9 less than 10, which is written $10 - 9$.

(c) Fifteen **is not equal to** eighteen. $15 \neq 18$

(d) Seven **is greater than** four. $7 > 4$

(e) Thirteen **is less than or equal to** forty. $13 \leq 40$

(f) Six **is greater than or equal to** six. $6 \geq 6$

‹‹‹ Work Problem 6 at the Side.

OBJECTIVE 6 Write a statement that changes the direction of an inequality symbol. Any statement with $<$ can be converted to one with $>$, and any statement with $>$ can be converted to one with $<$. We do this by reversing both the order of the numbers and the direction of the symbol. For example, the statement $6 < 10$ can be written as $10 > 6$.

$6 < 10$ becomes $10 > 6$

Interchange numbers.

Reverse symbol.

EXAMPLE 6 Converting between $<$ and $>$

Parts (a)–(d) show the same statements written in two equally correct ways. In each inequality, the symbol points toward the lesser number.

(a) $9 < 16$, $16 > 9$ (b) $5 > 2$, $2 < 5$

(c) $3 \leq 8$, $8 \geq 3$ (d) $12 \geq 5$, $5 \leq 12$

‹‹‹ Work Problem 7 at the Side.

Here is a summary of the symbols of equality and inequality.

Symbol	Meaning	Example
$=$	Is equal to	$.5 = \frac{1}{2}$ means .5 is equal to $\frac{1}{2}$.
$\neq$	Is not equal to	$3 \neq 7$ means 3 is not equal to 7.
$<$	Is less than	$6 < 10$ means 6 is less than 10.
$>$	Is greater than	$15 > 14$ means 15 is greater than 14.
$\leq$	Is less than or equal to	$4 \leq 8$ means 4 is less than or equal to 8.
$\geq$	Is greater than or equal to	$1 \geq 0$ means 1 is greater than or equal to 0.

CAUTION
The symbols of equality and inequality are used to write mathematical *sentences.* They differ from the symbols for operations ($+$, $-$, $\cdot$, and $\div$), discussed earlier, which are used to write mathematical *expressions* that represent a number. For example, compare the sentence $4 < 10$, which gives the relationship between 4 and 10, with the expression $4 + 10$, which tells how to operate on 4 and 10 to get the number 14.

1.1 Exercises

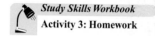
Decide whether each statement is true *or* false. *If it is* false, *explain why.*

1. Exponents are also called powers.

2. Some grouping symbols are $+$, $-$, $\cdot$, and $\div$.

3. When evaluated, $4 + 3(8 - 2)$ is equal to 42.

4. $3^3 = 9$

5. The statement "4 is 12 less than 16" is interpreted $4 = 12 - 16$.

6. The statement "6 is 4 less than 10" is interpreted $6 < 10 - 4$.

Find the value of each exponential expression. See Example 1.

7. 7^2

8. 4^2

9. 12^2

10. 14^2

11. 4^3

12. 5^3

13. 10^3

14. 11^3

15. 3^4

16. 6^4

17. 4^5

18. 3^5

19. $\left(\dfrac{2}{3}\right)^4$

20. $\left(\dfrac{3}{4}\right)^3$

21. $(.04)^3$

22. $(.05)^4$

23. When evaluating $(4^2 + 3^3)^4$, what is the *last* exponent that would be applied? Explain your answer.

24. Which are not grouping symbols—parentheses, brackets, fraction bars, exponents?

Find the value of each expression. See Examples 2 and 3.

25. $13 + 9 \cdot 5$

26. $11 + 7 \cdot 6$

27. $20 - 4 \cdot 3 + 5$

28. $18 - 7 \cdot 2 + 6$

29. $9 \cdot 5 - 13$

30. $7 \cdot 6 - 11$

31. $18 - 2 + 3$

32. $22 - 8 + 9$

33. $\dfrac{1}{4} \cdot \dfrac{2}{3} + \dfrac{2}{5} \cdot \dfrac{11}{3}$

34. $\dfrac{9}{4} \cdot \dfrac{2}{3} + \dfrac{4}{5} \cdot \dfrac{5}{3}$

35. $9 \cdot 4 - 8 \cdot 3$

36. $11 \cdot 4 + 10 \cdot 3$

37. $2.5(1.9) + 4.3(7.3)$

38. $4.3(1.2) + 2.1(8.5)$

39. $10 + 40 \div 5 \cdot 2$

40. $12 + 8^2 \div 8 - 4$

41. $18 - 2(3 + 4)$

42. $30 - 3(4 + 2)$

43. $5[3 + 4(2^2)]$

44. $6\left[\dfrac{3}{4} + 8\left(\dfrac{1}{2}\right)^3\right]$

45. $\left(\dfrac{3}{2}\right)^2\left[\left(11 + \dfrac{1}{3}\right) - 6\right]$

46. $4^2[(13 + 4) - 8]$

47. $\dfrac{8 + 6(3^2 - 1)}{3 \cdot 2 - 2}$

48. $\dfrac{8 + 2(8^2 - 4)}{4 \cdot 3 - 10}$

49. $\dfrac{4(7+2)+8(8-3)}{6(4-2)-2^2}$

50. $\dfrac{6(5+1)-9(1+1)}{5(8-4)-2^3}$

Tell whether each statement is true *or* false. *In Exercises 53–62, first simplify each expression involving an operation. See Example 4.*

51. $8 \geq 17$

52. $10 \geq 41$

53. $17 \leq 18-1$

54. $12 \geq 10+2$

55. $6 \cdot 8 + 6 \cdot 6 \geq 0$

56. $4 \cdot 20 - 16 \cdot 5 \geq 0$

57. $6[5+3(4+2)] \leq 70$

58. $6[2+3(2+5)] \leq 135$

59. $\dfrac{9(7-1)-8 \cdot 2}{4(6-1)} > 3$

60. $\dfrac{2(5+3)+2 \cdot 2}{2(4-1)} > 1$

61. $8 \leq 4^2 - 2^2$

62. $10^2 - 8^2 > 6^2$

Write each word statement in symbols. See Example 5.

63. Fifteen is equal to five plus ten.

64. Twelve is equal to twenty minus eight.

65. Nine is greater than five minus four.

66. Ten is greater than six plus one.

67. Sixteen is not equal to nineteen.

68. Three is not equal to four.

69. Two is less than or equal to three.

70. Five is less than or equal to nine.

Write each statement in words and decide whether it is true *or* false. *(Hint: To compare fractions, write them with the same denominator.)*

71. $7 < 19$

72. $9 < 10$

73. $\dfrac{1}{3} \neq \dfrac{3}{10}$

74. $\dfrac{10}{7} \neq \dfrac{3}{2}$

75. $8 \geq 11$

76. $4 \leq 2$

Write each statement with the inequality symbol reversed. See Example 6.

77. $5 < 30$

78. $8 > 4$

79. $12 \geq 3$

80. $25 \leq 41$

The table shows the number of pupils per teacher in selected states. Use this table to answer the questions in Exercises 81–83.

81. Which states had a figure greater than 13.9?

82. Which states had a figure that was at most 14.7?

83. For which states were scores not less than 13.9?

U.S. PUBLIC SCHOOLS, FALL 2001

State	Pupils per Teacher
Alaska	16.7
Texas	14.7
California	20.5
Wyoming	12.5
Maine	12.3
Idaho	17.8
Missouri	13.9

Source: National Center for Education Statistics.

1.2 Variables, Expressions, and Equations

To make general statements about numbers in algebra, letters called **variables** are used. Different numbers can replace the variables to form specific statements. For example, in **Section 1.7** we see that

$$a + b = b + a.$$

This statement is true for any replacements of the variables a and b, such as 2 for a and 5 for b, which gives the true statement

$$2 + 5 = 5 + 2.$$

An **algebraic expression** is a collection of numbers, variables, operation symbols, and grouping symbols, such as parentheses, square brackets, or fraction bars.

$$x + 5, \quad 2m - 9, \quad \text{and} \quad 8p^2 + 6(p - 2) \qquad \text{Algebraic expressions}$$

In $2m - 9$, the $2m$ means $2 \cdot m$, the product of 2 and m; $8p^2$ represents the product of 8 and p^2. Also, $6(p - 2)$ means the product of 6 and $p - 2$.

OBJECTIVE 1 Evaluate algebraic expressions, given values for the variables. An algebraic expression has different numerical values for different values of the variables.

EXAMPLE 1 Evaluating Expressions Given Values of the Variable

Find the value of each algebraic expression if $m = 5$ and then if $m = 9$.

(a) $8m$

$8m = 8 \cdot 5$	Let $m = 5$.	$8m = 8 \cdot 9$	Let $m = 9$.
$= 40$	Multiply.	$= 72$	Multiply.

(b) $3m^2$

$3m^2 = 3 \cdot 5^2$	Let $m = 5$.	$3m^2 = 3 \cdot 9^2$	Let $m = 9$.
$= 3 \cdot 25$	Square.	$= 3 \cdot 81$	Square.
$= 75$	Multiply.	$= 243$	Multiply.

CAUTION
In Example 1(b), notice that $3m^2$ means $3 \cdot m^2$; it *does not* mean $3m \cdot 3m$. ***Unless parentheses are used, the exponent refers only to the variable or number just before it.*** To write $3m \cdot 3m$ with exponents, use parentheses: $3m \cdot 3m = (3m)^2$.

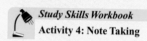

Work Problem 1 at the Side.

EXAMPLE 2 Evaluating Expressions with More Than One Variable

Find the value of each expression if $x = 5$ and $y = 3$.

(a) $2x + 5y = 2 \cdot 5 + 5 \cdot 3$ Replace x with 5 and y with 3.

$\qquad\qquad = 10 + 15$ Multiply.

$\qquad\qquad = 25$ Add.

Continued on Next Page

Study Skills Workbook
Activity 4: Note Taking

1 Find the value of each expression if $p = 3$.

(a) $6p$

(b) $p + 12$

(c) $5p^2$

ANSWERS
1. (a) 18   **(b)** 15   **(c)** 45

2 Find the value of each expression if $x = 6$ and $y = 9$.

(a) $4x + 7y$

(b) $\dfrac{9x - 8y}{2x - y} = \dfrac{9 \cdot 5 - 8 \cdot 3}{2 \cdot 5 - 3}$ Replace x with 5 and y with **3**.

$\qquad = \dfrac{45 - 24}{10 - 3}$ Multiply.

$\qquad = \dfrac{21}{7}$ Subtract.

$\qquad = 3$ Divide.

(c) $x^2 - 2y^2 = 5^2 - 2 \cdot 3^2$ Replace x with 5 and y with **3**.

$\qquad = 25 - 2 \cdot 9$ Use the exponents.

$\qquad = 25 - 18$ Multiply.

$\qquad = 7$ Subtract.

▸▸▸ **Work Problem 2 at the Side.**

Calculator Tip   An Introduction to Calculators in the front of this book explains how to perform arithmetic operations and evaluate exponentials with a calculator.

(b) $\dfrac{4x - 2y}{x + 1}$

OBJECTIVE 2 Convert phrases from words to algebraic expressions.

> **PROBLEM-SOLVING HINT**
> Sometimes variables must be used to change word phrases into algebraic expressions. This process will be important later for solving applied problems.

EXAMPLE 3 Using Variables to Change Word Phrases into Algebraic Expressions

Change each word phrase to an algebraic expression. Use x as the variable to represent the number.

(c) $2x^2 + y^2$

(a) The **sum** of a number and 9
   "Sum" is the answer to an addition problem. This phrase translates as

$$x + 9 \quad \text{or} \quad 9 + x.$$

(b) 7 **minus** a number
   "Minus" indicates subtraction, so the translation is

$$7 - x.$$

Note that $x - 7$ would *not* be correct because we cannot subtract in either order and get the same results.

(c) A number **subtracted from** 12
   Since a number is subtracted *from* 12, write this as

$$12 - x.$$

Compare this result with "12 subtracted from a number," which is $x - 12$.

Continued on Next Page

ANSWERS

2. (a) 87 (b) $\dfrac{6}{7}$ (c) 153

(d) The **product** of 11 and a number

$$11 \cdot x \quad \text{or} \quad 11x$$

(e) 5 **divided by** a number

$$5 \div x \quad \text{or} \quad \frac{5}{x} \qquad \frac{x}{5} \text{ would not be correct here.}$$

(f) The **product of** 2 and the **difference** between a number and 8

$$2(x - 8)$$

We are multiplying 2 times another number. This number is the difference between a number and 8, written $x - 8$. Using parentheses around this difference, the final expression is $2(x - 8)$.

> **CAUTION**
> Notice that in translating the words "the difference between a number and 8" the order is kept the same: $x - 8$. "The difference between 8 and a number" would be written $8 - x$.

> **Work Problem 3 at the Side.** ▶▶▶

OBJECTIVE 3 Identify solutions of equations. An **equation** is a statement that two expressions are equal. Examples of equations are

$$x + 4 = 11, \quad 2y = 16, \quad \text{and} \quad 4p + 1 = 25 - p. \qquad \text{Equations}$$

To **solve** an equation, we must find all values of the variable that make the equation true. Such values of the variable are called the **solutions** of the equation.

EXAMPLE 4 Deciding Whether a Number Is a Solution of an Equation

Decide whether the given number is a solution of the equation.

(a) Is 7 a solution of $5p + 1 = 36$?

$$5p + 1 = 36$$
$$5 \cdot 7 + 1 = 36 \qquad \text{Replace } p \text{ with 7.}$$
$$35 + 1 = 36 \qquad \text{Multiply.}$$
$$36 = 36 \qquad \text{True}$$

The number 7 is a solution of the equation.

(b) Is $\frac{14}{3}$ a solution of $9m - 6 = 32$?

$$9m - 6 = 32$$
$$9 \cdot \frac{14}{3} - 6 = 32 \qquad \text{Replace } m \text{ with } \frac{14}{3}.$$
$$42 - 6 = 32 \qquad \text{Multiply.}$$
$$36 = 32 \qquad \text{False}$$

The number $\frac{14}{3}$ is not a solution of the equation.

> **Work Problem 4 at the Side.** ▶▶▶

3 Write as an algebraic expression. Let x represent the variable.

(a) The sum of 5 and a number

(b) A number minus 4

(c) A number subtracted from 48

(d) The product of 6 and a number

(e) 9 multiplied by the sum of a number and 5

4 Decide whether the given number is a solution of the equation.

(a) $p - 1 = 3; 2$

(b) $2k + 3 = 15; 7$

(c) $8p - 11 = 5; 2$

ANSWERS
3. **(a)** $5 + x$ **(b)** $x - 4$ **(c)** $48 - x$
   (d) $6x$ **(e)** $9(x + 5)$
4. **(a)** no **(b)** no **(c)** yes

5 Change each sentence to an equation. Let x represent the number.

(a) Three times the sum of a number and 13 is 19.

(b) Five times a number is subtracted from 21, giving 15.

6 Decide whether each is an *equation* or an *expression*.

(a) $2x + 5y - 7$

(b) $\dfrac{3x - 1}{5}$

(c) $2x + 5 = 7$

(d) $\dfrac{x}{y - 3} = 4x$

OBJECTIVE 4 Translate word statements to equations. We have seen how to translate phrases from words to expressions. Sentences given in words are translated as equations.

EXAMPLE 5 Translating Word Sentences to Equations

Change each word sentence to an equation. Let x represent the number.

(a) Twice the sum of a number and four is six.
"Twice" means two times. The word *is* suggests equals. With x representing the number, translate as follows.

$$2(x + 4) = 6$$

(b) Nine more than five times a number is 49.
Use x to represent the unknown number. Start with $5x$ and then add 9 to it. The word *is* translates as $=$.

$$5x + 9 = 49$$

(c) Seven less than three times a number is eleven.
Here, 7 is *subtracted* from three times a number to get 11.

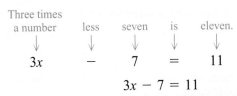

$$3x - 7 = 11$$

⫷⫷⫷ Work Problem 5 at the Side.

OBJECTIVE 5 Distinguish between *expressions* and *equations*. Students often have trouble distinguishing between equations and expressions. *Remember that an equation is a sentence (with an $=$ symbol); an expression is a phrase that represents a number.*

$$4x + 5 = 9 \qquad\qquad 4x + 5$$

Equation (to solve)   Expression (to simplify or evaluate)

EXAMPLE 6 Distinguishing between Equations and Expressions

Decide whether each is an *equation* or an *expression*.

(a) $2x - 5y$

There is no equals sign, so this is an expression.

(b) $2x = 5y$

Because of the equals sign, this is an equation.

⫷⫷⫷ Work Problem 6 at the Side.

ANSWERS
5. (a) $3(x + 13) = 19$ (b) $21 - 5x = 15$
6. (a) expression   (b) expression
(c) equation   (d) equation

1.2 Exercises

FOR EXTRA HELP Addison-Wesley Math Tutor Center   MathXL   Digital Video Tutor CD 1 Videotape 1   Student's Solutions Manual   *MyMathLab* MyMathLab   Interactmath.com

Fill in each blank with the correct response.

1. If $x = 3$, then the value of $x + 8$ is _____ .

2. If $x = 1$ and $y = 2$, then the value of $5xy$ is _____ .

3. "The sum of 13 and x" is represented by the expression _____ . If $x = 3$, the value of that expression is _____ .

4. Will the equation $x = x + 5$ ever have a solution? _____

5. $2x + 6$ is an _____ , while $2x + 6 = 8$ is an _____ .
   (equation/expression)   (equation/expression)

Exercises 6–10 cover some of the concepts introduced in this section. Give a short explanation for each.

6. Why is $2x^3$ not the same as $2x \cdot 2x \cdot 2x$? Explain, using an exponent to write $2x \cdot 2x \cdot 2x$.

7. If the words *more than* in Example 5(b) were changed to *less than,* how would the equation be changed?

8. Explain in your own words why, when evaluating the expression $4x^2$ for $x = 3$, 3 must be squared *before* multiplying by 4.

9. There are many pairs of values of x and y for which $2x + y$ will equal 6. Name two such pairs and describe how you determined them.

10. Suppose that for the equation $3x - y = 9$, the value of x is given as 4. What would be the corresponding value of y? How do you know this?

*Find the numerical value of each expression if **(a)** $x = 4$ and **(b)** $x = 6$. See Example 1.*

11. $4x^2$

(a)   (b)

12. $5x^2$

(a)   (b)

13. $\dfrac{3x - 5}{2x}$

(a)   (b)

14. $\dfrac{4x - 1}{3x}$

(a)   (b)

15. $\dfrac{6.459x}{2.7}$ (to the nearest thousandth)

(a)   (b)

16. $\dfrac{.74x^2}{.85}$ (to the nearest thousandth)

(a)   (b)

17. $3x^2 + x$

(a)   (b)

18. $2x + x^2$

(a)   (b)

*Find the numerical value of each expression if **(a)** $x = 2$ and $y = 1$ and **(b)** $x = 1$ and $y = 5$. See Example 2.*

19. $3(x + 2y)$

(a)   (b)

20. $2(2x + y)$

(a)   (b)

21. $x + \dfrac{4}{y}$

(a)   (b)

22. $y + \dfrac{8}{x}$

(a)   (b)

23. $\dfrac{x}{2} + \dfrac{y}{3}$

(a)   (b)

24. $\dfrac{x}{5} + \dfrac{y}{4}$

(a)   (b)

25. $\dfrac{2x + 4y - 6}{5y + 2}$

(a)   (b)

26. $\dfrac{4x + 3y - 1}{2x + y}$

(a)   (b)

27. $2y^2 + 5x$

(a)   (b)

28. $6x^2 + 4y$

(a)   (b)

29. $\dfrac{3x + y^2}{2x + 3y}$

(a)   (b)

30. $\dfrac{x^2 + 1}{4x + 5y}$

(a)   (b)

31. $.841x^2 + .32y^2$

    (a)   **(b)**

32. $.941x^2 + .2y^2$

    (a)   **(b)**

Change each word phrase to an algebraic expression. Use x to represent the number.
See Example 3.

33. Twelve times a number

34. Thirteen added to a number

35. Two subtracted from a number

36. Eight subtracted from a number

37. One-third of a number, subtracted from seven

38. One-fifth of a number, subtracted from fourteen

39. The difference between twice a number and 6

40. The difference between 6 and half a number

41. 12 divided by the sum of a number and 3

42. The difference between a number and 5, divided by 12

43. The product of 6 and four less than a number

$6(x-4)$

44. The product of 9 and five more than a number

45. In the phrase "four more than the product of a number and 6," does the word *and* signify the operation of addition? Explain.

46. Suppose that the directions on a test read "Solve the following expressions." How would you politely correct the person who wrote these directions?

Decide whether the given number is a solution of the equation. See Example 4.

47. Is 7 a solution of $x - 5 = 12$?

48. Is 10 a solution of $x + 6 = 15$?

49. Is 1 a solution of $5x + 2 = 7$?

50. Is 1 a solution of $3x + 5 = 8$?

51. Is $\frac{1}{5}$ a solution of $6x + 4x + 9 = 11$?

52. Is $\frac{12}{5}$ a solution of $2x + 3x + 8 = 20$?

53. Is 3 a solution of $2y + 3(y - 2) = 14$?

54. Is 2 a solution of $6a + 2(a + 3) = 14$?

55. Is $\dfrac{1}{3}$ a solution of $\dfrac{z + 4}{2 - z} = \dfrac{13}{5}$?

56. Is $\dfrac{13}{4}$ a solution of $\dfrac{x + 6}{x - 2} = \dfrac{37}{5}$?

57. Is 4.3 a solution of $3r^2 - 2 = 53.47$?

58. Is 3.7 a solution of $2x^2 + 1 = 28.38$?

Change each sentence to an equation. Use x to represent the number. See Example 5.

59. The sum of a number and 8 is 18.

60. A number minus three equals 1.

61. Five more than twice a number is 5.

62. The product of 2 and the sum of a number and 5 is 14.

63. Sixteen minus three-fourths of a number is 13.

64. The sum of six-fifths of a number and 2 is 14.

65. Three times a number is equal to 8 more than twice the number.

66. Twelve divided by a number equals $\frac{1}{3}$ times that number.

Identify each as an expression *or an* equation. *See Example 6.*

67. $3x + 2(x - 4)$

68. $5y - (3y + 6)$

69. $7t + 2(t + 1) = 4$

70. $9r + 3(r - 4) = 2$

RELATING CONCEPTS (EXERCISES 71–74) For Individual or Group Work

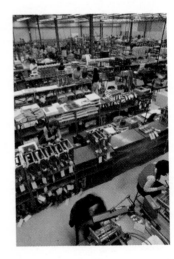

A **mathematical model** *is an equation that describes the relationship between two quantities. For example, based on data from the U.S. Bureau of Labor Statistics, average hourly earnings of production workers in manufacturing industries in the United States from 1996 through 2002 are approximated by the equation* $y = .494x - 974.0$, *where x represents the year and y represents the hourly earnings in dollars. Use this model to approximate the hourly earnings during each year. Compare with the actual earnings given in parentheses.*

71. 1997   ($12.49)

72. 2000   ($14.00)

73. 2001   ($14.53)

74. 2002   ($14.95)

1.3 Real Numbers and the Number Line

OBJECTIVE **1** **Classify numbers and graph them on number lines.**
The numbers used for counting are called the **natural numbers.** We use set braces, { }, to denote the elements of a set.

Natural Numbers

$$\{1, 2, 3, 4, 5, \dots\}$$

In **Chapter R,** we introduced the set of **whole numbers.**

Whole Numbers

$$\{0, 1, 2, 3, 4, 5, \dots\}$$

These numbers, along with many others, can be represented on a **number line** like the one in Figure 1. We draw a number line by choosing any point on the line and labeling it 0. Choose any point to the right of 0 and label it 1. The distance between 0 and 1 gives a unit of measure used to locate other points, as shown in Figure 1. The points labeled in Figure 1 correspond to the first few whole numbers.

The indicated points correspond to natural numbers.

The indicated points correspond to whole numbers.

Be sure that number lines are properly labeled.

Figure 1

The natural numbers are located to the right of 0 on the number line. But numbers may also be placed to the left of 0. For each natural number we can place a corresponding number to the left of 0. These numbers, written $-1, -2, -3, -4$, and so on, are shown in Figure 2. Each is the **opposite** or **negative** of a natural number. The natural numbers, their opposites, and 0 form a new set of numbers called the **integers.**

Integers

$$\{\dots, -3, -2, -1, 0, 1, 2, 3, \dots\}$$

Zero
(neither positive nor negative)

Negative numbers   Positive numbers

Opposites
The points correspond to integers.

Figure 2

❶ Use an integer to express the number(s) in each application.

(a) Erin discovers that she has spent $53 more than she has in her checking account.

There are many practical applications of negative numbers. For example, a Fahrenheit temperature on a cold January day might be $-10°$, and a business that spends more than it takes in has a negative "profit."

EXAMPLE 1 Using Negative Numbers in Applications

Use an integer to express the number in each application.

(a) The lowest Fahrenheit temperature ever recorded in meteorological records was 129° below zero at Vostok, Antarctica, on July 21, 1983. (*Source: World Almanac and Book of Facts, 2004.*)
Use $-129°$ because "below zero" indicates a negative number.

(b) The shore surrounding the Dead Sea is 1348 ft below sea level. (*Source: World Almanac and Book of Facts, 2004.*)
Again, "below sea level" indicates a negative number, -1348.

◀◀◀ **Work Problem 1 at the Side.**

(b) The record high Fahrenheit temperature in the United States was 134° in Death Valley, California on July 10, 1913. (*Source: World Almanac and Book of Facts, 2004.*)

Not all numbers are integers. For example, $\frac{1}{2}$ is not; it is a number halfway between the integers 0 and 1. Also, $3\frac{1}{4}$ is not an integer. These numbers and others that are quotients of integers are **rational numbers.** (The name comes from the word *ratio,* which indicates a quotient.)

Rational Numbers

{numbers that can be written as quotients of integers, with denominators not 0}

(c) A football team gained 5 yd, then lost 10 yd on the next play.

Since any integer can be written as the quotient of itself and 1, all integers are also rational numbers. For example, $-5 = \frac{-5}{1}$. A decimal number that comes to an end (terminates), such as .23, is a rational number. For example, $.23 = \frac{23}{100}$. Decimal numbers that repeat in a fixed block of digits, such as $.3333\ldots = .\overline{3}$ and $.454545\ldots = .\overline{45}$, are also rational numbers. For example, $.\overline{3} = \frac{1}{3}$.

As shown in Figures 1 and 2 on the preceding page, to **graph** a number, we place a dot on the number line at the point that corresponds to the number. The number is called the **coordinate** of the point. Think of the graph of a set of numbers as a picture of the set.

❷ Graph each number on the number line.

$$-3, \frac{17}{8}, -2.75, 1\frac{1}{2}, -\frac{3}{4}$$

EXAMPLE 2 Graphing Rational Numbers

Graph each number on the number line.

$$-\frac{3}{2}, \quad -\frac{2}{3}, \quad \frac{1}{2}, \quad 1\frac{1}{3}, \quad \frac{23}{8}, \quad 3\frac{1}{4}$$

To locate the improper fractions on the number line, write them as mixed numbers or decimals. The graph is shown in Figure 3.

Figure 3

◀◀◀ **Work Problem 2 at the Side.**

Although many numbers are rational, not all are. For example, a square that measures one unit on a side has a diagonal whose length is the square root of 2, written $\sqrt{2}$. See Figure 4. It can be shown that $\sqrt{2}$ cannot be written as a quotient of integers. Because of this, $\sqrt{2}$ is not rational; it is **irrational.** Other examples of irrational numbers are $\sqrt{3}$, $\sqrt{7}$, $-\sqrt{10}$, and π (the ratio of the circumference of a circle to its diameter).

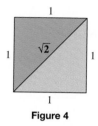

Figure 4

Irrational Numbers
{nonrational numbers represented by points on the number line}

The decimal form of an irrational number neither terminates nor repeats. Irrational numbers are discussed in **Chapter 8.**

Both rational and irrational numbers can be represented by points on the number line and are called **real numbers.**

Real Numbers
{all numbers that are either rational or irrational}

All the numbers mentioned so far are real numbers. The relationships between the various types of numbers are shown in Figure 5. Notice that any real number is either a rational number or an irrational number.

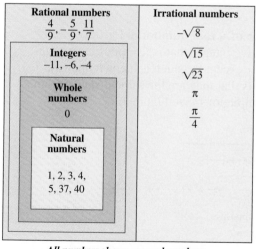

All numbers shown are real numbers.

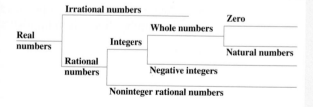

Figure 5

❸ Tell whether each statement is *true* or *false*.

(a) $-2 < 4$

(b) $6 > -3$

(c) $-9 < -12$

(d) $-4 \geq -1$

(e) $-6 \leq 0$

OBJECTIVE ❷ Tell which of two real numbers is less than the other. Given any two whole numbers, we can tell which number is less than the other. But what about two negative numbers, as in the set of integers? Moving from 0 to the right along a number line, the positive numbers corresponding to the points on the number line *increase*. For example, $8 < 12$, and 8 is to the left of 12 on a number line. We extend this ordering to all real numbers.

> **Ordering of the Real Numbers**
>
> For any two real numbers a and b, **a is less than b** if a is to the left of b on a number line.
>
>
>
> **a is to the left of b,**
> **$a < b$.**

This means that any negative number is less than 0, and any negative number is less than any positive number. Also, 0 is less than any positive number.

EXAMPLE 3 **Determining the Order of Real Numbers**

Is it true that $-3 < -1$?

To find out, locate -3 and -1 on a number line, as shown in Figure 6. Because -3 is to the left of -1 on the number line, -3 is less than -1. The statement $-3 < -1$ is true.

−3 is to the left of −1, so −3 < −1.

Figure 6

◀◀◀ Work Problem 3 at the Side.

OBJECTIVE ❸ Find the opposite of a real number. Earlier, we saw that every positive integer has a negative integer that is its opposite or negative. This is true for every real number except 0, which is its own opposite.* A characteristic of pairs of opposites is that they are the same distance from 0 on the number line but in opposite directions. See Figure 7.

Pairs of opposites

Figure 7

ANSWERS
3. **(a)** true **(b)** true **(c)** false
(d) false **(e)** true

_____

* The opposite (or negative) of a number is also called the *additive inverse* of the number, as we shall see in **Section 1.7.**

We indicate the opposite of a number by writing the symbol − in front of the number. For example, the opposite of 7 is −7 (read "negative 7"). We could write the opposite of −4 as −(−4), but we know that 4 is the opposite of −4. Since a number can have only one opposite, −(−4) and 4 must represent the same number, so

$$-(-4) = 4.$$

This idea can be generalized.

Double Negative Rule

For any real number a,

$$-(-a) = a.$$

The following chart shows several numbers and their opposites.

Number	Opposite
−4	−(−4), or 4
−3	3
0	0
5	−5
19	−19

The chart suggests the following rule.

Except for 0, the opposite of a number is found by changing the sign of the number.

> **Work Problem 4 at the Side.** ▶▶▶

OBJECTIVE 4 Find the absolute value of a real number. As previously mentioned, opposites are numbers the same distance from 0 on the number line but on opposite sides of 0. Another way to say this is to say that opposites have the same *absolute value*. The **absolute value** of a number is the undirected distance between 0 and the number on the number line. The symbol for the absolute value of the number a is $|a|$, read "the absolute value of a." For example, the distance between 2 and 0 on the number line is 2 units, so

$$|2| = 2.$$

Also, the distance between −2 and 0 on the number line is 2, so

$$|-2| = 2.$$

Since distance is a physical measurement, which is never negative, we can make the following statement.

The absolute value of a number can never be negative.

---

④ Find the opposite of each number.

(a) 6

(b) 15

(c) −9

(d) −12

(e) 0

5 Simplify.

(a) $|-6|$

(b) $|9|$

(c) $-|15|$

(d) $-|-9|$

(e) $|9-4|$

(f) $-|32-2|$

For example,

$$|12| = 12 \quad \text{and} \quad |-12| = 12$$

because both 12 and -12 lie at a distance of 12 units from 0 on the number line. Since the distance of 0 from 0 is 0 units, we have

$$|0| = 0.$$

EXAMPLE 4 Evaluating Absolute Value

Simplify.

(a) $|5| = 5$ **(b)** $|-5| = 5$

(c) $-|-5| = -(5) = -5$ Replace $|-5|$ with 5.

(d) $-|-13| = -(13) = -13$

(e) $|8 - 5|$

Simplify within the absolute value bars first.

$$|8 - 5| = |3| = 3$$

(f) $-|8 - 5| = -|3| = -3$

(g) $-|12 - 3| = -|9| = -9$

Parts (e)–(g) in Example 4 show that absolute value bars also act as grouping symbols. You must perform any operations within absolute value bars before finding the absolute value.

◀◀◀ **Work Problem 5 at the Side.**

ANSWERS
5. **(a)** 6 **(b)** 9 **(c)** -15 **(d)** -9
   (e) 5 **(f)** -30

1.3 Exercises

In Exercises 1–6, give an example of a number that satisfies each given condition.

1. An integer between 3.6 and 4.6

2. A rational number between 2.8 and 2.9

3. A whole number that is not positive and is less than 1

4. A whole number greater than 3.5

5. An irrational number that is between $\sqrt{12}$ and $\sqrt{14}$

6. A real number that is neither negative nor positive

List all numbers from each set that are (a) natural numbers, (b) whole numbers, (c) integers, (d) rational numbers, (e) irrational numbers, (f) real numbers.

7. $\left\{-9, -\sqrt{7}, -1\frac{1}{4}, -\frac{3}{5}, 0, \sqrt{5}, 3, 5.9, 7\right\}$

8. $\left\{-5.3, -5, -\sqrt{3}, -1, -\frac{1}{9}, 0, 1.2, 4, \sqrt{12}\right\}$

Use an integer to express each number representing a change in the following applications. See Example 1.

9. In all of 2003, there were 1.85 million housing starts. In December 2003, the number of housing starts in the United States increased from the previous month by about 40,000 units. (*Source:* http://money.cnn.com)

10. There were 16,900 fewer Honda Civics produced in the United States in 2002 compared to 2001. (*Source: Ward's AutoInfoBank.*)

11. Between 1995 and 2001, the population of the District of Columbia decreased by about 9000. (*Source:* U.S. Bureau of the Census.)

12. In 2002, Taiwan produced 129,313 more passenger cars than trucks. (*Source:* Automotive News Data Center and Marketing Systems.)

Graph each group of numbers on a number line. See Example 2.

13. $0, 3, -5, -6$

14. $2, 6, -2, -1$

15. $-2, -6, -4, 3, 4$

16. $-5, -3, -2, 0, 4$

17. $\frac{1}{4}, 2\frac{1}{2}, -3\frac{4}{5}, -4, -\frac{13}{8}$

18. $5\frac{1}{4}, \frac{41}{9}, -2\frac{1}{3}, 0, -3\frac{2}{5}$

Select the lesser number in each pair. See Example 3.

19. $-11, -4$

20. $-9, -16$

21. $-21, 1$

22. $-57, 3$

23. $0, -100$

24. $-215, 0$

25. $-\dfrac{2}{3}, -\dfrac{1}{4}$

26. $-\dfrac{3}{8}, -\dfrac{9}{16}$

Decide whether each statement is true *or* false. *See Example 3.*

27. $8 < -16$

28. $12 < -24$

29. $-3 < -2$

30. $-10 < -9$

*For each number, **(a)** find its opposite and **(b)** find its absolute value.*

31. -2

   (a)   **(b)**

32. -8

   (a)   **(b)**

33. 6

   (a)   **(b)**

34. 11

   (a)   **(b)**

35. $-\dfrac{3}{4}$

   (a)   **(b)**

36. $-\dfrac{1}{3}$

   (a)   **(b)**

Simplify. See Example 4.

37. $|-7|$

38. $|-3|$

39. $-|12|$

40. $-|23|$

41. $-\left|-\dfrac{2}{3}\right|$

42. $-\left|-\dfrac{4}{5}\right|$

43. $|13 - 4|$

44. $|8 - 7|$

Decide whether each statement is true *or* false.

45. $|-8| < 7$

46. $|-6| \geq -|6|$

47. $4 \leq |4|$

48. $-|-3| > 2$

49. Students often say "The absolute value of a number is always positive." Is this true? If not, explain.

50. If the absolute value of a number is equal to the number itself, what must be true about the number?

To answer the questions in Exercises 51–54, refer to the table, which gives the changes in producer price indexes for two recent periods.

51. What commodity for which period represents the greatest decrease?

52. What commodity for which period represents the least change?

Commodity	Change from 2000 to 2001	Change from 2001 to 2002
Food	.9	−1.4
Shelter	.4	0
Fuel/other utilities	1.8	−13.3
Apparel	−.5	−.8
Private transportation	−5.5	−1.4
Public transportation	−5.5	−2.0
Medical care	.5	.1

Source: U.S. Bureau of Labor Statistics.

53. Which has lesser absolute value, the change for apparel from 2000 to 2001 or from 2001 to 2002?

54. Which has greater absolute value, the change for public transportation from 2000 to 2001 or from 2001 to 2002?

1.4 Adding Real Numbers

OBJECTIVE 1 Add two numbers with the same sign. We can use the number line to explain addition of real numbers. Later, we will give the rules for addition. Recall that the answer to an addition problem is called the **sum.**

EXAMPLE 1 Adding with the Number Line

Use the number line to find the sum $2 + 3$.

Add the positive numbers 2 and 3 by starting at 0 and drawing an arrow two units to the *right,* as shown in Figure 8. This arrow represents the number 2 in the sum $2 + 3$. Next, from the right end of this arrow draw another arrow three units to the right. The number below the end of this second arrow is 5, so $2 + 3 = 5$.

Figure 8

EXAMPLE 2 Adding with the Number Line

Use the number line to find the sum $-2 + (-4)$. (Parentheses are placed around the -4 to avoid the confusing use of $+$ and $-$ next to each other.)

To add the negative numbers -2 and -4 on the number line, we start at 0 and draw an arrow two units to the *left,* as shown in Figure 9. From the left end of this first arrow, we draw a second arrow four units to the left. We draw the arrow to the left to represent the addition of the *negative* number, -4. The number below the end of this second arrow is -6, so $-2 + (-4) = -6$.

Figure 9

Work Problem 1 at the Side. ▶▶▶

In Example 2, we found that the sum of the two negative numbers -2 and -4 is a negative number whose distance from 0 is the sum of the distance of -2 from 0 and the distance of -4 from 0. That is, ***the sum of two negative numbers is the negative of the sum of their absolute values.***

$$-2 + (-4) = -(|-2| + |-4|) = -(2 + 4) = -6$$

To add two numbers having the same sign, add the absolute values of the numbers. Give the result the same sign as the numbers being added.

Example: $-4 + (-3) = -7$.

OBJECTIVES

1 Add two numbers with the same sign.

2 Add numbers with different signs.

3 Add mentally.

4 Use the order of operations with real numbers.

5 Translate words and phrases that indicate addition.

1 Use a number line to find each sum.

(a) $1 + 4$

(b) $-2 + (-5)$

ANSWERS

1. (a) $1 + 4 = 5$

(b) $-2 + (-5) = -7$

② Find each sum.

(a) $-7 + (-3)$

(b) $-12 + (-18)$

(c) $-15 + (-4)$

③ Use a number line to find each sum.

(a) $6 + (-3)$

(b) $-5 + 1$

EXAMPLE 3 Adding Two Negative Numbers

Find each sum.

(a) $-2 + (-9) = -11$ The sum of two negative numbers is negative.

(b) $-8 + (-12) = -20$

(c) $-15 + (-3) = -18$

◀◀◀ **Work Problem 2 at the Side.**

OBJECTIVE 2 Add numbers with different signs.   We use the number line again to illustrate the sum of a positive number and a negative number.

EXAMPLE 4 Adding Numbers with Different Signs

Use the number line to find the sum $-2 + 5$.

We find the sum $-2 + 5$ on the number line by starting at 0 and drawing an arrow two units to the left. From the left end of this arrow, we draw a second arrow five units to the right, as shown in Figure 10. The number below the end of this second arrow is 3, so $-2 + 5 = 3$.

Figure 10

◀◀◀ **Work Problem 3 at the Side.**

Addition of numbers with different signs also can be defined using absolute value.

> To add numbers with different signs, find the absolute values of the numbers, and subtract the smaller absolute value from the larger. Give the answer the same sign as the number with the larger absolute value.
>
> *Example:* $-12 + 6 = -6$.

For example, to add -12 and 5, we find their absolute values:

$$|-12| = 12 \quad \text{and} \quad |5| = 5.$$

Then we find the difference between these absolute values: $12 - 5 = 7$. Since $|-12| > |5|$, the sum will be negative, so

$$-12 + 5 = -7.$$

🖩 **Calculator Tip**   The ⊝ or ⊕⁄⊖ key is used to input a negative number in some scientific calculators. Try using your calculator to add negative numbers.

OBJECTIVE 3 Add mentally. While a number line is useful in showing the rules for addition, it is important to be able to find sums mentally.

EXAMPLE 5 **Adding a Positive Number and a Negative Number**

Check each answer, trying to work the addition mentally. If you have trouble, use a number line.

(a) $7 + (-4) = 3$

(b) $-8 + 12 = 4$

(c) $-\dfrac{1}{2} + \dfrac{1}{8} = -\dfrac{4}{8} + \dfrac{1}{8} = -\dfrac{3}{8}$ Remember to find a common denominator first.

(d) $\dfrac{5}{6} + \left(-1\dfrac{1}{3}\right) = \dfrac{5}{6} + \left(-\dfrac{4}{3}\right) = \dfrac{5}{6} + \left(-\dfrac{8}{6}\right) = -\dfrac{3}{6} = -\dfrac{1}{2}$

(e) $-4.6 + 8.1 = 3.5$

Work Problem 4 at the Side. ▶▶▶

The rules for adding signed numbers are summarized below.

Adding Signed Numbers

Same sign Add the absolute values of the numbers. Give the sum the same sign as the numbers being added.

Different signs Find the absolute values of the numbers, and subtract the smaller absolute value from the larger. Give the answer the sign of the number having the larger absolute value.

OBJECTIVE 4 Use the order of operations with real numbers. Sometimes a problem involves square brackets, [ ]. As we mentioned earlier, brackets are treated just like parentheses. We do the calculations inside the brackets until a single number is obtained. Remember to use the order of operations given in **Section 1.1** for adding more than two numbers.

EXAMPLE 6 **Adding with Brackets**

Find each sum.

(a) $-3 + [4 + (-8)]$

First work inside the brackets. Follow the order of operations given in **Section 1.1.**

$$-3 + [4 + (-8)] = -3 + (-4) = -7$$

(b) $8 + [(-2 + 6) + (-3)] = 8 + [4 + (-3)] = 8 + 1 = 9$

Work Problem 5 at the Side. ▶▶▶

OBJECTIVE 5 Translate words and phrases that indicate addition. We now look at the interpretation of words and phrases that involve addition. Problem solving often requires translating words and phrases into symbols. We began this process with translating simple phrases in **Section 1.1.**

4 Check each answer, trying to work the addition mentally. If you have trouble, use a number line.

(a) $-8 + 2 = -6$

(b) $-15 + 4 = -11$

(c) $17 + (-10) = 7$

(d) $\dfrac{3}{4} + \left(-1\dfrac{3}{8}\right) = -\dfrac{5}{8}$

(e) $-9.5 + 3.8 = -5.7$

5 Find each sum.

(a) $2 + [7 + (-3)]$

(b) $6 + [(-2 + 5) + 7]$

(c) $-9 + [-4 + (-8 + 6)]$

ANSWERS
4. All are correct.
5. **(a)** 6   **(b)** 16   **(c)** −15

6 Write a numerical expression for each phrase, and simplify the expression.

(a) 4 more than -12

(b) The sum of 6 and -7

(c) -12 added to -31

(d) 7 increased by the sum of 8 and -3

The word *sum* indicates addition. There are other key words and phrases that also indicate addition. Some of these are given in the chart below.

Word or Phrase	Example	Numerical Expression and Simplification
Sum of	The *sum of* -3 and 4	$-3 + 4 = 1$
Added to	5 *added to* -8	$-8 + 5 = -3$
More than	12 *more than* -5	$(-5) + 12 = 7$
Increased by	-6 *increased by* 13	$-6 + 13 = 7$
Plus	3 *plus* 14	$3 + 14 = 17$

EXAMPLE 7 Translating Words and Phrases

Write a numerical expression for each phrase, and simplify the expression.

(a) The **sum of** -8 and 4 and 6

$$-8 + 4 + 6 = (-8 + 4) + 6 = -4 + 6 = 2$$

Notice that parentheses were placed around $-8 + 4$, and this addition was done first, using the order of operations given earlier.

(b) 3 **more than** -5, **increased by** 12

$$-5 + 3 + 12 = (-5 + 3) + 12 = -2 + 12 = 10$$

◀◀◀ **Work Problem 6 at the Side.**

Gains (or increases) and losses (or decreases) sometimes appear in applied problems. When they do, the gains may be interpreted as positive numbers and the losses as negative numbers.

EXAMPLE 8 Interpreting Gains and Losses

The Carolina Panthers football team gained 3 yd on first down, lost 12 yd on second down, and then gained 13 yd on third down. How many yards did the team gain or lose altogether?

The gains are represented by positive numbers and the loss by a negative number.

$$3 + (-12) + 13$$

Add from left to right.

$$3 + (-12) + 13 = [3 + (-12)] + 13$$
$$= (-9) + 13$$
$$= 4$$

The team gained 4 yd altogether.

◀◀◀ **Work Problem 7 at the Side.**

7 Solve the problem.

A football team lost 8 yd on first down, lost 5 yd on second down, and then gained 7 yd on third down. How many yards did the team gain or lose altogether?

1.4 Exercises

By the order of operations, what is the first step you would use to simplify each expression?

1. $4[3(-2 + 5) - 1]$

2. $[-4 + 7(-6 + 2)]$

3. $9 + ([-1 + (-3)] + 5)$

4. $[(-8 + 4) + (-6)] + 5$

Find each sum. See Examples 1–6.

5. $6 + (-4)$

6. $8 + (-5)$

7. $12 + (-15)$

8. $4 + (-8)$

9. $-7 + (-3)$

10. $-11 + (-4)$

11. $-10 + (-3)$

12. $-16 + (-7)$

13. $-12.4 + (-3.5)$

14. $-21.3 + (-2.5)$

15. $10 + [-3 + (-2)]$

16. $13 + [-4 + (-5)]$

17. $5 + [14 + (-6)]$

18. $7 + [3 + (-14)]$

19. $-3 + [5 + (-2)]$

20. $-7 + [10 + (-3)]$

21. $-8 + [3 + (-1) + (-2)]$

22. $-7 + [5 + (-8) + 3]$

23. $\dfrac{9}{10} + \left(-\dfrac{3}{5}\right)$

24. $\dfrac{5}{8} + \left(-\dfrac{17}{12}\right)$

25. $-\dfrac{1}{6} + \dfrac{2}{3}$

26. $-\dfrac{6}{25} + \dfrac{19}{20}$

27. $2\dfrac{1}{2} + \left(-3\dfrac{1}{4}\right)$

28. $-4\dfrac{3}{8} + 6\dfrac{1}{2}$

29. $7.8 + (-9.4)$

30. $14.7 + (-10.1)$

31. $-7.1 + [3.3 + (-4.9)]$

32. $-9.5 + [-6.8 + (-1.3)]$

33. $[-8 + (-3)] + [-7 + (-7)]$

34. $[-5 + (-4)] + [9 + (-2)]$

35. $\left(-\dfrac{1}{2} + .25\right) - \left(-\dfrac{3}{4} + .75\right)$

36. $\left(-\dfrac{3}{2} - .75\right) - \left(2.25 - \dfrac{1}{2}\right)$

Perform each operation, and then determine whether the statement is true *or* false. *Try to do all work mentally. See Examples 5 and 6.*

37. $-11 + 13 = 13 + (-11)$

38. $16 + (-9) = -9 + 16$

39. $-10 + 6 + 7 = -3$

40. $-12 + 8 + 5 = -1$

41. $\dfrac{7}{3} + \left(-\dfrac{1}{3}\right) + \left(-\dfrac{6}{3}\right) = 0$

42. $-\dfrac{3}{2} + 1 + \dfrac{1}{2} = 0$

43. $|-8 + 10| = -8 + (-10)$

44. $|-4 + 6| = -4 + (-6)$

45. $2\dfrac{1}{5} + \left(-\dfrac{6}{11}\right) = -\dfrac{6}{11} + 2\dfrac{1}{5}$

46. $-1\dfrac{1}{2} + \dfrac{5}{8} = \dfrac{5}{8} + \left(-1\dfrac{1}{2}\right)$

47. $-7 + [-5 + (-3)] = [(-7) + (-5)] + 3$

48. $6 + [-2 + (-5)] = [(-4) + (-2)] + 5$

RELATING CONCEPTS (EXERCISES 49–52) For Individual or Group Work

Recall the rules for adding signed numbers introduced in this section, and **work Exercises 49–52 in order.**

49. Suppose that the sum of two numbers is negative, and you know that one of the numbers is positive. What can you conclude about the other number?

50. If you are solving the equation $x + 5 = -7$ from a set of numbers, why could you immediately eliminate any positive numbers as possible solutions? (Remember how you answered Exercise 49.)

51. Suppose that the sum of two numbers is positive, and you know that one of the numbers is negative. What can you conclude about the other number?

52. If you are solving the equation $x + (-8) = 2$ from a set of numbers, why could you immediately eliminate any negative numbers as possible solutions? (Remember how you answered Exercise 51.)

---

53. In your own words, explain how to add two negative numbers.

54. In your own words, explain how to add a positive number and a negative number. Give two cases.

Write a numerical expression for each phrase, and simplify the expression. See Example 7.

55. The sum of -5 and 12 and 6

56. The sum of -3 and 5 and -12

57. 14 added to the sum of -19 and -4

58. -2 added to the sum of -18 and 11

59. The sum of -4 and -10, increased by 12

60. The sum of -7 and -13, increased by 14

61. $\frac{2}{7}$ more than the sum of $\frac{5}{7}$ and $-\frac{9}{7}$

62. .85 more than the sum of -1.25 and -4.75

Solve each problem. See Example 8.

63. Kramer owed Jerry $10 for snacks raided from the refrigerator. Kramer later borrowed $70 from George to finance his latest get-rich scheme. What positive or negative number represents Kramer's financial status?

64. Bonika's checking account balance is $54.00. She then takes a gamble by writing a check for $89.00. What is her new balance? (Write the balance as a signed number.)

65. The surface, or rim, of a canyon is at altitude 0. On a hike down into the canyon, a party of hikers stops for a rest at 130 m below the surface. They then descend another 54 m. What is their new altitude? (Write the altitude as a signed number.)

130 m

54 m

66. A pilot announces to the passengers that the current altitude of their plane is 34,000 ft. Because of some unexpected turbulence, the pilot is forced to descend 2100 ft. What is the new altitude of the plane? (Write the altitude as a signed number.)

34,000 ft

2100 ft

67. On three consecutive passes, Brett Favre of the Green Bay Packers passed for a gain of 6 yd, was sacked for a loss of 12 yd, and passed for a gain of 43 yd. What positive or negative number represents the total net yardage for the plays?

68. On a series of three consecutive running plays, Peyton Manning of the Indianapolis Colts gained 4 yd, lost 3 yd, and lost 2 yd. What positive or negative number represents his total net yardage for the series of plays?

69. The lowest temperature ever recorded in Arkansas was −29°F. The highest temperature ever recorded there was 149°F more than the lowest. What was this highest temperature? (*Source: World Almanac and Book of Facts,* 2004.)

70. On January 23, 1943, the temperature rose 49°F in two minutes in Spearfish, South Dakota. If the starting temperature was −4°F, what was the temperature two minutes later?

71. Dana Weightman owes $153 to a credit card company. She makes a $14 purchase with the card, and then pays $60 on the account. What is her current balance as a signed number?

72. A female polar bear weighed 660 lb when she entered her winter den. She lost 45 lb during each of the first two months of hibernation, and another 205 lb before leaving the den with her two cubs in March. How much did she weigh when she left the den?

73. Based on census population projections for 2020, New York will lose 5 seats in the U.S. House of Representatives, Pennsylvania will lose 4 seats, and Ohio will lose 3. Write a signed number that represents the total number of seats these three states are projected to lose. (*Source:* Population Reference Bureau.)

74. Michigan is projected to lose 3 seats in the U.S. House of Representatives and Illinois 2 in 2020. The states projected to gain the most seats are California with 9, Texas with 5, Florida with 3, Georgia with 2, and Arizona with 2. Write a signed number that represents the algebraic sum of these changes. (*Source:* Population Reference Bureau.)

1.5 Subtracting Real Numbers

OBJECTIVE **1** **Find a difference.** In the operation $a - b$, a is called the **minuend** and b is called the **subtrahend.** As we mentioned earlier, the answer to a subtraction problem is called a **difference.** Differences between signed numbers can be found by using a number line. Addition and subtraction are opposite operations. Thus, because *addition* of a positive number on the number line is shown by drawing an arrow to the *right, subtraction* of a positive number is shown by drawing an arrow to the *left*.

EXAMPLE 1 **Subtracting with the Number Line**

Use the number line to find the difference $7 - 4$.

   To find the difference $7 - 4$ on the number line, begin at 0 and draw an arrow 7 units to the *right*. From the right end of this arrow, draw an arrow 4 units to the *left*, as shown in Figure 11. The number at the end of the second arrow shows that $7 - 4 = 3$.

Figure 11

Work Problem 1 at the Side. ▶▶▶

OBJECTIVE **2** **Use the definition of subtraction.** The procedure used in Example 1 to find $7 - 4$ is exactly the same procedure that would be used to find $7 + (-4)$, so

$$7 - 4 = 7 + (-4).$$

This shows that *subtracting* a positive number from a larger positive number is the same as *adding* the opposite of the smaller number to the larger. We use this idea to define subtraction for all real numbers.

Subtraction

For any real numbers a and b,

$$a - b = a + (-b).$$

Example: $4 - 9 = 4 + (-9) = -5$.

To subtract b from a, add the opposite (or negative) of b to a. In other words, change the subtrahend to its opposite, and add.

Subtracting Signed Numbers

Step 1 Change the subtraction symbol to addition and change the sign of the subtrahend.

Step 2 Add, as in the previous section.

---

1 Use the number line to find each difference.

(a) $5 - 1$

(b) $6 - 2$

ANSWERS
1. (a) $5 - 1 = 4$

(b) $6 - 2 = 4$

② Subtract.

(a) $6 - 10$

(b) $-2 - 4$

(c) $3 - (-5)$

(d) $-8 - (-12)$

(e) $\dfrac{5}{4} - \left(-\dfrac{3}{7}\right)$

EXAMPLE 2 **Using the Definition of Subtraction**

Subtract.

No change —— Change − to +. Opposite of 3

(a) $12 - 3 = 12 + (-3) = 9$

In practice, we usually do not change the sign as shown here, since this is the kind of subtraction done in basic arithmetic.

(b) $5 - 7 = 5 + (-7) = -2$

(c) $8 - 15 = 8 + (-15) = -7$

No change —— Change − to +. Opposite of −5

(d) $-3 - (-5) = -3 + (5) = 2$

(e) $\dfrac{3}{8} - \left(-\dfrac{4}{5}\right) = \dfrac{15}{40} - \left(-\dfrac{32}{40}\right) = \dfrac{15}{40} + \dfrac{32}{40} = \dfrac{47}{40}$

◀◀◀ Work Problem 2 at the Side.

Subtraction can be used to reverse the result of an addition problem. For example, if 4 is added to a number and then subtracted from the sum, the original number is the result.

$$12 + 4 = 16 \quad \text{and} \quad 16 - 4 = 12$$

The symbol − has now been used for three purposes:

1. to represent subtraction, as in $9 - 5 = 4$;

2. to represent negative numbers, such as -10, -2, and -3;

3. to represent the opposite (or negative) of a number, as in "the opposite (or negative) of 8 is -8."

We may see more than one use in the same problem, such as $-6 - (-9)$, where -9 is subtracted from -6. The meaning of the symbol depends on its position in the algebraic expression.

OBJECTIVE 3 **Work subtraction problems that involve brackets.** As before, with problems that have both parentheses and brackets, first do any operations inside the parentheses and brackets. Work from the inside out. Because subtraction is defined in terms of addition, the order of operations from **Section 1.1** can still be used.

EXAMPLE 3 **Subtracting with Grouping Symbols**

Perform each operation.

$$\begin{aligned}
\textbf{(a)} \ -6 - [2 - (8 + 3)] &= -6 - [2 - 11] \\
&= -6 - [2 + (-11)] \quad \text{Change} - \text{to} +. \\
&= -6 - (-9) \\
&= -6 + (9) = 3
\end{aligned}$$

Continued on Next Page

(b) $5 - \left[\left(-\dfrac{1}{3} - \dfrac{1}{2}\right) - (4 - 1)\right] = 5 - \left[\left(-\dfrac{1}{3} + \left(-\dfrac{1}{2}\right)\right) - 3\right]$

$= 5 - \left[\left(-\dfrac{5}{6}\right) - 3\right]$

$= 5 - \left[\left(-\dfrac{5}{6}\right) + (-3)\right]$

$= 5 - \left(-\dfrac{23}{6}\right)$

$= 5 + \dfrac{23}{6} = \dfrac{53}{6}$

Work Problem 3 at the Side. ⟩⟩⟩

3 Perform each operation.

(a) $2 - [(-3) - (4 + 6)]$

(b) $[(5 - 7) + 3] - 8$

(c) $6 - [(-1 - 4) - 2]$

OBJECTIVE 4 Translate words and phrases that indicate subtraction.
Now we translate words and phrases that involve subtraction of real numbers. *Difference* is one of them. Some others are given in the chart below.

Word or Phrase	Example	Numerical Expression and Simplification
Difference between	The *difference between* -3 and -8	$-3 - (-8) = -3 + 8 = 5$
Subtracted from	12 *subtracted from* 18	$18 - 12 = 6$
Less than	6 *less than* 5	$5 - 6 = 5 + (-6) = -1$
Decreased by	9 *decreased by* -4	$9 - (-4) = 9 + 4 = 13$
Minus	-8 *minus* 5	$-8 - 5 = -8 + (-5) = -13$

CAUTION
When you are subtracting two numbers, it is important that you write them in the correct order, because, in general, *a − b ≠ b − a.* For example, $5 - 3 \neq 3 - 5$. ***Think carefully before interpreting an expression involving subtraction!*** Subtracting a larger number from a smaller number *always* produces a negative number.

EXAMPLE 4 Translating Words and Phrases

Write a numerical expression for each phrase, and simplify the expression.

(a) The **difference between** -8 and 5
When "difference between" is used, write the numbers in the order they are given.

$$-8 - 5 = -8 + (-5) = -13$$

(b) 4 **subtracted from** the sum of 8 and -3
Here the operation of addition is also used, as indicated by the word *sum*. First, add 8 and -3. Next, subtract 4 from this sum.

$$[8 + (-3)] - 4 = 5 - 4 = 1$$

Continued on Next Page

4 Write a numerical expression for each phrase, and simplify the expression.

(a) The difference between −5 and −12

(b) −2 subtracted from the sum of 4 and −4

(c) 7 less than −2

(d) 9, decreased by 10 less than 7

5 Solve the problem.
The highest elevation in Argentina is Mt. Aconcagua, which is 6960 m above sea level. The lowest point in Argentina is the Valdes Peninsula, 40 m below sea level. Find the difference between the highest and lowest elevations.

(c) 4 less than −6
Be careful with order here. 4 must be taken *from* −6, so write −6 first.
$$-6 - 4 = -6 + (-4) = -10$$
Notice that "4 less than −6" differs from "4 *is less than* −6." The statement "4 is less than −6" is symbolized as $4 < -6$ (which is a false statement).

(d) 8, **decreased by** 5 **less than** 12
First, write "5 less than 12" as $12 - 5$. Next, subtract $12 - 5$ from 8.
$$8 - (12 - 5) = 8 - 7 = 1$$

◀◀◀ Work Problem 4 at the Side.

We have seen a few applications of signed numbers in earlier sections. The next example involves subtraction of signed numbers.

EXAMPLE 5 Solving a Problem Involving Subtraction

The record high temperature of 134°F in the United States was recorded at Death Valley, California, in 1913. The record low was −80°F, at Prospect Creek, Alaska, in 1971. See Figure 12. What is the difference between these highest and lowest temperatures? (*Source: World Almanac and Book of Facts*, 2004.)

Figure 12

We must subtract the lowest temperature from the highest temperature.
$$134 - (-80) = 134 + 80 \quad \text{Use the definition of subtraction.}$$
$$= 214 \quad \text{Add.}$$
The difference between the two temperatures is 214°F.

◀◀◀ Work Problem 5 at the Side.

1.5 Exercises

Fill in each blank with the correct response.

1. By the definition of subtraction, in order to perform the subtraction $-6 - (-8)$, we must add the opposite of _____ to _____.

2. By the order of operations, to simplify $8 - [3 - (-4 - 5)]$, the first step is to subtract _____ from _____.

3. "The difference between 7 and 12" translates as _____, while "the difference between 12 and 7" translates as _____.

4. $-9 - (-3) = -9 +$ _____

5. $-8 - 4 = -8 +$ _____

6. $-19 - 22 = -19 +$ _____

Find each difference. See Examples 1–3.

7. $-7 - 3$

8. $-12 - 5$

9. $-10 - 6$

10. $-13 - 16$

11. $7 - (-4)$

12. $9 - (-6)$

13. $6 - (-13)$

14. $13 - (-3)$

15. $-7 - (-3)$

16. $-8 - (-6)$

17. $3 - (4 - 6)$

18. $6 - (7 - 14)$

19. $-3 - (6 - 9)$

20. $-4 - (5 - 12)$

21. $\dfrac{1}{2} - \left(-\dfrac{1}{4}\right)$

22. $\dfrac{1}{3} - \left(-\dfrac{4}{3}\right)$

23. $-\dfrac{3}{4} - \dfrac{5}{8}$

24. $-\dfrac{5}{6} - \dfrac{1}{2}$

25. $\dfrac{5}{8} - \left(-\dfrac{1}{2} - \dfrac{3}{4}\right)$

26. $\dfrac{9}{10} - \left(\dfrac{1}{8} - \dfrac{3}{10}\right)$

27. $4.4 - (-9.2)$

28. $6.7 - (-12.6)$

29. $-7.4 - 4.5$

30. $-5.4 - 9.6$

31. $-5.2 - (8.4 - 10.8)$

32. $-9.6 - (3.5 - 12.6)$

33. $[(-3.1) - 4.5] - (.8 - 2.1)$

34. $[(-7.8) - 9.3] - (.6 - 3.5)$

35. $-12 - [(9 - 2) - (-6 - 3)]$

36. $-4 + [(-6 - 9) - (-7 + 4)]$

37. $-8 + [(-3 - 10) - (-4 + 1)]$

38. $\left(-\dfrac{3}{4} - \dfrac{5}{2}\right) - \left(-\dfrac{1}{8} - 1\right)$

39. $\left(-\dfrac{3}{8} - \dfrac{2}{3}\right) - \left(-\dfrac{9}{8} - 3\right)$

40. $[-34.99 + (6.59 - 12.25)] - 8.33$

41. $[-12.25 - (8.34 + 3.57)] - 17.88$

42. Explain in your own words how to subtract signed numbers.

43. We know that, in general, $a - b \neq b - a$. Find two pairs of values for a and b so that $a - b = b - a$.

Simplify each expression. Use the order of operations.

44. $-3 - (-4) - 5$

45. $8 - (-3) - 9 + 6$

46. $-5 - 2 + 4 - 8 - (-6)$

47. Make up a subtraction problem so that the difference between two negative numbers is a negative number.

48. Make up a subtraction problem so that the difference between two negative numbers is a positive number.

Write a numerical expression for each phrase and simplify. See Example 4.

49. The difference between 4 and −8

50. The difference between 7 and −14

51. 8 less than −2

52. 9 less than −13

53. The sum of 9 and −4, decreased by 7

54. The sum of 12 and −7, decreased by 14

55. 12 less than the difference between 8 and −5

56. 19 less than the difference between 9 and −2

Solve each problem. See Example 5.

57. The coldest temperature recorded in Chicago, Illinois, was −35°F in 1996. The record low in South Dakota was set in 1936 and was 23°F lower than −35°F. What was the record low in South Dakota? (*Source: World Almanac and Book of Facts*, 2004.)

58. No one knows just why humpback whales love to heave their 45-ton bodies out of the water, but leap they do. Mark and Debbie, two researchers based on the island of Maui, noticed that one of their favorite whales, "Pineapple," leaped 15 ft above the surface of the ocean while her mate cruised 12 ft below the surface. What is the difference between these two heights?

59. The top of Mount Whitney, visible from Death Valley, has an altitude of 14,494 ft above sea level. The bottom of Death Valley is 282 ft below sea level. Using 0 as sea level, find the difference between these two elevations. (*Source: World Almanac and Book of Facts*, 2004.)

60. A chemist is running an experiment under precise conditions. At first, she runs it at $-174.6°F$. She then lowers the temperature by $2.3°F$. What is the new temperature for the experiment?

61. Ben owed his brother $10. He later borrowed $70. What positive or negative number represents his present financial status?

62. Francesca has $15 in her purse, and Emilio has a debt of $12. Find the difference between these amounts.

63. For the year 2003, one health club showed a profit of $86,000, while another showed a loss of $19,000. Find the difference between these amounts.

64. At 2:00 A.M., a plant worker found that a dial reading was 7.904. At 3:00 A.M., she found the reading to be -3.291. Find the difference between these two readings.

65. J. D. Patin enjoys playing Triominoes every Wednesday night. Last Wednesday, on four successive turns, his scores were -19, 28, -5, and 13. What was his final score for the four turns?

66. Marie Aguillard also enjoys playing Triominoes. On five successive turns, her scores were -13, 15, -12, 24, and 14. What was her total score for the five turns?

67. In August, Alison Romike began with a checking account balance of $904.89. Her checks and deposits for August are given below:

Checks	Deposits
$35.84	$85.00
$26.14	$120.76
$3.12	

Assuming no other transactions, what was her account balance at the end of August?

68. In September, Carter Fenton began with a checking account balance of $904.89. His checks and deposits for September are given below:

Checks	Deposits
$41.29	$80.59
$13.66	$276.13
$84.40	

Assuming no other transactions, what was his account balance at the end of September?

69. A certain Greek mathematician was born in 426 B.C. His father was born 43 years earlier. In what year was his father born?

70. A certain Roman philosopher was born in 325 B.C. Her mother was born 35 years earlier. In what year was her mother born?

71. Kim Falgout owes $870.00 on her MasterCard account. She returns two items costing $35.90 and $150.00 and receives credits for these on the account. Next, she makes a purchase of $82.50, and then two more purchases of $10.00 each. She makes a payment of $500.00. She then incurs a finance charge of $37.23. How much does she still owe?

72. Charles Vosburg owes $679.00 on his Visa account. He returns three items costing $36.89, $29.40, and $113.55 and receives credits for these on the account. Next, he makes purchases of $135.78 and $412.88, and two purchases of $20.00 each. He makes a payment of $400. He then incurs a finance charge of $24.57. How much does he still owe?

73. Dean Baldus enjoys scuba diving. He dives to 34 ft below the surface of a lake. His partner, Jeff Balius, dives to 40 ft below the surface, but then ascends 20 ft. What is the vertical distance between Dean and Jeff?

74. Rhonda Alessi also enjoys scuba diving. She dives to 12 ft below the surface of False River. Her sister, Sandy, dives to 20 ft below the surface, but then ascends 10 ft. What is the vertical distance between Rhonda and Sandy?

75. The height of Mt. Foraker is 17,400 ft, while the depth of the Java Trench is 23,376 ft. What is the vertical distance between the top of Mt. Foraker and the bottom of the Java Trench? (*Source: World Almanac and Book of Facts*, 2004.)

76. The height of Mt. Wilson is 14,246 ft, while the depth of the Cayman Trench is 24,721 ft. What is the vertical distance between the top of Mt. Wilson and the bottom of the Cayman Trench? (*Source: World Almanac and Book of Facts*, 2004.)

The bar graph shown depicts the sales growth changes in various countries for McDonald's revenue during the years 2001 and 2002. The change from one year to the next can be represented by a signed number, found by subtracting the figure for 2001 from the figure for 2002. For example, in Latin America, the sales figure actually increased for the period: $-1.0\% - (-3.9\%) = 2.9\%.$

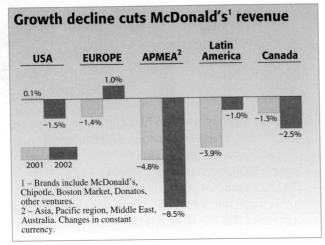

Growth decline cuts McDonald's[1] revenue

USA   EUROPE   APMEA[2]   Latin America   Canada

1.0%
0.1%
-1.5%   -1.4%
-1.0%   -1.3%
-2.5%
-3.9%
-4.8%
-8.5%

2001   2002

1 – Brands include McDonald's, Chipotle, Boston Market, Donatos, other ventures.
2 – Asia, Pacific region, Middle East, Australia. Changes in constant currency.

Source: McDonald's Corp.

Use a signed number to answer Exercises 77 and 78.

77. Find the percent change in the United States.

78. Find the percent change in Europe.

Median pricings for existing homes in the United States for the years 1997 through 2002 are shown in the table. Complete the table, determining the change from one year to the next by subtraction.

	Year	Median-Priced Existing Homes	Change from Previous Year
	1997	$121,800	
	1998	$128,400	$6600
79.	1999	$133,300	
80.	2000	$139,000	
81.	2001	$147,800	
82.	2002	$158,100	

Source: National Association of Realtors.

In Exercises 83–86, suppose that x represents a positive number and y represents a negative number. Determine whether the given expression must represent a positive number or a negative number.

83. $x - y$ **84.** $y - x$ **85.** $x + |y|$ **86.** $y - |x|$

1.6 Multiplying and Dividing Real Numbers

In this section we learn how to multiply positive and negative numbers. The result of multiplication is called the **product.** We already know how to multiply positive numbers and that the product of two positive numbers is positive. We also know that the product of 0 and any positive number is 0, and we extend that property to all real numbers.

Multiplication Property of 0

For any real number a,

$$a \cdot 0 = 0 \cdot a = 0.$$

OBJECTIVE 1 Find the product of numbers with different signs.   To define the product of numbers with different signs so that the result is consistent with multiplication of positive numbers, look at the following pattern.

$$3 \cdot 5 = 15$$
$$3 \cdot 4 = 12$$
$$3 \cdot 3 = 9$$
$$3 \cdot 2 = 6$$
$$3 \cdot 1 = 3$$
$$3 \cdot 0 = 0$$
$$3 \cdot (-1) = ?$$

The products decrease by 3.

What should $3(-1)$ equal? Since multiplication can also be considered repeated addition, the product $3(-1)$ represents the sum

$$-1 + (-1) + (-1) = -3,$$

so the product should be -3, which fits the pattern. Also,

$$3(-2) = -2 + (-2) + (-2) = -6.$$

> **Work Problem 1 at the Side.** ⟩⟩⟩

The results from Problem 1 maintain the pattern in the list above, which suggests the following rule.

> The product of a positive number and a negative number is negative.
>
> *Example:* $6(-3) = -18.$

EXAMPLE 1 Multiplying a Positive Number and a Negative Number

Find each product using the multiplication rule.

(a) $8(-5) = -(8 \cdot 5) = -40$ **(b)** $-7(2) = -(7 \cdot 2) = -14$

(c) $-9\left(\dfrac{1}{3}\right) = -3$ **(d)** $-6.2(4.1) = -25.42$

> **Work Problem 2 at the Side.** ⟩⟩⟩

OBJECTIVES

1 Find the product of numbers with different signs.

2 Find the product of two negative numbers.

3 Use the reciprocal of a number to apply the definition of division.

4 Use the order of operations when multiplying and dividing signed numbers.

5 Evaluate expressions involving variables.

6 Translate words and phrases involving multiplication and division.

7 Translate simple sentences into equations.

❶ Find each product by finding the sum of three numbers.

(a) $3(-3)$

(b) $3(-4)$

(c) $3(-5)$

❷ Find each product.

(a) $2(-6)$

(b) $7(-8)$

(c) $-9(2)$

(d) $-16\left(\dfrac{5}{32}\right)$

(e) $4.56(-10)$

ANSWERS
1. **(a)** -9 **(b)** -12 **(c)** -15
2. **(a)** -12 **(b)** -56 **(c)** -18
   (d) $-\dfrac{5}{2}$ **(e)** -45.6

❸ Find each product.

(a) $-5(-6)$

(b) $-7(-3)$

(c) $-8(-5)$

(d) $-11(-2)$

(e) $-17(3)(-7)$

(f) $-41(2)(-13)$

OBJECTIVE **2** **Find the product of two negative numbers.** The product of two positive numbers is positive, and the product of a positive number and a negative number is negative. What about the product of two negative numbers? Look at another pattern.

$$-5(4) = -20$$
$$-5(3) = -15$$
$$-5(2) = -10$$
$$-5(1) = -5$$
$$-5(0) = 0$$
$$-5(-1) = ?$$

The products increase by 5.

The numbers on the left of the equals signs (in color) decrease by 1 for each step down the list. The products on the right increase by 5 for each step down the list. To maintain this pattern, $-5(-1)$ should be 5 more than $-5(0)$, or 5 more than 0, so

$$-5(-1) = 5.$$

The pattern continues with

$$-5(-2) = 10$$
$$-5(-3) = 15$$
$$-5(-4) = 20$$
$$-5(-5) = 25,$$

and so on. This pattern suggests the next rule.

> The product of two negative numbers is positive.
>
> *Example:* $-5(-4) = 20.$

EXAMPLE 2 **Multiplying Two Negative Numbers**

Find each product using the multiplication rule.

(a) $-9(-2) = 18$ **(b)** $-6(-12) = 72$

(c) $-2(4)(-1) = -8(-1) = 8$ **(d)** $3(-5)(-2) = -15(-2) = 30$

◀◀◀ Work Problem 3 at the Side.

Here is a summary of the results for multiplying signed numbers.

> **Multiplying Signed Numbers**
>
> The product of two numbers having the *same* sign is *positive,* and the product of two numbers having *different* signs is *negative.*

OBJECTIVE **3** **Use the reciprocal of a number to apply the definition of division.** Recall that the result of division is called the **quotient.** In **Section 1.5** we saw that the difference between two numbers is found by adding the opposite of the subtrahend to the minuend. Similarly, the *quotient* of two numbers involves multiplying by the *reciprocal* of the second number.

Reciprocals

Pairs of numbers whose product is 1 are called **reciprocals** of each other.

Since $\quad 8 \cdot \dfrac{1}{8} = \dfrac{8}{8} = 1 \quad$ and $\quad \dfrac{5}{4} \cdot \dfrac{4}{5} = \dfrac{20}{20} = 1,$

the reciprocal of 8 is $\frac{1}{8}$, and that of $\frac{5}{4}$ is $\frac{4}{5}$. The following table shows several numbers and their reciprocals.

Number	Reciprocal
4	$\frac{1}{4}$
-5	$\frac{1}{-5}$ or $-\frac{1}{5}$
$\frac{3}{4}$	$\frac{4}{3}$
$-\frac{5}{8}$	$-\frac{8}{5}$
0	None

By definition, the product of a number and its reciprocal is 1. But the multiplication property of 0 says that the product of 0 and any number is 0. Thus,

0 has no reciprocal.

Work Problem 4 at the Side.

By definition, the quotient of a and b is the product of a and the reciprocal of b.

Division

The quotient $\frac{a}{b}$ of real numbers a and b, with $b \neq 0$, is

$$\frac{a}{b} = a \cdot \frac{1}{b}.$$

Example: $\quad \dfrac{8}{-4} = 8\left(-\dfrac{1}{4}\right) = -2.$

This definition indicates that b, the number to divide by, cannot be 0. Since 0 has no reciprocal,

$\frac{a}{0}$ **is not a number and** *division by 0 is undefined.* **If a division problem requires division by 0, write "undefined."**

To illustrate, $\frac{6}{2} = 3$ since $2 \cdot 3 = 6$, but there is no number to represent $\frac{6}{0}$, since there is no number that when multiplied by 0 gives 6 as a product.

NOTE

If $\quad a \neq 0, \quad$ then $\quad \dfrac{0}{a} = 0.$

4 Complete the table.

Number	Reciprocal
(a) 6	
(b) -2	
(c) $\frac{2}{3}$	
(d) $-\frac{1}{4}$	
(e) 0	

5 Find each quotient.

(a) $\dfrac{42}{7}$

(b) $\dfrac{-36}{(-2)(-3)}$

(c) $\dfrac{-12.56}{-.4}$

(d) $\dfrac{10}{7} \div \left(-\dfrac{24}{5}\right)$

(e) $\dfrac{-3}{0}$

(f) $\dfrac{0}{-53}$

Because division is defined in terms of multiplication, all the rules for multiplying signed numbers also apply to dividing them.

EXAMPLE 3 Using the Definition of Division

Find each quotient.

(a) $\dfrac{12}{3} = 12 \cdot \dfrac{1}{3} = 4$

(b) $\dfrac{5(-2)}{2} = -10 \cdot \dfrac{1}{2} = -5$

(c) $\dfrac{-1.47}{-7} = -1.47 \cdot \left(-\dfrac{1}{7}\right) = .21$

(d) $-\dfrac{2}{3} \div \left(-\dfrac{5}{4}\right) = -\dfrac{2}{3} \cdot \left(-\dfrac{4}{5}\right) = \dfrac{8}{15}$

(e) $\dfrac{-10}{0}$ Undefined

(f) $\dfrac{0}{13} = 0 \qquad \dfrac{0}{a} = 0 \quad (a \neq 0)$

Work Problem 5 at the Side.

When dividing fractions, multiplying by the reciprocal of the divisor works well. However, using the definition of division directly with integers is awkward. It is easier to divide in the usual way, then determine the sign of the answer. The following rule for division can be used instead of multiplying by the reciprocal.

Dividing Signed Numbers

The quotient of two numbers having the *same* sign is *positive;* the quotient of two numbers having *different* signs is *negative.*

Examples: $\dfrac{-15}{-5} = 3, \qquad \dfrac{15}{-5} = -3, \quad \text{and} \quad \dfrac{-15}{5} = -3.$

6 Find each quotient.

(a) $\dfrac{-8}{-2}$

(b) $\dfrac{-16.4}{2.05}$

(c) $\dfrac{1}{4} \div \left(-\dfrac{2}{3}\right)$

(d) $\dfrac{12}{-4}$

EXAMPLE 4 Dividing Signed Numbers

Find each quotient.

(a) $\dfrac{8}{-2} = -4$

(b) $\dfrac{-10}{2} = -5$

(c) $\dfrac{-4.5}{-.09} = 50$

(d) $-\dfrac{1}{8} \div \left(-\dfrac{3}{4}\right) = -\dfrac{1}{8} \cdot \left(-\dfrac{4}{3}\right) = \dfrac{1}{6}$

Work Problem 6 at the Side.

From the definitions of multiplication and division of real numbers,

$$\dfrac{-40}{8} = -40 \cdot \dfrac{1}{8} = -5 \quad \text{and} \quad \dfrac{40}{-8} = 40\left(\dfrac{1}{-8}\right) = -5, \text{ so}$$

$$\dfrac{-40}{8} = \dfrac{40}{-8}.$$

Based on this example, the quotient of a positive number and a negative number can be written in any of the following three forms.

For any positive real numbers a and b,

$$\dfrac{-a}{b} = \dfrac{a}{-b} = -\dfrac{a}{b}.$$

ANSWERS

5. (a) 6 (b) -6 (c) 31.4
   (d) $-\dfrac{25}{84}$ (e) undefined (f) 0

6. (a) 4 (b) -8 (c) $-\dfrac{3}{8}$ (d) -3

Similarly, the quotient of two negative numbers can be expressed as the quotient of two positive numbers.

> For any positive real numbers a and b,
>
> $$\frac{-a}{-b} = \frac{a}{b}.$$

OBJECTIVE 4 Use the order of operations when multiplying and dividing signed numbers.

EXAMPLE 5 Using the Order of Operations

Simplify.

(a) $-9(2) - (-3)(2)$

First find all products, working from left to right.

$$-9(2) - (-3)(2) = -18 - (-6)$$
$$= -18 + 6$$
$$= -12$$

(b) $-6(-2) - 3(-4) = 12 - (-12)$
$$= 12 + 12$$
$$= 24$$

(c) $\dfrac{5(-2) - 3(4)}{2(1 - 6)}$

Simplify the numerator and denominator separately.

$$\frac{5(-2) - 3(4)}{2(1 - 6)} = \frac{-10 - 12}{2(-5)} \quad \begin{array}{l}\text{Multiply in numerator.}\\ \text{Subtract in denominator.}\end{array}$$

$$= \frac{-22}{-10} \quad \begin{array}{l}\text{Subtract in numerator.}\\ \text{Multiply in denominator.}\end{array}$$

$$= \frac{11}{5} \quad \text{Write in lowest terms.}$$

Work Problem 7 at the Side.

The rules for operations with signed numbers are summarized here.

Operations with Signed Numbers

Addition

Same sign Add the absolute values of the numbers. The sum has the same sign as the numbers.

$$-4 + (-6) = -10$$

Different signs Find the absolute values of the numbers, and subtract the smaller absolute value from the larger. Give the sum the sign of the number having the larger absolute value.

$$4 + (-6) = -(6 - 4) = -2$$

(continued)

---

7 Perform the indicated operations.

(a) $-3(4) - 2(6)$

(b) $-8[-1 - (-4)(-5)]$

(c) $\dfrac{6(-4) - 2(5)}{3(2 - 7)}$

(d) $\dfrac{-6(-8) + 3(9)}{-2[4 - (-3)]}$

8 Evaluate each expression.

(a) $2x - 7(y + 1)$
if $x = -4$ and $y = 3$

(b) $2x^2 - 4y^2$
if $x = -2$ and $y = -3$

(c) $\dfrac{4x - 2y}{-3x}$
if $x = 2$ and $y = -1$

Subtraction

Add the opposite of the subtrahend to the minuend.

$$8 - (-3) = 8 + 3 = 11$$

Multiplication and Division

Same sign   The product or quotient of two numbers with the same sign is positive.

$$-5(-6) = 30 \quad \text{and} \quad \frac{-36}{-12} = 3$$

Different signs   The product or quotient of two numbers with different signs is negative.

$$-5(6) = -30 \quad \text{and} \quad \frac{18}{-6} = -3$$

Division by 0 is undefined.

OBJECTIVE 5 Evaluate expressions involving variables.

EXAMPLE 6 Evaluating Expressions for Numerical Values

Evaluate each expression, given that $x = -1$, $y = -2$, and $m = -3$.

(a) $(3x + 4y)(-2m)$

First substitute the given values for the variables. Then use the order of operations to find the value of the expression.

$(3x + 4y)(-2m) = [3(-1) + 4(-2)][-2(-3)]$ Put parentheses around the number for each variable.

$\quad = [-3 + (-8)][6]$ Find the products.

$\quad = (-11)(6)$ Add inside the brackets.

$\quad = -66$ Multiply.

(b) $2x^2 - 3y^2$

Use parentheses as shown.

$2(-1)^2 - 3(-2)^2 = 2(1) - 3(4)$ Substitute, then apply the exponents.

$\quad = 2 - 12$ Multiply.

$\quad = -10$ Subtract.

(c) $\dfrac{4y^2 + x}{m}$

$\dfrac{4(-2)^2 + (-1)}{-3} = \dfrac{4(4) + (-1)}{-3}$ Substitute, then apply the exponent.

$\quad = \dfrac{16 + (-1)}{-3}$ Multiply.

$\quad = \dfrac{15}{-3}$ Add.

$\quad = -5$ Divide.

Work Problem 8 at the Side.

ANSWERS

8. (a) -36 **(b)** -28 **(c)** $-\dfrac{5}{3}$

OBJECTIVE 6 Translate words and phrases involving multiplication and division. Just as there are words and phrases that indicate addition or subtraction, certain words and phrases indicate multiplication or division. The chart gives some phrases indicating multiplication.

Word or Phrase	Example	Numerical Expression and Simplification
Product of	The *product of* −5 and −2	$-5(-2) = 10$
Times	13 *times* −4	$13(-4) = -52$
Twice (meaning "2 times")	*Twice* 6	$2(6) = 12$
Of (used with fractions)	$\frac{1}{2}$ *of* 10	$\frac{1}{2}(10) = 5$
Percent of	12% *of* −16	$.12(-16) = -1.92$

EXAMPLE 7 Translating Words and Phrases

Write a numerical expression for each phrase, and simplify the expression.

(a) The **product of** 12 and the sum of 3 and −6
Here 12 is multiplied by "the sum of 3 and −6."

$$12[3 + (-6)] = 12(-3) = -36$$

(b) **Three times** the difference between 4 and −11

$$3[4 - (-11)] = 3(4 + 11) = 3(15) = 45$$

(c) Two-thirds **of** the sum of −5 and −3

$$\frac{2}{3}[-5 + (-3)] = \frac{2}{3}(-8) = -\frac{16}{3}$$

(d) 15% **of** the difference between 14 and −2
Remember from **Section R.2** that 15% = .15.

$$.15[14 - (-2)] = .15(14 + 2) = .15(16) = 2.4$$

> **Work Problem 9 at the Side.** ▶▶▶

The word *quotient* refers to the answer in a division problem. In algebra, a quotient is usually represented with a fraction bar; the symbol ÷ is seldom used. When translating an applied problem involving division, use a fraction bar. The chart gives some phrases associated with division.

Word or Phrase	Example	Numerical Expression and Simplification
Quotient of	The *quotient of* −24 and 3	$\frac{-24}{3} = -8$
Divided by	−16 *divided by* −4	$\frac{-16}{-4} = 4$
Ratio of	The *ratio of* 2 to 3	$\frac{2}{3}$

When translating a phrase involving division, we write the first number named as the numerator and the second as the denominator.

9 Write a numerical expression for each phrase and simplify.

(a) The product of 6 and the sum of −5 and −4

(b) Twice the difference between 8 and −4

(c) Three-fifths of the sum of 2 and −7

(d) 20% of the sum of 9 and −4

ANSWERS
9. (a) $6[(-5) + (-4)]$; −54
(b) $2[8 - (-4)]$; 24
(c) $\frac{3}{5}[2 + (-7)]$; −3
(d) $.20[9 + (-4)]$; 1

⑩ Write a numerical expression for each phrase, and simplify the expression.

(a) The quotient of 20 and the sum of 8 and −3

(b) The product of −9 and 2, divided by the difference between 5 and −1

⑪ Write each sentence in symbols, using x to represent the number.

(a) Twice a number is −6.

(b) The difference between −8 and a number is −11.

(c) The sum of 5 and a number is 8.

(d) The quotient of a number and −2 is 6.

ANSWERS

10. (a) $\dfrac{20}{8+(-3)}; 4$

   (b) $\dfrac{-9(2)}{5-(-1)}; -3$

11. (a) $2x = -6$
   (b) $-8 - x = -11$
   (c) $5 + x = 8$
   (d) $\dfrac{x}{-2} = 6$

EXAMPLE 8 **Translating Words and Phrases**

Write a numerical expression for each phrase, and simplify the expression.

(a) The **quotient** of 14 and the sum of −9 and 2

"Quotient" indicates division. The number 14 is the numerator and "the sum of −9 and 2" is the denominator.

$$\frac{14}{-9+2} = \frac{14}{-7} = -2$$

(b) The product of 5 and −6, **divided by** the difference between −7 and 8

The numerator of the fraction representing the division is obtained by multiplying 5 and −6. The denominator is found by subtracting −7 and 8.

$$\frac{5(-6)}{-7-8} = \frac{-30}{-15} = 2$$

◀◀◀ **Work Problem 10 at the Side.**

OBJECTIVE 7 **Translate simple sentences into equations.** In this section and the previous two sections, important words and phrases involving the four operations of arithmetic have been introduced. We can use these words and phrases to translate sentences into equations.

EXAMPLE 9 **Translating Sentences into Equations**

Write each sentence with symbols, using x to represent the number.

(a) Three **times** a number **is** −18.

The word *times* indicates multiplication, and the word *is* translates as the equals sign (=).

$$3x = -18$$

(b) The **sum** of a number and 9 **is** 12.

$$x + 9 = 12$$

(c) The **difference between** a number and 5 **is** 0.

$$x - 5 = 0$$

(d) The **quotient** of 24 and a number **is** −2.

$$\frac{24}{x} = -2$$

◀◀◀ **Work Problem 11 at the Side.**

CAUTION
It is important to recognize the distinction between the types of problems found in Example 8 and Example 9. In Example 8, the phrases translate as *expressions,* while in Example 9, the sentences translate as *equations.* Remember that an equation is a sentence, while an expression is a phrase.

$$\frac{5(-6)}{-7-8}$$
↑
Expression

$$3x = -18$$
↑
Equation

1.6 Exercises

Fill in each blank with one of the following: greater than 0, less than 0, equal to 0.

1. The product or the quotient of two numbers with the same sign is _____.

2. The product or the quotient of two numbers with different signs is _____.

3. If three negative numbers are multiplied together, the product is _____.

4. If two negative numbers are multiplied and then their product is divided by a negative number, the result is _____.

5. If a negative number is squared and the result is added to a positive number, the final answer is _____.

6. The reciprocal of a negative number is _____.

Find each product. See Examples 1 and 2.

7. $-7(4)$ **8.** $-8(5)$ **9.** $-5(-6)$ **10.** $-4(-20)$

11. $-8(0)$ **12.** $0(-12)$ **13.** $-\dfrac{3}{8}\left(-\dfrac{20}{9}\right)$ **14.** $-\dfrac{5}{4}\left(-\dfrac{6}{25}\right)$

15. $-6.8(.35)$ **16.** $-4.6(.24)$ **17.** $-6\left(-\dfrac{1}{4}\right)$ **18.** $-8\left(-\dfrac{1}{2}\right)$

Find each quotient. See Examples 3 and 4.

19. $\dfrac{-15}{5}$ **20.** $\dfrac{-18}{6}$ **21.** $\dfrac{20}{-10}$ **22.** $\dfrac{28}{-4}$

23. $\dfrac{-160}{-10}$ **24.** $\dfrac{-260}{-20}$ **25.** $\dfrac{0}{-3}$ **26.** $\dfrac{0}{-5}$

27. $\dfrac{-10.252}{0}$ **28.** $\dfrac{-29.584}{0}$ **29.** $\left(-\dfrac{3}{4}\right) \div \left(-\dfrac{1}{2}\right)$ **30.** $\left(-\dfrac{3}{16}\right) \div \left(-\dfrac{5}{8}\right)$

31. Which expression is undefined?

A. $\dfrac{5 - 5}{5 + 5}$ B. $\dfrac{5 + 5}{5 + 5}$ C. $\dfrac{5 - 5}{5 - 5}$ D. $\dfrac{5 - 5}{5}$

32. What is the reciprocal of .4?

Perform each indicated operation. See Example 5.

33. $\dfrac{-5(-6)}{9 - (-1)}$

34. $\dfrac{-12(-5)}{7 - (-5)}$

35. $\dfrac{-21(3)}{-3 - 6}$

36. $\dfrac{-40(3)}{-2 - 3}$

37. $\dfrac{-10(2) + 6(2)}{-3 - (-1)}$

38. $\dfrac{8(-1) + 6(-2)}{-6 - (-1)}$

39. $\dfrac{-27(-2) - (-12)(-2)}{-2(3) - 2(2)}$

40. $\dfrac{-13(-4) - (-8)(-2)}{(-10)(2) - 4(-2)}$

41. $\dfrac{3^2 - 4^2}{7(-8 + 9)}$

42. $\dfrac{5^2 - 7^2}{2(3 + 3)}$

43. If x and y are both replaced by negative numbers, is the value of $4x + 8y$ positive or negative? What about $4x - 8y$?

Evaluate each expression if $x = 6$, $y = -4$, and $a = 3$. See Example 6.

44. $5x - 2y + 3a$

45. $6x - 5y + 4a$

46. $(2x + y)(3a)$

47. $(5x - 2y)(-2a)$

48. $\left(\dfrac{1}{3}x - \dfrac{4}{5}y\right)\left(-\dfrac{1}{5}a\right)$

49. $\left(\dfrac{5}{6}x + \dfrac{3}{2}y\right)\left(-\dfrac{1}{3}a\right)$

50. $(-5 + x)(-3 + y)(3 - a)$

51. $(6 - x)(5 + y)(3 + a)$

52. $-2y^2 + 3a$

53. $5x - 4a^2$

54. $\dfrac{2y^2 - x}{a - 3}$

55. $\dfrac{xy + 9a}{x + y - 2}$

Write a numerical expression for each phrase and simplify. See Examples 7 and 8.

56. The product of -9 and 2, added to 9

57. The product of 4 and -7, added to -12

58. Twice the product of -1 and 6, subtracted from -4

59. Twice the product of -8 and 2, subtracted from -1

60. The product of 12 and the difference between 9 and -8

61. The product of -3 and the difference between 3 and -7

62. Four-fifths of the sum of -8 and -2

63. Three-tenths of the sum of -2 and -28

64. The quotient of -12 and the sum of -5 and -1

65. The quotient of -20 and the sum of -8 and -2

66. The sum of 15 and -3, divided by the product of 4 and -3

67. The sum of -18 and -6, divided by the product of 2 and -4

68. The product of $-\frac{1}{2}$ and $\frac{3}{4}$, divided by $-\frac{2}{3}$

69. The product of $-\frac{2}{3}$ and $-\frac{1}{5}$, divided by $\frac{1}{7}$

Write each sentence with symbols, using x to represent the number. See Example 9.

70. Seven times a number is -42.

71. Nine times a number is -36.

72. The quotient of a number and 3 is -3.

73. The quotient of a number and 4 is -1.

74. $\frac{1}{2}$ less than a number is 2.

75. $\frac{9}{11}$ less than a number is 5.

76. When 15 is divided by a number, the result is -5.

77. When 6 is divided by a number, the result is -3.

RELATING CONCEPTS (EXERCISES 78–83) For Individual or Group Work

*To find the average of a group of numbers, we add the numbers and then divide the sum by the number of terms added. **Work Exercises 78–81 in order,** to find the average of 23, 18, 13, -4, and -8. Then find the averages in Exercises 82 and 83.*

78. Find the sum of the given group of numbers.

79. How many numbers are in the group?

80. Divide your answer for Exercise 78 by your answer for Exercise 79. Give the quotient as a mixed number.

81. What is the average of the given group of numbers?

82. What is the average of all integers between -10 and 14, including both -10 and 14?

83. What is the average of the integers between -15 and -10, including -15 and -10?

Summary Exercises on Operations with Real Numbers

Operations with Signed Numbers

Addition

Same sign   Add the absolute values of the numbers. The sum has the same sign as the numbers.

Different signs   Find the absolute values of the numbers, and subtract the smaller absolute value from the larger. Give the sum the sign of the number having the larger absolute value.

Subtraction

Add the opposite of the subtrahend to the minuend.

Multiplication and Division

Same sign   The product or quotient of two numbers with the same sign is positive.

Different signs   The product or quotient of two numbers with different signs is negative.

Division by 0 is undefined.

Perform each indicated operation.

1. $14 - 3 \cdot 10$

2. $-3(8) - 4(-7)$

3. $(3 - 8)(-2) - 10$

4. $-6(7 - 3)$

5. $7 - (-3)(2 - 10)$

6. $-4[(-2)(6) - 7]$

7. $(-4)(7) - (-5)(2)$

8. $-5[-4 - (-2)(-7)]$

9. $40 - (-2)[8 - 9]$

10. $\dfrac{5(-4)}{-7 - (-2)}$

11. $\dfrac{-3 - (-9 + 1)}{-7 - (-6)}$

12. $\dfrac{5(-8 + 3)}{13(-2) + (-7)(-3)}$

13. $\dfrac{6^2 - 8}{-2(2) + 4(-1)}$

14. $\dfrac{16(-8 + 5)}{15(-3) + (-7 - 4)(-3)}$

15. $\dfrac{9(-6) - 3(8)}{4(-7) + (-2)(-11)}$

16. $\dfrac{2^2 + 4^2}{5^2 - 3^2}$

17. $\dfrac{(2 + 4)^2}{(5 - 3)^2}$

18. $\dfrac{4^3 - 3^3}{-5(-4 + 2)}$

19. $\dfrac{-9(-6) + (-2)(27)}{3(8 - 9)}$

20. $|-4(9)| - |-11|$

21. $\dfrac{6(-10 + 3)}{15(-2) - 3(-9)}$

22. $\dfrac{(-9)^2 - 9^2}{3^2 - 5^2}$

23. $\dfrac{(-10)^2 + 10^2}{-10(5)}$

24. $-\dfrac{3}{4} \div \left(-\dfrac{5}{8}\right)$

25. $\dfrac{1}{2} \div \left(-\dfrac{1}{2}\right)$

26. $\dfrac{8^2 - 12}{(-5)^2 + 2(6)}$

27. $\left[\dfrac{5}{8} - \left(-\dfrac{1}{16}\right)\right] + \dfrac{3}{8}$

28. $\left(\dfrac{1}{2} - \dfrac{1}{3}\right) - \dfrac{5}{6}$

29. $-.9(-3.7)$

30. $-5.1(-.2)$

31. $-3^2 - 2^2$

32. $|-2(3) + 4| - |-2|$

33. $40 - (-2)[-5 - 3]$

Evaluate each expression if $x = -2, y = 3,$ and $a = 4$.

34. $-x + y - 3a$

35. $(x + 6)^3 - y^3$

36. $(x - y) - (a - 2y)$

37. $\left(\dfrac{1}{2}x + \dfrac{2}{3}y\right)\left(-\dfrac{1}{4}a\right)$

38. $\dfrac{2x + 3y}{a - xy}$

39. $\dfrac{x^2 - y^2}{x^2 + y^2}$

40. $-x^2 + 3y$

41. $\dfrac{-x + 2y}{2x + a}$

42. $\dfrac{2x + a}{-x + 2y}$

1.7 Properties of Real Numbers

If you are asked to find the sum

$$3 + 89 + 97,$$

you might mentally add $3 + 97$ to get 100, and then add $100 + 89$ to get 189. While the order of operations guidelines say to add (or multiply) from left to right, the fact is we may change the order of the terms (or factors) and group them in any way we choose without affecting the sum (or product). This is an example of a shortcut we use in everyday mathematics that is justified by the properties of real numbers introduced in this section. In the following statements, *a*, *b*, and *c* represent real numbers.

OBJECTIVE 1 Use the commutative properties. The word *commute* means to go back and forth. Many people commute to work or to school. If you travel from home to work and follow the same route from work to home, you travel the same distance each time. The **commutative properties** say that if two numbers are added or multiplied in any order, they give the same result.

$$a + b = b + a \qquad \text{Addition}$$

$$ab = ba \qquad \text{Multiplication}$$

EXAMPLE 1 Using the Commutative Properties

Use a commutative property to complete each statement.

(a) $-8 + 5 = 5 +$ _____
  By the commutative property for addition, the missing number is -8 because $-8 + 5 = 5 + (-8)$.

(b) $-2(7) =$ _____ (-2)
  By the commutative property for multiplication, the missing number is 7, since $-2(7) = 7(-2)$.

Work Problem 1 at the Side.

OBJECTIVE 2 Use the associative properties. When we *associate* one object with another, we tend to think of those objects as being grouped together. The **associative properties** say that when we add or multiply three numbers, we can group them in any manner and get the same answer.

$$(a + b) + c = a + (b + c) \qquad \text{Addition}$$

$$(ab)c = a(bc) \qquad \text{Multiplication}$$

EXAMPLE 2 Using the Associative Properties

Use an associative property to complete each statement.

(a) $8 + (-1 + 4) = (8 +$ _____$) + 4$
  The missing number is -1.

(b) $[2(-7)]6 = 2$ _____
  The missing expression on the right should be $[(-7)6]$.

Work Problem 2 at the Side.

OBJECTIVES

1 Use the commutative properties.

2 Use the associative properties.

3 Use the identity properties.

4 Use the inverse properties.

5 Use the distributive property.

---

1 Complete each statement. Use a commutative property.

(a) $x + 9 = 9 +$ _____

(b) $-12(4) =$ _____(-12)

(c) $5x = x \cdot$ _____

2 Complete each statement. Use an associative property.

(a) $(9 + 10) + (-3)$
    $= 9 + [$_____$+ (-3)]$

(b) $-5 + (2 + 8)$
    $= ($_____$) + 8$

(c) $10[-8(-3)] =$ _____

ANSWERS
1. (a) x **(b)** 4 **(c)** 5
2. (a) 10 **(b)** $-5 + 2$ **(c)** $[10(-8)](-3)$

3 Decide whether each statement is an example of a commutative property, an associative property, or both.

(a) $2(4 \cdot 6) = (2 \cdot 4)6$

(b) $(2 \cdot 4)6 = (4 \cdot 2)6$

(c) $(2 + 4) + 6 = 4 + (2 + 6)$

By the associative property of addition, the sum of three numbers will be the same no matter how the numbers are "associated" in groups. For this reason, parentheses can be left out in many addition problems. For example, both

$$(-1 + 2) + 3 \quad \text{and} \quad -1 + (2 + 3)$$

can be written as

$$-1 + 2 + 3.$$

In the same way, parentheses also can be left out of many multiplication problems.

EXAMPLE 3 Distinguishing between Associative and Commutative Properties

(a) Is $(2 + 4) + 5 = 2 + (4 + 5)$ an example of an associative or a commutative property?

The order of the three numbers is the same on both sides of the equals sign. The only change is in the *grouping*, or association, of the numbers. Therefore, this is an example of an associative property.

(b) Is $6(3 \cdot 10) = 6(10 \cdot 3)$ an example of an associative or a commutative property?

The same numbers, 3 and 10, are grouped on each side. On the left, however, 3 appears first in $(3 \cdot 10)$. On the right, 10 appears first. Since the only change involves the *order* of the numbers, this statement is an example of a commutative property.

(c) Is $(8 + 1) + 7 = 8 + (7 + 1)$ an example of an associative or a commutative property?

In the statement, both the order and the grouping are changed. On the left, the order of the three numbers is 8, 1, and 7. On the right it is 8, 7, and 1. On the left, 8 and 1 are grouped, and on the right, 7 and 1 are grouped. Therefore, both associative and commutative properties are used.

◀◀◀ Work Problem 3 at the Side.

We can use commutative and associative properties to simplify expressions.

4 Find the sum.

$$5 + 18 + 29 + 31 + 12$$

EXAMPLE 4 Using Commutative and Associative Properties

The commutative and associative properties make it possible to choose pairs of numbers that are easy to add or multiply.

(a) $23 + 41 + 2 + 9 + 25 = (41 + 9) + (23 + 2) + 25$
$$= 50 + 25 + 25$$
$$= 100$$

(b) $25(69)(4) = 25(4)(69)$
$$= 100(69)$$
$$= 6900$$

◀◀◀ Work Problem 4 at the Side.

OBJECTIVE 3 Use the identity properties. The identity or value of a real number is left unchanged when identity properties are applied. The **identity properties** say that the sum of 0 and any number equals that number, and the product of 1 and any number equals that number.

$$a + 0 = a \quad \text{and} \quad 0 + a = a \quad \text{Addition}$$

$$a \cdot 1 = a \quad \text{and} \quad 1 \cdot a = a \quad \text{Multiplication}$$

The number 0 leaves the identity, or value, of any real number unchanged by addition. For this reason, 0 is called the **identity element for addition** or the **additive identity.** Since multiplication by 1 leaves any real number unchanged, 1 is the **identity element for multiplication** or the **multiplicative identity.**

EXAMPLE 5 Using Identity Properties

These statements are examples of identity properties.

(a) $-3 + 0 = -3$ Addition   **(b)** $1 \cdot 25 = 25$ Multiplication

Work Problem 5 at the Side. ▶▶▶

We use the identity property for multiplication to write fractions in lowest terms and to find common denominators.

EXAMPLE 6 Using the Identity Element for Multiplication to Simplify Expressions

Simplify each expression.

(a) $\dfrac{49}{35} = \dfrac{7 \cdot 7}{5 \cdot 7}$ Factor.

$$= \dfrac{7}{5} \cdot \dfrac{7}{7} \quad \text{Write as a product.}$$

$$= \dfrac{7}{5} \cdot 1 \quad \text{Property of 1}$$

$$= \dfrac{7}{5} \quad \text{Identity property}$$

(b) $\dfrac{3}{4} + \dfrac{5}{24} = \dfrac{3}{4} \cdot 1 + \dfrac{5}{24}$ Identity property

$$= \dfrac{3}{4} \cdot \dfrac{6}{6} + \dfrac{5}{24} \quad \text{Use } 1 = \tfrac{6}{6} \text{ to get a common denominator.}$$

$$= \dfrac{18}{24} + \dfrac{5}{24} \quad \text{Multiply.}$$

$$= \dfrac{23}{24} \quad \text{Add.}$$

Work Problem 6 at the Side. ▶▶▶

5 Use an identity property to complete each statement.

(a) $9 + 0 =$ _____

(b) _____ $+ (-7) = -7$

(c) _____ $\cdot 1 = 5$

6 Use an identity property to simplify each expression.

(a) $\dfrac{85}{105}$

(b) $\dfrac{9}{10} - \dfrac{53}{50}$

ANSWERS

5. **(a)** 9 **(b)** 0 **(c)** 5

6. **(a)** $\dfrac{17}{21}$ **(b)** $-\dfrac{4}{25}$

7 Complete each statement so that it is an example of either an identity property or an inverse property. Tell which property is used.

(a) $-6 + \underline{\quad\quad} = 0$

(b) $\dfrac{4}{3} \cdot \underline{\quad\quad} = 1$

(c) $-\dfrac{1}{9} \cdot \underline{\quad\quad} = 1$

(d) $275 + \underline{\quad\quad} = 275$

(e) $-.75 + \dfrac{3}{4} = \underline{\quad\quad}$

OBJECTIVE **4** **Use the inverse properties.** Each day before you go to work or school, you probably put on your shoes before you leave. Before you go to sleep at night, you probably take them off, and this leads to the same situation that existed before you put them on. These operations from everyday life are examples of inverse operations.

The **inverse properties** of addition and multiplication lead to the additive and multiplicative identities, respectively. The opposite of a, $-a$, is the **additive inverse** of a and the reciprocal of a, $\frac{1}{a}$, is the **multiplicative inverse** of the nonzero number a. The sum of the numbers a and $-a$ is 0, and the product of the nonzero numbers a and $\frac{1}{a}$, is 1.

$$a + (-a) = 0 \quad \text{and} \quad -a + a = 0 \qquad \text{Addition}$$

$$a \cdot \frac{1}{a} = 1 \quad \text{and} \quad \frac{1}{a} \cdot a = 1 \quad (a \neq 0) \qquad \text{Multiplication}$$

EXAMPLE 7 **Using Inverse Properties**

The following statements are examples of inverse properties.

(a) $\dfrac{2}{3} \cdot \dfrac{3}{2} = 1$ Multiplication   **(b)** $(-5)\left(-\dfrac{1}{5}\right) = 1$ Multiplication

(c) $-\dfrac{1}{2} + \dfrac{1}{2} = 0$ Addition   **(d)** $4 + (-4) = 0$ Addition

(e) $\dfrac{1}{2} + (-.5) = 0$ Addition

Work Problem 7 at the Side.

OBJECTIVE **5** **Use the distributive property.** The everyday meaning of the word *distribute* is "to give out from one to several." An important property of real number operations involves this idea.

Look at the value of the following expressions.

$$2(5 + 8) = 2(13) = 26$$

$$2(5) + 2(8) = 10 + 16 = 26$$

Since both expressions equal 26,

$$2(5 + 8) = 2(5) + 2(8).$$

This result is an example of the *distributive property of multiplication with respect to addition,* the only property involving *both* addition and multiplication. With this property, a product can be changed to a sum or difference. This idea is illustrated by the divided rectangle in Figure 13.

The area of the left part is 2(5) = 10.
The area of the right part is 2(8) = 16.
The total area is 2(5 + 8) = 26 or the total area is
2(5) + 2(8) = 10 + 16 = 26.
Thus, 2(5 + 8) = 2(5) + 2(8).
Figure 13

The **distributive property** says that multiplying a number a by a sum of numbers $b + c$ gives the same result as multiplying a by b and a by c and then adding the two products.

$$a(b + c) = ab + ac \qquad \text{and} \qquad (b + c)a = ba + ca$$

As the arrows show, the a outside the parentheses is "distributed" over the b and c inside. The distributive property is also valid for subtraction.

$$a(b - c) = ab - ac \qquad \text{and} \qquad (b - c)a = ba - ca$$

The distributive property also can be extended to the sum (or difference) of more than two numbers.

$$a(b + c + d) = ab + ac + ad$$

EXAMPLE 8 **Using the Distributive Property**

Use the distributive property to rewrite each expression.

(a) $5(9 + 6) = 5 \cdot 9 + 5 \cdot 6$ Distributive property

$\qquad\qquad = 45 + 30$ Multiply.

$\qquad\qquad = 75$ Add.

(b) $4(x + 5 + y) = 4x + 4 \cdot 5 + 4y$ Distributive property

$\qquad\qquad\quad = 4x + 20 + 4y$ Multiply.

(c) $-2(x + 3) = -2x + (-2)(3)$ Distributive property

$\qquad\qquad = -2x + (-6)$ Multiply.

$\qquad\qquad = -2x - 6$

(d) $3(k - 9) = 3k - 3 \cdot 9$ Distributive property

$\qquad\qquad = 3k - 27$ Multiply.

(e) $6 \cdot 8 + 6 \cdot 2$

The distributive property says that $a(b + c) = ab + ac$. This can be reversed to read

$$ab + ac = a(b + c).$$

We use this form of the distributive property to write a sum like $6 \cdot 8 + 6 \cdot 2$ with a common factor (of 6) as a product.

$\qquad ab + ac = a(b + c)$ Distributive property

$\quad 6 \cdot 8 + 6 \cdot 2 = 6(8 + 2)$ Let $a = 6$, $b = 8$, and $c = 2$.

$\qquad\qquad = 6(10)$

$\qquad\qquad = 60$

(f) $8(3r + 11t + 5z) = 8(3r) + 8(11t) + 8(5z)$ Distributive property

$\qquad\qquad = (8 \cdot 3)r + (8 \cdot 11)t + (8 \cdot 5)z$ Associative property

$\qquad\qquad = 24r + 88t + 40z$

Work Problem 8 at the Side. ▷▷▷

8 Use the distributive property to rewrite each expression.

(a) $2(p + 5)$

(b) $-4(y + 7)$

(c) $5(m - 4)$

(d) $9 \cdot k + 9 \cdot 5$

(e) $3a - 3b$

(f) $7(2y + 7k - 9m)$

ANSWERS

8. **(a)** $2p + 10$ **(b)** $-4y - 28$
(c) $5m - 20$ **(d)** $9(k + 5)$
(e) $3(a - b)$ **(f)** $14y + 49k - 63m$

9 Write without parentheses.

(a) $-(3k - 5)$

(b) $-(2 - r)$

(c) $-(-5y + 8)$

(d) $-(-z + 4)$

The symbol $-a$ may be interpreted as $-1 \cdot a$. Similarly, when a negative sign precedes an expression within parentheses, it may also be interpreted as a factor of -1. Thus, we can use the distributive property to remove (or clear) the parentheses from expressions such as $-(2y + 3)$. We do this by first writing $-(2y + 3)$ as $-1 \cdot (2y + 3)$.

$$-(2y + 3) = -1 \cdot (2y + 3) \qquad -a = -1 \cdot a$$
$$= -1 \cdot (2y) + (-1) \cdot (3) \qquad \text{Distributive property}$$
$$= -2y - 3 \qquad \text{Multiply.}$$

EXAMPLE 9 Using the Distributive Property to Remove Parentheses

Write without parentheses.

(a) $-(7r - 8) = -1(7r - 8)$
$$= -1(7r) + (-1)(-8) \qquad \text{Distributive property}$$
$$= -7r + 8 \qquad \text{Multiply.}$$

(b) $-(-9w + 2) = -1(-9w + 2)$
$$= 9w - 2$$

◀◀◀ **Work Problem 9 at the Side.**

The properties discussed here are the basic properties of real numbers that justify how we add and multiply in algebra. You should know them by name because we will be referring to them frequently. Here is a summary of these properties.

Properties of Addition and Multiplication

For any real numbers a, b, and c, the following properties hold.

Commutative properties $\qquad a + b = b + a \qquad ab = ba$

Associative properties $\qquad (a + b) + c = a + (b + c)$
$$(ab)c = a(bc)$$

Identity properties $\qquad$ There is a real number 0 such that
$$a + 0 = a \quad \text{and} \quad 0 + a = a.$$
There is a real number 1 such that
$$a \cdot 1 = a \quad \text{and} \quad 1 \cdot a = a.$$

Inverse properties $\qquad$ For each real number a, there is a single real number $-a$ such that
$$a + (-a) = 0 \quad \text{and} \quad (-a) + a = 0.$$
For each nonzero real number a, there is a single real number $\frac{1}{a}$ such that
$$a \cdot \frac{1}{a} = 1 \quad \text{and} \quad \frac{1}{a} \cdot a = 1.$$

Distributive property $\qquad a(b + c) = ab + ac$
$$(b + c)a = ba + ca$$

ANSWERS
9. (a) $-3k + 5$ (b) $-2 + r$
   (c) $5y - 8$ (d) $z - 4$

1.7 Exercises

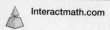
Match each item in Column I with the correct choice from Column II. Choices may be used once, more than once, or not at all.

I	**II**
1. Identity element for addition	**A.** $(5 \cdot 4) \cdot 3 = 5 \cdot (4 \cdot 3)$
2. Identity element for multiplication	**B.** 0
3. Additive inverse of a	**C.** $-a$
4. Multiplicative inverse, or reciprocal, of the nonzero number a	**D.** -1
5. The only number that has no multiplicative inverse	**E.** $5 \cdot 4 \cdot 3 = 60$
6. An example of an associative property	**F.** 1
7. An example of a commutative property	**G.** $(5 \cdot 4) \cdot 3 = 3 \cdot (5 \cdot 4)$
8. An example of the distributive property	**H.** $5(4 + 3) = 5 \cdot 4 + 5 \cdot 3$
	I. $\dfrac{1}{a}$

Decide whether each statement is an example of a commutative, associative, identity, or inverse property, or of the distributive property. See Examples 1, 2, 3, and 5–8.

9. $\dfrac{2}{3}(-4) = -4\left(\dfrac{2}{3}\right)$

10. $6\left(-\dfrac{5}{6}\right) = \left(-\dfrac{5}{6}\right)6$

11. $-6 + (12 + 7) = (-6 + 12) + 7$

12. $(-8 + 13) + 2 = -8 + (13 + 2)$

13. $-6 + 6 = 0$

14. $12 + (-12) = 0$

15. $\left(\dfrac{2}{3}\right)\left(\dfrac{3}{2}\right) = 1$

16. $\left(\dfrac{5}{8}\right)\left(\dfrac{8}{5}\right) = 1$

17. $2.34 \cdot 1 = 2.34$

18. $-8.456 \cdot 1 = -8.456$

19. $(4 + 17) + 3 = 3 + (4 + 17)$

20. $(-8 + 4) + (-12) = -12 + (-8 + 4)$

21. $6(x + y) = 6x + 6y$

22. $14(t + s) = 14t + 14s$

23. $-\dfrac{5}{9} = -\dfrac{5}{9} \cdot \dfrac{3}{3} = -\dfrac{15}{27}$

24. $\dfrac{13}{12} = \dfrac{13}{12} \cdot \dfrac{7}{7} = \dfrac{91}{84}$

25. $5(2x) + 5(3y) = 5(2x + 3y)$

26. $3(5t) - 3(7r) = 3(5t - 7r)$

27. What number(s) satisfy each condition? **(a)** a number that is its own additive inverse **(b)** two numbers that are their own multiplicative inverses

28. The distributive property holds for multiplication with respect to addition. Is there a distributive property for addition with respect to multiplication? That is, does $a + b \cdot c = (a + b)(a + c)$? If not, give an example to show why.

29. Evaluate $25 - (6 - 2)$ and $(25 - 6) - 2$. Use the results to explain why subtraction is or is not associative.

30. Suppose that a classmate shows you the following work.

$$-2(5 - 6) = -2(5) - 2(6) = -10 - 12 = -22$$

The classmate has made a very common error. Explain the error and then work the problem correctly.

Write a new expression that is equal to the given expression, using the given property. Then simplify the new expression if possible. See Examples 1, 2, 5, 7, and 8.

31. $r + 7$; commutative

32. $t + 9$; commutative

33. $s + 0$; identity

34. $w + 0$; identity

35. $-6(x + 7)$; distributive

36. $-5(y + 2)$; distributive

37. $(w + 5) + (-3)$; associative

38. $(b + 8) + (-10)$; associative

39. Explain how the procedure of changing $\frac{3}{4}$ to $\frac{9}{12}$ requires the use of the multiplicative identity element, 1.

Use the properties of this section to simplify each expression. See Example 4.

40. $26 + 8 - 26 + 12$

41. $-\frac{3}{8} + \frac{2}{5} + \frac{8}{5} + \frac{3}{8}$

42. $\frac{9}{7}(-.38)\left(\frac{7}{9}\right)$

Use the distributive property to rewrite each expression. Simplify if possible. See Example 8.

43. $5 \cdot 3 + 5 \cdot 17$

44. $15 \cdot 6 + 5 \cdot 6$

45. $4(t + 3)$

46. $5(w + 4)$

47. $-8(r + 3)$

48. $-11(x + 4)$

49. $-5(y - 4)$

50. $-9(g - 4)$

51. $-\frac{4}{3}(12y + 15z)$

52. $-\frac{2}{5}(10b + 20a)$

53. $8 \cdot z + 8 \cdot w$

54. $4 \cdot s + 4 \cdot r$

55. $7(2v) + 7(5r)$

56. $13(5w) + 13(4p)$

57. $8(3r + 4s - 5y)$

58. $2(5u - 3v + 7w)$

59. $-3(8x + 3y + 4z)$

60. $-5(2x - 5y + 6z)$

Use the distributive property to write each expression without parentheses. See Example 9.

61. $-(4t + 5m)$

62. $-(9x + 12y)$

63. $-(-5c - 4d)$

64. $-(-13x - 15y)$

65. $-(-3q + 5r - 8s)$

66. $-(-4z + 5w - 9y)$

67. "Starting a car" and "driving away in a car" are not commutative. Give an example of another pair of everyday activities that are not commutative.

68. Are "undressing" and "taking a shower" commutative?

69. *True* or *false:* "preparing a meal" and "eating a meal" are commutative.

70. The phrase "dog biting man" has two different meanings, depending on how the words are associated.

(dog biting) man   or   dog (biting man)

Give another example of a three-word phrase that has different meanings depending on how the words are associated.

71. Use parentheses to show how the associative property can be used to give two different meanings to "foreign sales clerk."

72. Use parentheses to show two different meanings for "hot pink pants."

RELATING CONCEPTS (EXERCISES 73–76)   For Individual or Group Work

*In **Section 1.6** we used a pattern to see that the product of two negative numbers is a positive number. In the exercises that follow, we show another justification for determining the sign of the product of two negative numbers.* **Work Exercises 73–76 in order.**

73. Evaluate the expression $-3[5 + (-5)]$ by using the order of operations.

74. Write the expression in Exercise 73 using the distributive property. Do not simplify the products.

75. The product $-3(5)$ should be one of the terms you wrote when answering Exercise 74. Based on the results in **Section 1.6,** what is this product?

76. In Exercise 73, you should have obtained 0 as the answer. Now, consider the following, using the results of Exercises 73 and 75.

$$-3[5 + (-5)] = -3(5) + (-3)(-5)$$
$$0 = -15 + ?$$

The question mark represents the product $-3(-5)$. When added to -15, it must give a sum of 0. Therefore, $-3(-5)$ must equal what?

1.8 Simplifying Expressions

OBJECTIVE 1 Simplify expressions. We now simplify expressions using the properties of addition and multiplication introduced in **Section 1.7.**

EXAMPLE 1 Simplifying Expressions

Simplify each expression.

(a) $4x + 8 + 9$

Since $8 + 9 = 17$, $4x + 8 + 9 = 4x + 17$.

(b) $4(3m - 2n)$

Use the distributive property.

$$4(3m - 2n) = 4(3m) - 4(2n)$$
$$= 12m - 8n$$

(c) $6 + 3(4k + 5) = 6 + 3(4k) + 3(5)$ Distributive property
$$= 6 + 12k + 15 \quad \text{Multiply.}$$
$$= 21 + 12k \quad \text{Add.}$$

(d) $5 - (2y - 8) = 5 - 1(2y - 8)$ $-a = -1 \cdot a$
$$= 5 - 2y + 8 \quad \text{Distributive property}$$
$$= 13 - 2y \quad \text{Add.}$$

NOTE

In Examples 1(c) and 1(d) we mentally used the commutative and associative properties to add in the last step. In practice, these steps are usually left out, but we should realize that they are used whenever the ordering and grouping in a sum are rearranged.

Work Problem 1 at the Side.

OBJECTIVE 2 Identify terms and numerical coefficients. A **term** is a number, a variable, or a product or quotient of a number and one or more variables raised to powers. Examples of terms include

$$-9x^2, \quad 15y, \quad -3, \quad 8m^2n, \quad \frac{2}{p}, \quad \text{and} \quad k. \quad \text{Terms}$$

The **numerical coefficient,** or simply coefficient, of the term $9m$ is 9; the numerical coefficient of $-15x^3y^2$ is -15; the numerical coefficient of x is 1; and the numerical coefficient of 8 is 8. In the expression $\frac{x}{3}$, the numerical coefficient of x is $\frac{1}{3}$ since $\frac{x}{3} = \frac{1x}{3} = \frac{1}{3}x$.

CAUTION

It is important to be able to distinguish between *terms* and *factors.* For example, in the expression $8x^3 + 12x^2$, there are two *terms,* $8x^3$ and $12x^2$. Terms are separated by a $+$ or $-$ sign. On the other hand, in the one-term expression $(8x^3)(12x^2)$, $8x^3$ and $12x^2$ are *factors.* Factors are multiplied.

OBJECTIVES

1 Simplify expressions.
2 Identify terms and numerical coefficients.
3 Identify like terms.
4 Combine like terms.
5 Simplify expressions from word phrases.

1 Simplify each expression.

(a) $9k + 12 - 5$

(b) $7(3p + 2q)$

(c) $2 + 5(3z - 1)$

(d) $-3 - (2 + 5y)$

ANSWERS
1. (a) $9k + 7$ **(b)** $21p + 14q$
(c) $15z - 3$ **(d)** $-5 - 5y$

② Give the numerical coefficient of each term.

(a) $15q$

(b) $-2m^3$

(c) $-18m^7q^4$

(d) $-r$

(e) $\dfrac{5x}{4}$

③ Identify each pair of terms as *like* or *unlike*.

(a) $9x, 4x$

(b) $-8y^3, 12y^2$

(c) $5x^2y^4, 5x^4y^2$

(d) $7x^2y^4, -7x^2y^4$

(e) $13kt, 4tk$

④ Combine like terms.

(a) $4k + 7k$

(b) $4r - r$

(c) $5z + 9z - 4z$

(d) $8p + 8p^2$

(e) $5x - 3y + 2x - 5y - 3$

ANSWERS

2. **(a)** 15 **(b)** -2 **(c)** -18
   (d) -1 **(e)** $\dfrac{5}{4}$
3. **(a)** like **(b)** unlike **(c)** unlike
   (d) like **(e)** like
4. **(a)** $11k$ **(b)** $3r$ **(c)** $10z$
   (d) cannot be combined **(e)** $7x - 8y - 3$

Here are some examples of terms and their numerical coefficients.

Term	Numerical Coefficient
$-7y$	-7
$34r^3$	34
$-26x^5yz^4$	-26
$-k$	-1
r	1
$\dfrac{3x}{8} = \dfrac{3}{8}x$	$\dfrac{3}{8}$

◀◀◀ Work Problem 2 at the Side.

OBJECTIVE ③ Identify like terms. Terms with exactly the same variables (including the same exponents) are called **like terms.** For example, $9m$ and $4m$ have the same variables and are like terms. Also, $6x^3$ and $-5x^3$ are like terms. The terms $-4y^3$ and $4y^2$ have different exponents and are **unlike terms.** Here are some additional examples.

$5x$ and $-12x$	$3x^2y$ and $5x^2y$	Like terms
$4xy^2$ and $5xy$	$8x^2y^3$ and $7x^3y^2$	Unlike terms

◀◀◀ Work Problem 3 at the Side.

OBJECTIVE ④ Combine like terms. Recall the distributive property:

$$x(y + z) = xy + xz.$$

As seen in the previous section, this statement can also be written as

$$xy + xz = x(y + z) \qquad \text{or} \qquad xy + xz = (y + z)x.$$

Thus the distributive property may be used to find the sum or difference of like terms. For example,

$$3x + 5x = (3 + 5)x = 8x.$$

This process is called **combining like terms.**

EXAMPLE 2 Combining Like Terms

Combine like terms in each expression.

(a) $9m + 5m$
Use the distributive property as given above.

$$9m + 5m = (9 + 5)m = 14m$$

(b) $6r + 3r + 2r = (6 + 3 + 2)r = 11r$ Distributive property

(c) $\dfrac{3}{4}x + x = \dfrac{3}{4}x + 1x = \left(\dfrac{3}{4} + 1\right)x = \dfrac{7}{4}x$ (Note: $x = 1x$.)

(d) $16y^2 - 9y^2 = (16 - 9)y^2 = 7y^2$

(e) $32y + 10y^2$ cannot be combined because $32y$ and $10y^2$ are unlike terms. The distributive property cannot be used here to combine coefficients.

◀◀◀ Work Problem 4 at the Side.

> **CAUTION**
> Remember that *only like terms may be combined.*

When an expression involves parentheses, the distributive property is used both "forward" and "backward" to combine like terms, as shown in the following example.

EXAMPLE 3 Simplifying Expressions Involving Like Terms

Simplify each expression.

(a) $14y + 2(6 + 3y) = 14y + 2(6) + 2(3y)$ Distributive property

$= 14y + 12 + 6y$ Multiply.

$= 20y + 12$ Combine like terms.

(b) $9k - 6 - 3(2 - 5k) = 9k - 6 - 3(2) - 3(-5k)$ Distributive property

$= 9k - 6 - 6 + 15k$ Multiply.

$= 24k - 12$ Combine like terms.

(c) $-(2 - r) + 10r = -1(2 - r) + 10r$ $-(2 - r) = -1(2 - r)$

$= -1(2) - 1(-r) + 10r$ Distributive property

$= -2 + r + 10r$ Multiply.

$= -2 + 11r$ Combine like terms.

(d) $5(2a^2 - 6a) - 3(4a^2 - 9) = 10a^2 - 30a - 12a^2 + 27$ Distributive property

$= -2a^2 - 30a + 27$ Combine like terms.

> **Work Problem 5 at the Side.**))))

OBJECTIVE 5 Simplify expressions from word phrases. Earlier we translated words, phrases, and statements into expressions and equations. Now we can simplify translated expressions by combining like terms.

EXAMPLE 4 Translating Words into a Mathematical Expression

Write the following phrase as a mathematical expression and simplify: four times a number, subtracted from the sum of twice the number and 4.

Let x represent the number. The expression is

The sum of twice the number and 4   Four times the number

$(2x + 4) - 4x$ Write with symbols.

which simplifies to

$-2x + 4.$ Combine like terms.

> **Work Problem 6 at the Side.**))))

> **CAUTION**
> In Example 4, we are dealing with an expression to be simplified, *not* an equation to be solved.

---

5 Simplify.

(a) $10p + 3(5 + 2p)$

(b) $7z - 2 - (1 + z)$

(c) $-(3k^2 + 5k) + 7(k^2 - 4k)$

6 Write each phrase as a mathematical expression, and simplify by combining like terms.

(a) Three times a number, subtracted from the sum of the number and 8

(b) Twice a number added to the sum of 6 and the number

Real-Data Applications

Algebraic Expressions and Tuition Costs

Algebraic expressions are useful in real-life scenarios in which the same set of instructions are repeated for different choices of numbers. Below is the description of how tuition and fees are calculated for "Resident of District" students at North Harris Montgomery Community College District (NHMCCD) in Texas for 2003–2004. The information is given in the college's schedule and can be found at the Web site www.nhmccd.edu.*

Fees Required at NHMCCD

[*Residents of the district pay*] tuition at the rate of $32 per credit hour, a $6 per credit hour technology fee, a $2 per credit hour student services fee, and a registration fee of $12.

For Group Discussion

1. Calculate the tuition and fees for a student who is a resident of the district and who enrolls at NHMCCD for the specified number of credit hours. Let x represent the number of credit hours. Pay attention to the *process* used in your calculations so that you can write the algebraic expression for x credit hours.

   (a) 3 credit hours: _____

   (b) 9 credit hours: _____

   (c) 12 credit hours: _____

   (d) x credit hours: _____ dollars

Write the algebraic expression that represents the tuition and fees for each institution for one semester. Let x represent the number of credit hours. If you have difficulty, first calculate the costs for 3 or 9 credit hours and focus on the process that you used to get the answer.

2. American River College, California (nonresident student) www.losrios.edu*
   Enrollment fee $18 per unit; nonresident tuition $149 per unit; parking permit $30 per semester; student representation fee $1 per semester

3. Austin Community College, Texas (in-state and out-of-district student) www.austin.cc.tx.us*
   Tuition $89 per credit; building fee $13 per credit; student activity fee $3 per term; parking fee $10 per year

4. Anoka Ramsey Community College, Minnesota (in-state resident) www.anokaramsey.edu*
   Tuition $93.12 per credit; technology fee $5.50 per credit; student activity fee $4.75 per credit; parking fee $2.00 per credit; student association fee $.28 per credit

5. Your own college

*Note that URLs sometimes change, although that is unlikely for academic institutions. If the Web address given does not work, use a search engine, such as www.yahoo.com, to find the new URL.

1.8 Exercises

 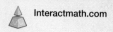

In Exercises 1–4, choose the letter of the correct response.

1. Which is true for all real numbers x?

   A. $6 + 2x = 8x$ **B.** $6 - 2x = 4x$

   C. $6x - 2x = 4x$ **D.** $3 + 8(4x - 6) = 11(4x - 6)$

2. Which is an example of a pair of like terms?

   A. $6t, 6w$ **B.** $-8x^2y, 9xy^2$

   C. $5ry, 6yr$ **D.** $-5x^2, 2x^3$

3. Which is an example of a term with numerical coefficient 5?

   A. $5x^3y^7$ **B.** x^5 **C.** $\dfrac{x}{5}$ **D.** 5^2xy^3

4. Which is a correct translation for "six times a number, subtracted from the product of eleven and the number" (if x represents the number)?

   A. $6x - 11x$ **B.** $11x - 6x$

   C. $(11 + x) - 6x$ **D.** $6x - (11 + x)$

Simplify each expression. See Example 1.

5. $3x + 12x$

6. $4y + 9y$

7. $8t - 5t + 2t$

8. $6s - 9s + 4s$

9. $4r + 19 - 8$

10. $7t + 18 - 4$

11. $5 + 2(x - 3y)$

12. $8 + 3(s - 6t)$

13. $-2 - (5 - 3p)$

14. $-10 - (7 - 14r)$

Give the numerical coefficient of each term.

15. $-12k$

16. $-23y$

17. $5m^2$

18. $-3n^6$

19. xw

20. pq

21. $-x$

22. $-t$

23. 74

24. 98

25. Give an example of a pair of like terms with the variable x, such that one of them has a negative numerical coefficient, one has a positive numerical coefficient, and their sum has a positive numerical coefficient.

26. Give an example of a pair of unlike terms such that each term has x as the only variable.

Identify each group of terms as like *or* unlike.

27. $8r, -13r$

28. $-7a, 12a$

29. $5z^4, 9z^3$

30. $8x^5, -10x^3$

31. $4, 9, -24$

32. $7, 17, -83$

33. x, y

34. t, s

35. There is an old saying "You can't add apples and oranges." Explain how this saying can be applied to Objective 3 in this section.

36. Explain how the distributive property is used in combining $6t + 5t$ to get $11t$.

Simplify each expression. See Examples 2 and 3.

37. $-5 - 2(x - 3)$

38. $-8 - 3(2x + 4)$

39. $-\dfrac{4}{3} + 2t + \dfrac{1}{3}t - 8 - \dfrac{8}{3}t$

40. $-\dfrac{5}{6} + 8x + \dfrac{1}{6}x - 7 - \dfrac{7}{6}$

41. $-5.3r + 4.9 - (2r + .7) + 3.2r$

42. $2.7b + 5.8 - (3b + .5) - 4.4b$

43. $2y^2 - 7y^3 - 4y^2 + 10y^3$

44. $9x^4 - 7x^6 + 12x^4 + 14x^6$

45. $13p + 4(4 - 8p)$

46. $5x + 3(7 - 2x)$

47. $-\dfrac{4}{3}(y - 12) - \dfrac{1}{6}y$

48. $-\dfrac{7}{5}(t - 15) - \dfrac{3}{2}$

49. $-5(5y - 9) + 3(3y + 6)$

50. $-3(2t + 4) + 8(2t - 4)$

Write each phrase as a mathematical expression. Use x to represent the number. Combine like terms when possible. See Example 4.

51. Five times a number, added to the sum of the number and three

52. Six times a number, added to the sum of the number and six

53. A number multiplied by -7, subtracted from the sum of 13 and six times the number

54. A number multiplied by 5, subtracted from the sum of 14 and eight times the number

55. Six times a number added to -4, subtracted from twice the sum of three times the number and 4

56. Nine times a number added to 6, subtracted from triple the sum of 12 and 8 times the number

57. Write the expression $9x - (x + 2)$ using words, as in Exercises 51–56.

58. Write the expression $2(3x + 5) - 2(x + 4)$ using words, as in Exercises 51–56.

RELATING CONCEPTS (EXERCISES 59–62) For Individual or Group Work

A manufacturer has fixed costs of $1000 to produce widgets. Each widget costs $5 to make. The fixed cost to produce gadgets is $750, and each gadget costs $3 to make. **Work Exercises 59–62 in order.**

59. Write an expression for the cost to make x widgets. (*Hint:* The cost will be the sum of the fixed cost and the cost per item times the number of items.)

60. Write an expression for the cost to make y gadgets.

61. Write an expression for the total cost to make x widgets and y gadgets.

62. Simplify the expression you wrote in Exercise 61.

Chapter 1
S U M M A R Y

KEY TERMS

1.1	**exponent**	An exponent, or **power**, is a number that indicates how many times a factor is repeated. $3^4 \leftarrow$ Exponent $\Big\}$ Exponential expression; $\llcorner$ Base
	base	The base is the number that is a repeated factor when written with an exponent.
	exponential expression	A number written with an exponent is an exponential expression.
1.2	**variable**	A variable is a symbol, usually a letter, used to represent an unknown number.
	algebraic expression	An algebraic expression is a collection of numbers, variables, operation symbols, and grouping symbols.
	equation	An equation is a statement that says two expressions are equal.
	solution	A solution of an equation is any value of the variable that makes the equation true.
1.3	**natural numbers**	The set of natural numbers is $\{1, 2, 3, 4, \ldots\}$.
	whole numbers	The set of whole numbers is $\{0, 1, 2, 3, 4, 5, \ldots\}$.
	number line	The number line shows the ordering of the real numbers on an infinite line.
	opposite	The opposite of a number a is the number that is the same distance from 0 on the number line as a, but on the opposite side of 0. This number is also called the **negative** of a or the **additive inverse** of a.
	integers	The set of integers is $\{\ldots, -3, -2, -1, 0, 1, 2, 3, \ldots\}$.
	negative number	A negative number is located to the *left* of 0 on the number line.
	positive number	A positive number is located to the *right* of 0 on the number line.
	rational numbers	A rational number is a number that can be written as the quotient of two integers, with denominator not 0.
	coordinate	The number that corresponds to a point on the number line is the coordinate of that point.
	irrational numbers	An irrational number is a real number that is not a rational number.
	real numbers	Real numbers are numbers that can be represented by points on the number line, or all rational and irrational numbers.
	absolute value	The absolute value of a number is the distance between 0 and the number on the number line.
1.4	**sum**	The answer to an addition problem is called the sum.
1.5	**minuend**	In the operation $a - b$, a is called the minuend.
	subtrahend	In the operation $a - b$, b is called the subtrahend.
	difference	The answer to a subtraction problem is called the difference.
1.6	**product**	The answer to a multiplication problem is called the product.
	quotient	The answer to a division problem is called the quotient.
	reciprocal	Pairs of numbers whose product is 1 are called reciprocals or **multiplicative inverses** of each other.
1.7	**identity element for addition**	When the identity element for addition, which is 0, is added to a number, the number is unchanged.
	identity element for multiplication	When a number is multiplied by the identity element for multiplication, which is 1, the number is unchanged.
1.8	**term**	A term is a number, a variable, or a product or quotient of a number and one or more variables raised to powers.
	numerical coefficient	The numerical factor in a term is its numerical coefficient.
	like terms	Terms with exactly the same variables (including the same exponents) are called like terms.

Number line

Negative numbers | Positive numbers

-3 -2 -1 0 1 2 3

Opposites

NEW SYMBOLS

a^n	n factors of a	$a(b)$, $(a)b$, $(a)(b)$, $a \cdot b$, or ab	a times b
$=$	is equal to	$\dfrac{a}{b}$, a/b, or $a \div b$	a divided by b
$\neq$	is not equal to	$\{\ \}$	set braces
$<$	is less than	$[\ \ ]$	square brackets
$\leq$	is less than or equal to	$|x|$	absolute value of x
$>$	is greater than	$\dfrac{1}{x}$	multiplicative inverse or reciprocal of x ($x \neq 0$)
$\geq$	is greater than or equal to		

TEST YOUR WORD POWER

See how well you have learned the vocabulary in this chapter. Answers, with examples, follow the Quick Review.

1. The **product** is
  A. the answer in an addition problem
  B. the answer in a multiplication problem
  C. one of two or more numbers that are added to get another number
  D. one of two or more numbers that are multiplied to get another number.

2. A number is **prime** if
  A. it cannot be factored
  B. it has just one factor
  C. it has only itself and 1 as factors
  D. it has at least two different factors.

3. An **exponent** is
  A. a symbol that tells how many numbers are being multiplied
  B. a number raised to a power
  C. a number that tells how many times a factor is repeated
  D. one of two or more numbers that are multiplied.

4. A **variable** is
  A. a symbol used to represent an unknown number
  B. a value that makes an equation true
  C. a solution of an equation
  D. the answer in a division problem.

5. An **integer** is
  A. a positive or negative number
  B. a natural number, its opposite, or zero
  C. any number that can be graphed on a number line
  D. the quotient of two numbers.

6. A **coordinate** is
  A. the number that corresponds to a point on a number line
  B. the graph of a number
  C. any point on a number line
  D. the distance from 0 on a number line.

7. The **absolute value** of a number is
  A. the graph of the number
  B. the reciprocal of the number
  C. the opposite of the number
  D. the distance between 0 and the number on a number line.

8. A **term** is
  A. a numerical factor
  B. a number, a variable, or a product or quotient of numbers and variables raised to powers
  C. one of several variables with the same exponents
  D. a sum of numbers and variables raised to powers.

9. A **numerical coefficient** is
  A. the numerical factor in a term
  B. the number of terms in an expression
  C. a variable raised to a power
  D. the variable factor in a term.

10. The **subtrahend** in $a - b = c$ is
  A. a
  B. b
  C. c
  D. $a - b$.

Concepts	Examples

QUICK REVIEW

1.1 *Exponents, Order of Operations, and Inequality*

Order of Operations

Simplify within any parentheses or brackets and above and below fraction bars, using the following steps.

Step 1 Apply all exponents.

Step 2 Multiply or divide from left to right.

Step 3 Add or subtract from left to right.

$$\frac{9(2+6)}{2} - 2(2^3 + 3) = 36 - 2(8+3)$$
$$= 36 - 2(11)$$
$$= 36 - 22$$
$$= 14$$

1.2 *Variables, Expressions, and Equations*

Evaluate an expression with a variable by substituting a given number for the variable.

Evaluate $2x + y^2$ if $x = 3$ and $y = -4$.
$$2x + y^2 = 2(3) + (-4)^2$$
$$= 6 + 16$$
$$= 22$$

Values of a variable that make an equation true are solutions of the equation.

Is 2 a solution of $5x + 3 = 18$?
$$5(2) + 3 = 18$$
$$13 = 18 \qquad \text{False}$$
2 is not a solution.

1.3 *Real Numbers and the Number Line*

Ordering Real Numbers

a is less than *b* if *a* is to the left of *b* on the number line.

The opposite or additive inverse of *a* is $-a$.

The absolute value of *a*, $|a|$, is the distance between *a* and 0 on the number line.

$$-2 < 3 \qquad 3 > 0 \qquad 0 < 3$$
$$-(5) = -5 \qquad -(-7) = 7 \qquad -0 = 0$$
$$|13| = 13 \qquad |0| = 0 \qquad |-5| = 5$$

1.4 *Adding Real Numbers*

To add two numbers with the same sign, add their absolute values. The sum has that same sign.

To add two numbers with different signs, subtract their absolute values. The sum has the sign of the number with larger absolute value.

$$9 + 4 = 13$$
$$-8 + (-5) = -13$$
$$7 + (-12) = -5$$
$$-5 + 13 = 8$$

1.5 *Subtracting Real Numbers*

To subtract signed numbers, change the subtraction symbol to addition, and change the sign of the subtrahend. Add as in the previous section.

$$5 - (-2) = 5 + 2 = 7$$
$$-3 - 4 = -3 + (-4) = -7$$
$$-2 - (-6) = -2 + 6 = 4$$

1.6 *Multiplying and Dividing Real Numbers*

The product (or quotient) of two numbers having the *same sign* is *positive*.

The product (or quotient) of two numbers having *different signs* is *negative*.

$$6 \cdot 5 = 30 \qquad (-7)(-8) = 56$$
$$\frac{10}{2} = 5 \qquad \frac{-24}{-6} = 4$$
$$-6(5) = -30 \qquad 6(-5) = -30$$
$$-18 \div 9 = \frac{-18}{9} = -2 \qquad 49 \div (-7) = \frac{49}{-7} = -7$$

(continued)

| **Concepts** | **Examples** |

1.6 Multiplying and Dividing Real Numbers (continued)

To divide a by b, multiply a by the reciprocal of b.

$$\frac{10}{\frac{2}{3}} = 10 \div \frac{2}{3} = 10 \cdot \frac{3}{2} = 15$$

0 divided by a nonzero number is 0. Division by 0 is undefined.

$$\frac{0}{5} = 0 \qquad \frac{5}{0} \text{ is undefined.}$$

1.7 Properties of Real Numbers

Commutative Properties
$$a + b = b + a$$
$$ab = ba$$

$$7 + (-1) = -1 + 7$$
$$5(-3) = (-3)5$$

Associative Properties
$$(a + b) + c = a + (b + c)$$
$$(ab)c = a(bc)$$

$$(3 + 4) + 8 = 3 + (4 + 8)$$
$$[-2(6)]4 = -2[6(4)]$$

Identity Properties
$$a + 0 = a \qquad 0 + a = a$$
$$a \cdot 1 = a \qquad 1 \cdot a = a$$

$$-7 + 0 = -7 \qquad 0 + (-7) = -7$$
$$9 \cdot 1 = 9 \qquad 1 \cdot 9 = 9$$

Inverse Properties
$$a + (-a) = 0 \qquad -a + a = 0$$
$$a \cdot \frac{1}{a} = 1 \qquad \frac{1}{a} \cdot a = 1 \ (a \neq 0)$$

$$7 + (-7) = 0 \qquad -7 + 7 = 0$$
$$-2\left(-\frac{1}{2}\right) = 1 \qquad -\frac{1}{2}(-2) = 1$$

Distributive Properties
$$a(b + c) = ab + ac$$
$$(b + c)a = ba + ca$$
$$a(b - c) = ab - ac$$

$$5(4 + 2) = 5(4) + 5(2)$$
$$(4 + 2)5 = 4(5) + 2(5)$$
$$9(5 - 4) = 9(5) - 9(4)$$

1.8 Simplifying Expressions

Only like terms may be combined.

$$-3y^2 + 6y^2 + 14y^2 = 17y^2$$
$$-8a^5b^3 + 2a^3b^5 - 6a^5b^3 + 5a^3b^5 = -14a^5b^3 + 7a^3b^5$$
$$4(3 + 2x) - 6(5 - x) = 12 + 8x - 30 + 6x$$
$$= 14x - 18$$

ANSWERS TO TEST YOUR WORD POWER

1. B; *Example:* The product of 2 and 5, or 2 times 5, is 10.
2. C; *Examples:* 2, 3, 11, 41, 53
3. C; *Example:* In 2^3, the number 3 is the exponent (or power), so 2 is a factor three times; $2^3 = 2 \cdot 2 \cdot 2 = 8$.
4. A; *Examples:* a, b, c
5. B; *Examples:* $-9, 0, 6$
6. A; *Example:* The point graphed three units to the right of 0 on a number line has coordinate 3.
7. D; *Examples:* $|2| = 2$ and $|-2| = 2$
8. B; *Examples:* $6, \frac{x}{2}, -4ab^2$
9. A; *Examples:* The term 3 has numerical coefficient 3, $8z$ has numerical coefficient 8, and $-10x^4y$ has numerical coefficient -10.
10. B; *Example:* In $5 - 3 = 2$, 5 is the minuend, 3 is the subtrahend, and 2 is the difference.

Chapter **1**

REVIEW EXERCISES

If you need help with any of these Review Exercises, look in the section indicated in brackets.

[1.1] *Find the value of each exponential expression.*

1. 5^4

2. $(.03)^4$

3. $.21^3$

4. $\left(\dfrac{5}{2}\right)^3$

Find the value of each expression.

5. $8 \cdot 5 - 13$

6. $5[4^2 + 3(2^3)]$

7. $\dfrac{7(3^2 - 5)}{16 - 2 \cdot 6}$

8. $\dfrac{3(9 - 4) + 5(8 - 3)}{2^3 - (5 - 3)}$

Write each word statement in symbols.

9. Thirteen is less than seventeen.

10. Five plus two is not equal to ten.

11. Write $6 < 15$ in words.

12. Construct a false statement that involves addition on the left side, the symbol $\geq$, and division on the right side.

[1.2] *Evaluate each expression if $x = 6$ and $y = 3$.*

13. $2x + 6y$

14. $4(3x - y)$

15. $\dfrac{x}{3} + 4y$

16. $\dfrac{x^2 + 3}{3y - x}$

Change each word phrase to an algebraic expression. Use x to represent the number.

17. Six added to a number

18. A number subtracted from eight

19. Nine subtracted from six times a number

20. Three-fifths of a number added to 12

Decide whether the given number is a solution of the equation.

21. $5x + 3(x + 2) = 22; \, 2$

22. $\dfrac{x + 5}{3x} = 1; \, 6$

Change each word sentence to an equation. Use x to represent the number.

23. Six less than twice a number is 10.

24. The product of a number and 4 is 8.

Identify each of the following as either an equation *or an* expression.

25. $5r - 8(r + 7) = 2$

26. $2y + (5y - 9) + 2$

[1.3] *Graph each group of numbers on a number line.*

27. $-4, -\dfrac{1}{2}, 0, 2.5, 5$

28. $-2, -3, |-3|, |-1|$

29. $-3\dfrac{1}{4}, \dfrac{14}{5}, -1\dfrac{1}{8}, \dfrac{5}{6}$

30. $|-4|, -|-3|, -|-5|, -6$

Select the lesser number in each pair.

31. $-10, 5$

32. $-8, -9$

33. $-\dfrac{2}{3}, -\dfrac{3}{4}$

34. $0, -|23|$

Decide whether each statement is true *or* false.

35. $12 > -13$

36. $0 > -5$

37. $-9 < -7$

38. $-13 > -13$

Simplify by finding the absolute value.

39. $-|3|$

40. $-|-19|$

41. $-|9 - 2|$

42. $|15 - 6|$

[1.4] *Find each sum.*

43. $-10 + 4$

44. $14 + (-18)$

45. $-8 + (-9)$

46. $\dfrac{4}{9} + \left(-\dfrac{5}{4}\right)$

47. $[-6 + (-8) + 8] + [9 + (-13)]$

48. $(-4 + 7) + (-11 + 3) + (-15 + 1)$

Write a numerical expression for each phrase, and simplify the expression.

49. 19 added to the sum of -31 and 12

50. 13 more than the sum of -4 and -8

Solve each problem.

51. Mohammed Hashemi has \$18 in his checking account. He then writes a check for \$26. What negative number represents his balance?

52. The temperature at noon on an August day in Houston was 93°F. After a thunderstorm, it dropped 6°. What was the new temperature?

[1.5] *Find each difference.*

53. $-7 - 4$ **54.** $-12 - (-11)$ **55.** $5 - (-2)$ **56.** $-\dfrac{3}{7} - \dfrac{4}{5}$

57. $2.56 - (-7.75)$ **58.** $(-10 - 4) - (-2)$ **59.** $(-3 + 4) - (-1)$ **60.** $|5 - 9| - |-3 + 6|$

Write a numerical expression for each phrase, and simplify the expression.

61. The difference between -4 and -6

62. Five less than the sum of 4 and -8

Solve each problem.

63. In the year 2000, the U.S. budget surplus was $236.4 billion. By 2004, this had changed to a deficit of $477.0 billion. By how much had the year 2000 amount decreased? (*Source:* White House; Congressional Budget Office.)

64. The 1994 Women's Olympic Downhill Skiing champion, Katja Seizinger, from West Germany, finished the course in 1 min, 35.93 sec. Seizinger won again in 1998. Her time decreased by 7.04 sec. What was Seizinger's winning time in 1998? (*Source: World Almanac and Book of Facts,* 2004.)

65. Explain in your own words how the subtraction problem $-8 - (-6)$ is performed.

66. Can the difference of two negative numbers be positive? Explain with an example.

The bar graph shows the federal budget outlays for national defense for the years 1993–2001. Use a signed number to represent the change in outlay for each time period. For example, the change from 1995 to 1996 was $253.3 - $259.6 = -$6.3 billion.

67. 2000–2001

68. 1993–1994

69. 1997–1998

70. 1996–1997

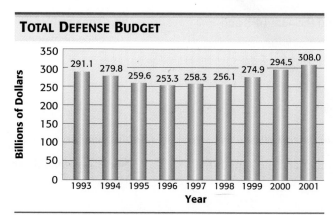

TOTAL DEFENSE BUDGET

Billions of Dollars

291.1 279.8 259.6 253.3 258.3 256.1 274.9 294.5 308.0

1993 1994 1995 1996 1997 1998 1999 2000 2001

Year

Source: U.S. Office of Management and Budget.

[1.6] *Perform the indicated operations.*

71. $(-12)(-3)$

72. $15(-7)$

73. $\left(-\dfrac{4}{3}\right)\left(-\dfrac{3}{8}\right)$

74. $(-4.8)(-2.1)$

75. $5(8-12)$

76. $(5-7)(8-3)$

77. $2(-6)-(-4)(-3)$

78. $3(-10)-5$

79. $\dfrac{-36}{-9}$

80. $\dfrac{220}{-11}$

81. $-\dfrac{1}{2} \div \dfrac{2}{3}$

82. $-33.9 \div (-3)$

83. $\dfrac{-5(3)-1}{8-4(-2)}$

84. $\dfrac{5(-2)-3(4)}{-2[3-(-2)]+10}$

85. $\dfrac{10^2-5^2}{8^2+3^2-(-2)}$

86. $\dfrac{4^2-8\cdot2}{(-1.2)^2-(-.56)}$

Evaluate each expression if $x = -5$, $y = 4$, and $z = -3$.

87. $6x-4z$

88. $5x+y-z$

89. $5x^2$

90. $z^2(3x-8y)$

Write a numerical expression for each phrase, and simplify the expression.

91. Nine less than the product of -4 and 5

92. Five-sixths of the sum of 12 and -6

93. The quotient of 12 and the sum of 8 and -4

94. The product of -20 and 12, divided by the difference between 15 and -15

Translate each sentence to an equation, using x to represent the number.

95. The quotient of a number and the sum of the number and 5 is -2.

96. 3 less than 8 times a number is -7.

[1.7] *Decide whether each statement is an example of a commutative, associative, identity, or inverse property, or of the distributive property.*

97. $6 + 0 = 6$

98. $5 \cdot 1 = 5$

99. $-\dfrac{2}{3}\left(-\dfrac{3}{2}\right) = 1$

100. $17 + (-17) = 0$

101. $5 + (-9 + 2) = [5 + (-9)] + 2$

102. $w(xy) = (wx)y$

103. $3x + 3y = 3(x + y)$

104. $(1 + 2) + 3 = 3 + (1 + 2)$

Use the distributive property to rewrite each expression. Simplify if possible.

105. $7y + y$

106. $-12(4 - t)$

107. $3(2s) + 3(4y)$

108. $-(-4r + 5s)$

[1.8] *Use the distributive property as necessary and combine like terms.*

109. $16p^2 - 8p^2 + 9p^2$

110. $4r^2 - 3r + 10r + 12r^2$

111. $-8(5k - 6) + 3(7k + 2)$

112. $2s - (-3s + 6)$

113. $-7(2t - 4) - 4(3t + 8) - 19(t + 1)$

114. $3.6t^2 + 9t - 8.1(6t^2 + 4t)$

Translate each phrase into a mathematical expression. Use x to represent the number, and combine like terms when possible.

115. Seven times a number, subtracted from the product of -2 and three times the number

116. The quotient of 9 more than a number and 6 less than the number

117. In Exercise 115, does the word *and* signify addition? Explain.

118. Write the expression $3(4x - 6)$ using words, as in Exercises 115 and 116.

MIXED REVIEW EXERCISES*

Perform the indicated operations.

119. $[(-2) + 7 - (-5)] + [-4 - (-10)]$

120. $\left(-\dfrac{5}{6}\right)^2$

121. $-|(-7)(-4)| - (-2)$

122. $\dfrac{6(-4) + 2(-12)}{5(-3) + (-3)}$

123. $\dfrac{3}{8} - \dfrac{5}{12}$

124. $\dfrac{12^2 + 2^2 - 8}{10^2 - (-4)(-15)}$

125. $\dfrac{8^2 + 6^2}{7^2 + 1^2}$

126. $-16(-3.5) - 7.2(-3)$

127. $2\dfrac{5}{6} - 4\dfrac{1}{3}$

128. $-8 + [(-4 + 17) - (-3 - 3)]$

129. $-\dfrac{12}{5} \div \dfrac{9}{7}$

130. $(-8 - 3) - 5(2 - 9)$

131. $[-7 + (-2) - (-3)] + [8 + (-13)]$

132. $\dfrac{15}{2} \cdot \left(-\dfrac{4}{5}\right)$

Write a numerical expression or an equation for each problem, and simplify any expressions if possible. Use x as the variable, and specify what it represents.

133. In 2003, a company spent $1400 less on advertising than in the previous year. The total spent for this purpose over these two years was $25,800.

134. The quotient of a number and 14 less than three times the number

---

*The order of exercises in this final group does not correspond to the order in which topics occur in the chapter. This random ordering should help you prepare for the chapter test in yet another way.

Chapter **1**

T E S T

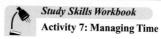
Study Skills Workbook
Activity 7: Managing Time

Decide whether the statement is true *or* false.

1. $4[-20 + 7(-2)] \leq -135$

1. _____

2. $\left(\dfrac{1}{2}\right)^2 + \left(\dfrac{2}{3}\right)^2 = \left(\dfrac{1}{2} + \dfrac{2}{3}\right)^2$

2. _____

3. Graph the numbers $-1, -3, |-4|,$ and $|-1|$ on the number line.

3. ![number line from -3 to 4]

Select the lesser number from each pair.

4. $6, -|-8|$

4. _____

5. $-.742, -1.277$

5. _____

6. Write in symbols: The quotient of -6 and the sum of 2 and -8. Simplify the expression.

6. _____

7. If a and b are both negative, is $\dfrac{a + b}{a \cdot b}$ positive or negative?

7. _____

Perform the indicated operations whenever possible.

8. $-2 - (5 - 17) + (-6)$

8. _____

9. $-5\dfrac{1}{2} + 2\dfrac{2}{3}$

9. _____

10. $-6.2 - [-7.1 + (2.0 - 3.1)]$

10. _____

11. $4^2 + (-8) - (2^3 - 6)$

11. _____

12. $(-5)(-12) + 4(-4) + (-8)^2$

12. _____

13. $\dfrac{-7 - |-6 + 2|}{-5 - (-4)}$

13. _____

14. _____

$$14. \quad \frac{30(-1-2)}{-9[3-(-2)]-12(-2)}$$

In Exercises 15 and 16, evaluate each expression if x = −2 and y = 4.

15. _____

15. $3x - 4y^2$

16. _____

$$16. \quad \frac{5x + 7y}{3(x + y)}$$

17. _____

17. The highest Fahrenheit temperature ever recorded in Idaho was 118°, while the lowest was −60°. What is the difference between these highest and lowest temperatures? (*Source: World Almanac and Book of Facts*, 2004.)

Match each example in Column I with a property in Column II.

I	II

18. _____D_____

18. $3x + \boxed{0} = 3x$ D   **A.** Commutative

19. _____A_____

19. $(5 + 2) + 8 = 8 + (5 + 2)$ A   **B.** Associative

20. _____E_____

20. $-3(x + y) = -3x + (-3y)$ E   **C.** Inverse

21. _____B_____

21. $-5 + (3 + 2) = (-5 + 3) + 2$ B   **D.** Identity

22. _____C_____

22. $-\frac{5}{3}\left(-\frac{3}{5}\right) = 1$ C   **E.** Distributive

23. _____

23. Simplify $-2(3x^2 + 4) - 3(x^2 + 2x)$ by using the distributive property and combining like terms.

24. _____

24. Which properties are used to show that $-(3x + 1) = -3x - 1$?

25. (a) _____

(b) _____

25. Consider the expression $-6[5 + (-2)]$.
   (a) Evaluate it by first working within the brackets.
   (b) Evaluate it by using the distributive property.
   (c) Why must the answers in parts (a) and (b) be the same?

(c) _____

Equations, Inequalities, and Applications

In 1896, 241 competitors (no women among them) from 14 countries gathered in Athens, Greece, for the first modern Olympic Games. In 2004, the XXVIII Olympic Summer Games returned to Athens as a truly international event, attracting 10,500 athletes from 202 countries.

One ceremonial aspect of the games is the flying of the Olympic flag with its five interlocking rings of different colors on a white background. First introduced at the 1920 Games in Antwerp, Belgium, the five rings on the flag symbolize unity among the nations of Africa, the Americas, Asia, Australia, and Europe. (*Source: USA Today,* August 13, 2004; *Microsoft Encarta Encyclopedia 2002.*)

Throughout this chapter we use linear equations to solve applications about the Olympics.

2.1 The Addition Property of Equality

OBJECTIVES

1 Identify linear equations.

2 Use the addition property of equality.

3 Simplify equations, and then use the addition property of equality.

Recall from **Section 1.2** that an *equation* is a statement that two algebraic expressions are equal. The simplest type of equation is a *linear equation*.

OBJECTIVE 1 Identify linear equations.

Linear Equation in One Variable
A **linear equation in one variable** can be written in the form

$$Ax + B = C$$

where A, B, and C are real numbers, with $A \neq 0$.

For example,

$$4x + 9 = 0, \quad 2x - 3 = 5, \quad \text{and} \quad x = 7 \qquad \text{Linear equations}$$

are linear equations in one variable (x). The final two can be written in the specified form using properties developed in this chapter. However,

$$x^2 + 2x = 5, \quad \frac{1}{x} = 6, \quad \text{and} \quad |2x + 6| = 0 \qquad \text{Nonlinear equations}$$

are *not* linear equations.

As we saw in **Section 1.2**, a *solution* of an equation is a number that makes the equation true when it replaces the variable. Equations that have exactly the same solutions are **equivalent equations.** Linear equations are solved by using a series of steps to produce a simpler equivalent equation of the form

$$x = \text{a number} \quad \text{or} \quad \text{a number} = x.$$

OBJECTIVE 2 Use the addition property of equality. In the equation $x - 5 = 2$, both $x - 5$ and 2 represent the same number because this is the meaning of the equals sign. To solve the equation, we change the left side from $x - 5$ to just x. We do this by adding 5 to $x - 5$. We use 5 because 5 is the opposite (additive inverse) of -5, and $-5 + 5 = 0$. To keep the two sides equal, we must also add 5 to the right side.

$x - 5 = 2$	Given equation
$x - 5 + 5 = 2 + 5$	Add 5 to each side.
$x + 0 = 7$	Additive inverse property
$x = 7$	Additive identity property

The solution of the given equation is 7. We check by replacing x with 7 in the original equation.

Check:

$x - 5 = 2$		Original equation
$7 - 5 = 2$	?	Let $x = 7$.
$2 = 2$		True

Since the final equation is true, 7 checks as the solution.

To solve the equation, we added the same number to each side. The **addition property of equality** justifies this step.

Addition Property of Equality

If A, B, and C are real numbers, then the equations

$$A = B \quad \text{and} \quad A + C = B + C$$

are equivalent equations.

In words, we can add the same number to each side of an equation without changing the solution.

In the addition property, C represents a real number. This means that any quantity that represents a real number can be added to each side of an equation to change it to an equivalent equation.

> **NOTE**
> Equations can be thought of in terms of a balance. Thus, adding the same quantity to each side does not affect the balance. See Figure 1.
>
>
>
> **Figure 1**

EXAMPLE 1 Using the Addition Property of Equality

Solve $x - 16 = 7$.

Our goal is to get an equivalent equation of the form x = a number. To do this, we use the addition property of equality and add 16 to each side.

$$x - 16 = 7$$
$$x - 16 + 16 = 7 + 16 \qquad \text{Add 16 to each side.}$$
$$x = 23 \qquad \text{Combine like terms.}$$

Note that we combined the steps that change $x - 16 + 16$ to $x + 0$ and $x + 0$ to x. We check by substituting 23 for x in the *original* equation.

Check:
$$x - 16 = 7 \qquad \text{Original equation}$$
$$23 - 16 = 7 \quad ? \qquad \text{Let } x = 23.$$
$$7 = 7 \qquad \text{True}$$

Since a true statement results, 23 is the solution.

Work Problem 1 at the Side. ▶▶▶

EXAMPLE 2 Using the Addition Property of Equality

Solve $x - 2.9 = -6.4$.

We use the addition property of equality to get x alone on the left side.

$$x - 2.9 = -6.4$$
$$x - 2.9 + 2.9 = -6.4 + 2.9 \qquad \text{Add 2.9 to each side.}$$
$$x = -3.5$$

Check:
$$x - 2.9 = -6.4 \qquad \text{Original equation}$$
$$-3.5 - 2.9 = -6.4 \quad ? \qquad \text{Let } x = -3.5.$$
$$-6.4 = -6.4 \qquad \text{True}$$

Since a true statement results, the solution is -3.5.

Work Problem 2 at the Side. ▶▶▶

---

1 Solve.

(a) $x - 12 = 9$

(b) $x - 25 = -18$

2 Solve.

(a) $x - 3.7 = -8.1$

(b) $a - 4.1 = 6.3$

ANSWERS
1. (a) 21 **(b)** 7
2. (a) -4.4 **(b)** 10.4

3 Solve.

(a) $-3 = a + 2$

The addition property of equality says that the same number may be *added* to each side of an equation. In **Section 1.5,** subtraction was defined as addition of the opposite. Thus, we can also use the following rule when solving an equation.

> The same number may be *subtracted* from each side of an equation without changing the solution.

For example, to solve the equation $x + 4 = 10$, we subtract 4 from each side to get $x = 6$.

EXAMPLE 3   **Using the Addition Property of Equality**

Solve $-7 = x + 22$.
    Here the variable x is on the right side of the equation. To get x alone on the right we must eliminate the 22 by subtracting 22 from each side.

$$-7 = x + 22$$

$$-7 - \mathbf{22} = x + 22 - \mathbf{22} \qquad \text{Subtract 22 from each side.}$$

$$-29 = x \quad \text{or} \quad x = -29$$

Check: $\qquad -7 = x + 22 \qquad\qquad$ Original equation

$$-7 = -\mathbf{29} + 22 \qquad ? \quad \text{Let } x = -29.$$

$$-7 = -7 \qquad\qquad\qquad \text{True}$$

The check confirms that the solution is -29.

(b) $22 = -16 + r$

Work Problem 3 at the Side.

CAUTION
The final line of the check does *not* give the solution to the problem, only a confirmation that the solution found is correct.

EXAMPLE 4   **Subtracting a Variable Expression**

Solve $\frac{3}{5}k + 12 = \frac{8}{5}k$.
    To get all terms with variables on the same side of the equation, subtract $\frac{3}{5}k$ from each side.

$$\frac{3}{5}k + 12 = \frac{8}{5}k$$

$$\frac{3}{5}k + 12 - \frac{3}{5}k = \frac{8}{5}k - \frac{3}{5}k \qquad \text{Subtract } \tfrac{3}{5}k \text{ from each side.}$$

$$12 = 1k \qquad\qquad \tfrac{3}{5}k - \tfrac{3}{5}k = 0; \tfrac{8}{5}k - \tfrac{3}{5}k = \tfrac{5}{5}k = 1k$$

$$12 = k \qquad\qquad \text{Multiplicative identity property}$$

From now on we will skip the step that changes $1k$ to k. Check the solution by replacing k with 12 in the original equation. The solution is 12.

What happens if we solve the equation in Example 4 by first subtracting $\frac{8}{5}k$ from each side?

$$\frac{3}{5}k + 12 = \frac{8}{5}k \qquad \text{Equation from Example 4}$$

$$\frac{3}{5}k + 12 - \frac{8}{5}k = \frac{8}{5}k - \frac{8}{5}k \qquad \text{Subtract } \tfrac{8}{5}k \text{ from each side.}$$

$$12 - k = 0 \qquad \tfrac{3}{5}k - \tfrac{8}{5}k = -\tfrac{5}{5}k = -1k = -k; \tfrac{8}{5}k - \tfrac{8}{5}k = 0$$

$$12 - k - 12 = 0 - 12 \qquad \text{Subtract 12 from each side.}$$

$$-k = -12 \qquad \text{Combine like terms; additive inverse}$$

This result gives the value of $-k$, but not of k itself. However, it does say that the additive inverse of k is -12, which means that k must be 12.

$$-k = -12$$
$$k = 12 \qquad \text{Same result as in Example 4}$$

(This result can also be justified using the multiplication property of equality, covered in **Section 2.2.**) We can make the following generalization.

> If a is a number and $-x = a$, then $x = -a$.

Work Problem 4 at the Side. ▶▶▶

OBJECTIVE ③ Simplify equations, and then use the addition property of equality. Sometimes an equation must be simplified as a first step in its solution.

EXAMPLE 5 Simplifying an Equation before Solving

Solve $3t - 12 + t + 2 = 5 + 3t + 2$.
  Begin by combining like terms on each side of the equation to get

$$4t - 10 = 7 + 3t.$$

Next, get all terms that contain variables on the same side of the equation and all terms without variables on the other side. One way to start is to subtract $3t$ from each side.

$$4t - 10 - 3t = 7 + 3t - 3t \qquad \text{Subtract } 3t \text{ from each side.}$$
$$t - 10 = 7 \qquad \text{Combine like terms.}$$
$$t - 10 + 10 = 7 + 10 \qquad \text{Add 10 to each side.}$$
$$t = 17 \qquad \text{Combine like terms.}$$

Check: Substitute 17 for t in the original equation.

$$3t - 12 + t + 2 = 5 + 3t + 2 \qquad \text{Original equation}$$
$$3(17) - 12 + 17 + 2 = 5 + 3(17) + 2 \quad ? \quad \text{Let } t = 17.$$
$$51 - 12 + 17 + 2 = 5 + 51 + 2 \quad ? \quad \text{Multiply.}$$
$$58 = 58 \qquad \text{True}$$

The check results in a true statement, so the solution is 17.

Work Problem 5 at the Side. ▶▶▶

---

④ (a) Solve $6m = 4 + 5m$.

(b) Solve $\frac{7}{2}m + 1 = \frac{9}{2}m$.

(c) What is the solution of $-x = 6$?

(d) What is the solution of $-x = -12$?

⑤ Solve.

(a) $4x + 6 + 2x - 3 = 9 + 5x - 4$

(b) $9r + 4r + 6 - 2 = 9r + 4 + 3r$

6 Solve.

(a) $4(r + 1) - (3r + 5) = 1$

(b) $-3(m - 4) + 2(5 + 2m) = 29$

EXAMPLE 6 Using the Distributive Property to Simplify an Equation before Solving

Solve $3(2 + 5x) - (1 + 14x) = 6$.

$$3(2 + 5x) - (1 + 14x) = 6$$

$$3(2 + 5x) - 1(1 + 14x) = 6 \qquad -(1 + 14x) = -1(1 + 14x)$$

$$3(2) + 3(5x) - 1(1) - 1(14x) = 6 \qquad \text{Distributive property}$$

$$6 + 15x - 1 - 14x = 6 \qquad \text{Multiply.}$$

$$x + 5 = 6 \qquad \text{Combine like terms.}$$

$$x + 5 - 5 = 6 - 5 \qquad \text{Subtract 5 from each side.}$$

$$x = 1 \qquad \text{Combine like terms.}$$

Check by substituting 1 for x in the original equation. The solution is 1.

CAUTION

Be careful to apply the distributive property correctly in a problem like that in Example 6, or a sign error may result.

⑪⑪⑪ Work Problem 6 at the side.

2.1 Exercises

FOR EXTRA HELP   Tutor Center Addison-Wesley Math Tutor Center   MathXL   Digital Video Tutor CD 2 Videotape 2   Student's Solutions Manual   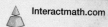 MyMathLab   Interactmath.com

1. Which of the pairs of equations are equivalent equations?

  A. $x + 2 = 6$ and $x = 4$ **B.** $10 - x = 5$ and $x = -5$

  C. $x + 3 = 9$ and $x = 6$ **D.** $4 + x = 8$ and $x = -4$

2. Decide whether each is an *expression* or an *equation*. If it is an expression, simplify it. If it is an equation, solve it.

  (a) $5x + 8 - 4x + 7$ **(b)** $-6y + 12 + 7y - 5$

  (c) $5x + 8 - 4x = 7$ **(d)** $-6y + 12 + 7y = -5$

3. Which of the following are not linear equations in one variable?

  A. $x^2 - 5x + 6 = 0$ **B.** $x^3 = x$

  C. $3x - 4 = 0$ **D.** $7x - 6x = 3 + 9x$

4. Explain how to check a solution of an equation.

Solve each equation, and check your solution. See Examples 1–4.

5. $x - 4 = 8$ **6.** $x - 8 = 9$ **7.** $x - 5 = -8$ **8.** $x - 7 = -9$

9. $r + 9 = 13$ **10.** $t + 6 = 10$ **11.** $x + 26 = 17$ **12.** $x + 45 = 24$

13. $x - 8.4 = -2.1$ **14.** $z - 15.5 = -5.1$ **15.** $t + 12.3 = -4.6$

16. $x + 21.5 = -13.4$ **17.** $7 + r = -3$ **18.** $8 + k = -4$

19. $2 = p + 15$ **20.** $3 = z + 17$ **21.** $-2 = x - 12$

22. $-6 = x - 21$ **23.** $3x = 2x + 7$ **24.** $5x = 4x + 9$

25. $10x + 4 = 9x$ **26.** $8t + 5 = 7t$ **27.** $\frac{9}{7}r - 3 = \frac{2}{7}r$

28. $\dfrac{8}{5}w - 6 = \dfrac{3}{5}w$

29. $5.6x + 2 = 4.6x$

30. $9.1x - 5 = 8.1x$

31. $3p + 6 = 10 + 2p$

32. $8x - 4 = -6 + 7x$

Solve each equation, and check your solution. See Examples 5 and 6.

33. $3x + 6 - 10 = 2x - 2$

34. $8k - 4 + 6 = 7k + 1$

35. $6x + 5 + 7x + 3 = 12x + 4$

36. $4x - 3 - 8x + 1 = -5x + 9$

37. $10x + 5x + 7 - 8 = 12x + 3 + 2x$

38. $7p + 4p + 13 - 7 = 7p + 9 + 3p$

39. $5.2q - 4.6 - 7.1q = -.9q - 4.6$

40. $-4.0x + 2.7 - 1.6x = -4.6x + 2.7$

41. $\dfrac{5}{7}x + \dfrac{1}{3} = \dfrac{2}{5} - \dfrac{2}{7}x + \dfrac{2}{5}$

42. $\dfrac{6}{7}s - \dfrac{3}{4} = \dfrac{4}{5} - \dfrac{1}{7}s + \dfrac{1}{6}$

43. $(5x + 6) - (3 + 4x) = 10$

44. $(8r - 3) - (7r + 1) = -6$

45. $2(p + 5) - (9 + p) = -3$

46. $4(k - 6) - (3k + 2) = -5$

47. $-6(2x + 1) + (13x - 7) = 0$

48. $-5(3w - 3) + (1 + 16w) = 0$

49. $10(-2x + 1) = -19(x + 1)$

50. $2(2 - 3r) = -5(r - 3)$

51. $-2(8p + 2) - 3(2 - 7p) = 2(4 + 2p)$

52. $-5(1 - 2z) + 4(3 - z) = 7(3 + z)$

53. Write an equation where 6 must be added to each side to solve the equation, and the solution is a negative number.

54. Write an equation where $\frac{1}{2}$ must be subtracted from each side, and the solution is a positive number.

2.2 The Multiplication Property of Equality

OBJECTIVE 1 Use the multiplication property of equality. The addition property of equality alone is not enough to solve some equations, such as $3x + 2 = 17$.

$$3x + 2 = 17$$
$$3x + 2 - 2 = 17 - 2 \qquad \text{Subtract 2 from each side.}$$
$$3x = 15 \qquad \text{Combine like terms.}$$

Notice that the coefficient of x on the left side is 3, not 1 as desired. We must develop a method that leads to an equation of the form

$$x = \text{a number.}$$

If $3x = 15$, then $3x$ and 15 both represent the same number. Multiplying both $3x$ and 15 by the same number will also result in an equality. The **multiplication property of equality** states that we can multiply each side of an equation by the same nonzero number without changing the solution.

> **Multiplication Property of Equality**
>
> If A, B, and C ($C \neq 0$) represent real numbers, then the equations
>
> $$A = B \quad \text{and} \quad AC = BC$$
>
> are equivalent equations.
>
> In words, we can multiply each side of an equation by the same nonzero number without changing the solution.

This property can be used to solve $3x = 15$. The $3x$ on the left must be changed to $1x$, or x, instead of $3x$. To isolate x, multiply each side of the equation by $\frac{1}{3}$. We use $\frac{1}{3}$ because $\frac{1}{3}$ is the reciprocal of 3, and $\frac{1}{3} \cdot 3 = \frac{3}{3} = 1$.

$$3x = 15$$
$$\frac{1}{3}(3x) = \frac{1}{3} \cdot 15 \qquad \text{Multiply each side by } \tfrac{1}{3}.$$
$$\left(\frac{1}{3} \cdot 3\right)x = \frac{1}{3} \cdot 15 \qquad \text{Associative property}$$
$$1x = 5 \qquad \text{Multiplicative inverse property}$$
$$x = 5 \qquad \text{Multiplicative identity property}$$

The solution of the equation is 5. We can check this result in the original equation. (We usually combine the last two steps shown above.)

Work Problem 1 at the Side.))))

Just as the addition property of equality permits *subtracting* the same number from each side of an equation, the multiplication property of equality permits *dividing* each side of an equation by the same nonzero number. For example, the equation $3x = 15$, which we just solved by multiplication, could also be solved by dividing each side by 3, as follows.

$$3x = 15$$
$$\frac{3x}{3} = \frac{15}{3} \qquad \text{Divide each side by 3.}$$
$$x = 5$$

OBJECTIVES

1 Use the multiplication property of equality.

2 Simplify equations, and then use the multiplication property of equality.

1 Check that 5 is the solution of $3x = 15$.

ANSWERS
1. Since $3(5) = 15$, the solution of $3x = 15$ is 5.

2 Solve.

(a) $-6p = -14$

We can divide each side of an equation by the same nonzero number without changing the solution. Do not, however, divide each side by a variable, since the variable might be equal to 0.

> **NOTE**
> In practice, it is usually easier to multiply on each side if the coefficient of the variable is a fraction, and divide on each side if the coefficient is an integer. For example, to solve
> $$-\frac{3}{4}x = 12,$$
> it is easier to multiply by $-\frac{4}{3}$, the reciprocal of $-\frac{3}{4}$, than to divide by $-\frac{3}{4}$. On the other hand, to solve
> $$-5x = -20,$$
> it is easier to divide by -5 than to multiply by $-\frac{1}{5}$.

(b) $3r = -12$

EXAMPLE 1 Dividing Each Side of an Equation by a Nonzero Number

Solve $25p = 30$.

Transform the equation so that p (instead of $25p$) is on the left by using the multiplication property of equality. Divide each side of the equation by 25, the coefficient of p.

$$25p = 30$$

$$\frac{25p}{25} = \frac{30}{25} \qquad \text{Divide by 25.}$$

(c) $-2m = 16$

$$p = \frac{30}{25} = \frac{6}{5} \qquad \text{Write in lowest terms.}$$

To check, substitute $\frac{6}{5}$ for p in the original equation.

Check: $$25p = 30$$

$$\frac{25}{1}\left(\frac{6}{5}\right) = 30 \quad ? \quad \text{Let } p = \frac{6}{5}.$$

$$30 = 30 \qquad \text{True}$$

3 Solve.

(a) $-.7m = -5.04$

The check confirms that the solution is $\frac{6}{5}$.

> ◀◀◀ **Work Problem 2 at the Side.**

EXAMPLE 2 Solving an Equation with Decimals

Solve $2.1x = 6.09$.

$$2.1x = 6.09$$

$$\frac{2.1x}{2.1} = \frac{6.09}{2.1} \qquad \text{Divide each side by 2.1.}$$

(b) $12.5k = -63.75$

$$x = 2.9 \qquad \text{Divide; you may use a calculator.}$$

Check that the solution is 2.9.

ANSWERS

2. (a) $\dfrac{7}{3}$ (b) -4 (c) -8

3. (a) 7.2 (b) -5.1

> ◀◀◀ **Work Problem 3 at the Side.**

In the next two examples, multiplication produces the solution more quickly than division would.

EXAMPLE 3 **Using the Multiplication Property of Equality**

Solve $\frac{a}{4} = 3$.

Replace $\frac{a}{4}$ by $\frac{1}{4}a$, since dividing by 4 is the same as multiplying by $\frac{1}{4}$. To get a alone on the left, multiply each side by 4, the reciprocal of the coefficient of a.

$$\frac{a}{4} = 3$$

$$\frac{1}{4}a = 3 \qquad \text{Change } \tfrac{a}{4} \text{ to } \tfrac{1}{4}a.$$

$$4 \cdot \frac{1}{4}a = 4 \cdot 3 \qquad \text{Multiply by 4.}$$

$$a = 12 \qquad \text{Multiplicative inverse property; multiplicative identity property}$$

Check:
$$\frac{a}{4} = 3 \qquad \text{Original equation}$$

$$\frac{12}{4} = 3 \qquad ? \quad \text{Let } a = 12.$$

$$3 = 3 \qquad \text{True}$$

The solution is 12.

> **Work Problem 4 at the Side.** ⟩⟩⟩

EXAMPLE 4 **Using the Multiplication Property of Equality**

Solve $\frac{3}{4}h = 6$.

Transform the equation so that h is alone on the left by multiplying each side of the equation by $\frac{4}{3}$. Use $\frac{4}{3}$ because $\frac{4}{3} \cdot \frac{3}{4}h = 1 \cdot h = h$.

$$\frac{3}{4}h = 6$$

$$\frac{4}{3}\left(\frac{3}{4}h\right) = \frac{4}{3} \cdot 6 \qquad \text{Multiply by } \tfrac{4}{3}.$$

$$1 \cdot h = \frac{4}{3} \cdot \frac{6}{1} \qquad \text{Multiplicative inverse property}$$

$$h = 8 \qquad \text{Multiplicative identity property; multiply fractions.}$$

Check:
$$\frac{3}{4}h = 6 \qquad \text{Original equation}$$

$$\frac{3}{4}(8) = 6 \qquad ? \quad \text{Let } h = 8.$$

$$6 = 6 \qquad \text{True}$$

The solution is 8.

> **Work Problem 5 at the Side.** ⟩⟩⟩

4 Solve.

(a) $\dfrac{y}{5} = 5$

(b) $\dfrac{p}{4} = -6$

5 Solve.

(a) $-\dfrac{5}{6}t = -15$

(b) $\dfrac{3}{4}k = -21$

ANSWERS
4. (a) 25 (b) −24
5. (a) 18 (b) −28

6 Solve.

(a) $-m = 2$

(b) $-p = -7$

In **Section 2.1**, we obtained the equation $-k = -12$ in our alternate solution to Example 4. We reasoned that since this equation says that the additive inverse (or opposite) of k is -12, then k must equal 12. We can also use the multiplication property of equality to obtain the same result, as shown in the next example.

┌─ **EXAMPLE 5** Using the Multiplication Property of Equality When the Coefficient of the Variable Is -1

Solve $-k = -12$.
    On the left side, change $-k$ to k by first writing $-k$ as $-1 \cdot k$.

$$-k = -12$$
$$-1 \cdot k = -12 \qquad\qquad -k = -1 \cdot k$$
$$-1(-1 \cdot k) = -1(-12) \qquad \text{Multiply by } -1, \text{ since } -1(-1) = 1.$$
$$[-1(-1)] \cdot k = 12 \qquad \text{Associative property; multiply.}$$
$$1 \cdot k = 12 \qquad \text{Multiplicative inverse property}$$
$$k = 12 \qquad \text{Multiplicative identity property}$$

Check: $\qquad -k = -12 \qquad\qquad$ Original equation
$$-(12) = -12 \qquad ? \quad \text{Let } k = 12.$$
$$-12 = -12 \qquad\qquad \text{True}$$

The solution, 12, checks.

◀◀◀ Work Problem 6 at the Side.

7 Solve.

(a) $4r - 9r = 20$

OBJECTIVE 2 Simplify equations, and then use the multiplication property of equality.   In the next example, it is necessary to simplify the equation before using the multiplication property of equality.

┌─ **EXAMPLE 6** Simplifying an Equation before Solving

Solve $5m + 6m = 33$.

$$5m + 6m = 33$$
$$11m = 33 \qquad \text{Combine like terms.}$$
$$\frac{11m}{11} = \frac{33}{11} \qquad \text{Divide by 11.}$$
$$1m = 3 \qquad \text{Divide.}$$
$$m = 3 \qquad \text{Multiplicative identity property}$$

(b) $7m - 5m = -12$

The solution, 3, checks.

◀◀◀ Work Problem 7 at the Side.

2.2 Exercises

FOR EXTRA HELP

Tutor Center Addison-Wesley Math Tutor Center

 MathXL

 Digital Video Tutor CD 2 Videotape 2

Student's Solutions Manual

 MyMathLab

Interactmath.com

By what number is it necessary to multiply each side of each equation in order to obtain just x on the left side? Do not actually solve these equations.

1. $\dfrac{2}{3}x = 8$ **2.** $\dfrac{4}{5}x = 6$ **3.** $.1x = 3$ **4.** $.01x = 8$

5. $-\dfrac{9}{2}x = -4$ **6.** $-\dfrac{8}{3}x = -11$ **7.** $-x = .36$ **8.** $-x = .29$

By what number is it necessary to divide each side of each equation in order to obtain just x on the left side? Do not actually solve these equations.

9. $6x = 5$ **10.** $7x = 10$ **11.** $-4x = 13$ **12.** $-13x = 6$

13. $.12x = 48$ **14.** $.21x = 63$ **15.** $-x = 23$ **16.** $-x = 49$

17. A student tried to solve the equation $4x = 8$ by dividing each side by 8. What is a better approach?

18. Which equation does *not* require the use of the multiplication property of equality?

A. $3x - 5x = 6$ **B.** $-\dfrac{1}{4}x = 12$ **C.** $5x - 4x = 7$ **D.** $\dfrac{x}{3} = -2$

Solve each equation, and check your solution. See Examples 1–6.

19. $5x = 30$ **20.** $7x = 56$ **21.** $2m = 15$ **22.** $3m = 10$

23. $3a = -15$ **24.** $5k = -70$ **25.** $10t = -36$ **26.** $4s = -34$

27. $-6x = -72$ **28.** $-8x = -64$ **29.** $2r = 0$ **30.** $5x = 0$

31. $-y = 12$

32. $-t = 14$

33. $.2t = 8$

34. $.9x = 18$

35. $-2.1m = 25.62$

36. $-3.9a = 31.2$

37. $\frac{1}{4}y = -12$

38. $\frac{1}{5}p = -3$

39. $\frac{x}{7} = -5$

40. $\frac{k}{8} = -3$

41. $\frac{z}{6} = 12$

42. $\frac{x}{5} = 15$

43. $\frac{2}{7}p = 4$

44. $\frac{3}{8}x = 9$

45. $-\frac{7}{9}c = \frac{3}{5}$

46. $-\frac{5}{6}d = \frac{4}{9}$

47. $4x + 3x = 21$

48. $9x + 2x = 121$

49. $3r - 5r = 10$

50. $9p - 13p = 24$

51. $5m + 6m - 2m = 63$

52. $11r - 5r + 6r = 168$

53. $-6x + 4x - 7x = 0$

54. $-5x + 4x - 8x = 0$

55. $.9w - .5w + .1w = -3$

56. $.5x - .6x + .3x = -1$

57. Write an equation that requires the use of the multiplication property of equality, where each side must be multiplied by $\frac{2}{3}$, and the solution is a negative number.

58. Write an equation that requires the use of the multiplication property of equality, where each side must be divided by 100, and the solution is not an integer.

Write an equation using the information given in the problem. Use x as the variable. Then solve the equation.

59. When a number is multiplied by -4, the result is 10. Find the number.

When a number is divided by -5, the result is 2. Find the number.

2.3 More on Solving Linear Equations

OBJECTIVE 1 Learn the four steps for solving a linear equation, and apply them. In this section, we solve more complicated equations using the following four-step method.

OBJECTIVES

1 Learn the four steps for solving a linear equation, and apply them.

2 Solve equations with fractions or decimals as coefficients.

3 Solve equations that have no solution or infinitely many solutions.

4 Write expressions for two related unknown quantities.

Solving Linear Equations

Step 1 **Simplify each side separately.** Clear parentheses using the distributive property, if needed, and combine terms.

Step 2 **Isolate the variable term on one side.** Use the addition property if necessary so that the variable term is on one side of the equation and a number is on the other.

Step 3 **Isolate the variable.** Use the multiplication property if necessary to get the equation in the form $x = $ a number.

Step 4 **Check.** Substitute the proposed solution into the *original* equation to see if a true statement results.

1 Solve.

(a) $5y - 7y + 6y - 9$
$= 3 + 2y$

EXAMPLE 1 Using the Four Steps to Solve an Equation

Solve $3r + 4 - 2r - 7 = 4r + 3$.
  Our goal is to isolate the variable, r.

Step 1 $3r + 4 - 2r - 7 = 4r + 3$

$r - 3 = 4r + 3$ Combine terms.

Step 2 $r - 3 + 3 = 4r + 3 + 3$ Add 3.

$r = 4r + 6$ Combine terms.

$r - 4r = 4r + 6 - 4r$ Subtract $4r$.

$-3r = 6$ Combine terms.

Step 3 $\dfrac{-3r}{-3} = \dfrac{6}{-3}$ Divide by -3.

$r = -2$ $\frac{-3}{-3} = 1; 1r = r$

Step 4   Substitute -2 for r in the original equation to check.

$3r + 4 - 2r - 7 = 4r + 3$

$3(-2) + 4 - 2(-2) - 7 = 4(-2) + 3$?   Let $r = -2$.

$-6 + 4 + 4 - 7 = -8 + 3$?   Multiply.

$-5 = -5$ True

The solution of the equation is -2.

(b) $-3k - 5k - 6 + 11$
$= 2k - 5$

NOTE
In Step 2 of Example 1, we added and subtracted the terms in such a way that the variable term ended up on the left side of the equation. Choosing differently would have put the variable term on the right side of the equation. Either way, the same solution results.

Work Problem 1 at the Side.)))

② Solve.

(a) $7(p - 2) + p = 2p + 4$

(b) $11 + 3(x + 1) = 5x + 16$

EXAMPLE 2 **Using the Four Steps to Solve an Equation**

Solve $4(k - 3) - k = k - 6$.

Step 1 Clear parentheses using the distributive property.

$$4(k - 3) - k = k - 6$$

$4(k) + 4(-3) - k = k - 6$	Distributive property
$4k - 12 - k = k - 6$	Multiply.
$3k - 12 = k - 6$	Combine terms.

Step 2
$3k - 12 + 12 = k - 6 + 12$	Add 12.
$3k = k + 6$	Combine terms.
$3k - k = k + 6 - k$	Subtract k.
$2k = 6$	Combine terms.

Step 3
$\dfrac{2k}{2} = \dfrac{6}{2}$	Divide by 2.
$k = 3$	

Step 4 Check by substituting 3 for k in the original equation.

$4(k - 3) - k = k - 6$		
$4(3 - 3) - 3 = 3 - 6$	?	Let $k = 3$.
$4(0) - 3 = 3 - 6$	?	Work inside the parentheses.
$-3 = -3$		True

The solution of the equation is 3.

◄◄◄ Work Problem 2 at the Side.

EXAMPLE 3 **Using the Four Steps to Solve an Equation**

Solve $8a - (3 + 2a) = 3a + 1$.

Step 1
$8a - (3 + 2a) = 3a + 1$	
$8a - 1(3 + 2a) = 3a + 1$	Multiplicative identity property
$8a - 3 - 2a = 3a + 1$	Distributive property
$6a - 3 = 3a + 1$	Combine terms.

Step 2
$6a - 3 + 3 = 3a + 1 + 3$	Add 3.
$6a = 3a + 4$	Combine terms.
$6a - 3a = 3a + 4 - 3a$	Subtract $3a$.
$3a = 4$	Combine terms.

Step 3
$\dfrac{3a}{3} = \dfrac{4}{3}$	Divide by 3.
$a = \dfrac{4}{3}$	

Step 4 Check that the solution is $\frac{4}{3}$.

CAUTION
Be very careful with signs when solving an equation like the one in Example 3. When clearing parentheses in the expression

$$8a - (3 + 2a),$$

remember that the $-$ sign acts like a factor of -1 and affects the sign of *every* term in the parentheses. Thus,

$$8 - (3 + 2a) = 8 - 3 - 2a.$$

Change to $-$ in *both* terms.

Work Problem 3 at the Side. ▶▶▶

EXAMPLE 4 Using the Four Steps to Solve an Equation

Solve $4(8 - 3t) = 32 - 8(t + 2)$.

Step 1
$$4(8 - 3t) = 32 - 8(t + 2)$$
$$32 - 12t = 32 - 8t - 16 \qquad \text{Distributive property}$$
$$32 - 12t = 16 - 8t \qquad \text{Combine terms.}$$

Step 2 $32 - 12t - 32 = 16 - 8t - 32 \qquad \text{Subtract 32.}$
$$-12t = -16 - 8t \qquad \text{Combine terms.}$$
$$-12t + 8t = -16 - 8t + 8t \qquad \text{Add } 8t.$$
$$-4t = -16 \qquad \text{Combine terms.}$$

Step 3 $\dfrac{-4t}{-4} = \dfrac{-16}{-4} \qquad \text{Divide by } -4.$
$$t = 4$$

Step 4 Check this solution in the original equation.
$$4(8 - 3t) = 32 - 8(t + 2)$$
$$4(8 - 3 \cdot 4) = 32 - 8(4 + 2) \qquad ? \qquad \text{Let } t = 4.$$
$$4(8 - 12) = 32 - 8(6) \qquad ?$$
$$4(-4) = 32 - 48 \qquad ?$$
$$-16 = -16 \qquad \text{True}$$

The solution, 4, checks.

Work Problem 4 at the Side. ▶▶▶

OBJECTIVE 2 **Solve equations with fractions or decimals as coefficients.**   We clear an equation of fractions by multiplying each side by the least common denominator (LCD) of all the fractions in the equation. It is a good idea to do this to avoid messy computations.

CAUTION
When clearing an equation of fractions, be sure to multiply every term on each side of the equation by the LCD.

3 Solve.

(a) $7m - (2m - 9) = 39$

(b) $4x - (x + 7) = 9$

4 Solve.

(a) $2(4 + 3r) = 3(r + 1) + 11$

(b) $2 - 3(2 + 6z) = 4(z + 1) + 18$

ANSWERS

3. (a) 6 (b) $\dfrac{16}{3}$

4. (a) 2 (b) $-\dfrac{13}{11}$

⑤ Solve $\dfrac{1}{4}x - 4 = \dfrac{3}{2}x + \dfrac{3}{4}x$.

EXAMPLE 5 Solving an Equation with Fractions as Coefficients

Solve $\frac{2}{3}x - \frac{1}{2}x = -\frac{1}{6}x - 2$.

The LCD of all the fractions in the equation is 6, so multiply each side by 6 to clear the fractions.

$$\frac{2}{3}x - \frac{1}{2}x = -\frac{1}{6}x - 2$$

$$6\left(\frac{2}{3}x - \frac{1}{2}x\right) = 6\left(-\frac{1}{6}x - 2\right) \qquad \text{Multiply by 6.}$$

$$6\left(\frac{2}{3}x\right) + 6\left(-\frac{1}{2}x\right) = 6\left(-\frac{1}{6}x\right) + 6(-2) \qquad \text{Distributive property}$$

$$4x - 3x = -x - 12$$

Now use the four steps to solve this equivalent equation.

Step 1 $x = -x - 12$ Combine terms.

Step 2 $x + x = -x - 12 + x$ Add x.

$\qquad\qquad 2x = -12$ Combine terms.

Step 3 $\dfrac{2x}{2} = \dfrac{-12}{2}$ Divide by 2.

$\qquad\qquad x = -6$

Step 4   Check by substituting -6 for x in the original equation.

$$\frac{2}{3}(-6) - \frac{1}{2}(-6) = -\frac{1}{6}(-6) - 2 \quad ? \qquad \text{Let } x = -6.$$

$$-4 + 3 = 1 - 2 \qquad\qquad ?$$

$$-1 = -1 \qquad\qquad\qquad \text{True}$$

The solution of the equation is -6.

⑥ Solve $.06(100 - x) + .04x = .05(92)$.

$\blacktriangleleft\!\blacktriangleleft\!\blacktriangleleft$ **Work Problem 5 at the Side.**

EXAMPLE 6 Solving an Equation with Decimals as Coefficients

Solve $.1t + .05(20 - t) = .09(20)$.

The decimals here are expressed as tenths (.1, which equals .10) and hundredths (.05 and .09). Choose the least exponent on 10 needed to eliminate the decimals; in this case, use $10^2 = 100$. A number can be multiplied by 100 by moving the decimal point two places to the right.

$$.10t + .05(20 - t) = .09(20) \qquad .1 = .10$$

$$10t + 5(20 - t) = 9(20) \qquad \text{Multiply by 100.}$$

Step 1 $10t + 5(20) + 5(-t) = 180$ Distributive property

$\qquad\qquad 10t + 100 - 5t = 180$

$\qquad\qquad 5t + 100 = 180$ Combine terms.

Step 2 $5t + 100 - 100 = 180 - 100$ Subtract 100.

$\qquad\qquad 5t = 80$ Combine terms.

Step 3 $\dfrac{5t}{5} = \dfrac{80}{5}$ Divide by 5.

$\qquad\qquad t = 16$

Step 4   Check to confirm that 16 is the solution.

$\blacktriangleleft\!\blacktriangleleft\!\blacktriangleleft$ **Work Problem 6 at the Side.**

OBJECTIVE 3 Solve equations that have no solution or infinitely many solutions.   Every equation solved so far has had exactly one solution. Sometimes this is not the case, as shown in the next examples.

7 Solve each equation.

(a) $2(x - 6) = 2x - 12$

EXAMPLE 7 Solving an Equation That Has Infinitely Many Solutions

Solve $5x - 15 = 5(x - 3)$.

$$5x - 15 = 5(x - 3)$$

$$5x - 15 = 5x - 15 \qquad \text{Distributive property}$$

$$5x - 15 + 15 = 5x - 15 + 15 \qquad \text{Add 15.}$$

$$5x = 5x \qquad \text{Combine terms.}$$

$$5x - 5x = 5x - 5x \qquad \text{Subtract } 5x.$$

$$0 = 0 \qquad \text{True}$$

The final step leads to an equation that contains no variables ($0 = 0$ in this case). Whenever such a statement is true, as it is in this example, *any* real number is a solution. (Try several replacements for x in the given equation to see that they all satisfy the equation.)

An equation with both sides exactly the same, like $0 = 0$, is called an **identity.** An identity is true for all replacements of the variables. We indicate this by writing ***all real numbers.***

CAUTION

When you are solving an equation like the one in Example 7, do not write "0" as the solution. While 0 is a solution, there are infinitely many other solutions.

(b) $3x + 6(x + 1) = 9x - 4$

EXAMPLE 8 Solving an Equation That Has No Solution

Solve $2x + 3(x + 1) = 5x + 4$.

$$2x + 3(x + 1) = 5x + 4$$

$$2x + 3x + 3 = 5x + 4 \qquad \text{Distributive property}$$

$$5x + 3 = 5x + 4 \qquad \text{Combine terms.}$$

$$5x + 3 - 5x = 5x + 4 - 5x \qquad \text{Subtract } 5x.$$

$$3 = 4 \qquad \text{False}$$

Again, the variable has disappeared, but this time a false statement ($3 = 4$) results. Whenever this happens in solving an equation, it is a signal that the equation has no solution and we write ***no solution.***

Work Problem 7 at the Side. ▶▶▶

ANSWERS

7. (a) all real numbers   (b) no solution

8 One number is 5 more than twice another. If the first number is represented by x, write an expression for the second number.

OBJECTIVE **4** Write expressions for two related unknown quantities. Often we are given a problem in which the sum of two quantities is a particular number, and we are asked to find the values of the two quantities. Example 9 shows how to express the unknown quantities in terms of a single variable.

EXAMPLE 9 **Translating a Phrase into an Algebraic Expression**

Two numbers have a sum of 23. If one of the numbers is represented by k, find an expression for the other number.

First, suppose that the sum of two numbers is 23, and one of the numbers is **10**. How would you find the other number? You would subtract **10** from 23 to get 13.

$$23 - 10 = 13$$

So instead of using **10** as one of the numbers, use k as stated in the problem. The other number would be obtained in the same way. You must subtract k from 23. Therefore, an expression for the other number is

$$23 - k.$$

CAUTION
Since the sum of the two numbers in Example 9 is 23, the expression for the other number must be $23 - k$, *not $k - 23$*. To check, find the sum of the two numbers:
$$k + (23 - k) = 23, \quad \text{as required.}$$

Work Problem 8 at the Side.

2.3 Exercises

FOR EXTRA HELP

Tutor Center Addison-Wesley Math Tutor Center

Math XL MathXL

Digital Video Tutor CD 2 Videotape 2

Student's Solutions Manual

MyMathLab MyMathLab

Interactmath.com

Solve each equation, and check your solution. See Examples 1–4, 7, and 8.

1. $5m + 8 = 7 + 4m$

2. $4r + 2 = 3r - 6$

3. $10p + 6 = 12p - 4$

4. $-5x + 8 = -3x + 10$

5. $7r - 5r + 2 = 5r - r$

6. $9p - 4p + 6 = 7p - 3p$

7. $x + 3 = -(2x + 2)$

8. $2x + 1 = -(x + 3)$

9. $4(2x - 1) = -6(x + 3)$

10. $6(3w + 5) = 2(10w + 10)$

11. $6(4x - 1) = 12(2x + 3)$

12. $6(2x + 8) = 4(3x - 6)$

13. $3(2x - 4) = 6(x - 2)$

14. $3(6 - 4x) = 2(-6x + 9)$

15. Which linear equation does *not* have all real numbers as solutions?

A. $5x = 4x + x$ **B.** $2(x + 6) = 2x + 12$ **C.** $\frac{1}{2}x = .5x$ **D.** $3x = 2x$

16. After correctly working through several steps of the solution of a linear equation, a student obtains the equation $7x = 3x$. Then the student divides each side by x to get $7 = 3$ and gives "no solution" as the answer. Is this correct? If not, explain why.

17. Explain in your own words the major steps used in solving a linear equation that does not contain fractions or decimals as coefficients.

18. Explain in your own words the major steps used in solving a linear equation that contains fractions or decimals as coefficients.

Solve each equation, and check your solution. See Examples 5 and 6.

19. $-\dfrac{2}{7}r + 2r = \dfrac{1}{2}r + \dfrac{17}{2}$

20. $\dfrac{3}{5}t - \dfrac{1}{10}t = t - \dfrac{5}{2}$

21. $\dfrac{1}{9}(x + 18) + \dfrac{1}{3}(2x + 3) = x + 3$

22. $-\dfrac{1}{4}(x - 12) + \dfrac{1}{2}(x + 2) = x + 4$

23. $-\dfrac{5}{6}q - \left(q - \dfrac{1}{2}\right) = \dfrac{1}{4}(q + 1)$

24. $\dfrac{2}{3}k - \left(k + \dfrac{1}{4}\right) = \dfrac{1}{12}(k + 4)$

25. $.30(30) + .15x = .20(30 + x)$

26. $.20(60) + .05x = .10(60 + x)$

27. $.92x + .98(12 - x) = .96(12)$

28. $1.00x + .05(12 - x) = .10(63)$

29. $.02(5000) + .03x = .025(5000 + x)$

30. $.06(10{,}000) + .08x = .072(10{,}000 + x)$

RELATING CONCEPTS (EXERCISES 31–36) For Individual or Group Work

Work Exercises 31–36 in order.

31. Evaluate the term $100ab$ for $a = 2$ and $b = 4$.

32. Will you get the same answer as in Exercise 31 if you evaluate $(100a)b$ for $a = 2$ and $b = 4$? Why or why not?

33. Is the term $(100a)(100b)$ equivalent to $100ab$? Why or why not?

34. If your answer to Exercise 33 is *no,* explain why the distributive property is not involved.

35. The simplest way to solve the equation $.05(x + 2) + .10x = 2.00$ is to begin by multiplying each side by 100. If we do this, the first term on the left becomes $100(.05)(x + 2)$. Is this expression equivalent to $[100(.05)](x + 2)$? Explain. (*Hint:* Compare to Exercises 31 and 32 with $a = .05$ and $b = x + 2$.)

36. Students often want to "distribute" the 100 to both .05 and $(x + 2)$ in the expression $100(.05)(x + 2)$. Is this correct? (*Hint:* See Exercises 34 and 35.)

Solve each equation, and check your solution. See Examples 1–8.

37. $-3(5z + 24) + 2 = 2(3 - 2z) - 4$

38. $-2(2s - 4) - 8 = -3(4s + 4) - 1$

39. $-(6k - 5) - (-5k + 8) = -3$

40. $-(4y + 2) - (-3y - 5) = 3$

41. $\frac{1}{3}(x + 3) + \frac{1}{6}(x - 6) = x + 3$

42. $\frac{1}{2}(x + 2) + \frac{3}{4}(x + 4) = x + 5$

43. $.30(x + 15) + .40(x + 25) = 25$

44. $.10(x + 80) + .20x = 14$

45. $4(x + 3) = 2(2x + 8) - 4$

46. $4(x + 8) = 2(2x + 6) + 20$

47. $8(t - 3) + 4t = 6(2t + 1) - 10$

48. $9(v + 1) - 3v = 2(3v + 1) - 8$

Write the answer to each problem as an algebraic expression. See Example 9.

49. Two numbers have a sum of 12. One number is q. Find the other number.

50. The product of two numbers is 13. One number is k. What is the other number?

51. Mary is a years old. How old will she be in 12 yr? How old was she 5 yr ago?

52. Tom has r quarters. Find the value of the quarters in cents.

53. A bank teller has t dollars in ten-dollar bills. How many ten-dollar bills does the teller have?

54. A plane ticket costs b dollars for an adult and d dollars for a child. Find the total cost of 5 adult and 3 child tickets.

Summary Exercises on Solving Linear Equations

This section of miscellaneous linear equations provides practice in solving all the types introduced in **Sections 2.1–2.3.** Refer to the examples in these sections to review the various solution methods.

Solve each equation, and check your solution.

1. $a + 2 = -3$

2. $2m + 8 = 16$

3. $16.5k = -84.15$

4. $-x = -25$

5. $\dfrac{4}{5}x = -20$

6. $9x - 7x = -12$

7. $5x - 9 = 4(x - 3)$

8. $\dfrac{a}{-2} = 8$

9. $-3(t - 5) + 2(7 + 2t) = 36$

10. $\dfrac{2}{3}x + 8 = \dfrac{1}{4}x$

11. $.08x + .06(x + 9) = 1.24$

12. $x - 16.2 = 7.5$

13. $4x + 2(3 - 2x) = 6$

14. $-.3x + 2.1(x - 4) = -6.6$

15. $-x = 16$

16. $3(m + 5) - 1 + 2m = 5(m + 2)$

17. $10m - (5m - 9) = 39$

18. $7(p - 2) + p = 2(p + 2)$

19. $-2t + 5t - 9 = 3(t - 4) - 5$

20. $-9z = -21$

21. $.02(50) + .08r = .04(50 + r)$

22. $2.3x + 13.7 = 1.3x + 2.9$

23. $2(3 + 7x) - (1 + 15x) = 2$

24. $6q - 9 = 12 + 3q$

25. $2(5 + 3x) = 3(x + 1) + 13$

26. $r + 9 + 7r = 4(3 + 2r) - 3$

27. $\dfrac{5}{6}x + \dfrac{1}{3} = 2x + \dfrac{2}{3}$

28. $.06x + .09(15 - x) = .07(15)$

29. $\dfrac{3}{4}(a - 2) - \dfrac{1}{3}(5 - 2a) = -2$

30. $2 - (m + 4) = 3m + 8$

31. $5.2x - 4.6 - 7.1x = -2.1 - 1.9x - 2.5$

32. $9(2m - 3) - 4(5 + 3m) = 5(4 + m) - 3$

2.4 An Introduction to Applications of Linear Equations

OBJECTIVE 1 Learn the six steps for solving applied problems. We now look at how algebra is used to solve applied problems. Since many meaningful applications of mathematics require concepts that are beyond the level of this book, some of the problems you encounter will seem contrived, and to some extent they are. But the skills you develop in solving simple problems will help you solve more realistic problems in chemistry, physics, biology, business, and other fields.

While there is not one specific method that enables you to solve all kinds of applied problems, the following six-step method is suggested.*

OBJECTIVES

1 Learn the six steps for solving applied problems.

2 Solve problems involving unknown numbers.

3 Solve problems involving sums of quantities.

4 Solve problems involving supplementary and complementary angles.

5 Solve problems involving consecutive integers.

Solving an Applied Problem

Step 1 **Read** the problem, several times if necessary, until you *understand* what is given and what is to be found.

Step 2 **Assign a variable** to represent the unknown value, using diagrams or tables as needed. Write down what the variable represents. Express any other unknown values in terms of the variable.

Step 3 **Write an equation** using the variable expression(s).

Step 4 **Solve** the equation.

Step 5 **State the answer.** Does it seem reasonable?

Step 6 **Check** the answer in the words of the *original* problem.

OBJECTIVE 2 Solve problems involving unknown numbers. Some of the simplest applied problems involve unknown numbers.

> **PROBLEM-SOLVING HINT**
> The third step in solving an applied problem is often the hardest. To translate the problem into an equation, write the given phrases as mathematical expressions. Replace any words that mean *equal* or *same* with an = sign. Other forms of the verb "to be," such as *is, are, was,* and *were,* also translate as an = sign. The = sign leads to an equation to be solved.

EXAMPLE 1 Finding the Value of an Unknown Number

The product of 4, and a number decreased by 7, is 100. What is the number?

Step 1 **Read** the problem carefully. We are asked to find a number.

Step 2 **Assign a variable** to represent the unknown quantity. In this problem, we are asked to find a number, so we write

$$\text{Let } x = \text{the number.}$$

There are no other unknown quantities to find.

Continued on Next Page

---

* **Appendix A** Strategies for Problem Solving introduces additional methods and tips for solving applied problems.

1 Use the six steps to solve the problem. Give the equation, using x as the variable, and give the answer.

If 5 is added to the product of 9 and a number, the result is 19 less than the number. Find the number.

Step 3 **Write an equation.**

The product of 4, and a number decreased by 7, is 100.

$$4 \cdot (x - 7) = 100$$

(Because of the commas in the given problem, writing the equation as $4x - 7 = 100$ is incorrect. The equation $4x - 7 = 100$ corresponds to the statement "The product of 4 and a number, decreased by 7, is 100.")

Step 4 **Solve** the equation.

$$4(x - 7) = 100$$

$$4x - 28 = 100 \qquad \text{Distributive property}$$

$$4x - 28 + 28 = 100 + 28 \qquad \text{Add 28.}$$

$$4x = 128 \qquad \text{Combine terms.}$$

$$\frac{4x}{4} = \frac{128}{4} \qquad \text{Divide by 4.}$$

$$x = 32$$

Step 5 **State the answer.** The number is 32.

Step 6 **Check.** When 32 is decreased by 7, we get $32 - 7 = 25$. If 4 is multiplied by 25, we get 100, as required. The answer, 32, is correct.

◀◀◀ Work Problem 1 at the Side.

OBJECTIVE 3 **Solve problems involving sums of quantities.** A common type of problem in elementary algebra involves finding two quantities when the sum of the quantities is known.

> **PROBLEM-SOLVING HINT**
> In general, to solve problems involving sums of quantities, choose a variable to represent one of the unknowns and then represent the other quantity in terms of the same variable. (See Example 9 in **Section 2.3.**)

EXAMPLE 2 **Finding Numbers of Olympic Medals**

In the 2002 Winter Olympics in Salt Lake City, the United States won 10 more medals than Norway. The two countries won a total of 58 medals. How many medals did each country win? (*Source:* U.S. Olympic Committee.)

Step 1 **Read** the problem. We are given information about the total number of medals and asked to find the number each country won.

Step 2 **Assign a variable.**

Let $x =$ the number of medals Norway won.

Then $x + 10 =$ the number of medals the U.S. won.

—— **Continued on Next Page**

Step 3 **Write an equation.**

The total	is	the number of medals Norway won	plus	the number of medals the U.S. won.
↓	↓	↓	↓	↓
58	=	x	+	$(x + 10)$

Step 4 **Solve** the equation.

$$58 = 2x + 10 \qquad \text{Combine terms.}$$

$$58 - 10 = 2x + 10 - 10 \qquad \text{Subtract 10.}$$

$$48 = 2x \qquad \text{Combine terms.}$$

$$\frac{48}{2} = \frac{2x}{2} \qquad \text{Divide by 2.}$$

$$24 = x \quad \text{or} \quad x = 24$$

Step 5 **State the answer.** The variable x represents the number of medals Norway won, so Norway won 24 medals. Then the number of medals the United States won is $x + 10 = 24 + 10 = 34$.

Step 6 **Check.** Since the United States won 34 medals and Norway won 24, the total number of medals was $34 + 24 = 58$. Because $34 - 24 = 10$, the United States won 10 more medals than Norway. This information agrees with what is given in the problem, so the answer checks.

PROBLEM-SOLVING HINT

The problem in Example 2 could also be solved by letting x represent the number of medals the United States won. Then $x - 10$ would represent the number of medals Norway won. The equation would be

$$58 = x + (x - 10).$$

The solution of this equation is 34, which is the number of U.S. medals. The number of Norwegian medals would be $34 - 10 = 24$. The answers are the same, whichever approach is used.

Work Problem 2 at the Side. ❯❯❯

EXAMPLE 3 Analyzing a Gasoline/Oil Mixture

A lawn trimmer uses a mixture of gasoline and oil. The mixture contains 16 oz of gasoline for each ounce of oil. If the tank holds 68 oz of the mixture, how many ounces of oil and how many ounces of gasoline does it require when it is full?

Step 1 **Read** the problem. We must find how many ounces of oil and gasoline are needed to fill the tank.

Step 2 **Assign a variable.** Let x = the number of ounces of oil required. Then $16x$ = the number of ounces of gasoline required.

Continued on Next Page

2 Solve the problem.

On one day of their vacation, Annie drove three times as far as Jim. Altogether they drove 84 mi that day. Find the number of miles driven by each.

3 Solve the problem.

At a meeting of the local stamp club, each member brought two nonmembers. If a total of 27 people attended, how many were members and how many were nonmembers?

Meeting

| Members x | Nonmembers $2x$ | = 27 |

A diagram like the following is sometimes helpful.

Tank

| Oil x | Gasoline $16x$ | = 68 |

Step 3 **Write an equation.**

Amount of gasoline → Amount of oil → is → Total amount in tank →

$$16x + x = 68$$

Step 4 **Solve.**

$$17x = 68 \quad \text{Combine terms.}$$

$$\frac{17x}{17} = \frac{68}{17} \quad \text{Divide by 17.}$$

$$x = 4$$

Step 5 **State the answer.** The lawn trimmer requires 4 oz of oil and $16(4) = 64$ oz of gasoline when full.

Step 6 **Check.** Since $4 + 64 = 68$, and 64 is 16 times 4, the answer checks.

◀◀◀ **Work Problem 3 at the Side.**

PROBLEM-SOLVING HINT

Sometimes it is necessary to find three unknown quantities in an applied problem. Frequently the three unknowns are compared in *pairs*. When this happens, it is usually easiest to let the variable represent the unknown found in both pairs. The next example illustrates this.

EXAMPLE 4 **Dividing a Board into Pieces**

The instructions for a woodworking project call for three pieces of wood. The longest piece must be twice the length of the middle-sized piece, and the shortest piece must be 10 in. shorter than the middle-sized piece. Maria Gonzales has a board 70 in. long that she wishes to use. How long must each piece be?

Step 1 **Read** the problem. Three lengths must be found.

Step 2 **Assign a variable.** Since the middle-sized piece appears in both pairs of comparisons, let x represent the length, in inches, of the middle-sized piece. We have

$$x = \text{the length of the middle-sized piece,}$$

$$2x = \text{the length of the longest piece, and}$$

$$x - 10 = \text{the length of the shortest piece.}$$

Continued on Next Page

A sketch is helpful here. See Figure 2.

Figure 2

Step 3 **Write an equation.**

Longest		Middle-sized		Shortest	is	Total length
$2x$	$+$	x	$+$	$(x - 10)$	$=$	70

Step 4 **Solve.**

$$4x - 10 = 70 \qquad \text{Combine terms.}$$
$$4x - 10 + 10 = 70 + 10 \qquad \text{Add 10.}$$
$$4x = 80 \qquad \text{Combine terms.}$$
$$\frac{4x}{4} = \frac{80}{4} \qquad \text{Divide by 4.}$$
$$x = 20$$

Step 5 **State the answer.** The middle-sized piece is 20 in. long, the longest piece is 2(20) = 40 in. long, and the shortest piece is 20 − 10 = 10 in. long.

Step 6 **Check.** The sum of the lengths is 70 in. All conditions of the problem are satisfied.

Work Problem 4 at the Side.))))

OBJECTIVE **4** **Solve problems involving supplementary and complementary angles.** An angle can be measured by a unit called the degree (°), which is $\frac{1}{360}$ of a complete rotation. Two angles whose sum is 90° are said to be **complementary,** or *complements* of each other. An angle that measures 90° is a **right angle.** Two angles whose sum is 180° are said to be **supplementary,** or supplements of each other. One angle *supplements* the other to form a **straight angle** of 180°. See Figure 3.

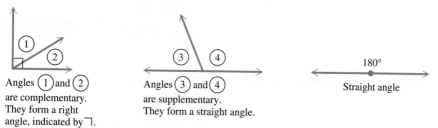

Figure 3

PROBLEM-SOLVING HINT

If x represents the degree measure of an angle, then

90 − x represents the degree measure of its complement, and

180 − x represents the degree measure of its supplement.

4 Solve the problem.

A piece of pipe is 50 in. long. It is cut into three pieces. The longest piece is 10 in. longer than the middle-sized piece, and the shortest piece measures 5 in. less than the middle-sized piece. Find the lengths of the three pieces.

ANSWERS
4. longest: 25 in.; middle: 15 in.; shortest: 10 in.

5 Find each angle measure.

(a) Fill in the blank below the figure. Then find the supplement of an angle that measures 92°.

Supplement

x | 92°

$x + 92 = $ _____

(b) Fill in the blank below the figure. Then find an angle whose complement has twice its measure.

Complement

$2x$

x

$2x + x = $ _____

(c) Find the measure of an angle such that twice its complement is 30° less than its supplement.

EXAMPLE 5 Finding the Measure of an Angle

Find the measure of an angle whose supplement is 10° more than twice its complement.

Step 1 **Read** the problem. We are to find the measure of an angle, given information about its complement and its supplement.

Step 2 **Assign a variable.**

Let $x = $ the degree measure of the angle.

Then $90 - x = $ the degree measure of its complement;

$180 - x = $ the degree measure of its supplement.

We can visualize this information using a sketch. See Figure 4.

Complement
of x:
$90 - x$

Supplement of x:
$180 - x$

x x x

Figure 4

Step 3 **Write an equation.**

Supplement is 10 more than twice its complement.

$180 - x = 10 + 2 \cdot (90 - x)$

Step 4 **Solve.**

$180 - x = 10 + 180 - 2x$ Distributive property

$180 - x = 190 - 2x$ Combine terms.

$180 - x + 2x = 190 - 2x + 2x$ Add $2x$.

$180 + x = 190$ Combine terms.

$180 + x - 180 = 190 - 180$ Subtract 180.

$x = 10$

Step 5 **State the answer.** The measure of the angle is 10°.

Step 6 **Check.** The complement of 10° is 80° and the supplement of 10° is 170°. Also, 170° is equal to 10° more than twice 80° (that is, $170 = 10 + 2(80)$ is true). Therefore, the answer is correct.

Work Problem 5 at the Side.

OBJECTIVE 5 Solve problems involving consecutive integers. Two integers that differ by 1 are called **consecutive integers.** For example, 3 and 4, 6 and 7, and -2 and -1 are pairs of consecutive integers. In general, if x represents an integer, $x + 1$ represents the next larger consecutive integer.

Consecutive *even* integers, such as 8 and 10, differ by 2. Similarly, **consecutive *odd* integers,** such as 9 and 11, also differ by two. In general, if x represents an even integer, $x + 2$ represents the next larger consecutive even integer. The same holds true for odd integers; that is, if x is an odd integer, $x + 2$ is the next larger odd integer.

ANSWERS

5. (a) 180; 88°   (b) 90; 30°   (c) 30°

PROBLEM-SOLVING HINT

When solving consecutive integer problems, if x = the first integer, then for any

two consecutive integers, use $\quad x, \quad x + 1;$

two consecutive *even* integers, use $\quad x, \quad x + 2;$

two consecutive *odd* integers, use $\quad x, \quad x + 2.$

6 Solve the problem.

Find two consecutive integers whose sum is -45.

EXAMPLE 6 Finding Consecutive Integers

Two pages that face each other in this book have 277 as the sum of their page numbers. What are the page numbers?

Step 1 **Read** the problem. Because the two pages face each other, they must have page numbers that are consecutive integers.

Step 2 **Assign a variable.**

Let $\qquad x$ = the first page number.

Then $\quad x + 1$ = the next page number.

Step 3 **Write an equation.** The sum of the page numbers is 277, so

$$x + (x + 1) = 277.$$

Step 4 **Solve.** $\qquad 2x + 1 = 277 \qquad$ Combine terms.

$$2x = 276 \qquad \text{Subtract 1.}$$

$$x = 138 \qquad \text{Divide by 2.}$$

Step 5 **State the answer.** The first page number is 138, and the next page number is $138 + 1 = 139$. (Your book is opened to these two pages!)

Step 6 **Check.** The sum of 138 and 139 is 277. The answer is correct.

> **Work Problem 6 at the Side.** ▶▶▶

7 Solve the problem.

Find two consecutive even integers such that six times the smaller added to the larger gives a sum of 86.

In Example 7, see if you can identify the six steps.

EXAMPLE 7 Finding Consecutive Odd Integers

If the smaller of two consecutive odd integers is doubled, the result is 7 more than the larger of the two integers. Find the two integers.

Let x be the smaller integer. Since the two numbers are consecutive *odd* integers, then $x + 2$ is the larger. Now write an equation.

If the smaller is doubled,	the result is	7	more than	the larger.
↓	↓	↓	↓	↓
$2x$	$=$	7	$+$	$x + 2$

$$2x = 9 + x \qquad \text{Combine terms.}$$

$$x = 9 \qquad \text{Subtract } x.$$

The first integer is 9 and the second is $9 + 2 = 11$. To check, we see that when 9 is doubled, we get 18, which is 7 more than the larger odd integer, 11. The answer is correct.

> **Work Problem 7 at the Side.** ▶▶▶

Real-Data Applications

The Magic Number in Sports

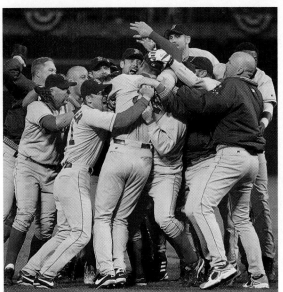

The climax of any sports season is the play-offs. Baseball fans eagerly debate predictions of which team will win the pennant for their division. The *magic number* for each first-place team is often used to predict the division winner. The **magic number** is the combined number of wins by the first-place team and losses by the second-place team that would clinch the title for the first-place team.

For Group Discussion

To calculate the magic number, consider the following conditions.

The number of wins for the first-place team (W_1) *plus the magic number (M) is one more than the sum of the number of wins to date* (W_2) *and the number of games remaining in the season* (N_2) *for the second-place team.*

1. First, use the variable definitions to write an equation involving the magic number. Second, solve the equation for the magic number. Write the formula for the magic number.

American League

East Division

	W	L	Pct.	GB
New York	94	58	.618	—
Boston	89	63	.586	5
Toronto	79	73	.520	15
Baltimore	68	83	.450	25½
Tampa Bay	60	92	.395	34

Central Division

	W	L	Pct.	GB
Minnesota	84	69	.549	—
Chicago	80	72	.526	3½
Kansas City	79	73	.520	4½
Cleveland	66	88	.429	18½
Detroit	38	114	.250	45½

West Division

	W	L	Pct.	GB
Oakland	92	61	.601	—
Seattle	87	66	.569	5
Anaheim	72	81	.471	20
Texas	68	85	.444	24

Source: USA Today.

2. The American League standings with about 10 games left in the 2003 baseball season are shown at the left. There were 162 regulation games in the 2003 season. Find the magic number for each team. The number of games remaining in the season for the second-place team is calculated as

$$N_2 = 162 - (W_2 + L_2).$$

(a) AL East: New York vs Boston

Magic No. _____

(b) AL Central: Minnesota vs Chicago

Magic No. _____

(c) AL West: Oakland vs Seattle

Magic No. _____

[*Note:* For the National League in the 2003 season, Atlanta and San Francisco were runaway winners of the Eastern and Western Divisions, respectively. Chicago, Houston, and St. Louis were locked in a dead heat for the Central Division lead, which was eventually won by Chicago.]

2.4 Exercises

1. In your own words, write the general procedure for solving applications as outlined in this section.

2. List some of the words that translate as "=" when writing an equation to solve an applied problem.

3. Suppose that a problem requires you to find the number of cars on a dealer's lot. Which one of the following would not be a reasonable answer? Justify your answer.

   A. 0   **B.** 45   **C.** 1   **D.** $6\frac{1}{2}$

4. Suppose that a problem requires you to find the number of hours a light bulb is on during a day. Which one of the following would not be a reasonable answer? Justify your answer.

   A. 0   **B.** 4.5   **C.** 13   **D.** 25

5. Suppose that a problem requires you to find the distance traveled in miles. Which one of the following would not be a reasonable answer? Justify your answer.

   A. -10 **B.** 1.8   **C.** $10\frac{1}{2}$ **D.** 50

6. Suppose that a problem requires you to find the time in minutes. Which one of the following would not be a reasonable answer? Justify your answer.

   A. 0   **B.** 10.5   **C.** -5 **D.** 90

Solve each problem. See Example 1.

7. The product of 8, and a number increased by 6, is 104. What is the number?

8. The product of 5, and 3 more than twice a number, is 85. What is the number?

9. Two less than three times a number is equal to 14 more than five times the number. What is the number?

10. Nine more than five times a number is equal to 3 less than seven times the number. What is the number?

11. If 2 is subtracted from a number and this difference is tripled, the result is 6 more than the number. Find the number.

12. If 3 is added to a number and this sum is doubled, the result is 2 more than the number. Find the number.

13. The sum of three times a number and 7 more than the number is the same as the difference between −11 and twice the number. What is the number?

14. If 4 is added to twice a number and this sum is multiplied by 2, the result is the same as if the number is multiplied by 3 and 4 is added to the product. What is the number?

Solve each problem. See Example 2.

15. The number of drive-in movie screens has declined steadily in the United States since the 1960s. California and New York were two of the states with the most remaining drive-in movie screens in 2001. California had 11 more screens than New York, and there were 107 screens total in the two states. How many drive-in movie screens remained in each state? (*Source:* National Association of Theatre Owners.)

16. Thursday is the most-watched night for the major broadcast TV networks (ABC, CBS, NBC, and Fox), with 20 million more viewers than Saturday, the least-watched night. The total for the two nights is 102 million viewers. How many viewers of the major networks are there on each of these nights? (*Source:* Nielsen Media Research.)

17. During the 108th session (2002–2003), the U.S. Senate had a total of 99 Democrats and Republicans. There were 3 more Republicans than Democrats. How many Democrats and Republicans were there in the Senate? (*Source: World Almanac and Book of Facts,* 2004.)

18. The total number of Democrats and Republicans in the U.S. House of Representatives during the 108th session was 434. There were 24 more Republicans than Democrats. How many members of each party were there? (*Source: World Almanac and Book of Facts,* 2004.)

19. Bruce Springsteen and the E Street Band generated top revenue on the concert circuit in 2003. Springsteen and second-place Céline Dion together took in $196.4 million from ticket sales. If Céline Dion took in $35.4 million less than Bruce Springsteen and the E Street Band, how much revenue did each generate? (*Source: Parade,* February 15, 2004.)

20. The Toyota Camry was the top-selling passenger car in the United States in 2003, followed by the Honda Accord. Honda Accord sales were 35 thousand less than Toyota Camry sales, and 833 thousand of these two cars were sold. How many of each make of car were sold? (*Source:* Ward's Communications.)

21. In the 2002–2003 NBA regular season, the Sacramento Kings won 13 more than twice as many games as they lost. The Kings played 82 games. How many wins and losses did the team have? (*Source:* nba.com)

22. In the 2003 regular baseball season, the Atlanta Braves won 21 less than twice as many games as they lost. They played 162 regular season games. How many wins and losses did the team have? (*Source: World Almanac and Book of Facts,* 2004.)

Solve each problem. See Example 3.

23. The value of a "Mint State-63" (uncirculated) 1950 Jefferson nickel minted at Denver is $\frac{8}{7}$ the value of a similar condition 1945 nickel minted at Philadelphia. Together the total value of the two coins is $15.00. What is the value of each coin? (*Source:* Yeoman, R., *A Guide Book of United States Coins,* edited by K. Bressett, 56th edition, 2003.)

24. The largest sheep ranch in the world is located in Australia. The number of sheep on the ranch is $\frac{8}{3}$ the number of uninvited kangaroos grazing on the pastureland. Together, herds of these two animals number 88,000. How many sheep and how many kangaroos roam the ranch? (*Source: The Guinness Book of Records.*)

25. In 1988, a dairy in Alberta, Canada, created a sundae with approximately 1 lb of topping for every 83.2 lb of ice cream. The total of the two ingredients weighed approximately 45,225 lb. To the nearest tenth of a pound, how many pounds of ice cream and how many pounds of topping were there? (*Source: The Guinness Book of Records,* 2000.)

26. A husky running the Iditarod (a thousand-mile race between Anchorage and Nome, Alaska) burns $5\frac{3}{8}$ calories in exertion for every 1 calorie burned in thermoregulation in extreme cold. According to one scientific study, a husky in top condition burns an amazing total of 11,200 calories per day. How many calories are burned for exertion, and how many are burned for regulation of body temperature? Round answers to the nearest whole number.

27. In a mixture of concrete, there are 3 lb of cement mix for each pound of gravel. If the mixture contains a total of 140 lb of these two ingredients, how many pounds of gravel are there?

28. A mixture of nuts contains only peanuts and cashews. For every ounce of cashews there are 5 oz of peanuts. If the mixture contains a total of 27 oz, how many ounces of each type of nut does the mixture contain?

Solve each problem. See Example 4.

29. In one day, Akilah Cadet received 13 packages. Federal Express delivered three times as many as Airborne Express, while United Parcel Service delivered 2 fewer than Airborne Express. How many packages did each service deliver to Akilah?

30. In his job at the post office, Eddie Thibodeaux works a 6.5-hr day. He sorts mail, sells stamps, and does supervisory work. One day he sold stamps twice as long as he sorted mail, and he supervised .5 hr longer than he sorted mail. How many hours did he spend at each task?

31. The United States earned 103 medals at the 2004 Summer Olympics in Athens. The number of silver medals earned was 4 more than the number of gold medals. The number of bronze medals earned was 6 less than the number of gold medals. How many of each kind of medal did the United States earn? (*Source: The Gazette,* August 30, 2004.)

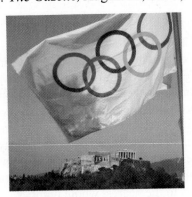

32. Nagaraj Nanjappa has a party-length submarine sandwich 59 in. long. He wants to cut it into three pieces so that the middle piece is 5 in. longer than the shortest piece and the shortest piece is 9 in. shorter than the longest piece. How long should the three pieces be?

33. Venus is 31.2 million mi farther from the sun than Mercury, while Earth is 57 million mi farther from the sun than Mercury. If the total of the distances from these three planets to the sun is 196.2 million mi, how far away from the sun is Mercury? (All distances given here are mean (*average*) distances.) (*Source: The Universal Almanac.*)

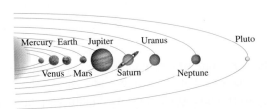

34. Together, Saturn, Jupiter, and Uranus have a total of 113 natural satellites (moons). Jupiter has 30 more satellites than Saturn, and Uranus has 10 fewer satellites than Saturn. How many known satellites does Saturn have? (*Source: World Almanac and Book of Facts,* 2004.)

35. The sum of the measures of the angles of any triangle is 180°. In triangle *ABC*, angles *A* and *B* have the same measure, while the measure of angle *C* is 60° larger than each of *A* and *B*. What are the measures of the three angles?

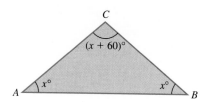

36. In triangle *ABC*, the measure of angle *A* is 141° more than the measure of angle *B*. The measure of angle *B* is the same as the measure of angle *C*. Find the measure of each angle. (*Hint:* See Exercise 35.)

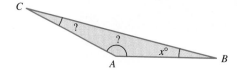

Use the concepts of this section to answer each question.

37. Is there an angle whose supplement is equal to its complement? If so, what is the measure of the angle?

38. Is there an angle that is equal to its supplement? Is there an angle that is equal to its complement? If the answer is yes to either question, give the measure of the angle.

39. If *x* represents an integer, how can you express the next smaller consecutive integer in terms of *x*?

40. If *x* represents an integer, how can you express the next smaller even integer in terms of *x*?

Solve each problem. See Example 5.

41. Find the measure of an angle whose complement is four times its measure.

42. Find the measure of an angle whose supplement is three times its measure.

43. Find the measure of an angle whose supplement measures 39° more than twice its complement.

44. Find the measure of an angle whose supplement measures 38° less than three times its complement.

45. Find the measure of an angle such that the difference between the measures of its supplement and three times its complement is 10°.

46. Find the measure of an angle such that the sum of the measures of its complement and its supplement is 160°.

Solve each problem. See Examples 6 and 7.

47. The numbers on two consecutively numbered gym lockers have a sum of 137. What are the locker numbers?

48. The sum of two consecutive checkbook check numbers is 357. Find the numbers.

49. Two pages that are back-to-back in this book have 293 as the sum of their page numbers. What are the page numbers?

50. Find two consecutive odd integers such that twice the larger is 17 more than the smaller.

51. Find two consecutive even integers such that the smaller added to three times the larger gives a sum of 46.

52. Two houses on the same side of the street have house numbers that are consecutive even integers. The sum of the integers is 58. What are the two house numbers?

53. When the smaller of two consecutive integers is added to three times the larger, the result is 43. Find the integers.

54. If five times the smaller of two consecutive integers is added to three times the larger, the result is 59. Find the integers.

Apply the ideas of this section to solve Exercises 55 and 56, based on the graphs.

55. In a recent year, the funding for Head Start programs increased by .61 billion dollars from the funding in the previous year. The following year, the increase was .93 billion dollars more. For those three years, the total funding was 16.13 billion dollars. How much was funded in each of these years? (*Source:* U.S. Department of Health and Human Services.)

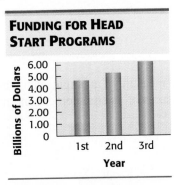

56. According to data provided by the National Safety Council for a recent year, the number of serious injuries per 100,000 participants in football, bicycling, and golf is illustrated in the graph. There were 800 more in bicycling than in golf, and there were 1267 more in football than in bicycling. Altogether there were 3179 serious injuries per 100,000 participants. How many such serious injuries were there in each sport?

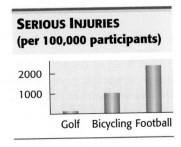

2.5 Formulas and Applications from Geometry

Many applied problems can be solved with *formulas*. A **formula** is a mathematical expression in which variables are used to describe a relationship. Formulas exist for geometric figures, for distance, and for money earned on bank savings. The formulas used in this book are given on the inside covers.

O B J E C T I V E S

1 Solve a formula for one variable, given the values of the other variables.

2 Use a formula to solve an applied problem.

3 Solve problems involving vertical angles and straight angles.

4 Solve a formula for a specified variable.

OBJECTIVE 1 Solve a formula for one variable, given the values of the other variables. Given the values of all but one of the variables in a formula, we can find the value of the remaining variable. In Example 1, we use the idea of *area*. The **area** of a plane (two-dimensional) geometric figure is a measure of the surface covered by the figure.

EXAMPLE 1 Using Formulas to Evaluate Variables

Find the value of the remaining variable in each formula.

(a) $A = LW$; $A = 64, L = 10$

As shown in Figure 5, this formula gives the area of a rectangle with length L and width W.

Rectangle
$A = LW$
Figure 5

Substitute the given values into the formula and then solve for W.

$$A = LW$$

$$64 = 10W \qquad \text{Let } A = 64 \text{ and } L = 10.$$

$$6.4 = W \qquad \text{Divide by 10.}$$

The width is 6.4. Since $10(6.4) = 64$, the given area, the answer checks.

(b) $A = \dfrac{1}{2}h(b + B)$; $A = 210, B = 27, h = 10$

This formula gives the area of a trapezoid with parallel sides of lengths b and B and distance h between the parallel sides. See Figure 6.

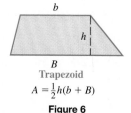

Trapezoid
$A = \frac{1}{2}h(b + B)$
Figure 6

Again, begin by substituting the given values into the formula.

$$A = \frac{1}{2}h(b + B)$$

$$210 = \frac{1}{2}(10)(b + 27) \qquad A = 210, h = 10, B = 27$$

Continued on Next Page

1 Find the value of the remaining variable in each formula.

(a) $I = prt$; $I = \$246$, $r = .06$, $t = 2$

(b) $P = 2L + 2W$; $P = 126$, $W = 25$

2 Solve the problem.

A farmer has 800 m of fencing material to enclose a rectangular field. The width of the field is 175 m. Find the length of the field.

Now solve for b.

$$210 = 5(b + 27) \qquad \text{Multiply.}$$
$$210 = 5b + 135 \qquad \text{Distributive property}$$
$$210 - \mathbf{135} = 5b + 135 - \mathbf{135} \qquad \text{Subtract 135.}$$
$$75 = 5b \qquad \text{Combine terms.}$$
$$\frac{75}{5} = \frac{5b}{5} \qquad \text{Divide by 5.}$$
$$15 = b$$

Check that the length of the shorter parallel side, b, is 15.

Work Problem 1 at the Side.

OBJECTIVE 2 Use a formula to solve an applied problem. Formulas are often used to solve applied problems. *It is a good idea to draw a sketch when a geometric figure is involved.* Example 2 uses the idea of *perimeter*. The **perimeter** of a plane (two-dimensional) geometric figure is the distance around the figure, that is, the sum of the lengths of its sides.

EXAMPLE 2 Finding the Width of a Rectangular Lot

A rectangular lot has perimeter 80 m and length 25 m. Find the width of the lot.

Step 1 **Read.** We are told to find the width of the lot.

Step 2 **Assign a variable.** Let $W =$ the width of the lot in meters. See Figure 7.

25 m

Figure 7

Step 3 **Write an equation.** We use the formula for the perimeter of a rectangle, and find the width by substituting 80 for P and 25 for L.

$$P = 2L + 2W \qquad \text{Perimeter formula}$$
$$\mathbf{80} = 2(\mathbf{25}) + 2W \qquad P = 80, L = 25$$

Step 4 **Solve.**
$$80 = 50 + 2W \qquad \text{Multiply.}$$
$$80 - \mathbf{50} = 50 + 2W - \mathbf{50} \qquad \text{Subtract 50.}$$
$$30 = 2W \qquad \text{Combine terms.}$$
$$\frac{30}{2} = \frac{2W}{2} \qquad \text{Divide by 2.}$$
$$15 = W$$

Step 5 **State the answer.** The width is 15 m.

Step 6 **Check.** If the width is 15 m and the length is 25 m, the perimeter is $2(25) + 2(15) = 50 + 30 = 80$ m, as required.

Work Problem 2 at the Side.

EXAMPLE 3 **Finding the Height of a Triangular Sail**

The area of a triangular sail of a sailboat is 126 ft^2. (Recall that ft^2 means "square feet.") The base of the sail is 12 ft. Find the height of the sail.

Step 1 **Read.** We must find the height of the triangular sail.

Step 2 **Assign a variable.** Let h = the height of the sail in feet. See Figure 8.

Figure 8

Step 3 **Write an equation.** The formula for the area of a triangle is $A = \frac{1}{2}bh$, where A is the area, b is the base, and h is the height. Using the information given in the problem, substitute 126 for A and 12 for b in the formula.

$$A = \frac{1}{2}bh$$

$$\mathbf{126} = \frac{1}{2}(\mathbf{12})h \qquad A = 126, b = 12$$

Step 4 **Solve** the equation.

$$126 = 6h \qquad \text{Multiply.}$$

$$21 = h \qquad \text{Divide by 6.}$$

Step 5 **State the answer.** The height of the sail is 21 ft.

Step 6 **Check** to see that the values $A = 126$, $b = 12$, and $h = 21$ satisfy the formula for the area of a triangle.

Work Problem 3 at the Side. ▶▶▶

OBJECTIVE **3** **Solve problems involving vertical angles and straight angles.**   Figure 9 shows two intersecting lines forming angles that are numbered ①, ②, ③, and ④. Angles ① and ③ lie "opposite" each other. They are called **vertical angles.** Another pair of vertical angles is ② and ④. In geometry, it is shown that *vertical angles have equal measures.*

Now look at angles ① and ②. When their measures are added, we get the measure of a **straight angle,** which is **180°.** There are three other such pairs of angles: ② and ③, ③ and ④, and ① and ④.

The next example uses these ideas.

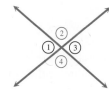

Figure 9

3 Solve the problem.
    The area of a triangle is 120 m^2. The height is 24 m. Find the length of the base of the triangle.

4 Find the measure of each marked angle.

(a)

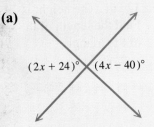

$(2x + 24)°$ $(4x - 40)°$

(b)

$(5x + 12)°$ $(3x)°$

EXAMPLE 4 Finding Angle Measures

Refer to the appropriate figure in each part.

(a) Find the measure of each marked angle in Figure 10.

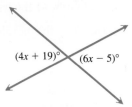

$(4x + 19)°$ $(6x - 5)°$

Figure 10

Since the marked angles are vertical angles, they have equal measures.

$$4x + 19 = 6x - 5 \qquad \text{Set } 4x + 19 \text{ equal to } 6x - 5.$$
$$4x + 19 - 4x = 6x - 5 - 4x \qquad \text{Subtract } 4x.$$
$$19 = 2x - 5$$
$$19 + 5 = 2x - 5 + 5 \qquad \text{Add 5.}$$
$$24 = 2x$$
$$\frac{24}{2} = \frac{2x}{2} \qquad \text{Divide by 2.}$$
$$12 = x$$

Since $x = 12$, one angle has measure $4(12) + 19 = 67$ degrees. The other has the same measure, since $6(12) - 5 = 67$ as well. Each angle measures $67°$.

(b) Find the measure of each marked angle in Figure 11.

$(3x - 30)°$ $(4x)°$

Figure 11

The measures of the marked angles must add to $180°$ because together they form a straight angle. The equation to solve is

$$(3x - 30) + 4x = 180.$$
$$7x - 30 = 180 \qquad \text{Combine terms.}$$
$$7x = 210 \qquad \text{Add 30.}$$
$$x = 30 \qquad \text{Divide by 7.}$$

To find the measures of the angles, replace x with 30 in the two expressions.

$$3x - 30 = 3(30) - 30 = 90 - 30 = 60$$
$$4x = 4(30) = 120$$

The two angle measures are $60°$ and $120°$.

CAUTION
In Example 4, the answer is *not* the value of x. Remember to substitute the value of the variable into the expression given for each angle.

OBJECTIVE **4** **Solve a formula for a specified variable.** Sometimes it is necessary to solve a large number of problems that use the same formula. For example, a surveying class might need to solve several problems that involve the formula for the area of a rectangle, $A = LW$. Suppose that in each problem the area (A) and the length (L) of a rectangle are given, and the width (W) must be found. Rather than solving for W each time the formula is used, it would be simpler to *rewrite the formula* so that it is solved for W. This process is called **solving for a specified variable** or **solving a literal equation.**

In solving a formula for a specified variable, we treat the specified variable as if it were the *only* variable in the equation, and treat the other variables as if they were numbers. We use the same steps to solve the equation for the specified variable that we have used to solve equations with just one variable.

5 Solve $I = prt$ for t.

EXAMPLE 5 **Solving for a Specified Variable**

Solve $A = LW$ for W.

Our goal is to get W alone on one side of the equation. To do this, think of undoing what has been done to W. Since W is multiplied by L, undo the multiplication by dividing each side of $A = LW$ by L.

$$A = LW$$

$$\frac{A}{L} = \frac{LW}{L} \qquad \text{Divide by } L.$$

$$\frac{A}{L} = W \quad \text{or} \quad W = \frac{A}{L} \qquad \tfrac{L}{L} = 1; 1W = W$$

The formula is now solved for W.

Work Problem 5 at the Side.))⟩

6 Solve $P = a + b + c$ for a.

EXAMPLE 6 **Solving for a Specified Variable**

Solve $P = 2L + 2W$ for L.

We want to get L alone on one side of the equation. We begin by subtracting $2W$ from each side.

$$P = 2L + 2W$$

$$P - 2W = 2L + 2W - 2W \qquad \text{Subtract } 2W.$$

$$P - 2W = 2L \qquad \text{Combine terms.}$$

$$\frac{P - 2W}{2} = \frac{2L}{2} \qquad \text{Divide by 2.}$$

$$\frac{P - 2W}{2} = L \quad \text{or} \quad L = \frac{P - 2W}{2} \qquad \tfrac{2}{2} = 1; 1L = L$$

The last step gives the formula solved for L, as required.

Work Problem 6 at the Side.))⟩

7 (a) Solve $A = p + prt$ for t.

EXAMPLE 7 **Solving for a Specified Variable**

Solve $F = \frac{9}{5}C + 32$ for C. (This is the formula for converting temperatures from Celsius to Fahrenheit.)

We need to isolate C on one side of the equation. First undo the addition of 32 to $\frac{9}{5}C$ by subtracting 32 from each side.

$$F = \frac{9}{5}C + 32$$

$$F - 32 = \frac{9}{5}C + 32 - 32 \qquad \text{Subtract 32.}$$

$$F - 32 = \frac{9}{5}C$$

Now multiply each side by $\frac{5}{9}$. Use parentheses on the left.

$$\frac{5}{9}(F - 32) = \frac{5}{9} \cdot \frac{9}{5}C \qquad \text{Multiply by } \tfrac{5}{9}.$$

$$\frac{5}{9}(F - 32) = C \quad \text{or} \quad C = \frac{5}{9}(F - 32)$$

This last result is the formula for converting temperatures from Fahrenheit to Celsius.

Work Problem 7 at the Side.

(b) Solve $Ax + By = C$ for y.

ANSWERS

7. (a) $t = \dfrac{A - p}{pr}$ (b) $y = \dfrac{C - Ax}{B}$

2.5 Exercises

1. In your own words, explain what is meant by each term.

   (a) Perimeter of a plane geometric figure

   (b) Area of a plane geometric figure

2. The distance around a circle is called the _____ of the circle.

3. If a formula has exactly five variables, how many values would you need to be given in order to find the value of any one variable?

4. The formula for changing Celsius temperature to Fahrenheit is given in Example 7 as $F = \frac{9}{5}C + 32$. Sometimes it is seen as $F = \frac{9C}{5} + 32$. These are both correct. Why is it true that $\frac{9}{5}C$ is equal to $\frac{9C}{5}$?

Decide whether perimeter or area would be used to solve a problem concerning the measure of the quantity.

5. Sod for a lawn

6. Carpeting for a bedroom

7. Baseboards for a living room

8. Fencing for a yard

9. Fertilizer for a garden

10. Tile for a bathroom

11. Determining the cost of planting rye grass in a lawn for the winter

12. Determining the cost of replacing a linoleum floor with a wood floor

In the following exercises a formula is given, along with the values of all but one of the variables in the formula. Find the value of the variable that is not given. (When necessary, use 3.14 as an approximation for π (pi).) See Example 1.

13. $P = 2L + 2W$ (perimeter of a rectangle); $L = 8$, $W = 5$

14. $P = 2L + 2W$; $L = 6$, $W = 4$

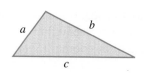

15. $A = \frac{1}{2}bh$ (area of a triangle); $b = 8$, $h = 16$

16. $A = \frac{1}{2}bh$; $b = 10$, $h = 14$

17. $P = a + b + c$ (perimeter of a triangle); $P = 12$, $a = 3$, $c = 5$

18. $P = a + b + c$; $P = 15$, $a = 3$, $b = 7$

19. $d = rt$ (distance formula); $d = 252, r = 45$

20. $d = rt; d = 100, t = 2.5$

21. $I = prt$ (simple interest); $p = 7500, r = .035, t = 6$

22. $I = prt; p = 5000, r = .025, t = 7$

23. $C = 2\pi r$ (circumference of a circle); $C = 16.328$

24. $C = 2\pi r; C = 8.164$

25. $A = \pi r^2$ (area of a circle); $r = 4$

26. $A = \pi r^2; r = 12$

*The **volume** of a three-dimensional object is a measure of the space occupied by the object. For example, we would need to know the volume of a gasoline tank in order to know how many gallons of gasoline it would take to completely fill the tank. In the following exercises, a formula for the volume (V) of a three-dimensional object is given, along with values for the other variables. Evaluate V. (Use 3.14 as an approximation for π.) See Example 1.*

27. $V = LWH$ (volume of a rectangular box); $L = 10, W = 5, H = 3$

28. $V = LWH; L = 12, W = 8, H = 4$

29. $V = \frac{1}{3}Bh$ (volume of a pyramid); $B = 12, h = 13$

30. $V = \frac{1}{3}Bh; B = 36, h = 4$

31. $V = \frac{4}{3}\pi r^3$ (volume of a sphere); $r = 12$

32. $V = \frac{4}{3}\pi r^3; r = 6$

*Use a formula to write an equation for each application, and then use the problem-solving method of **Section 2.4** to solve. (Use 3.14 as an approximation for π.) **Formulas are found on the inside covers of this book.** See Examples 2 and 3.*

33. A prehistoric ceremonial site dating to about 3000 B.C. was discovered at Stanton Drew in southwestern England. The site, which is larger than Stonehenge, is a nearly perfect circle, consisting of nine concentric rings that probably held upright wooden posts. Around this timber temple is a wide, encircling ditch enclosing an area with a diameter of 443 ft. Find this enclosed area to the nearest thousand square feet. (*Source: Archaeology,* vol. 51, no. 1, Jan./Feb. 1998.)

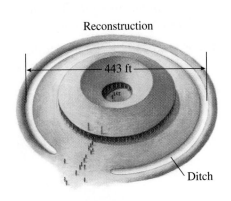

Reconstruction

443 ft

Ditch

34. The Skydome in Toronto, Canada, is the first stadium with a hard-shell, retractable roof. The steel dome is 630 ft in diameter. To the nearest foot, what is the circumference of this dome? (*Source:* www.4ballparks.com)

630 ft

35. The *Daily Banner,* published in Roseberg, Oregon, in the 19th century, had page size 3 in. by 3.5 in. What was the perimeter? What was the area? (*Source: The Guinness Book of Records.*)

36. The newspaper *The Constellation,* printed in 1859 in New York City as part of the Fourth of July celebration, had length 51 in. and width 35 in. What was the perimeter? What was the area? (*Source: The Guinness Book of Records.*)

37. The largest drum ever constructed was made from Japanese cedar and cowhide, with diameter 15.74 ft. It was built in Ishikawa, Japan, and completed on January 1, 2001. What was the area of the circular face of the drum? Round your answer to the nearest hundredth of a square foot. (*Hint:* Use $A = \pi r^2$.) (*Source:* www.guinnessworldrecords.com)

38. What was the circumference of the drum described in Exercise 37? Round your answer to the nearest hundredth of a foot. (*Hint:* Use $C = 2\pi r$.)

39. The survey plat depicted here shows two lots that form a trapezoid. The measures of the parallel sides are 115.80 ft and 171.00 ft. The height of the trapezoid is 165.97 ft. Find the combined area of the two lots. Round your answer to the nearest hundredth of a square foot.

40. Lot A in the figure is in the shape of a trapezoid. The parallel sides measure 26.84 ft and 82.05 ft. The height of the trapezoid is 165.97 ft. Find the area of Lot A. Round your answer to the nearest hundredth of a square foot.

Source: Property survey in New Roads, Louisiana.

41. The U.S. Postal Service requires that any box sent through the mail have length plus girth (distance around) totaling no more than 108 in. The maximum volume that meets this condition is contained by a box with a square end 18 in. on each side. What is the length of the box? What is the maximum volume?

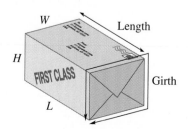

42. The largest box of popcorn was filled by students in Jacksonville, Florida. The box was approximately 40 ft long, $20\frac{2}{3}$ ft wide, and 8 ft high. To the nearest cubic foot, what was the volume of the box? (*Source: The Guinness Book of Records.*)

Find the measure of each marked angle. See Example 4.

43.

$(x + 1)°$ $(4x - 56)°$

44.

$(10x + 7)°$ $(7x + 3)°$

45.

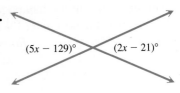

$(5x - 129)°$ $(2x - 21)°$

46.

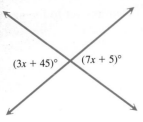

$(3x + 45)°$ $(7x + 5)°$

47.

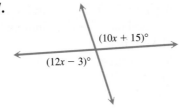

$(10x + 15)°$

$(12x - 3)°$

48.

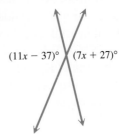

$(11x - 37)°$ $(7x + 27)°$

Solve each formula for the specified variable. See Examples 5–7.

49. $d = rt$ for t

50. $d = rt$ for r

51. $V = LWH$ for H

52. $A = LW$ for L

53. $P = a + b + c$ for b

54. $P = a + b + c$ for c

55. $I = prt$ for r

56. $I = prt$ for p

57. $A = \dfrac{1}{2}bh$ for h

58. $A = \dfrac{1}{2}bh$ for b

59. $P = 2L + 2W$ for W

60. $A = p + prt$ for r

61. $V = \dfrac{1}{3}\pi r^2 h$ for h

62. $V = \pi r^2 h$ for h

63. $y = mx + b$ for m

64. $y = mx + b$ for x

65. $M = C(1 + r)$ for r

66. $C = \dfrac{5}{9}(F - 32)$ for F

2.6 Ratio, Proportion, and Percent

OBJECTIVE 1 Write ratios. A **ratio** is a comparison of two quantities using a quotient.

OBJECTIVES

1 Write ratios.

2 Solve proportions.

3 Solve applied problems using proportions.

4 Find percentages and percents.

> **Ratio**
>
> The ratio of the number a to the number b is written
>
> $$a \text{ to } b, \quad a:b, \quad \text{or} \quad \frac{a}{b}.$$

This last way of writing a ratio is most common in algebra.

1 Write each ratio.

(a) 9 women to 5 women

EXAMPLE 1 Writing a Word Phrase as a Ratio

Write a ratio for each word phrase.

(a) The ratio of 5 hr to 3 hr is

$$\frac{5 \text{ hr}}{3 \text{ hr}} = \frac{5}{3}.$$

(b) To find the ratio of 6 hr to 3 days, first convert 3 days to hours.

$$3 \text{ days} = 3 \cdot 24$$
$$= 72 \text{ hr}$$

The ratio of 6 hr to 3 days is thus

$$\frac{6 \text{ hr}}{3 \text{ days}} = \frac{6 \text{ hr}}{72 \text{ hr}} = \frac{6}{72} = \frac{1}{12}.$$

> **Work Problem 1 at the Side.** ▶▶▶

(b) 4 in. to 1 ft

An application of ratios is in unit pricing, to see which size of an item offered in different sizes produces the best price per unit. To do this, set up the ratio of the price of the item to the number of units on the label. Then divide to obtain the price per unit.

EXAMPLE 2 Finding the Price per Unit

The Cub Foods supermarket in Coon Rapids, Minnesota, charges the following prices for a jar of extra crunchy peanut butter.

PEANUT BUTTER

Size	Price
18-oz	$1.50
40-oz	$4.14
64-oz	$6.29

Which size is the best buy? That is, which size has the lowest unit price?

Continued on Next Page

ANSWERS

1. (a) $\frac{9}{5}$ (b) $\frac{4}{12} = \frac{1}{3}$

2 Solve the problem.

The local supermarket charges the following prices for a popular brand of pancake syrup.

PANCAKE SYRUP

Size	Price
36-oz	$3.89
24-oz	$2.79
12-oz	$1.89

Which size is the best buy? What is the unit cost for that size?

To find the best buy, write ratios comparing the price for each size jar to the number of units (ounces) per jar. The results in the following table are rounded to the nearest thousandth.

Size	Unit Cost (dollars per ounce)	
18-oz	$\dfrac{\$1.50}{18} = \$.083$	← The best buy
40-oz	$\dfrac{\$4.14}{40} = \$.104$	
64-oz	$\dfrac{\$6.29}{64} = \$.098$	

Because the 18-oz size produces the lowest unit cost, it is the best buy. This example shows that buying the largest size does not always provide the best buy, although this is often true.

)))(Work Problem 2 at the Side.

OBJECTIVE 2 Solve proportions. A ratio is used to compare two numbers or amounts. A **proportion** says that two ratios are equal, so it is a special type of equation. For example,

$$\frac{3}{4} = \frac{15}{20} \qquad \text{Proportion}$$

is a proportion that says that the ratios $\frac{3}{4}$ and $\frac{15}{20}$ are equal. In the proportion

$$\frac{a}{b} = \frac{c}{d} \qquad (b, d \neq 0),$$

a, b, c, and d are the **terms** of the proportion. The a and d terms are called the **extremes**, and the b and c terms are called the **means**. We read the proportion $\frac{a}{b} = \frac{c}{d}$ as "a is to b as c is to d." Multiplying each side of this proportion by the common denominator, bd, gives

$$bd \cdot \frac{a}{b} = bd \cdot \frac{c}{d}$$

$$\frac{b}{b}(d \cdot a) = \frac{d}{d}(b \cdot c) \qquad \text{Associative and commutative properties}$$

$$ad = bc. \qquad \text{Commutative and identity properties}$$

We can also find the products ad and bc by multiplying diagonally.

$$\frac{a}{b} \overset{bc}{\underset{ad}{\times}} \frac{c}{d}$$

For this reason, ad and bc are called **cross products.**

If $\dfrac{a}{b} = \dfrac{c}{d}$, then the cross products ad and bc are equal.

Also, if $ad = bc$, then $\dfrac{a}{b} = \dfrac{c}{d}$ $(b, d \neq 0)$.

From this rule, if $\frac{a}{b} = \frac{c}{d}$ then $ad = bc$; that is, *the product of the extremes equals the product of the means.*

> **NOTE**
>
> If $\frac{a}{c} = \frac{b}{d}$, then $ad = cb$, or $ad = bc$. This means that the two proportions are equivalent, and
>
> $$\text{the proportion } \frac{a}{b} = \frac{c}{d} \text{ can always be written as } \frac{a}{c} = \frac{b}{d}.$$
>
> Sometimes one form is more convenient to work with than the other.

Four numbers are used in a proportion. If any three of these numbers are known, the fourth can be found.

EXAMPLE 3 **Finding an Unknown in a Proportion**

Solve the proportion.

$$\frac{5}{9} = \frac{x}{63}$$

$$5 \cdot 63 = 9 \cdot x \qquad \text{Cross products must be equal.}$$

$$315 = 9x \qquad \text{Multiply.}$$

$$35 = x \qquad \text{Divide by 9.}$$

Check by substituting 35 for x in the proportion. The solution is 35.

Work Problem 3 at the Side. ❱❱❱

> **CAUTION**
>
> The cross product method cannot be used directly if there is more than one term on either side.

EXAMPLE 4 **Solving an Equation Using Cross Products**

Solve the equation.

$$\frac{m-2}{5} = \frac{m+1}{3}$$

$$3(m-2) = 5(m+1) \qquad \text{Find the cross products; use parentheses.}$$

$$3m - 6 = 5m + 5 \qquad \text{Distributive property}$$

$$3m = 5m + 11 \qquad \text{Add 6.}$$

$$-2m = 11 \qquad \text{Subtract } 5m.$$

$$m = -\frac{11}{2} \qquad \text{Divide by } -2.$$

Check that the solution is $-\frac{11}{2}$.

Work Problem 4 at the Side. ❱❱❱

> **NOTE**
>
> When you set cross products equal to each other, you are really multiplying each ratio in the proportion by a common denominator.

❸ Solve each proportion.

(a) $\dfrac{y}{6} = \dfrac{35}{42}$

(b) $\dfrac{a}{24} = \dfrac{15}{16}$

❹ Solve each equation.

(a) $\dfrac{z}{2} = \dfrac{z+1}{3}$

(b) $\dfrac{p+3}{3} = \dfrac{p-5}{4}$

ANSWERS

3. **(a)** 5 **(b)** $\dfrac{45}{2}$

4. **(a)** 2 **(b)** -27

5 Solve the problem.

Twelve gal of diesel fuel costs $20.88. How much would 16.5 gal of the same fuel cost?

OBJECTIVE 3 Solve applied problems using proportions. Proportions are useful in many practical applications. We continue to use the six-step method, although the steps are not numbered here.

EXAMPLE 5 Applying Proportions

After Lee Ann Spahr pumped 5.0 gal of gasoline, the display showing the price read $9.40. When she finished pumping the gasoline, the price display read $25.38. How many gallons did she pump?

To solve this problem, set up a proportion, with prices in the numerators and gallons in the denominators. Make sure that the corresponding numbers appear together.

Let x = the number of gallons she pumped.

$$\begin{array}{c} \text{Price} \rightarrow \\ \text{Gallons} \rightarrow \end{array} \frac{\$9.40}{5.0} = \frac{\$25.38}{x} \begin{array}{c} \leftarrow \text{Price} \\ \leftarrow \text{Gallons} \end{array}$$

$$9.40x = 5.0(25.38) \qquad \text{Cross products}$$

$$9.40x = 126.90 \qquad \text{Multiply.}$$

$$x = 13.5 \qquad \text{Divide by 9.40.}$$

She pumped a total of 13.5 gal. Check this answer. Notice that the way the proportion was set up uses the fact that the unit price is the same, no matter how many gallons are purchased.

▦ **Calculator Tip** Using a calculator to perform the arithmetic in Example 5 reduces the possibility of errors.

◀◀◀ **Work Problem 5 at the Side.**

OBJECTIVE 4 Find percentages and percents. Percents are ratios where the second number is always 100. For example, 50% represents the ratio of 50 to 100, 27% represents the ratio of 27 to 100, and so on. We can use the techniques for solving proportions to solve percent problems. Recall from **Section R.2** that the decimal point is moved two places to the left to change a percent to a decimal number. For example, 75% can be written as the decimal .75.

▦ **Calculator Tip** Many calculators have a percent key that does this automatically.

We can solve a percent problem by writing it as the proportion

$$\frac{amount}{base} = \frac{percent}{100} \qquad \text{or} \qquad \frac{a}{b} = \frac{p}{100}.$$

The amount, or **percentage,** is compared to the **base** (the whole amount). Since *percent* means *per 100,* we compare the numerical value of the percent to 100. Thus, we write 50% as

$$\frac{p}{100} = \frac{50}{100}. \qquad p = 50$$

EXAMPLE 6 Finding Percentages

Solve each problem.

(a) Find 15% of 600.

Here, the base is 600, the percent is 15, and we must find the percentage.

$$\frac{a}{b} = \frac{p}{100}$$

$$\frac{a}{600} = \frac{15}{100}$$

$$100a = 600(15) \quad \text{Cross products}$$

$$a = \frac{600(15)}{100} \quad \text{Divide by 100.}$$

$$a = 90$$

Thus, 15% of 600 is 90.

(b) A DVD with a regular price of $18 is on sale this week at 22% off. Find the amount of the discount and the sale price of the disc.

The discount is 22% of $18. We want to find a, given b is 18 and p is 22.

$$\frac{a}{b} = \frac{p}{100}$$

$$\frac{a}{18} = \frac{22}{100}$$

$$100a = 18(22) \quad \text{Cross products}$$

$$100a = 396$$

$$a = 3.96 \quad \text{Divide by 100.}$$

The amount of the discount on the DVD is $3.96, and the sale price is $18.00 − $3.96 = $14.04.

Work Problem 6 at the Side. ▶▶▶

EXAMPLE 7 Solving an Applied Percent Problem

A newspaper ad offered a set of tires at a sale price of $258. The regular price was $300. What percent of the regular price was the savings?

The savings amounted to $300 − $258 = $42. We can now restate the problem: What percent of 300 is 42? Substitute into the percent proportion. We have $a = 42$, $b = 300$, and p is to be found.

$$\frac{a}{b} = \frac{p}{100}$$

$$\frac{42}{300} = \frac{p}{100}$$

$$300p = 4200 \quad \text{Cross products}$$

$$p = 14 \quad \text{Divide by 300.}$$

The sale price represented a 14% savings.

Work Problem 7 at the Side. ▶▶▶

6 Solve each problem.

(a) Find 20% of 70.

(b) Find the discount on a television set with a regular price of $270 if the set is on sale at 25% off. Find the sale price of the set.

7 Solve each problem.

(a) 90 is what percent of 360?

(b) The interest in 1 yr on deposits of $11,000 was $682. What percent interest was paid?

ANSWERS
6. (a) 14 **(b)** $67.50; $202.50
7. (a) 25% **(b)** 6.2%

Real-Data Applications

Currency Exchange

When you travel between countries, you need to exchange your U.S. dollars (USD) for the local currency. The exchange rate between currencies changes daily, and you can easily find the updated rates using the Internet. The table shown here was taken from the Bloomberg Currency Calculator Web page.

WESTERN EUROPE CURRENCY RATES

Currency	Currency per 1 unit of USD	
	Symbol	Value
British Pound	GBP	.5456
Euro	EUR	.7968
Danish Krone	DKK	5.9373

Source: Bloomberg L.P.

On February 4, 2004, the currency exchange rate from U.S. dollars to British pounds was given as follows:

$1.00 U.S. was equivalent to £.5456 (British pounds).

You can set up a proportion to convert dollars to British pounds. For example, suppose you want to determine how many British pounds is equivalent to $50.

$$\frac{\$1}{£.5456} = \frac{\$50}{£x} \quad \text{or} \quad \frac{1}{.5456} = \frac{50}{x}$$

$$1(x) = .5456(50)$$

$$x = 27.28$$

So at this exchange rate, 27.28 British pounds equals 50 U.S. dollars.

For Group Discussion

1. Based on the currency exchange rates in the table above, find the amount of the local currency equivalent to $50 U.S. and find the number of U.S. dollars equivalent to 200 units of the local currency. Round to the nearest hundredth as necessary.

    (a) $50 = _____ Danish Krone and 200 Krone = _____ dollars

    (b) $50 = _____ Euros and 200 Euros = _____ dollars

2. Set up a proportion to find the number of U.S. dollars equivalent to £1 (British pound).

    £1 (British) was equivalent to $_____ (U.S.).

3. From Problem 2, you should recognize the conversion rate based on £1 as the expression $\frac{1}{.5456}$. What is the mathematical term that describes the relationship between the conversion rates .5456 and $\frac{1}{.5456}$?

2.6 Exercises

FOR EXTRA HELP

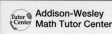 Addison-Wesley Math Tutor Center

Math**XL** MathXL

Digital Video Tutor CD 3 Videotape 3

Student's Solutions Manual

 MyMathLab

 Interactmath.com

1. Match each ratio in Column I with the ratio equivalent to it in Column II.

I	II
(a) 75 to 100	**A.** 80 to 100
(b) 5 to 4	**B.** 50 to 100
(c) $\dfrac{1}{2}$	**C.** 3 to 4
(d) 4 to 5	**D.** 15 to 12

2. Which one of the following represents a ratio of 3 days to 2 weeks?

A. $\dfrac{3}{2}$ **B.** $\dfrac{3}{7}$

C. $\dfrac{1.5}{1}$ **D.** $\dfrac{3}{14}$

Write a ratio for each word phrase. In Exercises 7–10, first write the amounts with the same units. Write fractions in lowest terms. See Example 1.

3. 60 ft to 70 ft

4. 40 mi to 30 mi

5. 72 dollars to 220 dollars

6. 120 people to 90 people

7. 30 in. to 8 ft

8. 20 yd to 8 ft

9. 16 min to 1 hr

10. 24 min to 2 hr

Find the best buy (based on price per unit) for each item. Give the unit price to the nearest thousandth for that size. See Example 2. (Source: Cub Foods.)

11. GRANULATED SUGAR

Size	Price
4-lb	$1.78
10-lb	$4.39

12. GROUND COFFEE

Size	Price
13-oz	$2.58
39-oz	$4.44

13. SALAD DRESSING

Size	Price
16-oz	$2.44
32-oz	$2.98
48-oz	$4.95

14. BLACK PEPPER

Size	Price
2-oz	$1.79
4-oz	$2.59
8-oz	$5.59

15. VEGETABLE OIL

Size	Price
16-oz	$1.54
24-oz	$2.08
64-oz	$3.63
128-oz	$5.65

16. MOUTHWASH

Size	Price
8.5-oz	$.99
16.9-oz	$1.87
33.8-oz	$2.49
50.7-oz	$2.99

17. TOMATO KETCHUP

Size	Price
14-oz	$1.39
24-oz	$1.55
36-oz	$1.78
64-oz	$3.99

18. GRAPE JELLY

Size	Price
12-oz	$1.05
18-oz	$1.73
32-oz	$1.84
48-oz	$2.88

19. Explain how percent and ratio are related.

20. Explain the distinction between *ratio* and *proportion*.

Solve each equation. See Examples 3 and 4.

21. $\dfrac{k}{4} = \dfrac{175}{20}$

22. $\dfrac{x}{6} = \dfrac{18}{4}$

23. $\dfrac{49}{56} = \dfrac{z}{8}$

24. $\dfrac{20}{100} = \dfrac{z}{80}$

25. $\dfrac{z}{4} = \dfrac{z+1}{6}$

26. $\dfrac{m}{5} = \dfrac{m-2}{2}$

27. $\dfrac{3y-2}{5} = \dfrac{6y-5}{11}$

28. $\dfrac{2r+8}{4} = \dfrac{3r-9}{3}$

29. $\dfrac{5k+1}{6} = \dfrac{3k-2}{3}$

30. $\dfrac{x+4}{6} = \dfrac{x+10}{8}$

31. $\dfrac{2p+7}{3} = \dfrac{p-1}{4}$

32. $\dfrac{3m-2}{5} = \dfrac{4-m}{3}$

Solve each problem. See Example 5.

33. If 6 gal of premium unleaded gasoline cost $11.34, how much would it cost to completely fill a 15-gal tank?

34. If sales tax on a $16.00 compact disc is $1.32, how much would the sales tax be on a $120.00 compact disc player?

35. The distance between Kansas City, Missouri, and Denver is 600 mi. On a certain wall map, this is represented by a length of 2.4 ft. On the map, how many feet would there be between Memphis and Philadelphia, two cities that are actually 1000 mi apart?

36. The distance between Singapore and Tokyo is 3300 mi. On a certain wall map, this distance is represented by 11 in. The actual distance between Mexico City and Cairo is 7700 mi. How far apart are they on the same map?

37. As of December 2002, there were 19 vehicles for every 10 U.S. households. How many vehicles were there for the 107 million U.S. households? (*Source:* U.S. Transportation Department.)

38. For the first time, more vehicles are parked in the average American driveway than there are licensed drivers in the house. If there are 18 drivers for every 10 U.S. households, how many drivers are there in the 107 million U.S. households? (*Source:* U.S. Transportation Department.)

39. A chain saw requires a mixture of 2-cycle engine oil and gasoline. According to the directions on a bottle of Oregon 2-cycle Engine Oil, for a 50 to 1 ratio requirement, approximately 2.5 fluid oz of oil are required for 1 gal of gasoline. For 2.75 gal, how many fluid ounces of oil are required?

40. The directions on the bottle mentioned in Exercise 39 indicate that if the ratio requirement is 24 to 1, approximately 5.5 oz of oil are required for 1 gal of gasoline. If gasoline is to be mixed with 22 oz of oil, how much gasoline is to be used?

41. On February 4, 2004, the exchange rate between British pounds and U.S. dollars was 1 pound to $1.8329. Margaret went to London and exchanged her U.S. currency for British pounds, and received 400 pounds. How much in U.S. dollars did Margaret exchange? (*Source:* Bloomberg L.P.)

42. If 3 U.S. dollars can be exchanged for 3.75 Swiss francs, how many Swiss francs can be obtained for $49.50? Round to the nearest hundredth. (*Source:* Bloomberg L.P.)

Answer each question about percent. See Example 6.

43. What is 48.6% of 19?

44. What is 26% of 480?

45. What percent of 48 is 96?

46. What percent of 30 is 36?

47. 12% of what number is 3600?

48. 25% of what number is 150?

49. 78.84 is what percent of 292?

50. .392 is what percent of 28?

Use mental techniques to answer the questions in Exercises 51 and 52.

51. The 2000 U.S. Census showed that the population of Alabama was 4,447,000, with 26.0% represented by African-Americans. What is the best estimate of the African-American population in Alabama? (*Source:* U.S. Bureau of the Census.)

    A. 500,000   **B.** 750,000

    C. 1,000,000   **D.** 1,500,000

52. The 2000 U.S. Census showed that the population of New Mexico was 1,819,000, with 42.1% being Hispanic. What is the best estimate of the Hispanic population of New Mexico? (*Source:* U.S. Bureau of the Census.)

    A. 720,000   **B.** 72,000

    C. 650,000   **D.** 36,000

Work each problem. Round all money amounts to the nearest dollar and percents to the nearest tenth. See Examples 6 and 7.

53. In 2002, the U.S. civilian labor force consisted of 144,863,000 persons. Of this total, 8,378,000 were unemployed. What was the percent of unemployment? (*Source:* U.S. Bureau of Labor Statistics.)

54. In 2002, the U.S. labor force (excluding agricultural employees, self-employed persons, and the unemployed) consisted of 122,007,000 persons. Of this total, 16,107,000 were union members. What percent of this labor force belonged to unions? (*Source:* U.S. Bureau of Labor Statistics.)

55. As of June 2003, there were 844,000 eateries in the United States. Of these, 177,000 served fast food. What percent of the eateries were *not* fast food establishments? (*Source:* National Restaurant Association.)

56. During 1999 and 2000, the total public and private school enrollment in the United States was 52,885,000. Of this total, 11.4% of the students were enrolled in private schools. How many students were enrolled in public schools? (*Source:* National Center for Education Statistics.)

57. A family of four with a monthly income of $3800 plans to spend 8% of this amount on entertainment. How much will be spent on entertainment?

58. Quinhon Dac Ho earns $3200 per month. He wants to save 12% of this amount. How much will he save?

59. The 1916 dime minted in Denver is quite rare. The 1979 edition of *A Guide Book of United States Coins* listed its value in Extremely Fine condition as $625. The 2003 value had increased to $2400. What was the percent increase in the value of this coin?

60. Here is a common business problem. If the sales tax rate is 6.5% and I have collected $3400 in sales tax, how much were my sales?

The Consumer Price Index, issued by the U.S. Bureau of Labor Statistics, provides a means of determining the purchasing power of the U.S. dollar from one year to the next. Using the period from 1982 to 1984 as a measure of 100.0, the Consumer Price Index for selected years from 1991 to 2003 is shown here. To use the Consumer Price Index to predict a price in a particular year, we can set up a proportion and compare it with a known price in another year, as follows:

$$\frac{\text{price in year } A}{\text{index in year } A} = \frac{\text{price in year } B}{\text{index in year } B}.$$

Year	Consumer Price Index
1991	136.2
1993	144.5
1995	152.4
1997	160.5
1999	166.6
2001	177.1
2003	183.9

Source: U.S. Bureau of Labor Statistics.

Use the Consumer Price Index figures in the table to find the amount that would be charged for the use of the same amount of electricity that cost $225 in 1991. Give your answer to the nearest dollar.

61. in 1995   **62.** in 1999   **63.** in 2001   **64.** in 2003

RELATING CONCEPTS (EXERCISES 65–68) For Individual or Group Work

*In **Section 2.3** we solved equations with fractions by first multiplying each side of the equation by the common denominator. A proportion with a variable is this kind of equation. **Work Exercises 65–68 in order.** The steps justify the method of solving a proportion by cross products.*

65. What is the LCD of the fractions in the equation $\dfrac{x}{6} = \dfrac{2}{5}$?

66. Solve the equation in Exercise 65 as follows.

  (a) Multiply each side by the LCD. What equation do you get?

  (b) Solve the equation from part (a) by dividing each side by the coefficient of x.

67. Solve the equation in Exercise 65 using cross products.

68. Compare your solutions from Exercises 66 and 67. What do you notice?

Summary Exercises on Solving Applied Problems

*The following problems are of the various types discussed in this chapter. Solve each problem. The problem-solving steps from **Section 2.4** are repeated here.*

Solving an Applied Problem

Step 1   **Read** the problem, several times if necessary, until you *understand* what is given and what is to be found.

Step 2   **Assign a variable** to represent the unknown value, using diagrams or tables as needed. Write down what the variable represents. Express any other unknown values in terms of the variable.

Step 3   **Write an equation** using the variable expression(s).

Step 4   **Solve** the equation.

Step 5   **State the answer.** Does it seem reasonable?

Step 6   **Check** the answer in the words of the *original* problem.

1. Nevaraz and Smith were opposing candidates in the school board election. Nevaraz received 30 more votes than Smith, with 516 votes cast. How many votes did Smith receive?

2. On an algebra test, the highest grade was 42 points more than the lowest grade. The sum of the two grades was 138. Find the lowest grade.

3. A certain lawn mower uses 3 tanks of gas to cut 10 acres of lawn. How many tanks of gas would be needed for 30 acres?

4. If 2 lb of fertilizer will cover 50 ft^2 of garden, how many pounds would be needed for 225 ft^2?

5. The perimeter of a certain square is seven times the length of a side, decreased by 12. Find the length of a side.

6. The perimeter of a certain rectangle is 16 times the width. The length is 12 cm more than the width. Find the width of the rectangle.

7. Find the measure of an angle whose measure is 70° more than its complement.

8. Find the measure of an angle whose measure is 20° more than its supplement.

9. If 2 is added to five times a number, the result is equal to 5 more than four times the number. Find the number.

10. If four times a number is added to 8, the result is three times the number added to 5. Find the number.

11. The smallest of three consecutive integers is added to twice the largest, producing a result 15 less than four times the middle integer. Find the smallest integer.

12. If the middle of three consecutive even integers is added to 100, the result is 42 more than the sum of the largest integer and twice the smallest. Find the smallest integer.

13. A store has 39 qt of milk, some in pint cartons and some in quart cartons. There are six times as many quart cartons as pint cartons. How many quart cartons are there? (*Hint:* 1 qt = 2 pt.)

14. A rectangular table is three times as long as it is wide. If it were 3 ft shorter and 3 ft wider, it would be square (with all sides equal). How long and how wide is it?

15. Find the measures of the marked angles.

$(9x - 4)°$

$(6x + 32)°$

16. Find the measures of the marked angles.

$(10x + 50)°$ $(4x + 4)^c$

17. Grant Wood painted his most famous work, *American Gothic*, in 1930 on composition board with perimeter 108.44 in. If the width of the painting is 29.88 in., find the length. (*Source: The Gazette*, March 12, 2004.)

18. Refer to Exercise 17. What is the area of *American Gothic*? Round your answer to the nearest hundredth.

19. If the radius of a certain circle is tripled, and then 8.2 cm are added, the result is the circumference of the circle. Find the radius of the circle. (Use 3.14 as the approximation for π.) Round your answer to the nearest tenth.

C

r

20. A fully inflated professional basketball has a circumference of 78 cm. What is the radius of a circular cross section through the center of the ball? (Use 3.14 as the approximation for π.) Round your answer to the nearest hundredth.

78 cm

21. Mr. Silvester is 5 yr older than his wife. Five years ago his age was $\frac{4}{3}$ her age. What are their ages now?

22. Chris is 10 yr older than Josh. Next year, Chris will be twice as old as Josh. What are their ages now?

23. An MP-3 player that normally sells for $180 is on sale for $150. What is the percent discount on the player?

24. A grocer marks up cereal boxes by 20%. If a box of Raisin Bran costs the grocer $2.49, what is the grocer's selling price to the nearest cent?

25. Athletes in vigorous training programs can eat 50 calories per day for every 2.2 lb of body weight. To the nearest hundred, how many calories can a 175 lb athlete consume per day? (*Source: The Gazette*, March 23, 2002.)

26. The distance between two cities on a road map is 11 in. The cities are actually 308 mi apart. The distance between two other cities on the map is 15 in. What is the actual distance between those cities?

27. The fountain sculpture *Spoonbridge and Cherry* weighs about 7000 lb. The spoon weighs 200 lb less than five times the weight of the cherry. How much does each part of the sculpture weigh? (*Source:* Minneapolis Sculpture Garden brochure.)

28. In the 2003 Masters Golf Tournament in Augusta, Georgia, Tiger Woods finished with a score of 9 more than the winner, Mike Weir. The sum of their scores was 571. Find their scores. (*Source: World Almanac and Book of Facts*, 2004.)

29. Two slices of bacon contain 85 calories. How many calories are there in twelve slices of bacon?

30. Three ounces of liver contain 22 g of protein. How many ounces of liver provide 121 g of protein?

31. The average cost of a traditional Thanksgiving dinner for 10 people, featuring turkey, stuffing, cranberries, pumpkin pie, and trimmings, was $34.56 in 2002. This price increased 5.0% in 2003. What was the price of this traditional Thanksgiving dinner in 2003? Round your answer to the nearest cent. (*Source:* American Farm Bureau.)

32. Refer to Exercise 31. The cost of a traditional Thanksgiving dinner in 1987, the year this information was first collected, was $26.24. What percent increase is the 2003 cost over the 1987 cost? Round your answer to the nearest tenth. (*Source:* American Farm Bureau.)

33. According to *The Guinness Book of World Records*, the longest recorded voyage in a paddleboat is 2226 mi in 103 days; the boat was propelled down the Mississippi River by the foot power of two boaters. Assuming a constant rate, how far would they have gone in 120 days? Round your answer to the nearest mile.

34. In the 2000 Summer Olympics held in Sydney, Australia, Russian athletes earned 88 medals. Four of every 11 medals were gold. How many gold medals did Russia earn? (*Source: Times Picayune,* October 2, 2000.)

In Exercises 35 and 36, find the best buy based on unit pricing. Give the unit price to the nearest thousandth for that size. (Source: Cub Foods.)

35. SPAGHETTI SAUCE

Size	Price
$15\frac{1}{2}$-oz	$1.19
32-oz	$1.69
48-oz	$2.69

36. DISH SOAP

Size	Price
12.6-oz	$1.39
25-oz	$2.44
50-oz	$4.68

2.7 Solving Linear Inequalities

Inequalities are statements with algebraic expressions related by

$<$	"is less than,"	$\leq$	"is less than or equal to,"
$>$	"is greater than,"	$\geq$	"is greater than or equal to."

We solve an inequality by finding all real number solutions for it. For example, the solutions of $x \leq 2$ include all *real numbers* that are less than or equal to 2, not just the *integers* less than or equal to 2.

OBJECTIVE 1 Graph the solutions of inequalities on a number line.
Graphing is a good way to show the solutions of an inequality. To graph all real numbers satisfying $x \leq 2$, we place a closed circle at 2 on a number line and draw an arrow extending from the closed circle to the left (to represent the fact that all numbers less than 2 are also part of the graph). The graph is shown in Figure 12.

Figure 12

EXAMPLE 1 Graphing the Solutions of an Inequality

Graph $x > -5$.

The statement $x > -5$ says that x can take any value greater than -5, but x cannot equal -5 itself. We show this on a graph by placing an open circle at -5 and drawing an arrow to the right, as in Figure 13. The open circle at -5 shows that -5 is not part of the graph.

Figure 13

EXAMPLE 2 Graphing the Solutions of an Inequality

Graph $3 > x$.

The statement $3 > x$ means the same as $x < 3$. The graph of $x < 3$ is shown in Figure 14.

Figure 14

NOTE
To graph an inequality like the one in Example 2, first rewrite it with the variable on the left. Fewer errors occur this way.

> **Work Problem 1 at the Side.** ▶▶▶

OBJECTIVES

1 Graph the solutions of inequalities on a number line.

2 Use the addition property of inequality.

3 Use the multiplication property of inequality.

4 Solve inequalities using both properties of inequality.

5 Use inequalities to solve applied problems.

---

1 Graph each inequality.

(a) $x \leq 3$

_____

(b) $x > -4$

_____

(c) $-4 \geq x$

_____

(d) $0 < x$

_____

ANSWERS

1. (a)

(b)

(c)

(d)

2 Graph each inequality.

(a) $-7 < x < -2$

⎯⎯⎯⎯⎯⎯⎯⎯→

(b) $-6 < x \leq -4$

⎯⎯⎯⎯⎯⎯⎯⎯→

EXAMPLE 3 Graphing the Solutions of an Inequality

Graph $-3 \leq x < 2$.

The statement $-3 \leq x < 2$ is read "-3 is less than or equal to x *and* x is less than 2." We graph the solutions of this inequality by placing a closed circle at -3 (because -3 is part of the graph) and an open circle at 2 (because 2 is not part of the graph), then drawing a line segment between the two circles. Notice that the graph includes all points *between* -3 and 2 and includes -3 as well. See Figure 15.

Figure 15

⟪⟪⟪ **Work Problem 2 at the Side.** ⟫

OBJECTIVE 2 Use the addition property of inequality. Solving inequalities is similar to solving equations.

> **Linear Inequality in One Variable**
>
> A **linear inequality in one variable** can be written in the form
>
> $$Ax + B < C,$$
>
> where A, B, and C are real numbers, with $A \neq 0$.

Examples of linear inequalities in one variable include

$$x + 5 < 2, \quad t - 3 \geq 5, \quad \text{and} \quad 2k + 5 \leq 10. \quad \text{Linear inequalities}$$

(All definitions and rules are also valid for $>$, $\leq$, and $\geq$.)

Consider the inequality $2 < 5$. If 4 is added to each side of this inequality, the result is

$$2 + 4 < 5 + 4$$
$$6 < 9,$$

a true sentence. Now subtract 8 from each side:

$$2 - 8 < 5 - 8$$
$$-6 < -3.$$

The result is again a true sentence. These examples suggest the **addition property of inequality.**

> **Addition Property of Inequality**
>
> For any real numbers A, B, and C, the inequalities
>
> $$A < B \quad \text{and} \quad A + C < B + C$$
>
> have exactly the same solutions.
>
> In words, the same number may be added to each side of an inequality without changing the solutions.

As with the addition property of equality, the same number may be *subtracted* from each side of an inequality.

ANSWERS

2. **(a)** ⊢+⊕+++++⊕+⊢→
      $-8 \ -6 \ -4 \ -2 \quad 0$

   (b) ⊢+⊕⎯+⎯●+⊢→
      $-7 \ -6 \ -5 \ -4 \ -3$

EXAMPLE 4 **Using the Addition Property of Inequality**

Solve $7 + 3k > 2k - 5$.

$$7 + 3k > 2k - 5$$

$$7 + 3k - 2k > 2k - 5 - 2k \qquad \text{Subtract } 2k.$$

$$7 + k > -5 \qquad \text{Combine terms.}$$

$$7 + k - 7 > -5 - 7 \qquad \text{Subtract } 7.$$

$$k > -12 \qquad \text{Combine terms.}$$

A graph of the solutions, $k > -12$, is shown in Figure 16.

Figure 16

Work Problem 3 at the Side.

OBJECTIVE 3 Use the multiplication property of inequality. The addition property of inequality alone cannot be used to solve inequalities such as $4x \geq 28$. These inequalities require the *multiplication property of inequality.* To see how this property works, we look at some examples.

Multiply each side of the inequality $3 < 7$ by the positive number 2.

$$3 < 7$$

$$2(3) < 2(7) \qquad \text{Multiply by 2.}$$

$$6 < 14 \qquad \text{True}$$

Now multiply each side of $3 < 7$ by the negative number -5.

$$3 < 7$$

$$-5(3) < -5(7) \qquad \text{Multiply by } -5.$$

$$-15 < -35 \qquad \text{False}$$

To get a true statement when multiplying each side by -5, we must reverse the direction of the inequality symbol.

$$3 < 7$$

$$-5(3) > -5(7) \qquad \text{Multiply by } -5; \text{ reverse the symbol.}$$

$$-15 > -35 \qquad \text{True}$$

Take the inequality $-6 < 2$ as another example. Multiply each side by the positive number 4.

$$-6 < 2$$

$$4(-6) < 4(2) \qquad \text{Multiply by 4.}$$

$$-24 < 8 \qquad \text{True}$$

Multiplying each side of $-6 < 2$ by -5 *and at the same time reversing the direction of the inequality symbol* gives

$$-6 < 2$$

$$-5(-6) > -5(2) \qquad \text{Multiply by } -5; \text{ reverse the symbol.}$$

$$30 > -10. \qquad \text{True}$$

Work Problem 4 at the Side.

3 Solve each inequality, and graph the solutions.

(a) $-1 + 8r < 7r + 2$

(b) $5m - \dfrac{4}{3} \leq 4m$

4 **(a)** Multiply each side of $-2 < 8$ by 6 and then by -5. Reverse the direction of the inequality symbol if necessary to make a true statement.

(b) Multiply each side of $-4 > -9$ by 2 and then by -8. Reverse the direction of the inequality symbol if necessary to make a true statement.

ANSWERS

3. (a) $r < 3$

(b) $m \leq \dfrac{4}{3}$

4. (a) $-12 < 48$; $10 > -40$
  (b) $-8 > -18$; $32 < 72$

In summary, the **multiplication property of inequality** has two parts.

Multiplication Property of Inequality

For any real numbers A, B, and C ($C \neq 0$),

1. if C is *positive*, then the inequalities

$$A < B \quad \text{and} \quad AC < BC$$

have exactly the same solutions;

2. if C is *negative*, then the inequalities

$$A < B \quad \text{and} \quad AC > BC$$

have exactly the same solutions.

In words, each side of an inequality may be multiplied by the same positive number without changing the solutions. ***If the multiplier is negative, we must reverse the direction of the inequality symbol**.*

We can replace $<$ in the multiplication property of inequality with $>$, $\leq$, or $\geq$. As with the multiplication property of equality, the same nonzero number may be divided into each side.

It is important to remember the differences in the multiplication property for positive and negative numbers.

1. When each side of an inequality is multiplied or divided by a positive number, the direction of the inequality symbol *does not change*. (Adding or subtracting terms on each side also does not change the symbol.)

2. When each side of an inequality is multiplied or divided by a negative number, the direction of the symbol *does change*. ***Reverse the direction of the inequality symbol only when multiplying or dividing each side by a negative number.***

EXAMPLE 5 **Using the Multiplication Property of Inequality**

Solve $3r < -18$.

Using the multiplication property of inequality, we divide each side by 3. Since 3 is a positive number, the direction of the inequality symbol *does not* change. ***It does not matter that the number on the right side of the inequality is negative.***

$$3r < -18$$

$$\frac{3r}{3} < \frac{-18}{3} \qquad \text{Divide by 3.}$$

$$r < -6$$

The graph of the solutions is shown in Figure 17.

Figure 17

EXAMPLE 6 Using the Multiplication Property of Inequality

Solve $-4t \geq 8$.

Here each side of the inequality must be divided by -4, a negative number, which *does* require changing the direction of the inequality symbol.

$$-4t \geq 8$$

$$\frac{-4t}{-4} \leq \frac{8}{-4} \qquad \text{Divide by } -4; \text{ reverse the symbol.}$$

$$t \leq -2$$

The solutions are graphed in Figure 18.

Figure 18

> **Work Problem 5 at the Side.** ▶▶▶

OBJECTIVE 4 Solve inequalities using both properties of inequality.
The steps to solve an inequality are summarized below.

Solving Inequalities

Step 1 **Simplify each side separately.** Use the distributive property to clear parentheses and combine terms on each side as needed.

Step 2 **Isolate the variable term on one side.** Use the addition property to get all terms with variables on one side of the inequality and all numbers on the other side.

Step 3 **Isolate the variable.** Use the multiplication property to write the inequality in the form $x < c$ or $x > c$.

EXAMPLE 7 Solving an Inequality

Solve $5(k - 3) - 7k \geq 4(k - 3) + 9$.

Step 1 Clear parentheses; then combine like terms.

$$5(k - 3) - 7k \geq 4(k - 3) + 9$$

$$5k - 15 - 7k \geq 4k - 12 + 9 \qquad \text{Distributive property}$$

$$-2k - 15 \geq 4k - 3 \qquad \text{Combine terms.}$$

Step 2 Use the addition property.

$$-2k - 15 - 4k \geq 4k - 3 - 4k \qquad \text{Subtract } 4k.$$

$$-6k - 15 \geq -3 \qquad \text{Combine terms.}$$

$$-6k - 15 + 15 \geq -3 + 15 \qquad \text{Add } 15.$$

$$-6k \geq 12 \qquad \text{Combine terms.}$$

Step 3 Divide each side by -6, a negative number. Change the direction of the inequality symbol.

$$\frac{-6k}{-6} \leq \frac{12}{-6} \qquad \text{Divide by } -6; \text{ reverse the symbol.}$$

$$k \leq -2$$

Continued on Next Page

---

5 Solve each inequality. Graph the solutions.

(a) $9x < -18$

(b) $-2r > -12$

(c) $-5p \leq 0$

ANSWERS

5. (a) $x < -2$

$$-5\,-4\,-3\,-2\,-1\ \ 0\ \ 1$$

(b) $r < 6$

$$3\ \ 4\ \ 5\ \ 6\ \ 7\ \ 8\ \ 9$$

(c) $p \geq 0$

$$-3\,-2\,-1\ \ 0\ \ 1\ \ 2\ \ 3$$

6 Solve each inequality. Graph the solutions.

(a) $5r - r + 2 < 7r - 5$

_____

(b) $4(x - 1) - 3x > -15 - (2x + 1)$

_____

A graph of the solutions is shown in Figure 19.

Figure 19

>>> **Work Problem 6 at the Side.**

OBJECTIVE 5 **Use inequalities to solve applied problems.** The chart below gives some of the more common phrases that suggest inequality, along with examples and translations.

Phrase	Example	Inequality
Is greater than	A number *is greater than* 4	$x > 4$
Is less than	A number *is less than* -12	$x < -12$
Is at least	A number *is at least* 6	$x \geq 6$
Is at most	A number *is at most* 8	$x \leq 8$

CAUTION
Do not confuse phrases like "5 less than a number" and statements like "5 *is* less than a number." The first of these is expressed as $x - 5$ while the second is expressed as $5 < x$.

The next application is relevant to anyone who has ever asked, "What score can I make on my next test and have a (particular grade) in this course?" It uses the idea of finding the average of a number of grades. In general, to find the average of n numbers, add the numbers and divide by n.

7 Solve the problem.

Maggie has scores of 98, 86, and 88 on her first three tests in algebra. If she wants an average of at least 90 after her fourth test, what score must she make on her fourth test?

EXAMPLE 8 **Finding an Average Test Score**

Brent has test grades of 86, 88, and 78 on his first three tests in geometry. If he wants an average of at least 80 after his fourth test, what score must he make on his fourth test?

Let x represent Brent's score on his fourth test. To find the average of the four scores, add them and divide by 4.

$$\overset{\text{Average}}{\overset{\downarrow}{\frac{86 + 88 + 78 + x}{4}}} \overset{\substack{\text{is at} \\ \text{least 80.} \\ \downarrow \ \downarrow}}{\geq 80}$$

$$4\left(\frac{252 + x}{4}\right) \geq 4(80) \qquad \text{Add in the numerator; multiply by 4.}$$

$$252 + x \geq 320$$

$$252 - 252 + x \geq 320 - 252 \qquad \text{Subtract 252.}$$

$$x \geq 68 \qquad \text{Combine terms.}$$

He must score 68 or more on the fourth test to have an average of *at least* 80.

>>> **Work Problem 7 at the Side.**

2.7 Exercises

Write an inequality using the variable x that corresponds to each graph of solutions on a number line.

1. ![number line from -4 to 3]

2. ![number line from -4 to 4]

3. ![number line from -2 to 5]

4. ![number line from -2 to 5]

5. ![number line from -1 to 2]

6. ![number line from -1 to 2]

7. ![number line from -1 to 2]

8. ![number line from -1 to 2]

9. How can you determine whether to use an open circle or a closed circle at an endpoint when graphing an inequality on a number line?

10. How does the graph of $t \geq -7$ differ from the graph of $t > -7$?

Graph each inequality on the given number line. See Examples 1–3.

11. $k \leq 4$![number line]

12. $r \leq -11$![number line]

13. $x > -3$![number line]

14. $x > 3$![number line]

15. $8 \leq x \leq 10$![number line]

16. $3 \leq x \leq 5$![number line]

17. $0 < x \leq 10$![number line]

18. $-3 \leq x < 5$![number line]

19. Why is it *wrong* to write $3 < x < -2$ to indicate that x is between -2 and 3?

20. Your friend tells you that when solving the inequality $6x < -42$, he reversed the direction of the inequality because of the presence of -42. How would you respond?

Solve each inequality, and graph the solutions. See Example 4.

21. $z - 8 \geq -7$![number line]

22. $p - 3 \geq -11$![number line]

23. $2k + 3 \geq k + 8$![number line]

24. $3x + 7 \geq 2x + 11$![number line]

25. $3n + 5 < 2n - 6$![number line]

26. $5x - 2 < 4x - 5$![number line]

27. Under what conditions must the inequality symbol be reversed when using the multiplication property of inequality?

28. Explain the steps you would use to solve the inequality $-5x > 20$.

Solve each inequality, and graph the solutions. See Examples 5 and 6.

29. $3x < 18$![number line]

30. $5x < 35$![number line]

31. $2x \geq -20$![number line]

32. $6m \geq -24$![number line]

33. $-8t > 24$![number line]

34. $-7x > 49$![number line]

35. $-x \geq 0$![number line]

36. $-k < 0$![number line]

37. $-\dfrac{3}{4}r < -15$![number line]

38. $-\dfrac{7}{8}t < -14$![number line]

39. $-.02x \leq .06$![number line]

40. $-.03v \geq -.12$![number line]

Solve each inequality, and graph the solutions. See Example 7.

41. $5r + 1 \geq 3r - 9$

![number line]

42. $6t + 3 < 3t + 12$

![number line]

43. $6x + 3 + x < 2 + 4x + 4$

44. $-4w + 12 + 9w \geq w + 9 + w$

![number line]

45. $-x + 4 + 7x \leq -2 + 3x + 6$

46. $14x - 6 + 7x > 4 + 10x - 10$

47. $5(x + 3) - 6x \leq 3(2x + 1) - 4x$

48. $2(x - 5) + 3x < 4(x - 6) + 1$

49. $\dfrac{2}{3}(p + 3) > \dfrac{5}{6}(p - 4)$

50. $\dfrac{7}{9}(n - 4) \leq \dfrac{4}{3}(n + 5)$

51. $4x - (6x + 1) \leq 8x + 2(x - 3)$

52. $2x - (4x + 3) < 6x + 3(x + 4)$

53. $5(2k + 3) - 2(k - 8) > 3(2k + 4) + k - 2$

54. $2(3z - 5) + 4(z + 6) \geq 2(3z + 2) + 3z - 15$

Solve each application of inequalities. See Example 8.

55. John Douglas has grades of 84 and 98 on his first two history tests. What must he score on his third test so that his average is at least 90?

56. Elizabeth Gainey has scores of 74 and 82 on her first two algebra tests. What must she score on her third test so that her average is at least 80?

57. When 2 is added to the difference between six times a number and 5, the result is greater than 13 added to 5 times the number. Find all such numbers.

58. When 8 is subtracted from the sum of three times a number and 6, the result is less than 4 more than the number. Find all such numbers.

59. The formula for converting Celsius temperature to Fahrenheit is

$$F = \frac{9}{5}C + 32.$$

The Fahrenheit temperature of Providence, Rhode Island, has never exceeded 104°. How would you describe this using Celsius temperature?

60. The formula for converting Fahrenheit temperature to Celsius is

$$C = \frac{5}{9}(F - 32).$$

If the Celsius temperature on a certain day in San Diego, California, is never more than 25°, how would you describe the corresponding Fahrenheit temperature?

61. For what values of x would the rectangle have perimeter of at least 400?

$4x + 3$

$x + 37$

62. For what values of x would the triangle have perimeter of at least 72?

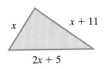

x $x + 11$

$2x + 5$

63. A long-distance phone call costs $2.00 for the first three minutes plus $.30 per minute for each minute or fractional part of a minute after the first three minutes. If x represents the number of minutes of the length of the call after the first three minutes, then $2 + .30x$ represents the cost of the call. If Jorge has $5.60 to spend on a call, what is the maximum total time he can use the phone?

64. At the Speedy Gas 'n Go, a car wash costs $3.00, and gasoline is selling for $1.50 per gal. Terri Hoelker has $17.25 to spend, and her car is so dirty that she must have it washed. What is the maximum number of gallons of gasoline that she can purchase?

RELATING CONCEPTS (EXERCISES 65–69) For Individual or Group Work

Work Exercises 65–69 in order, to see the connection between the solution of an equation and the solutions of the corresponding inequalities. Graph the solutions in Exercises 65–67.

65. $3x + 2 = 14$

66. $3x + 2 < 14$

67. $3x + 2 > 14$

68. Now graph all the solutions together on the following number line.

How would you describe the graph?

69. Based on your results from Exercises 65–68, if you were to graph the solutions of

$$-4x + 3 = -1, \quad -4x + 3 > -1,$$
$$\text{and} \quad -4x + 3 < -1$$

on the same number line, what do you think the graph would be?

Chapter 2
SUMMARY

2.1	**linear equation**	A linear equation in one variable is an equation that can be written in the form $Ax + B = C$, where A, B, and C are real numbers, with $A \neq 0$.
	equivalent equations	Equations that have the same solutions are equivalent equations.
2.3	**identity**	An identity is an equation that is true for all replacements of the variable.
2.4	**complementary angles**	Two angles whose measures have a sum of 90° are complementary angles.
	right angle	A right angle measures 90°.
	supplementary angles	Two angles whose measures have a sum of 180° are supplementary angles.
	straight angle	A straight angle measures 180°.
	consecutive integers	Two integers that differ by 1 are consecutive integers.
2.5	**formula**	A formula is a mathematical expression in which variables are used to describe a relationship.
	area	The area of a plane geometric figure is a measure of the surface covered by the figure.
	perimeter	The perimeter of a plane geometric figure is the distance around the figure, that is, the sum of the length of its sides.
	vertical angles	Vertical angles are angles formed by intersecting lines. They have the same measure.
2.6	**ratio**	A ratio is a comparison of two quantities using a quotient.
	proportion	A proportion is a statement that two ratios are equal.
	cross products	The method of cross products provides a way of determining whether a proportion is true.

$$\frac{a}{b} = \frac{c}{d} \qquad ad \text{ and } bc \text{ are cross products.}$$

	terms	In the proportion $\frac{a}{b} = \frac{c}{d}$, a, b, c, and d are the terms. The a and d terms are called the **extremes,** and the b and c terms are called the **means.**
2.7	**inequality**	Inequalities are statements with algebraic expressions related by $<$, $\leq$, $>$, or $\geq$.
	linear inequality	A linear inequality in one variable can be written in the form $Ax + B < C$, $Ax + B \leq C$, $Ax + B > C$, or $Ax + B \geq C$, where A, B, and C are real numbers, with $A \neq 0$.

NEW SYMBOLS

1°   one degree a to b, $a:b$, or $\dfrac{a}{b}$ the ratio of a to b

TEST YOUR WORD POWER

See how well you have learned the vocabulary in this chapter. Answers, with examples, follow the Quick Review.

1. A **solution** of an equation is a number that
   A. makes an expression undefined
   B. makes the equation false
   C. makes the equation true
   D. makes an expression equal to 0.

2. **Complementary angles** are angles
   A. formed by two parallel lines
   B. whose sum is 90°
   C. whose sum is 180°
   D. formed by perpendicular lines.

3. **Supplementary angles** are angles
   A. formed by two parallel lines
   B. whose sum is 90°
   C. whose sum is 180°
   D. formed by perpendicular lines.

4. A **ratio**
   A. compares two quantities using a quotient
   B. says that two quotients are equal
   C. is a product of two quantities
   D. is a difference between two quantities.

5. A **proportion**
   A. compares two quantities using a quotient
   B. says that two ratios are equal
   C. is a product of two quantities
   D. is a difference between two quantities.

6. An **inequality** is
   A. a statement that two algebraic expressions are equal
   B. a point on a number line
   C. an equation with no solutions
   D. a statement with algebraic expressions related by $<$, $\leq$, $>$, or $\geq$.

QUICK REVIEW

Concepts	Examples
2.1 *The Addition Property of Equality* The same number may be added to (or subtracted from) each side of an equation without changing the solution.	Solve. $x - 6 = 12$ $x - 6 + 6 = 12 + 6$ Add 6. $x = 18$ Combine terms.
2.2 *The Multiplication Property of Equality* Each side of an equation may be multiplied (or divided) by the same nonzero number without changing the solution.	Solve. $\dfrac{3}{4}x = -9$ $\dfrac{4}{3} \cdot \dfrac{3}{4}x = \dfrac{4}{3}(-9)$ Multiply by $\frac{4}{3}$. $x = -12$
2.3 *More on Solving Linear Equations* *Step 1* Simplify each side separately. *Step 2* Isolate the variable term on one side. *Step 3* Isolate the variable. *Step 4* Check.	Solve. $2x + 2(x + 1) = 14 + x$ $2x + 2x + 2 = 14 + x$ Distributive property $4x + 2 = 14 + x$ Combine terms. $4x + 2 - x - 2 = 14 + x - x - 2$ Subtract x; subtract 2. $3x = 12$ Combine terms. $\dfrac{3x}{3} = \dfrac{12}{3}$ Divide by 3. $x = 4$ *Check:* $2(4) + 2(4 + 1) = 14 + 4$? Let $x = 4$. $18 = 18$ True The solution is 4.

Concepts	**Examples**
2.4 *An Introduction to Applications of Linear Equations*	One number is 5 more than another. Their sum is 21. What are the numbers?
Step 1 Read.	We are looking for two numbers.
Step 2 Assign a variable.	Let x represent the smaller number. Then $x + 5$ represents the larger number.
Step 3 Write an equation.	
Step 4 Solve the equation.	

$$x + (x + 5) = 21$$

$$2x + 5 = 21 \qquad \text{Combine terms.}$$

$$2x + 5 - 5 = 21 - 5 \qquad \text{Subtract 5.}$$

$$2x = 16 \qquad \text{Combine terms.}$$

$$\frac{2x}{2} = \frac{16}{2} \qquad \text{Divide by 2.}$$

$$x = 8$$

Step 5 State the answer.
Step 6 Check.

The numbers are 8 and 13.
13 is 5 more than 8, and $8 + 13 = 21$. It checks.

2.5 *Formulas and Applications from Geometry*

To find the value of one of the variables in a formula, given values for the others, substitute the known values into the formula.

Find L if $A = LW$, given that $A = 24$ and $W = 3$.

$$24 = L \cdot 3 \qquad A = 24,\ W = 3$$

$$\frac{24}{3} = \frac{L \cdot 3}{3} \qquad \text{Divide by 3.}$$

$$8 = L$$

To solve a formula for one of the variables, isolate that variable by treating the other variables as numbers and using the steps for solving equations.

Solve $P = 2L + 2W$ for W.

$$P - 2L = 2L + 2W - 2L \qquad \text{Subtract } 2L.$$

$$P - 2L = 2W \qquad \text{Combine terms.}$$

$$\frac{P - 2L}{2} = \frac{2W}{2} \qquad \text{Divide by 2.}$$

$$\frac{P - 2L}{2} = W \quad \text{or} \quad W = \frac{P - 2L}{2}$$

2.6 *Ratio, Proportion, and Percent*

To write a ratio, express quantities in the same units.

4 ft to 8 in. = 48 in. to 8 in. = $\dfrac{48}{8} = \dfrac{6}{1}$

To solve a proportion, use the method of cross products.

Solve $\dfrac{x}{12} = \dfrac{35}{60}$.

$$60x = 12 \cdot 35 \qquad \text{Cross products}$$

$$60x = 420 \qquad \text{Multiply.}$$

$$\frac{60x}{60} = \frac{420}{60} \qquad \text{Divide by 60.}$$

$$x = 7$$

To solve a percent problem, use the proportion

$$\frac{\text{amount}}{\text{base}} = \frac{\text{percent}}{100}.$$

Concepts

2.7 Solving Linear Inequalities
Step 1 Simplify each side separately.

Step 2 Isolate the variable term on one side.

Step 3 Isolate the variable.

(Be sure to reverse the direction of the inequality symbol when multiplying or dividing by a negative number.)

Examples

Solve and graph the solutions.

$$3(1 - x) + 5 - 2x > 9 - 6$$

$3 - 3x + 5 - 2x > 9 - 6$	Distributive property
$8 - 5x > 3$	Combine terms.
$8 - 5x - 8 > 3 - 8$	Subtract 8.
$-5x > -5$	Combine terms.
$\dfrac{-5x}{-5} < \dfrac{-5}{-5}$	Divide by -5; change $>$ to $<$.
$x < 1$	

ANSWERS TO TEST YOUR WORD POWER

1. C; *Example:* 8 is the solution of $2x + 5 = 21$.
2. B; *Example:* Angles with measures 35° and 55° are complementary angles.
3. C; *Example:* Angles with measures 112° and 68° are supplementary angles.
4. A; *Example:* $\dfrac{7 \text{ in.}}{12 \text{ in.}} = \dfrac{7}{12}$
5. B; *Example:* $\dfrac{2}{3} = \dfrac{8}{12}$
6. D; *Examples:* $x < 5, 7 + 2y \geq 11$

Chapter 2

REVIEW EXERCISES

[2.1–2.3] *Solve each equation. Check the solution.*

1. $x - 7 = 2$

2. $4r - 6 = 10$

3. $5x + 8 = 4x + 2$

4. $8t = 7t + \dfrac{3}{2}$

5. $(4r - 8) - (3r + 12) = 0$

6. $7(2x + 1) = 6(2x - 9)$

7. $-\dfrac{6}{5}y = -18$

8. $\dfrac{1}{2}r - \dfrac{1}{6}r + 3 = 2 + \dfrac{1}{6}r + 1$

9. $3x - (-2x + 6) = 4(x - 4) + x$

10. $.10(x + 80) + .20x = 8 + .30x$

[2.4] *Solve each problem.*

11. If 7 is added to five times a number, the result is equal to three times the number. Find the number.

12. If 4 is subtracted from twice a number, the result is 36. Find the number.

13. The land area of Hawaii is 5213 mi² greater than that of Rhode Island. Together, the areas total 7637 mi². What is the area of each state?

14. The height of Seven Falls in Colorado is $\frac{5}{2}$ the height (in feet) of Twin Falls in Idaho. The sum of the heights is 420 ft. Find the height of each.

15. The supplement of an angle measures 10 times the measure of its complement. What is the measure of the angle (in degrees)?

16. Find two consecutive odd integers such that when the smaller is added to twice the larger, the result is 24 more than the larger integer.

[2.5] *A formula is given in each exercise, along with the values for all but one of the variables. Find the value of the variable that is not given. (For Exercises 19 and 20, use 3.14 as an approximation for π.)*

17. $A = \dfrac{1}{2}bh;\ A = 44,\ b = 8$

18. $A = \dfrac{1}{2}h(b + B);\ b = 3,\ B = 4,\ h = 8$

19. $C = 2\pi r;\ C = 29.83$

20. $V = \dfrac{4}{3}\pi r^3;\ r = 9$

Solve each formula for the specified variable.

21. $A = LW$ for W

22. $A = \dfrac{1}{2}h(b + B)$ for h

Find the measure of each marked angle.

23.

24.

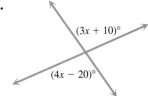

⊞ *Solve each application of geometry.*

25. A cinema screen in Indonesia has length 92.75 ft and width 70.5 ft. What is the perimeter? What is the area? (*Source: The Guinness Book of Records.*)

26. There is a Montezuma cypress in Mexico that is 137 ft tall and has a circumference of about 146.9 ft. What is the diameter of the tree? What is the radius of the tree? Use 3.14 as an approximation for π. Round your answers to the nearest hundredth. (*Source: The Guinness Book of Records, 2003.*)

[2.6] *Write a ratio for each word phrase. Write fractions in lowest terms.*

27. 60 cm to 40 cm

28. 5 days to 2 weeks

29. 90 in. to 10 ft

30. 3 months to 3 yr

Solve each proportion.

31. $\dfrac{p}{21} = \dfrac{5}{30}$

32. $\dfrac{5 + x}{3} = \dfrac{2 - x}{6}$

33. $\dfrac{y}{5} = \dfrac{6y - 5}{11}$

34. Explain how 40% can be expressed as a ratio of two whole numbers.

Solve each problem.

35. If 2 lb of fertilizer will cover 150 ft² of lawn, how many pounds would be needed to cover 500 ft²?

36. If 8 oz of medicine must be mixed with 20 oz of water, how many ounces of medicine must be mixed with 90 oz of water?

37. Biologists tagged 500 fish in Willow Lake on February 18. At a later date they found 7 tagged fish in a sample of 700. Estimate the total number of fish in Willow Lake to the nearest hundred.

38. The distance between two cities on a road map is 32 cm. The two cities are actually 150 km apart. The distance on the map between two other cities is 80 cm. How far apart are these cities?

39. What is 23% of 76?

40. What percent of 12 is 21?

41. 6 is what percent of 18?

42. 36% of what number is 900?

43. Terry paid $18,690, including tax, for her 2003 Chrysler Sebring LX. The sales tax rate was 5%. What was the actual price of the car? (*Source: Author McGinnis' sales receipt.*)

44. Lauren, from the mathematics editorial division of Addison-Wesley, took the mathematics faculty from a community college out to dinner. The bill was $304.75. Lauren added a 15% tip, and paid for the meal with her corporate credit card. What was the total price she paid?

[2.7] *Graph each inequality on the number line provided.*

45. $p \geq -4$

46. $x < 7$

47. $-5 \leq k < 6$

48. $r \geq \dfrac{1}{2}$

Solve each inequality. Graph the solutions.

49. $x + 6 \geq 3$

50. $5t < 4t + 2$

51. $-6x \leq -18$

52. $8(k - 5) - (2 + 7k) \geq 4$

53. $4x - 3x > 10 - 4x + 7x$

54. $3(2w + 5) + 4(8 + 3w) < 5(3w + 2) + 2w$

55. Justin Sudak has grades of 94 and 88 on his first two calculus tests. What possible scores on a third test will give him an average of at least 90?

56. If nine times a number is added to 6, the result is at most 3. Find all such numbers.

MIXED REVIEW EXERCISES

Solve.

57. $\dfrac{y}{7} = \dfrac{y - 5}{2}$

58. $C = \pi d$ for d

59. $-2x > -4$

60. $2k - 5 = 4k + 13$

61. $.05x + .02x = 4.9$

62. $2 - 3(t - 5) = 4 + t$

63. $9x - (7x + 2) = 3x + (2 - x)$

64. $\dfrac{1}{3}s + \dfrac{1}{2}s + 7 = \dfrac{5}{6}s + 5 + 2$

65. On May 13 researchers at Argyle Lake tagged 840 fish. When they returned a few weeks later, their sample of 1000 fish contained 18 that were tagged. Give an approximation of the fish population in Argyle Lake to the nearest hundred.

66. Two-thirds of a number added to the number is 10. What is the number?

67. In the 2002 Winter Olympic Games in Salt Lake City, the United States and Canada earned a total of 51 medals. The United States earned twice as many medals as Canada. How many medals did each country earn? (*Source: The Gazette,* February 2, 2002.)

68. Of the 58 medals earned by the host country, Australia, in the 2000 Summer Olympics, there were 9 more silver than gold medals, and 8 fewer bronze than silver medals. How many of each medal did Australia earn? (*Source: Times Picayune,* October 2, 2000.)

69. The perimeter of a triangle is 96 m. One side is twice as long as another, and the third side is 30 m long. What is the length of the longest side?

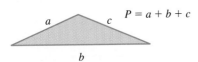

$P = a + b + c$

70. The perimeter of a rectangle is 288 ft. The length is 4 ft longer than the width. Find the width.

$P = 2L + 2W$

71. Find the best buy. Give the unit price to the nearest thousandth for that size. (*Source: Cub Foods.*)

LAUNDRY DETERGENT

Size	Price
87-oz	$7.88
131-oz	$10.98
263-oz	$19.96

72. If nine pairs of jeans cost $121.50, find the cost of five pairs. (Assume all are equally priced.)

73. Latarsha has grades of 82 and 96 on her first two English tests. What must she make on her third test so that her average will be at least 90?

74. Find the measure of each marked angle.

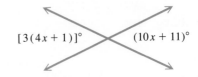

$[3(4x + 1)]°$ $(10x + 11)°$

Chapter **2**

TEST

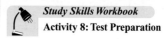

Study Skills Workbook
Activity 8: Test Preparation

Solve each equation, and check the solution.

1. $3x - 7 = 11$

1. _____

2. $5x + 9 = 7x + 21$

2. _____

3. $2 - 3(x - 5) = 3 + (x + 1)$

3. _____

4. $2.3x + 13.7 = 1.3x + 2.9$

4. _____

5. $7 - (m - 4) = -3m + 2(m + 1)$

5. _____

6. $-\dfrac{4}{7}x = -12$

6. _____

7. $.06(x + 20) + .08(x - 10) = 4.6$

7. _____

8. $-8(2x + 4) = -4(4x + 8)$

8. _____

Solve each problem.

9. (a) The San Antonio Spurs beat the New Jersey Nets by 11 points in the final 2003 NBA Championship game held June 15 in San Antonio. The total of the two team scores was 165. What was the final score of the game?

9. (a) _____

   (b) The high scorer for the Nets during the finals was Jason Kidd. He made 10 fewer field goals than Tim Duncan, the high scorer for the Spurs. The two players made a total of 98 field goals. How many field goals did Kidd make?

   (b) _____

   (*Source: World Almanac and Book of Facts*, 2004.)

10. The three largest islands in the Hawaiian island chain are Hawaii (the Big Island), Maui, and Kauai. Together, their areas total 5300 mi². The island of Hawaii is 3293 mi² larger than the island of Maui, and Maui is 177 mi² larger than Kauai. What is the area of each island?

10. _____

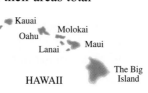

Kauai
Oahu
Molokai
Lanai
Maui
HAWAII
The Big Island

11. Find the measure of an angle if its supplement measures 10° more than three times its complement.

11. _____

12. The formula for the perimeter of a rectangle is $P = 2L + 2W$.

    (a) Solve for W.

    (b) If $P = 116$ and $L = 40$, find the value of W.

12. (a) _____

    (b) _____

Find the measure of each marked angle.

13. _____

13.

14.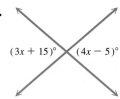

14. _____

Solve each proportion.

15. _____

15. $\dfrac{z}{8} = \dfrac{12}{16}$

16. $\dfrac{x + 5}{3} = \dfrac{x - 3}{4}$

16. _____

17. Find the best buy. Give the unit price to the nearest thousandth for that size.

17. _____

PROCESSED CHEESE SLICES

Size	Price
12-oz	$1.99
16-oz	$2.49
24-oz	$3.49

18. _____

18. The distance between Milwaukee and Boston is 1050 mi. On a certain map, this distance is represented by 42 in. On the same map, Seattle and Cincinnati are 92 in. apart. What is the actual distance between Seattle and Cincinnati?

19. _____

19. The Anaheim Mighty Ducks of the NHL finished the 2002–2003 season with 95 points, up from 69 points in the 2001–2002 season. What was the percent of increase in points? Round your answer to the nearest tenth. (*Source: World Almanac and Book of Facts*, 2004.)

20. (a) _____

    (b) _____

20. Write an inequality involving x that describes the numbers graphed.

    (a)

Solve each inequality, and graph the solutions.

21. $\longleftrightarrow$

21. $-3x > -33$

22. $\longleftrightarrow$

22. $-.04x \le .12$

23. $\longleftrightarrow$

23. $-4x + 2(x - 3) \ge 4x - (3 + 5x) - 7$

24. _____

24. Shania Johnson has grades of 76 and 81 on her first two algebra tests. If she wants an average of at least 80 after her third test, what score must she make on her third test?

25. _____

25. Write a short explanation of the additional (extra) rule that must be remembered when solving an inequality (as opposed to solving an equation).

Cumulative Review Exercises

CHAPTERS R–2

Write each fraction in lowest terms.

1. $\dfrac{15}{40}$

2. $\dfrac{108}{144}$

Perform the indicated operations.

3. $\dfrac{5}{6} + \dfrac{1}{4} + \dfrac{7}{15}$

4. $16\dfrac{7}{8} - 3\dfrac{1}{10}$

5. $\dfrac{9}{8} \cdot \dfrac{16}{3}$

6. $\dfrac{3}{4} \div \dfrac{5}{8}$

7. $4.8 + 12.5 + 16.73$

8. $56.3 - 28.99$

9. $67.8(.45)$

10. $236.46 \div 4.2$

11. In making dresses, Earth Works uses $\frac{5}{8}$ yd of trim per dress. How many yards of trim would be used to make 56 dresses?

12. A cook wants to increase a recipe for Quaker Quick Grits that serves 4 to make enough for 10 people. The recipe calls for 3 cups of water. How much water will be needed to serve 10?

13. Buster weighs $27\frac{1}{4}$ lb and Sofi weighs $39\frac{7}{8}$ lb. How much do the two dogs weigh together?

14. A small business owner bought 3 computer workstations of various sizes for \$329.99, \$379.99, and \$439.99 and 3 ergonomic office chairs for \$249.99 each. What was the final bill (without tax)? (*Source:* Staples "Furniture Values" catalog, January 2004.)

Tell whether each inequality is true *or* false.

15. $\dfrac{8(7) - 5(6 + 2)}{3 \cdot 5 + 1} \geq 1$

16. $\dfrac{4(9 + 3) - 8(4)}{2 + 3 - 3} \geq 2$

Perform the indicated operations.

17. $-11 + 20 + (-2)$

18. $13 + (-19) + 7$

19. $9 - (-4)$

20. $-2(-5)(-4)$

21. $\dfrac{4 \cdot 9}{-3}$

22. $\dfrac{8}{7 - 7}$

23. $(-5 + 8) + (-2 - 7)$

24. $(-7 - 1)(-4) + (-4)$

25. $\dfrac{-3 - (-5)}{1 - (-1)}$

26. $\dfrac{6(-4) - (-2)(12)}{3^2 + 7^2}$

27. $\dfrac{(-3)^2 - (-4)(2^4)}{5 \cdot 2 - (-2)^3}$

28. $\dfrac{-2(5^3) - 6}{4^2 + 2(-5) + (-2)}$

Find the value of each expression when $x = -2$, $y = -4$, and $z = 3$.

29. $xz^3 - 5y^2$

30. $\dfrac{xz - y^3}{-4z}$

Name the property illustrated by each equation.

31. $7(k + m) = 7k + 7m$

32. $3 + (5 + 2) = 3 + (2 + 5)$

33. $7 + (-7) = 0$

34. $3.5(1) = 3.5$

Simplify each expression.

35. $4p - 6 + 3p - 8$

36. $-4(k + 2) + 3(2k - 1)$

Solve each equation, and check the solution.

37. $2r - 6 = 8$

38. $2(p - 1) = 3p + 2$

39. $4 - 5(a + 2) = 3(a + 1) - 1$

40. $2 - 6(z + 1) = 4(z - 2) + 10$ **41.** $-(m - 1) = 3 - 2m$

42. $\dfrac{x - 2}{3} = \dfrac{2x + 1}{5}$

43. $\dfrac{2x + 3}{5} = \dfrac{x - 4}{2}$

44. $\dfrac{2}{3}x + \dfrac{3}{4}x = -17$

Solve each formula for the indicated variable.

45. $P = a + b + c$ for c

46. $P = 4s$ for s

Solve each inequality. Graph the solutions.

47. $-5z \geq 4z - 18$

48. $6(r - 1) + 2(3r - 5) < -4$

Solve each problem.

49. The small business owner in Exercise 14 paid a sales tax of $6\frac{1}{4}\%$ on his purchase. What was the final bill, including tax, to the nearest cent?

50. A car has a price of $5000. For trading in her old car, Shannon d'Hemecourt will get 25% off. Find the price of the car with the trade-in.

51. Jennifer Johnston bought textbooks at the college bookstore for $244.33, including 6% sales tax. What did the books cost?

52. Carter Fenton received a bill from his credit card company for $104.93. The bill included interest at $1\frac{1}{2}\%$ per month for one month and a $5.00 late charge. How much did his purchases amount to?

53. The perimeter of a rectangle is 98 cm. The width is 19 cm. Find the length.

?

☐ 19 cm

54. The area of a triangle is 104 in.^{2}. The base is 13 in. Find the height.

13 in.

Graphs of Linear Equations and Inequalities in Two Variables

3

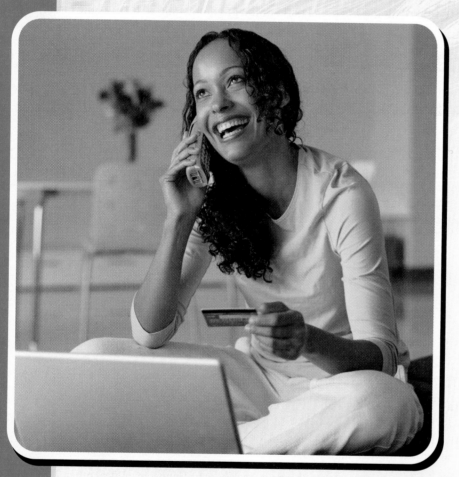

The use and abuse of credit cards is putting college students deeper in debt than ever before. College campuses have become fertile territory as credit card companies pitch their plastic to students at bookstores, student unions, and sporting events. According to federal loan provider Nellie Mae, an estimated 83% of college students have credit cards with an average balance of more than $2300. (*Source:* ISU Extension, *Family Living in Farm Country,* April 2003.)

In Example 6 of Section 3.2 we examine a linear equation that models credit card debt in the United States.

193

3.1 Reading Graphs; Linear Equations in Two Variables

OBJECTIVES

1. Interpret graphs.
2. Write a solution as an ordered pair.
3. Decide whether a given ordered pair is a solution of a given equation.
4. Complete ordered pairs for a given equation.
5. Complete a table of values.
6. Plot ordered pairs.

We live in an age of information. Graphs provide a quick way to organize and communicate much of this information. They can also be used to analyze data, make predictions, or simply entertain us.

OBJECTIVE 1 Interpret graphs. There are many ways to represent the relationship between two quantities. *Circle graphs, bar graphs*, and *line graphs* are often used for this purpose.

In a **circle graph** or **pie chart,** a circle is used to indicate the total of all the categories represented. The circle is divided into *sectors*, or wedges (like pieces of a pie), whose sizes show the relative magnitudes of the categories. The sum of all the fractional parts of the graph must be 1 (for 1 whole circle).

EXAMPLE 1 Interpreting a Circle Graph

The 2003 market share for satellite-TV home subscribers is shown in the circle graph in Figure 1.

SATELLITE-TV HOME SUBSCRIBERS

Echostar 43%

DirecTV 55%

C-Band 2%

Source: Skyreport.com; *USA Today.*

Figure 1

1 Refer to the circle graph in Figure 1.

(a) Which provider had the smallest market share in December 2003?

(b) Estimate the number of home subscribers to DirecTV.

(c) How many actual home subscribers to DirecTV were there?

The number of subscribers reached 22 million in December 2003.

(a) Which provider had the largest share of the home subscriber market in December 2003? What was that share?

In the circle graph, the sector for DirecTV is the largest, so DirecTV had the largest market share, 55%.

(b) Estimate the number of home subscribers to Echostar in December 2003.

A market share of 43% can be rounded to 40%, or .4. We multiply .4 by the total number of subscribers, 22 million. A good estimate for the number of Echostar subscribers would be

$$.4(22) = 8.8 \approx 9 \text{ million.}$$

(c) How many actual home subscribers to Echostar were there?

To find the answer, we multiply the actual percent from the graph for Echostar, 43% or .43, by the number of subscribers, 22 million:

$$.43(22) = 9.46.$$

Thus, 9.46 million homes subscribed to Echostar. This is reasonable given our estimate in part (b).

Work Problem 1 at the Side.

ANSWERS
1. **(a)** C-Band
   (b) 60% of 22 million = 13.2 million
   (c) 12.1 million

A **bar graph** is used to show comparisons. It consists of a series of bars (or simulations of bars) arranged either vertically or horizontally. In a bar graph, values from two categories are paired with each other.

EXAMPLE 2 Interpreting a Bar Graph

The bar graph in Figure 2 illustrates the amount of personal savings, in billions of dollars, accumulated during the years 1997 through 2001.

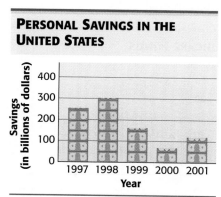

PERSONAL SAVINGS IN THE UNITED STATES

Source: U.S. Bureau of Economic Analysis.

Figure 2

(a) Which year had the greatest amount of savings? Which had the least?

The tallest bar corresponds to 1998, so the largest amount was in 1998. The year 2000, with the shortest bar, had the least.

(b) Which years had amounts greater than $200 billion?

Locate 200 on the vertical scale and follow the line across to the right. Two years, 1997 and 1998, have bars that extend above the line for 200, so they had amounts greater than $200 billion.

(c) Estimate the amounts for 1997 and 1998.

Locate the top of the bar for 1997 and move horizontally across to the vertical scale to see that it lies about halfway between 200 and 300. The amount for 1997 was about $250 billion.

Follow the top of the bar for 1998 across to the vertical scale to see that it is about 300. The amount for 1998 was about $300 billion.

(d) Estimate the difference between the amounts for the years 1997 and 1998. Interpret this result.

Based on the results of part (c), the difference is approximately

$300 billion − $250 billion = $50 billion.

The amount of personal savings increased from 1997 to 1998 by about $50 billion. (However, during the next two years, it decreased each year.)

(e) How did personal savings in 1998 compare to personal savings in 1999?

Comparing the heights of the bars for 1998 and 1999, we see that the bar for 1998 is about twice as tall as the bar for 1999. Therefore, personal savings in 1998 was about twice that for 1999.

Also, if we estimate the amounts of personal savings for 1998 and 1999 as about $300 billion and about $150 billion respectively, we see that personal savings in 1998 was about twice that for 1999.

> **Work Problem 2 at the Side.** ⟩⟩⟩

2 Refer to the bar graph in Figure 2.

(a) Which years had amounts less than $200 billion?

(b) Estimate the amounts of personal savings for 2000 and 2001.

3 Refer to the line graph in Figure 3.

(a) Which year has the greatest amount of Medicare funds?

A **line graph** is used to show changes or trends in data over time. To form a line graph, we connect a series of points representing data with line segments.

EXAMPLE 3 Interpreting a Line Graph

Current projections indicate that funding for Medicare will not cover its costs unless the program changes. The line graph in Figure 3 shows projections for the years 2004 through 2013.

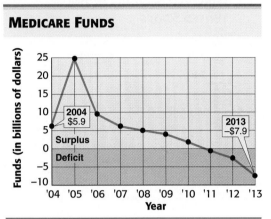

Source: Centers for Medicare and Medicaid Services.

Figure 3

(b) Estimate Medicare funds for 2008. Is there a surplus or a deficit in 2008?

(a) Which is the only period in which Medicare funds are predicted to increase?

Because the graph *rises* from 2004 to 2005 and falls in every other case, funds are predicted to increase between these two years.

(b) What will be the general trend from 2005 to 2013?

Funds will decrease, since the graph *falls* during this period.

(c) In which year will funds first show a deficit?

From 2004 to 2010, the graph is always above 0, but in 2011, it falls below 0 for the first time, indicating a deficit.

(c) About how much will funds decrease from 2006 to 2011?

(d) Based on the figures shown in the graph, what is the difference in Medicare funds from 2004 to 2013?

$$\underbrace{-\$7.9 \text{ billion}}_{\text{2013 amount}} - \underbrace{\$5.9 \text{ billion}}_{\text{2004 amount}} = \underbrace{-\$13.8 \text{ billion}}_{\text{Difference}}$$

The fund amount will have *decreased* $13.8 billion (as indicated by the negative sign in $-\$13.8$).

◀◀◀ Work Problem 3 at the Side.

Many everyday situations, such as those illustrated in Examples 2 and 3, involve two quantities that are related. The equations and applications we discussed in **Chapter 2** had only one variable. In this chapter, we extend those ideas to *linear equations in two variables.*

ANSWERS
3. (a) 2005
    (b) $5 billion; surplus
    (c) $10 billion

Linear Equation in Two Variables

A **linear equation in two variables** is an equation that can be written in the form

$$Ax + By = C,$$

where A, B, and C are real numbers and A and B are not both 0.

Some examples of linear equations in two variables in this form, called *standard form*, are

$$3x + 4y = 9, \quad x - y = 0, \quad \text{and} \quad x + 2y = -8.$$ Linear equations in two variables

> **NOTE**
> Other linear equations in two variables, such as
>
> $$y = 4x + 5 \quad \text{and} \quad 3x = 7 - 2y,$$
>
> are not written in standard form but could be. We will discuss the forms of linear equations in more detail in **Section 3.4.**

OBJECTIVE 2 Write a solution as an ordered pair. Recall from **Section 1.2** that a *solution* of an equation is a number that makes the equation true when it replaces the variable. For example, the linear equation in one variable $x - 2 = 5$ has solution 7, since replacing x with 7 gives a true statement.

A solution of a linear equation in *two* variables requires *two* numbers, one for each variable. For example, a true statement results when we replace x with 2 and y with 13 in the equation $y = 4x + 5$ since

$$13 = 4(2) + 5. \quad \text{Let } x = 2, y = 13.$$

The pair of numbers $x = 2$ and $y = 13$ gives one solution of the equation $y = 4x + 5$. The phrase "$x = 2$ and $y = 13$" is abbreviated

x-value ⟶   ⟵ y-value
$$(2, 13)$$
Ordered pair

with the x-value, 2, and the y-value, 13, given as a pair of numbers written inside parentheses. ***The x-value is always given first.*** A pair of numbers such as $(2, 13)$ is called an **ordered pair.** As the name indicates, the order in which the numbers are written is important. The ordered pairs $(2, 13)$ and $(13, 2)$ are not the same. The second pair indicates that $x = 13$ and $y = 2$. For two ordered pairs to be equal, their x-coordinates must be equal *and* their y-coordinates must be equal.

> **Work Problem 4 at the Side.** ▶▶▶

OBJECTIVE 3 Decide whether a given ordered pair is a solution of a given equation. We substitute the x- and y-values of an ordered pair into a linear equation in two variables to see whether the ordered pair is a solution.

---

4 Write each solution as an ordered pair.

(a) $x = 5$ and $y = 7$

(b) $y = 6$ and $x = -1$

(c) $y = 4$ and $x = -3$

(d) $x = 3$ and $y = -12$

ANSWERS
4. (a) $(5, 7)$ **(b)** $(-1, 6)$ **(c)** $(-3, 4)$
(d) $(3, -12)$

5 Decide whether each ordered pair is a solution of the equation $5x + 2y = 20$.

(a) $(0, 10)$

$$5x + 2y = 20$$
$$5(\quad) + 2(\quad) = 20$$
$$\underline{\qquad} + 20 = 20$$
$$\underline{\qquad} = 20$$

Is $(0, 10)$ a solution?

(b) $(2, -5)$

(c) $(3, 2)$

(d) $(-4, 20)$

6 Complete each ordered pair for the equation $y = 2x - 9$.

(a) $(5, \quad)$

$$y = 2(\quad) - 9$$
$$y = \underline{\qquad} - 9$$
$$y = \underline{\qquad}$$

The ordered pair is _____.

(b) $(2, \quad)$

(c) $(\quad, 7)$

(d) $(\quad, -13)$

EXAMPLE 4 **Deciding Whether Ordered Pairs Are Solutions of an Equation**

Decide whether each ordered pair is a solution of the equation $2x + 3y = 12$.

(a) $(3, 2)$

To see whether $(3, 2)$ is a solution of the given equation $2x + 3y = 12$, substitute 3 for x and 2 for y in the equation.

$$2x + 3y = 12$$
$$2(3) + 3(2) = 12 \quad ? \quad \text{Let } x = 3; \text{ let } y = 2.$$
$$6 + 6 = 12 \quad ?$$
$$12 = 12 \quad\quad \text{True}$$

This result is true, so $(3, 2)$ is a solution of $2x + 3y = 12$.

(b) $(-2, -7)$

$$2x + 3y = 12$$
$$2(-2) + 3(-7) = 12 \quad ? \quad \text{Let } x = -2; \text{ let } y = -7.$$
$$-4 + (-21) = 12 \quad ?$$
$$-25 = 12 \quad\quad \text{False}$$

This result is false, so $(-2, -7)$ is *not* a solution of $2x + 3y = 12$.

> **Work Problem 5 at the Side.**

OBJECTIVE 4 **Complete ordered pairs for a given equation.** Choosing a number for one variable in a linear equation makes it possible to find the value of the other variable.

EXAMPLE 5 **Completing Ordered Pairs**

Complete each ordered pair for the equation $y = 4x + 5$.

(a) $(7, \quad)$

In this ordered pair, $x = 7$. (Remember that x always comes first.) To find the corresponding value of y, replace x with 7 in the equation.

$$y = 4x + 5$$
$$y = 4(7) + 5 \quad \text{Let } x = 7.$$
$$y = 28 + 5$$
$$y = 33$$

The ordered pair is $(7, 33)$.

(b) $(\quad, -3)$

In this ordered pair, $y = -3$. Find the value of x by replacing y with -3 in the equation; then solve for x.

$$y = 4x + 5$$
$$-3 = 4x + 5 \quad \text{Let } y = -3.$$
$$-8 = 4x \quad\quad \text{Subtract 5 from each side.}$$
$$-2 = x \quad\quad \text{Divide each side by 4.}$$

The ordered pair is $(-2, -3)$.

> **Work Problem 6 at the Side.**

OBJECTIVE 5 Complete a table of values. Ordered pairs are often displayed in a **table of values.** The table may be written either vertically or horizontally.

EXAMPLE 6 **Completing Tables of Values**

Complete the table of values for each equation.

(a) $x - 2y = 8$

x	y
2	
10	
	0
	-2

To complete the first two ordered pairs of the table, let $x = 2$ and $x = 10$, respectively.

If $x = 2$,
then $x - 2y = 8$
becomes $2 - 2y = 8$
$-2y = 6$
$y = -3.$

If $x = 10$,
then $x - 2y = 8$
becomes $10 - 2y = 8$
$-2y = -2$
$y = 1.$

Now complete the last two ordered pairs by letting $y = 0$ and $y = -2$, respectively.

If $y = 0$,
then $x - 2y = 8$
becomes $x - 2(0) = 8$
$x - 0 = 8$
$x = 8.$

If $y = -2$,
then $x - 2y = 8$
becomes $x - 2(-2) = 8$
$x + 4 = 8$
$x = 4.$

The completed table of values follows.

x	y
2	-3
10	1
8	0
4	-2

The corresponding ordered pairs are $(2, -3)$, $(10, 1)$, $(8, 0)$, and $(4, -2)$. Notice that each ordered pair is a solution of the given equation.

(b) $x = 5$

x	y
	-2
	6
	3

The given equation is $x = 5$. No matter which value of y is chosen, the value of x is always 5.

x	y
5	-2
5	6
5	3

The corresponding ordered pairs are $(5, -2)$, $(5, 6)$, and $(5, 3)$.

Work Problem 7 at the Side.

7 Complete the table of values for each equation.

(a) $2x - 3y = 12$

x	y
0	
	0
3	
	-3

(b) $y = 4$

x	y
-3	
2	
5	

ANSWERS
7. (a)

x	y
0	-4
6	0
3	-2
$\frac{3}{2}$	-3

(b)

x	y
-3	4
2	4
5	4

8 Name the quadrant in which each point in the figure is located.

NOTE
We can think of $x = 5$ in Example 6(b) as an equation in two variables by rewriting $x = 5$ as $x + 0y = 5$. This form of the equation shows that for any value of y, the value of x is 5. Similarly, $y = 4$ in Problem 7(b) in the margin on the preceding page is the same as $0x + y = 4$.

OBJECTIVE **6** **Plot ordered pairs.** In **Section 2.3,** we saw that linear equations in *one* variable had either one, zero, or an infinite number of real number solutions. These solutions could be graphed on *one* number line. Every linear equation in *two* variables has an infinite number of ordered pairs as solutions. Each choice of a number for one variable leads to a particular real number for the other variable.

To graph these solutions, represented as the ordered pairs (x, y), we need *two* number lines, one for each variable. These two number lines are drawn as shown in Figure 4. The horizontal number line is called the **x-axis,** and the vertical line is called the **y-axis.** Together, the x-axis and y-axis form a **rectangular coordinate system**, also called the **Cartesian coordinate system,** in honor of René Descartes (1596–1650), the French mathematician who is credited with its invention.

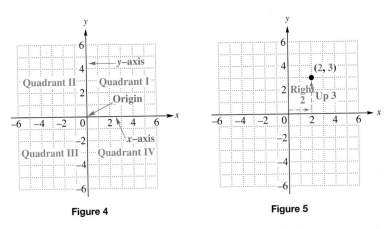

Figure 4   Figure 5

The coordinate system is divided into four regions, called **quadrants.** These quadrants are numbered counterclockwise, as shown in Figure 4. *Points on the axes themselves are not in any quadrant.* The point at which the x-axis and y-axis meet is called the **origin.** The origin, which is labeled 0 in Figure 4, is the point corresponding to $(0, 0)$.

(((Work Problem 8 at the Side.

The x-axis and y-axis determine a **plane,** a flat surface illustrated by a sheet of paper. By referring to the two axes, every point in the plane can be associated with an ordered pair. The numbers in the ordered pair are called the **coordinates** of the point. For example, locate the point associated with the ordered pair $(2, 3)$ by starting at the origin. Since the x-coordinate is 2, go 2 units to the right along the x-axis. Then, since the y-coordinate is 3, turn and go up 3 units on a line parallel to the y-axis. The point $(2, 3)$ is **plotted** in Figure 5. From now on, we will refer to the point with x-coordinate 2 and y-coordinate 3 as the point $(2, 3)$.

ANSWERS
8. *A*, II; *B*, IV; *C*, I; *D*, II; *E*, no quadrant

> **NOTE**
> When we graph on a number line, one number corresponds to each point. On a plane, however, both numbers in the ordered pair are needed to locate a point. The ordered pair is a name for the point.

EXAMPLE 7 Plotting Ordered Pairs

Plot each ordered pair on a coordinate system.

(a) $(1, 5)$ **(b)** $(-2, 3)$ **(c)** $(-1, -4)$ **(d)** $(7, -2)$

(e) $\left(\frac{3}{2}, 2\right)$ **(f)** $(5, 0)$ **(g)** $(0, -3)$

See Figure 6. In part (c), locate the point $(-1, -4)$ by first going 1 unit to the left along the x-axis. Then turn and go 4 units down, parallel to the y-axis. Plot the point $\left(\frac{3}{2}, 2\right)$ in part (e) by first going $\frac{3}{2}$ (or $1\frac{1}{2}$) units to the right along the x-axis. Then turn and go 2 units up, parallel to the y-axis.

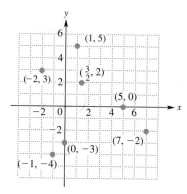

Figure 6

Work Problem 9 at the Side. ▶▶▶

Sometimes we can use a linear equation to mathematically describe, or *model*, a real-life situation, as shown in the next example.

EXAMPLE 8 Completing Ordered Pairs to Estimate Annual Costs of Doctors' Visits

The amount Americans pay annually for doctors' visits increased from 1990 through 2000. This amount can be approximated by the linear equation

Cost ⎯⎯⎯⎯⎯⎯ Year

$$y = 34.3x - 67{,}693,$$

which relates x, the year, and y, the cost in dollars. (*Source:* U.S. Health Care Financing Administration.)

(a) Complete the table of values for this linear equation.

x (Year)	y (Cost)
1990	
1996	
2000	

Continued on Next Page

---

9 Plot each ordered pair on a coordinate system.

(a) $(3, 5)$ **(b)** $(-2, 6)$

(c) $(-4, 0)$ **(d)** $(-5, -2)$

(e) $(5, -2)$ **(f)** $(0, -6)$

ANSWERS
9.

10 Refer to the linear equation in Example 8.

(a) Find the y-value for $x = 1996$. Round to the nearest whole number.

To find y when $x = 1990$, substitute into the equation.

$$y = 34.3(1990) - 67,693 \qquad \text{Let } x = 1990.$$

$$y = 564 \qquad \text{Use a calculator.}$$

This means that in 1990, Americans each spent about $564 on doctors' visits.

◀◀◀ Work Problem 10 at the Side. ▶

Including the results from Problem 10 at the side gives the completed table that follows.

x (Year)	y (Cost)
1990	564
1996	770
2000	907

We can write the results from the table of values as ordered pairs (x, y). Each year x is paired with its cost y:

$$(1990, 564), \quad (1996, 770), \quad \text{and} \quad (2000, 907).$$

(b) Graph the ordered pairs found in part (a).

The ordered pairs are graphed in Figure 7. This graph of ordered pairs of data is called a **scatter diagram.** Notice how the axes are labeled: x represents the year, and y represents the cost in dollars. Different scales are used on the two axes. Here, each square represents two units in the horizontal direction and 100 units in the vertical direction. Because the numbers in the first ordered pair are so large, we show a break in the axes near the origin.

(b) Find the y-value for $x = 2000$. Interpret your result.

COSTS OF DOCTORS' VISITS

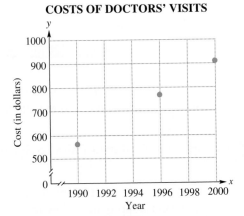

Figure 7

A scatter diagram enables us to tell whether two quantities are related to each other. In Figure 7, the plotted points could be connected to form a straight *line*, so the variables x (year) and y (cost) have a *linear* relationship. The increase in costs is also reflected.

CAUTION

The equation in Example 8 is valid only for the years 1990 through 2000 because it was based on data for those years. Do not assume that this equation would provide reliable data for other years since the data for those years may not follow the same pattern.

3.1 Exercises

FOR
EXTRA
HELP

 Addison-Wesley
Math Tutor Center

 MathXL

 Digital Video Tutor CD 3
Videotape 3

Student's
Solutions
Manual

MyMathLab
MyMathLab

 Interactmath.com

On February 13, 2000, Peanuts *fans bid farewell to new segments of this popular comic strip (which is still being printed as* Classic Peanuts*). The circle graph shows the results of a survey of adults to determine their favorite* Peanuts *characters. Use the circle graph to work Exercises 1–4. See Example 1.*

1. Which *Peanuts* character was most popular? What percent of those surveyed named this character as their favorite?

2. A random sample of 5000 adults is surveyed.

   (a) Estimate how many would be expected to name Lucy as their favorite *Peanuts* character. (*Hint:* To estimate, round 8% to 10%.)

   (b) Use the actual figure from the graph to determine how many adults would name Lucy as their favorite character.

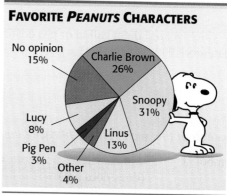

FAVORITE *PEANUTS* CHARACTERS

No opinion 15%
Charlie Brown 26%
Snoopy 31%
Lucy 8%
Linus 13%
Pig Pen 3%
Other 4%

Source: *USA Today*/CNN/Gallup Poll conducted nationwide February 4–6, 2000.

3. Regardless of the number of adults surveyed, how many would we expect to name Charlie Brown as their favorite *Peanuts* character compared to Linus?

4. Using the group of 5000 adults, confirm your answer to Exercise 3.

The bar graph compares egg production in millions of eggs for six states in the year 2002. Use the bar graph to work Exercises 5–8. See Example 2.

5. Name the top two egg-producing states. Estimate their production.

6. Which states had egg production less than 5000 million eggs?

7. Which state had the least production? Estimate this production.

8. How did egg production in Texas (TX) compare to egg production in Iowa (IA)?

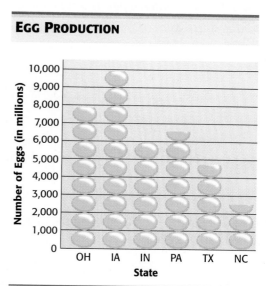

EGG PRODUCTION

Number of Eggs (in millions)

OH IA IN PA TX NC
State

Source: U.S. Department of Agriculture.

The line graph shows the average price, adjusted for inflation, that Americans have paid for a gallon of gasoline for selected years since 1970. Use the line graph to work Exercises 9–12. See Example 3.

9. Over which period of years did the greatest increase in the price of a gallon of gas occur? About how much was this increase?

10. Estimate the price of a gallon of gas during 1985, 1990, 1995, and 2000.

11. Describe the trend in gas prices from 1980 to 1995.

12. During which year(s) did a gallon of gas cost approximately $1.50?

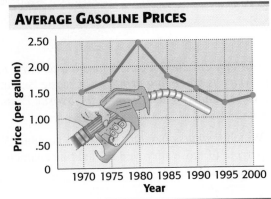

AVERAGE GASOLINE PRICES

Source: American Petroleum Institute; AP research.

Use the concepts of this section to fill in each blank with the correct response.

13. The symbol (x, y) _____ represent an ordered pair, while the
    (does/does not)

    symbols $[x, y]$ and $\{x, y\}$ _____ represent ordered pairs.
    (do/do not)

14. The point whose graph has coordinates $(-4, 2)$ is in quadrant _____.

15. The point whose graph has coordinates $(0, 5)$ lies on the _____-axis.

16. The ordered pair $(4, $ _____$)$ is a solution of the equation $y = 3$.

17. The ordered pair $($ _____$, -2)$ is a solution of the equation $x = 6$.

18. The ordered pair $(3, 2)$ is a solution of the equation $2x - 5y = $ _____.

Decide whether each ordered pair is a solution of the given equation. See Example 4.

19. $x + y = 9; (0, 9)$

20. $x + y = 8; (0, 8)$

21. $2x - y = 6; (4, 2)$

22. $2x + y = 5; (3, -1)$

23. $4x - 3y = 6; (2, 1)$

24. $5x - 3y = 15; (5, 2)$

25. $y = \dfrac{2}{3}x; (-6, -4)$

26. $y = -\dfrac{1}{4}x; (-8, 2)$

27. $x = -6; (5, -6)$

28. $y = 2; (2, 4)$

29. Do $(4, -1)$ and $(-1, 4)$ represent the same ordered pair? Explain.

30. Explain why it would be easier to find the corresponding y-value for $x = \frac{1}{3}$ in the equation $y = 6x + 2$ than it would be for $x = \frac{1}{7}$.

Complete each ordered pair for the equation $y = 2x + 7$. *See Example 5.*

31. (2,)   **32.** (0,)   **33.** (, 0)   **34.** (, −3)

Complete each ordered pair for the equation $y = -4x - 4$. *See Example 5.*

35. (0,)   **36.** (, 0)   **37.** (, 16)   **38.** (, 24)

Complete each table of values. In Exercises 39–42, write the results as ordered pairs.
See Example 6.

39. $2x + 3y = 12$

x	y
0	
	0
	8

(   )

40. $4x + 3y = 24$

x	y
0	
	0
	4

41. $3x - 5y = -15$

x	y
0	
	0
	−6

(   ) (   )

42. $4x - 9y = -36$

x	y
	0
0	
	8

(   )

43. $x = -9$

x	y
	6
	2
	−3

44. $x = 12$

x	y
	3
	8
	0

45. $y = -6$

x	y
8	
4	
−2	

46. $y = -10$

x	y
4	
0	
−4	

47. $x - 8 = 0$

x	y
	8
	3
	0

48. $y + 2 = 0$

x	y
9	
2	
0	

Give the ordered pairs for the points labeled A–F in the figure.

49. *A*   **50.** *B*   **51.** *C*

52. *D*   **53.** *E*   **54.** *F*

Fill in each blank with the word positive *or the word* negative.

The point with coordinates (x, y) is in

55. quadrant III if x is _____ and y is _____.

56. quadrant II if x is _____ and y is _____.

57. quadrant IV if x is _____ and y is _____.

58. quadrant I if x is _____ and y is _____.

59. A point (x, y) has the property that $xy < 0$. In which quadrant(s) must the point lie? Explain.

60. A point (x, y) has the property that $xy > 0$. In which quadrant(s) must the point lie? Explain.

Plot each ordered pair on the rectangular coordinate system provided. See Example 7.

61. $(6, 2)$ **62.** $(5, 3)$ **63.** $(-4, 2)$

64. $(-3, 5)$ **65.** $\left(-\dfrac{4}{5}, -1\right)$ **66.** $\left(-\dfrac{3}{2}, -4\right)$

67. $(0, 4)$ **68.** $(0, -3)$ **69.** $(4, 0)$ **70.** $(-3, 0)$

Complete each table of values, and then plot the ordered pairs. See Examples 6 and 7.

71. $x - 2y = 6$

x	y
0	
	0
2	
	-1

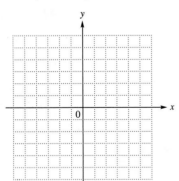

72. $2x - y = 4$

x	y
0	
	0
1	
	-6

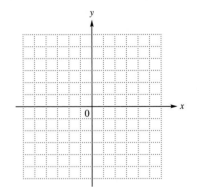

73. $3x - 4y = 12$

x	y
0	
	0
-4	
	-4

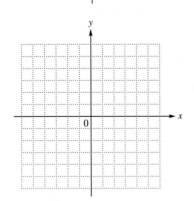

74. $2x - 5y = 10$

x	y
0	
	0
-5	
	-3

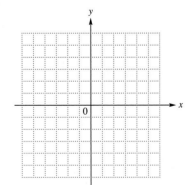

75. $y + 4 = 0$

x	y
0	
5	
-2	
-3	

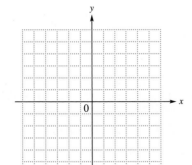

76. $x - 5 = 0$

x	y
	1
	0
	6
	-4

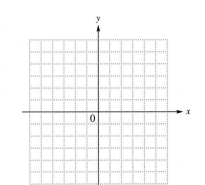

77. Look at the graphs of the ordered pairs in Exercises 71–76. Describe the pattern indicated by the plotted points.

Work each problem. See Example 8.

78. The table shows the amount of e-commerce in billions of dollars.

Year	Amount (in billions)
1996	.7
1997	2.6
1998	7.8
1999	18.9
2000	38.2
2001	45.7

Source: Jupiter Research.

(a) Write the data from the table as ordered pairs (x, y), where x represents the year and y represents the amount of e-commerce in billions of dollars.

(b) What does the ordered pair (2002, 62.0) mean in the context of this discussion?

(c) Make a scatter diagram of the data using the ordered pairs from part (a).

E-COMMERCE

(d) Describe what is happening to the amount of e-commerce during these years.

79. The table shows the rate (in percent) at which 4-year college students (both private and public) graduate within 5 years.

Year	Percent
1996	53.3
1997	52.8
1998	52.1
1999	51.6
2000	51.2
2001	50.9

Source: ACT.

(a) Write the data from the table as ordered pairs (x, y), where x represents the year and y represents graduation percent.

(b) What does the ordered pair (2002, 51.0) mean in the context of this discussion?

(c) Make a scatter diagram of the data using the ordered pairs from part (a).

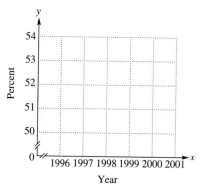

4-YEAR COLLEGE STUDENTS GRADUATING WITHIN 5 YEARS

(d) Describe the pattern indicated by the points on the scatter diagram. What is happening to graduation rates for 4-year college students within 5 years?

80. The maximum benefit for the heart from exercising occurs if the heart rate is in the target heart rate zone. The lower limit of this target zone can be approximated by the linear equation

$$y = -.5x + 108,$$

where *x* represents age and *y* represents heartbeats per minute. (*Source:* www.fitresource.com)

(a) Complete the table of values for this linear equation.

Age	Heartbeats (per minute)
20	
40	
60	
80	

(b) Write the data from the table of values as ordered pairs.

(c) Make a scatter diagram of the data. Do the points lie in an approximately linear pattern?

TARGET HEART RATE ZONE
(Lower Limit)

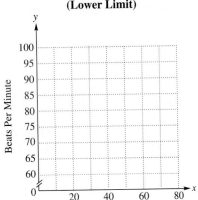

81. (See Exercise 80.) The upper limit of the target heart rate zone can be approximated by the linear equation

$$y = -.8x + 173,$$

where *x* represents age and *y* represents heartbeats per minute. (*Source:* www.fitresource.com)

(a) Complete the table of values for this linear equation.

Age	Heartbeats (per minute)
20	
40	
60	
80	

(b) Write the data from the table of values as ordered pairs.

(c) Make a scatter diagram of the data. Describe the pattern indicated by the data.

TARGET HEART RATE ZONE
(Upper Limit)

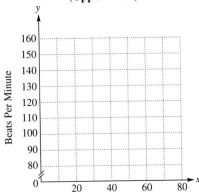

82. Refer to Exercises 80 and 81. What is the target heart rate zone for age 20? age 40?

3.2 Graphing Linear Equations in Two Variables

OBJECTIVES

1. Graph linear equations by plotting ordered pairs.
2. Find intercepts.
3. Graph linear equations where the intercepts coincide.
4. Graph linear equations of the form $y = k$ or $x = k$.
5. Use a linear equation to model data.

OBJECTIVE 1 **Graph linear equations by plotting ordered pairs.** There are infinitely many ordered pairs that satisfy an equation in two variables. We find ordered pairs that are solutions of the equation $x + 2y = 7$ by choosing as many values of x (or y) as we wish and then completing each ordered pair.

For example, if we choose $x = 1$, then $y = 3$, so the ordered pair $(1, 3)$ is a solution of the equation $x + 2y = 7$.

$$1 + 2(3) = 1 + 6 = 7$$

> **Work Problem 1 at the Side.** ▶▶▶

Figure 8 shows a graph of all the ordered pairs found for $x + 2y = 7$ above and in Problem 1 at the side.

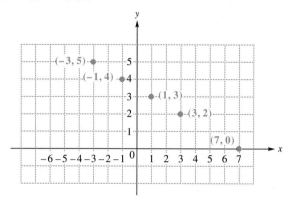

Figure 8

Notice that the points plotted in this figure all appear to lie on a straight line. The line that goes through these points is shown in Figure 9. In fact, all ordered pairs satisfying the equation $x + 2y = 7$ correspond to points that lie on this same straight line. This line gives a "picture" of all the solutions of the equation $x + 2y = 7$. Only a portion of the line is shown here, but it extends indefinitely in both directions, as suggested by the arrowhead on each end of the line.

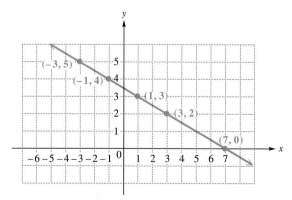

Figure 9

The line in Figure 9 is called the **graph** of the equation $x + 2y = 7$, and the process of plotting the ordered pairs and drawing the line through the corresponding points is called **graphing.** The preceding discussion can be generalized.

1. Complete each ordered pair for the equation $x + 2y = 7$.

   (a) $(-3, \quad)$

   (b) $(3, \quad)$

   (c) $(-1, \quad)$

   (d) $(7, \quad)$

ANSWERS
1. **(a)** $(-3, 5)$ **(b)** $(3, 2)$
   (c) $(-1, 4)$ **(d)** $(7, 0)$

> The graph of any linear equation in two variables is a straight line.

(Notice that the word *line* appears in the term "*line*ar equation.")

Because two distinct points determine a line, a straight line can be graphed by finding any two different points on the line. However, it is a good idea to plot a third point as a check.

EXAMPLE 1 **Graphing a Linear Equation**

Graph the linear equation $y = -\frac{3}{2}x + 3$.

Although this equation is not in the form $Ax + By = C$, it *could* be written in that form, so it is a linear equation. Two different points on the graph can be found by first letting $x = 0$ and then letting $y = 0$.

If $x = 0$, then

$$y = -\frac{3}{2}x + 3$$

$$y = -\frac{3}{2}(0) + 3 \qquad \text{Let } x = 0.$$

$$y = 0 + 3$$

$$y = 3.$$

If $y = 0$, then

$$y = -\frac{3}{2}x + 3$$

$$0 = -\frac{3}{2}x + 3 \qquad \text{Let } y = 0.$$

$$\frac{3}{2}x = 3$$

$$x = 2. \qquad \text{Multiply by } \frac{2}{3}.$$

This gives the ordered pairs $(0, 3)$ and $(2, 0)$. Find a third point (as a check) by letting x or y equal some other number. For example, let $x = -2$. (Any number could be used, but a multiple of 2 makes multiplying by $-\frac{3}{2}$ easier.)

$$y = -\frac{3}{2}x + 3$$

$$y = -\frac{3}{2}(-2) + 3 \qquad \text{Let } x = -2.$$

$$y = 3 + 3$$

$$y = 6$$

These three ordered pairs are shown in the table with Figure 10. Plot the corresponding points, then draw a line through them. This line, shown in Figure 10, is the graph of $y = -\frac{3}{2}x + 3$.

x	y
0	3
2	0
−2	6

Figure 10

CAUTION

When graphing a linear equation as in Example 1, all three points should lie on the same straight line. If they don't, double-check the ordered pairs you found.

Work Problem 2 at the Side. ▶▶▶

EXAMPLE 2 Graphing a Linear Equation

Graph the linear equation $4x = 5y + 20$.

As before, at least two different points are needed to draw the graph. First let $x = 0$ and then let $y = 0$ to complete two ordered pairs.

$4x = 5y + 20$	$4x = 5y + 20$
$4(0) = 5y + 20$ Let $x = 0$.	$4x = 5(0) + 20$ Let $y = 0$.
$0 = 5y + 20$	$4x = 0 + 20$
$-5y = 20$	$4x = 20$
$y = -4$	$x = 5$

The ordered pairs are $(0, -4)$ and $(5, 0)$. Get a third ordered pair (as a check) by choosing some number other than 0 for x or y. We choose $y = 2$. Replacing y with 2 in the equation $4x = 5y + 20$ leads to the ordered pair $\left(\frac{15}{2}, 2\right)$, or $\left(7\frac{1}{2}, 2\right)$.

Plot the three ordered pairs $(0, -4)$, $(5, 0)$, and $\left(7\frac{1}{2}, 2\right)$, and draw a line through them. This line, shown in Figure 11, is the graph of $4x = 5y + 20$.

x	y
0	-4
5	0
$7\frac{1}{2}$	2

Figure 11

Work Problem 3 at the Side. ▶▶▶

OBJECTIVE 2 Find intercepts. In Figure 11, the graph crosses or intersects the y-axis at $(0, -4)$ and the x-axis at $(5, 0)$. For this reason, $(0, -4)$ is called the **y-intercept,** and $(5, 0)$ is called the **x-intercept** of the graph. The intercepts are particularly useful for graphing linear equations. (In general, any point on the y-axis has x-coordinate 0; any point on the x-axis has y-coordinate 0.) The intercepts are found by replacing, in turn, each variable with 0 in the equation and solving for the value of the other variable.

Finding Intercepts

To find the **x-intercept,** let $y = 0$ in the given equation and solve for x. Then $(x, 0)$ is the x-intercept.

To find the **y-intercept,** let $x = 0$ in the given equation and solve for y. Then $(0, y)$ is the y-intercept.

2 Complete the table of values, and graph the linear equation.

$x + y = 6$

x	y
0	
	0
2	

3 Make a table of values, and graph the linear equation.

$2x = 3y + 6$

x	y

ANSWERS

2.

x	y
0	6
6	0
2	4

$x + y = 6$

3.

$2x = 3y + 6$

4 Find the intercepts for the graph of $5x + 2y = 10$. Then draw the graph. (Be sure to get a third point as a check.)

EXAMPLE 3 Finding Intercepts

Find the intercepts for the graph of $2x + y = 4$. Then draw the graph.
To find the y-intercept, let $x = 0$; to find the x-intercept, let $y = 0$.

$$2x + y = 4$$
$$2(0) + y = 4 \quad \text{Let } x = 0.$$
$$0 + y = 4$$
$$y = 4$$

$$2x + y = 4$$
$$2x + 0 = 4 \quad \text{Let } y = 0.$$
$$2x = 4$$
$$x = 2$$

The y-intercept is $(0, 4)$. The x-intercept is $(2, 0)$. The graph with the two intercepts shown in color is given in Figure 12. Find a third point as a check. For example, choosing $x = 1$ gives $y = 2$. Plot $(0, 4)$, $(2, 0)$, and $(1, 2)$ and draw a line through them. This line, shown in Figure 12, is the graph.

x	y
0	4
2	0
1	2

y-intercept $(0, 4)$

$(1, 2)$ is used as a check.

x-intercept $(2, 0)$

$2x + y = 4$

Figure 12

◀◀◀ **Work Problem 4 at the Side.**

OBJECTIVE 3 Graph linear equations where the intercepts coincide. In the preceding examples, the x- and y-intercepts were used to help draw the graphs. This is not always possible. Example 4 shows what to do when the x- and y-intercepts are the same point (that is, coincide).

EXAMPLE 4 Graphing an Equation of the Form $Ax + By = 0$

Graph the linear equation $x - 3y = 0$.
If we let $x = 0$, then $y = 0$, giving the ordered pair $(0, 0)$. Letting $y = 0$ also gives $(0, 0)$. This is the same ordered pair, so choose two *other* values for x or y. Choosing 2 for y gives $x - 3 \cdot 2 = 0$, or $x = 6$, so another ordered pair is $(6, 2)$. Choosing -6 for x gives -2 for y. The ordered pairs $(-6, -2)$, $(0, 0)$, and $(6, 2)$ are used to sketch the graph in Figure 13.

x	y
0	0
6	2
−6	−2

$x - 3y = 0$

$(6, 2)$

x-intercept and y-intercept

$(0, 0)$

$(-6, -2)$

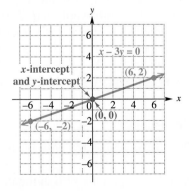

Figure 13

ANSWERS
4. x-intercept $(2, 0)$; y-intercept $(0, 5)$

$5x + 2y = 10$

Example 4 can be generalized as follows.

If A and B are nonzero real numbers, the graph of a linear equation of the form

$$Ax + By = 0$$

passes through the origin $(0, 0)$.

Work Problem 5 at the Side. ▶▶▶

OBJECTIVE 4 Graph linear equations of the form $y = k$ or $x = k$.
The equation $y = -4$ is a linear equation in which the coefficient of x is 0.
(To see this, write $y = -4$ as $0x + y = -4$.) Also, $x = 3$ is a linear equation in which the coefficient of y is 0. These equations lead to horizontal or vertical straight lines, as the next example shows.

EXAMPLE 5 Graphing Equations of the Form $y = k$ and $x = k$

(a) Graph the linear equation $y = -4$.
As the equation states, for any value of x, y is always equal to -4. Three ordered pairs that satisfy the equation are shown in the table of values. Drawing a line through these points gives the horizontal line in Figure 14. The y-intercept is $(0, -4)$; there is no x-intercept.

x	y
-2	-4
0	-4
3	-4

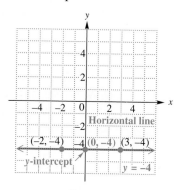

Figure 14

(b) Graph $x - 3 = 0$.
First add 3 to each side of $x - 3 = 0$ to get $x = 3$. All the ordered pairs that satisfy this equation have x-coordinate 3. Any number can be used for y. See Figure 15 for the graph of this vertical line, along with a table of values. The x-intercept is $(3, 0)$; there is no y-intercept.

x	y
3	3
3	0
3	-2

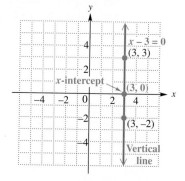

Figure 15

5 Graph each equation.

(a) $2x - y = 0$

(b) $x = -4y$

ANSWERS
5. (a)

6 Graph each equation.

(a) $y = -5$

(b) $x + 4 = 6$

6. (a)

$y = -5$

(b)

$x + 4 = 6$

From the results in Example 5, we make the following observations.

Horizontal and Vertical Lines

The graph of the linear equation $y = k$, where k is a real number, is the horizontal line with y-intercept $(0, k)$ and no x-intercept.

The graph of the linear equation $x = k$, where k is a real number, is the vertical line with x-intercept $(k, 0)$ and no y-intercept.

Work Problem 6 at the Side.

The different forms of linear equations from this section and the methods of graphing them are summarized below.

Graphing Linear Equations

Equation	Graphing Method	Example
$y = k$	Draw a horizontal line through $(0, k)$.	
$x = k$	Draw a vertical line through $(k, 0)$.	
$Ax + By = 0$	Graph passes through $(0, 0)$. To get additional points that lie on the graph, choose any values for x or y, except 0.	

(continued)

$Ax + By = C$
$A, B,$ and $C \neq 0$

Find any two points on the line. A good choice is to find the intercepts. Let $x = 0$, and find the corresponding value of y; then let $y = 0$, and find x. As a check, get a third point by choosing a value of x or y that has not yet been used.

$3x - 2y = 6$

$(2, 0)$
$(0, -3)$

7 Match the information about the graphs with the linear equations in A–D.

A. $x = 5$
B. $2x - 5y = 8$
C. $y - 2 = 3$
D. $x + 4y = 0$

(a) The graph of the equation is a horizontal line.

Work Problem 7 at the Side. ⟩⟩⟩

NOTE
Another method of graphing linear equations, using the concepts of slope and y-intercept, will be covered in Objective 2 of **Section 3.4.**

(b) The graph of the equation passes through the origin.

OBJECTIVE 5 Use a linear equation to model data.

EXAMPLE 6 Using a Linear Equation to Model Credit Card Debt

Credit card debt in households in the United States increased steadily during the 1990s. The amount of debt y in billions of dollars can be modeled by the linear equation

$$y = 47.3x + 281,$$

where $x = 0$ represents the year 1992, $x = 1$ represents 1993, and so on. (*Source:* Board of Governors of the Federal Reserve System.)

(a) Use the equation to approximate credit card debt in the years 1992, 1993, and 1999.
    Substitute the appropriate value for each year x to find credit card debt in that year.

For 1992: $y = 47.3(0) + 281$ Replace x with 0.
          $y = 281$ billion dollars

For 1993: $y = 47.3(1) + 281$ Replace x with 1.
          $y = 328.3$ billion dollars

For 1999: $y = 47.3(7) + 281$ Replace x with 7.
          $y = 612.1$ billion dollars

(c) The graph of the equation is a vertical line.

(d) The graph of the equation passes through $(9, 2)$.

—— **Continued on Next Page**

8 Use the graph and then the equation in Example 6 to approximate credit card debt in 1997.

(b) Write the information from part (a) as three ordered pairs, and use them to graph the given linear equation.

Since x represents the year and y represents the debt in billions of dollars, the ordered pairs are (0, 281), (1, 328.3), and (7, 612.1). Figure 16 shows a graph of these ordered pairs and the line through them. (Note that arrowheads are not included with the graphed line since the data are for the years 1992 to 1999 only, that is, from $x = 0$ to $x = 7$.)

U.S. CREDIT CARD DEBT

Figure 16

(c) Use the graph and then the equation to approximate credit card debt in 1996.

For 1996, $x = 4$. On the graph, find 4 on the horizontal axis and move up to the graphed line, then across to the vertical axis. It appears that credit card debt in 1996 was about 465 billion dollars.

To use the equation, substitute 4 for x.

$$y = 47.3x + 281$$

$$y = 47.3(4) + 281 \qquad \text{Let } x = 4.$$

$$y = 470.2 \text{ billion dollars}$$

This result for 1996 is close to our estimate using the graph.

◀◀◀ **Work Problem 8 at the Side.**

3.2 Exercises

FOR EXTRA HELP

 Addison-Wesley Math Tutor Center   MathXL   Digital Video Tutor CD 3 Videotape 3   Student's Solutions Manual   MyMathLab   Interactmath.com

Complete the given ordered pairs for each equation. Then graph each equation by plotting the points and drawing a line through them. See Examples 1 and 2.

1. $y = -x + 5$

$(0, \ ), (\ , 0), (2, \ )$

2. $y = x - 2$

$(0, \ ), (\ , 0), (5, \ )$

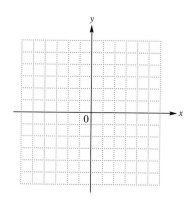

3. $y = \dfrac{2}{3}x + 1$

$(0, \ ), (3, \ ), (-3, \ )$

4. $y = -\dfrac{3}{4}x + 2$

$(0, \ ), (4, \ ), (-4, \ )$

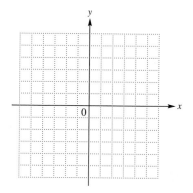

5. $3x = -y - 6$

$(0, \ ), (\ , 0), \left(-\dfrac{1}{3}, \ \right)$

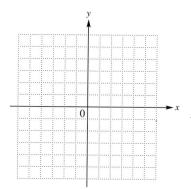

6. $x = 2y + 3$

$(\ , 0), (0, \ ), \left(\ , \dfrac{1}{2}\right)$

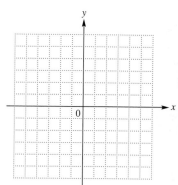

Match the information about each graph in Column I with the correct linear equation in Column II.

<table>
<tr><td align="center">**I**</td><td align="center">**II**</td></tr>
</table>

7. The graph of the equation has y-intercept $(0, -4)$.

A. $3x + y = -4$

8. The graph of the equation has $(0, 0)$ as x-intercept and y-intercept.

B. $x - 4 = 0$

9. The graph of the equation does not have an x-intercept.

C. $y = 4x$

10. The graph of the equation has x-intercept $(4, 0)$.

D. $y = 4$

Find the intercepts for the graph of each equation. See Example 3.

11. $2x - 3y = 24$

    x-intercept:

    y-intercept:

12. $-3x + 8y = 48$

    x-intercept:

    y-intercept:

13. $x + 6y = 0$

    x-intercept:

    y-intercept:

14. $3x - y = 0$

    x-intercept:

    y-intercept:

15. A student attempted to graph $4x + 5y = 0$ by finding intercepts. She first let $x = 0$ and found y; then she let $y = 0$ and found x. In both cases, the resulting point was $(0, 0)$. She knew that she needed at least two points to graph the line, but was unsure what to do next because finding intercepts gave her only one point. How would you explain to her what to do next?

16. What is the equation of the x-axis? What is the equation of the y-axis?

Graph each linear equation. See Examples 1–5.

17. $x = y + 2$

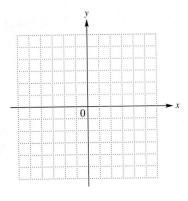

18. $x = -y + 6$

19. $x - y = 4$

20. $x - y = 5$

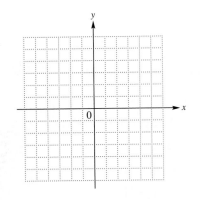

21. $2x + y = 6$

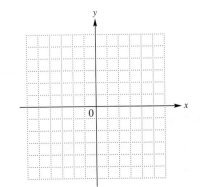

22. $-3x + y = -6$

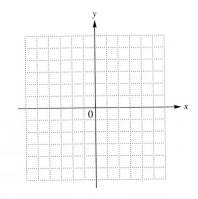

23. $3x + 7y = 14$

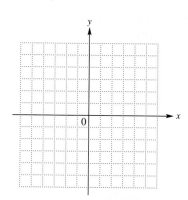

24. $6x - 5y = 18$

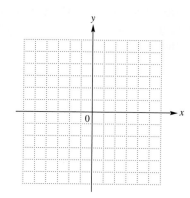

25. $y - 2x = 0$

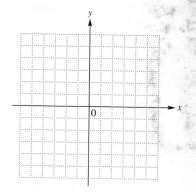

26. $y + 3x = 0$

27. $y = -6x$

28. $x = 4$

29. $x = -2$

30. $y + 1 = 0$

31. $y - 3 = 0$

32. Write a few sentences summarizing how to graph a linear equation in two variables.

Solve each problem. See Example 6.

33. The height y (in centimeters) of a woman is related to the length of her radius bone x (from the wrist to the elbow) and is approximated by the linear equation

$$y = 3.9x + 73.5.$$

(a) Use the equation to find the approximate heights of women with radius bones of lengths 20 cm, 26 cm, and 22 cm.

(b) Graph the equation using the data from part (a).

HEIGHTS OF WOMEN

Length of Radius Bone (in cm)

(c) Use the graph to estimate the length of the radius bone in a woman who is 167 cm tall. Then use the equation to find the length of this radius bone to the nearest centimeter. (*Hint:* Substitute for y in the equation.)

34. The weight y (in pounds) of a man taller than 60 in. can be roughly approximated by the linear equation

$$y = 5.5x - 220,$$

where x is the height of the man in inches.

(a) Use the equation to approximate the weights of men whose heights are 62 in., 66 in., and 72 in.

(b) Graph the equation using the data from part (a).

WEIGHTS OF MEN

Height (in inches)

(c) Use the graph to estimate the height of a man who weighs 155 lb. Then use the equation to find the height of this man to the nearest inch. (*Hint:* Substitute for y in the equation.)

35. Refer to **Section 3.1** Exercise 80. Draw a line through the points you plotted in the scatter diagram there.

(a) Use the graph to estimate the lower limit of the target heart rate zone for age 30.

(b) Use the linear equation given there to approximate the lower limit for age 30.

(c) How does the approximation using the equation compare to the estimate from the graph?

36. Refer to **Section 3.1** Exercise 81. Draw a line through the points you plotted in the scatter diagram there.

(a) Use the graph to estimate the upper limit of the target heart rate zone for age 30.

(b) Use the linear equation given there to approximate the upper limit for age 30.

(c) How does the approximation using the equation compare to the estimate from the graph?

37. Use the results of Exercises 35(b) and 36(b) to determine the target heart rate zone for age 30.

38. Should the graphs of the target heart rate zone in the **Section 3.1** exercises be used to estimate the target heart rate zone for ages below 20 or above 80? Why or why not?

39. Per capita consumption of coffee increased for the years 1995 through 2000 as shown in the graph. If $x = 0$ represents 1995, $x = 1$ represents 1996, and so on, per capita consumption y in gallons can be modeled by the linear equation

$$y = 1.13x + 20.67.$$

COFFEE CONSUMPTION

Source: U.S. Department of Agriculture.

(a) Use the equation to approximate consumption in 1995, 1996, and 1998 to the nearest tenth.

(b) Use the graph to estimate consumption for the same years.

(c) How do the approximations using the equation compare to the estimates from the graph?

40. Sporting goods sales y (in billions of dollars) from 1995 through 2000 are modeled by the linear equation

$$y = 3.606x + 41.86,$$

where $x = 5$ corresponds to 1995, $x = 6$ corresponds to 1996, and so on.

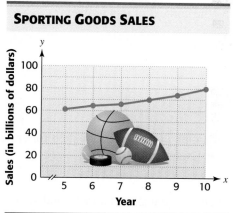

SPORTING GOODS SALES

Source: U.S. Bureau of the Census.

(a) Use the equation to approximate sporting goods sales in 1995, 1997, and 2000. Round your answers to the nearest billion dollars.

(b) Use the graph to estimate sales for the same years.

(c) How do the approximations using the equation compare to the estimates using the graph?

41. The graph shows the value of a certain sport-utility vehicle over the first 5 yr of ownership.

SUV VALUE

Use the graph to do the following.

(a) Determine the initial value of the SUV.

(b) Find the *depreciation* (loss in value) from the original value after the first 3 yr.

(c) What is the annual or yearly depreciation in each of the first 5 yr?

(d) What does the ordered pair (5, 5000) mean in the context of this problem?

42. Demand for an item is often closely related to its price. As price increases, demand decreases, and as price decreases, demand increases. Suppose demand for a video game is 2000 units when the price is $40, and demand is 2500 units when the price is $30.

(a) Let x be the price and y be the demand for the game. Graph the two given pairs of prices and demands.

VIDEO GAME PRICE/DEMAND

(b) Assume the relationship is linear. Draw a line through the two points from part (a). From your graph, estimate the demand if the price drops to $20.

(c) Use the graph to estimate the price if the demand is 3500 units.

43. The graph of the linear equation for credit card debt from Example 6,

$$y = 47.3x + 281,$$

where $x = 0$ represents 1992, and so on, and y is in billions of dollars, is shown in the figure. The actual data for 1992 through 1999 is also plotted.

(a) In general, how well does the linear equation model the actual data?

(b) Use the plotted points to estimate the actual credit card debt for 1996. How does it compare to the answer in Example 6(c)?

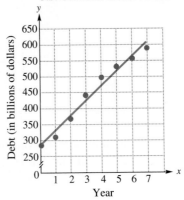

U.S. CREDIT CARD DEBT

Source: Board of Governors of the Federal Reserve System.

(c) Should this equation be used to predict credit card debt for the year 2002? Why or why not?

3.3 Slope of a Line

An important characteristic of the lines we graphed in the previous section is their slant or "steepness", as viewed from left to right. See Figure 17.

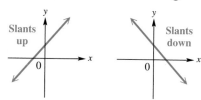

Figure 17

One way to measure the steepness of a line is to compare the vertical change in the line to the horizontal change while moving along the line from one fixed point to another. This measure of steepness is called the *slope* of the line.

OBJECTIVE 1 Find the slope of a line given two points. Figure 18 shows a line through two nonspecific points (x_1, y_1) and (x_2, y_2). (This notation is called **subscript notation.** Read x_1 as "x-sub-one" and x_2 as "x-sub-two.")

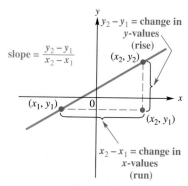

Figure 18

Moving along the line from the point (x_1, y_1) to the point (x_2, y_2) causes y to change by $y_2 - y_1$ units. This is the vertical change or **rise.** Similarly, x changes by $x_2 - x_1$ units, which is the horizontal change or **run.** (In both cases, the change is expressed as a *difference*.) Remember from **Section 2.6** that one way to compare two numbers is by using a ratio. **Slope** is the ratio of the vertical change in y to the horizontal change in x.

EXAMPLE 1 Comparing Rise to Run

Find the slope ratio of the rise to the run for each line shown in Figures 19(a) and 19(b).

We use the two points shown on each line. For the line in Figure 19(a), we find the rise from point Q to point P by determining the vertical change from -4 to 4, the difference $4 - (-4) = \mathbf{8}$. Similarly, we find the run by determining the horizontal change from Q to P, $5 - (-5) = \mathbf{10}$. Slope is the ratio

$$\frac{\text{rise}}{\text{run}} = \frac{8}{10} \text{ or } \frac{4}{5}.$$

Continued on Next Page

(a)

Figure 19

1 Find the slope ratio of the rise to the run for each line.

(a)

(b)

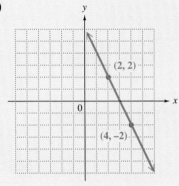

2 Find $\dfrac{y_2 - y_1}{x_2 - x_1}$ for the following values.

(a) $y_2 = 4, y_1 = -1,$
$x_2 = 3, x_1 = 4$

(b) $x_1 = 3, x_2 = -5,$
$y_1 = 7, y_2 = -9$

(c) $x_1 = 2, x_2 = 7,$
$y_1 = 4, y_2 = 9$

ANSWERS

1. **(a)** $\dfrac{3}{2}$ **(b)** -2

2. **(a)** -5 **(b)** 2 **(c)** 1

Moving from Q to P, the line in Figure 19(b) has rise $3 - (-1) = 4$ and run $2 - 6 = -4$, so the slope is the ratio

$$\frac{\text{rise}}{\text{run}} = \frac{4}{-4} = \frac{1}{-1} \quad \text{or} \quad -1.$$

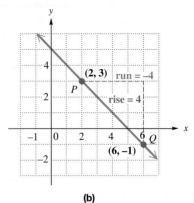

(b)

Figure 19

To confirm our slope ratios, count grid squares from one point on the line to another. For example, starting at the point $(5, 0)$ in Figure 19(b), count up 1 square (the rise in the slope ratio $\frac{1}{-1}$) and then 1 square to the *left* (the run) to arrive at the point $(4, 1)$ on the line.

◀◀◀ **Work Problem 1 at the Side.**

The idea of slope is used in many everyday situations. See Figure 20. For example, a highway with a 10% or $\frac{1}{10}$ grade (or slope) rises 1 m for every 10 m horizontally. Architects specify the pitch of a roof using slope; a $\frac{5}{12}$ roof means that the roof rises 5 ft for every 12 ft in the horizontal direction. The slope of a stairwell also indicates the ratio of the vertical rise to the horizontal run. In the figure, the slope of the stairwell is $\frac{8}{10}$ or $\frac{4}{5}$.

Figure 20

If we know the coordinates of two points on a line, we can find its slope, traditionally designated m, using the slope formula.

Slope Formula

The **slope** of the line through the points (x_1, y_1) and (x_2, y_2) is

$$m = \frac{\text{change in } y}{\text{change in } x} = \frac{y_2 - y_1}{x_2 - x_1}, \qquad \text{if } x_1 \neq x_2.$$

◀◀◀ **Work Problem 2 at the Side.**

The slope of a line tells how fast y changes for each unit of change in x; that is, the slope gives the rate of change in y for each unit of change in x.

EXAMPLE 2 **Using the Slope Formula**

Find the slope of each line.

(a) The line through $(1, -2)$ and $(-4, 7)$

Use the slope formula. Let $(-4, 7) = (x_2, y_2)$ and $(1, -2) = (x_1, y_1)$. Then

$$\text{slope } m = \frac{\text{change in } y}{\text{change in } x} = \frac{y_2 - y_1}{x_2 - x_1} = \frac{7 - (-2)}{-4 - 1} = \frac{9}{-5} = -\frac{9}{5}.$$

See Figure 21(a).

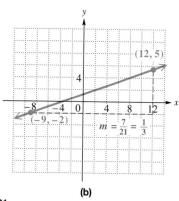

(a) (b)

Figure 21

(b) The line through $(-9, -2)$ and $(12, 5)$

$$m = \frac{y_2 - y_1}{x_2 - x_1} = \frac{5 - (-2)}{12 - (-9)} = \frac{7}{21} = \frac{1}{3}$$

See Figure 21(b). The same slope is obtained by subtracting in reverse order.

$$m = \frac{-2 - 5}{-9 - 12} = \frac{-7}{-21} = \frac{1}{3}$$

CAUTION
It makes no difference which point is (x_1, y_1) or (x_2, y_2); however, it is important to be consistent. Start with the x- and y-values of one point (either one) and subtract the corresponding values of the other point. Also, the slope of a line is the same for *any* two points on the line.

Work Problem 3 at the Side. ▶▶▶

In Example 2(a) the slope is negative and the corresponding line in Figure 21(a) falls from left to right. The slope in Example 2(b) is positive and the corresponding line in Figure 21(b) rises from left to right. These facts can be generalized.

---

3 Find the slope of each line.

(a) Through $(6, -2)$ and $(5, 4)$

(b) Through $(-3, 5)$ and $(-4, -7)$

(c) Through $(6, -8)$ and $(-2, 4)$
(Find this slope in two different ways as in Example 2(b).)

ANSWERS
3. **(a)** -6 **(b)** 12 **(c)** $-\dfrac{3}{2}$; $-\dfrac{3}{2}$

Positive and Negative Slopes

A line with positive slope rises from left to right.

A line with negative slope falls from left to right.

EXAMPLE 3 **Showing that the Slope of a Horizontal Line Is Zero**

Find the slope of the line through $(-8, 4)$ and $(2, 4)$.

$$m = \frac{y_2 - y_1}{x_2 - x_1} = \frac{4 - 4}{-8 - 2} = \frac{0}{-10} = 0 \qquad \text{Zero slope}$$

As shown in Figure 22, the line through the given points is horizontal. ***All horizontal lines have slope 0*** since the difference in y-values is always 0.

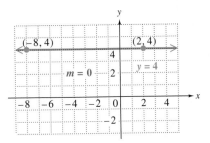

Figure 22

EXAMPLE 4 **Showing that a Vertical Line Has Undefined Slope**

Find the slope of the line through $(6, 2)$ and $(6, -4)$.

$$m = \frac{y_2 - y_1}{x_2 - x_1} = \frac{2 - (-4)}{6 - 6} = \frac{6}{0} \qquad \text{Undefined slope}$$

Because division by 0 is undefined, this line has undefined slope. (This is why the slope formula at the beginning of this section had the restriction $x_1 \neq x_2$.) The graph in Figure 23 shows that this line is vertical. All points on a vertical line have the same x-value, so ***all vertical lines have undefined slope.***

Figure 23

Slopes of Horizontal and Vertical Lines

Horizontal lines, which have equations of the form $y = k$, have **slope 0.**

Vertical lines, which have equations of the form $x = k$, have **undefined slope.**

> **Work Problem 4 at the Side.** ⟩⟩⟩

OBJECTIVE **2** **Find the slope from the equation of a line.** The slope of a line can be found directly from its equation. For example, the slope of the line

$$y = -3x + 5$$

can be found using any two points on the line. We get these two points by first choosing two different values of x and then finding the corresponding values of y. Choose $x = -2$ and $x = 4$.

$$y = -3x + 5 \qquad\qquad y = -3x + 5$$
$$y = -3(-2) + 5 \quad \text{Let } x = -2. \qquad y = -3(4) + 5 \quad \text{Let } x = 4.$$
$$y = 6 + 5 \qquad\qquad\qquad\qquad y = -12 + 5$$
$$y = 11 \qquad\qquad\qquad\qquad\qquad y = -7$$

The ordered pairs are $(-2, 11)$ and $(4, -7)$. Now use the slope formula.

$$m = \frac{11 - (-7)}{-2 - 4} = \frac{18}{-6} = -3$$

The slope, -3, is the same number as the coefficient of x in the equation $y = -3x + 5$. It can be shown that this always happens, *as long as the equation is solved for y*. This fact is used to find the slope of a line from its equation.

Finding the Slope of a Line from Its Equation

Step 1 Solve the equation for y.

Step 2 The slope is given by the coefficient of x.

NOTE

We will see in the next section that the equation $y = -3x + 5$ is written using a special form of the equation of a line,

$$y = mx + b,$$

called *slope-intercept form.*

---

4 Find the slope of each line.

(a) Through $(2, 5)$ and $(-1, 5)$

(b) Through $(3, 1)$ and $(3, -4)$

(c) With equation $y = -1$

(d) With equation $x - 4 = 0$

⑤ Find the slope of each line.

(a) $y = -\dfrac{7}{2}x + 1$

(b) $3x + 2y = 9$

(c) $y + 4 = 0$

(d) $x + 3 = 7$

EXAMPLE 5 Finding Slopes from Equations

Find the slope of each line.

(a) $2x - 5y = 4$

Step 1 Solve the equation for y.

$$2x - 5y = 4$$
$$-5y = -2x + 4 \qquad \text{Subtract } 2x.$$
$$y = \frac{2}{5}x - \frac{4}{5} \qquad \text{Divide by } -5.$$

Step 2 The slope is given by the coefficient of x, so the slope is $\frac{2}{5}$.

(b) $8x + 4y = 1$
  Solve for y.

$$8x + 4y = 1$$
$$4y = -8x + 1 \qquad \text{Subtract } 8x.$$
$$y = -2x + \frac{1}{4} \qquad \text{Divide by } 4.$$

The slope of this line is given by the coefficient of x, which is -2.

◀◀◀ Work Problem 5 at the Side.

OBJECTIVE ③ Use slope to determine whether two lines are parallel, perpendicular, or neither. Two lines in a plane that never intersect are **parallel.** We use slopes to tell whether two lines are parallel. For example, Figure 24 shows the graphs of $x + 2y = 4$ and $x + 2y = -6$. These lines appear to be parallel. Solving for y, we find that both $x + 2y = 4$ and $x + 2y = -6$ have slope $-\frac{1}{2}$. *Nonvertical parallel lines always have equal slopes.*

Figure 24

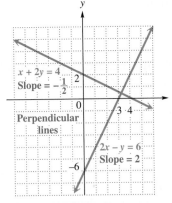

Figure 25

Figure 25 shows the graphs of $x + 2y = 4$ and $2x - y = 6$. These lines appear to be **perpendicular** (that is, they intersect at a 90° angle). Solving for y shows that the slope of $x + 2y = 4$ is $-\frac{1}{2}$, while the slope of $2x - y = 6$ is 2. The product of $-\frac{1}{2}$ and 2 is

$$-\frac{1}{2}(2) = -1.$$

This is true in general; *the product of the slopes of two perpendicular lines (neither of which is vertical) is always -1.*

ANSWERS

5. **(a)** $-\dfrac{7}{2}$ **(b)** $-\dfrac{3}{2}$ **(c)** 0 **(d)** undefined

Slopes of Parallel and Perpendicular Lines

Two lines with the same slope are parallel.

Two lines whose slopes have a product of -1 are perpendicular.

EXAMPLE 6 Deciding Whether Lines Are Parallel, Perpendicular, or Neither

Decide whether each pair of lines is *parallel, perpendicular,* or *neither.*

(a) $x + 2y = 7$

$-2x + y = 3$

Find the slope of each line by first solving each equation for y.

$$x + 2y = 7 \qquad\qquad -2x + y = 3$$
$$2y = -x + 7 \qquad\qquad y = 2x + 3$$
$$y = -\frac{1}{2}x + \frac{7}{2}$$

Slope is $-\frac{1}{2}$. $\qquad\qquad$ Slope is 2.

Because the slopes are not equal, the lines are not parallel. Check the product of the slopes: $-\frac{1}{2}(2) = -1$. The two lines are perpendicular because the product of their slopes is -1. See Figure 26.

Figure 26

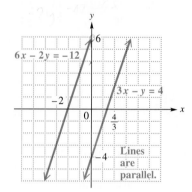

Figure 27

(b) $3x - y = 4$ $\qquad$ Solve for y. $\qquad$ $y = 3x - 4$

$6x - 2y = -12$ $\xrightarrow{\qquad}$ $y = 3x + 6$

Both lines have slope 3, so the lines are parallel. See Figure 27.

(c) $4x + 3y = 6$ $\qquad\qquad\qquad\; y = -\frac{4}{3}x + 2$

$\qquad\qquad\qquad$ Solve for y.

$2x - y = 5$ $\qquad\qquad\qquad\quad y = 2x - 5$

Here the slopes are $-\frac{4}{3}$ and 2. Because $-\frac{4}{3} \neq 2$ and $-\frac{4}{3}(2) \neq -1$, these lines are neither parallel nor perpendicular.

(d) $5x - y = 1$ $\qquad\qquad\qquad\; y = 5x - 1$

$\qquad\qquad\qquad$ Solve for y.

$x - 5y = -10$ $\xrightarrow{\qquad}$ $y = \frac{1}{5}x + 2$

The slopes are 5 and $\frac{1}{5}$. The lines are not parallel, nor are they perpendicular. *(Be careful! $5\left(\frac{1}{5}\right) = 1$, not -1.)*

Work Problem 6 at the Side.

6 Decide whether each pair of lines is *parallel, perpendicular,* or *neither.*

(a) $x + y = 6$

$x + y = 1$

(b) $3x - y = 4$

$x + 3y = 9$

(c) $2x - y = 5$

$2x + y = 3$

(d) $3x - 7y = 35$

$7x - 3y = -6$

ANSWERS

6. (a) parallel **(b)** perpendicular
(c) neither **(d)** neither

Real-Data Applications

Linear or Nonlinear? That Is the Question about Windchill

The **windchill factor** measures the cooling effect that the wind has on one's skin. The table gives the windchill factor for various wind speeds and temperatures.

WINDCHILL FACTOR

		Air Temperature (°Fahrenheit)													
		35	30	25	20	15	10	5	0	−5	−10	−15	−20	−25	−30	−35
Wind Speed (mph)	4	35	30	25	20	15	10	5	0	−5	−10	−15	−20	−25	−30	−35
	5	32	27	22	16	11	6	0	−5	−10	−15	−21	−26	−31	−36	−42
	10	22	16	10	3	−3	−9	−15	−22	−27	−34	−40	−46	−52	−58	−64
	15	16	9	2	−5	−11	−18	−25	−31	−38	−45	−51	−58	−65	−72	−78
	20	12	4	−3	−10	−17	−24	−31	−39	−46	−53	−60	−67	−74	−81	−88
	25	8	1	−7	−15	−22	−29	−36	−44	−51	−59	−66	−74	−81	−88	−96
	30	6	−2	−10	−18	−25	−33	−41	−49	−56	−64	−71	−79	−86	−93	−101
	35	4	−4	−12	−20	−27	−35	−43	−52	−58	−67	−74	−82	−89	−97	−105
	40	3	−5	−13	−21	−29	−37	−45	−53	−60	−69	−76	−84	−92	−100	−107
	45	2	−6	−14	−22	−30	−38	−46	−54	−62	−70	−78	−85	−93	−102	−109

Source: USA Today.

The data in the table represents the relationships between two different sets of variable quantities: Windchill versus Air Temperature and Windchill versus Wind Speed. The question is whether either of these relationships is linear, that is, whether the data points, when graphed, could be connected to form a straight line.

Example 1 Windchill versus Air Temperature   Choose one measure of wind speed to keep constant, such as 15 mph. Complete the table with Air Temperature (AT) as the *input* and Windchill (WC) as the *output*. Both variables are measured in degrees Fahrenheit.

AT	35	30	25	20	15	10	5	0	−5	−10	−15			
WC	16	9	2	−5	−11	−18	−25	−31	−38					

Example 2 Windchill versus Wind Speed   Choose one measure of air temperature to keep constant, such as 10°F. Complete the table with Wind Speed (WS) as the *input* and Windchill (WC) as the *output*. Wind speed is measured in mph.

WS	4	5	10	15	20	25	30			
WC	10	6	−9	−18	−24					

For Group Discussion

1. Refer to the Windchill versus Air Temperature data (Example 1).
   (a) Write the data as ordered pairs.

   (b) On a sheet of graph paper, draw and label a rectangular coordinate system. Use a scale of 5 on the *x*-axis and the *y*-axis. Make a scatter diagram of the data. Does the graph represent a linear relationship?

2. Repeat Problem 1 using the Windchill versus Wind Speed data (Example 2).

3.3 Exercises

FOR EXTRA HELP   Addison-Wesley Math Tutor Center   *Math XL* MathXL   Digital Video Tutor CD 3 Videotape 3   Student's Solutions Manual   *MyMathLab* MyMathLab   Interactmath.com

Use the coordinates of the indicated points to find the slope of each line. See Example 1.

1.

2.

3.

4.

5.

6.
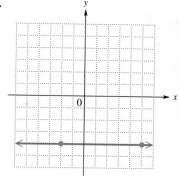

7. In the context of the graph of a straight line, what is meant by "rise"? What is meant by "run"?

8. Look at the graph in Exercise 1, and answer the following.

(a) Start at the point $(-1, -4)$ and count vertically up to the horizontal line that goes through the other plotted point. What is this vertical change? (Remember: "up" means positive, "down" means negative.) _____

(b) From this new position, count horizontally to the other plotted point. What is this horizontal change? (Remember: "right" means positive, "left" means negative.) _____

(c) What is the quotient of the numbers found in parts (a) and (b)? _____
What do we call this number? _____

9. Refer to Exercise 8. If we were to *start* at the point (3, 2) and *end* at the point (−1, −4), would the answer to part (c) be the same? Explain why or why not.

On the given coordinate system, sketch the graph of a straight line with the indicated slope.

10. Negative

11. Positive

12. Undefined

13. Zero

14. Explain in your own words what is meant by the *slope* of a line.

15. A student found the slope of the line through the points (2, 5) and (−1, 3) and got $-\frac{2}{3}$ as his answer. He showed his work as

$$\frac{3-5}{2-(-1)} = \frac{-2}{3} = -\frac{2}{3}.$$

Is he correct? If not, find his error and give the correct slope.

Find the slope of the line through each pair of points. See Examples 1–4.

16. (4, −1) and (−2, −8)   **17.** (1, −2) and (−3, −7)   **18.** (−8, 0) and (0, −5)

19. (0, 3) and (−2, 0)   **20.** (−4, −5) and (−5, −8)   **21.** (−2, 4) and (−3, 7)

22. (6, −5) and (−12, −5)   **23.** (4, 3) and (−6, 3)   **24.** (−8, 6) and (−8, −1)

25. (−12, 3) and (−12, −7)   **26.** (3.1, 2.6) and (1.6, 2.1)   **27.** $\left(-\frac{7}{5}, \frac{3}{10}\right)$ and $\left(\frac{1}{5}, -\frac{1}{2}\right)$

Find the slope of each line. See Example 5.

28. $y = 2x - 3$ **29.** $y = 5x + 12$ **30.** $2y = -x + 4$ **31.** $4y = x + 1$

32. $-6x + 4y = 4$ **33.** $3x - 2y = 3$ **34.** $y = 4$ **35.** $y = 6$

36. $x = 5$ **37.** $x = -2$ **38.** $x + y = 0$ **39.** $x - y = 0$

The figure at the right shows a line that has a positive slope (because it rises from left to right) and a positive y-value for the y-intercept (because it intersects the y-axis above the origin).

*For each figure in Exercises 40–45, decide whether **(a)** the slope is* positive, negative, *or* 0 *and whether **(b)** the y-value of the y-intercept is* positive, negative, *or* 0.

40. (a) _____   **41. (a)** _____   **42. (a)** _____
   (b) _____   **(b)** _____   **(b)** _____

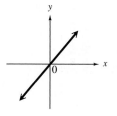

43. (a) _____   **44. (a)** _____   **45. (a)** _____
   (b) _____   **(b)** _____   **(b)** _____

In each pair of equations, give the slope of each line, and then determine whether the two lines are parallel, perpendicular, *or* neither parallel nor perpendicular. *See Example 6.*

46. $2x + 5y = 4$ **47.** $-4x + 3y = 4$ **48.** $8x - 9y = 6$
   $4x + 10y = 1$ $-8x + 6y = 0$ $8x + 6y = -5$

49. $5x - 3y = -2$ **50.** $3x - 2y = 6$ **51.** $3x - 5y = -1$
   $3x - 5y = -8$ $2x + 3y = 3$ $5x + 3y = 2$

52. What is the slope (or pitch) of this roof?

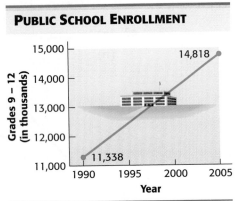

6 ft

20 ft

53. What is the slope (or grade) of this hill?

32 m

108 m

RELATING CONCEPTS (EXERCISES 54–59) For Individual or Group Work

Figure A gives public school enrollment (in thousands) in grades 9–12 in the United States. Figure B gives the (average) number of public school students per computer.

PUBLIC SCHOOL ENROLLMENT

14,818

11,338

Grades 9 – 12 (in thousands)

15,000
14,000
13,000
12,000
11,000

1990   1995   2000   2005

Year

Source: Digest of Educational Statistics, annual, and *Projections of Educational Statistics,* annual.

Figure A

STUDENTS PER COMPUTER

22

5.4

Number of Students per Computer

25
20
15
10
5
0

1990 1992 1994 1996 1998 2000

Year

Source: Quality Education Data.

Figure B

Work Exercises 54–59 in order.

54. Use the ordered pairs (1990, 11,338) and (2005, 14,818) to find the slope of the line in Figure A.

55. The slope of the line in Figure A is _____. This means that during
(positive/negative)

the period represented, enrollment _____.
(increased/decreased)

56. The slope of a line represents its *rate of change*. Based on Figure A, what was the increase in students *per year* during the period shown?

57. Use the given information to find the slope of the line in Figure B.

58. The slope of the line in Figure B is _____. This means that during
(positive/negative)

the period represented, the number of students per computer _____.
(increased/decreased)

59. Based on Figure B, what was the decrease in students per computer *per year* during the period shown?

3.4 Equations of Lines

In **Section 3.3,** we found the slope (steepness) of a line from the equation of the line by solving the equation for y. In that form, the slope is the coefficient of x. For example, the slope of the line with equation $y = 2x + 3$ is 2, the coefficient of x. What does the number 3 represent? If $x = 0$, the equation becomes

$$y = 2(0) + 3 = 0 + 3 = 3.$$

Since $y = 3$ corresponds to $x = 0$, $(0, 3)$ is the y-intercept of the graph of $y = 2x + 3$. An equation like $y = 2x + 3$ that is solved for y is said to be in **slope-intercept form** because both the slope and the y-intercept of the line can be read directly from the equation.

Slope-Intercept Form

The slope-intercept form of the equation of a line with slope m and y-intercept $(0, b)$ is

$$y = mx + b.$$

Slope _____↑   ↑_____ $(0, b)$ is the
                          y-intercept.

Remember that the intercept in the slope-intercept form is the y-intercept.

> **NOTE**
> The slope-intercept form is the most useful form for a linear equation because of the information we can determine from it. It is also the form used by graphing calculators and the one that describes a *linear function*, an important concept in mathematics.

OBJECTIVE 1 Write an equation of a line given its slope and *y*-intercept. Given the slope and y-intercept of a line, we can use the slope-intercept form to find an equation of the line.

EXAMPLE 1 Finding an Equation of a Line

Find an equation of the line with slope $\frac{2}{3}$ and y-intercept $(0, -1)$.
Here $m = \frac{2}{3}$ and $b = -1$, so an equation is

Slope _____↓   ↓_____ y-intercept

$$y = mx + b$$

$$y = \frac{2}{3}x - 1.$$

Work Problem 1 at the Side. ▶▶▶

OBJECTIVE 2 Graph a line given its slope and a point on the line. We can use the slope and y-intercept to graph any line. If a linear equation is given in standard form $Ax + By = C$, it can be graphed using the following procedure.

OBJECTIVES

1 Write an equation of a line given its slope and y-intercept.

2 Graph a line given its slope and a point on the line.

3 Write an equation of a line given its slope and any point on the line.

4 Write an equation of a line given two points on the line.

5 Find an equation of a line that fits a data set.

1 Find an equation of the line with the given slope and y-intercept.

(a) slope $\frac{1}{2}$; y-intercept $(0, -4)$

(b) slope -1; y-intercept $(0, 8)$

(c) slope 3; y-intercept $(0, 0)$

(d) slope 0; y-intercept $(0, 2)$

ANSWERS

1. (a) $y = \frac{1}{2}x - 4$ **(b)** $y = -x + 8$

  (c) $y = 3x$ **(d)** $y = 2$

2 Graph $3x - 4y = 8$ using the slope and y-intercept.

Graphing Using Slope and y-Intercept

Step 1 Solve for y to obtain the $y = mx + b$ form of the equation.

Step 2 Identify the y-intercept from the form just obtained. Graph the point $(0, b)$.

Step 3 The slope of the line is m. Use the geometric interpretation of slope ("rise over run") to find another point on the graph by counting from the y-intercept.

Step 4 Join the two points with a line to obtain the graph of the equation.

EXAMPLE 2 **Graphing a Line Using Slope and y-Intercept**

Graph $2x - 3y = 3$.

Step 1 Begin by solving for y.

$$2x - 3y = 3 \qquad \text{Given equation}$$
$$-3y = -2x + 3 \qquad \text{Subtract } 2x.$$
$$y = \frac{2}{3}x - 1 \qquad \text{Divide by } -3.$$

Step 2 The y-intercept is $(0, -1)$. Graph this point. See Figure 28.

Step 3 The slope is $\frac{2}{3}$. By the definition of slope,

$$m = \frac{\text{change in } y}{\text{change in } x} = \frac{2}{3}.$$

Counting from the y-intercept 2 units up and 3 units to the right, we obtain another point on the graph, $(3, 1)$.

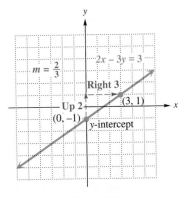

Figure 28

Step 4 Draw the line through the points $(0, -1)$ and $(3, 1)$ to obtain the graph of $2x - 3y = 3$. See Figure 28.

◀◀◀ **Work Problem 2 at the Side.**

The method of Example 2 can be extended to graph a line given its slope and *any* point on the line.

EXAMPLE 3 **Graphing a Line Given a Point and the Slope**

Graph the line through $(-2, 3)$ with slope -4.

First, locate the point $(-2, 3)$. See Figure 29. Write the slope -4 as

$$m = \frac{\text{change in } y}{\text{change in } x} = \frac{-4}{1}.$$

Continued on Next Page

Locate another point on the line by counting 4 units down (because of the negative sign) from $(-2, 3)$ and then 1 unit to the right. Finally, draw the line through this new point P and the given point $(-2, 3)$. See Figure 29.

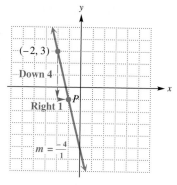

Figure 29

③ Graph the line passing through $(2, -3)$, with slope $-\frac{1}{3}$.

NOTE

In Example 3, we could have written the slope as $\frac{4}{-1}$ instead. In this case, we would move 4 units up from $(-2, 3)$ and then 1 unit to the left (because of the negative sign). Verify that this produces the same line.

Work Problem 3 at the Side. ▷▷▷

OBJECTIVE 3 **Write an equation of a line given its slope and any point on the line.** Let m represent the slope of a line and (x_1, y_1) represent a given point on the line. Let (x, y) represent any other point on the line. Then by the slope formula,

$$\frac{y - y_1}{x - x_1} = m$$

$$y - y_1 = m(x - x_1). \qquad \text{Multiply by } x - x_1.$$

This result is the **point-slope form** of the equation of a line.

Point-Slope Form

The point-slope form of the equation of a line with slope m going through (x_1, y_1) is

$$y - y_1 = m(x - x_1).$$

EXAMPLE 4 **Using the Point-Slope Form to Write Equations**

Find an equation of each line. Write the equation in slope-intercept form.

(a) Through $(-2, 4)$, with slope -3

The given point is $(-2, 4)$ so $x_1 = -2$ and $y_1 = 4$. Also, $m = -3$. Substitute these values into the point-slope form.

$$y - y_1 = m(x - x_1) \qquad \text{Point-slope form}$$

$$y - 4 = -3\left[x - (-2)\right] \qquad \text{Let } x_1 = -2, y_1 = 4, m = -3.$$

$$y - 4 = -3(x + 2)$$

$$y - 4 = -3x - 6 \qquad \text{Distributive property}$$

$$y = -3x - 2 \qquad \text{Add 4.}$$

Continued on Next Page

ANSWERS
3.

4 Find an equation for each line. Write answers in slope-intercept form.

(a) Through $(-1, 3)$, with slope -2

$$y - y_1 = m(x - x_1)$$

$$y - \underline{\quad} = \underline{\quad}[x - (\quad)]$$

$$y - 3 = -2(x + \underline{\quad})$$

$$y - 3 = -2x - \underline{\quad}$$

$$y = \underline{\quad}$$

(b) Through $(5, 2)$, with slope $-\frac{1}{3}$

5 Write an equation in slope-intercept form for the line through each pair of points.

(a) $(-3, 1)$ and $(2, 4)$

(b) $(2, 5)$ and $(-1, 6)$

(b) Through $(4, 2)$, with slope $\frac{3}{5}$

$$y - y_1 = m(x - x_1) \qquad \text{Point-slope form}$$

$$y - 2 = \frac{3}{5}(x - 4) \qquad \text{Let } x_1 = 4, y_1 = 2, m = \frac{3}{5}.$$

$$y - 2 = \frac{3}{5}x - \frac{12}{5} \qquad \text{Distributive property}$$

$$y = \frac{3}{5}x - \frac{12}{5} + \frac{10}{5} \qquad \text{Add } 2 = \frac{10}{5}.$$

$$y = \frac{3}{5}x - \frac{2}{5} \qquad \text{Combine terms.}$$

We did not clear fractions after the substitution step because we want the equation in slope-intercept form—that is, solved for y.

◀◀◀ Work Problem 4 at the Side.

OBJECTIVE **4** **Write an equation of a line given two points on the line.** We can also use the point-slope form to find an equation of a line when two points on the line are known.

EXAMPLE 5 **Finding the Equation of a Line Given Two Points**

Find an equation of the line through the points $(-2, 5)$ and $(3, 4)$. Write the equation in slope-intercept form.

First, find the slope of the line, using the slope formula.

$$\text{slope } m = \frac{y_2 - y_1}{x_2 - x_1} = \frac{5 - 4}{-2 - 3} = \frac{1}{-5} = -\frac{1}{5}$$

Now use either $(-2, 5)$ or $(3, 4)$ and the point-slope form. Using $(3, 4)$ gives

$$y - y_1 = m(x - x_1)$$

$$y - 4 = -\frac{1}{5}(x - 3) \qquad \text{Let } x_1 = 3, y_1 = 4, m = -\frac{1}{5}.$$

$$y - 4 = -\frac{1}{5}x + \frac{3}{5} \qquad \text{Distributive property}$$

$$y = -\frac{1}{5}x + \frac{3}{5} + \frac{20}{5} \qquad \text{Add } 4 = \frac{20}{5}.$$

$$y = -\frac{1}{5}x + \frac{23}{5}. \qquad \text{Combine terms.}$$

The same result would be found using $(-2, 5)$ for (x_1, y_1).

◀◀◀ Work Problem 5 at the Side.

Many of the linear equations in **Sections 3.1–3.3** were given in the form $Ax + By = C$, called **standard form,** which we define as follows.

Standard Form

A linear equation is in standard form if it is written as

$$Ax + By = C,$$

where A, B, and C are integers and $A > 0$, $B \neq 0$.

ANSWERS

4. **(a)** $3; -2; -1; 1; 2; -2x + 1$
   (b) $y = -\frac{1}{3}x + \frac{11}{3}$

5. **(a)** $y = \frac{3}{5}x + \frac{14}{5}$ **(b)** $y = -\frac{1}{3}x + \frac{17}{3}$

> **NOTE**
> The preceding definition of standard form is not the same in all texts.
> A linear equation can be written in this form in many different, equally
> correct, ways. For example,
>
> $$3x + 4y = 12, \quad 6x + 8y = 24, \quad \text{and} \quad 9x + 12y = 36$$
>
> all represent the same set of ordered pairs. Let us agree that
> $3x + 4y = 12$ is preferable to the other forms because the greatest
> common factor of 3, 4, and 12 is 1.

A summary of the types of linear equations follows.

Linear Equations

$x = k$

    Vertical line
    Slope is undefined; x-intercept is $(k, 0)$.

$y = k$

    Horizontal line
    Slope is 0; y-intercept is $(0, k)$.

$y = mx + b$

    Slope-intercept form
    Slope is m; y-intercept is $(0, b)$.

$y - y_1 = m(x - x_1)$

    Point-slope form
    Slope is m; line passes through (x_1, y_1).

$Ax + By = C$

    Standard form
    Slope is $-\frac{A}{B}$; x-intercept is $\left(\frac{C}{A}, 0\right)$; y-intercept
    is $\left(0, \frac{C}{B}\right)$.

OBJECTIVE 5 Find an equation of a line that fits a data set. Earlier
in this chapter, we gave linear equations that modeled real data, such as
annual costs of doctors' visits and amounts of credit card debt, and then used
these equations to estimate or predict values. We now develop a procedure
to find such an equation if the given set of data fits a linear pattern—that is,
its graph consists of points lying close to a straight line.

EXAMPLE 6 Finding an Equation of a Line That Describes Data

The table lists the average annual cost (in dollars) of tuition and fees at
public 4-year colleges and universities for selected years. Year 1 represents
1994, year 3 represents 1996, and so on. Plot the data and find an equation
that approximates it.

Year	Cost (in dollars)
1	2537
3	2849
5	3110
7	3349
9	3746

Source: U.S. Department of
Education.

Letting y represent the cost in year x, we plot the data as shown in
Figure 30 on the next page.

Continued on Next Page

6 Use the points (1, 2537) and (9, 3746) to find an equation in slope-intercept form that approximates the data of Example 6. How well does this equation approximate the cost in 1998?

AVERAGE ANNUAL COSTS AT PUBLIC 4-YEAR COLLEGES AND UNIVERSITIES

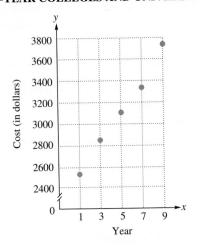

Figure 30

The points appear to lie approximately in a straight line. We can use two of the data pairs and the point-slope form of the equation of a line to get an equation that describes the relationship between the year and the cost. We choose the ordered pairs (3, 2849) and (7, 3349) from the table on the preceding page and find the slope of the line through these points.

$$m = \frac{y_2 - y_1}{x_2 - x_1} = \frac{3349 - 2849}{7 - 3} = 125 \qquad \begin{array}{l}\text{Let } (7, 3349) = (x_2, y_2) \\ \text{and } (3, 2849) = (x_1, y_1).\end{array}$$

As we might expect, the slope, 125, is positive, indicating that tuition and fees increased $125 each year. Now use this slope and the point (3, 2849) in the point-slope form to find an equation of the line.

$$y - y_1 = m(x - x_1) \qquad \text{Point-slope form}$$

$$y - 2849 = 125(x - 3) \qquad \text{Substitute for } x_1, y_1, \text{ and } m.$$

$$y - 2849 = 125x - 375 \qquad \text{Distributive property}$$

$$y = 125x + 2474 \qquad \text{Add 2849.}$$

To see how well this equation approximates the ordered pairs in the data table, let $x = 9$ (for 2002) and find y.

$$y = 125x + 2474 \qquad \text{Equation of the line}$$

$$y = 125(9) + 2474 \qquad \text{Substitute 9 for } x.$$

$$y = 3599$$

The corresponding value in the table for $x = 9$ is 3746, so the equation gives a value that is a bit lower than the actual value. With caution, the equation could be used to predict values for years between 1 and 9 that are not included in the table.

> **NOTE**
> In Example 6, if we had chosen two different data points, we would have gotten a slightly different equation.

ANSWERS
6. $y = 151.125x + 2385.875$;
The equation gives $y \approx 3142$
when $x = 5$, which is a very good
approximation.

◀◀◀ Work Problem 6 at the Side.

3.4 **Exercises**

FOR EXTRA HELP

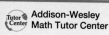 Addison-Wesley Math Tutor Center

Math **XL** MathXL

Digital Video Tutor CD 3 Videotape 3

Student's Solutions Manual

MyMathLab MyMathLab

Interactmath.com

Match the correct equation in Column II with the description given in Column I.

I	II

I

1. Slope $= -2$, through the point $(4, 1)$

2. Slope $= -2$, y-intercept $(0, 1)$

3. Through the points $(0, 0)$ and $(4, 1)$

4. Through the points $(0, 0)$ and $(1, 4)$

II

A. $y = 4x$

B. $y = \dfrac{1}{4}x$

C. $y = -2x + 1$

D. $y - 1 = -2(x - 4)$

*Use the geometric interpretation of slope (rise divided by run, from **Section 3.3**) to find the slope of each line. Then, by identifying the y-intercept from the graph, write the slope-intercept form of the equation of the line.*

5.

6.

7.

8.

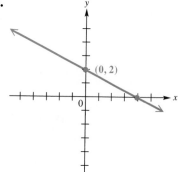

Write the equation of the line with the given slope and y-intercept. See Example 1.

9. slope 4;
    y-intercept $(0, -3)$

10. slope -5;
    y-intercept $(0, 6)$

11. slope 0;
    y-intercept $(0, 3)$

12. slope 3;
    y-intercept $(0, 0)$

13. Explain why the equation of a vertical line cannot be written in the form $y = mx + b$.

14. Match each equation with the graph that would most closely resemble its graph.

    (a) $y = x + 3$

    (b) $y = -x + 3$

    (c) $y = x - 3$

    (d) $y = -x - 3$

A.

B.

C.

D.

Graph each equation by finding the slope and y-intercept, and using their definitions to find two points on the line. See Example 2.

15. $y = 3x + 2$

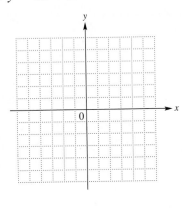

16. $y = 4x - 4$

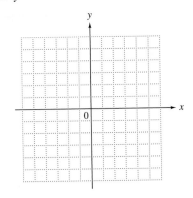

17. $2x + y = -5$

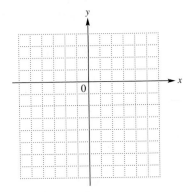

18. $3x + y = -2$

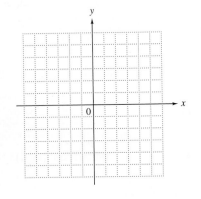

19. $x + 2y = 4$

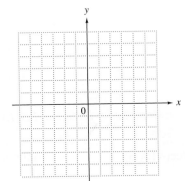

20. $x + 3y = 12$

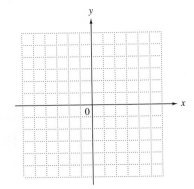

Graph the line through the given point with the given slope. (In Exercises 25–28, recall the types of lines having slope 0 and undefined slope.) Give the slope-intercept form of the equation of the line if possible. See Example 3.

21. $(-2, 3), m = \dfrac{1}{2}$

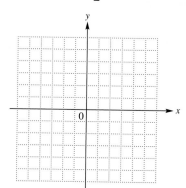

22. $(-4, -1), m = \dfrac{3}{4}$

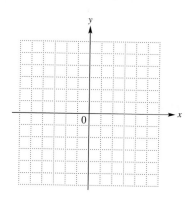

23. $(1, -5), m = -\dfrac{2}{5}$

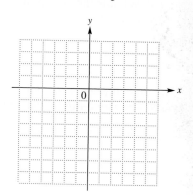

24. $(2, -1), m = -\dfrac{1}{3}$

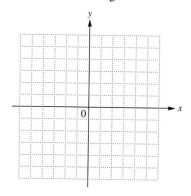

25. $(3, 2), m = 0$

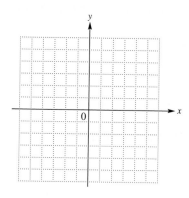

26. $(-2, 3), m = 0$

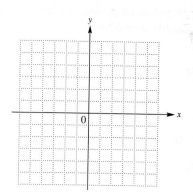

27. $(3, -2)$, undefined slope

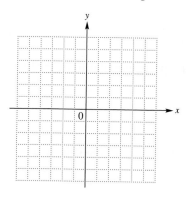

28. $(2, 4)$, undefined slope

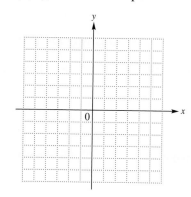

29. $(0, 0), m = \dfrac{2}{3}$

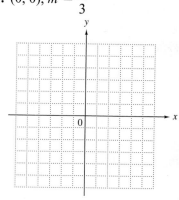

30. (a) What is the common name given to the vertical line whose x-intercept is the origin?

(b) What is the common name given to the line with slope 0 whose y-intercept is the origin?

Write an equation of the line through the given point with the given slope. Write the equation in slope-intercept form. See Example 4.

31. $(4, 1), m = 2$

32. $(2, 7), m = 3$

33. $(3, -10), m = -2$

34. $(2, -5), m = -4$

35. $(-2, 5), m = \dfrac{2}{3}$

36. $(-4, 1), m = \dfrac{3}{4}$

Write an equation, in slope-intercept form if possible, of the line through each pair of points. See Example 5.

37. $(8, 5)$ and $(9, 6)$

38. $(4, 10)$ and $(6, 12)$

39. $(-1, -7)$ and $(-8, -2)$

40. $(-2, -1)$ and $(3, -4)$

41. $(0, -2)$ and $(-3, 0)$

42. $(-4, 0)$ and $(0, 2)$

43. $(3, 5)$ and $(3, -2)$

44. $(3, -5)$ and $(-1, -5)$

45. $\left(\dfrac{1}{2}, \dfrac{3}{2}\right)$ and $\left(-\dfrac{1}{4}, \dfrac{5}{4}\right)$

46. $\left(-\dfrac{2}{3}, \dfrac{8}{3}\right)$ and $\left(\dfrac{1}{3}, \dfrac{7}{3}\right)$

Write an equation in slope-intercept form of the line satisfying the given conditions.

47. Through $(2, -3)$, parallel to $3x = 4y + 5$

48. Through $(-1, 4)$, perpendicular to $2x + 3y = 8$

49. Perpendicular to $x - 2y = 7$, y-intercept $(0, -3)$

50. Parallel to $5x = 2y + 10$, y-intercept $(0, 4)$

RELATING CONCEPTS (EXERCISES 51–58) For Individual or Group Work

If we think of ordered pairs of the form (C, F), then the two most common methods of measuring temperature, Celsius and Fahrenheit, can be related as follows: When C = 0, F = 32, and when C = 100, F = 212. **Work Exercises 51–58 in order.**

51. Write two ordered pairs relating these two temperature scales.

52. Find the slope of the line through the two points.

53. Use the point-slope form to find an equation of the line. (Your variables should be C and F rather than x and y.)

54. Write an equation for F in terms of C.

55. Use the equation from Exercise 54 to write an equation for C in terms of F.

56. Use the equation from Exercise 54 to find the Fahrenheit temperature when $C = 30$.

57. Use the equation from Exercise 55 to find the Celsius temperature when $F = 50$.

58. For what temperature is $F = C$?

*The cost to produce x items is, in some cases, expressed as y = mx + b. The number b gives the **fixed cost** (the cost that is the same no matter how many items are produced), and the number m is the **variable cost** (the cost to produce an additional item). Use this information to work Exercises 59 and 60.*

59. It costs $400 to start up a business of selling snow cones. Each snow cone costs $.25 to produce.

(a) What is the fixed cost?

(b) What is the variable cost?

(c) Write the cost equation.

(d) What will be the cost to produce 100 snow cones, based on the cost equation?

(e) How many snow cones will be produced if total cost is $775?

60. It costs $2000 to purchase a copier, and each copy costs $.02 to make.

(a) What is the fixed cost?

(b) What is the variable cost?

(c) Write the cost equation.

(d) What will be the cost to produce 10,000 copies, based on the cost equation?

(e) How many copies will be produced if total cost is $2600?

Solve each problem. See Example 6.

61. The table lists the average annual cost (in dollars) of tuition and fees at 2-year colleges for selected years, where year 1 represents 1994, year 3 represents 1996, and so on.

Year	Cost (in dollars)
1	1125
3	1239
5	1314
7	1338
9	1379

Source: U.S. Department of Education.

(a) Write five ordered pairs for the data.

(b) Plot the ordered pairs. Do the points lie approximately in a straight line?

AVERAGE ANNUAL COSTS AT 2-YEAR COLLEGES

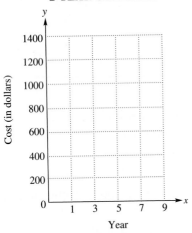

(c) Use the ordered pairs (3, 1239) and (9, 1379) to find the equation of a line that approximates the data. Write the equation in slope-intercept form. (Round the slope to the nearest hundredth and the *y*-intercept to the nearest whole number.)

(d) Use the equation from part (c) to predict the average annual cost at 2-year colleges in 2004 to the nearest dollar.

62. The table gives heavy-metal nuclear waste (in thousands of metric tons) from spent reactor fuel now stored temporarily at reactor sites, awaiting permanent storage. (*Source:* "Burial of Radioactive Nuclear Waste Under the Seabed," *Scientific American*, January 1998.)

Year x	Waste y
1995	32
2000*	42
2010*	61
2020*	76

*Estimates by the U.S. Department of Energy.

Let $x = 0$ represent 1995, $x = 5$ represent 2000 (since $2000 - 1995 = 5$), and so on.

(a) For 1995, the ordered pair is (0, 32). Write ordered pairs for the data for the other years given in the table.

(b) Plot the ordered pairs (*x, y*). Do the points lie approximately in a straight line?

HEAVY-METAL NUCLEAR WASTE AWAITING STORAGE

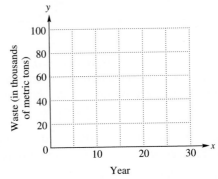

(c) Use the ordered pairs (0, 32) and (25, 76) to find the equation of a line that approximates the other ordered pairs. Write the equation in slope-intercept form.

(d) Use the equation from part (c) to estimate the amount of nuclear waste in 2005. (*Hint:* What is the value of *x* for 2005?)

Summary Exercises on Graphing Linear Equations

Identify the slope and the y-intercept of the graph of each equation.

1. $3x + y = -6$

2. $2x + y = -4$

3. $-4x - y = 3$

4. $-5x - y = 8$

5. $-3x + 2y = 12$

6. $-5x + 3y = 15$

Graph each equation using its slope and y-intercept.

7. $m = 1, b = -2$

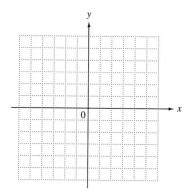

8. $m = 1, b = -4$

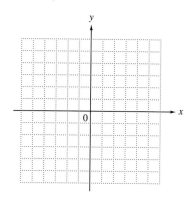

9. $m = -2, b = 6$

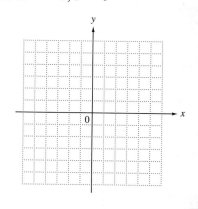

10. $m = -1, b = 6$

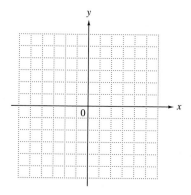

11. $m = -\dfrac{2}{3}, b = -2$

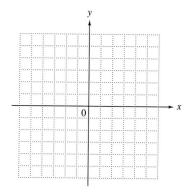

12. $m = -\dfrac{3}{4}, b = -1$

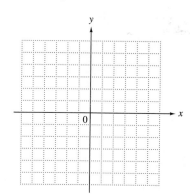

*For each equation **(a)** find the slope, **(b)** find the y-intercept, and **(c)** sketch the graph. Label two points on the graph.*

13. $-x + y = -3$

14. $-x + y = -5$

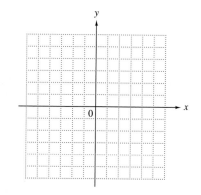

15. $x + 2y = 4$

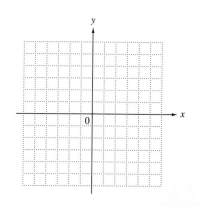

16. $x + 3y = -6$

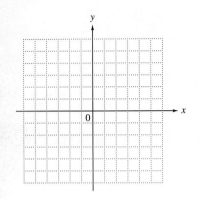

17. $4x - 5y = 20$

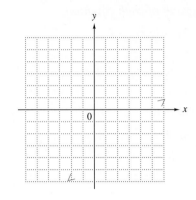

18. $6x - 5y = 30$

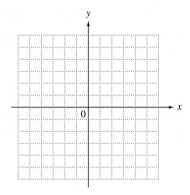

19. $2x + 3y = 12$

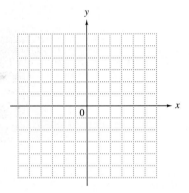

20. $5x + 2y = 10$

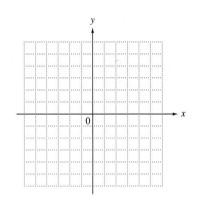

21. $x - 3y = 6$

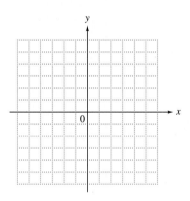

22. $x - 2y = -4$

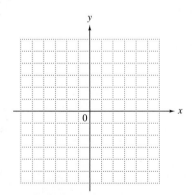

23. $x - 4y = 0$

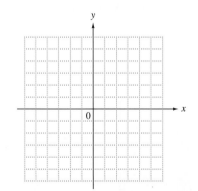

24. $x + 5y = 0$

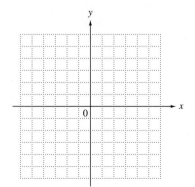

3.5 Graphing Linear Inequalities in Two Variables

In **Section 3.2** we graphed linear equations, such as $2x + 3y = 6$. Now this work is extended to **linear inequalities in two variables,** such as

$$2x + 3y \leq 6.$$

(Recall that $\leq$ is read "is less than or equal to.")

OBJECTIVE 1 Graph linear inequalities involving $\leq$ or $\geq$. The inequality $2x + 3y \leq 6$ means that

$$2x + 3y < 6 \quad \text{or} \quad 2x + 3y = 6.$$

As we found earlier, the graph of $2x + 3y = 6$ is a line. This **boundary line** divides the plane into two regions. The graph of the solutions of the inequality $2x + 3y < 6$ will include only *one* of these regions. We find the required region by solving the given inequality for y.

$$2x + 3y \leq 6$$
$$3y \leq -2x + 6 \qquad \text{Subtract } 2x.$$
$$y \leq -\frac{2}{3}x + 2 \qquad \text{Divide by 3.}$$

By this last statement, ordered pairs in which y is *less than or equal to* $-\frac{2}{3}x + 2$ will be solutions of the inequality. The ordered pairs in which y is equal to $-\frac{2}{3}x + 2$ are on the boundary line, so the ordered pairs in which y *is less than* $-\frac{2}{3}x + 2$ will be *below* that line. (This is because as we move *down* vertically, the y-values *decrease.*) To indicate the solutions, we shade the region below the line, as in Figure 31. The shaded region, along with the line, is the desired graph.

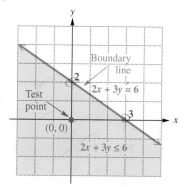

Figure 31

> **Work Problem 1 at the Side.** ▷▷▷

Alternatively, a test point gives a quick way to find the correct region to shade. We choose any point *not* on the boundary line. Because $(0, 0)$ is easy to substitute into an inequality, it is often a good choice, and we will use it here. We substitute 0 for x and 0 for y in the given inequality to see whether the resulting statement is true or false. In the example above,

$$2x + 3y \leq 6$$
$$2(0) + 3(0) \leq 6 \quad ? \qquad \text{Let } x = 0 \text{ and } y = 0.$$
$$0 + 0 \leq 6 \quad ?$$
$$0 \leq 6. \qquad \text{True}$$

Since the last statement is true, we shade the region that includes the test point $(0, 0)$. This agrees with the result shown in Figure 31.

---

1 Shade the appropriate region for each linear inequality.

(a) $x + 2y \geq 6$

(b) $3x + 4y \leq 12$

ANSWERS

1. (a)

$x + 2y \geq 6$

(b)

$3x + 4y \leq 12$

◀◀◀ **Work Problem 2 at the Side.**

② Use $(0, 0)$ as a test point to shade the proper region for the inequality $4x - 5y \leq 20$.

③ Use $(1, 1)$ as a test point to shade the proper region for the inequality $3x + 5y > 15$.

O B J E C T I V E **2** **Graph other linear inequalities.** An inequality that does not include the equals sign is graphed in a similar way.

EXAMPLE 1 **Graphing a Linear Inequality**

Graph the inequality $x - y > 5$.

This inequality does not include the equals sign. Therefore, the points on the line

$$x - y = 5$$

do *not* belong to the graph. However, the line still serves as a boundary for two regions, one of which satisfies the inequality. To graph the inequality, first graph the equation $x - y = 5$. Use a *dashed line* to show that the points on the line are *not* solutions of the inequality $x - y > 5$. Then choose a test point not on the line to see which side of the line satisfies the inequality. We choose $(1, -2)$ this time.

$$x - y > 5$$
$$1 - (-2) > 5 \quad ? \quad \text{Let } x = 1 \text{ and } y = -2.$$
$$3 > 5 \quad \text{False}$$

Because $3 > 5$ is false, the graph of the inequality is the region that does *not* contain $(1, -2)$. We shade the region that does not include the test point $(1, -2)$, as in Figure 32. This shaded region is the desired graph. To check that the proper region is shaded, we select a point in the shaded region and substitute for x and y in the inequality $x - y > 5$. For example, we use $(4, -3)$ from the shaded region as follows.

$$x - y > 5$$
$$4 - (-3) > 5 \quad ? \quad \text{Let } x = 4 \text{ and } y = -3.$$
$$7 > 5 \quad \text{True}$$

This verifies that the correct region is shaded in Figure 32.

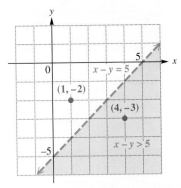

Figure 32

◀◀◀ **Work Problem 3 at the Side.**

ANSWERS

2.

$4x - 5y \leq 20$

3.

$3x + 5y > 15$

A summary of the steps used to graph a linear inequality in two variables follows.

Graphing a Linear Inequality

Step 1 **Graph the boundary.** Graph the line that is the boundary of the region. Use the methods of **Section 3.2.** Draw a solid line if the inequality has $\leq$ or $\geq$; draw a dashed line if the inequality has $<$ or $>$.

Step 2 **Shade the appropriate side.** Use any point not on the line as a test point. Substitute for x and y in the *inequality*. If a true statement results, shade the side containing the test point. If a false statement results, shade the other side.

4 Graph $2x - y \geq -4$.

EXAMPLE 2 **Graphing a Linear Inequality**

Graph the inequality $2x - 5y \geq 10$.

Start by graphing the equation

$$2x - 5y = 10.$$

Use a solid line to show that the points on the line are solutions of the inequality $2x - 5y \geq 10$. Choose any test point not on the line. Again, we choose $(0, 0)$.

$$2x - 5y \geq 10$$

$$2(0) - 5(0) \geq 10 \qquad ? \quad \text{Let } x = 0 \text{ and } y = 0.$$

$$0 - 0 \geq 10 \qquad ?$$

$$0 \geq 10 \qquad \text{False}$$

Because $0 \geq 10$ is false, shade the region *not* containing $(0, 0)$. See Figure 33. Verify that a point in the shaded region satisfies the inequality.

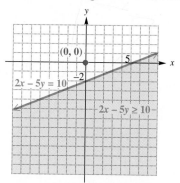

Figure 33

> **Work Problem 4 at the Side.** ▶▶▶

EXAMPLE 3 **Graphing a Linear Inequality with a Vertical Boundary Line**

Graph the inequality $x \leq 3$.

First graph $x = 3$, a vertical line through the point $(3, 0)$. Use a solid line. (Why?) Choose $(0, 0)$ as a test point.

$$x \leq 3$$

$$0 \leq 3 \qquad ? \quad \text{Let } x = 0.$$

$$0 \leq 3 \qquad \text{True}$$

Continued on Next Page

ANSWERS

4.

$2x - y \geq -4$

⑤ Graph $y < 4$.

Because $0 \le 3$ is true, shade the region containing $(0, 0)$, as in Figure 34.

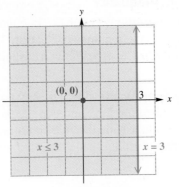

Figure 34

⟨⟨⟨ **Work Problem 5 at the Side.**

OBJECTIVE 3 Graph an inequality with boundary through the origin. If the graph of an inequality has a boundary line through the origin, $(0, 0)$ cannot be used as a test point.

⑥ Graph $x \ge -3y$.

EXAMPLE 4 Graphing a Linear Inequality

Graph the inequality $x \le 2y$.

We begin by graphing $x = 2y$, using a solid line. Some ordered pairs that can be used to graph this line are $(0, 0)$, $(6, 3)$, and $(4, 2)$. We cannot use $(0, 0)$ as a test point because $(0, 0)$ is on the line $x = 2y$. Instead, we choose a test point off the line, $(1, 3)$.

$$x \le 2y$$
$$1 \le 2(3) \qquad ? \quad \text{Let } x = 1 \text{ and } y = 3.$$
$$1 \le 6 \qquad \text{True}$$

Because $1 \le 6$ is true, we shade the side of the graph containing the test point $(1, 3)$. See Figure 35.

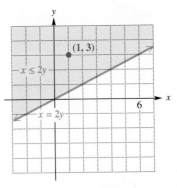

Figure 35

⟨⟨⟨ **Work Problem 6 at the Side.**

ANSWERS

5.

$y < 4$

6.

$x \ge -3y$

3.5 Exercises

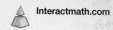

Decide whether each statement is true *or* false.

1. The point (4, 0) lies on the graph of $3x - 4y < 12$.

2. The point (4, 0) lies on the graph of $3x - 4y \leq 12$.

3. Both points (4, 1) and (0, 0) lie on the graph of $3x - 2y \geq 0$.

4. The graph of $y > x$ does not contain points in quadrant IV.

The following statements were taken from articles in newspapers or magazines. Each includes a phrase that can be symbolized with one of the inequality symbols $<$, $\leq$, $>$, or $\geq$. In Exercises 5–8, give the inequality symbol for the bold-faced words.

5. According to the Kaiser Family Foundation, in January 2001, (about) one-quarter of Medicare beneficiaries spent **more than** $2000 a year on drugs.

6. By 1937, a population of as many as a million Attwater's prairie-chickens had been cut to **less than** 9000. (*Source: National Geographic*, March 2002.)

7. In one study, 9 percent of pregnant women had active hepatitis, meaning that **at most** 9 percent of children could get it at birth. (*Source: 2000 Dow Jones & Company, Inc.*)

8. Forty percent of Americans keep **at least** one gun at home. (*Source:* Gallup Organization, quoted in *Reader's Digest*, March 2002.)

In Exercises 9–16, the straight-line boundary has been drawn. Complete each graph by shading the correct region. See Examples 1–4.

9. $x + y \geq 4$

10. $x + y \leq 2$

11. $x + 2y \geq 7$

12. $2x + y \geq 5$

13. $-3x + 4y > 12$

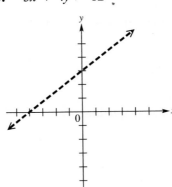

14. $4x - 5y < 20$

15. $x > 4$

16. $y < -1$

17. Explain how to determine whether to use a dashed line or a solid line when graphing a linear inequality in two variables.

18. Explain why the point $(0, 0)$ is not an appropriate choice for a test point when graphing an inequality whose boundary goes through the origin.

Graph each linear inequality. See Examples 1–4.

19. $x + y \leq 5$

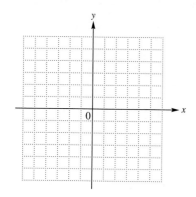

20. $x + y \geq 3$

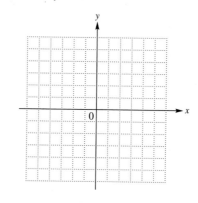

21. $x + 2y < 4$

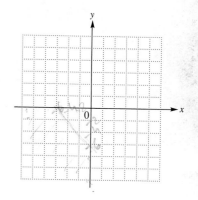

22. $x + 3y > 6$

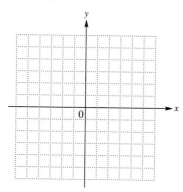

23. $2x + 6 > -3y$

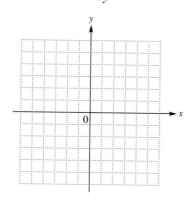

24. $-4y > 3x - 12$

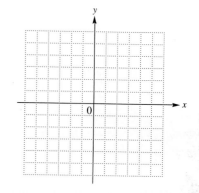

25. $y \geq 2x + 1$

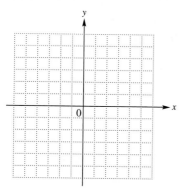

26. $y < -3x + 1$

27. $x \leq -2$

28. $x \geq 1$

29. $y < 5$

30. $y < -3$

31. $y \geq 4x$

32. $y \leq 2x$

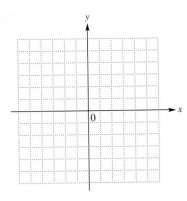

33. Explain why the graph of $y > x$ cannot lie in quadrant IV.

34. Explain why the graph of $y < x$ cannot lie in quadrant II.

Solve each problem. In part (a), $x \geq 0$ and $y \geq 0$, so graph only the part of the inequality in quadrant I.

35. A company will ship x units of merchandise to outlet I and y units of merchandise to outlet II. The company must ship a total of at least 500 units to these two outlets. This can be expressed by writing

$$x + y \geq 500.$$

(a) Graph the inequality.

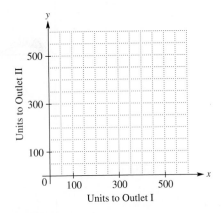

(b) Give two ordered pairs that satisfy the inequality.

36. A toy manufacturer makes stuffed bears and geese. It takes 20 min to sew a bear and 30 min to sew a goose. There is a total of 480 min of sewing time available to make x bears and y geese. These restrictions lead to the inequality

$$20x + 30y \leq 480.$$

(a) Graph the inequality.

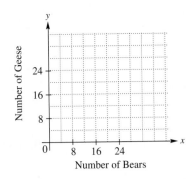

(b) Give two ordered pairs that satisfy the inequality.

Chapter 3
SUMMARY

3.1

circle graph   A circle graph is a circle divided into sectors (or wedges) whose sizes show the relative magnitudes of the categories of data represented.

bar graph   A bar graph is a series of bars used to show comparisons between two categories of data.

line graph   A line graph consists of a series of points that are connected with line segments and is used to show changes or trends in data.

linear equation in two variables   An equation that can be written in the form $Ax + By = C$ is a linear equation in two variables. (A and B are real numbers that cannot both be 0.)

ordered pair   A pair of numbers written between parentheses in which order is important is called an ordered pair.

table of values   A table showing selected ordered pairs of numbers that satisfy an equation is called a table of values.

x-axis   The horizontal axis in a coordinate system is called the x-axis.

y-axis   The vertical axis in a coordinate system is called the y-axis.

rectangular (Cartesian) coordinate system   An x-axis and y-axis at right angles form a coordinate system.

quadrants   A coordinate system divides the plane into four regions called quadrants.

origin   The point at which the x-axis and y-axis intersect is called the origin.

plane   A flat surface determined by two intersecting lines is a plane.

coordinates   The numbers in an ordered pair are called the coordinates of the corresponding point.

plot   To plot an ordered pair is to find the corresponding point on a coordinate system.

scatter diagram   A graph of ordered pairs of data is a scatter diagram.

3.2

graph   The graph of an equation is the set of all points that correspond to the ordered pairs that satisfy the equation.

graphing   The process of plotting the ordered pairs that satisfy a linear equation and drawing a line through them is called graphing.

y-intercept   If a graph intersects the y-axis at k, then the y-intercept is $(0, k)$.

x-intercept   If a graph intersects the x-axis at k, then the x-intercept is $(k, 0)$.

3.3

rise   Rise is the vertical change between two different points on a line.

run   Run is the horizontal change between two different points on a line.

slope   The slope of a line is the ratio of the change in y compared to the change in x when moving along the line from one point to another.

parallel lines   Two lines in a plane that never intersect are parallel.

perpendicular lines   Perpendicular lines intersect at a 90° angle.

3.5

linear inequality in two variables   An inequality that can be written in the form $Ax + By < C$, $Ax + By > C$, $Ax + By \leq C$, or $Ax + By \geq C$ is a linear inequality in two variables.

boundary line   In the graph of a linear inequality, the boundary line separates the region that satisfies the inequality from the region that does not satisfy the inequality.

NEW SYMBOLS

(x, y) ordered pair (x_1, y_1) subscript notation; m slope
x-sub-one, y-sub-one

TEST YOUR WORD POWER

See how well you have learned the vocabulary in this chapter. Answers, with examples, follow the Quick Review.

1. An **ordered pair** is a pair of numbers written
   A. in numerical order between brackets
   B. between parentheses or brackets
   C. between parentheses in which order is important
   D. between parentheses in which order does not matter.

2. The **coordinates** of a point are
   A. the numbers in the corresponding ordered pair
   B. the solution of an equation
   C. the values of the x- and y-intercepts
   D. the graph of the point.

3. An **intercept** is
   A. the point where the x-axis and y-axis intersect
   B. a pair of numbers written in parentheses in which order is important
   C. one of the four regions determined by a rectangular coordinate system
   D. a point where a graph intersects the x-axis or the y-axis.

4. The **slope** of a line is
   A. the measure of the run over the rise of the line
   B. the distance between two points on the line
   C. the ratio of the change in y to the change in x along the line
   D. the horizontal change compared to the vertical change of two points on the line.

5. Two lines in a plane are **parallel** if
   A. they represent the same line
   B. they never intersect
   C. they intersect at a 90° angle
   D. one has a positive slope and one has a negative slope.

6. Two lines in a plane are **perpendicular** if
   A. they represent the same line
   B. they never intersect
   C. they intersect at a 90° angle
   D. one has a positive slope and one has a negative slope.

QUICK REVIEW

Concepts	Examples

3.1 *Reading Graphs; Linear Equations in Two Variables*
Circle graphs, bar graphs, and line graphs are several ways to represent the relationship between two variables.

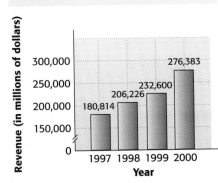

COMMUNICATIONS INDUSTRY REVENUE

Source: Veronis Suhler Stevenson, *Communications Industry Report,* annual.

The bar graph illustrates communications industry revenue for the years 1997–2000 in millions of dollars.

Concepts	Examples

3.1 Reading Graphs; Linear Equations in Two Variables (continued)

An ordered pair is a solution of an equation if it makes the equation a true statement.

Is $(2, -5)$ or $(0, -6)$ a solution of $4x - 3y = 18$?

$$4(2) - 3(-5) = 23 \neq 18 \qquad 4(0) - 3(-6) = 18$$

$(2, -5)$ is not a solution. $\qquad (0, -6)$ is a solution.

If a value of either variable in an equation is given, the value of the other variable can be found by substitution.

Complete the ordered pair $(0, \ \ )$ for $3x = y + 4$.

$$3(0) = y + 4 \qquad \text{Let } x = 0.$$

$$0 = y + 4$$

$$-4 = y$$

The ordered pair is $(0, -4)$.

To plot the ordered pair $(-3, 4)$, start at the origin, go 3 units to the left, and from there go 4 units up.

3.2 Graphing Linear Equations in Two Variables

To graph a linear equation:

Step 1 Find at least two ordered pairs that are solutions of the equation.

Step 2 Plot the corresponding points.

Step 3 Draw a straight line through the points.

Graph $x - 2y = 4$.

x	y
0	-2
4	0

3.3 Slope of a Line

The slope of the line through (x_1, y_1) and (x_2, y_2) is

$$m = \frac{\text{change in } y}{\text{change in } x} = \frac{y_2 - y_1}{x_2 - x_1} \quad (x_1 \neq x_2).$$

Horizontal lines have slope 0.

Vertical lines have undefined slope.

To find the slope of a line from its equation, solve for y. The slope is the coefficient of x.

The line through $(-2, 3)$ and $(4, -5)$ has slope

$$m = \frac{-5 - 3}{4 - (-2)} = \frac{-8}{6} = -\frac{4}{3}.$$

The line $y = -2$ has slope 0.

The line $x = 4$ has undefined slope.

Find the slope of the graph of

$$3x - 4y = 12.$$

$$-4y = -3x + 12$$

$$y = \frac{3}{4}x - 3$$

The slope is $\frac{3}{4}$.

Concepts	Examples

3.4 *Equations of Lines*

Slope-Intercept Form

$y = mx + b$

m is the slope.

$(0, b)$ is the y-intercept.

Find an equation of the line with slope **2** and y-intercept $(0, -5)$.

$$y = 2x - 5$$

Point-Slope Form

$y - y_1 = m(x - x_1)$

m is the slope.

(x_1, y_1) is a point on the line.

Find an equation of the line with slope $-\frac{1}{2}$ through $(-4, 5)$.

$$y - 5 = -\frac{1}{2}[x - (-4)]$$

$$y - 5 = -\frac{1}{2}(x + 4)$$

$$y - 5 = -\frac{1}{2}x - 2$$

$$y = -\frac{1}{2}x + 3$$

Standard Form

$Ax + By = C$

A, B, and C are integers and $A > 0, B \neq 0$.

This equation is written in standard form as

$$x + 2y = 6,$$

with $A = 1, B = 2$, and $C = 6$.

3.5 *Graphing Linear Inequalities in Two Variables*

Step 1 Graph the line that is the boundary of the region. Make it solid if the inequality is $\leq$ or $\geq$; make it dashed if the inequality is $<$ or $>$.

Step 2 Use any point not on the line as a test point. Substitute for x and y in the inequality. If the result is true, shade the side of the line containing the test point; if the result is false, shade the other side.

Graph $2x + y \leq 5$.

Graph the line $2x + y = 5$. Make it solid because the symbol $\leq$ includes equality.

Use $(1, 0)$ as a test point.

$$2(1) + 0 \leq 5 \qquad ?$$

$$2 \leq 5 \qquad \text{True}$$

Shade the side of the line containing $(1, 0)$.

ANSWERS TO TEST YOUR WORD POWER

1. C; *Examples:* $(0, 3), (3, 8), (4, 0)$
2. A; *Example:* The point associated with the ordered pair $(1, 2)$ has x-coordinate 1 and y-coordinate 2.
3. D; *Example:* The graph of the equation $4x - 3y = 12$ has x-intercept at $(3, 0)$ and y-intercept at $(0, -4)$.
4. C; *Example:* The line through $(3, 6)$ and $(5, 4)$ has slope $\dfrac{4 - 6}{5 - 3} = \dfrac{-2}{2} = -1$.
5. B; *Example:* See Figure 24 in **Section 3.3**.
6. C; *Example:* See Figure 25 in **Section 3.3**.

Chapter **3**
REVIEW EXERCISES

[3.1] The percents of four-year college students in private institutions who earned a degree within five years of entry between 1996 and 2001 are shown in the graph.

1. What was the total percent decrease for the period from 1996 to 2001?

2. Write ordered pairs to reflect the data shown in the graph.

3. In what year did the percent show the greatest decrease from the previous year? What was this decrease?

PERCENTS OF STUDENTS GRADUATING WITHIN 5 YEARS (PRIVATE INSTITUTIONS)

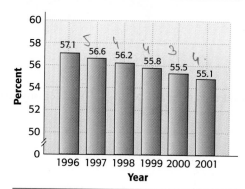

Source: ACT.

4. Describe the general trend seen in the graph.

Complete the given ordered pairs for each equation.

5. $y = 3x + 2$ $(-1,\ ), (0,\ ), (\ , 5)$

6. $4x + 3y = 6$ $(0,\ ), (\ , 0), (-2,\ )$

7. $x = 3y$ $(0,\ ), (8,\ ), (\ , -3)$

8. $x - 7 = 0$ $(\ , -3) (\ , 0), (\ , 5)$

Decide whether each ordered pair is a solution of the given equation.

9. $x + y = 7; (2, 5)$

10. $2x + y = 5; (-1, 3)$

11. $3x - y = 4; \left(\dfrac{1}{3}, -3\right)$

Plot each ordered pair on the given coordinate system.

12. $(2, 3)$ **13.** $(-4, 2)$

14. $(3, 0)$ **15.** $(0, -6)$

16. If $x > 0$ and $y < 0$, in what quadrant(s) must (x, y) lie? Explain.

17. On what axis does the point $(k, 0)$ lie for any real value of k? the point $(0, k)$? Explain.

Without plotting the given point, name the quadrant in which each point lies.

18. $(-2, 3)$ **19.** $(-1, -4)$ **20.** $\left(0, -5\dfrac{1}{2}\right)$

[3.2] *Find the intercepts for each equation.*

21. $y = 2x + 5$ **22.** $2x + y = -7$ **23.** $3x + 2y = 8$

    x-intercept: x-intercept: x-intercept:

    y-intercept: y-intercept: y-intercept:

Graph each linear equation.

24. $2x - y = 3$ **25.** $x + 2y = -4$ **26.** $x + y = 0$

  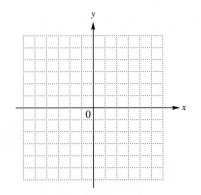

[3.3] *Find the slope of each line.*

27. Through $(2, 3)$ and $(-4, 6)$　　**28.** Through $(0, 0)$ and $(-3, 2)$　　**29.** Through $(0, 6)$ and $(1, 6)$

30. Through $(2, 5)$ and $(2, 8)$　　**31.** $y = 3x - 4$　　**32.** $y = \dfrac{2}{3}x + 1$

33.

34.

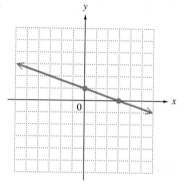

35. $x = 0$

36. $y = 4$

37. The line having these points

x	y
0	1
2	4
6	10

38. **(a)** A line parallel to the graph of $y = 2x + 3$

(b) A line perpendicular to the graph of $y = -3x + 3$

Decide whether each pair of lines is parallel, perpendicular, *or* neither.

39. $3x + 2y = 6$
$6x + 4y = 8$

40. $x - 3y = 1$
$3x + y = 4$

41. $x - 2y = 8$
$x + 2y = 8$

42. What is the slope of a line perpendicular to a line with undefined slope?

[3.4] *Write an equation in slope-intercept form (if possible) for each line.*

43. $m = -1; b = \dfrac{2}{3}$

44. The line in Exercise 34

45. Through $(4, -3); m = 1$

46. Through $(-1, 4); m = \dfrac{2}{3}$

47. Through $(1, -1); m = -\dfrac{3}{4}$

48. Through $(2, 1)$ and $(-2, 2)$

49. Through $(-4, 1)$ with slope 0

50. Through $\left(\dfrac{1}{3}, -\dfrac{3}{4}\right)$ with undefined slope

51. Consider the equation $x + 3y = 15$.

   (a) Write it in the form $y = mx + b$.

   (b) What is the slope? What is the y-intercept?

   (c) Use the slope and the y-intercept to graph the line. Indicate two points on the graph.

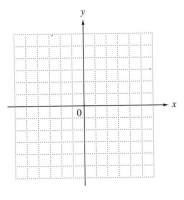

[3.5] *Graph each linear inequality.*

52. $3x + 5y > 9$

53. $2x - 3y > -6$

54. $x \geq -4$

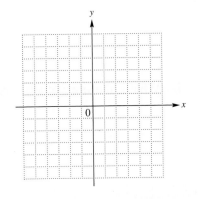

MIXED REVIEW EXERCISES

In Exercises 55–60, match each statement to the appropriate graph or graphs in
A–D. Graphs may be used more than once.

A.

B.

C.

D.

55. The line shown in the graph has undefined slope.

56. The graph of the equation has y-intercept $(0, -3)$.

57. The graph of the equation has x-intercept $(-3, 0)$.

58. The line shown in the graph has negative slope.

59. The graph is that of the equation $y = -3$.

60. The line shown in the graph has slope 1.

Find the intercepts and the slope of each line. Then graph the line.

61. $y = -2x - 5$

    x-intercept:

    y-intercept:

    slope:

62. $x + 3y = 0$

    x-intercept:

    y-intercept:

    slope:

63. $y - 5 = 0$

    x-intercept:

    y-intercept:

    slope:

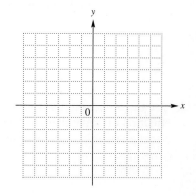

Write an equation in slope-intercept form for each line.

64. $m = -\dfrac{1}{4}; b = -\dfrac{5}{4}$

65. Through $(8, 6)$; $m = -3$

66. Through $(3, -5)$ and $(-4, -1)$

Graph each inequality.

67. $y < -4x$

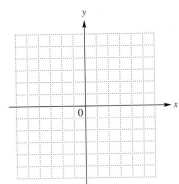

68. $x - 2y \le 6$

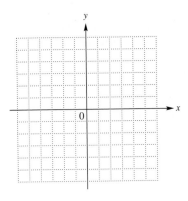

RELATING CONCEPTS (EXERCISES 69–75)   For Individual or Group Work

The percents of four-year college students in public schools who earned a degree within five years of entry between 1997 and 2002 are shown in the graph. Use the graph to **work** *Exercises 69–75 in order.*

69. What was the percent decrease from 1997 to 2002?

70. Since the points of the graph lie approximately in a linear pattern, a straight line can be used to model the data. Will this line have positive or negative slope? Explain.

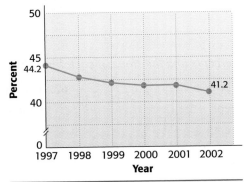

Source: ACT.

71. Write two ordered pairs for the data for 1997 and 2002.

72. Use the ordered pairs from Exercise 71 to find the equation of a line that models the data. Write the equation in slope-intercept form.

73. Based on the equation you found in Exercise 72, what is the slope of the line? Does it agree with your answer in Exercise 70?

74. Use the equation from Exercise 72 to approximate the percents for 1998 through 2001, and complete the table. Round your answers to the nearest tenth.

75. Use the equation from Exercise 72 to predict the percent for 2003. Can we be sure that this prediction is accurate?

Year	Percent
1998	
1999	
2000	
2001	

Chapter **3**

T E S T

Study Skills Workbook
Activity 9: Taking a Test

The line graph shows the average prices for a gallon of gasoline in the United States for the years 1998 to 2002. Use the graph to work Exercises 1–3.

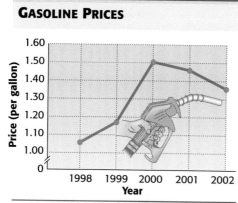

GASOLINE PRICES

Source: U.S. Department of Energy.

1. About how much did a gallon of gasoline cost in 1998?

2. About how much did the price of a gallon of gasoline increase from 1998 to 2000?

3. During which years did the price decrease?

Graph each linear equation. Give the x- and y-intercepts.

4. $3x + y = 6$

5. $y - 2x = 0$

1. _____

2. _____

3. _____

4. *x*-intercept: _____

   y-intercept: _____

5. *x*-intercept: _____

   y-intercept: _____

6. *x*-intercept: _____

   y-intercept: _____

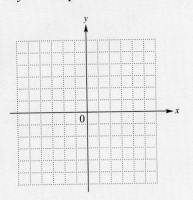

6. $x + 3 = 0$

7. *x*-intercept: _____

   y-intercept: _____

7. $y = 1$

8. *x*-intercept: _____

   y-intercept: _____

8. $x - y = 4$

Find the slope of each line.

9. _____

9. Through $(-4, 6)$ and $(-1, -2)$

10. _____

10. $2x + y = 10$

11. _____

11. $x + 12 = 0$

12.

13. A line parallel to the graph of $y - 4 = 6$

Write an equation in slope-intercept form for each line.

14. Through $(-1, 4)$; $m = 2$

15. The line in Exercise 12

16. Through $(2, -6)$ and $(1, 3)$

17. x-intercept: $(3, 0)$; y-intercept: $\left(0, \dfrac{9}{2}\right)$

Graph each linear inequality.

18. $x + y \leq 3$

12. _____

13. _____

14. _____

15. _____

16. _____

17. _____

18.

19.

19. $3x - y > 0$

The graph shows total food and drink sales at U.S. restaurants from 1970 through 2000, where 1970 corresponds to $x = 0$. Use the graph to work Exercises 20–22.

WHAT'S FOR DINNER?

Source: National Restaurant Association.

20. _____

20. Is the slope of the line in the graph positive or negative? Explain.

21. _____

21. Write two ordered pairs for the data points shown in the graph. Use them to find the slope of the line.

22. The linear equation

$$y = 11.1x + 43$$

approximates food and drink sales y in billions of dollars, where $x = 0$ again represents 1970.

22. (a) _____

(a) Use the equation to approximate food and drink sales for 1990 and 1995.

(b) _____

(b) What does the ordered pair (30, 376) mean in the context of this problem?

Cumulative Review Exercises

CHAPTERS R–3

Perform the indicated operations.

1. $10\dfrac{5}{8} - 3\dfrac{1}{10}$

2. $\dfrac{3}{4} \div \dfrac{1}{8}$

3. $5 - (-4) + (-2)$

4. $\dfrac{(-3)^2 - (-4)(2^4)}{5(2) - (-2)^3}$

5. True or false? $\dfrac{4(3-9)}{2-6} \geq 6$

6. Find the value of $xz^3 - 5y^2$ when $x = -2$, $y = -3$, and $z = -1$.

7. What property does $3(-2 + x) = -6 + 3x$ illustrate?

8. Simplify $-4p - 6 + 3p + 8$ by combining terms.

Solve.

9. $V = \dfrac{1}{3}\pi r^2 h$ for h

10. $6 - 3(1 + a) = 2(a + 5) - 2$

11. $-(m - 3) = 5 - 2m$

12. $\dfrac{y-2}{3} = \dfrac{2y+1}{5}$

Solve each inequality, and graph the solution.

13. $-2.5x < 6.5$

14. $4(x + 3) - 5x < 12$

15. $\dfrac{2}{3}t - \dfrac{1}{6}t \leq -2$

Solve each problem.

16. The gap in average annual earnings by level of education continues to increase. Based on the most recent statistics available, a person with a bachelor's degree can expect to earn $29,200 more each year than someone with a high school diploma. Together the individuals would earn $102,644. How much can a person at each level of education expect to earn? (*Source*: U.S. Bureau of the Census.)

17. Mount Mayon in the Philippines is the most perfectly shaped conical volcano in the world. Its base is a perfect circle with circumference 80 mi, and it has a height of about 8200 ft. (One mile is 5280 ft.) Find the radius of the circular base to the nearest mile. (*Hint*: This problem has some unneeded information.) (*Source*: Microsoft Encarta Encyclopedia 2000.)

Circumference = 80 mi

18. The winning times in seconds for the women's 1000 m speed skating event in the Winter Olympics for the years 1960 through 2002 can be closely approximated by the linear equation

$$y = -.5075x + 95.4179,$$

where x is the number of years since 1960. That is, $x = 4$ represents 1964, $x = 8$ represents 1968, and so on. (*Source: World Almanac and Book of Facts,* 2004.)

(a) Use this equation to complete the table of values. Round times to the nearest hundredth of a second.

x	y
12	
28	
34	

(b) Based on this equation, what does the ordered pair (20, 85.27) mean?

19. Baby boomers are expected to inherit $10.4 trillion from their parents over the next 45 yr, an average of $50,000 each. The circle graph shows how they plan to spend their inheritances.

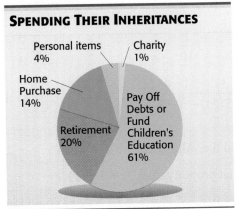

SPENDING THEIR INHERITANCES

Personal items 4%
Charity 1%
Home Purchase 14%
Pay Off Debts or Fund Children's Education 61%
Retirement 20%

Source: First Interstate Bank Trust and Private Banking Group.

(a) How much of the $50,000 is expected to go toward home purchase?

(b) How much is expected to go toward retirement?

(c) Use the answer from part (b) to estimate the amount expected to go toward paying off debts or funding children's education.

Consider the linear equation $-3x + 4y = 12.$ *Find the following.*

20. The x- and y-intercepts

21. The slope

22. The graph

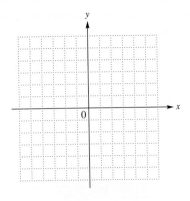

23. The y-value of the point having x-value 4

24. Are the lines with equations $x + 5y = -6$ and $y = 5x - 8$ *parallel, perpendicular,* or *neither?*

Write an equation in slope-intercept form for each line.

25. Through $(2, -5)$ with slope 3

26. Through $(0, 4)$ and $(2, 4)$

Systems of Linear Equations and Inequalities

Although Americans continued their fascination with Hollywood and the movies in 2003, movie attendance and revenues dipped for the first time since 1991. Nonetheless, some 1.52 billion tickets were sold and revenues exceeded $9 billion for the second year in a row. The top box office draws of the year—*The Lord of the Rings: The Return of the King* and *Finding Nemo*—attracted scores of adults and children wishing to get away from it all for a few hours. (*Source:* Exhibitor Relations Co., Nielsen EDI.)

In Exercise 13 of Section 4.4, we use a *system of linear equations* to find out how much money these top films earned.

4.1 Solving Systems of Linear Equations by Graphing

OBJECTIVES

1 Decide whether a given ordered pair is a solution of a system.

2 Solve linear systems by graphing.

3 Solve special systems by graphing.

A **system of linear equations,** often called a **linear system,** consists of two or more linear equations with the same variables. Examples of systems of two linear equations include

$$2x + 3y = 4 \qquad x + 3y = 1 \qquad x - y = 1$$
$$3x - y = -5 \qquad -y = 4 - 2x \qquad y = 3.$$

Linear systems

In the system on the right, think of $y = 3$ as an equation in two variables by writing it as $0x + y = 3$.

OBJECTIVE 1 Decide whether a given ordered pair is a solution of a system. A **solution of a system** of linear equations is an ordered pair that makes both equations true at the same time. A solution of an equation is said to *satisfy* the equation.

1 Fill in the blanks, and decide whether the given ordered pair is a solution of the system.

(a) $(2, 5)$

$$3x - 2y = -4$$
$$5x + y = 15$$

$$3x - 2y = -4$$
$$3(\underline{}) - 2(\underline{}) = -4$$

$$5x + y = 15$$
$$5(2) + \underline{} = \underline{}$$

$(2, 5)$ _____ a solution.
     (is/is not)

EXAMPLE 1 Determining Whether an Ordered Pair Is a Solution

Is $(4, -3)$ a solution of each system?

(a) $x + 4y = -8$
$3x + 2y = 6$

To decide whether or not $(4, -3)$ is a solution of the system, substitute 4 for x and -3 for y in each equation.

$x + 4y = -8$		$3x + 2y = 6$	
$4 + 4(-3) = -8$	?	$3(4) + 2(-3) = 6$	?
$4 + (-12) = -8$	? Multiply.	$12 + (-6) = 6$	? Multiply.
$-8 = -8$	True	$6 = 6$	True

Because $(4, -3)$ satisfies both equations, it is a solution of the system.

(b) $2x - 5y = -7$
$3x + 4y = 2$

Again, substitute 4 for x and -3 for y in both equations.

$2x + 5y = -7$		$3x + 4y = 2$	
$2(4) + 5(-3) = -7$	?	$3(4) + 4(-3) = 2$	?
$8 + (-15) = -7$	? Multiply.	$12 + (-12) = 2$	? Multiply.
$-7 = -7$	True	$0 = 2$	False

The ordered pair $(4, -3)$ is not a solution of this system because it does not satisfy the second equation.

(b) $(1, -2)$

$$x - 3y = 7$$
$$4x + y = 5$$

$(1, -2)$ _____ a solution.
     (is/is not)

◀◀◀ **Work Problem 1 at the Side.**

OBJECTIVE 2 Solve linear systems by graphing. One way to find the solution of a system of two linear equations is to graph both equations on the same axes. The graph of each line shows points whose coordinates satisfy the equation of that line. Any intersection point would be on both lines and would therefore be a solution of *both* equations. ***Thus, the coordinates of any point where the lines intersect give a solution of the system.***

The graph in Figure 1 shows that the solution of the system in Example 1(a) is the intersection point $(4, -3)$. Because *two different* straight lines can intersect at no more than one point, there can never be more than one solution for such a system.

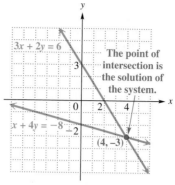

Figure 1

EXAMPLE 2 Solving a System by Graphing

Solve the system of equations by graphing both equations on the same axes.

$$2x + 3y = 4$$
$$3x - y = -5$$

We graph these two equations by plotting several points for each line. Recall from **Section 3.2** that the intercepts are often convenient choices. It is a good idea to find a third ordered pair as a check.

$2x + 3y = 4$

x	y
0	$\frac{4}{3}$
2	0
-2	$\frac{8}{3}$

$3x - y = -5$

x	y
0	5
$-\frac{5}{3}$	0
-2	-1

The lines in Figure 2 suggest that the graphs intersect at the point $(-1, 2)$. We check this by substituting -1 for x and 2 for y in both equations. Because $(-1, 2)$ satisfies both equations, the solution of this system is $(-1, 2)$.

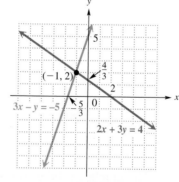

Figure 2

Work Problem 2 at the Side. ▷▷▷

② Solve each system of equations by graphing both equations on the same axes. Check your solutions.

(a) $5x - 3y = 9$
$x + 2y = 7$
(One of the lines is already graphed.)

(b) $x + y = 4$
$2x - y = -1$

NOTE

We can also graph a linear system by writing each equation in the system in slope-intercept form and using the slope and y-intercept to graph each line. For Example 2,

$2x + 3y = 4$ becomes $y = -\frac{2}{3}x + \frac{4}{3}$ y-intercept $(0, \frac{4}{3})$; slope $-\frac{2}{3}$ or $-\frac{2}{3}$

$3x - y = -5$ becomes $y = 3x + 5$. y-intercept $(0, 5)$; slope 3 or $\frac{3}{1}$

Confirm that graphing these equations results in the same lines and the same solution shown in Figure 2.

ANSWERS
2. (a) $(3, 2)$ **(b)** $(1, 3)$

3 Solve each system of equations by graphing both equations on the same axes.

(a) $3x - y = 4$
$6x - 2y = 12$
(One of the lines is already graphed.)

(b) $-x + 3y = 2$
$2x - 6y = -4$

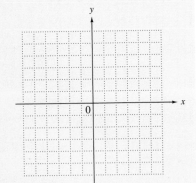

CAUTION
A difficulty with the graphing method of solution is that it may not be possible to determine from the graph the exact coordinates of the point that represents the solution, particularly if these coordinates are not integers. For this reason, algebraic methods of solution are explained later in this chapter. The graphing method does, however, show geometrically how solutions are found and is useful when approximate answers will do.

OBJECTIVE 3 Solve special systems by graphing. Sometimes the graphs of the two equations in a system either do not intersect at all or are the same line, as in the systems in Example 3.

EXAMPLE 3 Solving Special Systems

Solve each system by graphing.

(a) $2x + y = 2$
$2x + y = 8$

The graphs of these lines are shown in Figure 3. The two lines are parallel and have no points in common. For such a system, we will write "*no solution.*"

Figure 3

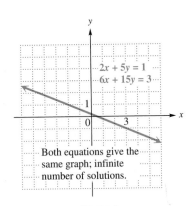

Figure 4

(b) $2x + 5y = 1$
$6x + 15y = 3$

The graphs of these two equations are the same line. See Figure 4. The second equation can be obtained by multiplying each side of the first equation by 3. In this case, every point on the line is a solution of the system, and the solutions are the infinite number of ordered pairs that satisfy the equations. We will write "*infinite number of solutions*" to indicate this case.

Work Problem 3 at the Side.

The system in Example 2 has exactly one solution. A system with at least one solution is called a **consistent system.** A system of equations with no solutions, such as the one in Example 3(a), is called an **inconsistent system.** The equations in Example 2 are **independent equations** with different graphs. The equations of the system in Example 3(b) have the same graph and are equivalent. Because they are different forms of the same equation, these equations are called **dependent equations.**

ANSWERS
3. (a) no solution
 (b) infinite number of solutions

Examples 2 and 3 show the three cases that may occur when solving a system of two equations with two variables.

Possible Types of Solutions

1. The graphs intersect at exactly one point, which gives the (single) ordered pair solution of the system. The **system is consistent,** and the **equations are independent.**

2. The graphs are parallel lines, so there is no solution. The **system is inconsistent.**

3. The graphs are the same line. The solution is an infinite number of ordered pairs. The **equations are dependent.**

Real-Data Applications

Estimating Fahrenheit Temperature

When traveling in countries other than the United States, you will hear the daily high and low temperatures reported in degrees Celsius, instead of degrees Fahrenheit. The following information may help you interpret these Celsius temperatures.

- The linear equation to convert degrees Celsius to degrees Fahrenheit is $F = \frac{9}{5}C + 32$.
- Travel books advise you to use a *rule of thumb* to estimate Fahrenheit temperature that says "*Double the temperature (degrees Celsius) and add 30.*" This rule of thumb is written mathematically as $F = 2C + 30$.

For Group Discussion

Suppose you are interested in knowing for what temperature the rule of thumb and the actual formulas give the same result. You also want to know if the rule of thumb formula is predicting temperatures that are lower or higher than the actual temperature.

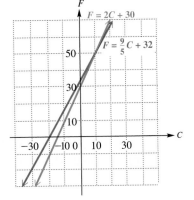

1. The two formulas can be written as the system of equations

$$F = \frac{9}{5}C + 32$$

$$F = 2C + 30.$$

   (a) Use the graph of the system of equations to find the point of intersection. (*Hint:* To check your answer, use substitution to see if it satisfies both formulas.)

   (b) For what temperature in degrees Celsius do the two formulas agree?

   (c) For what temperature in degrees Fahrenheit do the two formulas agree?

2. (a) Complete the table of values to compare the *actual* and the *rule of thumb* formulas for temperature conversion.

°C	°F (*Actual*)	°F (*Rule of Thumb*)
0		
5		
10		
15		
20		
30		

   (b) If the daily low is predicted to be 5°C, then is the rule of thumb estimate too high or too low?

   (c) If the daily high is predicted to be 20°C, then is the rule of thumb estimate too high or too low?

   (d) If the daily high is predicted to be 30°C, then is the rule of thumb estimate too high or too low?

   (e) How many degrees "off" is the rule of thumb estimate for the boiling point of water?

   (f) Comment on the accuracy of using the rule of thumb as an estimate of the actual Fahrenheit temperature.

4.1 Exercises

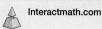

1. Which ordered pair could be a solution of the system graphed? Why is it the only valid choice?
   - A. $(2, 2)$
   - B. $(-2, 2)$
   - C. $(-2, -2)$
   - D. $(2, -2)$

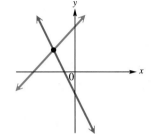

2. Which ordered pair could be a solution of the system graphed? Why is it the only valid choice?
   - A. $(2, 0)$
   - B. $(0, 2)$
   - C. $(-2, 0)$
   - D. $(0, -2)$

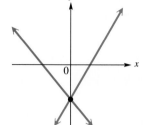

3. How can you tell without graphing that this system has no solution?

$$x + y = 2$$
$$x + y = 4$$

4. Explain why a system of two linear equations cannot have exactly two solutions.

Decide whether the given ordered pair is a solution of the given system. See Example 1.

5. $(2, -3)$
   $x + y = -1$
   $2x + 5y = 19$

6. $(4, 3)$
   $x + 2y = 10$
   $3x + 5y = 3$

7. $(-1, -3)$
   $3x + 5y = -18$
   $4x + 2y = -10$

8. $(-9, -2)$
   $2x - 5y = -8$
   $3x + 6y = -39$

9. $(7, -2)$
   $4x = 26 - y$
   $3x = 29 + 4y$

10. $(9, 1)$
    $2x = 23 - 5y$
    $3x = 24 + 3y$

11. $(6, -8)$
    $-2y = x + 10$
    $3y = 2x + 30$

12. $(-5, 2)$
    $5y = 3x + 20$
    $3y = -2x - 4$

Solve each system of equations by graphing. If the two equations produce parallel lines, write no solution. *If the two equations produce the same line, write* infinite number of solutions. *See Examples 2 and 3.*

13. $x - y = 2$
$x + y = 6$

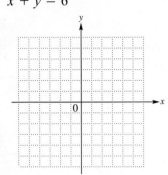

14. $x - y = 3$
$x + y = -1$

15. $x + y = 4$
$y - x = 4$

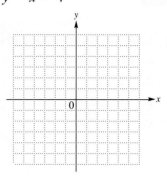

16. $x + y = -5$
$x - y = 5$

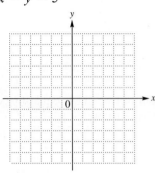

17. $x - 2y = 6$
$x + 2y = 2$

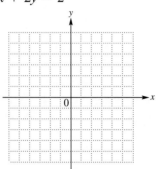

18. $2x - y = 4$
$4x + y = 2$

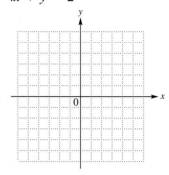

19. $3x - 2y = -3$
$-3x - y = -6$

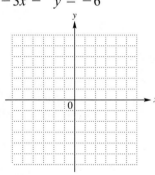

20. $2x - y = 4$
$2x + 3y = 12$

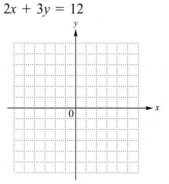

21. $2x - 3y = -6$
$y = -3x + 2$

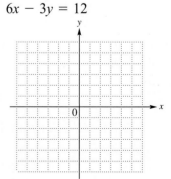

22. $-3x + y = -3$
$y = x - 3$

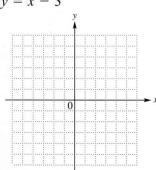

23. $x + 2y = 6$
$2x + 4y = 8$

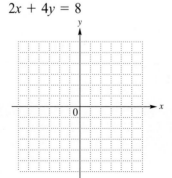

24. $2x - y = 6$
$6x - 3y = 12$

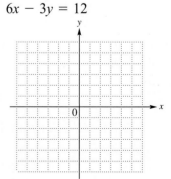

25. $2x - y = 4$
$4x = 2y + 8$

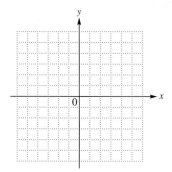

26. $3x = 5 - y$
$6x + 2y = 10$

27. $3x - 4y = 24$
$y = -\dfrac{3}{2}x + 3$

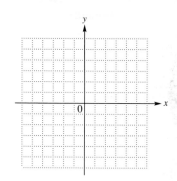

28. $3x - 2y = 12$
$y = -4x + 5$

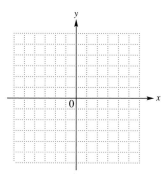

29. $3x = y + 5$
$6x - 5 = 2y$

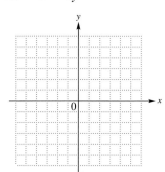

30. $2x = y - 4$
$4x - 2y = -4$

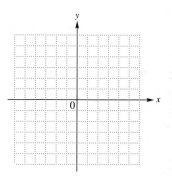

RELATING CONCEPTS (EXERCISES 31–34) For Individual or Group Work

In Exercises 31–33, first write each equation in slope-intercept form. (See the Note following Example 2.) Then use what you learned in **Chapter 3** *about slope and the y-intercept to describe the graphs of each system of equations.* ***Work Exercises 31–34 in order.***

31. $3x + 2y = 6$
$-2y = 3x - 5$

32. $2x - y = 4$
$x = .5y + 2$

33. $x - 3y = 5$
$2x + y = 8$

34. Use the results of Exercises 31–33 to determine the number of solutions of each system.

The graph shows network share (the percentage of TV sets in use) for the early evening news programs for the three major broadcast networks from 1986 through 2000.

35. Between what years did the ABC early evening news dominate?

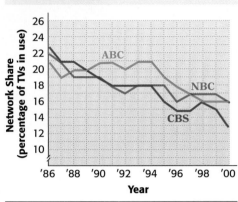

WHO'S WATCHING THE EVENING NEWS?

36. During what year did ABC's dominance end? Which network equaled ABC's share that year? What was that share?

37. During what years did ABC and CBS have equal network share? What was the share for each of these years?

Source: Nielsen Media Research.

38. Which networks most recently had equal share? Write their share as an ordered pair of the form (year, share).

39. Explain one of the drawbacks of solving a system of equations graphically.

40. If the two lines that are the graphs of the equations in a system are parallel, how many solutions does the system have? If the two lines coincide, how many solutions does the system have?

41. Find a system of equations with the solution $(-2, 3)$, and show the graph.

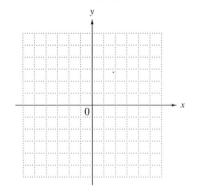

42. Solve the system

$$2x + 3y = 6$$
$$x - 3y = 5$$

by graphing. Can you check your answer? Why or why not?

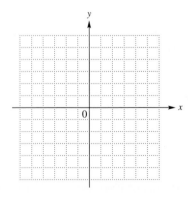

4.2 Solving Systems of Linear Equations by Substitution

OBJECTIVE 1 Solve linear systems by substitution. Graphing to solve a system of equations has a serious drawback: It is difficult to accurately find a solution such as $\left(\frac{1}{3}, -\frac{5}{6}\right)$ from a graph. One algebraic method for solving a system of equations is the **substitution method.** This method is particularly useful for solving systems where one equation is already solved, or can be solved quickly, for one of the variables.

> **OBJECTIVES**
>
> **1** Solve linear systems by substitution.
>
> **2** Solve special systems.
>
> **3** Solve linear systems with fractions.

EXAMPLE 1 Using the Substitution Method

Solve the system

$$3x + 5y = 26$$
$$y = 2x.$$

The second equation is already solved for y. This equation says that $y = 2x$. Substituting $2x$ for y in the first equation gives

$$3x + 5y = 26$$
$3x + 5(2x) = 26$	Let $y = 2x$.
$3x + 10x = 26$	Multiply.
$13x = 26$	Combine terms.
$x = 2.$	Divide by 13.

Because $x = 2$, we find y from the equation $y = 2x$ by substituting 2 for x.

$$y = 2(2) = 4 \qquad \text{Let } x = 2.$$

Check that the solution of the given system is $(2, 4)$ by substituting 2 for x and 4 for y in *both* equations.

> **Work Problem 1 at the Side.** ▶▶▶

1 Fill in the blanks to solve by the substitution method. Check your solution.

$$3x + 5y = 69$$
$$y = 4x$$
$$3x + 5(\underline{\quad}) = 69$$
$$\underline{\quad} = 69$$
$$x = \underline{\quad}$$
$$y = 4(\underline{\quad}) = \underline{\quad}$$

The solution is \underline{\quad}.

EXAMPLE 2 Using the Substitution Method

Solve the system

$$2x + 5y = 7$$
$$x = -1 - y.$$

The second equation gives x in terms of y. Substitute $-1 - y$ for x in the first equation.

$$2x + 5y = 7$$
$2(-1 - y) + 5y = 7$	Let $x = -1 - y$.
$-2 - 2y + 5y = 7$	Distributive property
$-2 + 3y = 7$	Combine terms.
$3y = 9$	Add 2.
$y = 3$	Divide by 3.

To find x, substitute 3 for y in the equation $x = -1 - y$ to get

$$x = -1 - 3 = -4.$$

Check that the solution of the given system is $(-4, 3)$.

> **Work Problem 2 at the Side.** ▶▶▶

2 Solve by the substitution method. Check your solution.

$$2x + 7y = -12$$
$$x = 3 - 2y$$

ANSWERS
1. $4x$; $23x$; 3; 3; 12; (3, 12)
2. $(15, -6)$

3 Solve each system by substitution. Check each solution.

(a) Fill in the blanks to solve

$$x + 4y = -1$$
$$2x - 5y = 11.$$

Solve the first equation for x.

$$x = -1 - \underline{\quad}$$

Substitute into the second equation to find y.

$$2(\underline{\quad}) - 5y = 11$$
$$-2 - 8y - 5y = 11$$
$$-2 - \underline{\quad} y = 11$$
$$\underline{\quad} y = 13$$
$$y = \underline{\quad}$$

Find x.

$$x = -1 - \underline{\quad}$$
$$x = \underline{\quad}$$

The solution is $\underline{\quad}$.

(b) $2x + 5y = 4$
$x + y = -1$

CAUTION

Even though we found y first in Example 2, *the x-coordinate is always written first in the ordered pair solution of a system.*

To solve a system by substitution, follow these steps.

Solving a Linear System by Substitution

Step 1 **Solve one equation for either variable.** If one of the variables has coefficient 1 or -1, choose it.

Step 2 **Substitute** for that variable in the other equation. The result should be an equation with just one variable.

Step 3 **Solve** the equation from Step 2.

Step 4 **Substitute** the result from Step 3 into the equation from Step 1 to find the value of the other variable.

Step 5 **Check** the solution in both of the original equations. Then write the solution as an ordered pair.

EXAMPLE 3 Using the Substitution Method

Use substitution to solve the system

$$2x = 4 - y \qquad (1)$$
$$5x + 3y = 10. \qquad (2)$$

Step 1 For the substitution method, we must solve one of the equations for either x or y. Because the coefficient of y in equation (1) is -1, we choose equation (1) and solve for y.

$$2x = 4 - y \qquad (1)$$
$$2x - 4 = -y \qquad \text{Subtract 4.}$$
$$-2x + 4 = y \qquad \text{Multiply by } -1.$$

Step 2 Now substitute $-2x + 4$ for y in equation (2).

$$5x + 3y = 10 \qquad (2)$$
$$5x + 3(-2x + 4) = 10 \qquad \text{Let } y = -2x + 4.$$

Step 3 Now solve the equation from Step 2.

$$5x - 6x + 12 = 10 \qquad \text{Distributive property}$$
$$-x + 12 = 10 \qquad \text{Combine terms.}$$
$$-x = -2 \qquad \text{Subtract 12.}$$
$$x = 2 \qquad \text{Multiply by } -1.$$

Step 4 Since $y = -2x + 4$ and $x = 2$, $y = -2(2) + 4 = 0$.

Step 5 Check that $(2, 0)$ is the solution.

$$\begin{array}{ll} 2x = 4 - y \qquad (1) & 5x + 3y = 10 \qquad (2) \\ 2(2) = 4 - 0 \quad ? & 5(2) + 3(0) = 10 \quad ? \\ 4 = 4 \qquad \text{True} & 10 = 10 \qquad \text{True} \end{array}$$

The solution of the system is $(2, 0)$.

Work Problem 3 at the Side.

EXAMPLE 4 **Using the Substitution Method**

Use substitution to solve the system

$$2x + 3y = 10 \qquad (1)$$
$$-3x - 2y = 0. \qquad (2)$$

Step 1   To use the substitution method, we must solve one of the equations for one of the variables. We choose equation (1) and solve for x.

$$2x + 3y = 10 \qquad (1)$$
$$2x = 10 - 3y \qquad \text{Subtract } 3y.$$
$$x = 5 - \frac{3}{2}y \qquad \text{Divide by 2.}$$

Step 2   Substitute this expression for x in equation (2).

$$-3x - 2y = 0 \qquad (2)$$
$$-3\left(5 - \frac{3}{2}y\right) - 2y = 0 \qquad \text{Let } x = 5 - \tfrac{3}{2}y.$$

Step 3
$$-15 + \frac{9}{2}y - 2y = 0 \qquad \text{Distributive property}$$
$$-15 + \frac{5}{2}y = 0 \qquad \text{Combine terms.}$$
$$\frac{5}{2}y = 15 \qquad \text{Add 15.}$$
$$y = \frac{30}{5} = 6 \qquad \text{Multiply by } \tfrac{2}{5}.$$

Step 4   Find x by substituting **6** for y in $x = 5 - \tfrac{3}{2}y$.

$$x = 5 - \frac{3}{2}(6) = -4$$

Step 5   Check that $(-4, 6)$ is the solution.

$2x + 3y = 10$		$-3x - 2y = 0$	
$2(-4) + 3(6) = 10$	?	$-3(-4) - 2(6) = 0$	?
$-8 + 18 = 10$	?	$12 - 12 = 0$	?
$10 = 10$	True	$0 = 0$	True

The solution of the system is $(-4, 6)$.

NOTE

In Example 4, we could have started the solution by solving the second equation for either x or y and then substituting the result into the first equation. The solution would be the same.

4 Solve the system by substitution. Check your solution.

$$3x + 2y = 1$$
$$3x - 4y = -11$$

Work Problem 4 at the Side. ▶▶▶

OBJECTIVE **2** **Solve special systems.** We can solve inconsistent systems with graphs that are parallel lines and systems of dependent equations with graphs that are the same line using the substitution method.

EXAMPLE 5 **Solving an Inconsistent System by Substitution**

Use substitution to solve the system

$$x = 5 - 2y \quad (1)$$
$$2x + 4y = 6. \quad (2)$$

Substitute $5 - 2y$ for x in equation (2).

$$2x + 4y = 6 \quad (2)$$
$$2(5 - 2y) + 4y = 6 \quad \text{Let } x = 5 - 2y.$$
$$10 - 4y + 4y = 6 \quad \text{Distributive property}$$
$$10 = 6 \quad \text{False}$$

This false result means that the equations in the system have graphs that are parallel lines. The system is inconsistent and has no solution. See Figure 5.

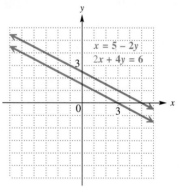

Figure 5

CAUTION

It is a common error to give "false" as the answer to an inconsistent system. The correct response is "no solution."

EXAMPLE 6 **Solving a System with Dependent Equations by Substitution**

Solve the system by the substitution method.

$$3x - y = 4 \quad (1)$$
$$-9x + 3y = -12 \quad (2)$$

Begin by solving equation (1) for y to get $y = 3x - 4$. Substitute $3x - 4$ for y in equation (2) and solve the resulting equation.

$$-9x + 3y = -12 \quad (2)$$
$$-9x + 3(3x - 4) = -12 \quad \text{Let } y = 3x - 4.$$
$$-9x + 9x - 12 = -12 \quad \text{Distributive property}$$
$$0 = 0 \quad \text{Add 12; combine terms.}$$

Continued on Next Page

This true result means that every solution of one equation is also a solution of the other, so the system has an infinite number of solutions: all the ordered pairs corresponding to points that lie on the common graph. A graph of the equations of this system is shown in Figure 6.

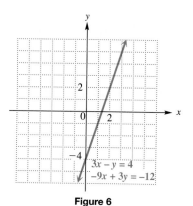

Figure 6

5 Solve each system by substitution.

(a) $8x - y = 4$
$y = 8x + 4$

> **CAUTION**
> It is a common error to give "true" as the answer to a system of dependent equations. The correct response is "infinite number of solutions."

Work Problem 5 at the Side. ⟫

OBJECTIVE 3 Solve linear systems with fractions. When a system includes an equation with fractions as coefficients, eliminate the fractions by multiplying each side of the equation by a common denominator. Then solve the resulting system.

(b) $7x - 6y = 10$
$-14x + 20 = -12y$

EXAMPLE 7 **Using the Substitution Method with Fractions as Coefficients**

Solve the system by the substitution method.

$$3x + \frac{1}{4}y = 2 \qquad (1)$$

$$\frac{1}{2}x + \frac{3}{4}y = -\frac{5}{2} \qquad (2)$$

Clear equation (1) of fractions by multiplying each side by 4.

$$4\left(3x + \frac{1}{4}y\right) = 4(2) \qquad \text{Multiply by 4.}$$

$$4(3x) + 4\left(\frac{1}{4}y\right) = 4(2) \qquad \text{Distributive property}$$

$$12x + y = 8 \qquad (3)$$

Now clear equation (2) of fractions by multiplying each side by the common denominator 4.

Continued on Next Page

6 Solve the system by substitution. First clear all fractions. Check your solution.

$$\frac{2}{3}x + \frac{1}{2}y = 6$$

$$\frac{1}{2}x - \frac{3}{4}y = 0$$

$$\frac{1}{2}x + \frac{3}{4}y = -\frac{5}{2} \qquad (2)$$

$$4\left(\frac{1}{2}x + \frac{3}{4}y\right) = 4\left(-\frac{5}{2}\right) \qquad \text{Multiply by 4.}$$

$$4\left(\frac{1}{2}x\right) + 4\left(\frac{3}{4}y\right) = 4\left(-\frac{5}{2}\right) \qquad \text{Distributive property}$$

$$2x + 3y = -10 \qquad (4)$$

The given system of equations has been simplified to the equivalent system

$$12x + y = 8 \qquad (3)$$

$$2x + 3y = -10. \qquad (4)$$

Solve this system by the substitution method. Equation (3) can be solved for y by subtracting $12x$ from each side.

$$12x + y = 8 \qquad (3)$$

$$y = -12x + 8 \qquad \text{Subtract } 12x.$$

Now substitute this result for y in equation (4).

$$2x + 3y = -10 \qquad (4)$$

$$2x + 3(-12x + 8) = -10 \qquad \text{Let } y = -12x + 8.$$

$$2x - 36x + 24 = -10 \qquad \text{Distributive property}$$

$$-34x = -34 \qquad \text{Combine terms; subtract 24.}$$

$$x = 1 \qquad \text{Divide by } -34.$$

Substitute 1 for x in $y = -12x + 8$ to get

$$y = -12(1) + 8 = -4.$$

The solution is $(1, -4)$. Check by substituting 1 for x and -4 for y in both of the original equations.

◀◀◀ Work Problem 6 at the Side.

4.2 Exercises

| FOR
EXTRA
HELP | Addison-Wesley
Math Tutor Center |
MathXL | 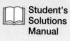 Digital Video Tutor CD 4
Videotape 4 | Student's
Solutions
Manual | *MyMathLab*
MyMathLab | Interactmath.com |

1. A student solves the system

$$5x - y = 15$$
$$7x + y = 21$$

and finds that $x = 3$, which is the correct value for x. The student gives the solution as "$x = 3$." Is this correct? Explain.

2. When you use the substitution method, how can you tell that a system has

  (a) no solution?   **(b)** an infinite number of solutions?

Solve each system by the substitution method. Check each solution. See Examples 1–7.

3. $x + y = 12$
    $y = 3x$

4. $x + 3y = -28$
    $y = -5x$

5. $3x + 2y = 27$
    $x = y + 4$

6. $4x + 3y = -5$
    $x = y - 3$

7. $3x + 5y = 14$
    $x - 2y = -10$

8. $5x + 2y = -1$
    $2x - y = -13$

9. $3x + 4 = -y$
    $2x + y = 0$

10. $2x - 5 = -y$
    $x + 3y = 0$

11. $7x + 4y = 13$
    $x + y = 1$

12. $3x - 2y = 19$
    $x + y = 8$

13. $3x - y = 5$
    $y = 3x - 5$

14. $4x - y = -3$
    $y = 4x + 3$

15. $6x - 8y = 6$
    $2y = -2 + 3x$

16. $3x + 2y = 6$
    $6x = 8 + 4y$

17. $2x + 8y = 3$
    $x = 8 - 4y$

18. $2x + 10y = 3$
  $x = 1 - 5y$

19. $12x - 16y = 8$
  $3x = 4y + 2$

20. $6x + 9y = 6$
  $2x = 2 - 3y$

21. $5x + 4y = 40$
  $x + y = 1$

22. $x - 5y = 7$
  $2x - y = 14$

23. $3x = 6 - 4y$
  $9x + 12y = 10$

24. $\dfrac{1}{3}x - \dfrac{1}{2}y = \dfrac{1}{6}$
  $3x - 2y = 9$

25. $\dfrac{1}{5}x + \dfrac{2}{3}y = -\dfrac{8}{5}$
  $3x - y = 9$

26. $\dfrac{1}{6}x + \dfrac{1}{6}y = 2$
  $-\dfrac{1}{2}x - \dfrac{1}{3}y = -8$

27. $\dfrac{x}{2} - \dfrac{y}{3} = 9$
  $\dfrac{x}{5} - \dfrac{y}{4} = 5$

28. $\dfrac{x}{3} - \dfrac{3y}{4} = -\dfrac{1}{2}$
  $\dfrac{x}{6} + \dfrac{y}{8} = \dfrac{3}{4}$

29. $\dfrac{x}{5} + 2y = \dfrac{16}{5}$
  $\dfrac{3x}{5} + \dfrac{y}{2} = -\dfrac{7}{5}$

RELATING CONCEPTS (EXERCISES 30–33) For Individual or Group Work

A system of linear equations can be used to model the cost and the revenue of a business.
Work Exercises 30–33 in order.

30. Suppose that you start a business manufacturing and selling bicycles, and it costs you $5000 to get started. You determine that each bicycle will cost $400 to manufacture. Explain why the linear equation $y_1 = 400x + 5000$ gives your *total* cost to manufacture x bicycles (y_1 in dollars).

31. You decide to sell each bike for $600. What expression in x represents the revenue you will take in if you sell x bikes? Write an equation using y_2 to express your revenue when you sell x bikes (y_2 in dollars).

32. Form a system from the two equations in Exercises 30 and 31, and then solve the system, assuming $y_1 = y_2$, that is, cost = revenue.

33. The value of x from Exercise 32 is the number of bikes it takes to *break even*. Fill in the blanks: When _____ bikes are sold, the break-even point is reached. At that point, you have spent _____ dollars and taken in _____ dollars.

4.3 Solving Systems of Linear Equations by Elimination

OBJECTIVE 1 Solve linear systems by elimination.   An algebraic method that depends on the addition property of equality can be used to solve systems. As mentioned earlier, adding the same quantity to each side of an equation results in equal sums.

$$\text{If} \quad A = B, \quad \text{then} \quad A + C = B + C.$$

This addition can be taken a step further. Adding *equal* quantities, rather than the *same* quantity, to both sides of an equation also results in equal sums.

$$\text{If} \quad A = B \quad \text{and} \quad C = D, \quad \text{then} \quad A + C = B + D.$$

Using the addition property to solve systems is called the **elimination method.** When using this method, the idea is to *eliminate* one of the variables. To do this, one of the variables in the two equations must have coefficients that are opposites.

EXAMPLE 1 Using the Elimination Method

Use the elimination method to solve the system

$$x + y = 5$$
$$x - y = 3.$$

Each equation in this system is a statement of equality, so the sum of the left sides equals the sum of the right sides. Adding in this way gives

$$(x + y) + (x - y) = 5 + 3.$$

Combine terms and simplify to get

$$2x = 8$$
$$x = 4. \qquad \text{Divide by 2.}$$

Notice that y has been eliminated. The result, $x = 4$, gives the x-value of the solution of the given system. To find the y-value of the solution, substitute 4 for x in either of the two equations of the system.

Work Problem 1 at the Side. ▶▶▶

The solution found at the side, (4, 1), can be checked by substituting 4 for x and 1 for y in both equations of the given system.

Check:
$x + y = 5$	$x - y = 3$
$4 + 1 = 5$?	$4 - 1 = 3$?
$5 = 5$ True	$3 = 3$ True

Since both results are true, the solution of the system is (4, 1).

CAUTION

A system is not completely solved until values for both x and y are found. Do not stop after finding the value of only one variable. Remember to write the solution as an ordered pair.

---

1 **(a)** Substitute 4 for x in the equation $x + y = 5$ to find the value of y.

(b) Give the solution of the system.

◀◀◀ **Work Problem 2 at the Side.**

2 Solve each system by the elimination method. Check each solution.

(a) Fill in the blanks to find the solution.

$$x + y = 8$$
$$x - y = 2$$

Add.

$$(x + y) + (x - y) = 8 + \underline{\qquad}$$
$$2 \underline{\qquad} = \underline{\qquad}$$
$$x = \underline{\qquad}$$

Find y.

$$x - y = 2$$
$$\underline{\qquad} - y = 2$$
$$-y = \underline{\qquad}$$
$$y = \underline{\qquad}$$

The solution is $\underline{\qquad}$.

In general, to solve a system by elimination, follow these steps.

Solving a Linear System by Elimination

Step 1 **Write both equations in standard form** $Ax + By = C$.

Step 2 **Transform so that the coefficients of one pair of variable terms are opposites.** Multiply one or both equations by appropriate numbers so that the sum of the coefficients of either the x- or y-terms is 0.

Step 3 **Add** the new equations to eliminate a variable. The sum should be an equation with just one variable.

Step 4 **Solve** the equation from Step 3 for the remaining variable.

Step 5 **Substitute** the result from Step 4 into either of the original equations and solve for the other variable.

Step 6 **Check** the solution in both of the original equations. Then write the solution as an ordered pair.

It does not matter which variable is eliminated first. Usually we choose the one that is more convenient to work with.

EXAMPLE 2 **Using the Elimination Method**

Solve the system

$$y + 11 = 2x$$
$$5x = y + 26.$$

Step 1 Rewrite both equations in the form $Ax + By = C$ to get the system

$$-2x + y = -11 \qquad \text{Subtract } 2x \text{ and } 11.$$
$$5x - y = 26. \qquad \text{Subtract } y.$$

Step 2 Because the coefficients of y are 1 and -1, adding will eliminate y. It is not necessary to multiply either equation by a number.

(b) $3x - y = 7$
$2x + y = 3$

Step 3 Add the two equations. This time we use vertical addition.

$$\begin{array}{rcl} -2x + y &=& -11 \\ 5x - y &=& 26 \\ \hline 3x &=& 15 \end{array} \qquad \text{Add in columns.}$$

Step 4 Solve the equation.

$$3x = 15$$
$$x = 5 \qquad \text{Divide by 3.}$$

Step 5 Find the value of y by substituting 5 for x in either of the original equations. Choosing the first gives

$$y + 11 = 2x$$
$$y + 11 = 2(5) \qquad \text{Let } x = 5.$$
$$y + 11 = 10$$
$$y = -1. \qquad \text{Subtract 11.}$$

Continued on Next Page

Step 6   Check the solution by substituting $x = 5$ and $y = -1$ into both of the original equations.

$$y + 11 = 2x$$
$$(-1) + 11 = 2(5) \quad ?$$
$$10 = 10 \qquad \text{True}$$

$$5x = y + 26$$
$$5(5) = -1 + 26 \quad ?$$
$$25 = 25 \qquad \text{True}$$

The solution $(5, -1)$ is correct.

Work Problem 3 at the Side. ▶▶▶

OBJECTIVE 2   Multiply when using the elimination method.   Sometimes we need to multiply each side of one or both equations in a system by some number before adding the equations will eliminate a variable.

EXAMPLE 3   Multiplying Both Equations When Using the Elimination Method

Solve the system

$$2x + 3y = -15 \qquad (1)$$
$$5x + 2y = 1. \qquad (2)$$

Adding the two equations gives $7x + 5y = -14$, which does not eliminate either variable. However, we can multiply each equation by a suitable number so that the coefficients of one of the two variables are opposites. For example, to eliminate x, multiply each side of equation (1) by 5, and each side of equation (2) by -2.

$$\begin{array}{ll} 10x + 15y = -75 & \text{Multiply equation (1) by 5.} \\ \underline{-10x - 4y = -2} & \text{Multiply equation (2) by } -2. \\ 11y = -77 & \text{Add.} \\ y = -7 & \text{Divide by 11.} \end{array}$$

Substituting -7 for y in either equation (1) or (2) gives $x = 3$. Check that the solution of the system is $(3, -7)$.

Work Problem 4 at the Side. ▶▶▶

OBJECTIVE 3   Use an alternative method to find the second value in a solution.   Sometimes it is easier to find the value of the second variable in a solution by using the elimination method twice.

EXAMPLE 4   Finding the Second Value Using an Alternative Method

Solve the system

$$4x = 9 - 3y \qquad (1)$$
$$5x - 2y = 8. \qquad (2)$$

Rearrange the terms in equation (1) so that like terms are aligned in columns. To do this, add $3y$ to each side to get the following system.

$$4x + 3y = 9 \qquad (3)$$
$$5x - 2y = 8 \qquad (2)$$

One way to proceed is to eliminate y by multiplying each side of equation (3) by 2 and each side of equation (2) by 3, and then adding.

— **Continued on Next Page**

3 Solve each system by the elimination method. Check each solution.

(a) $2x - y = 2$
$4x + y = 10$

(b) $8x - 5y = 32$
$4x + 5y = 4$

4 (a) Solve the system in Example 3 by first eliminating the variable y. Check your solution.

(b) Solve

$$6x + 7y = 4$$
$$5x + 8y = -1,$$

and check your solution.

ANSWERS

3. (a) $(2, 2)$ (b) $\left(3, -\dfrac{8}{5}\right)$

4. (a) $(3, -7)$ (b) $(3, -2)$

5 Solve each system of equations.

(a) $5x = 7 + 2y$
$5y = 5 - 3x$

(b) $3y = 8 + 4x$
$6x = 9 - 2y$

$$8x + 6y = 18 \qquad \text{Multiply equation (3) by 2.}$$
$$\underline{15x - 6y = 24} \qquad \text{Multiply equation (2) by 3.}$$
$$23x \qquad = 42 \qquad \text{Add.}$$
$$x = \frac{42}{23} \qquad \text{Divide by 23.}$$

Substituting $\frac{42}{23}$ for x in one of the given equations would give y, but the arithmetic involved would be messy. Instead, solve for y by starting again with the original equations and eliminating x. Multiply each side of equation (3) by 5 and each side of equation (2) by -4, and then add.

$$20x + 15y = \quad 45 \qquad \text{Multiply equation (3) by 5.}$$
$$\underline{-20x + \; 8y = -32} \qquad \text{Multiply equation (2) by } -4.$$
$$23y = \quad 13 \qquad \text{Add.}$$
$$y = \frac{13}{23} \qquad \text{Divide by 23.}$$

Check that the solution is $\left(\frac{42}{23}, \frac{13}{23}\right)$.

>>> **Work Problem 5 at the Side.**

When the value of the first variable is a fraction, the method used in Example 4 helps avoid arithmetic errors. Of course, this method could be used to solve any system of equations.

OBJECTIVE 4 Use the elimination method to solve special systems.

6 Solve each system by the elimination method.

(a) $4x + 3y = 10$
$2x + \dfrac{3}{2}y = 12$

(b) $\quad 4x - \; 6y = 10$
$-10x + 15y = -25$

EXAMPLE 5 Using the Elimination Method for an Inconsistent System or Dependent Equations

Solve each system by the elimination method.

(a) $2x + 4y = 5$
$4x + 8y = -9$
Multiply each side of $2x + 4y = 5$ by -2; then add to $4x + 8y = -9$.

$$-4x - 8y = -10$$
$$\underline{4x + 8y = \quad -9}$$
$$0 = -19 \qquad \text{False}$$

The false statement $0 = -19$ shows that the given system has no solution.

(b) $\quad 3x - \; y = 4$
$-9x + 3y = -12$
Multiply each side of the first equation by 3; then add the two equations.

$$9x - 3y = \quad 12$$
$$\underline{-9x + 3y = -12}$$
$$0 = \quad 0 \qquad \text{True}$$

A true statement occurs when the equations are equivalent. As before, this indicates that every solution of one equation is also a solution of the other; there are an infinite number of solutions. (See **Section 4.2,** Example 6, where the same system was solved using substitution.)

>>> **Work Problem 6 at the Side.**

4.3 Exercises

FOR EXTRA HELP

Tutor Center Addison-Wesley Math Tutor Center

Math XL MathXL

Digital Video Tutor CD 4 Videotape 4

Student's Solutions Manual

MyMathLab MyMathLab

Interactmath.com

In Exercises 1–3, answer true *or* false *for each statement. If* false, *tell why.*

1. The ordered pair (0, 0) *must* be a solution of a system of the form

$$Ax + By = 0$$
$$Cx + Dy = 0.$$

2. To eliminate the *y*-terms in the system

$$2x + 12y = 7$$
$$3x + 4y = 1,$$

we should multiply the bottom equation by 3 and then add.

3. The system

$$x + y = 1$$
$$x + y = 2$$

has no solution.

4. Which one of the following systems would be easier to solve using the elimination method? Why?

$$5x - 3y = 7 \qquad 7x + 2y = 4$$
$$2x + 8y = 3 \qquad -7x + 3y = 1$$

Solve each system by the elimination method. Check each solution. See Examples 1 and 2.

5. $x + y = 2$
    $2x - y = -5$

6. $3x - y = -12$
    $x + y = 4$

7. $2x + y = -5$
    $x - y = 2$

8. $2x + y = -15$
    $-x - y = 10$

9. $3x + 2y = 0$
    $-3x - y = 3$

10. $5x - y = 5$
    $-5x + 2y = 0$

11. $6x - y = -1$
    $5y = 17 + 6x$

12. $y = 9 - 6x$
    $-6x + 3y = 15$

Solve each system by the elimination method. Check each solution. See Examples 3–5.

13. $2x - y = 12$
$3x + 2y = -3$

14. $x + y = 3$
$-3x + 2y = -19$

15. $x + 3y = 19$
$2x - y = 10$

16. $4x - 3y = -19$
$2x + y = 13$

17. $x + 4y = 16$
$3x + 5y = 20$

18. $2x + y = 8$
$5x - 2y = -16$

19. $5x - 3y = -20$
$-3x + 6y = 12$

20. $4x + 3y = -28$
$5x - 6y = -35$

21. $2x - 8y = 0$
$4x + 5y = 0$

22. $3x - 15y = 0$
$6x + 10y = 0$

23. $x + y = 7$
$x + y = -3$

24. $x - y = 4$
$x - y = -3$

25. $-x + 3y = 4$
$-2x + 6y = 8$

26. $6x - 2y = 24$
$-3x + y = -12$

27. $4x - 3y = -19$
$3x + 2y = 24$

28. $5x + 4y = 12$
$3x + 5y = 15$

29. $3x - 7 = -5y$
$5x + 4y = -10$

30. $2x + 3y = 13$
$6 + 2y = -5x$

31. $2x + 3y = 0$
$4x + 12 = 9y$

32. $-4x + 3y = 2$
$5x + 3 = -2y$

33. $24x + 12y = -7$
$16x - 17 = 18y$

34. $9x + 4y = -3$
$6x + 7 = -6y$

35. $3x = 3 + 2y$
$-\dfrac{4}{3}x + y = \dfrac{1}{3}$

36. $3x = 27 + 2y$
$x - \dfrac{7}{2}y = -25$

37. $5x - 2y = 3$
$10x - 4y = 5$

38. $3x - 5y = 1$
$6x - 10y = 4$

39. $6x + 3y = 0$
$-18x - 9y = 0$

40. $3x - 5y = 0$
$9x - 15y = 0$

RELATING CONCEPTS (EXERCISES 41–46) For Individual or Group Work

Attending the movies is one of America's favorite forms of entertainment. The graph shows movie attendance from 1991 to 1999. In 1991, attendance was 1141 million, as represented by the point P(1991, 1141). In 1999, attendance was 1465 million, as represented by the point Q(1999, 1465). We can find an equation of line segment PQ using a system of equations, and then we can use the equation to approximate the attendance in any of the years between 1991 and 1999. **Work Exercises 41–46 in order.**

Source: Motion Picture Association of America.

41. The line segment has an equation that can be written in the form $y = ax + b$. Using the coordinates of point P with $x = 1991$ and $y = 1141$, write an equation in the variables a and b.

42. Using the coordinates of point Q with $x = 1999$ and $y = 1465$, write a second equation in the variables a and b.

43. Write the system of equations formed from the two equations in Exercises 41 and 42, and solve the system using the elimination method.

44. What is the equation of the segment PQ?

45. Let $x = 1998$ in the equation of Exercise 44, and solve for y. How does the result compare with the actual figure of 1481 million?

46. The data points for the years 1991 through 1999 do not lie in a perfectly straight line. Explain the pitfalls of relying too heavily on using the equation in Exercise 44 to predict attendance.

Summary Exercises on Solving Systems of Linear Equations

The exercises in this summary include a variety of problems on solving systems of linear equations. Since we do not usually specify the method of solution, use the following guidelines to help you decide whether to use substitution or elimination.

Choosing a Method When Solving a System of Linear Equations

1. If one of the equations of the system is already solved for one of the variables, as in the systems

$$3x + 4y = 9 \qquad \text{or} \qquad -5x + 3y = 9$$
$$y = 2x - 6 \qquad\qquad\qquad x = 3y - 7,$$

the substitution method is the better choice.

2. If both equations are in standard $Ax + By = C$ form, as in

$$4x - 11y = 3$$
$$-2x + 3y = 4,$$

and none of the variables has coefficient -1 or 1, the elimination method is the better choice.

3. If one or both of the equations are in standard form and the coefficient of one of the variables is -1 or 1, as in the systems

$$3x + y = -2 \qquad\qquad -x + 3y = -4$$
$$-5x + 2y = 4 \qquad \text{or} \qquad 3x - 2y = 8,$$

either method is appropriate.

Use the information in the preceding box to solve each problem.

1. Assuming you want to minimize the amount of work required, tell whether you would use the substitution or elimination method to solve each system. Explain your answers. *Do not actually solve.*

   (a) $3x + 2y = 18$
   $y = 3x$

   (b) $3x + y = -7$
   $x - y = -5$

   (c) $3x - 2y = 0$
   $9x + 8y = 7$

2. Which one of the following systems would be easier to solve using the substitution method? Why?

$$5x - 3y = 7 \qquad\qquad 7x + 2y = 4$$
$$2x + 8y = 3 \qquad\qquad y = -3x + 1$$

*In Exercises 3 and 4, **(a)** solve the system by the elimination method, **(b)** solve the system by the substitution method, and **(c)** tell which method you prefer for that particular system and why.*

3. $4x - 3y = -8$
    $x + 3y = 13$

4. $2x + 5y = 0$
    $x = -3y + 1$

Solve each system by the method of your choice. (For Exercises 5–7, see your answers for Exercise 1.)

5. $3x + 2y = 18$
    $y = 3x$

6. $3x + y = -7$
    $x - y = -5$

7. $3x - 2y = 0$
    $9x + 8y = 7$

8. $x + y = 7$
    $x = -3 - y$

9. $5x - 4y = 15$
    $-3x + 6y = -9$

10. $4x + 2y = 3$
    $y = -x$

11. $3x = 7 - y$
    $2y = 14 - 6x$

12. $3x - 5y = 7$
    $2x + 3y = 30$

13. $3y = 4x + 2$
    $5x - 2y = -3$

14. $4x + 3y = 1$
    $3x + 2y = 2$

15. $2x - 3y = 7$
    $-4x + 6y = 14$

16. $2x + 3y = 10$
    $-3x + y = 18$

17. $6x + 5y = 13$
    $3x + 3y = 4$

18. $x - 3y = 7$
    $4x + y = 5$

Solve each system by any method. First clear all fractions.

19. $\dfrac{1}{4}x - \dfrac{1}{5}y = 9$
    $y = 5x$

20. $\dfrac{1}{2}x + \dfrac{1}{3}y = -\dfrac{1}{3}$
    $\dfrac{1}{2}x + 2y = -7$

21. $\dfrac{1}{6}x + \dfrac{1}{6}y = 1$
    $-\dfrac{1}{2}x - \dfrac{1}{3}y = -5$

22. $\dfrac{x}{5} + 2y = \dfrac{8}{5}$
    $\dfrac{3x}{5} + \dfrac{y}{2} = -\dfrac{7}{10}$

23. $\dfrac{x}{5} + y = \dfrac{6}{5}$
    $\dfrac{x}{10} + \dfrac{y}{3} = \dfrac{5}{6}$

24. $\dfrac{1}{6}x + \dfrac{1}{3}y = 8$
    $\dfrac{1}{4}x + \dfrac{1}{2}y = 12$

4.4 Applications of Linear Systems

Recall from **Section 2.4** the six-step method for solving applied problems. We modify those steps slightly to allow for two variables and two equations.

OBJECTIVES

1 Solve problems about unknown numbers.

2 Solve problems about quantities and their costs.

3 Solve problems about mixtures.

4 Solve problems about distance, rate (or speed), and time.

Solving Applied Problems with Two Variables

Step 1   **Read** the problem, several times if necessary, until you understand what is given and what is to be found.

Step 2   **Assign variables** to represent the unknown values, using diagrams or tables as needed. Write down what each variable represents.

Step 3   **Write two equations** using both variables.

Step 4   **Solve** the system of two equations.

Step 5   **State the answer** to the problem. Is the answer reasonable?

Step 6   **Check** the answer in the words of the original problem.

1 Solve the system
$$x = 1954 + y$$
$$x + y = 24{,}098.$$

OBJECTIVE 1 Solve problems about unknown numbers.

EXAMPLE 1 Solving a Problem about Two Unknown Numbers

In 2000, sales of athletic/sport footwear were $1954 million more than sales of athletic/sport clothing. Together, total sales for these items were $24,098 million. (*Source:* National Sporting Goods Association.) What were the sales for each?

Step 1   **Read** the problem carefully. We must find the 2000 sales (in millions of dollars) for athletic/sport clothing and footwear. We know how much more footwear sales were than clothing sales. Also, we know the total sales.

Step 2   **Assign variables.**

Let x = sales of footwear in millions of dollars,

and y = sales of clothing in millions of dollars.

Step 3   **Write two equations.**

$x = 1954 + y$ Sales of footwear were $1954 million more than sales of clothing.

$x + y = 24{,}098$ Total sales were $24,098 million.

Step 4   **Solve** the system from Step 3. The substitution method works well here since the first equation is already solved for x.

> **Work Problem 1 at the Side.** ▶▶▶

Step 5   **State the answer.** Footwear sales were $13,026 million, and clothing sales were $11,072 million.

Step 6   **Check** the answer in the original problem. Since

$$13{,}026 - 11{,}072 = 1954 \quad \text{and} \quad 13{,}026 + 11{,}072 = 24{,}098,$$

the answer satisfies the information in the problem.

2 Set up a system of equations for the following problem. Do not solve the system.

Two top-grossing Disney movies in 2002 were *Lilo and Stitch* and *The Santa Clause 2*. Together they grossed $284.2 million. *The Santa Clause 2* grossed $7.4 million less than *Lilo and Stitch*. How much did each movie gross? (*Source: Variety.*)

Let x = the amount (in millions) that *Lilo and Stitch* grossed,

and y = the amount (in millions) that _____ grossed.

> **CAUTION**
> If an applied problem asks for *two* values as in Example 1, be sure to give both of them in your answer.

◀◀◀ **Work Problem 2 at the Side.**

OBJECTIVE 2 Solve problems about quantities and their costs. We can also use a linear system to solve an applied problem involving two quantities and their costs.

EXAMPLE 2 Solving a Problem about Quantities and Costs

The all-time top-grossing movie *Titanic** earned more in Europe than in the United States. This may be because average movie prices in Europe exceed those of the United States. (*Source: Parade* magazine, September 13, 1998.)

For example, while the average movie ticket (to the nearest dollar) in 1997–1998 cost $5 in the United States, it cost an equivalent of $11 in London. Suppose that a group of 41 Americans and Londoners who paid these average prices spent a total of $307 for tickets. How many from each country were in the group?

Step 1 **Read** the problem several times.

Step 2 **Assign variables.**

Let x = the number of Americans in the group,

and y = the number of Londoners in the group.

Summarize the information given in the problem in a table. The entries in the first two rows of the Total Value column were found by multiplying the number of tickets sold by the price per ticket.

	Number of Tickets	Price per Ticket in dollars	Total Value
Americans	x	5	$5x$
Londoners	y	11	$11y$
Total	41		307

Step 3 **Write two equations.** The total number of tickets was 41, so

$$x + y = 41. \quad \text{Total number of tickets}$$

Since the total value was $307, the final column leads to

$$5x + 11y = 307. \quad \text{Total value of tickets}$$

These two equations form the system

$$x + y = 41 \quad (1)$$
$$5x + 11y = 307. \quad (2)$$

Step 4 **Solve** the system using the elimination method. To eliminate the x-terms, multiply each side of equation (1) by -5 to get

$$-5x - 5y = -205.$$

Continued on Next Page

* Through September 2003, *Titanic* was still number one. (*Source: Variety.*)

Then add this result to equation (2).

$$
\begin{array}{rcl}
-5x - 5y &=& -205 \\
\underline{5x + 11y} &=& \underline{307} \quad (2) \\
6y &=& 102 \quad \text{Add.} \\
y &=& 17 \quad \text{Divide by 6.}
\end{array}
$$

Substitute 17 for y in equation (1) to get

$$
\begin{array}{rcl}
x + y &=& 41 \\
x + 17 &=& 41 \quad \text{Let } y = 17. \\
x &=& 24.
\end{array}
$$

Step 5 **State the answer.** There were 24 Americans and 17 Londoners in the group.

Step 6 **Check.** The sum of 24 and 17 is 41, so the number of moviegoers is correct. Since 24 Americans paid $5 each and 17 Londoners paid $11 each, the total of the admission prices is

$$
\$5(24) + \$11(17) = \$307,
$$

which agrees with the total amount stated in the problem.

> **Work Problem 3 at the Side.** ▶▶▶

OBJECTIVE 3 Solve problems about mixtures. In **Section 2.6** we solved percent problems using one variable. Many problems about mixtures that involve percent can be solved using a system of two equations in two variables.

EXAMPLE 3 Solving a Mixture Problem Involving Percent

A pharmacist needs 100 L of 50% alcohol solution. She has on hand 30% alcohol solution and 80% alcohol solution, which she can mix. How many liters of each will be required to make the 100 L of 50% alcohol solution?

Step 1 **Read** the problem. Note the percent of each solution and of the mixture.

Step 2 **Assign variables.**

Let x = the number of liters of 30% alcohol needed,

and y = the number of liters of 80% alcohol needed.

Summarize the information in a table. Percents are represented in decimal form.

Percent	Liters of Mixture	Liters of Pure Alcohol
.30	x	$.30x$
.80	y	$.80y$
.50	100	$.50(100)$

Continued on Next Page

---

③ The average movie ticket (to the nearest U.S. dollar) costs $10 in Geneva and $8 in Paris. (*Source: Parade* magazine, September 13, 1998.) If a group of 36 people from these two cities paid $298 for tickets to see *Cheaper by the Dozen*, how many people from each city were there?

(a) Complete the table.

	Number of Tickets Sold	Price (in dollars)	Total Value
Genevans	x		
Parisians	y		
Total			

(b) Write a system of equations.

(c) Solve the system and check your answer in the words of the original problem.

ANSWERS
3. **(a)**

	Number of Tickets Sold	Price (in dollars)	Total Value
Genevans	x	10	$10x$
Parisians	y	8	$8y$
Total	36		298

(b) $x + y = 36$
$10x + 8y = 298$
(c) Genevans: 5; Parisians: 31

4 Solve the system

$$x + y = 100$$
$$.30x + .80y = 50.$$

5 How many liters of 25% alcohol solution must be mixed with 12% solution to get 13 L of 15% solution?

(a) Complete the table.

Percent	Liters	Liters of Pure Alcohol
.25	x	$.25x$
.12	y	
.15	13	

(b) Write a system of equations, and solve it.

6 Solve the problem.

Joe needs 100 cc (cubic centimeters) of 20% acid solution for a chemistry experiment. The lab has on hand only 10% and 25% solutions. How much of each should he mix to get the desired amount of 20% solution?

7 Solve using the distance formula.

A small plane traveled from Warsaw to Rome, averaging 164 mph. The trip took 2.5 hr. What is the distance from Warsaw to Rome?

ANSWERS

4. $(60, 40)$

5. **(a)**

Percent	Liters	Liters of Pure Alcohol
.25	x	$.25x$
.12	y	$.12y$
.15	13	$.15(13)$

(b) $x + y = 13$
$.25x + .12y = .15(13)$

3 L of 25%, 10 L of 12%

6. $33\frac{1}{3}$ cc of 10%, $66\frac{2}{3}$ cc of 25%

7. 410 mi

Figure 7 gives an idea of what is actually happening in this problem.

Figure 7

Step 3 **Write two equations.** Since the total number of liters in the final mixture will be 100, the first equation is

$$x + y = 100.$$

To find the amount of pure alcohol in each mixture, multiply the number of liters by the concentration. The amount of pure alcohol in the 30% solution added to the amount of pure alcohol in the 80% solution will equal the amount of pure alcohol in the final 50% solution. This gives the second equation,

$$.30x + .80y = .50(100).$$

These two equations form the system

$$x + y = 100$$
$$.30x + .80y = 50. \qquad .50(100) = 50$$

Step 4 **Solve** this system.

▶◀◀ Work Problem 4 at the Side.

Step 5 **State the answer.** From Problem 4 at the side, the pharmacist should use 60 L of the 30% solution and 40 L of the 80% solution.

Step 6 Since $60 + 40 = 100$ and $.30(60) + .80(40) = 50$, this mixture will give the 100 L of 50% solution, as required in the original problem.

▶◀◀ Work Problems 5 and 6 at the Side.

OBJECTIVE 4 **Solve problems about distance, rate (or speed), and time.** If an automobile travels at an average rate of 50 mph for 2 hr, then it travels $50 \times 2 = 100$ mi. This is an example of the basic relationship between distance, rate, and time:

$$\text{distance} = \text{rate} \times \text{time}.$$

This relationship is given by the formula $d = rt$.

▶◀◀ Work Problem 7 at the Side.

We can solve problems involving the distance formula with systems of two linear equations. Keep in mind that setting up a table and drawing a sketch will help you solve such problems.

EXAMPLE 4 Solving a Problem about Distance, Rate, and Time

Two executives in cities 400 mi apart drive to a business meeting at a location on the line between their cities. They meet after 4 hr. Find the speed of each car if one car travels 20 mph faster than the other.

Step 1 **Read** the problem carefully.

Step 2 **Assign variables.** Let x = the speed of the faster car,

and y = the speed of the slower car.

We use the formula $d = rt$. Since each car travels for 4 hr, the time, t, for each car is 4. See the table. The distance is found by using the formula $d = rt$ and the expressions already entered in the table.

	r	t	d
Faster Car	x	4	$4x$
Slower Car	y	4	$4y$

Find d from $d = rt$.

Figure 8 shows what is happening in the problem.

Figure 8

Step 3 **Write two equations.** As shown in the figure, since the total distance traveled by both cars is 400 mi, one equation is

$$4x + 4y = 400.$$

Because the faster car goes 20 mph faster than the slower car, the second equation is

$$x = 20 + y.$$

Step 4 **Solve** the system of equations,

$$4x + 4y = 400 \quad (1)$$
$$x = 20 + y, \quad (2)$$

by substitution. Replace x with $20 + y$ in equation (1) and then solve for y.

$4(20 + y) + 4y = 400$	Let $x = 20 + y$.
$80 + 4y + 4y = 400$	Distributive property
$80 + 8y = 400$	Combine like terms.
$8y = 320$	Subtract 80.
$y = 40$	Divide by 8.

Since $x = 20 + y$, and $y = 40$,

$$x = 20 + 40 = 60.$$

Step 5 **State the answer.** The speeds of the two cars are 40 mph and 60 mph.

Step 6 **Check** the answer. Since each car travels for 4 hr, total distance is

$$4(60) + 4(40) = 240 + 160 = 400 \text{ mi}, \qquad \text{as required.}$$

Work Problem 8 at the Side. ▶▶▶

8 Two cars that were 450 mi apart traveled toward each other. They met after 5 hr. If one car traveled twice as fast as the other, what were their speeds?

(a) Complete this table.

	r	t	d
Faster Car	x	5	
Slower Car	y	5	

(b) Write a system, and solve it.

ANSWERS
8. **(a)**

	r	t	d
Faster Car	x	5	$5x$
Slower Car	y	5	$5y$

(b) $5x + 5y = 450$
$x = 2y$

faster car: $x = 60$ mph
slower car: $y = 30$ mph

⑨ Solve the system

$$x + y = 320$$
$$x - y = 280.$$

EXAMPLE 5 Solving a Problem about Distance, Rate, and Time

A plane flies 560 mi in 1.75 hr traveling with the wind. The return trip against the same wind takes the plane 2 hr. Find the speed of the plane and the speed of the wind.

Step 1 **Read** the problem several times.

Step 2 **Assign variables.**

Let x = the speed of the plane,

and y = the speed of the wind.

The speed (rate) of the plane *with* the wind is $x + y$ mph, and the speed (rate) of the plane *against* the wind is $x - y$ mph. See Figure 9.

$x - y$ mph
against wind

$x + y$ mph
with wind

Figure 9

⑩ Solve the problem.
In 1 hr, Ann can row 2 mi against the current or 10 mi with the current. Find the speed of the current and Ann's speed in still water. (*Hint:* Let x = the speed of the current and y = Ann's speed in still water. Then her rate against the current is $y - x$, and her rate with the current is $y + x$.)

We use this information and the formula $d = rt$ (or $rt = d$) to complete a table.

	r	t	d
With Wind	$x + y$	1.75	560
Against Wind	$x - y$	2	560

Step 3 **Write two equations.** From the table,

$$1.75(x + y) = 560 \xrightarrow{\text{Divide by 1.75.}} x + y = 320 \quad (1)$$

$$2(x - y) = 560 \xrightarrow{\text{Divide by 2.}} x - y = 280. \quad (2)$$

Step 4 **Solve** the system of equations (1) and (2).

◀◀◀ Work Problem 9 at the Side.

Step 5 **State the answer.** From Problem 9 at the side, the speed of the plane is 300 mph and the speed of the wind is 20 mph.

Step 6 **Check.** The answer seems reasonable, and true statements result when the values are substituted into the equations of the system.

◀◀◀ Work Problem 10 at the Side.

4.4 Exercises

Choose the correct response in Exercises 1–7.

1. Which expression represents the monetary value of x 20-dollar bills?

   A. $\dfrac{x}{20}$ dollars   **B.** $\dfrac{20}{x}$ dollars   **C.** $20 + x$ dollars   **D.** $20x$ dollars

2. Which expression represents the cost of t pounds of candy that sells for $1.95 per lb?

   A. $1.95t$ **B.** $\dfrac{\$1.95}{t}$ **C.** $\dfrac{t}{\$1.95}$ **D.** $1.95 + t$

3. Which expression represents the amount of interest earned on d dollars at an interest rate of 2%?

   A. $2d$ dollars   **B.** $.02d$ dollars   **C.** $.2d$ dollars   **D.** $200d$ dollars

4. Suppose that x liters of a 40% acid solution are mixed with y liters of a 35% solution to obtain 100 L of a 38% solution. One equation in a system for solving this problem is $x + y = 100$. Which one of the following is the other equation?
   A. $.35x + .40y = .38(100)$ **B.** $.40x + .35y = .38(100)$
   C. $35x + 40y = 38$ **D.** $40x + 35y = .38(100)$

5. According to *Natural History* magazine, the speed of a cheetah is 70 mph. If a cheetah runs for x hours, how many miles does the cheetah cover?

   A. $70 + x$ miles   **B.** $70 - x$ miles   **C.** $\dfrac{70}{x}$ miles   **D.** $70x$ miles

6. What is the speed of a plane that travels at a rate of 560 mph *against* a wind of r mph?

   A. $560 + r$ mph   **B.** $\dfrac{560}{r}$ mph   **C.** $560 - r$ mph   **D.** $r - 560$ mph

7. What is the speed of a plane that travels at a rate of 560 mph *with* a wind of r mph?

   A. $\dfrac{r}{560}$ mph   **B.** $560 - r$ mph   **C.** $560 + r$ mph   **D.** $r - 560$ mph

8. Using the list of steps for solving an applied problem with two variables, write a short paragraph describing the general procedure you will use to solve the problems that follow in this exercise set.

Exercises 9 and 10 are good warm-up problems. In each case, refer to the six-step problem-solving method, fill in the blanks for Steps 2 and 3, and then complete the solution by applying Steps 4–6.

9. The sum of two numbers is 98 and the difference between them is 48. Find the two numbers.

Step 1 **Read** the problem carefully.

Step 2 **Assign variables.**

Let x = the first number and let

y = _____.

Step 3 **Write two equations.**

First equation: $x + y = 98$

Second equation: _____

10. The sum of two numbers is 201 and the difference between them is 11. Find the two numbers.

Step 1 **Read** the problem carefully.

Step 2 **Assign variables.**

Let x = the first number and let

y = _____.

Step 3 **Write two equations.**

First equation: $x + y = 201$

Second equation: _____

Write a system of equations for each problem, and then solve the problem. See Example 1.

11. During 2002, two of the top-grossing concert tours were by the Rolling Stones and Cher. Together the two tours visited 117 cities. Cher visited 51 more cities than the Rolling Stones. How many cities did each tour visit? (*Source:* Pollstar.)

12. In 2003, the two top formats of U.S. commercial radio stations were country and news/talk. There were 288 fewer news/talk stations than country stations, and together they comprised a total of 3912 stations. How many stations of each format were there? (*Source:* M Street Corporation.)

13. The two top-grossing movies of 2003 were *The Lord of the Rings: The Return of the King* and *Finding Nemo*. *Finding Nemo* grossed $21.4 million less than *The Lord of the Rings: The Return of the King*, and together the two films took in $700.8 million. How much did each of these movies earn? (*Source:* Nielsen EDI.)

14. The life span of a $100 bill is 80 months longer than the life span of a $1 bill. If the combined life span of a $1 bill and a $100 bill is 124 months, what is the life span of each bill? (*Source:* Bureau of Engraving and Printing.)

15. The Terminal Tower in Cleveland, Ohio, is 242 ft shorter than the Key Tower, also in Cleveland. The total of the heights of the two buildings is 1658 ft. Find the heights of the buildings. (*Source: World Almanac and Book of Facts, 2004.*)

Terminal Tower   Key Tower

16. In 2003, a total of 943.8 thousand people lived in the cities of Las Vegas, Nevada, and Sacramento, California. Sacramento had 73.4 thousand fewer residents than Las Vegas. What was the population of each city? (*Source:* Bureau of the Census.)

If x units of a product cost C dollars to manufacture and earn revenue of R dollars, the value of x where the expressions for C and R are equal is called the **break-even quantity,** *the number of units that produce 0 profit. In Exercises 17 and 18,* **(a)** *find the break-even quantity, and* **(b)** *decide whether the product should be produced based on whether it will earn a profit. (Profit equals revenue minus cost.)*

17. $C = 85x + 900$; $R = 105x$; no more than 38 units can be sold.

18. $C = 105x + 6000$; $R = 255x$; no more than 400 units can be sold.

Write a system of equations for each problem, and then solve the system. See Example 2.

19. A motel clerk counts his $1 and $10 bills at the end of a day. He finds that he has a total of 74 bills having a combined monetary value of $326. Find the number of bills of each denomination that he has.

Denomination of Bill	Number of Bills	Total Value
$1	x	
$10	y	
Totals	74	$326

20. Letarsha is a bank teller. At the end of a day, she has a total of 69 $5 and $10 bills. The total value of the money is $590. How many of each denomination does she have?

Denomination of Bill	Number of Bills	Total Value
$5	x	$5x$
$10	y	
Totals		

21. A newspaper advertised DVDs and CDs. Tracy Sudak went shopping and bought each of her seven nephews a gift, either a DVD of the movie *Miracle* or the latest Linkin Park CD. The DVD cost $14.95 and the CD cost $16.88, and she spent a total of $114.30. How many DVDs and how many CDs did she buy?

22. Terry Wong saw the ad (see Exercise 21) and he, too, went shopping. He bought each of his five nieces a gift, either a DVD of *Home on the Range* or the CD soundtrack to *Scooby Doo 2: Monsters Unleashed.* The DVD cost $14.99 and the soundtrack cost $13.88, and he spent a total of $70.51. How many DVDs and CDs did he buy?

23. Maria Lopez has twice as much money invested at 5% simple annual interest as she does at 4%. If her yearly income from these two investments is $350, how much does she have invested at each rate?

24. Charles Miller invested his textbook royalty income in two accounts, one paying 3% annual simple interest and the other paying 2% interest. He earned a total of $11 interest. If he invested three times as much in the 3% account as he did in the 2% account, how much did he invest at each rate?

25. Average movie ticket prices in the United States are, in general, lower than in other countries. It would cost $77.87 to buy three tickets in Japan plus two tickets in Switzerland. Three tickets in Switzerland plus two tickets in Japan would cost $73.83. How much does an average movie ticket cost in each of these countries? (*Source:* Business Traveler International.)

26. (See Exercise 25.) Four movie tickets in Germany plus three movie tickets in France would cost $62.27. Three tickets in Germany plus four tickets in France would cost $62.19. How much does an average movie ticket cost in each of these countries? (*Source:* Business Traveler International.)

Write a system of equations for each problem, and then solve the system. See Example 3.

27. A 40% dye solution is to be mixed with a 70% dye solution to get 120 L of a 50% solution. How many liters of the 40% and 70% solutions will be needed?

Percent (as a Decimal)	Liters of Solution	Liters of Pure Dye
.40	x	
.70	y	
.50	120	

28. A 90% antifreeze solution is to be mixed with a 75% solution to make 120 L of a 78% solution. How many liters of the 90% and 75% solutions will be used?

Percent (as a Decimal)	Liters of Solution	Liters of Pure Antifreeze
.90	x	
.75	y	
.78	120	

29. A merchant wishes to mix coffee worth $6 per lb with coffee worth $3 per lb to get 90 lb of a mixture worth $4 per lb. How many pounds of the $6 and the $3 coffees will be needed?

Dollars per Pound	Pounds	Cost
6	x	
	y	
	90	

30. A grocer wishes to blend candy selling for $1.20 per lb with candy selling for $1.80 per lb to get a mixture that will be sold for $1.40 per lb. How many pounds of the $1.20 and the $1.80 candies should be used to get 45 lb of the mixture?

Dollars per Pound	Pounds	Cost
	x	
1.80	y	
	45	

31. How many barrels of pickles worth $40 per barrel and pickles worth $60 per barrel must be mixed to obtain 50 barrels of a mixture worth $48 per barrel?

32. The owner of a nursery wants to mix some fertilizer worth $70 per bag with some worth $90 per bag to obtain 40 bags of mixture worth $77.50 per bag. How many bags of each type should she use?

Write a system of equations for each problem, and then solve the system. See Examples 4 and 5.

33. RAGBRAI®, the Des Moines **R**egister's **A**nnual **G**reat **B**icycle **R**ide **A**cross **I**owa, is the longest and oldest touring bicycle ride in the world. Suppose a cyclist began the 490 mi ride on July 25, 2004 in western Iowa at the same time that a car traveling toward it left eastern Iowa. If the bicycle and the car met after 7 hr and the car traveled 40 mph faster than the bicycle, find the average speed of each. (*Source:* www.ragbrai.org)

RAGBRAI XXXII ROUTE
July 25 – 31, 2004

34. In 2002, Atlanta's Hartsfield Airport was the nation's busiest. Suppose two planes leave the airport at the same time, one traveling east and the other traveling west. If the planes are 2100 mi apart after 2 hr and one plane travels 50 mph faster than the other, find the speed of each plane. (*Source:* Airports Council International—North America.)

35. Toledo and Cincinnati are 200 mi apart. A car leaves Toledo traveling toward Cincinnati, and another car leaves Cincinnati at the same time, traveling toward Toledo. The car leaving Toledo averages 15 mph faster than the other, and they meet after 1 hr and 36 min. What are the rates of the cars?

36. Kansas City and Denver are 600 mi apart. Two cars start from these cities, traveling toward each other. They meet after 6 hr. Find the rate of each car if one travels 30 mph slower than the other.

37. At the beginning of a bicycle ride for charity, Roberto and Juana are 30 mi apart. If they leave at the same time and ride in the same direction, Roberto overtakes Juana in 6 hr. If they ride toward each other, they meet in 1 hr. What are their speeds?

38. Mr. Abbot left Farmersville in a plane at noon to travel to Exeter. Mr. Baker left Exeter in his automobile at 2 P.M. to travel to Farmersville. It is 400 mi from Exeter to Farmersville. If the sum of their speeds was 120 mph, and if they crossed paths at 4 P.M., find the speed of each.

39. A boat takes 3 hr to go 24 mi upstream. It can go 36 mi downstream in the same time. Find the speed of the current and the speed of the boat in still water if x = the speed of the boat in still water and y = the speed of the current.

	d	r	t
Downstream	36	$x + y$	
Upstream	24	$x - y$	

40. It takes a boat $1\frac{1}{2}$ hr to go 12 mi downstream, and 6 hr to return. Find the speed of the boat in still water and the speed of the current. Let x = the speed of the boat in still water and y = the speed of the current.

	d	r	t
Downstream	12	$x + y$	$\frac{3}{2}$
Upstream			6

Downstream   Upstream
$x + y$ $x - y$

41. If a plane can travel 440 mph against the wind and 500 mph with the wind, find the speed of the wind and the speed of the plane in still air.

440 mph
against wind

500 mph
with wind

42. A small plane travels 200 mph with the wind and 120 mph against it. Find the speed of the wind and the speed of the plane in still air.

4.5 Solving Systems of Linear Inequalities

We graphed the solutions of a linear inequality in **Section 3.5.** Recall that to graph the solutions of $x + 3y > 12$, for example, we first graph $x + 3y = 12$ by finding and plotting a few ordered pairs that satisfy the equation. Because the points on the line do *not* satisfy the inequality, we use a dashed line. To decide which side of the line includes the points that are solutions, we choose a test point not on the line, such as $(0, 0)$. Substituting these values for x and y in the inequality gives

$$x + 3y > 12$$
$$0 + 3(0) > 12$$
$$0 > 12,$$

a false result. This indicates that the solutions are those points on the side of the line that does not include $(0, 0)$, as shown in Figure 10.

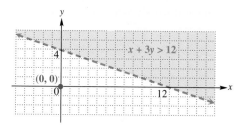

Figure 10

Now we use the same techniques to solve systems of linear inequalities.

OBJECTIVE 1 Solve systems of linear inequalities by graphing. A **system of linear inequalities** consists of two or more linear inequalities. The **solution of a system of linear inequalities** includes all points that make all inequalities of the system true at the same time. To solve a system of linear inequalities, use the following steps.

Solving a System of Linear Inequalities

Step 1 **Graph the inequalities.** Graph each inequality using the method of **Section 3.5.**

Step 2 **Choose the intersection.** Indicate the solution of the system by shading the intersection of the graphs (the region where the graphs overlap).

EXAMPLE 1 Solving a System of Two Linear Inequalities

Graph the solution of the system

$$3x + 2y \leq 6$$
$$2x - 5y \geq 10.$$

To graph $3x + 2y \leq 6$, graph the solid boundary line $3x + 2y = 6$ and shade the region containing $(0, 0)$, as shown in Figure 11(a) on the next page. Then graph $2x - 5y \geq 10$ with the solid boundary line $2x - 5y = 10$. The test point $(0, 0)$ makes this inequality false, so shade the region on the other side of the boundary line. See Figure 11(b).

Continued on Next Page

1 Graph the solution of the system

$$x - 2y \leq 8$$
$$3x + y \geq 6.$$

To get you started, the graphs of $x - 2y = 8$ and $3x + y = 6$ are shown.

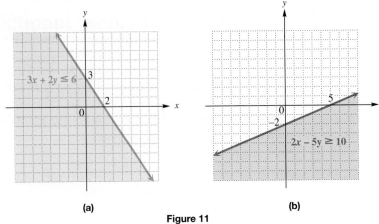

(a)   (b)

Figure 11

The solution of this system includes all points in the intersection (overlap) of the graphs of the two inequalities. It includes the shaded region and portions of the two boundary lines shown in Figure 12.

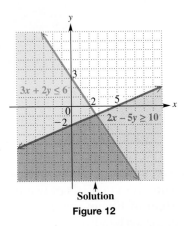

Solution

Figure 12

◀◀◀ **Work Problem 1 at the Side.**

NOTE

We usually do all the work on one set of axes. In the following examples, only one graph is shown. Be sure that the region of the final solution is clearly indicated.

EXAMPLE 2 **Solving a System of Two Linear Inequalities**

Graph the solution of the system

$$x - y > 5$$
$$2x + y < 2.$$

Figure 13 shows the graphs of both $x - y > 5$ and $2x + y < 2$. Dashed lines show that the graphs of the inequalities do not include their boundary lines. The solution of the system is the region with the darkest shading. The solution does not include either boundary line.

Continued on Next Page

ANSWERS
1.

$x - 2y \leq 8$
$3x + y \geq 6$

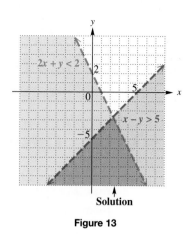

Figure 13

2 Graph the solution of each system.

(a) $x + 2y < 0$
$3x - 4y < 12$

(b) $3x + 2y \leq 12$
$x \leq 2$
$y \leq 4$

EXAMPLE 3 **Solving a System of Three Linear Inequalities**

Graph the solution of the system

$$4x - 3y \leq 8$$
$$x \geq 2$$
$$y \leq 4.$$

Recall that $x = 2$ is a vertical line through the point $(2, 0)$, and $y = 4$ is a horizontal line through $(0, 4)$. The graph of the solution is the shaded region in Figure 14, including all boundary lines.

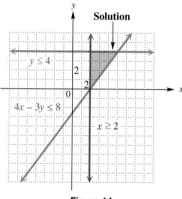

Figure 14

Work Problem 2 at the Side. ❱❱❱

ANSWERS
2. (a)

(b)

Real-Data Applications

Sales of Compact Discs versus Cassettes

Sales of compact discs (CDs) and cassettes for the years 1990 through 2000 are given in the table. The number of years since 1990 is represented by x. Sales of compact discs and cassettes can be modeled by linear equations.

- A linear model for the sales of compact discs is

$$y = 74.523x + 289.3.$$

- A linear model for the sales of cassettes is

$$y = -34.107x + 434.49.$$

y is sales in millions. The actual data and the linear models are graphed below.

Year	x	CD Sales (in millions)	Cassette Sales (in millions)
1990	0	286.5	442.2
1991	1	333.4	360.1
1992	2	407.5	366.4
1993	3	495.4	339.5
1994	4	662.1	345.4
1995	5	722.9	272.6
1996	6	778.9	225.3
1997	7	753.1	172.6
1998	8	847.0	158.5
1999	9	938.9	123.6
2000	10	942.5	76.0

Source: World Almanac and Book of Facts, 2004.

SALES OF CDs VERSUS CASSETTES

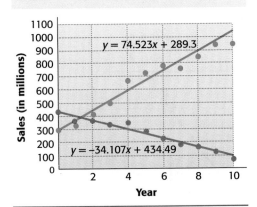

For Group Discussion

1. Shade the region on the graph that corresponds to the solution of the following system.

$$y \leq 74.523x + 289.3$$
$$y \geq -34.107x + 434.49$$

Interpret the solution in the context of sales of compact discs and cassettes.

2. Solve the linear inequality $74.523x + 289.3 > -34.107x + 434.49$. Round your answer to the nearest hundredth.

3. What does the solution to the inequality in Problem 2 represent in the context of sales of CDs and cassettes?

4.5 Exercises

FOR EXTRA HELP

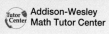 Addison-Wesley Math Tutor Center   *Math* XL MathXL   Digital Video Tutor CD 4 Videotape 4   Student's Solutions Manual   *MyMathLab* MyMathLab   Interactmath.com

Match each system of inequalities with the correct graph from choices A–D.

1. $x \geq 5$
$y \leq -3$

2. $x \leq 5$
$y \geq -3$

3. $x > 5$
$y < -3$

4. $x < 5$
$y > -3$

A.

B.

C.

D.

Graph the solution of each system of linear inequalities. See Examples 1–3.

5. $x + y \leq 6$
$x - y \geq 1$

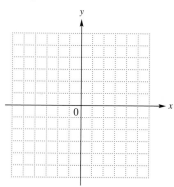

6. $x + y \leq 2$
$x - y \geq 3$

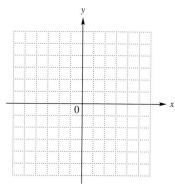

7. $4x + 5y \geq 20$
$x - 2y \leq 5$

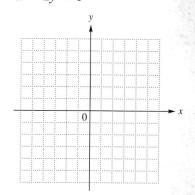

8. $x + 4y \leq 8$
$2x - y \geq 4$

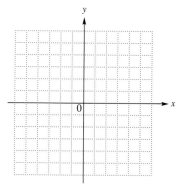

9. $2x + 3y < 6$
$x - y < 5$

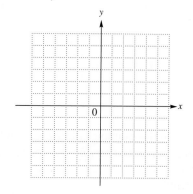

10. $x + 2y < 4$
$x - y < -1$

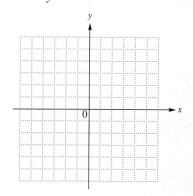

11. $y \leq 2x - 5$
    $x < 3y + 2$

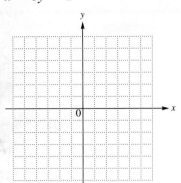

12. $x \geq 2y + 6$
    $y > -2x + 4$

13. $4x + 3y < 6$
    $x - 2y > 4$

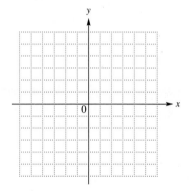

14. $3x + y > 4$
    $x + 2y < 2$

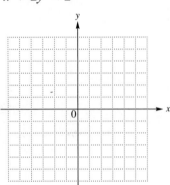

15. $x \leq 2y + 3$
    $x + y < 0$

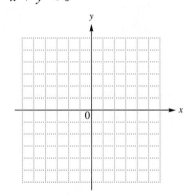

16. $x \leq 4y + 3$
    $x + y > 0$

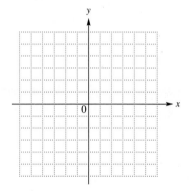

17. $4x + 5y < 8$
    $y > -2$
    $x > -4$

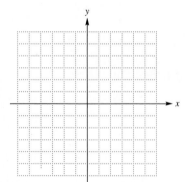

18. $x + y \geq -3$
    $x - y \leq 3$
    $y \leq 3$

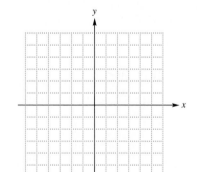

19. $3x - 2y \geq 6$
    $x + y \leq 4$
    $x \geq 0$
    $y \geq -4$

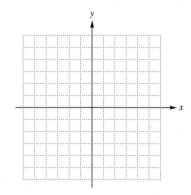

20. Every system of inequalities illustrated in the examples of this section has infinitely many solutions. Explain why this is so. Does this mean that *any* ordered pair is a solution?

Chapter 4

KEY TERMS

4.1

system of linear equations
A system of linear equations (or **linear system**) consists of two or more linear equations with the same variables.

solution of a system
The solution of a system of linear equations includes all the ordered pairs that make all the equations of the system true at the same time.

consistent system
A system of equations with at least one solution is a consistent system.

inconsistent system
An inconsistent system of equations is a system with no solution.

independent equations
Equations of a system that have different graphs are called independent equations.

dependent equations
Equations of a system that have the same graph (because they are different forms of the same equation) are called dependent equations.

4.5

system of linear inequalities
A system of linear inequalities contains two or more linear inequalities (and no other kinds of inequalities).

solution of a system of linear inequalities
The solution of a system of linear inequalities includes all points that make all inequalities of the system true at the same time.

TEST YOUR WORD POWER

See how well you have learned the vocabulary in this chapter. Answers, with examples, follow the Quick Review.

1. A **system of linear equations** consists of
   A. at least two linear equations with different variables
   B. two or more linear equations that have an infinite number of solutions
   C. two or more linear equations with the same variables
   D. two or more linear inequalities.

2. A **solution of a system** of linear equations is
   A. an ordered pair that makes one equation of the system true

   B. an ordered pair that makes all the equations of the system true at the same time
   C. any ordered pair that makes one or the other or both equations of the system true
   D. the set of values that make all the equations of the system false.

3. A **consistent system** is a system of equations
   A. with one solution
   B. with no solution
   C. with two solutions
   D. that has parallel lines at its graph.

4. An **inconsistent system** is a system of equations
   A. with one solution
   B. with no solution
   C. with an infinite number of solutions
   D. that have the same graph.

5. **Dependent equations**
   A. have different graphs
   B. have no solution
   C. have one solution
   D. are different forms of the same equation.

| **Concepts** | **Examples** |

4.1 *Solving Systems of Linear Equations by Graphing*

An ordered pair is a solution of a system if it makes all equations of the system true at the same time.

Is $(4, -1)$ a solution of the system $\quad\begin{aligned}x + y &= 3\\2x - y &= 9\end{aligned}$?

Yes, because $4 + (-1) = 3$ and $2(4) - (-1) = 9$ are both true.

If the graphs of the equations of a system are both sketched on the same axes, then the points of intersection, if any, are solutions of the system.

Solve by graphing.

$$x + y = 5$$
$$2x - y = 4$$

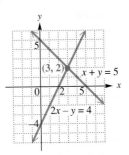

If the graphs of the equations do not intersect (that is, the lines are parallel), then the system has no solution.

If the graphs of the equations are the same line, then the system has an infinite number of solutions.

The ordered pair $(3, 2)$ satisfies both equations, so $(3, 2)$ is the solution of the system.

4.2 *Solving Systems of Linear Equations by Substitution*

Step 1 Solve one equation for either variable.

Solve by substitution.

$$x + 2y = -5 \quad (1)$$
$$y = -2x - 1 \quad (2)$$

Equation (2) is already solved for y.

Step 2 Substitute for that variable in the other equation to get an equation in one variable.

Substitute $-2x - 1$ for y in equation (1).

$$x + 2(-2x - 1) = -5$$

Step 3 Solve the equation from Step 2.

$$x - 4x - 2 = -5$$
$$-3x - 2 = -5$$
$$-3x = -3$$
$$x = 1$$

Step 4 Substitute the result into the equation from Step 1 to get the value of the other variable.

To find y, let $x = 1$ in equation (2):

$$y = -2(1) - 1 = -3.$$

Step 5 Check. Write the solution as an ordered pair.

The solution $(1, -3)$ checks.

4.3 *Solving Systems of Linear Equations by Elimination*

Step 1 Write both equations in standard form $Ax + By = C$.

Solve by elimination.

$$x + 3y = 7 \quad (1)$$
$$3x - y = 1 \quad (2)$$

Step 2 If necessary, multiply one or both equations by appropriate numbers so that the sum of the coefficients of either the x- or y-terms is 0.

Multiply equation (1) by -3 to eliminate the x-terms.

Step 3 Add the equations to get an equation with only one variable (or no variable).

$$\begin{aligned}-3x - 9y &= -21\\\underline{3x - y =\quad 1}\\-10y &= -20 \quad \text{Add.}\end{aligned}$$

Step 4 Solve the equation from Step 3.

$$y = 2 \qquad \text{Divide by } -10.$$

Concepts	Examples

4.3 *Solving Systems of Linear Equations by Elimination (continued)*

Step 5   Substitute the solution from Step 4 into either of the original equations to find the value of the remaining variable.

Substitute to get the value of x.

$$x + 3(2) = 7 \qquad (1)$$
$$x + 6 = 7$$
$$x = 1$$

Step 6   Check. Write the solution as an ordered pair.

Since $1 + 3(2) = 7$ and $3(1) - 2 = 1$, the solution $(1, 2)$ checks.

4.4 *Applications of Linear Systems*

Use the modified six-step method.

Step 1   **Read** the problem carefully.

Step 2   **Assign variables** for each unknown value. Use diagrams or tables as needed.

Step 3   **Write two equations** using both variables.

Step 4   **Solve** the system.

Step 5   **State the answer.**

Step 6   **Check** the answer in the words of the original problem.

The sum of two numbers is 30. Their difference is 6. Find the numbers.

Let x represent one number.

Let y represent the other number.

$$x + y = 30$$
$$\underline{x - y = 6}$$
$$2x = 36 \qquad \text{Add.}$$
$$x = 18 \qquad \text{Divide by 2.}$$

Let $x = 18$ in the first equation: $18 + y = 30$. Solve to get $y = 12$. The numbers are 18 and 12.

The sum of 18 and 12 is 30, and the difference between 18 and 12 is 6, so the answer checks.

4.5 *Solving Systems of Linear Inequalities*

To solve a system of two or more linear inequalities, graph the inequalities on the same axes. (This was explained in **Section 3.5.**) The solution of the system is the intersection (overlap) of the regions of the graphs. The portions of the boundary lines that bound the region of solutions are included for a $\leq$ or $\geq$ inequality and excluded for a $<$ or $>$ inequality.

The shaded region is the solution of the system

$$2x + 4y \geq 5$$
$$x \geq 1.$$

---

1. C; *Example:* $2x + y = 7, \quad 3x - y = 3$
2. B; *Example:* The ordered pair $(2, 3)$ satisfies both equations of the system in the Answer 1 example, so it is a solution of the system.
3. A; *Example:* The system in the Answer 1 example is consistent. The graphs of the equations intersect at exactly one point, in this case the solution $(2, 3)$.
4. B; *Example:* The equations of two parallel lines make up an inconsistent system; their graphs never intersect, so there is no solution to the system.
5. D; *Example:* The equations $4x - y = 8$ and $8x - 2y = 16$ are dependent because their graphs are the same line.

Real-Data Applications

Systems of Linear Equations and Modeling

A system of linear equations is an efficient tool for finding a linear *model,* or the equation for data that is known to be linear. Recall that the slope-intercept form of the equation of a line is $y = mx + b$. Once we know the values of the slope, *m,* and the *y*-intercept, *b,* we can then write the exact model. If we know two ordered pairs, then we can write a system of linear equations in which the unknown quantities are *m* and *b*.

For example, to find the formula to convert from Kelvin (K), the most commonly used thermodynamic temperature scale, as the *input* to degrees Fahrenheit (°F) as the *output,* we only need to know the data presented in the table. The linear equation has the form $F = mK + b$, and ordered pairs have the format (K, F).

	K	°F
Water Freezes	273	32
Water Boils	373	212

The system of linear equations to be solved is

$$32 = m(273) + b$$
$$212 = m(373) + b.$$

For Group Discussion

Use systems of linear equations to find the model for each problem.

1. Solve the system of linear equations given above to find the conversion formula from K to °F.

2. Water freezes at 0°C and boils at 100°C. Write the system of linear equations to find the model for converting from degrees Celsius as the input to degrees Fahrenheit as the output.

3. Suppose you begin a carefully managed weight-loss program in which you expect your weight to decline steadily. (A constant weight loss means that it is reasonable to assume that the relationship between number of weeks on the program and weight is linear.) After two weeks you weigh 179 lb, and after six weeks you weigh 169 lb. Use *x* to represent the number of weeks on the program and *y* to represent your weight in pounds at the end of *x* weeks. Write the linear model for your weight-loss program.

Extension: Suppose a line contains the distinct points (x_1, y_1) and (x_2, y_2), where $x_1 \neq x_2$. Use the method of this activity to derive the slope formula.

Chapter **4**

R E V I E W   E X E R C I S E S

[4.1] *Decide whether the given ordered pair is a solution of the given system.*

1. $(3, 4)$
$$4x - 2y = 4$$
$$5x + y = 19$$

2. $(-5, 2)$
$$x - 4y = -13$$
$$2x + 3y = 4$$

Solve each system by graphing.

3. $x + y = 4$
$2x - y = 5$

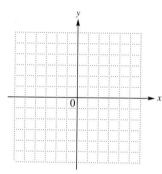

4. $x - 2y = 4$
$2x + y = -2$

5. $x - 2 = 2y$
$2x - 4y = 4$

6. $2x + 4 = 2y$
$y - x = -3$

7. When a student was asked to determine whether the ordered pair $(1, -2)$ is a solution of the system

$$x + y = -1$$
$$2x + y = 4,$$

he answered "yes." His reasoning was that the ordered pair satisfies the equation $x + y = -1$; that is, $1 + (-2) = -1$ is true. Why is the student's answer wrong?

[4.2] *Solve each system by the substitution method.*

8. $3x + y = 7$
    $x = 2y$

9. $2x - 5y = -19$
    $y = x + 2$

10. $4x + 5y = 44$
    $x + 2 = 2y$

11. $5x + 15y = 3$
    $x + 3y = 2$

[4.3] *Solve each system by the elimination method.*

12. $2x - y = 13$
    $x + y = 8$

13. $3x - y = -13$
    $x - 2y = -1$

14. $-4x + 3y = 25$
    $6x - 5y = -39$

15. $3x - 4y = 9$
    $6x - 8y = 18$

16. For the system

$$2x + 12y = 7$$
$$3x + 4y = 1,$$

if we were to multiply the first (top) equation by -3, by what number would we have to multiply the second (bottom) equation in order to

(a) eliminate the x-terms when solving by the elimination method?

(b) eliminate the y-terms when solving by the elimination method?

Solve each system by any method.

17. $x - 2y = 5$
    $y = x - 7$

18. $5x - 3y = 11$
    $2y = x - 4$

19. $\dfrac{x}{2} + \dfrac{y}{3} = 7$

  $\dfrac{x}{4} + \dfrac{2y}{3} = 8$

20. $\dfrac{3x}{4} - \dfrac{y}{3} = \dfrac{7}{6}$

  $\dfrac{x}{2} + \dfrac{2y}{3} = \dfrac{5}{3}$

[4.4] *Solve each problem by using a system of equations.*

21. At the end of 2001, Subway topped McDonald's as the largest restaurant chain in the United States. Subway operated 148 more restaurants than McDonald's, and together the two chains had 26,346 restaurants. How many restaurants did each company operate? (*Source: USA Today,* February 4, 2002.)

22. Two of the most popular magazines in the United States are *Modern Maturity* and *Reader's Digest.* Together, the average total circulation for these two magazines during a recent 6-month period was 35.6 million. *Reader's Digest* circulation was 5.4 million less than that of *Modern Maturity.* What were the circulation figures for each magazine? (*Source:* Audit Bureau of Circulations and Magazine Publishers of America.)

23. The perimeter of a rectangle is 90 m. Its length is $1\frac{1}{2}$ times its width. Find the length and width of the rectangle.

24. A cashier has 20 bills, all of which are $10 or $20 bills. The total value of the money is $330. How many of each type does the cashier have?

Denomination of Bill	Number of Bills	Total Value
$10	10 x	10x
$20	y	20y
Totals	20	$330

25. Candy that sells for $1.30 per lb is to be mixed with candy selling for $.90 per lb to get 100 lb of a mix that will sell for $1 per lb. How much of each type should be used?

26. A certain plane flying with the wind travels 540 mi in 2 hr. Later, flying against the same wind, the plane travels 690 mi in 3 hr. Find the speed of the plane in still air and the speed of the wind.

27. After taxes, Ms. Cesar's game show winnings were $18,000. She invested part of it at 3% annual simple interest and the rest at 4%. Her interest income for the first year was $650. How much did she invest at each rate?

Percent	Amount of Principal	Interest
.03	x	
.04	y	
Totals	$18,000	

28. A 40% antifreeze solution is to be mixed with a 70% solution to get 90 L of a 50% solution. How many liters of the 40% and 70% solutions will be needed?

Percent	Number of Liters	Amount of Pure Antifreeze
.40	x	
.70	y	
.50	90	

[4.5] *Graph the solution for each system of linear inequalities.*

29. $x + y \geq 2$
$x - y \leq 4$

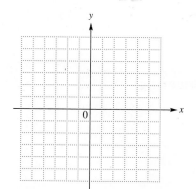

30. $y \geq 2x$
$2x + 3y \leq 6$

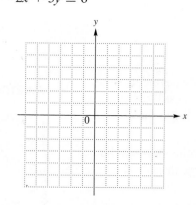

31. $x + y < 3$
$2x > y$

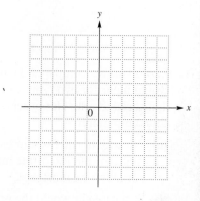

32. Which system of linear inequalities is graphed in the figure?

A. $x \leq 3$
$\quad y \leq 1$

B. $x \leq 3$
$\quad y \geq 1$

C. $x \geq 3$
$\quad y \leq 1$

D. $x \geq 3$
$\quad y \geq 1$

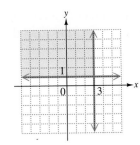

33. Without actually graphing, determine which system of inequalities has no solution.

A. $x \geq 4$
$\quad y \leq 3$

B. $x + y > 4$
$\quad x + y < 3$

C. $x > 2$
$\quad y < 1$

D. $x + y > 4$
$\quad x - y < 3$

MIXED REVIEW EXERCISES

Solve each system.

34. $3x + 4y = 6$
$\quad 4x - 5y = 8$

35. $\dfrac{3x}{2} + \dfrac{y}{5} = -3$

$\quad 4x + \dfrac{y}{3} = -11$

36. $x + 6y = 3$
$\quad 2x + 12y = 2$

37. $x + y < 5$
$\quad x - y \geq 2$

38. $y \leq 2x$
$\quad x + 2y > 4$

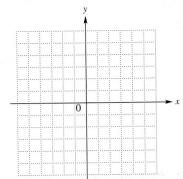

39. $y < -4x$
$\quad y < -2$

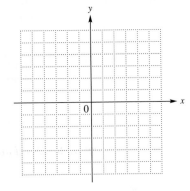

40. The perimeter of an isosceles triangle is 29 in. One side of the triangle is 5 in. longer than each of the two equal sides. Find the lengths of the sides of the triangle.

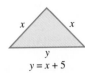

$y = x + 5$

41. In the 2004 National Football League AFC finals, the New England Patriots beat the Indianapolis Colts by 10 points, and the winning score was 4 less than twice the losing score. What was the final score of the game? (*Source:* NFL.)

42. Eboni Perkins compared the monthly payments she would incur for two types of mortgages; fixed-rate and variable-rate. Her observations led to the following graph.

(a) For which years would the monthly payment be more for the fixed-rate mortgage than for the variable-rate mortgage?

(b) In what year would the payments be the same, and what would those payments be?

Chapter 4

TEST

Study Skills Workbook
Activity 10: Using Test Results

1. Solve the system by graphing.

$$2x + y = 1$$
$$3x - y = 9$$

2. Suppose that the graph of a system of two linear equations consists of lines that have the same slope but different y-intercepts. How many solutions does the system have?

Solve each system by the substitution method.

3. $2x + y = -4$
$\quad x = y + 7$

4. $4x + 3y = -35$
$\quad x + y = 0$

Solve each system by the elimination method.

5. $2x - y = 4$
$\quad 3x + y = 21$

6. $4x + 2y = 2$
$\quad 5x + 4y = 7$

7. $\quad 6x - 5y = 0$
$\quad -2x + 3y = 0$

8. $\quad 4x + 5y = 2$
$\quad -8x - 10y = 6$

Solve each system by any method.

9. $3x = 6 + y$
$\quad 6x - 2y = 12$

10. $\dfrac{x}{2} - \dfrac{y}{4} = 7$

$\quad \dfrac{2x}{3} + \dfrac{5y}{4} = 3$

1. _____

2. _____

3. _____

4. _____

5. _____

6. _____

7. _____

8. _____

9. _____

10. _____

Solve each problem.

11. _____

11. The distance between Memphis and Atlanta is 782 mi less than the distance between Minneapolis and Houston. Together, the two distances total 1570 mi. How far is it between Memphis and Atlanta? How far is it between Minneapolis and Houston? (*Source: Rand McNally Road Atlas.*)

12. _____

12. In 2002, the two most popular amusement parks in the United States were Disneyland and the Magic Kingdom at Walt Disney World. Disneyland had 1.3 million fewer visitors than the Magic Kingdom, and together they had 26.7 million visitors. How many visitors did each park have? (*Source: Amusement Business.*)

13. _____

13. A 25% solution of alcohol is to be mixed with a 40% solution to get 50 L of a final mixture that is 30% alcohol. How much of each of the original solutions should be used?

14. _____

15.

14. Two cars leave from Perham, Minnesota, and travel in the same direction. One car travels $1\frac{1}{3}$ times as fast as the other. After 3 hr they are 45 mi apart. What are the speeds of the cars?

Graph the solution of each system of inequalities.

16.

15. $2x + 7y \leq 14$
$x - y \geq 1$

16. $2x - y > 6$
$4y + 12 \geq -3x$

Cumulative Review Exercises

CHAPTERS R–4

1. List all integer factors of 40.

2. Find the value of the expression if $x = 1$ and $y = 5$.

$$\frac{3x^2 + 2y^2}{10y + 3}$$

Name the property that justifies each statement.

3. $5 + (-4) = (-4) + 5$

4. $r(s - k) = rs - rk$

5. $-\dfrac{2}{3} + \dfrac{2}{3} = 0$

6. Evaluate $-2 + 6[3 - (4 - 9)]$.

Solve each linear equation.

7. $2 - 3(6x + 2) = 4(x + 1) + 18$

8. $\dfrac{3}{2}\left(\dfrac{1}{3}x + 4\right) = 6\left(\dfrac{1}{4} + x\right)$

Solve each linear inequality.

9. $-\dfrac{5}{6}x < 15$

10. $-8 < 2x + 3$

11. No baseball fan should be without a copy of *The Sports Encyclopedia: Baseball 2004* by David S. Neft and Richard M. Cohen. It provides the history of every player, team, and season from 1902–2003, and includes exhaustive statistics. The book has a perimeter of 37.8 in., and its width measures 2.58 in. less than its length. What are its dimensions? (*Source:* www.amazon.com)

Graph each linear equation.

12. $x - y = 4$

13. $3x + y = 6$

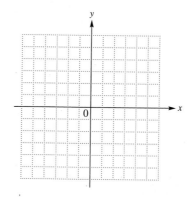

Find the slope of each line.

14. Through $(-5, 6)$ and $(1, -2)$

15. Perpendicular to the line $y = 4x - 3$

Write an equation for each line in slope-intercept form.

16. Through $(-4, 1)$ with slope $\frac{1}{2}$

17. Through the points $(1, 3)$ and $(-2, -3)$

18. (a) Write an equation of the vertical line through $(9, -2)$.

(b) Write an equation of the horizontal line through $(4, -1)$.

Solve each system by any method.

19. $2x - y = -8$
   $x + 2y = 11$

20. $4x + 5y = -8$
   $3x + 4y = -7$

21. $3x + 4y = 2$
   $6x + 8y = 1$

Use a system of equations to solve each problem.

22. Admission prices at a football game were \$6 for adults and \$2 for children. The total value of the tickets sold was \$2528, and 454 tickets were sold. How many adults and how many children attended the game?

Kind of Ticket	Number Sold	Cost of Each (in dollars)	Total Value (in dollars)
Adult	x	6	$6x$
Child	y		
Total	454		

23. The perimeter of a triangle is 53 in. If two sides are of equal length, and the third side measures 4 in. less than each of the equal sides, what are the lengths of the three sides?

24. Graph the solution of the system

$x + 2y \leq 12$

$2x - y \leq 8.$

Exponents and Polynomials

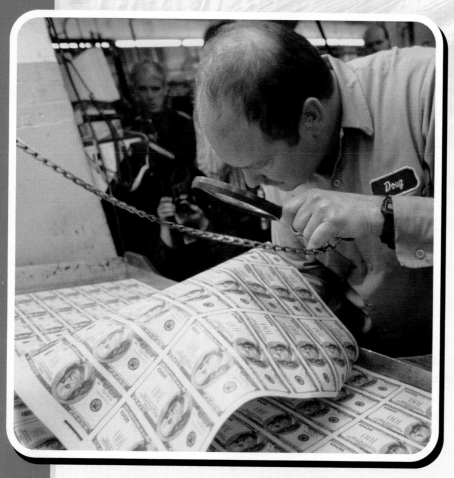

Just how much is a trillion? A trillion, which is written 1,000,000,000,000, is an incredibly huge number. A trillion is a million million or a thousand billion. A trillion seconds would last more than 31,000 years, that is, 310 centuries. To be a trillionaire, a person would need a stack of $1000 bills over 67 miles high.

The U.S. budget first exceeded $1 trillion in 1987 and topped $2 trillion for the 2003 fiscal year. (*Source: The Gazette*, February 5, 2002.) In Exercise 1 of Section 5.8, we use exponents to write large numbers like the amount of the NASA budget for the international space station using scientific notation.

5.1 Adding and Subtracting Polynomials

OBJECTIVES

1 Review combining like terms.

2 Know the vocabulary for polynomials.

3 Evaluate polynomials.

4 Add polynomials.

5 Subtract polynomials.

6 Add and subtract polynomials with more than one variable.

Recall from **Section 1.8** that in an expression such as

$$4x^3 + 6x^2 + 5x + 8,$$

the quantities that are added, $4x^3$, $6x^2$, $5x$, and 8 are called *terms*. In the term $4x^3$, the number 4 is called the *numerical coefficient,* or simply the *coefficient,* of x^3. In the same way, 6 is the coefficient of x^2 in the term $6x^2$, 5 is the coefficient of x in the term $5x$, and 8 is the *constant* term.

OBJECTIVE 1 **Review combining like terms.** In **Section 1.8,** we saw that *like terms* are terms with exactly the same variables, with the same exponents on the variables, such as $2x^2$ and $-5x^2$. Only the coefficients may differ. Like terms are combined, or *added,* by adding their coefficients using the distributive property.

EXAMPLE 1 **Adding Like Terms**

Simplify each expression by adding like terms.

(a) $-4x^3 + 6x^3 = (-4 + 6)x^3$ Distributive property

$\qquad\qquad\qquad\quad = 2x^3$

(b) $9x^6 - 14x^6 + x^6 = (9 - 14 + 1)x^6$ $x^6 = 1x^6$

$\qquad\qquad\qquad\qquad\quad = -4x^6$

(c) $12m^2 + 5m + 4m^2 = (12 + 4)m^2 + 5m$

$\qquad\qquad\qquad\qquad\quad\ = 16m^2 + 5m$

(d) $3x^2y + 4x^2y - x^2y = (3 + 4 - 1)x^2y$

$\qquad\qquad\qquad\qquad\qquad = 6x^2y$

---

1 Add like terms.

(a) $5x^4 + 7x^4$

(b) $9pq + 3pq - 2pq$

(c) $r^2 + 3r + 5r^2$

(d) $8t + 6w$

In Example 1(c), we cannot combine $16m^2$ and $5m$. These two terms are unlike because the exponents on the variables are different. *Unlike terms* have different variables or different exponents on the same variables.

◀◀◀ **Work Problem 1 at the Side.**

OBJECTIVE 2 **Know the vocabulary for polynomials.** A **polynomial in x** is a term or the sum of a finite number of terms of the form ax^n, for any real number a and any whole number n. For example,

$$16x^8 - 7x^6 + 5x^4 - 3x^2 + 4 \qquad \text{Polynomial}$$

is a polynomial in x. This polynomial is written in **descending powers,** because the exponents on x decrease from left to right. On the other hand,

$$2x^3 - x^2 + \frac{4}{x} \qquad \text{Not a polynomial}$$

is not a polynomial, since a variable appears in a denominator. Of course, we could define a *polynomial* using any variable, not just x, as in Example 1(c). In fact, polynomials may have terms with more than one variable, as in Example 1(d).

2 Choose all descriptions that apply for each of the expressions in parts (a)–(d).

A. Polynomial
B. Polynomial written in descending powers
C. Not a polynomial

(a) $3m^5 + 5m^2 - 2m + 1$

(b) $2p^4 + p^6$

(c) $\dfrac{1}{x} + 2x^2 + 3$

(d) $x - 3$

◀◀◀ **Work Problem 2 at the Side.**

ANSWERS
1. (a) $12x^4$ (b) $10pq$ (c) $6r^2 + 3r$
   (d) cannot be added—unlike terms
2. (a) A and B   (b) A   (c) C   (d) A and B

The **degree of a term** is the sum of the exponents on the variables. A constant term has degree 0. For example, $3x^4$ has degree **4**, while $6x^{17}$ has degree **17**. The term $5x$ (or $5x^1$) has degree **1**, -7 has degree 0, and $2x^2y$ has degree $2 + 1 = 3$ (y has an exponent of 1). The **degree of a polynomial** is the greatest degree of any nonzero term of the polynomial. For example, $3x^4 - 5x^2 + 6$ is of degree 4, the polynomial $5x + 7$ is of degree 1, 3 is of degree 0, and $x^2y + xy - 5xy^2$ is of degree 3.

Three types of polynomials are very common and are given special names. A polynomial with only one term is called a **monomial.** (*Mono*- means "one," as in *mono*rail.) Examples are

$$9m, \quad -6y^5, \quad a^2, \quad \text{and} \quad 6. \quad \text{Monomials}$$

A polynomial with exactly two terms is called a **binomial.** (*Bi*- means "two," as in *bi*cycle.) Examples are

$$-9x^4 + 9x^3, \quad 8m^2 + 6m, \quad \text{and} \quad 3m^5 - 9m^2. \quad \text{Binomials}$$

A polynomial with exactly three terms is called a **trinomial.** (*Tri*- means "three," as in *tri*angle.) Examples are

$$9m^3 - 4m^2 + 6, \quad \frac{19}{3}y^2 + \frac{8}{3}y + 5, \quad \text{and} \quad -3m^5 - 9m^2 + 2. \quad \text{Trinomials}$$

EXAMPLE 2 Classifying Polynomials

For each polynomial, first simplify if possible by combining like terms. Then give the degree and tell whether the polynomial is a *monomial*, a *binomial*, a *trinomial*, or *none of these.*

(a) $2x^3 + 5$

  The polynomial cannot be simplified. The degree is 3. The polynomial is a binomial.

(b) $4x - 5x + 2x$

  Add like terms to simplify: $4x - 5x + 2x = x$. The degree is 1 (since $x = x^1$). The simplified polynomial is a monomial.

> **Work Problem 3 at the Side.** ▷▷▷

OBJECTIVE 3 Evaluate polynomials. A polynomial usually represents different numbers for different values of the variable.

EXAMPLE 3 Evaluating a Polynomial

Find the value of $3x^4 + 5x^3 - 4x - 4$ when $x = -2$ and when $x = 3$.

  First, substitute -2 for x.

$$3x^4 + 5x^3 - 4x - 4 = 3(-2)^4 + 5(-2)^3 - 4(-2) - 4$$
$$= 3 \cdot 16 + 5(-8) - 4(-2) - 4 \quad \text{Apply exponents.}$$
$$= 48 - 40 + 8 - 4 \quad \text{Multiply.}$$
$$= 12 \quad \text{Add and subtract.}$$

Next, replace x with 3.

$$3x^4 + 5x^3 - 4x - 4 = 3(3)^4 + 5(3)^3 - 4(3) - 4$$
$$= 3 \cdot 81 + 5 \cdot 27 - 4(3) - 4$$
$$= 243 + 135 - 12 - 4$$
$$= 362$$

3 For each polynomial, first simplify if possible. Then give the degree and tell whether the polynomial is a *monomial, binomial, trinomial,* or *none of these.*

(a) $3x^2 + 2x - 4$

(b) $x^3 + 4x^3$

(c) $x^8 - x^7 + 2x^8$

ANSWERS

3. **(a)** degree 2; trinomial
   (b) degree 3; monomial (simplify to $5x^3$)
   (c) degree 8; binomial (simplify to $3x^8 - x^7$)

4 Find the value of
$2y^3 + 8y - 6$ in each case.

(a) when $y = -1$

(b) when $y = 4$

⫸⫸⫸ Work Problem 4 at the Side.

OBJECTIVE 4 Add polynomials. Polynomials may be added, subtracted, multiplied, and divided.

> **Adding Polynomials**
> To add two polynomials, add like terms.

EXAMPLE 4 **Adding Polynomials Vertically**

(a) Add $6x^3 - 4x^2 + 3$ and $-2x^3 + 7x^2 - 5$.
Write like terms in columns.

$$6x^3 - 4x^2 + 3$$
$$-2x^3 + 7x^2 - 5$$

Now add, column by column.

$$\begin{array}{ccc} 6x^3 & -4x^2 & 3 \\ -2x^3 & 7x^2 & -5 \\ \hline 4x^3 & 3x^2 & -2 \end{array}$$

Add the three sums together.

$$4x^3 + 3x^2 + (-2) = 4x^3 + 3x^2 - 2$$

(b) Add $2x^2 - 4x + 3$ and $x^3 + 5x$.
Write like terms in columns and add column by column.

$$2x^2 - 4x + 3$$
$$\underline{x^3 \qquad + 5x}$$
$$x^3 + 2x^2 + x + 3$$

Leave spaces for missing terms.

⫸⫸⫸ Work Problem 5 at the Side.

5 Add each pair of polynomials.

(a) $4x^3 - 3x^2 + 2x$
    $\underline{6x^3 + 2x^2 - 3x}$

(b) $x^2 - 2x + 5$
    $\underline{4x^2 \qquad - 2}$

The polynomials in Example 4 also could be added horizontally.

EXAMPLE 5 **Adding Polynomials Horizontally**

(a) Add $6x^3 - 4x^2 + 3$ and $-2x^3 + 7x^2 - 5$.
Combine like terms.

$$(6x^3 - 4x^2 + 3) + (-2x^3 + 7x^2 - 5) = 4x^3 + 3x^2 - 2,$$

the same answer found in Example 4(a).

Continued on Next Page

(b) Add $2x^2 - 4x + 3$ and $x^3 + 5x$.

$$
\begin{aligned}
(2x^2 - 4x + 3) + (x^3 + 5x) &= 2x^2 - 4x + 3 + x^3 + 5x \\
&= x^3 + 2x^2 + x + 3 \qquad \text{Combine like terms.}
\end{aligned}
$$

▶ **Work Problem 6 at the Side.** ▷▷▷

OBJECTIVE 5 Subtract polynomials.   In **Section 1.5,** the difference $x - y$ was defined as $x + (-y)$. (We find the difference $x - y$ by adding x and the opposite of y.) For example,

$$7 - 2 = 7 + (-2) = 5 \quad \text{and} \quad -8 - (-2) = -8 + 2 = -6.$$

A similar method is used to subtract polynomials.

> **Subtracting Polynomials**
>
> To subtract two polynomials, change all the signs of the second polynomial and add the result to the first polynomial.

EXAMPLE 6 Subtracting Polynomials

(a) Perform the subtraction $(5x - 2) - (3x - 8)$.
Change the signs in the second polynomial and add like terms.

$$
\begin{aligned}
(5x - 2) - (3x - 8) &= (5x - 2) + (-3x + 8) \\
&= 2x + 6
\end{aligned}
$$

(b) Subtract $6x^3 - 4x^2 + 2$ from $11x^3 + 2x^2 - 8$.
Write the problem.

$$(11x^3 + 2x^2 - 8) - (6x^3 - 4x^2 + 2)$$

Change all the signs in the second polynomial and add the two polynomials.

$$(11x^3 + 2x^2 - 8) + (-6x^3 + 4x^2 - 2) = 5x^3 + 6x^2 - 10$$

To check a subtraction problem, use the fact that if

$$a - b = c, \quad \text{then} \quad a = b + c.$$

For example, $6 - 2 = 4$, so we check by writing $6 = 2 + 4$, which is correct. Check the polynomial subtraction above by adding $6x^3 - 4x^2 + 2$ and $5x^3 + 6x^2 - 10$.

$$(6x^3 - 4x^2 + 2) + (5x^3 + 6x^2 - 10) = 11x^3 + 2x^2 - 8$$

Since the sum is $11x^3 + 2x^2 - 8$, the subtraction was performed correctly.

▶ **Work Problem 7 at the Side.** ▷▷▷

Subtraction also can be done in columns. We will use vertical subtraction in **Section 5.7** when we study polynomial division.

---

6 Find each sum.

(a) $(2x^4 - 6x^2 + 7)$
$\qquad + (-3x^4 + 5x^2 + 2)$

(b) $(3x^2 + 4x + 2)$
$\qquad + (6x^3 - 5x - 7)$

7 Subtract, and check your answers by addition.

(a) $(14y^3 - 6y^2 + 2y - 5)$
$\qquad - (2y^3 - 7y^2 - 4y + 6)$

(b) Subtract

$$\left(-\frac{3}{2}y^2 + \frac{4}{3}y + 6 \right)$$

$$\text{from } \left(\frac{7}{2}y^2 - \frac{11}{3}y + 8 \right).$$

ANSWERS
6. (a) $-x^4 - x^2 + 9$
   (b) $6x^3 + 3x^2 - x - 5$
7. (a) $12y^3 + y^2 + 6y - 11$
   (b) $5y^2 - 5y + 2$

8 Subtract, using the method of subtracting by columns.

$$(4y^3 - 16y^2 + 2y) \\ - (12y^3 - 9y^2 + 16)$$

EXAMPLE 7 Subtracting Polynomials Vertically

Use the method of subtracting by columns to find

$$(14y^3 - 6y^2 + 2y - 5) - (2y^3 - 7y^2 - 4y + 6).$$

Arrange like terms in columns.

$$14y^3 - 6y^2 + 2y - 5$$
$$\underline{2y^3 - 7y^2 - 4y + 6}$$

Change all signs in the second row, and then add.

$$14y^3 - 6y^2 + 2y - 5$$
$$\underline{-2y^3 + 7y^2 + 4y - 6} \quad \text{Change signs.}$$
$$12y^3 + y^2 + 6y - 11 \quad \text{Add.}$$

‹‹‹ Work Problem 8 at the Side.

---

9 Perform the indicated operations.

$$(6p^4 - 8p^3 + 2p - 1) \\ - (-7p^4 + 6p^2 - 12) \\ + (p^4 - 3p + 8)$$

Either the horizontal or the vertical method may be used for adding or subtracting polynomials.

EXAMPLE 8 Adding and Subtracting More Than Two Polynomials

Perform the indicated operations to simplify the expression

$$(4 - x + 3x^2) - (2 - 3x + 5x^2) + (8 + 2x - 4x^2).$$

Rewrite, changing the subtraction to adding the opposite.

$$(4 - x + 3x^2) - (2 - 3x + 5x^2) + (8 + 2x - 4x^2)$$
$$= (4 - x + 3x^2) + (-2 + 3x - 5x^2) + (8 + 2x - 4x^2)$$
$$= (2 + 2x - 2x^2) + (8 + 2x - 4x^2) \quad \text{Combine like terms.}$$
$$= 10 + 4x - 6x^2 \quad \text{Combine like terms.}$$

‹‹‹ Work Problem 9 at the Side.

---

10 Add or subtract.

(a) $(3mn + 2m - 4n) \\ + (-mn + 4m + n)$

OBJECTIVE 6 **Add and subtract polynomials with more than one variable.** Polynomials in more than one variable are added and subtracted by combining like terms, just as with single-variable polynomials.

EXAMPLE 9 Adding and Subtracting Multivariable Polynomials

Add or subtract as indicated.

(a) $(4a + 2ab - b) + (3a - ab + b)$
$$= 4a + 2ab - b + 3a - ab + b$$
$$= 7a + ab \quad \text{Combine like terms.}$$

(b) $(2x^2y + 3xy + y^2) - (3x^2y - xy - 2y^2)$
$$= 2x^2y + 3xy + y^2 - 3x^2y + xy + 2y^2$$
$$= -x^2y + 4xy + 3y^2$$

(b) $(5p^2q^2 - 4p^2 + 2q) \\ - (2p^2q^2 - p^2 - 3q)$

‹‹‹ Work Problem 10 at the Side.

5.1 Exercises

Fill in each blank with the correct response.

1. In the term $7x^5$, the coefficient is _____ and the exponent is _____.

2. The expression $5x^3 - 4x^2$ has _____ term(s).
        (how many?)

3. The degree of the term $-4x^8$ is _____.

4. The polynomial $4x^2 - y^2$ _____ an example of a trinomial.
        (is/is not)

5. When $x^2 + 10$ is evaluated for $x = 4$, the result is _____.

6. _____ is an example of a monomial with coefficient 5, in the variable x, having degree 9.

For each polynomial, determine the number of terms, and name the coefficient of each term.

7. $6x^4$

8. $-9y^5$

9. t^4

10. s^7

11. $-19r^2 - r$

12. $2y^3 - y$

13. $x + 8x^2$

14. $v - 2v^3$

In each polynomial, combine like terms whenever possible. Write the result with descending powers.

15. $-3m^5 + 5m^5$

16. $-4y^3 + 3y^3$

17. $2r^5 + (-3r^5)$

18. $-19y^2 + 9y^2$

19. $.2m^5 - .5m^2$

20. $-.9y + .9y^2$

21. $-3x^5 + 2x^5 - 4x^5$

22. $6x^3 - 8x^3 + 9x^3$

23. $-4p^7 + 8p^7 + 5p^9$

24. $-3a^8 + 4a^8 - 3a^2$

25. $-4y^2 + 3y^2 - 2y^2 + y^2$

26. $3r^5 - 8r^5 + r^5 + 2r^5$

For each polynomial, first simplify, if possible, and write it with descending powers. Then give the degree of the resulting polynomial, and tell whether it is a monomial, *a* binomial, *a* trinomial, *or* none of these. *See Example 2.*

27. $6x^4 - 9x$

28. $7t^3 - 3t$

29. $5m^4 - 3m^2 + 6m^5 - 7m^3$

30. $6p^5 + 4p^3 - 8p^4 + 10p^2$ **31.** $\dfrac{5}{3}x^4 - \dfrac{2}{3}x^4 + \dfrac{1}{3}x^2 - 4$ **32.** $\dfrac{4}{5}r^6 + \dfrac{1}{5}r^6 - r^4 + \dfrac{2}{5}r$

33. $.8x^4 - .3x^4 - .5x^4 + 7$ **34.** $1.2t^3 - .9t^3 - .3t^3 + 9$

*Find the value of each polynomial (**a**) when $x = 2$ and (**b**) when $x = -1$. See Example 3.*

35. $-2x + 3$ **36.** $5x - 4$ **37.** $2x^2 + 5x + 1$ **38.** $-3x^2 + 14x - 2$

39. $2x^5 - 4x^4 + 5x^3 - x^2$ **40.** $x^4 - 6x^3 + x^2 + 1$ **41.** $-4x^5 + x^2$ **42.** $2x^6 - 4x$

RELATING CONCEPTS (EXERCISES 43–46) For Individual or Group Work

A polynomial can model the distance in feet that a car going approximately 68 mph will skid in t seconds. If we let D represent this distance, then

$$D = 100t - 13t^2.$$

*Each time we evaluate this polynomial for a value of t, we get one and only one output value D. This idea is basic to the concept of a **function,** an important concept in mathematics. Exercises 43–46 illustrate this idea with this polynomial and two others. **Work them in order.***

43. Use the given polynomial to approximate the skidding distance in feet if $t = 5$ sec.

44. Use the polynomial equation $D = 100t - 13t^2$ to find the distance the car will skid in 1 sec. Write an ordered pair of the form (t, D).

45. If gasoline costs \$1.80 per gal, then the monomial $1.80x$ gives the cost, in dollars, of x gallons. How much would 4 gal cost?

46. If it costs \$15 plus \$2 per day to rent a chain saw, the binomial $2x + 15$ gives the cost in dollars to rent the chain saw for x days. How much would it cost to rent the saw for 6 days?

Add or subtract as indicated. See Examples 4 and 7.

47. Add.
$$3m^2 + 5m$$
$$\underline{2m^2 - 2m}$$

48. Add.
$$4a^3 - 4a^2$$
$$\underline{6a^3 + 5a^2}$$

49. Subtract.
$$12x^4 - x^2$$
$$\underline{8x^4 + 3x^2}$$

50. Subtract.
$$13y^5 - y^3$$
$$\underline{7y^5 + 5y^3}$$

51. Add.
$$\frac{2}{3}x^2 + \frac{1}{5}x + \frac{1}{6}$$
$$\underline{\frac{1}{2}x^2 - \frac{1}{3}x + \frac{2}{3}}$$

52. Add.
$$\frac{4}{7}y^2 - \frac{1}{5}y + \frac{7}{9}$$
$$\underline{\frac{1}{3}y^2 - \frac{1}{3}y + \frac{2}{5}}$$

53. Subtract.
$$12m^3 - 8m^2 + 6m + 7$$
$$\underline{ 5m^2 - 4}$$

54. Subtract.
$$5a^4 - 3a^3 + 2a^2 - a + 6$$
$$\underline{-6a^4 - a^2 + a - 1}$$

Perform the indicated operations. See Examples 5, 6, and 8.

55. $(2r^2 + 3r - 12) + (6r^2 + 2r)$

56. $(3r^2 + 5r - 6) + (2r - 5r^2)$

57. $(8m^2 - 7m) - (3m^2 + 7m - 6)$

58. $(x^2 + x) - (3x^2 + 2x - 1)$

59. $(16x^3 - x^2 + 3x) + (-12x^3 + 3x^2 + 2x)$

60. $(-2b^6 + 3b^4 - b^2) + (b^6 + 2b^4 + 2b^2)$

61. $(7y^4 + 3y^2 + 2y) - (18y^5 - 5y^3 + y)$

62. $(8t^5 + 3t^3 + 5t) - (19t^4 - 6t^2 + t)$

63. $[(8m^2 + 4m - 7) - (2m^3 - 5m + 2)] - (m^2 + m)$

64. $[(9b^3 - 4b^2 + 3b + 2) - (-2b^3 + b)] - (8b^3 + 6b + 4)$

Find the perimeter of each geometric figure.

65.

$4x^2 + 3x + 1$

$x + 2$

66.

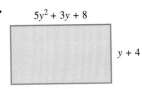

$5y^2 + 3y + 8$

$y + 4$

67.

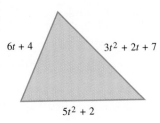

$6t + 4$ $3t^2 + 2t + 7$

$5t^2 + 2$

68.

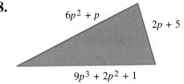

$6p^2 + p$ $2p + 5$

$9p^3 + 2p^2 + 1$

69. Subtract $9x^2 - 3x + 7$ from $-2x^2 - 6x + 4$.

70. Subtract $-5w^3 + 5w^2 - 7$ from $6w^3 + 8w + 5$.

71. Explain why the degree of the term 3^4 is not 4. What is its degree?

72. Can the sum of two polynomials in x, both of degree 3, be of degree 2? If so, give an example.

Add or subtract as indicated. See Example 9.

73. $(9a^2b - 3a^2 + 2b) + (4a^2b - 4a^2 - 3b)$

74. $(4xy^3 - 3x + y) + (5xy^3 + 13x - 4y)$

75. $(2c^4d + 3c^2d^2 - 4d^2) - (c^4d + 8c^2d^2 - 5d^2)$

76. $(3k^2h^3 + 5kh + 6k^3h^2) - (2k^2h^3 - 9kh + k^3h^2)$

77. Subtract. $9m^3n - 5m^2n^2 + 4mn^2$
$\underline{-3m^3n + 6m^2n^2 + 8mn^2}$

78. Subtract. $12r^5t + 11r^4t^2 - 7r^3t^3$
$\underline{-8r^5t + 10r^4t^2 + 3r^3t^3}$

5.2 The Product Rule and Power Rules for Exponents

OBJECTIVES

1 Use exponents.

2 Use the product rule for exponents.

3 Use the rule $(a^m)^n = a^{mn}$.

4 Use the rule $(ab)^m = a^m b^m$.

5 Use the rule $\left(\dfrac{a}{b}\right)^m = \dfrac{a^m}{b^m}$.

6 Use combinations of the rules for exponents.

7 Use the rules for exponents in an application of geometry.

OBJECTIVE 1 Use exponents. In **Section 1.1** we used exponents to write repeated products. Recall that in the expression 5^2, the number 5 is called the *base* and 2 is called the *exponent* or *power*. The expression 5^2 is called an *exponential expression*. Although we do not usually write a quantity with an exponent of 1, in general, for any quantity a, $a = a^1$.

EXAMPLE 1 Using Exponents

Write $3 \cdot 3 \cdot 3 \cdot 3 \cdot 3$ in exponential form and evaluate.

Since 3 occurs as a factor five times, the base is **3** and the exponent is **5**. The exponential expression is 3^5, read "3 to the fifth power" or simply "3 to the fifth." The value is

$$3^5 = 3 \cdot 3 \cdot 3 \cdot 3 \cdot 3 = 243.$$

Work Problem 1 at the Side.

EXAMPLE 2 Evaluating Exponential Expressions

Evaluate each exponential expression. Name the base and the exponent.

	Base	Exponent
(a) $5^4 = 5 \cdot 5 \cdot 5 \cdot 5 = 625$	5	4
(b) $-5^4 = -1 \cdot 5^4 = -1 \cdot (5 \cdot 5 \cdot 5 \cdot 5) = -625$	5	4
(c) $(-5)^4 = (-5)(-5)(-5)(-5) = 625$	-5	4

CAUTION

Notice the difference between Examples 2(b) and (c). In -5^4 the lack of parentheses shows that the exponent 4 applies only to the base 5, and not -5. In $(-5)^4$ the parentheses show that the exponent 4 applies to the base -5. In summary, $-a^n$ and $(-a)^n$ are not always the same.

Expression	Base	Exponent	Example
$-a^n$	a	n	$-3^2 = -(3 \cdot 3) = -9$
$(-a)^n$	$-a$	n	$(-3)^2 = (-3)(-3) = 9$

Work Problem 2 at the Side.

OBJECTIVE 2 Use the product rule for exponents. To develop the product rule, we use the definition of an exponential expression.

$$2^4 \cdot 2^3 = \overbrace{(2 \cdot 2 \cdot 2 \cdot 2)}^{4 \text{ factors}} \overbrace{(2 \cdot 2 \cdot 2)}^{3 \text{ factors}}$$
$$= \underbrace{2 \cdot 2 \cdot 2 \cdot 2 \cdot 2 \cdot 2 \cdot 2}_{4 + 3 = 7 \text{ factors}}$$
$$= 2^7$$

1 Write $2 \cdot 2 \cdot 2 \cdot 2$ in exponential form and evaluate.

2 Evaluate each exponential expression. Name the base and the exponent.

(a) $(-2)^5$ **(b)** -2^5

(c) -4^2 **(d)** $(-4)^2$

ANSWERS
1. $2^4 = 16$
2. **(a)** -32; -2; 5   **(b)** -32; 2; 5
 (c) -16; 4; 2   **(d)** 16; -4; 2

3 Find each product by the product rule, if possible.

(a) $8^2 \cdot 8^5$

(b) $(-7)^5 \cdot (-7)^3$

(c) $y^3 \cdot y$

(d) $4^2 \cdot 3^5$

(e) $6^4 + 6^2$

Also,
$$6^2 \cdot 6^3 = (6 \cdot 6)(6 \cdot 6 \cdot 6)$$
$$= 6 \cdot 6 \cdot 6 \cdot 6 \cdot 6$$
$$= 6^5.$$

Generalizing from these examples, $2^4 \cdot 2^3 = 2^{4+3} = 2^7$ and $6^2 \cdot 6^3 = 6^{2+3} = 6^5$. In each case, adding the exponents gives the exponent of the product, suggesting the **product rule for exponents.**

> **Product Rule for Exponents**
>
> For any positive integers m and n,
> $$a^m \cdot a^n = a^{m+n}.$$
>
> (Keep the same base and add the exponents.)
>
> *Example:* $6^2 \cdot 6^5 = 6^{2+5} = 6^7$.

> **CAUTION**
> Avoid the common error of multiplying the bases when using the product rule.
> $$6^2 \cdot 6^5 \neq 36^7$$
> *Keep the same base and add the exponents.*

EXAMPLE 3 Using the Product Rule

Use the product rule for exponents to find each product, if possible.

(a) $6^3 \cdot 6^5 = 6^{3+5} = 6^8$ by the product rule.

(b) $(-4)^7(-4)^2 = (-4)^{7+2} = (-4)^9$ by the product rule.

(c) $x^2 \cdot x = x^2 \cdot x^1 = x^{2+1} = x^3$

(d) $m^4 \cdot m^3 = m^{4+3} = m^7$

(e) $2^3 \cdot 3^2$
The product rule does not apply to the product $2^3 \cdot 3^2$ because the bases are different.
$$2^3 \cdot 3^2 = 8 \cdot 9 = 72$$

(f) $2^3 + 2^4$
The product rule does not apply to $2^3 + 2^4$ because it is a *sum*, not a *product*.
$$2^3 + 2^4 = 8 + 16 = 24$$

> **CAUTION**
> *The bases of the factors must be the same* before we can apply the product rule for exponents.

◀◀◀ Work Problem 3 at the Side.

EXAMPLE 4 **Using the Product Rule**

Multiply $2x^3$ and $3x^7$.

We use the associative and commutative properties and the product rule.

$$2x^3 \cdot 3x^7 = 2 \cdot 3 \cdot x^3 \cdot x^7 = 6x^{10} \quad 2x^3 = 2 \cdot x^3;\, 3x^7 = 3 \cdot x^7$$

CAUTION

Be sure you understand the difference between *adding* and *multiplying* exponential expressions. For example,

$$8x^3 + 5x^3 = (8 + 5)x^3 = 13x^3, \quad \text{Add.}$$

but

$$(8x^3)(5x^3) = (8 \cdot 5)x^{3+3} = 40x^6. \quad \text{Multiply.}$$

Work Problem 4 at the Side. ▶▶▶

OBJECTIVE **3** **Use the rule $(a^m)^n = a^{mn}$.** We can simplify an expression such as $(8^3)^2$ with the product rule for exponents, as follows.

$$(8^3)^2 = (8^3)(8^3) = 8^{3+3} = 8^6$$

The product of the exponents in $(8^3)^2$, $3 \cdot 2$, gives the exponent in 8^6. Also,

$$(5^2)^4 = 5^2 \cdot 5^2 \cdot 5^2 \cdot 5^2 \quad \text{Definition of exponent}$$
$$= 5^{2+2+2+2} \quad \text{Product rule}$$
$$= 5^8,$$

and $2 \cdot 4 = 8$. These examples suggest **power rule (a) for exponents.**

Power Rule (a) for Exponents

For any positive integers m and n,
$$(a^m)^n = a^{mn}.$$
(Raise a power to a power by multiplying exponents.)

Example: $(3^2)^4 = 3^{2 \cdot 4} = 3^8.$

EXAMPLE 5 **Using Power Rule (a)**

Use power rule (a) for exponents to simplify each expression.

(a) $(2^5)^3 = 2^{5 \cdot 3} = 2^{15}$ **(b)** $(5^7)^2 = 5^{7 \cdot 2} = 5^{14}$

(c) $(x^2)^5 = x^{2 \cdot 5} = x^{10}$ **(d)** $(n^3)^2 = n^{3 \cdot 2} = n^6$

Work Problem 5 at the Side. ▶▶▶

OBJECTIVE **4** **Use the rule $(ab)^m = a^m b^m$.** We can rewrite the expression $(4x)^3$ as shown below.

$$(4x)^3 = (4x)(4x)(4x) \quad \text{Definition of exponent}$$
$$= 4 \cdot 4 \cdot 4 \cdot x \cdot x \cdot x \quad \text{Commutative and associative properties}$$
$$= 4^3 x^3 \quad \text{Definition of exponent}$$

This example suggests **power rule (b) for exponents.**

---

4 Multiply.

(a) $5m^2 \cdot 2m^6$

(b) $3p^5 \cdot 9p^4$

(c) $-7p^5 \cdot (3p^8)$

5 Simplify each expression.

(a) $(5^3)^4$

(b) $(6^2)^5$

(c) $(3^2)^4$

(d) $(a^6)^5$

6 Simplify.

(a) $5(mn)^3$

(b) $(3a^2b^4)^5$

(c) $(-5m^2)^3$

Power Rule (b) for Exponents

For any positive integer m,

$$(ab)^m = a^m b^m.$$

(Raise a product to a power by raising each factor to the power.)

Example: $(2p)^5 = 2^5 p^5.$

EXAMPLE 6 Using Power Rule (b)

Use power rule (b) to simplify each expression.

(a) $(3xy)^2 = 3^2 x^2 y^2$ Power rule (b)
$$= 9x^2 y^2$$

(b) $9(pq)^2 = 9(p^2 q^2)$ Power rule (b)
$$= 9p^2 q^2$$

(c) $5(2m^2 p^3)^4 = 5[2^4 (m^2)^4 (p^3)^4]$ Power rule (b)
$$= 5(2^4 m^8 p^{12})$$ Power rule (a)
$$= 5 \cdot 2^4 m^8 p^{12}$$
$$= 80 m^8 p^{12}$$ $5 \cdot 2^4 = 5 \cdot 16 = 80$

(d) $(-5^6)^3 = (-1 \cdot 5^6)^3$ $-a = -1 \cdot a$
$$= (-1)^3 (5^6)^3$$ Power rule (b)
$$= -1 \cdot 5^{18}$$ Power rule (a)
$$= -5^{18}$$

CAUTION
Power rule (b) does not *apply to a* sum.
$$(x + 4)^2 \neq x^2 + 4^2$$

◄◄◄ Work Problem 6 at the Side.

OBJECTIVE 5 Use the rule $\left(\frac{a}{b}\right)^m = \frac{a^m}{b^m}$. Since the quotient $\frac{a}{b}$ can be written as $a \cdot \frac{1}{b}$, we can use power rule (b), together with some of the properties of real numbers, to get **power rule (c) for exponents.**

Power Rule (c) for Exponents

For any positive integer m,

$$\left(\frac{a}{b}\right)^m = \frac{a^m}{b^m} \quad (b \neq 0).$$

(Raise a quotient to a power by raising both the numerator and the denominator to the power.)

Example: $\left(\frac{5}{3}\right)^2 = \frac{5^2}{3^2}.$

EXAMPLE 7 Using Power Rule (c)

Simplify each expression.

(a) $\left(\dfrac{2}{3}\right)^5 = \dfrac{2^5}{3^5}$ or $\dfrac{32}{243}$　　　　**(b)** $\left(\dfrac{m}{n}\right)^4 = \dfrac{m^4}{n^4}, \quad n \neq 0$

Work Problem 7 at the Side. ▶▶▶

Next we list the rules for exponents discussed in this section. These rules are basic to the study of algebra and should be *memorized*.

Rules for Exponents

For positive integers m and n:　　　　　　　　*Examples*

Product rule　　$a^m \cdot a^n = a^{m+n}$　　　　$6^2 \cdot 6^5 = 6^{2+5} = 6^7$

Power rules　　**(a)** $(a^m)^n = a^{mn}$　　　　$(3^2)^4 = 3^{2 \cdot 4} = 3^8$

　　　　　　　(b) $(ab)^m = a^m b^m$　　　　$(2p)^5 = 2^5 p^5$

　　　　　　　(c) $\left(\dfrac{a}{b}\right)^m = \dfrac{a^m}{b^m}$　$(b \neq 0)$.　　$\left(\dfrac{5}{3}\right)^2 = \dfrac{5^2}{3^2}$

OBJECTIVE 6 **Use combinations of the rules for exponents.** As shown in the next example, more than one rule may be needed to simplify an expression.

EXAMPLE 8 Using Combinations of Rules

Simplify each expression.

(a) $\left(\dfrac{2}{3}\right)^2 \cdot 2^3 = \dfrac{2^2}{3^2} \cdot \dfrac{2^3}{1}$　　Power rule (c)

$= \dfrac{2^2 \cdot 2^3}{3^2 \cdot 1}$　　Multiply fractions.

$= \dfrac{2^5}{3^2}$　　Product rule

(b) $(5x)^3 (5x)^4 = (5x)^7$　　Product rule

$= 5^7 x^7$　　Power rule (b)

(c) $(2x^2 y^3)^4 (3xy^2)^3 = 2^4 (x^2)^4 (y^3)^4 \cdot 3^3 x^3 (y^2)^3$　　Power rule (b)

$= 2^4 \cdot x^8 \cdot y^{12} \cdot 3^3 \cdot x^3 \cdot y^6$　　Power rule (a)

$= 2^4 \cdot 3^3 x^8 x^3 y^{12} y^6$　　Commutative and associative properties

$= 16 \cdot 27 x^{11} y^{18}$　　Product rule

$= 432 x^{11} y^{18}$

Notice that

$$(2x^2 y^3)^4 = 2^4 x^{2 \cdot 4} y^{3 \cdot 4}, \quad \textbf{not} \quad (2 \cdot 4) x^{2 \cdot 4} y^{3 \cdot 4}.$$

Do not multiply the coefficient 2 and the exponent 4.

Continued on Next Page

7 Simplify. Assume all variables represent nonzero real numbers.

(a) $\left(\dfrac{5}{2}\right)^4$

(b) $\left(\dfrac{p}{q}\right)^2$

(c) $\left(\dfrac{r}{t}\right)^3$

ANSWERS

7. **(a)** $\dfrac{5^4}{2^4}$ or $\dfrac{625}{16}$　**(b)** $\dfrac{p^2}{q^2}$　**(c)** $\dfrac{r^3}{t^3}$

8 Simplify.

(a) $(2m)^3(2m)^4$

(b) $\left(\dfrac{5k^3}{3}\right)^2$

(c) $\left(\dfrac{1}{5}\right)^4 (2x)^2$

(d) $(-3xy^2)^3(x^2y)^4$

9 Find the area.

(d) $(-x^3y)^2(-x^5y^4)^3$

Think of the negative sign in each factor as -1.

$$\begin{aligned}
(-1x^3y)^2(-1x^5y^4)^3 &= (-1)^2(x^3)^2y^2 \cdot (-1)^3(x^5)^3(y^4)^3 &&\text{Power rule (b)}\\
&= (-1)^2(x^6)(y^2)(-1)^3(x^{15})(y^{12}) &&\text{Power rule (a)}\\
&= (-1)^5(x^{21})(y^{14}) &&\text{Product rule}\\
&= -1x^{21}y^{14}\\
&= -x^{21}y^{14}
\end{aligned}$$

◀◀◀ Work Problem 8 at the Side.

OBJECTIVE 7 Use the rules for exponents in an application of geometry.

EXAMPLE 9 Using an Area Formula

Find an expression that represents the area of each geometric figure in Figure 1.

(a)   **(b)**

Figure 1

(a) Use the formula for the area of a rectangle, $A = LW$.

$$\begin{aligned}
A &= (6x^4)(5x^3) &&\text{Area formula}\\
A &= 30x^7 &&\text{Product rule}
\end{aligned}$$

(b) This is a triangle with base $6m^4$ and height $3m^3$.

$$\begin{aligned}
A &= \frac{1}{2}bh &&\text{Area formula}\\
&= \frac{1}{2}(6m^4)(3m^3) &&\text{Substitute.}\\
&= \frac{1}{2}(18m^7) &&\text{Product rule}\\
&= 9m^7
\end{aligned}$$

◀◀◀ Work Problem 9 at the Side.

5.2 Exercises

1. What exponent is understood on the base x in the expression xy^2?

2. How are the expressions 3^2, 5^3, and 7^4 read?

Decide whether each statement is true *or* false.

3. $3^3 = 9$

4. $(-2)^4 = 2^4$

5. $(a^2)^3 = a^5$

6. $\left(\dfrac{1}{4}\right)^2 = \dfrac{1}{4^2}$

Write each expression using exponents. See Example 1.

7. $(-2)(-2)(-2)(-2)(-2)$

8. $w \cdot w \cdot w \cdot w \cdot w \cdot w$

9. $\left(\dfrac{1}{2}\right)\left(\dfrac{1}{2}\right)\left(\dfrac{1}{2}\right)\left(\dfrac{1}{2}\right)\left(\dfrac{1}{2}\right)\left(\dfrac{1}{2}\right)$

10. $\left(-\dfrac{1}{4}\right)\left(-\dfrac{1}{4}\right)\left(-\dfrac{1}{4}\right)\left(-\dfrac{1}{4}\right)\left(-\dfrac{1}{4}\right)$

11. $(-8p)(-8p)$

12. $(-7x)(-7x)(-7x)(-7x)$

13. Explain how the expressions $(-3)^4$ and -3^4 are different.

14. Explain how the expressions $(5x)^3$ and $5x^3$ are different.

Identify the base and the exponent for each exponential expression. In Exercises 15–18, also evaluate the expression. See Example 2.

15. 3^5

16. 2^7

17. $(-3)^5$

18. $(-2)^7$

19. $(-6x)^4$

20. $(-8x)^4$

21. $-6x^4$

22. $-8x^4$

23. Explain why the product rule does not apply to the expression $5^2 + 5^3$. Then evaluate the expression by finding the individual powers and adding the results.

24. Explain why the product rule does not apply to the expression $3^2 \cdot 4^3$. Then evaluate the expression by finding the individual powers and multiplying the results.

Use the product rule to simplify each expression. Write each answer in exponential form. See Examples 3 and 4.

25. $5^2 \cdot 5^6$

26. $3^6 \cdot 3^7$

27. $4^2 \cdot 4^7 \cdot 4^3$

28. $5^3 \cdot 5^8 \cdot 5^2$

29. $(-7)^3(-7)^6$

30. $(-9)^8(-9)^5$

31. $t^3 \cdot t^8 \cdot t^{13}$

32. $n^5 \cdot n^6 \cdot n^9$

33. $(-8r^4)(7r^3)$

34. $(10a^7)(-4a^3)$

35. $(-6p^5)(-7p^5)$

36. $(-5w^8)(-9w^8)$

Use the power rules for exponents to simplify each expression. Write each answer in exponential form. See Examples 5–7.

37. $(4^3)^2$

38. $(8^3)^6$

39. $(t^4)^5$

40. $(y^6)^5$

41. $(7r)^3$

42. $(11x)^4$

43. $(5xy)^5$

44. $(9pq)^6$

45. $8(qr)^3$

46. $4(vw)^5$

47. $\left(\dfrac{1}{2}\right)^3$

48. $\left(\dfrac{1}{3}\right)^5$

49. $\left(\dfrac{a}{b}\right)^3 \ (b \neq 0)$

50. $\left(\dfrac{r}{t}\right)^4 \ (t \neq 0)$

51. $\left(\dfrac{9}{5}\right)^8$

52. $\left(\dfrac{12}{7}\right)^3$

53. $(-2x^2y)^3$

54. $(-5m^4p^2)^3$

55. $(3a^3b^2)^2$

56. $(4x^3y^5)^4$

Use a combination of the rules for exponents introduced in this section to simplify each expression. See Example 8.

57. $\left(\dfrac{5}{2}\right)^3 \cdot \left(\dfrac{5}{2}\right)^2$

58. $\left(\dfrac{3}{4}\right)^5 \cdot \left(\dfrac{3}{4}\right)^6$

59. $\left(\dfrac{9}{8}\right)^3 \cdot 9^2$

60. $\left(\dfrac{8}{5}\right)^4 \cdot 8^3$

61. $(2x)^9(2x)^3$

62. $(6y)^5(6y)^8$

63. $(-6p)^4(-6p)$

64. $(-13q)^3(-13q)$

65. $(6x^2y^3)^5$

66. $(5r^5t^6)^7$

67. $(x^2)^3(x^3)^5$

68. $(y^4)^5(y^3)^5$

69. $(2w^2x^3y)^2(x^4y)^5$

70. $(3x^4y^2z)^3(yz^4)^5$

71. $(-r^4s)^2(-r^2s^3)^5$

72. $(-ts^6)^4(-t^3s^5)^3$

73. $\left(\dfrac{5a^2b^5}{c^6}\right)^3 \ (c \neq 0)$

74. $\left(\dfrac{6x^3y^9}{z^5}\right)^4 \ (z \neq 0)$

75. $(-5m^3p^4q)^2(p^2q)^3$

76. $(-a^4b^5)(-6a^3b^3)^2$

77. $(2x^2y^3z)^4(xy^2z^3)^2$

Find the area of each figure. See Example 9.

78.

$3x^2$

$4x^3$

79.

$3x^2$

$10x^5$

80.

m^2

$3m^4$

5.3 Multiplying Polynomials

OBJECTIVE 1 Multiply a monomial and a polynomial. As shown in Section 5.2, we find the product of two monomials by using the rules for exponents and the commutative and associative properties. For example,

$$(-8m^6)(-9n^6) = (-8)(-9)(m^6)(n^6) = 72m^6n^6.$$

OBJECTIVES

1 Multiply a monomial and a polynomial.

2 Multiply two polynomials.

3 Multiply binomials by the FOIL method.

> **CAUTION**
> *Do not confuse addition of terms with multiplication of terms.*
> $$7q^5 + 2q^5 = 9q^5, \quad \text{but} \quad (7q^5)(2q^5) = 7 \cdot 2q^{5+5} = 14q^{10}.$$

To find the product of a monomial and a polynomial with more than one term, we use the distributive property and multiplication of monomials.

1 Find each product.

(a) $5m^3(2m + 7)$

EXAMPLE 1 Multiplying a Monomial and a Polynomial

Use the distributive property to find each product.

(a) $4x^2(3x + 5)$

$$4x^2(3x + 5) = 4x^2(3x) + 4x^2(5) \qquad \text{Distributive property}$$
$$= 12x^3 + 20x^2 \qquad \text{Multiply monomials.}$$

(b) $-8m^3(4m^3 + 3m^2 + 2m - 1)$
$$= -8m^3(4m^3) + (-8m^3)(3m^2)$$
$$+ (-8m^3)(2m) + (-8m^3)(-1) \qquad \text{Distributive property}$$
$$= -32m^6 - 24m^5 - 16m^4 + 8m^3 \qquad \text{Multiply monomials.}$$

(b) $2x^4(3x^2 + 2x - 5)$

> **Work Problem 1 at the Side.** ▶▶▶

OBJECTIVE 2 Multiply two polynomials. We can use the distributive property repeatedly to find the product of any two polynomials. For example, to find the product of the polynomials $x^2 + 3x + 5$ and $x - 4$, think of $x - 4$ as a single quantity and use the distributive property as follows.

$$(x^2 + 3x + 5)(x - 4) = x^2(x - 4) + 3x(x - 4) + 5(x - 4)$$

Now use the distributive property three more times to find the products $x^2(x - 4)$, $3x(x - 4)$, and $5(x - 4)$.

$$x^2(x - 4) + 3x(x - 4) + 5(x - 4)$$
$$= x^2(x) + x^2(-4) + 3x(x) + 3x(-4) + 5(x) + 5(-4)$$
$$= x^3 - 4x^2 + 3x^2 - 12x + 5x - 20 \qquad \text{Multiply monomials.}$$
$$= x^3 - x^2 - 7x - 20 \qquad \text{Combine terms.}$$

This example suggests the following rule.

(c)
$-4y^2(3y^3 + 2y^2 - 4y + 8)$

Multiplying Polynomials

To multiply two polynomials, multiply each term of the second polynomial by each term of the first polynomial and add the products.

② Multiply.

(a) $(m^3 - 2m + 1)$
$\cdot (2m^2 + 4m + 3)$

(b) $(6p^2 + 2p - 4)(3p^2 - 5)$

③ Find the product.

$$3x^2 + 4x - 5$$
$$\underline{\qquad x + 4}$$

EXAMPLE 2 Multiplying Two Polynomials

Multiply $(m^2 + 5)(4m^3 - 2m^2 + 4m)$.

Multiply each term of the second polynomial by each term of the first.

$(m^2 + 5)(4m^3 - 2m^2 + 4m)$
$= m^2(4m^3) + m^2(-2m^2) + m^2(4m) + 5(4m^3) + 5(-2m^2) + 5(4m)$
$= 4m^5 - 2m^4 + 4m^3 + 20m^3 - 10m^2 + 20m$
$= 4m^5 - 2m^4 + 24m^3 - 10m^2 + 20m$ Combine like terms.

◄◄◄ **Work Problem 2 at the Side.**

When at least one of the factors in a product of polynomials has three or more terms, the multiplication can be performed alternatively by writing one polynomial above the other vertically.

EXAMPLE 3 Multiplying Polynomials Vertically

Multiply $(x^3 + 2x^2 + 4x + 1)(3x + 5)$ using the vertical method.

Write the polynomials as follows.

$$x^3 + 2x^2 + 4x + 1$$
$$\underline{\qquad\qquad 3x + 5}$$

It is not necessary to line up terms in columns, because any terms may be multiplied (not just like terms). Begin by multiplying each of the terms in the top row by 5.

$$x^3 + 2x^2 + 4x + 1$$
$$\underline{\qquad\qquad 3x + 5}$$
$$5x^3 + 10x^2 + 20x + 5 \qquad 5(x^3 + 2x^2 + 4x + 1)$$

Notice how this process is similar to multiplication of whole numbers. Now multiply each term in the top row by $3x$. Be careful to place like terms in columns, since the final step will involve addition (as in multiplying two whole numbers).

$$x^3 + 2x^2 + 4x + 1$$
$$\underline{\qquad\qquad 3x + 5}$$
$$5x^3 + 10x^2 + 20x + 5$$
$$3x^4 + 6x^3 + 12x^2 + \ 3x \qquad 3x(x^3 + 2x^2 + 4x + 1)$$

Add like terms.

$$x^3 + 2x^2 + 4x + 1$$
$$\underline{\qquad\qquad 3x + 5}$$
$$5x^3 + 10x^2 + 20x + 5$$
$$\underline{3x^4 + \ 6x^3 + 12x^2 + \ 3x}$$
$$3x^4 + 11x^3 + 22x^2 + 23x + 5$$

The product is $3x^4 + 11x^3 + 22x^2 + 23x + 5$.

◄◄◄ **Work Problem 3 at the Side.**

ANSWERS

2. (a) $2m^5 + 4m^4 - m^3 - 6m^2 - 2m + 3$
   (b) $18p^4 + 6p^3 - 42p^2 - 10p + 20$
3. $3x^3 + 16x^2 + 11x - 20$

EXAMPLE 4 **Multiplying Polynomials Vertically**

Find the product of $4m^3 - 2m^2 + 4m$ and $\frac{1}{2}m^2 + \frac{5}{2}$.

$$
\begin{array}{r}
4m^3 - 2m^2 + 4m \\
\frac{1}{2}m^2 + \frac{5}{2} \\
\hline
10m^3 - 5m^2 + 10m \\
2m^5 - m^4 + 2m^3 \\
\hline
2m^5 - m^4 + 12m^3 - 5m^2 + 10m
\end{array}
$$

Terms of top row multiplied by $\frac{5}{2}$

Terms of top row multiplied by $\frac{1}{2}m^2$

Add.

Work Problem 4 at the Side. ▷▷▷

We can use a rectangle to model polynomial multiplication. For example, to find the product

$$(2x + 1)(3x + 2),$$

label a rectangle with each term as shown below on the left. Then put the product of each pair of monomials in the appropriate box as shown on the right.

	3x	2
2x		
1		

	3x	2
2x	$6x^2$	$4x$
1	$3x$	2

The product of the binomials is the sum of these four monomial products.

$$(2x + 1)(3x + 2) = 6x^2 + 4x + 3x + 2$$
$$= 6x^2 + 7x + 2$$

Work Problem 5 at the Side. ▷▷▷

OBJECTIVE 3 Multiply binomials by the FOIL method. In algebra, many of the polynomials to be multiplied are both binomials (with just two terms). For these products, the **FOIL method** reduces the rectangle method to a systematic approach without the rectangle. To develop the FOIL method, we use the distributive property to find $(x + 3)(x + 5)$.

$$(x + 3)(x + 5) = (x + 3)x + (x + 3)5$$
$$= x(x) + 3(x) + x(5) + 3(5)$$
$$= x^2 + 3x + 5x + 15$$
$$= x^2 + 8x + 15$$

Here is where the letters of the word FOIL originate.

$(x + 3)(x + 5)$ Multiply the **First terms**: $x(x)$.   **F**

$(x + 3)(x + 5)$ Multiply the **Outer terms**: $x(5)$.   **O**
This is the **outer product**.

$(x + 3)(x + 5)$ Multiply the **Inner terms**: $3(x)$.   **I**
This is the **inner product**.

$(x + 3)(x + 5)$ Multiply the **Last terms**: $3(5)$.   **L**

The inner product and the outer product should be added mentally so that the three terms of the answer can be written without extra steps as

$$(x + 3)(x + 5) = x^2 + 8x + 15.$$

---

4 Find each product.

(a)
$$
\begin{array}{r}
k^3 - k^2 + k + 1 \\
\frac{2}{3}k - \frac{1}{3} \\
\hline
\end{array}
$$

(b)
$$
\begin{array}{r}
a^3 + 3a - 4 \\
2a^2 + 6a + 5 \\
\hline
\end{array}
$$

5 Use the rectangle method to find each product.

(a) $(4x + 3)(x + 2)$

	x	2
4x	$4x^2$	
3		

(b) $(x + 5)(x^2 + 3x + 1)$

⑥ For the product $(2p - 5)(3p + 7)$, find the following.

(a) Product of first terms

(b) Outer product

(c) Inner product

(d) Product of last terms

(e) Complete product in simplified form

⑦ Use the FOIL method to find each product.

(a) $(m + 4)(m - 3)$

(b) $(y + 7)(y + 2)$

(c) $(r - 8)(r - 5)$

A summary of the steps in the FOIL method follows.

Multiplying Binomials by the FOIL Method

Step 1 Multiply the two **First** terms of the binomials to get the first term of the answer.

Step 2 Find the **Outer** product and the **Inner** product and combine them (when possible) to get the middle term of the answer.

Step 3 Multiply the two **Last** terms of the binomials to get the last term of the answer.

$$\mathbf{F} = x^2 \qquad\qquad \mathbf{L} = 15$$

$$(x + 3)(x + 5)$$

$$\mathbf{I} = 3x$$
$$\mathbf{O} = 5x$$
$$\overline{8x} \qquad \text{Add.}$$

◀◀◀ Work Problem 6 at the Side.

EXAMPLE 5 Using the FOIL Method

Use the FOIL method to find the product $(x + 8)(x - 6)$.

Step 1 **F** Multiply the **first** terms.

$$x(x) = x^2$$

Step 2 **O** Find the **outer** product.

$$x(-6) = -6x$$

I Find the **inner** product.

$$8(x) = 8x$$

Add the outer and inner products mentally.

$$-6x + 8x = 2x$$

Step 3 **L** Multiply the **last** terms.

$$8(-6) = -48$$

The product of $x + 8$ and $x - 6$ is the sum of the terms found in the three steps above, so

$$(x + 8)(x - 6) = x^2 + 2x - 48.$$

As a shortcut, this product can be found in the following manner.

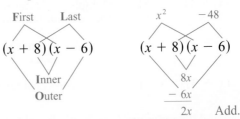

First   Last

$$(x + 8)(x - 6)$$

Inner
Outer

$$x^2 \qquad -48$$

$$(x + 8)(x - 6)$$

$$8x$$
$$\underline{-6x}$$
$$2x \qquad \text{Add.}$$

◀◀◀ Work Problem 7 at the Side.

ANSWERS
6. (a) $2p(3p) = 6p^2$ **(b)** $2p(7) = 14p$
(c) $-5(3p) = -15p$ **(d)** $-5(7) = -35$
(e) $6p^2 - p - 35$
7. (a) $m^2 + m - 12$ **(b)** $y^2 + 9y + 14$
(c) $r^2 - 13r + 40$

It is not possible to add the inner and outer products of the FOIL method if unlike terms result, as shown in the next example.

EXAMPLE 6 Using the FOIL Method

Multiply $(9x - 2)(3y + 1)$.

First	$(9x - 2)(3y + 1)$	$27xy$
Outer	$(9x - 2)(3y + 1)$	$9x$
Inner	$(9x - 2)(3y + 1)$	$-6y$
Last	$(9x - 2)(3y + 1)$	-2

Unlike terms

$$\begin{array}{cccc} & F & O & I & L \\ (9x - 2)(3y + 1) = & 27xy & + 9x & - 6y & - 2 \end{array}$$

Work Problem 8 at the Side. ▶▶▶

EXAMPLE 7 Using the FOIL Method

Find each product.

$$\begin{array}{cccc} & F & O & I & L \end{array}$$

(a) $(2k + 5y)(k + 3y) = 2k(k) + 2k(3y) + 5y(k) + 5y(3y)$

$$= 2k^2 + 6ky + 5ky + 15y^2$$

$$= 2k^2 + 11ky + 15y^2$$

(b) $(7p + 2q)(3p - q) = 21p^2 - pq - 2q^2$ FOIL

(c) $2x^2(x - 3)(3x + 4) = 2x^2(3x^2 - 5x - 12)$ FOIL

$$= 6x^4 - 10x^3 - 24x^2$$ Distributive property

Work Problem 9 at the Side. ▶▶▶

NOTE
Example 7(c) showed one way to multiply three polynomials. We could have multiplied $2x^2$ and $x - 3$ first, then multiplied that product and $3x + 4$ as follows.

$$2x^2(x - 3)(3x + 4) = (2x^3 - 6x^2)(3x + 4)$$

$$= 6x^4 - 10x^3 - 24x^2$$

8 Find the product.

$$(4x - 3)(2y + 5)$$

9 Find each product.

(a) $(6m + 5)(m - 4)$

(b) $(3r + 2t)(3r + 4t)$

(c) $y^2(8y + 3)(2y + 1)$

Real-Data Applications

Algebra as Generalized Arithmetic

The rules of algebra are consistent with those for arithmetic. To learn a method for multiplying binomial factors, such as $(3x + 2)(4x + 1)$, we can observe the method for multiplying two-digit numbers, such as $32 \cdot 41$. The number 32 is shorthand for the expanded number $3 \cdot 10 + 2$, and the number 41 is shorthand for $4 \cdot 10 + 1$. So, multiplying $32 \cdot 41$ is the same as multiplying $(3 \cdot 10 + 2)(4 \cdot 10 + 1)$.

1. An expanded version of the usual algorithm is shown in the first column below. Each partial product, such as 1×2 and 40×30, is shown to clarify how it contributes to the process.

2. In the standard algorithm, it is clear that the 32 represents the sum of 1×2 and 1×30, and 1280 represents the sum of 40×2 and 40×30.

3. When FOIL is used to multiply the numbers, the term $11 \cdot 10$ represents the sum of the partial products 1×30 and 40×2. When we simplify $12 \cdot 10^2 + 11 \cdot 10 + 2$, the result is 1312.

4. When FOIL is used to multiply the binomials, each term exactly matches the corresponding term from the multiplication of the numbers.

Partial Products Multiplication Algorithm	Standard Algorithm	FOIL Method for Numbers	FOIL Method for Variables
32	32	$(3 \cdot 10 + 2)(4 \cdot 10 + 1)$	$(3x + 2)(4x + 1)$
$\times\ 41$	$\times\ 41$	$12 \cdot 10^2 + 3 \cdot 10 + 8 \cdot 10 + 2$	$12x^2 + 3x + 8x + 2$
$2 = 1 \times 2$	32	$12 \cdot 10^2 + 11 \cdot 10 + 2$	$12x^2 + 11x + 2$
$30 = 1 \times 30$	1280	$1200 + 110 + 2$	
$80 = 40 \times 2$	1312	1312	
$1200 = 40 \times 30$			
1312			

For Group Discussion

Use FOIL to compute each binomial product and corresponding arithmetic product. Verify that the results of the arithmetic product are valid. For the numerical problems, write the correct *signed* product for each term.

1. $(2x + 1)(2x - 3)$ and $(2 \cdot 10 + 1)(2 \cdot 10 - 3)$, which is $21 \cdot 17$
   Does the arithmetic FOIL result simplify to the correct answer?

2. $(4x - 2)(2x + 5)$ and $(4 \cdot 10 - 2)(2 \cdot 10 + 5)$, which is $38 \cdot 25$
   Does the arithmetic FOIL result simplify to the correct answer?

3. $(7x - 3)(5x - 4)$ and $(7 \cdot 10 - 3)(5 \cdot 10 - 4)$, which is $67 \cdot 46$
   Does the arithmetic FOIL result simplify to the correct answer?

4. A mental trick for multiplying two-digit numbers, such as $27 \cdot 18$, follows: "Multiply the ones $(7 \times 8 = 56)$. Write the 6 in the ones place, and carry the 5. Add the inner product (7×1), the outer product (2×8), and the carried 5 $(7 + 16 + 5 = 28)$. Write the 8 in the tens place, and carry the 2. Multiply the tens (2×1), and add to the carried 2. Write 4 in the hundreds place. The answer is 486." Why does the trick work?

5.3 **Exercises**

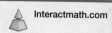
Find each product using the rectangle method shown in the text.

1. $(x + 3)(x + 4)$ 　　　**2.** $(x + 5)(x + 2)$ 　　　**3.** $(2x + 1)(x^2 + 3x + 2)$ 　　**4.** $(x + 4)(3x^2 + 2x + 1)$

5. In multiplying a monomial by a polynomial, such as in $4x(3x^2 + 7x^3) = 4x(3x^2) + 4x(7x^3)$, the first property that is used is the _____ property.

6. Match each product in parts (a)–(d) with the correct polynomial in choices A–D.

 　(a) $(x - 5)(x + 3)$ 　　**(b)** $(x + 5)(x + 3)$ 　　**(c)** $(x - 5)(x - 3)$ 　　**(d)** $(x + 5)(x - 3)$

 　A. $x^2 + 8x + 15$ 　　**B.** $x^2 - 8x + 15$ 　　**C.** $x^2 - 2x - 15$ 　　**D.** $x^2 + 2x - 15$

Find each product. See Example 1.

7. $-2m(3m + 2)$ 　　　　　**8.** $-5p(6 + 3p)$ 　　　　　**9.** $\dfrac{3}{4}p(8 - 6p + 12p^3)$

10. $\dfrac{4}{3}x(3 + 2x + 5x^3)$ 　　　**11.** $2y^5(3 + 2y + 5y^4)$ 　　　**12.** $2m^4(3m^2 + 5m + 6)$

Find each product. See Examples 2–4.

13. $(6x + 1)(2x^2 + 4x + 1)$ 　　　　　　**14.** $(9y - 2)(8y^2 - 6y + 1)$

15. $(4m + 3)(5m^3 - 4m^2 + m - 5)$ 　　　　**16.** $(y + 4)(3y^3 - 2y^2 + y + 3)$

17. $(2x - 1)(3x^5 - 2x^3 + x^2 - 2x + 3)$ 　　　**18.** $(2a + 3)(a^4 - a^3 + a^2 - a + 1)$

19. $(5x^2 + 2x + 1)(x^2 - 3x + 5)$ 　　　　　**20.** $(2m^2 + m - 3)(m^2 - 4m + 5)$

Find each binomial product using the FOIL method. See Examples 5–7.

21. $(n - 2)(n + 3)$ 　　　　**22.** $(r - 6)(r + 8)$ 　　　　　**23.** $(4r + 1)(2r - 3)$

24. $(5x + 2)(2x - 7)$ 　　　**25.** $(3x + 2)(3x - 2)$ 　　　　**26.** $(7x + 3)(7x - 3)$

27. $(3q + 1)(3q + 1)$

28. $(4w + 7)(4w + 7)$

29. $(3t + 4s)(2t + 5s)$

30. $(8v + 5w)(2v + 3w)$

31. $(-.3t + .4)(t + .6)$

32. $(-.5x + .9)(x - .2)$

33. $\left(x - \dfrac{2}{3}\right)\left(x + \dfrac{1}{4}\right)$

34. $\left(-\dfrac{8}{3} + 3k\right)\left(-\dfrac{2}{3} - k\right)$

35. $\left(-\dfrac{5}{4} + 2r\right)\left(-\dfrac{3}{4} - r\right)$

36. $2m^3(4m - 1)(2m + 3)$

37. $3y^3(2y + 3)(y - 5)$

38. $5t^4(t + 3)(3t - 1)$

RELATING CONCEPTS (EXERCISES 39–44) For Individual or Group Work

Work Exercises 39–44 in order. (All units are in yards.) Refer to the figure as necessary.

39. Find a polynomial that represents the area of the rectangle.

40. Suppose you know that the area of the rectangle is 600 yd². Use this information and the polynomial from Exercise 39 to write an equation in x, and solve it.

41. What are the dimensions of the rectangle?

42. Suppose the rectangle represents a lawn and it costs \$3.50 per square yard to lay sod on the lawn. How much will it cost to sod the entire lawn?

43. Use the result of Exercise 41 to find the perimeter of the lawn.

44. Again, suppose the rectangle represents a lawn and it costs \$9.00 per yard to fence the lawn. How much will it cost to fence the lawn?

---

45. Perform the following multiplications: $(x + 4)(x - 4)$; $(y + 2)(y - 2)$; $(r + 7)(r - 7)$. Observe your answers, and explain the pattern that can be found in the answers.

46. Repeat Exercise 45 for the following: $(x + 4)(x + 4)$; $(y - 2)(y - 2)$; $(r + 7)(r + 7)$.

5.4 Special Products

In this section, we develop shortcuts to find certain binomial products that occur frequently.

OBJECTIVE **1** **Square binomials.** The square of a binomial can be found quickly by using the method shown in Example 1.

EXAMPLE 1 **Squaring a Binomial**

Find $(m + 3)^2$.
    Squaring $m + 3$ by the FOIL method gives
$$(m + 3)(m + 3) = m^2 + 3m + 3m + 9$$
$$= m^2 + 6m + 9.$$

This result has the squares of the first and the last terms of the binomial:
$$m^2 = m^2 \quad \text{and} \quad 3^2 = 9.$$

The middle term, $6m$, is twice the product of the two terms of the binomial, since the outer and inner products are $m(3)$ and $3(m)$, and
$$m(3) + 3(m) = 2(m)(3) = 6m.$$

Work Problem 1 at the Side. ▶▶▶

Example 1 suggests the following rules.

Square of a Binomial

The square of a binomial is a trinomial consisting of the square of the first term, plus twice the product of the two terms, plus the square of the last term of the binomial. For a and b,
$$(a + b)^2 = a^2 + 2ab + b^2.$$
Also, $\qquad (a - b)^2 = a^2 - 2ab + b^2.$

EXAMPLE 2 **Squaring Binomials**

Use the rules to square each binomial.

$$(a \; - \; b)^2 \; = \quad a^2 \; - \; 2 \cdot a \cdot b \; + \; b^2$$
$$\downarrow \quad \downarrow \qquad \downarrow \quad \downarrow \; \downarrow \; \downarrow \qquad \downarrow$$

(a) $(5z - 1)^2 = (5z)^2 - 2(5z)(1) + (1)^2$
$$= 25z^2 - 10z + 1 \qquad (5z)^2 = 5^2 z^2 = 25z^2$$

(b) $(3b + 5r)^2 = (3b)^2 + 2(3b)(5r) + (5r)^2$
$$= 9b^2 + 30br + 25r^2$$

(c) $(2a - 9x)^2 = 4a^2 - 36ax + 81x^2$

(d) $\left(4m + \dfrac{1}{2}\right)^2 = (4m)^2 + 2(4m)\left(\dfrac{1}{2}\right) + \left(\dfrac{1}{2}\right)^2$
$$= 16m^2 + 4m + \dfrac{1}{4}$$

1 Consider the binomial $x + 4$.

(a) What is the first term of the binomial? Square it.

(b) What is the last term of the binomial? Square it.

(c) Find twice the product of the two terms of the binomial.

(d) Find $(x + 4)^2$.

2 Find each square by using the rules for the square of a binomial.

(a) $(t + u)^2$

(b) $(2m - p)^2$

(c) $(4p + 3q)^2$

(d) $(5r - 6s)^2$

(e) $\left(3k - \dfrac{1}{2}\right)^2$

Notice that in the square of a sum, all of the terms are positive, as in Examples 2(b) and (d). In the square of a difference, the middle term is negative, as in Examples 2(a) and (c).

CAUTION
A common error when squaring a binomial is to forget the middle term of the product. In general,
$$(a + b)^2 \neq a^2 + b^2.$$

◀◀◀ **Work Problem 2 at the Side.**

OBJECTIVE 2 Find the product of the sum and difference of two terms. Binomial products of the form $(a + b)(a - b)$ also occur frequently. In these products, one binomial is the sum of two terms, and the other is the difference of the same two terms. For example, the product of $x + 2$ and $x - 2$ is
$$(x + 2)(x - 2) = x^2 - 2x + 2x - 4$$
$$= x^2 - 4.$$

As this example suggests, the product of $a + b$ and $a - b$ is the difference between two squares.

Product of the Sum and Difference of Two Terms
$$(a + b)(a - b) = a^2 - b^2$$

EXAMPLE 3 Finding the Product of the Sum and Difference of Two Terms

Find each product.

(a) $(x + 4)(x - 4)$
Use the rule for the product of the sum and difference of two terms.
$$(x + 4)(x - 4) = x^2 - 4^2$$
$$= x^2 - 16$$

(b) $\left(\dfrac{2}{3} - w\right)\left(\dfrac{2}{3} + w\right)$
By the commutative property, this product is the same as $\left(\frac{2}{3} + w\right)\left(\frac{2}{3} - w\right)$.
$$\left(\dfrac{2}{3} - w\right)\left(\dfrac{2}{3} + w\right) = \left(\dfrac{2}{3} + w\right)\left(\dfrac{2}{3} - w\right)$$
$$= \left(\dfrac{2}{3}\right)^2 - w^2$$
$$= \dfrac{4}{9} - w^2$$

(c) $x(x + 2)(x - 2) = x(x^2 - 4)$
$$= x^3 - 4x$$

EXAMPLE 4 Finding the Product of the Sum and Difference of Two Terms

Find each product.

$$\underset{\downarrow}{(a} \quad \underset{\downarrow}{+ \; b)} \; \underset{\downarrow}{(a} \quad \underset{\downarrow}{- \; b)}$$

(a) $(5m + 3)(5m - 3)$

Use the rule for the product of the sum and difference of two terms.

$$(5m + 3)(5m - 3) = (5m)^2 - 3^2$$
$$= 25m^2 - 9$$

(b) $(4x + y)(4x - y) = (4x)^2 - y^2$
$$= 16x^2 - y^2$$

(c) $\left(z - \dfrac{1}{4}\right)\left(z + \dfrac{1}{4}\right) = z^2 - \dfrac{1}{16}$

(d) $2p(p^2 + 3)(p^2 - 3) = 2p(p^4 - 9)$
$$= 2p^5 - 18p$$

> **Work Problem 3 at the Side.** ▶▶▶

The product rules of this section will be important later, particularly in **Chapters 6** and **7.** Therefore, it is important to learn these rules and practice using them.

OBJECTIVE 3 Find greater powers of binomials.   The methods used in the previous section and this section can be combined to find greater powers of binomials.

EXAMPLE 5 Finding Greater Powers of Binomials

Find each product.

(a) $(x + 5)^3 = (x + 5)^2(x + 5)$ $a^3 = a^2 \cdot a$
$$= (x^2 + 10x + 25)(x + 5) \quad \text{Square the binomial.}$$
$$= x^3 + 10x^2 + 25x + 5x^2 + 50x + 125 \quad \text{Multiply polynomials.}$$
$$= x^3 + 15x^2 + 75x + 125 \quad \text{Combine like terms.}$$

(b) $(2y - 3)^4 = (2y - 3)^2(2y - 3)^2$ $a^4 = a^2 \cdot a^2$
$$= (4y^2 - 12y + 9)(4y^2 - 12y + 9) \quad \text{Square each binomial.}$$
$$= 16y^4 - 48y^3 + 36y^2 - 48y^3 + 144y^2 \quad \text{Multiply polynomials.}$$
$$\quad - 108y + 36y^2 - 108y + 81$$
$$= 16y^4 - 96y^3 + 216y^2 - 216y + 81 \quad \text{Combine like terms.}$$

(c) $-2r(r + 2)^3 = -2r(r + 2)(r + 2)^2$
$$= -2r(r + 2)(r^2 + 4r + 4)$$
$$= -2r(r^3 + 4r^2 + 4r + 2r^2 + 8r + 8)$$
$$= -2r(r^3 + 6r^2 + 12r + 8)$$
$$= -2r^4 - 12r^3 - 24r^2 - 16r$$

> **Work Problem 4 at the Side.** ▶▶▶

3 Find each product by using the rule for the sum and difference of two terms.

(a) $(6a + 3)(6a - 3)$

(b) $(10m + 7)(10m - 7)$

(c) $(7p + 2q)(7p - 2q)$

(d) $\left(3r - \dfrac{1}{2}\right)\left(3r + \dfrac{1}{2}\right)$

(e) $3x(x^3 - 4)(x^3 + 4)$

4 Find each product.

(a) $(m + 1)^3$

(b) $(3k - 2)^4$

(c) $-3x(x - 4)^3$

ANSWERS
3. (a) $36a^2 - 9$ **(b)** $100m^2 - 49$
  (c) $49p^2 - 4q^2$ **(d)** $9r^2 - \dfrac{1}{4}$
  (e) $3x^7 - 48x$
4. (a) $m^3 + 3m^2 + 3m + 1$
  (b) $81k^4 - 216k^3 + 216k^2 - 96k + 16$
  (c) $-3x^4 + 36x^3 - 144x^2 + 192x$

Real-Data Applications

Using a Rule of Thumb

A Dynamic Homes neighborhood features variations of three models of houses. Each buyer has an option to purchase a concrete patio extension, constructed to his or her choice of size. Each of the three models is designed so that the patio will be in the shape of a large square that is missing a corner square, similar to the diagram shown on the left. The size of the removed corner and the length of the patio vary from model to model, as does the size of the entire patio. To determine the dimensions of the patio, the rectangle of size $b \times (a - b)$ in the middle patio diagram can be rotated and repositioned to form the rectangle shown on the right, with length $a + b$ and width $a - b$.

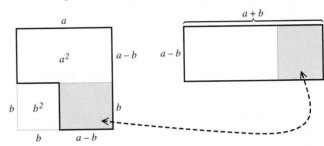

Since every time a house is sold the salesperson must ask the construction supervisor to calculate the cost of the patio extension, the supervisor devises a *rule of thumb* based on the quantity $(a + b)(a - b)$. There are only three possible choices for the value of b, one for each model house. This means that the salesperson needs to know only one additional measurement—the distance from the corner H to the edge of the patio E, which is $a - b$. The thickness of the patio is $\frac{1}{3}$ ft. The cost of concrete is $58.00 per yd^3. (*Source:* Dunham Price, Inc., Westlake, LA.) There is a 100% markup in price to cover profit as well as costs for ground preparation, building forms, and finishing the concrete, giving a cost factor of $116.00 per yd^3.

For Group Discussion

1. Why is knowing the values for b and $a - b$ sufficient for finding the quantity $a + b$?

2. Explain why the area of the patio can be written both as $(a + b)(a - b)$ and $a^2 - b^2$.

3. Apply the construction supervisor's rule of thumb to the three examples given in the table. To calculate the total cost for a patio with long side of length a feet, use the table and work from left to right. The second-to-last column is the volume of concrete needed, and the last column is the total cost of the patio. Round to the next tenth.

House Model	Corner Length b ft	Corner Length Doubled $2b$	Distance from Corner H to Patio Edge E $a - b$	Add Previous Two Columns $2b + (a - b)$	Multiply Previous Two Columns $(a + b)(a - b)$	VOLUME Multiply Previous Column by $\frac{1}{3}$ and Divide by 27	COST Multiply Previous Column by Cost Factor of $116.00
A	5		10				
B	6		12				
C	8		14				

5.4 Exercises

1. Consider the square $(2x + 3)^2$.

   (a) What is the square of the first term, $(2x)^2$? _____

   (b) What is twice the product of the two terms, $2(2x)(3)$? _____

   (c) What is the square of the last term, 3^2? _____

   (d) Write the final product, which is a trinomial, using your results from parts (a)–(c). _____

2. Repeat Exercise 1 for the square $(3x - 2)^2$.

Find each square. See Examples 1 and 2.

3. $(a - c)^2$ **4.** $(p - y)^2$ **5.** $(p + 2)^2$ **6.** $(r + 5)^2$

7. $(4x - 3)^2$ **8.** $(5y + 2)^2$ **9.** $(.8t + .7s)^2$ **10.** $(.7z - .3w)^2$

11. $\left(5x + \dfrac{2}{5}y\right)^2$ **12.** $\left(6m - \dfrac{4}{5}n\right)^2$ **13.** $\left(4a - \dfrac{3}{2}b\right)^2$ **14.** $x(2x + 5)^2$

15. $-(4r - 2)^2$ **16.** $-(3y - 8)^2$

17. Consider the product $(7x + 3y)(7x - 3y)$.

   (a) What is the product of the first terms, $7x(7x)$? _____

   (b) Multiply the outer terms, $7x(-3y)$. Then multiply the inner terms, $3y(7x)$. Add the results. What is this sum? _____

   (c) What is the product of the last terms, $3y(-3y)$? _____

   (d) Write the complete product using your answers in parts (a) and (c). _____ Why is the sum found in part (b) omitted here?

18. Repeat Exercise 17 for the product $(5x + 7y)(5x - 7y)$.

Find each product. See Examples 3 and 4.

19. $(q + 2)(q - 2)$ **20.** $(x + 8)(x - 8)$ **21.** $(2w + 5)(2w - 5)$ **22.** $(3z + 8)(3z - 8)$

23. $(10x + 3y)(10x - 3y)$ **24.** $(13r + 2z)(13r - 2z)$ **25.** $(2x^2 - 5)(2x^2 + 5)$ **26.** $(9y^2 - 2)(9y^2 + 2)$

27. $\left(7x + \dfrac{3}{7}\right)\left(7x - \dfrac{3}{7}\right)$ **28.** $\left(9y + \dfrac{2}{3}\right)\left(9y - \dfrac{2}{3}\right)$ **29.** $p(3p + 7)(3p - 7)$ **30.** $q(5q - 1)(5q + 1)$

RELATING CONCEPTS (EXERCISES 31–40)   For Individual or Group Work

*Special products can be illustrated by using areas of rectangles. Use the figure and **work Exercises 31–36 in order,** to justify the special product* $(a + b)^2 = a^2 + 2ab + b^2$.

31. Express the area of the large square as the square of a binomial.

32. Give the monomial that represents the area of the red square.

33. Give the monomial that represents the sum of the areas of the blue rectangles.

34. Give the monomial that represents the area of the yellow square.

35. What is the sum of the monomials you obtained in Exercises 32–34?

36. Explain why the binomial square you found in Exercise 31 must equal the polynomial you found in Exercise 35.

To understand how the special product $(a + b)^2 = a^2 + 2ab + b^2$ *can be applied to a purely numerical problem,* **work Exercises 37–40 in order.**

37. Evaluate 35^2 using either traditional paper-and-pencil methods or a calculator.

38. The number 35 can be written as $30 + 5$. Therefore, $35^2 = (30 + 5)^2$. Use the special product for squaring a binomial with $a = 30$ and $b = 5$ to write an expression for $(30 + 5)^2$. Do not simplify at this time.

39. Use the order of operations to simplify the expression you found in Exercise 38.

40. How do the answers in Exercises 37 and 39 compare?

Find each product. See Example 5.

41. $(m - 5)^3$ **42.** $(p + 3)^3$ **43.** $(2a + 1)^3$

44. $(3m - 1)^3$ **45.** $(3r - 2t)^4$ **46.** $(2z + 5y)^4$

47. $3x^2(x - 3)^3$ **48.** $4p^3(p + 4)^3$ **49.** $-8x^2y(x + y)^4$

In Exercises 50 and 51, refer to the figure shown here.

50. Find a polynomial that represents the volume of the cube.

51. If the value of x is 6, what is the volume of the cube?

5.5 Integer Exponents and the Quotient Rule

In all our earlier work, exponents were positive integers. Now we want to develop meaning for exponents that are not positive integers.

Consider the following list of exponential expressions.

$$2^4 = 16$$
$$2^3 = 8$$
$$2^2 = 4$$

Do you see the pattern in the values? Each time we reduce the exponent by 1, the value is divided by 2 (the base). Using this pattern, we can continue the list to smaller and smaller integer exponents.

$$2^1 = 2$$
$$2^0 = 1$$
$$2^{-1} = \frac{1}{2}$$

> **Work Problem 1 at the Side.** ▶▶▶

From the preceding list and the answers to Problem 1, it appears that we should define 2^0 as 1 and negative exponents as reciprocals.

OBJECTIVE 1 Use 0 as an exponent. We want the definitions of 0 and negative exponents to satisfy the rules for exponents from **Section 5.2.** For example, if $6^0 = 1$,

$$6^0 \cdot 6^2 = 1 \cdot 6^2 = 6^2 \quad \text{and} \quad 6^0 \cdot 6^2 = 6^{0+2} = 6^2,$$

so the product rule is satisfied. Check that the power rules are also valid for a 0 exponent. Thus, we define a 0 exponent as follows.

Zero Exponent

For any nonzero real number a, $a^0 = 1$.

Example: $17^0 = 1$.

EXAMPLE 1 Using Zero Exponents

Evaluate each exponential expression.

(a) $60^0 = 1$

(b) $(-60)^0 = 1$

(c) $-60^0 = -(1) = -1$

(d) $y^0 = 1, \quad y \neq 0$

(e) $6y^0 = 6(1) = 6, \quad y \neq 0$

(f) $(6y)^0 = 1, \quad y \neq 0$

CAUTION

Look again at Examples 1(b) and (c). In $(-60)^0$, the base is -60 and the exponent is 0. Any nonzero base raised to the exponent 0 is 1. In -60^0, the base is 60. Then $60^0 = 1$, and $-60^0 = -1$.

> **Work Problem 2 at the Side.** ▶▶▶

OBJECTIVES

OBJECTIVES

1 Use 0 as an exponent.

2 Use negative numbers as exponents.

3 Use the quotient rule for exponents.

4 Use combinations of rules.

1 Continue the list of exponentials using $-2, -3,$ and -4 as exponents.

$2^{-2} = $ _____

$2^{-3} = $ _____

$2^{-4} = $ _____

2 Evaluate.

(a) 28^0

(b) $(-16)^0$

(c) -7^0

(d) $m^0, \quad m \neq 0$

(e) $-p^0, \quad p \neq 0$

ANSWERS

1. $2^{-2} = \frac{1}{4}; 2^{-3} = \frac{1}{8}; 2^{-4} = \frac{1}{16}$

2. **(a)** 1 **(b)** 1 **(c)** -1 **(d)** 1 **(e)** -1

OBJECTIVE 2 Use negative numbers as exponents. From the lists at the beginning of this section and margin problem 1, since $2^{-2} = \frac{1}{4}$ and $2^{-3} = \frac{1}{8}$, we can deduce that 2^{-n} should equal $\frac{1}{2^n}$. Is the product rule valid in such cases? For example, if we multiply 6^{-2} by 6^2, we get

$$6^{-2} \cdot 6^2 = 6^{-2+2} = 6^0 = 1.$$

The expression 6^{-2} behaves as if it were the reciprocal of 6^2, because their product is 1. The reciprocal of 6^2 may be written $\frac{1}{6^2}$, leading us to define 6^{-2} as $\frac{1}{6^2}$. This is a particular case of the definition of negative exponents.

> **Negative Exponents**
>
> For any nonzero real number a and any integer n,
>
> $$a^{-n} = \frac{1}{a^n}.$$
>
> *Example:* $3^{-2} = \frac{1}{3^2}$.

By definition, a^{-n} and a^n are reciprocals, since

$$a^n \cdot a^{-n} = a^n \cdot \frac{1}{a^n} = 1.$$

Since $1^n = 1$, the definition of a^{-n} can also be written

$$a^{-n} = \frac{1}{a^n} = \frac{1^n}{a^n} = \left(\frac{1}{a}\right)^n.$$

For example, $6^{-3} = \left(\frac{1}{6}\right)^3$ and $\left(\frac{1}{3}\right)^{-2} = 3^2.$

EXAMPLE 2 Using Negative Exponents

Simplify by writing each expression with positive exponents.

(a) $3^{-2} = \frac{1}{3^2} = \frac{1}{9}$

(b) $5^{-3} = \frac{1}{5^3} = \frac{1}{125}$

(c) $\left(\frac{1}{2}\right)^{-3} = 2^3 = 8$ $\frac{1}{2}$ and 2 are reciprocals.

Notice that we can change the base to its reciprocal if we also change the sign of the exponent.

(d) $\left(\frac{2}{5}\right)^{-4} = \left(\frac{5}{2}\right)^4$ $\frac{2}{5}$ and $\frac{5}{2}$ are reciprocals.   **(e)** $\left(\frac{4}{3}\right)^{-5} = \left(\frac{3}{4}\right)^5$

(f) $4^{-1} - 2^{-1} = \frac{1}{4} - \frac{1}{2} = \frac{1}{4} - \frac{2}{4} = -\frac{1}{4}$

Apply the exponents first, then subtract.

Continued on Next Page

(g) $p^{-2} = \dfrac{1}{p^2}, \quad p \neq 0$

(h) $\dfrac{1}{x^{-4}}, \quad x \neq 0$

$$\frac{1}{x^{-4}} = \frac{1^{-4}}{x^{-4}} \qquad 1^{-4} = 1$$

$$= \left(\frac{1}{x}\right)^{-4} \qquad \text{Power rule (c)}$$

$$= x^4 \qquad \tfrac{1}{x} \text{ and } x \text{ are reciprocals.}$$

CAUTION

A negative exponent does not indicate a negative number; negative exponents lead to reciprocals.

Expression	Example	
a^{-n}	$3^{-2} = \dfrac{1}{3^2} = \dfrac{1}{9}$	Not negative
$-a^{-n}$	$-3^{-2} = -\dfrac{1}{3^2} = -\dfrac{1}{9}$	Negative

---

Work Problem 3 at the Side. ▶▶▶

The definition of negative exponents allows us to move factors in a fraction if we also change the signs of the exponents. For example,

$$\frac{2^{-3}}{3^{-4}} = \frac{\dfrac{1}{2^3}}{\dfrac{1}{3^4}} = \frac{1}{2^3} \div \frac{1}{3^4} = \frac{1}{2^3} \cdot \frac{3^4}{1} = \frac{3^4}{2^3},$$

so that

$$\frac{2^{-3}}{3^{-4}} = \frac{3^4}{2^3}.$$

Changing from Negative to Positive Exponents

For any nonzero numbers a and b, and any integers m and n,

$$\frac{a^{-m}}{b^{-n}} = \frac{b^n}{a^m} \quad \text{and} \quad \left(\frac{a}{b}\right)^{-m} = \left(\frac{b}{a}\right)^m.$$

Examples: $\dfrac{3^{-5}}{2^{-4}} = \dfrac{2^4}{3^5} \quad \text{and} \quad \left(\dfrac{4}{5}\right)^{-3} = \left(\dfrac{5}{4}\right)^3.$

---

3 Write with positive exponents.

(a) 4^{-3}

(b) 6^{-2}

(c) $\left(\dfrac{2}{3}\right)^{-2}$

(d) $2^{-1} + 5^{-1}$

(e) $m^{-5}, \quad m \neq 0$

(f) $\dfrac{1}{z^{-4}}, \quad z \neq 0$

4 Write with only positive exponents. Assume all variables represent nonzero real numbers.

(a) $\dfrac{7^{-1}}{5^{-4}}$

(b) $\dfrac{x^{-3}}{y^{-2}}$

(c) $\dfrac{4h^{-5}}{m^{-2}k}$

(d) $p^2 q^{-5}$

(e) $\left(\dfrac{3m}{p}\right)^{-2}$

EXAMPLE 3 Changing from Negative to Positive Exponents

Write with only positive exponents. Assume all variables represent nonzero real numbers.

(a) $\dfrac{4^{-2}}{5^{-3}} = \dfrac{5^3}{4^2}$

(b) $\dfrac{m^{-5}}{p^{-1}} = \dfrac{p^1}{m^5} = \dfrac{p}{m^5}$

(c) $\dfrac{a^{-2}b}{3d^{-3}} = \dfrac{bd^3}{3a^2}$

Notice that b in the numerator and the coefficient 3 in the denominator were not affected.

(d) $x^3 y^{-4} = \dfrac{x^3 y^{-4}}{1} = \dfrac{x^3}{y^4}$

(e) $\left(\dfrac{x}{2y}\right)^{-4} = \left(\dfrac{2y}{x}\right)^4 = \dfrac{2^4 y^4}{x^4}$

Work Problem 4 at the Side.

CAUTION
Be careful. We cannot change negative exponents to positive exponents using this rule if the exponents occur in a *sum* of terms. For example,

$$\dfrac{5^{-2} + 3^{-1}}{7 - 2^{-3}}$$

cannot be written with positive exponents using the rule given here. We would have to use the definition of a negative exponent to rewrite this expression with positive exponents, as

$$\dfrac{\dfrac{1}{5^2} + \dfrac{1}{3}}{7 - \dfrac{1}{2^3}}.$$

OBJECTIVE 3 Use the quotient rule for exponents. We now consider the quotient of exponential expressions with the same base. We know that

$$\dfrac{6^5}{6^3} = \dfrac{6 \cdot 6 \cdot 6 \cdot 6 \cdot 6}{6 \cdot 6 \cdot 6} = 6^2.$$

Notice that the difference between the exponents, $5 - 3 = 2$, is the exponent in the quotient. Also,

$$\dfrac{6^2}{6^4} = \dfrac{6 \cdot 6}{6 \cdot 6 \cdot 6 \cdot 6} = \dfrac{1}{6^2} = 6^{-2}.$$

Here, $2 - 4 = -2$. These examples suggest the **quotient rule for exponents.**

ANSWERS

4. (a) $\dfrac{5^4}{7}$ (b) $\dfrac{y^2}{x^3}$ (c) $\dfrac{4m^2}{h^5 k}$

(d) $\dfrac{p^2}{q^5}$ (e) $\dfrac{p^2}{3^2 m^2}$

Quotient Rule for Exponents

For any nonzero real number a and any integers m and n,

$$\frac{a^m}{a^n} = a^{m-n}.$$

(Keep the same base and subtract the exponents.)

Example: $\dfrac{5^8}{5^4} = 5^{8-4} = 5^4.$

CAUTION

A common **error** is to write $\dfrac{5^8}{5^4} = 1^{8-4} = 1^4$. Notice that by the quotient rule, the quotient should have the *same base*, 5. That is,

$$\frac{5^8}{5^4} = 5^{8-4} = 5^4.$$

If you are not sure, use the definition of an exponent to write out the factors:

$$5^8 = 5 \cdot 5 \cdot 5 \cdot 5 \cdot 5 \cdot 5 \cdot 5 \cdot 5 \quad \text{and} \quad 5^4 = 5 \cdot 5 \cdot 5 \cdot 5.$$

Then it is clear that the quotient is 5^4.

EXAMPLE 4 Using the Quotient Rule for Exponents

Simplify, using the quotient rule for exponents. Write answers with positive exponents.

(a) $\dfrac{5^8}{5^6} = 5^{8-6} = 5^2$

(b) $\dfrac{4^2}{4^9} = 4^{2-9} = 4^{-7} = \dfrac{1}{4^7}$

(c) $\dfrac{5^{-3}}{5^{-7}} = 5^{-3-(-7)} = 5^4$

(d) $\dfrac{q^5}{q^{-3}} = q^{5-(-3)} = q^8, \quad q \neq 0$

(e) $\dfrac{3^2 x^5}{3^4 x^3} = \dfrac{3^2}{3^4} \cdot \dfrac{x^5}{x^3} = 3^{2-4} \cdot x^{5-3} = 3^{-2} x^2 = \dfrac{x^2}{3^2}, \quad x \neq 0$

(f) $\dfrac{(m+n)^{-2}}{(m+n)^{-4}} = (m+n)^{-2-(-4)} = (m+n)^{-2+4} = (m+n)^2, \ m \neq -n$

(g) $\dfrac{7 x^{-3} y^2}{2^{-1} x^2 y^{-5}} = \dfrac{7 \cdot 2^1 y^2 y^5}{x^2 x^3} = \dfrac{14 y^7}{x^5}, \quad x \neq 0$

Work Problem 5 at the Side. ▶▶▶

5 Simplify. Write answers with positive exponents.

(a) $\dfrac{5^{11}}{5^8}$

(b) $\dfrac{4^7}{4^{10}}$

(c) $\dfrac{6^{-5}}{6^{-2}}$

(d) $\dfrac{8^4 m^9}{8^5 m^{10}}, \quad m \neq 0$

(e) $\dfrac{3^{-1}(x+y)^{-3}}{2^{-2}(x+y)^{-4}}, \quad x \neq -y$

ANSWERS

5. (a) 5^3 **(b)** $\dfrac{1}{4^3}$ **(c)** $\dfrac{1}{6^3}$ **(d)** $\dfrac{1}{8m}$

(e) $\dfrac{4}{3}(x+y)$

The definitions and rules for exponents given in this section and **Section 5.2** are summarized below.

Definitions and Rules for Exponents

For any integers m and n: **Examples**

Product rule	$a^m \cdot a^n = a^{m+n}$	$7^4 \cdot 7^5 = 7^9$
Zero exponent	$a^0 = 1 \quad (a \neq 0)$	$(-3)^0 = 1$
Negative exponent	$a^{-n} = \dfrac{1}{a^n} \quad (a \neq 0)$	$5^{-3} = \dfrac{1}{5^3}$
Quotient rule	$\dfrac{a^m}{a^n} = a^{m-n} \quad (a \neq 0)$	$\dfrac{2^2}{2^5} = 2^{2-5} = 2^{-3} = \dfrac{1}{2^3}$
Power rules (a)	$(a^m)^n = a^{mn}$	$(4^2)^3 = 4^6$
(b)	$(ab)^m = a^m b^m$	$(3k)^4 = 3^4 k^4$
(c)	$\left(\dfrac{a}{b}\right)^m = \dfrac{a^m}{b^m} \quad (b \neq 0)$	$\left(\dfrac{2}{3}\right)^2 = \dfrac{2^2}{3^2}$
Negative-to-positive rules	$\dfrac{a^{-m}}{b^{-n}} = \dfrac{b^n}{a^m} \quad (a, b \neq 0)$	$\dfrac{2^{-4}}{5^{-3}} = \dfrac{5^3}{2^4}$
	$\left(\dfrac{a}{b}\right)^{-m} = \left(\dfrac{b}{a}\right)^m .$	$\left(\dfrac{4}{7}\right)^{-2} = \left(\dfrac{7}{4}\right)^2$

OBJECTIVE 4 **Use combinations of rules.** We sometimes need to use more than one rule to simplify an expression.

EXAMPLE 5 **Using a Combination of Rules**

Use a combination of the rules for exponents to simplify each expression. Assume all variables represent nonzero real numbers.

(a) $\dfrac{(4^2)^3}{4^5} = \dfrac{4^6}{4^5}$ Power rule (a)

$\phantom{\dfrac{(4^2)^3}{4^5}} = 4^{6-5}$ Quotient rule

$\phantom{\dfrac{(4^2)^3}{4^5}} = 4^1 = 4$

(b) $(2x)^3 (2x)^2 = (2x)^5$ Product rule

$ = 2^5 x^5 \quad \text{or} \quad 32x^5$ Power rule (b)

(c) $\left(\dfrac{2x^3}{5}\right)^{-4} = \left(\dfrac{5}{2x^3}\right)^4$ Negative-to-positive rule

$\phantom{\left(\dfrac{2x^3}{5}\right)^{-4}} = \dfrac{5^4}{2^4 x^{12}} \quad \text{or} \quad \dfrac{625}{16x^{12}}$ Power rules (a)–(c)

(d) $\left(\dfrac{3x^{-2}}{4^{-1}y^3}\right)^{-3} = \dfrac{3^{-3}x^6}{4^3 y^{-9}}$ Power rules (a)–(c)

$\phantom{\left(\dfrac{3x^{-2}}{4^{-1}y^3}\right)^{-3}} = \dfrac{x^6 y^9}{4^3 \cdot 3^3} \quad \text{or} \quad \dfrac{x^6 y^9}{1728}$ Negative-to-positive rule

Continued on Next Page

(e) $\dfrac{(4m)^{-3}}{(3m)^{-4}} = \dfrac{4^{-3}m^{-3}}{3^{-4}m^{-4}}$ Power rule (b)

$\quad = \dfrac{3^4 m^4}{4^3 m^3}$ Negative-to-positive rule

$\quad = \dfrac{3^4 m^{4-3}}{4^3}$ Quotient rule

$\quad = \dfrac{3^4 m}{4^3}$ or $\dfrac{81m}{64}$

NOTE

Since the steps can be done in several different orders, there are many equally correct ways to simplify expressions like those in Examples 5(d) and 5(e).

Work Problem 6 at the Side. ▷▷▷

6 Simplify. Assume all variables represent nonzero real numbers.

(a) $12^5 \cdot 12^{-7} \cdot 12^6$

(b) $y^{-2} \cdot y^5 \cdot y^{-8}$

(c) $\dfrac{(6x)^{-1}}{(3x^2)^{-2}}$

(d) $\dfrac{3^9 \cdot (x^2 y)^{-2}}{3^3 \cdot x^{-4} y}$

ANSWERS

6. (a) 12^4 or $20{,}736$ **(b)** $\dfrac{1}{y^5}$ **(c)** $\dfrac{3x^3}{2}$

(d) $\dfrac{3^6}{y^3}$ or $\dfrac{729}{y^3}$

Real-Data Applications

Numbers BIG and SMALL

The ancient Egyptians used the *astonished man* symbol to represent a million. We now use exponents to write very big and very small numbers efficiently. Columbia University professor Edward Kasner asked his nine-year-old nephew to think of a name for the exceedingly large number 10^{100}, which is a 1 followed by 100 zeros. His nephew proclaimed it to be a **googol.** Kasner then called the unimaginably large number 10^{googol} a **googolplex.**

A googol is 10^{100} or

10,000,000,000,000,000,000,000,000,000,000,

000,000,000,000,000,000,000,000,000,000,

000,000,000,000,000,000,000,000,000,000.

Real-world examples of very big and very small numbers are described in Howard Eves's book *Mathematical Circles Revisited*. A few such examples are listed here.

- The total number of electrons in the universe is, according to an estimate by Sir Arthur Eddington, about 10^{79}.
- The number of grains of sand on the beach at Coney Island, New York, is about 10^{20}.
- The total number of printed words since the Gutenberg Bible appeared is approximately 10^{16}.
- The temperature at the center of an atomic bomb explosion is 2×10^8 degrees Fahrenheit.
- The diameter of a human hair is about 10^{-4} millimeters.
- The diameter of a nucleus of a cell is about 10^{-6} millimeters (1 micron).
- The probability of winning a lottery by choosing 6 numbers from among 50 is about 6.3×10^{-8}.
- The size of a quark is approximately 10^{-18} millimeters.

Interestingly enough, the Web search engine Google™ is named after a googol. Sergey Brin, president and co-founder of Google, Inc., was a math major. He chose the name Google to describe the vast reach of this search engine. (*Source: The Gazette,* March 2, 2001.)

For Group Discussion

Suppose that you have been offered a new job with "salary negotiable." You present to your new employer the following offer: You will work for 30 days and will be paid 1¢ on day one, 2¢ on day two, 4¢ on day three, 8¢ on day four, and so on, doubling your pay each day for the month. Your employer accepts your proposal, and you begin work on the first day of the next month.

1. On which day will you have received half of your month's wages?

2. When will you have received one-fourth of your total month's wages?

3. What do you think your approximate monthly salary will be?

4. How many days would it take you to become a "googolaire"?

5.5 Exercises

FOR EXTRA HELP   Addison-Wesley Math Tutor Center   MathXL   Digital Video Tutor CD 5 Videotape 5   Student's Solutions Manual   MyMathLab   Interactmath.com

Decide whether each expression is positive, negative, or 0.

1. $(-2)^{-3}$

2. $(-3)^{-2}$

3. -2^4

4. -3^6

5. $\left(\dfrac{1}{4}\right)^{-2}$

6. $\left(\dfrac{1}{5}\right)^{-2}$

7. $1 - 5^0$

8. $1 - 7^0$

Each expression is equal to either 0, 1, or −1. Decide which is correct. See Example 1.

9. $(-4)^0$

10. $(-10)^0$

11. -9^0

12. -5^0

13. $(-2)^0 - 2^0$

14. $(-8)^0 - 8^0$

15. $\dfrac{0^{10}}{10^0}$

16. $\dfrac{0^5}{5^0}$

Evaluate each expression. See Examples 1 and 2.

17. $7^0 + 9^0$

18. $8^0 + 6^0$

19. 4^{-3}

20. 5^{-4}

21. $\left(\dfrac{1}{2}\right)^{-4}$

22. $\left(\dfrac{1}{3}\right)^{-3}$

23. $\left(\dfrac{6}{7}\right)^{-2}$

24. $\left(\dfrac{2}{3}\right)^{-3}$

25. $5^{-1} + 3^{-1}$

26. $6^{-1} + 2^{-1}$

27. $-2^{-1} + 3^{-2}$

28. $(-3)^{-2} + (-4)^{-1}$

RELATING CONCEPTS (EXERCISES 29–32) For Individual or Group Work

In Objective 1, we used the product rule to motivate the definition of a 0 exponent. We can also use the quotient rule. To see this, **work Exercises 29–32 in order.**

29. Consider the expression $\frac{25}{25}$. What is its simplest form?

30. Write the quotient in Exercise 29 using the fact that $25 = 5^2$.

31. Apply the quotient rule for exponents to your answer for Exercise 30. Give the answer as a power of 5.

32. Because your answers for Exercises 29 and 31 both represent $\frac{25}{25}$, they must be equal. Write this equality. What definition does it support?

Use the quotient rule to simplify each expression. Write each expression with positive exponents. Assume that all variables represent nonzero real numbers. See Examples 2–4.

33. $\dfrac{9^4}{9^5}$

34. $\dfrac{7^3}{7^4}$

35. $\dfrac{6^{-3}}{6^2}$

36. $\dfrac{4^{-2}}{4^3}$

37. $\dfrac{1}{6^{-3}}$

38. $\dfrac{1}{5^{-2}}$

39. $\dfrac{2}{r^{-4}}$

40. $\dfrac{3}{s^{-8}}$

41. $\dfrac{4^{-3}}{5^{-2}}$

42. $\dfrac{6^{-2}}{5^{-4}}$

43. $p^5 q^{-8}$

44. $x^{-8} y^4$

45. $\dfrac{r^5}{r^{-4}}$

46. $\dfrac{a^6}{a^{-4}}$

47. $\dfrac{6^4 x^8}{6^5 x^3}$

48. $\dfrac{3^8 y^5}{3^{10} y^2}$

49. $\dfrac{6y^3}{2y}$

50. $\dfrac{5m^2}{m}$

51. $\dfrac{3x^5}{3x^2}$

52. $\dfrac{10p^8}{2p^4}$

Use a combination of the rules for exponents to simplify each expression. Write answers with only positive exponents. Assume that all variables represent nonzero real numbers. See Example 5.

53. $\dfrac{(7^4)^3}{7^9}$

54. $\dfrac{(5^3)^2}{5^2}$

55. $x^{-3} \cdot x^5 \cdot x^{-4}$

56. $y^{-8} \cdot y^5 \cdot y^{-2}$

57. $\dfrac{(3x)^{-2}}{(4x)^{-3}}$

58. $\dfrac{(2y)^{-3}}{(5y)^{-4}}$

59. $\left(\dfrac{x^{-1}y}{z^2}\right)^{-2}$

60. $\left(\dfrac{p^{-4}q}{r^{-3}}\right)^{-3}$

61. $(6x)^4 (6x)^{-3}$

62. $(10y)^9 (10y)^{-8}$

63. $\dfrac{(m^7 n)^{-2}}{m^{-4} n^3}$

64. $\dfrac{(m^8 n^{-4})^2}{m^{-2} n^5}$

65. $\dfrac{5x^{-3}}{(4x)^2}$

66. $\dfrac{-3k^5}{(2k)^2}$

67. $\left(\dfrac{2p^{-1}q}{3^{-1}m^2}\right)^2$

68. $\left(\dfrac{4xy^2}{x^{-1}y}\right)^{-2}$

Summary Exercises on the Rules for Exponents

Use the rules for exponents to simplify each expression. Use only positive exponents in your answers. Assume that all variables represent nonzero real numbers.

1. $\left(\dfrac{6x^2}{5}\right)^{12}$

2. $\left(\dfrac{rs^2t^3}{3t^4}\right)^6$

3. $(10x^2y^4)^2(10xy^2)^3$

4. $(-2ab^3c)^4(-2a^2b)^3$

5. $\left(\dfrac{9wx^3}{y^4}\right)^3$

6. $(4x^{-2}y^{-3})^{-2}$

7. $\dfrac{c^{11}(c^2)^4}{(c^3)^3(c^2)^{-6}}$

8. $\left(\dfrac{k^4t^2}{k^2t^{-4}}\right)^{-2}$

9. $5^{-1}+6^{-1}$

10. $\dfrac{(3y^{-1}z^3)^{-1}(3y^2)}{(y^3z^2)^{-3}}$

11. $\dfrac{(2xy^{-1})^3}{2^3x^{-3}y^2}$

12. $-8^0+(-8)^0$

13. $(z^4)^{-3}(z^{-2})^{-5}$

14. $\left(\dfrac{r^2st^5}{3r}\right)^{-2}$

15. $\dfrac{(3^{-1}x^{-3}y)^{-1}(2x^2y^{-3})^2}{(5x^{-2}y^2)^{-2}}$

16. $\left(\dfrac{5x^2}{3x^{-4}}\right)^{-1}$

17. $\left(\dfrac{-2x^{-2}}{2x^2}\right)^{-2}$

18. $\dfrac{(x^{-4}y^2)^3(x^2y)^{-1}}{(xy^2)^{-3}}$

19. $\dfrac{(a^{-2}b^3)^{-4}}{(a^{-3}b^2)^{-2}(ab)^{-4}}$

20. $(2a^{-30}b^{-29})(3a^{31}b^{30})$

21. $5^{-2}+6^{-2}$

22. $\left(\dfrac{(x^{47}y^{23})^2}{x^{-26}y^{-42}}\right)^0$

23. $\left(\dfrac{7a^2b^3}{2}\right)^3$

24. $-(-12^0)$

25. $-(-12)^0$

26. $\dfrac{0^{12}}{12^0}$

27. $\dfrac{(2xy^{-3})^{-2}}{(3x^{-2}y^4)^{-3}}$

28. $\left(\dfrac{a^2b^3c^4}{a^{-2}b^{-3}c^{-4}}\right)^{-2}$

29. $(6x^{-5}z^3)^{-3}$

30. $(2p^{-2}qr^{-3})(2p)^{-4}$

31. $\dfrac{(xy)^{-3}(xy)^5}{(xy)^{-4}}$

32. $42^0 - (-12)^0$

33. $\dfrac{(7^{-1}x^{-3})^{-2}(x^4)^{-6}}{7^{-1}x^{-3}}$

34. $\left(\dfrac{3^{-4}x^{-3}}{3^{-3}x^{-6}}\right)^{-2}$

35. $(5p^{-2}q)^{-3}(5pq^3)^4$

36. $8^{-1} + 6^{-1}$

37. $\left(\dfrac{4r^{-6}s^{-2}t}{2r^8s^{-4}t^2}\right)^{-1}$

38. $(13x^{-6}y)(13x^{-6}y)^{-1}$

39. $\dfrac{(8pq^{-2})^4}{(8p^{-2}q^{-3})^3}$

40. $\left(\dfrac{mn^{-2}p}{m^2np^4}\right)^{-2}\left(\dfrac{mn^{-2}p}{m^2np^4}\right)^3$

41. $-(-3^0)^0$

42. $5^{-1} - 8^{-1}$

5.6 Dividing a Polynomial by a Monomial

OBJECTIVE 1 **Divide a polynomial by a monomial.** We add two fractions with a common denominator as follows.

$$\frac{a}{c} + \frac{b}{c} = \frac{a+b}{c}$$

Looking at this statement in reverse gives us a rule for dividing a polynomial by a monomial.

Dividing a Polynomial by a Monomial

To divide a polynomial by a monomial, divide each term of the polynomial by the monomial:

$$\frac{a+b}{c} = \frac{a}{c} + \frac{b}{c} \quad (c \neq 0).$$

Examples: $\quad \dfrac{2+5}{3} = \dfrac{2}{3} + \dfrac{5}{3} \quad$ and $\quad \dfrac{x+3z}{2y} = \dfrac{x}{2y} + \dfrac{3z}{2y}.$

The parts of a division problem are named here.

$$\text{Dividend} \to \frac{12x^2 + 6x}{6x} = 2x + 1 \leftarrow \text{Quotient}$$
$$\text{Divisor} \to$$

EXAMPLE 1 Dividing a Polynomial by a Monomial

Divide $5m^5 - 10m^3$ by $5m^2$.

Use the preceding rule, with $+$ replaced by $-$. Then use the quotient rule.

$$\frac{5m^5 - 10m^3}{5m^2} = \frac{5m^5}{5m^2} - \frac{10m^3}{5m^2} = m^3 - 2m$$

Check by multiplying: $\quad 5m^2(m^3 - 2m) = 5m^5 - 10m^3.$

Because division by 0 is undefined, the quotient

$$\frac{5m^5 - 10m^3}{5m^2}$$

is undefined if $m = 0$. From now on, we assume that no denominators are 0.

Work Problem 1 at the Side. ⟩⟩⟩

EXAMPLE 2 Dividing a Polynomial by a Monomial

Divide: $\dfrac{16a^5 - 12a^4 + 8a^2}{4a^3}.$

Divide each term of $16a^5 - 12a^4 + 8a^2$ by $4a^3$.

$$\frac{16a^5 - 12a^4 + 8a^2}{4a^3} = \frac{16a^5}{4a^3} - \frac{12a^4}{4a^3} + \frac{8a^2}{4a^3}$$

$$= 4a^2 - 3a + \frac{2}{a} \qquad \text{Quotient rule}$$

Continued on Next Page

OBJECTIVE

1 Divide a polynomial by a monomial.

1 Divide.

(a) $\dfrac{6p^4 + 18p^7}{3p^2}$

(b) $\dfrac{12m^6 + 18m^5 + 30m^4}{6m^2}$

(c) $(18r^7 - 9r^2) \div (3r)$

ANSWERS
1. (a) $2p^2 + 6p^5$ (b) $2m^4 + 3m^3 + 5m^2$
(c) $6r^6 - 3r$

2 Divide.

(a) $\dfrac{20x^4 - 25x^3 + 5x}{5x^2}$

(b) $\dfrac{50m^4 - 30m^3 + 20m}{10m^3}$

3 Divide.

(a) $\dfrac{8y^7 - 9y^6 - 11y - 4}{y^2}$

(b) $\dfrac{12p^5 + 8p^4 + 3p^3 - 5p^2}{3p^3}$

4 Divide.

$\dfrac{45x^4y^3 + 30x^3y^2 - 60x^2y}{-15x^2y}$

The quotient $4a^2 - 3a + \frac{2}{a}$ is not a polynomial because of the expression $\frac{2}{a}$, which has a variable in the denominator. While the sum, difference, and product of two polynomials are always polynomials, the quotient of two polynomials may not be.

Again, *check* by multiplying.

$$4a^3\left(4a^2 - 3a + \frac{2}{a}\right) = 4a^3(4a^2) - 4a^3(3a) + 4a^3\left(\frac{2}{a}\right)$$

$$= 16a^5 - 12a^4 + 8a^2$$

◀◀◀ **Work Problem 2 at the Side.**

EXAMPLE 3 **Dividing a Polynomial by a Monomial**

Divide $12x^4 - 7x^3 + 4x$ by $4x$.

$$\frac{12x^4 - 7x^3 + 4x}{4x} = \frac{12x^4}{4x} - \frac{7x^3}{4x} + \frac{4x}{4x}$$

$$= 3x^3 - \frac{7x^2}{4} + 1 \qquad \text{Quotient rule}$$

Check by multiplying.

> **CAUTION**
>
> In Example 3, notice that the quotient $\frac{4x}{4x} = 1$. It is a common error to leave the 1 out of the answer. Multiplying to check will show that the answer $3x^3 - \frac{7x^2}{4}$ is not correct.

◀◀◀ **Work Problem 3 at the Side.**

EXAMPLE 4 **Dividing a Polynomial by a Monomial**

Divide the polynomial

$$180x^4y^{10} - 150x^3y^8 + 120x^2y^6 - 90xy^4 + 100y$$

by the monomial $-30xy^2$.

$$\frac{180x^4y^{10} - 150x^3y^8 + 120x^2y^6 - 90xy^4 + 100y}{-30xy^2}$$

$$= \frac{180x^4y^{10}}{-30xy^2} - \frac{150x^3y^8}{-30xy^2} + \frac{120x^2y^6}{-30xy^2} - \frac{90xy^4}{-30xy^2} + \frac{100y}{-30xy^2}$$

$$= -6x^3y^8 + 5x^2y^6 - 4xy^4 + 3y^2 - \frac{10}{3xy}$$

◀◀◀ **Work Problem 4 at the Side.**

ANSWERS

2. (a) $4x^2 - 5x + \dfrac{1}{x}$ **(b)** $5m - 3 + \dfrac{2}{m^2}$

3. (a) $8y^5 - 9y^4 - \dfrac{11}{y} - \dfrac{4}{y^2}$

(b) $4p^2 + \dfrac{8p}{3} + 1 - \dfrac{5}{3p}$

4. $-3x^2y^2 - 2xy + 4$

5.6 Exercises

| FOR EXTRA HELP | Tutor Center Addison-Wesley Math Tutor Center | Math XL MathXL | Digital Video Tutor CD 5 Videotape 5 | Student's Solutions Manual | MyMathLab MyMathLab | Interactmath.com |

Fill in each blank with the correct response.

1. In the statement $\dfrac{6x^2 + 8}{2} = 3x^2 + 4$, _____ is the dividend, _____ is the divisor, and _____ is the quotient.

2. The expression $\dfrac{3x + 12}{x}$ is undefined if $x =$ _____.

3. To check the division shown in Exercise 1, multiply _____ by _____ and show that the product is _____.

4. The expression $5x^2 - 3x + 6 + \frac{2}{x}$ _____ a polynomial.
   (is/is not)

5. Explain why the division problem $\dfrac{16m^3 - 12m^2}{4m}$ can be performed using the method of this section, while the division problem $\dfrac{4m}{16m^3 - 12m^2}$ cannot.

6. Evaluate $\dfrac{5y + 6}{2}$ when $y = 2$. Evaluate $5y + 3$ when $y = 2$. Does $\dfrac{5y + 6}{2}$ equal $5y + 3$?

Perform each division. See Examples 1–4.

7. $\dfrac{60x^4 - 20x^2 + 10x}{2x}$

8. $\dfrac{120x^6 - 60x^3 + 80x^2}{2x}$

9. $\dfrac{20m^5 - 10m^4 + 5m^2}{-5m^2}$

10. $\dfrac{12t^5 - 6t^3 + 6t^2}{-6t^2}$

11. $\dfrac{8t^5 - 4t^3 + 4t^2}{2t}$

12. $\dfrac{8r^4 - 4r^3 + 6r^2}{2r}$

13. $\dfrac{4a^5 - 4a^2 + 8}{4a}$

14. $\dfrac{5t^8 + 5t^7 + 15}{5t}$

15. $\dfrac{12x^5 - 4x^4 + 6x^3}{-6x^2}$

16. $\dfrac{24x^6 - 12x^5 + 30x^4}{-6x^2}$

17. $\dfrac{4x^2 + 20x^3 - 36x^4}{4x^2}$

18. $\dfrac{5x^2 - 30x^4 + 30x^5}{5x^2}$

19. $\dfrac{4x^4 + 3x^3 + 2x}{3x^2}$

20. $\dfrac{5x^4 - 6x^3 + 8x}{3x^2}$

21. $\dfrac{27r^4 - 36r^3 - 6r^2 + 3r - 2}{3r}$

22. $\dfrac{8k^4 - 12k^3 - 2k^2 - 2k - 3}{2k}$

23. $\dfrac{2m^5 - 6m^4 + 8m^2}{-2m^3}$

24. $\dfrac{6r^5 - 8r^4 + 10r^2}{-2r^4}$

25. $(20a^4b^3 - 15a^5b^2 + 25a^3b) \div (-5a^4b)$

26. $(16y^5z - 8y^2z^2 + 12yz^3) \div (-4y^2z^2)$

27. $(120x^{11} - 60x^{10} + 140x^9 - 100x^8) \div (10x^{12})$

28. $(120x^{12} - 84x^9 + 60x^8 - 36x^7) \div (12x^9)$

29. The quotient in Exercise 19 is $\dfrac{4x^2}{3} + x + \dfrac{2}{3x}$. Notice how the third term is written with x in the denominator. Would $\frac{2}{3}x$ be an acceptable form for this term? Explain why or why not. Is $\frac{4}{3}x^2$ an acceptable form for the first term? Why or why not?

30. What expression represents the length of the rectangle?

$2x$ ▭

Area $= 12x^2 - 4x + 2$

31. What polynomial, when divided by $5x^3$, yields $3x^2 - 7x + 7$ as a quotient?

32. The quotient of a certain polynomial and $-12y^3$ is $6y^3 - 5y^2 + 2y - 3 + \frac{7}{y}$. Find the polynomial.

RELATING CONCEPTS (EXERCISES 33–36) For Individual or Group Work

Our system of numeration is called a decimal system. It is based on powers of ten. In a whole number such as 2846, each digit is understood to represent the number of powers of ten for its place value. The 2 represents two thousands (2×10^3), the 8 represents eight hundreds (8×10^2), the 4 represents four tens (4×10^1), and the 6 represents six ones (or units) (6×10^0). In expanded form we write

$$2846 = (2 \times 10^3) + (8 \times 10^2) + (4 \times 10^1) + (6 \times 10^0).$$

*Keeping this information in mind, **work Exercises 33–36 in order.***

33. Divide 2846 by 2, using paper-and-pencil methods: $2\overline{)2846}$.

34. Write your answer in Exercise 33 in expanded form.

35. Use the methods of this section to divide the polynomial $2x^3 + 8x^2 + 4x + 6$ by 2.

36. Compare your answers in Exercises 34 and 35. How are they similar? How are they different? For what value of x does the answer in Exercise 35 equal the answer in Exercise 34?

5.7 Dividing a Polynomial by a Polynomial

OBJECTIVE 1 Divide a polynomial by a polynomial. We use a method of "long division" to divide a polynomial by a polynomial (other than a monomial), similar to that used for dividing two whole numbers. Both polynomials must be written in descending powers.

OBJECTIVES

1 Divide a polynomial by a polynomial.

2 Apply division to a geometry problem.

Dividing Whole Numbers

Step 1

Divide 6696 by 27.

$$27\overline{)6696}$$

Step 2

66 divided by 27 = 2;
2 · 27 = **54**.

$$\begin{array}{r} 2 \\ 27\overline{)6696} \\ 54 \end{array}$$

Step 3

Subtract; then bring down the next digit.

$$\begin{array}{r} 2 \\ 27\overline{)6696} \\ 54\downarrow \\ \hline 129 \end{array}$$

Step 4

129 divided by 27 = 4;
4 · 27 = **108**.

$$\begin{array}{r} 24 \\ 27\overline{)6696} \\ 54 \\ \hline 129 \\ 108 \end{array}$$

Step 5

Subtract; then bring down the next digit.

$$\begin{array}{r} 24 \\ 27\overline{)6696} \\ 54\downarrow \\ \hline 129 \\ 108\downarrow \\ \hline 216 \end{array}$$

Dividing Polynomials

Divide $8x^3 - 4x^2 - 14x + 15$ by $2x + 3$.

$$2x + 3\overline{)8x^3 - 4x^2 - 14x + 15}$$

$8x^3$ divided by $2x = 4x^2$;
$4x^2(2x + 3) = 8x^3 + 12x^2$.

$$\begin{array}{r} 4x^2 \\ 2x + 3\overline{)8x^3 - 4x^2 - 14x + 15} \\ 8x^3 + 12x^2 \end{array}$$

Subtract; then bring down the next term.

$$\begin{array}{r} 4x^2 \\ 2x + 3\overline{)8x^3 - 4x^2 - 14x + 15} \\ \underline{8x^3 + 12x^2} \\ -16x^2 - 14x \end{array}$$

(To subtract two polynomials, change the signs of the second and then add.)

$-16x^2$ divided by $2x = -8x$;
$-8x(2x + 3) = -16x^2 - 24x$.

$$\begin{array}{r} 4x^2 - 8x \\ 2x + 3\overline{)8x^3 - 4x^2 - 14x + 15} \\ \underline{8x^3 + 12x^2} \\ -16x^2 - 14x \\ -16x^2 - 24x \end{array}$$

Subtract; then bring down the next term.

$$\begin{array}{r} 4x^2 - 8x \\ 2x + 3\overline{)8x^3 - 4x^2 - 14x + 15} \\ \underline{8x^3 + 12x^2} \\ -16x^2 - 14x \\ \underline{-16x^2 - 24x} \\ 10x + 15 \end{array}$$

(continued)

Step 6

216 divided by 27 = **8**;
8 · 27 = **216**.

$$
\begin{array}{r}
248 \\
27\overline{)6696} \\
54 \\
\overline{129} \\
108 \\
\overline{216} \\
216 \\
\overline{0}
\end{array}
$$

6696 divided by 27 is 248.
The remainder is zero.

10x divided by 2x = **5**;
5(2x + 3) = **10x + 15.**

$$
\begin{array}{r}
4x^2 - 8x + 5 \\
2x+3\overline{)8x^3 - 4x^2 - 14x + 15} \\
8x^3 + 12x^2 \\
\overline{-16x^2 - 14x } \\
-16x^2 - 24x \\
\overline{10x + 15} \\
10x + 15 \\
\overline{0}
\end{array}
$$

$8x^3 - 4x^2 - 14x + 15$ divided by
$2x + 3$ is $4x^2 - 8x + 5$. The
remainder is zero.

Step 7

Check by multiplying.

27 · 248 = 6696

Check by multiplying.

$(2x + 3)(4x^2 - 8x + 5)$
$= 8x^3 - 4x^2 - 14x + 15$

EXAMPLE 1 **Dividing a Polynomial by a Polynomial**

Divide $5x + 4x^3 - 8 - 4x^2$ by $2x - 1$.

Both polynomials must be written with the exponents in descending order. Rewrite the first polynomial as $4x^3 - 4x^2 + 5x - 8$. Then begin the division process.

Divide $4x^3 - 4x^2 + 5x - 8$ by $2x - 1$.

$$
\begin{array}{r}
2x^2 - x + 2 \\
2x-1\overline{)4x^3 - 4x^2 + 5x - 8} \\
4x^3 - 2x^2 \\
\overline{-2x^2 + 5x } \\
-2x^2 + x \\
\overline{4x - 8} \\
4x - 2 \\
\overline{-6} \leftarrow \text{Remainder}
\end{array}
$$

Step 1 $4x^3$ divided by $2x = 2x^2$; $2x^2(2x - 1) = 4x^3 - 2x^2$.

Step 2 Subtract; bring down the next term.

Step 3 $-2x^2$ divided by $2x = -x$; $-x(2x - 1) = -2x^2 + x$.

Step 4 Subtract; bring down the next term.

Step 5 $4x$ divided by $2x = 2$; $2(2x - 1) = 4x - 2$.

Step 6 Subtract. The remainder is -6. Write the remainder as the numerator of a fraction that has $2x - 1$ as its denominator. The answer is not a polynomial because of the nonzero remainder.

$$
\frac{4x^3 - 4x^2 + 5x - 8}{2x - 1} = 2x^2 - x + 2 + \frac{-6}{2x - 1}
$$

Continued on Next Page

Step 7 Check by multiplying.

$$(2x - 1)\left(2x^2 - x + 2 + \frac{-6}{2x - 1}\right)$$

$$= (2x - 1)(2x^2) + (2x - 1)(-x) + (2x - 1)(2)$$

$$+ (2x - 1)\left(\frac{-6}{2x - 1}\right)$$

$$= 4x^3 - 2x^2 - 2x^2 + x + 4x - 2 - 6$$

$$= 4x^3 - 4x^2 + 5x - 8$$

Work Problem 1 at the Side.

EXAMPLE 2 **Dividing into a Polynomial with Missing Terms**

Divide $x^3 - 1$ by $x - 1$.

Here the polynomial $x^3 - 1$ is missing the x^2-term and the x-term. When terms are missing, use 0 as the coefficient for each missing term. (Zero acts as a placeholder here, just as it does in our number system.)

$$x^3 - 1 = x^3 + 0x^2 + 0x - 1$$

Now divide.

$$
\begin{array}{r}
x^2 + x + 1 \\
x - 1{\overline{\smash{\big)}\,x^3 + 0x^2 + 0x - 1}} \\
\underline{x^3 - x^2} \\
x^2 + 0x \\
\underline{x^2 - x} \\
x - 1 \\
\underline{x - 1} \\
0
\end{array}
$$

The remainder is 0. The quotient is $x^2 + x + 1$. *Check* by multiplying.

$$(x - 1)(x^2 + x + 1) = x^3 - 1$$

Work Problem 2 at the Side.

EXAMPLE 3 **Dividing by a Polynomial with Missing Terms**

Divide $x^4 + 2x^3 + 2x^2 - x - 1$ by $x^2 + 1$.

Since $x^2 + 1$ has a missing x-term, write it as $x^2 + 0x + 1$. Then go through the division process as follows.

$$
\begin{array}{r}
x^2 + 2x + 1 \\
x^2 + 0x + 1{\overline{\smash{\big)}\,x^4 + 2x^3 + 2x^2 - x - 1}} \\
\underline{x^4 + 0x^3 + x^2} \\
2x^3 + x^2 - x \\
\underline{2x^3 + 0x^2 + 2x} \\
x^2 - 3x - 1 \\
\underline{x^2 + 0x + 1} \\
-3x - 2 \leftarrow \text{Remainder}
\end{array}
$$

Continued on Next Page

1 Divide.

(a) $(x^3 + x^2 + 4x - 6)$ $\div (x - 1)$

(b) $\dfrac{p^3 - 2p^2 - 5p + 9}{p + 2}$

2 Divide.

(a) $\dfrac{r^2 - 5}{r + 4}$

(b) $(x^3 - 8) \div (x - 2)$

ANSWERS
1. (a) $x^2 + 2x + 6$
   (b) $p^2 - 4p + 3 + \dfrac{3}{p + 2}$
2. (a) $r - 4 + \dfrac{11}{r + 4}$
   (b) $x^2 + 2x + 4$

❸ Divide.

(a)

$$(2x^4 + 3x^3 - x^2 + 6x + 5)$$
$$\div (x^2 - 1)$$

(b)

$$\frac{2m^5 + m^4 + 6m^3 - 3m^2 - 18}{m^2 + 3}$$

When the result of subtracting ($-3x - 2$, in this case) is a polynomial of lesser degree than the divisor ($x^2 + 0x + 1$), that polynomial is the remainder. Write the answer as

$$x^2 + 2x + 1 + \frac{-3x - 2}{x^2 + 1}.$$

Multiply to check that this is the correct quotient.

◀◀◀ **Work Problem 3 at the Side.**

EXAMPLE 4 Dividing a Polynomial with a Quotient That Has Fractional Coefficients

Divide $4x^3 + 2x^2 + 3x + 1$ by $4x - 4$.

$$
\begin{array}{r}
x^2 + \frac{3}{2}x + \frac{9}{4} \\
4x - 4\overline{)4x^3 + 2x^2 + 3x + 1} \\
\underline{4x^3 - 4x^2} \\
6x^2 + 3x \\
\underline{6x^2 - 6x} \\
9x + 1 \\
\underline{9x - 9} \\
10
\end{array}
$$

The answer is $x^2 + \frac{3}{2}x + \frac{9}{4} + \frac{10}{4x - 4}$.

◀◀◀ **Work Problem 4 at the Side.**

❹ Divide $3x^3 + 7x^2 + 7x + 10$ by $3x + 6$.

OBJECTIVE **2** Apply division to a geometry problem.

EXAMPLE 5 Using an Area Formula

The area of the rectangle in Figure 2 is given by $x^3 + 4x^2 + 8x + 8$ sq. units and the width by $x + 2$ units. What is its length?

Length = ?

Width = $x + 2$

Area = $x^3 + 4x^2 + 8x + 8$

Figure 2

❺ Divide $x^3 + 4x^2 + 8x + 8$ by $x + 2$.

Since $A = LW$, solving for L gives $L = \frac{A}{W}$. Divide $x^3 + 4x^2 + 8x + 8$ by the width, $x + 2$.

◀◀◀ **Work Problem 5 at the Side.**

The quotient from Problem 5, $x^2 + 2x + 4$, represents the length of the rectangle in units.

ANSWERS

3. **(a)** $2x^2 + 3x + 1 + \frac{9x + 6}{x^2 - 1}$

(b) $2m^3 + m^2 - 6$

4. $x^2 + \frac{1}{3}x + \frac{5}{3}$

5. $x^2 + 2x + 4$

5.7 Exercises

FOR
EXTRA
HELP
 Addison-Wesley Math Tutor Center   MathXL   Digital Video Tutor CD 5 Videotape 5   Student's Solutions Manual   MyMathLab   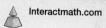 Interactmath.com

1. In the division problem $(4x^4 + 2x^3 - 14x^2 + 19x + 10) \div (2x + 5) = 2x^3 - 4x^2 + 3x + 2$, which polynomial is the divisor? Which is the quotient?

2. When dividing one polynomial by another, how do you know when to stop dividing?

3. In dividing $12m^2 - 20m + 3$ by $2m - 3$, what is the first step?

4. In the division in Exercise 3, what is the second step?

Perform each division. See Example 1.

5. $\dfrac{x^2 - x - 6}{x - 3}$

6. $\dfrac{m^2 - 2m - 24}{m - 6}$

7. $\dfrac{2y^2 + 9y - 35}{y + 7}$

8. $\dfrac{2y^2 + 9y + 7}{y + 1}$

9. $\dfrac{p^2 + 2p + 20}{p + 6}$

10. $\dfrac{x^2 + 11x + 16}{x + 8}$

11. $(r^2 - 8r + 15) \div (r - 3)$

12. $(t^2 + 2t - 35) \div (t - 5)$

13. $\dfrac{4a^2 - 22a + 32}{2a + 3}$

14. $\dfrac{9w^2 + 6w + 10}{3w - 2}$

15. $\dfrac{8x^3 - 10x^2 - x + 3}{2x + 1}$

16. $\dfrac{12t^3 - 11t^2 + 9t + 18}{4t + 3}$

Perform each division. See Examples 2–4.

17. $\dfrac{3y^3 + y^2 + 2}{y + 1}$

18. $\dfrac{2r^3 - 6r - 36}{r - 3}$

19. $\dfrac{3k^3 - 4k^2 - 6k + 10}{k^2 - 2}$

20. $\dfrac{5z^3 - z^2 + 10z + 2}{z^2 + 2}$

21. $(x^4 - x^2 - 2) \div (x^2 - 2)$

22. $(r^4 + 2r^2 - 3) \div (r^2 - 1)$

23. $\dfrac{6p^4 - 15p^3 + 14p^2 - 5p + 10}{3p^2 + 1}$

24. $\dfrac{6r^4 - 10r^3 - r^2 + 15r - 8}{2r^2 - 3}$

25. $\dfrac{2x^5 + x^4 + 11x^3 - 8x^2 - 13x + 7}{2x^2 + x - 1}$

26. $\dfrac{4t^5 - 11t^4 - 6t^3 + 5t^2 - t + 3}{4t^2 + t - 3}$

27. $\dfrac{x^4 - 1}{x^2 - 1}$

28. $\dfrac{y^3 + 1}{y + 1}$

29. $(10x^3 + 13x^2 + 4x + 1) \div (5x + 5)$

30. $(6x^3 - 19x^2 - 19x - 4) \div (2x - 8)$

Work each problem. See Example 5.

31. Give the length of the rectangle.

$5x + 2$

The area is $5x^3 + 7x^2 - 13x - 6$ sq. units.

32. Find the measure of the base of the parallelogram.

$x - 1$

The area is $2x^3 + 2x^2 - 3x - 1$ sq. units.

RELATING CONCEPTS (EXERCISES 33–36)   For Individual or Group Work

We can find the value of a polynomial in x for a given value of x by substituting that number for x. Surprisingly, we can accomplish the same thing by division. For example, to find the value of $2x^2 - 4x + 3$ for $x = -3$, we would divide $2x^2 - 4x + 3$ by $x - (-3)$. The remainder will give the value of the polynomial for $x = -3$. **Work Exercises 33–36 in order.**

33. Find the value of $2x^2 - 4x + 3$ for $x = -3$ by substitution.

34. Divide $2x^2 - 4x + 3$ by $x + 3$. Give the remainder.

35. Compare your answers to Exercises 33 and 34. What do you notice?

36. Choose another polynomial and evaluate it both ways for some value of the variable. Do the answers agree?

5.8 An Application of Exponents: Scientific Notation

OBJECTIVES

1 Express numbers in scientific notation.

2 Convert numbers in scientific notation to numbers without exponents.

3 Use scientific notation in calculations.

OBJECTIVE 1 Express numbers in scientific notation. One example of the use of exponents comes from science. The numbers occurring in science are often extremely large (such as the distance from Earth to the sun, 93,000,000 mi) or extremely small (the wavelength of yellow-green light, approximately .0000006 m). Because of the difficulty of working with many zeros, scientists often express such numbers with exponents. Each number is written as

$$a \times 10^n, \text{ where } 1 \leq |a| < 10 \text{ and } n \text{ is an integer.}$$

This form is called **scientific notation.** There is always one nonzero digit before the decimal point. This is shown in the following examples.

> **NOTE**
> In work with scientific notation, the times symbol, $\times$, is commonly used.

$3.19 \times 10^1 = 3.19 \times 10 = 31.9$ Decimal point moves 1 place to the right.

$3.19 \times 10^2 = 3.19 \times 100 = 319.$ Decimal point moves 2 places to the right.

$3.19 \times 10^3 = 3.19 \times 1000 = 3190.$ Decimal point moves 3 places to the right.

$3.19 \times 10^{-1} = 3.19 \times .1 = .319$ Decimal point moves 1 place to the left.

$3.19 \times 10^{-2} = 3.19 \times .01 = .0319$ Decimal point moves 2 places to the left.

$3.19 \times 10^{-3} = 3.19 \times .001 = .00319$ Decimal point moves 3 places to the left.

A number in scientific notation is always written with the decimal point after the first nonzero digit and then multiplied by the appropriate power of 10. For example, 35 is written 3.5×10^1, or 3.5×10; 56,200 is written 5.62×10^4, since

$$56,200 = 5.62 \times 10,000 = 5.62 \times 10^4.$$

To write a number in scientific notation, follow these steps.

Writing a Number in Scientific Notation

Step 1 Move the decimal point to the right of the first nonzero digit.

Step 2 Count the number of places you moved the decimal point.

Step 3 The number of places in Step 2 is the absolute value of the exponent on 10.

Step 4 The exponent on 10 is positive if the original number is greater than the number in Step 1; the exponent is negative if the original number is less than the number in Step 1. If the decimal point is not moved, the exponent is 0.

For negative numbers, follow these steps using the absolute value of the number; then make the result negative.

1 Write each number in scientific notation.

(a) 63,000

(b) 5,870,000

(c) .0571

(d) −.000062

2 Write without exponents.

(a) 4.2×10^3

(b) 8.7×10^5

(c) 6.42×10^{-3}

EXAMPLE 1 Using Scientific Notation

Write each number in scientific notation.

(a) 93,000,000
Move the decimal point to follow the first nonzero digit. Count the number of places the decimal point was moved.

9.3 000 000   7 places

The number will be written in scientific notation as 9.3×10^n. To find the value of *n*, first compare 9.3 with 93,000,000. Since 93,000,000 is *greater* than 9.3, we must multiply by a *positive* power of 10 so the product 9.3×10^n will equal the larger number.
Since the decimal point was moved 7 places, and since *n* is positive,

$$93,000,000 = 9.3 \times 10^7.$$

(b) $463,000,000,000,000 = 4.63\ 000\ 000\ 000\ 000$ 14 places
$$= 4.63 \times 10^{14}$$

(c) $3.021 = 3.021 \times 10^0$

(d) .00462
Move the decimal point to the right of the first nonzero digit and count the number of places the decimal point was moved.

004.62   3 places

Because .00462 is *less* than 4.62, the exponent must be *negative*.
$$.00462 = 4.62 \times 10^{-3}$$

(e) $-.0000762 = -7.62 \times 10^{-5}$

Work Problem 1 at the Side.

OBJECTIVE 2 Convert numbers in scientific notation to numbers without exponents. To convert a number written in scientific notation to a number without exponents, work in reverse. *Multiplying a number by a positive power of 10 will make the number greater; multiplying by a negative power of 10 will make the number less.*

EXAMPLE 2 Writing Numbers without Exponents

Write each number without exponents.

(a) 6.2×10^3
Since the exponent is positive, make 6.2 greater by moving the decimal point 3 places to the right. It is necessary to attach two 0s.
$$6.2 \times 10^3 = 6.200 = 6200$$

(b) $4.283 \times 10^5 = 4.28300 = 428,300$ Move 5 places to the right; attach 0s as necessary.

(c) $-9.73 \times 10^{-2} = -09.73 = -.0973$ Move 2 places to the left.

As these examples show, *the exponent tells the number of places and the direction that the decimal point is moved.*

Work Problem 2 at the Side.

OBJECTIVE 3 Use scientific notation in calculations. The next example shows how scientific notation can be used with products and quotients.

EXAMPLE 3 Multiplying and Dividing with Scientific Notation

Write each product or quotient without exponents.

(a) $(6 \times 10^3)(5 \times 10^{-4})$

$= (6 \times 5)(10^3 \times 10^{-4})$ Commutative and associative properties

$= 30 \times 10^{-1}$ Product rule for exponents

$= 30. = 3$ Write without exponents.

(b) $\dfrac{6 \times 10^{-5}}{2 \times 10^3} = \dfrac{6}{2} \times \dfrac{10^{-5}}{10^3} = 3 \times 10^{-8} = .00000003$

Work Problem 3 at the Side.

Calculator Tip Calculators usually have a key labeled EE or EXP for scientific notation. See An Introduction to Calculators at the front of this book for more information.

EXAMPLE 4 Applying Scientific Notation

Convert to scientific notation, calculate each computation, then give the result without scientific notation.

(a) In determining helium usage at Kennedy Space Center, the product 70,000(.0283)(1000) must be calculated. (*Source: NASA-AMATYC-NSF Mathematics Explorations II*, Capital Community College, 2000.)

$70,000(.0283)(1000) = (7 \times 10^4)(2.83 \times 10^{-2})(1 \times 10^3)$

$= (7 \times 2.83 \times 1)(10^{4-2+3})$

$= 19.81 \times 10^5$

$= 1,981,000$

(b) The ratio of the tidal force exerted by the moon compared to that exerted by the sun is given by

$$\frac{73.5 \times 10^{21} \times (1.5 \times 10^8)^3}{1.99 \times 10^{30} \times (3.84 \times 10^5)^3}.$$

(*Source:* Kastner, Bernice, *Space Mathematics*, NASA.)

$\dfrac{7.35 \times 10^1 \times 10^{21} \times 1.5^3 \times 10^{24}}{1.99 \times 10^{30} \times 3.84^3 \times 10^{15}} \approx .22 \times 10^{1+21+24-30-15}$

$= .22 \times 10^1$

$= 2.2$

Work Problem 4 at the Side.

---

3 Simplify, and write without exponents.

(a) $(2.6 \times 10^4)(2 \times 10^{-6})$

(b) $\dfrac{4.8 \times 10^2}{2.4 \times 10^{-3}}$

4 The speed of light is approximately 3.0×10^5 km per sec. (*Source: World Almanac and Book of Facts.*) Write answers without exponents.

(a) How far does light travel in 6.0×10^1 sec?

(b) How many seconds does it take light to travel approximately 1.5×10^8 km from the sun to Earth?

ANSWERS
3. (a) .052 **(b)** 200,000
4. (a) 18,000,000 km **(b)** 500 sec

Real-Data Applications

Earthquake Intensities Measured by the Richter Scale

Charles F. Richter devised a scale in 1935 to compare the intensities, or relative power, of earthquakes. The **intensity** of an earthquake is measured relative to the intensity of a standard **zero-level** earthquake of intensity I_0. The relationship is equivalent to $I = I_0 \times 10^R$, where R is the **Richter scale** measure. For example, if an earthquake has magnitude 5.0 on the Richter scale, then its intensity is calculated as $I = I_0 \times 10^{5.0} = I_0 \times 100,000$, which is 100,000 times as intense as a zero-level earthquake. The following diagram illustrates the intensities of earthquakes and their Richter scale magnitudes.

Intensity	I_0	$I_0 \times 10^1$	$I_0 \times 10^2$	$I_0 \times 10^3$	$I_0 \times 10^4$	$I_0 \times 10^5$	$I_0 \times 10^6$	$I_0 \times 10^7$	$I_0 \times 10^8$
Richter Scale	0	1	2	3	4	5	6	7	8

To compare two earthquakes to each other, a ratio of the intensities is calculated. For example, to compare an earthquake that measures 8.0 on the Richter scale to one that measures 5.0, simply find the ratio of the intensities:

$$\frac{\text{intensity } 8.0}{\text{intensity } 5.0} = \frac{I_0 \times 10^{8.0}}{I_0 \times 10^{5.0}} = \frac{10^8}{10^5} = 10^{8-5} = 10^3 = 1000.$$

Therefore an earthquake that measures 8.0 on the Richter scale is 1000 times as intense as one that measures 5.0.

For Group Discussion

The table gives Richter scale measurements for several earthquakes.

Earthquake		Richter Scale Measurement
1960	Concepción, Chile	9.5
1906	San Francisco, California	8.3
1939	Erzincan, Turkey	8.0
1998	Sumatra, Indonesia	7.0
1998	Adana, Turkey	6.3

Source: World Almanac and Book of Facts, 2004.

1. Compare the intensity of the 1939 Erzincan earthquake to the 1998 Sumatra earthquake.

2. Compare the intensity of the 1998 Adana earthquake to the 1906 San Francisco earthquake.

3. Compare the intensity of the 1939 Erzincan earthquake to the 1998 Adana earthquake.

4. Suppose an earthquake measures 7.2 on the Richter scale. How would the intensity of a second earthquake compare if its Richter scale measure differed by $+3.0$? By -1.0?

5.8 Exercises

 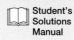
Write the numbers (other than dates) mentioned in the following statements in scientific notation.

1. NASA has budgeted $6,130,900,000 for 2003 and $5,868,900,000 for 2004 for the international space station. (*Source:* U.S. National Aeronautics and Space Administration.)

2. The mass of Pluto, the smallest planet, is .0021 times that of Earth; the mass of Jupiter, the largest planet, is 317.83 times that of Earth. (*Source: World Almanac and Book of Facts.*)

3. In 2000, the federal government spent $69,627,000,000 on research and development. Industry spent $181,040,000,000 in that same year. (*Source:* U.S. National Science Foundation.)

4. The risk to industrial workers at the Hansom Landfill at the Kennedy Space Center depends on the reference doses of materials dumped there. For thallium, the reference dose is 700,000 mg/kg per day, and the reference dose for beryllium is 5000 mg/kg per day. (*Source: NASA-AMATYC-NSF Math Explorations I*, Capital Community College, 1999.)

Determine whether or not the given number is written in scientific notation as defined in Objective 1. If it is not, write it as such.

5. 4.56×10^3
6. 7.34×10^5
7. 5,600,000
8. 34,000

9. .004
10. .0007
11. $.8 \times 10^2$
12. $.9 \times 10^3$

13. Explain in your own words what it means for a number to be written in scientific notation.

14. Explain how to multiply a number by a positive power of ten. Then explain how to multiply a number by a negative power of ten.

Write each number in scientific notation. See Example 1.

15. 5,876,000,000
16. 9,994,000,000
17. 82,350
18. 78,330

19. .000007
20. .0000004
21. $-.00203$
22. $-.0000578$

Write each number without exponents. See Example 2.

23. 7.5×10^5

24. 8.8×10^6

25. 5.677×10^{12}

26. 8.766×10^9

27. -6.21×10^0

28. -8.56×10^0

29. 7.8×10^{-4}

30. 8.9×10^{-5}

31. 5.134×10^{-9}

32. 7.123×10^{-10}

Perform the indicated operations. Write the answers in scientific notation and then without exponents. See Example 3.

33. $(2 \times 10^8) \times (3 \times 10^3)$

34. $(4 \times 10^7) \times (3 \times 10^3)$

35. $(5 \times 10^4) \times (3 \times 10^2)$

36. $(8 \times 10^5) \times (2 \times 10^3)$

37. $(3.15 \times 10^{-4}) \times (2.04 \times 10^8)$

38. $(4.92 \times 10^{-3}) \times (2.25 \times 10^7)$

Perform the indicated operations, and write the answers in scientific notation. See Example 3.

39. $\dfrac{9 \times 10^{-5}}{3 \times 10^{-1}}$

40. $\dfrac{12 \times 10^{-4}}{4 \times 10^{-3}}$

41. $\dfrac{8 \times 10^3}{2 \times 10^2}$

42. $\dfrac{5 \times 10^4}{1 \times 10^3}$

43. $\dfrac{2.6 \times 10^{-3} \times 7.0 \times 10^{-1}}{2 \times 10^2 \times 3.5 \times 10^{-3}}$

44. $\dfrac{9.5 \times 10^{-1} \times 2.4 \times 10^4}{5 \times 10^3 \times 1.2 \times 10^{-2}}$

▦ *Work each problem. Give answers without exponents. See Example 4.*

45. There are 10^9 social security numbers. The population of the U.S. is about 3×10^8. How many social security numbers are available for each person? (*Source:* U.S. Bureau of the Census.)

46. The number of possible hands in contract bridge is about 6.35×10^{11}. The probability of being dealt one particular hand is $\dfrac{1}{6.35 \times 10^{11}}$. Express this number without scientific notation.

47. The top-grossing movie of all time is *Titanic*. During its first year, box office receipts were about 6×10^8 dollars. That amount represented a fraction of about 9.5×10^{-3} of the total receipts for motion pictures in that year. (*Source:* U.S. Bureau of the Census.) What were the total receipts?

48. In a recent year, the state of Texas had about 1.3×10^6 farms with an average of 7.1×10^2 acres per farm. What was the total number of acres devoted to farmland in Texas that year? (*Source:* National Agricultural Statistics Service, U.S. Department of Agriculture.)

49. The body of a 150-lb person contains about 2.3×10^{-4} lb of copper. How much copper is contained in the bodies of 1200 such people?

50. It takes about 3.6×10^1 sec at a speed of 3.0×10^5 km per sec for light from the sun to reach Venus. (*Source: World Almanac and Book of Facts*, 2004.) How far is Venus from the sun?

Chapter 5
SUMMARY

KEY TERMS

5.1	**polynomial**	A polynomial is a term or the sum of a finite number of terms with whole number exponents.
	descending powers	A polynomial in x is written in descending powers if the exponents on x in its terms are in decreasing order.
	degree of a term	The degree of a term is the sum of the exponents on the variables.
	degree of a polynomial	The degree of a polynomial is the greatest degree of any term of the polynomial.
	monomial	A monomial is a polynomial with one term.
	binomial	A binomial is a polynomial with two terms.
	trinomial	A trinomial is a polynomial with three terms.
5.3	**FOIL**	FOIL is a shortcut method for finding the product of two binomials.
	outer product	The outer product of $(2x + 3)(x - 5)$ is $2x(-5)$.
	inner product	The inner product of $(2x + 3)(x - 5)$ is $3x$.
5.8	**scientific notation**	A number written as $a \times 10^n$, where $1 \le |a| < 10$ and n is an integer, is in scientific notation.

NEW SYMBOLS

x^{-n} x to the negative n power

TEST YOUR WORD POWER

See how well you have learned the vocabulary in this chapter. Answers, with examples, follow the Quick Review.

1. A **polynomial** is an algebraic expression made up of
   A. a term or a finite product of terms with positive coefficients and exponents
   B. a term or a finite sum of terms with real coefficients and whole number exponents
   C. the product of two or more terms with positive exponents
   D. the sum of two or more terms with whole number coefficients and exponents.

2. The **degree of a term** is
   A. the number of variables in the term
   B. the product of the exponents on the variables
   C. the least exponent on the variables
   D. the sum of the exponents on the variables.

3. A **trinomial** is a polynomial with
   A. only one term
   B. exactly two terms
   C. exactly three terms
   D. more than three terms.

4. A **binomial** is a polynomial with
   A. only one term
   B. exactly two terms
   C. exactly three terms
   D. more than three terms.

5. A **monomial** is a polynomial with
   A. only one term
   B. exactly two terms
   C. exactly three terms
   D. more than three terms.

6. **FOIL** is a method for
   A. adding two binomials
   B. adding two trinomials
   C. multiplying two binomials
   D. multiplying two trinomials.

Concepts	Examples

5.1 *Adding and Subtracting Polynomials*

Addition
Add like terms.

Add.
$$2x^2 + 5x - 3$$
$$5x^2 - 2x + 7$$
$$\overline{7x^2 + 3x + 4}$$

Subtraction
Change the signs of the terms in the second polynomial and add to the first polynomial.

Subtract. $(2x^2 + 5x - 3) - (5x^2 - 2x + 7)$
$$= (2x^2 + 5x - 3) + (-5x^2 + 2x - 7)$$
$$= -3x^2 + 7x - 10$$

5.2 *The Product Rule and Power Rules for Exponents*
For any integers m and n:

Product rule $a^m \cdot a^n = a^{m+n}$

Power rules **(a)** $(a^m)^n = a^{mn}$

(b) $(ab)^m = a^m b^m$

(c) $\left(\dfrac{a}{b}\right)^m = \dfrac{a^m}{b^m}$ $(b \neq 0)$.

$$2^4 \cdot 2^5 = 2^9$$
$$(3^4)^2 = 3^8$$
$$(6a)^5 = 6^5 a^5$$
$$\left(\frac{2}{3}\right)^4 = \frac{2^4}{3^4}$$

5.3 *Multiplying Polynomials*
Multiply each term of the first polynomial by each term of the second polynomial. Then add like terms.

Multiply.
$$3x^3 - 4x^2 + 2x - 7$$
$$4x + 3$$
$$\overline{9x^3 - 12x^2 + 6x - 21}$$
$$12x^4 - 16x^3 + 8x^2 - 28x$$
$$\overline{12x^4 - 7x^3 - 4x^2 - 22x - 21}$$

FOIL Method
Step 1 Multiply the two first terms to get the first term of the answer.

Step 2 Find the outer product and the inner product and mentally add them, when possible, to get the middle term of the answer.

Step 3 Multiply the two last terms to get the last term of the answer.

Add the terms found in Steps 1–3.

Multiply $(2x + 3)(5x - 4)$.
$$2x(5x) = 10x^2$$

$$2x(-4) + 3(5x) = 7x$$

$$3(-4) = -12$$

$$(2x + 3)(5x - 4) = 10x^2 + 7x - 12$$

5.4 *Special Products*

Square of a Binomial
$$(a + b)^2 = a^2 + 2ab + b^2$$
$$(a - b)^2 = a^2 - 2ab + b^2$$

$$(3x + 1)^2 = 9x^2 + 6x + 1$$
$$(2m - 5n)^2 = 4m^2 - 20mn + 25n^2$$

Product of the Sum and Difference of Two Terms
$$(a + b)(a - b) = a^2 - b^2$$

$$(4a + 3)(4a - 3) = 16a^2 - 9$$

Concepts	Examples

5.5 *Integer Exponents and the Quotient Rule*
If $a, b \neq 0$, for integers m and n:

Zero exponent $a^0 = 1$

$$15^0 = 1$$

Negative exponent $a^{-n} = \dfrac{1}{a^n}$

$$5^{-2} = \dfrac{1}{5^2} = \dfrac{1}{25}$$

Quotient rule $\dfrac{a^m}{a^n} = a^{m-n}$

$$\dfrac{4^8}{4^3} = 4^5$$

Negative-to-positive rules $\dfrac{a^{-m}}{b^{-n}} = \dfrac{b^n}{a^m}$ $\left(\dfrac{a}{b}\right)^{-m} = \left(\dfrac{b}{a}\right)^m$.

$$\dfrac{6^{-2}}{7^{-3}} = \dfrac{7^3}{6^2}$$ $\left(\dfrac{5}{3}\right)^{-4} = \left(\dfrac{3}{5}\right)^4$

5.6 *Dividing a Polynomial by a Monomial*
Divide each term of the polynomial by the monomial:

$$\dfrac{a+b}{c} = \dfrac{a}{c} + \dfrac{b}{c}.$$

Divide. $\dfrac{4x^3 - 2x^2 + 6x - 8}{2x} = \dfrac{4x^3}{2x} - \dfrac{2x^2}{2x} + \dfrac{6x}{2x} - \dfrac{8}{2x}$

$$= 2x^2 - x + 3 - \dfrac{4}{x}$$

5.7 *Dividing a Polynomial by a Polynomial*
Use "long division."

Divide.

$$
\begin{array}{r}
2x - 5 + \dfrac{-1}{3x+4} \\[4pt]
3x + 4\overline{\smash{)}6x^2 - 7x - 21} \\
\underline{6x^2 + 8x} \\
-15x - 21 \\
\underline{-15x - 20} \\
-1 \leftarrow \text{Remainder}
\end{array}
$$

5.8 *An Application of Exponents: Scientific Notation*
To write a number in scientific notation (as $a \times 10^n$), move the decimal point to the right of the first nonzero digit. If the decimal point is moved n places, and this makes the number smaller, n is positive; otherwise, n is negative. If the decimal point is not moved, n is 0.

$$247 = 2.47 \times 10^2$$
$$.0051 = 5.1 \times 10^{-3}$$
$$4.8 = 4.8 \times 10^0$$
$$3.25 \times 10^5 = 325{,}000$$
$$8.44 \times 10^{-6} = .00000844$$

ANSWERS TO TEST YOUR WORD POWER

1. B; *Example:* $5x^3 + 2x^2 - 7$
2. D; *Examples:* The term 6 has degree 0, $3x$ has degree 1, $-2x^8$ has degree 8, and $5x^2y^4$ has degree 6.
3. C; *Example:* $2a^2 - 3ab + b^2$
4. B; *Example:* $3t^3 + 5t$
5. A; *Examples:* -5 and $4xy^5$

$$\text{F}\text{O}\text{I}\text{L}$$
6. C; *Example:* $(m+4)(m-3) = m(m) - 3m + 4m + 4(-3) = m^2 + m - 12$

Real-Data Applications

Algebra in Euclid's *Elements*

The word *algebra* is derived from *Al-jabr wa'l muqabalah*, a ninth-century treatise written by the Arabic mathematician al-Khwarizmi. The notation that we use today, including the use of letters to represent variables and the symbols $+$ for addition and $-$ for subtraction, was introduced in the sixteenth century by François Viète. In Book II of Euclid's *Elements*, algebraic relationships were written in terms of geometric figures. The following proposition is an example.

Proposition 4: "If a straight line is cut at random, the square on the whole equals the squares on the segments plus twice the rectangle contained by the segments."

This proposition can be viewed geometrically. The straight line segment has length $a + b$. The "square on the whole" is the large outer square, $(a + b)^2$. The "squares on the segments" are a^2 and b^2, and the "rectangle contained by the segments" is ab, as shown in the figure. The algebraic statement equivalent to Proposition 4 is $(a + b)^2 = a^2 + b^2 + 2ab$. You should recognize this as the formula for computing the square of a binomial. We usually write it in the form $(a + b)^2 = a^2 + 2ab + b^2$.

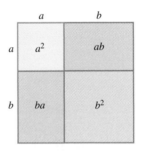

For Group Discussion

Consider the following propositions from Book II of Euclid's *Elements*. An equivalent algebraic statement accompanies each proposition.

Proposition 1: "If there are two straight lines and one of them is cut into any number of segments whatever [2 in the example], then the rectangle contained by the two straight lines equals the sum of the rectangles contained by the uncut straight line and each of the segments."

The equivalent algebraic form is $a(b + c) = ab + ac$.

1. By what name do we know this property?

Proposition 7: "If a straight line is cut at random, then the sum of the square on the whole [a] and that on one of the segments [b] equals twice the rectangle contained by the whole and the said segment plus the square on the remaining segment [$a - b$]."

The equivalent algebraic form is $a^2 + b^2 = 2ab + (a - b)^2$.

2. How is this property written in your textbook?

Proposition 8: An equivalent algebraic form of this proposition is $4ab + (a - b)^2 = (a + b)^2$.

3. Expand both the left and right sides of the formula. Are they the same expression?

Chapter **5**

R E V I E W   E X E R C I S E S

[5.1] *Combine terms where possible in each polynomial. Write the answer in descending powers of the variable. Give the degree of the answer. Identify the polynomial as a* monomial, binomial, trinomial, *or* none of these.

1. $9m^2 + 11m^2 + 2m^2$

2. $-4p + p^3 - p^2 + 8p + 2$

3. $12a^5 - 9a^4 + 8a^3 + 2a^2 - a + 3$

4. $-7y^5 - 8y^4 - y^5 + y^4 + 9y$

Add or subtract as indicated.

5. Add.

$$-2a^3 + 5a^2$$
$$\underline{-3a^3 -\ a^2}$$

6. Add.

$$4r^3 - 8r^2 + 6r$$
$$\underline{-2r^3 + 5r^2 + 3r}$$

7. Subtract.

$$6y^2 - 8y + 2$$
$$\underline{-5y^2 + 2y - 7}$$

8. Subtract.

$$-12k^4 - 8k^2 +\ 7k - 5$$
$$\underline{\ k^4 + 7k^2 + 11k + 1}$$

9. $(2m^3 - 8m^2 + 4) + (8m^3 + 2m^2 - 7)$

10. $(-5y^2 + 3y + 11) + (4y^2 - 7y + 15)$

11. $(6p^2 - p - 8) - (-4p^2 + 2p + 3)$

12. $(12r^4 - 7r^3 + 2r^2) - (5r^4 - 3r^3 + 2r^2 + 1)$

[5.2] *Use the product rule or power rules to simplify each expression. Write the answer in exponential form.*

13. $4^3 \cdot 4^8$

14. $(-5)^6(-5)^5$

15. $(-8x^4)(9x^3)$

16. $(2x^2)(5x^3)(x^9)$

17. $(19x)^5$

18. $(-4y)^7$

19. $5(pt)^4$

20. $\left(\dfrac{7}{5}\right)^6$

21. $(3x^2y^3)^3$

22. $(t^4)^8(t^2)^5$

23. $(6x^2z^4)^2(x^3yz^2)^4$

24. Explain why the product rule for exponents does not apply to the expression $7^2 + 7^4$.

[5.3] *Find each product.*

25. $5x(2x + 14)$

26. $-3p^3(2p^2 - 5p)$

27. $(3r - 2)(2r^2 + 4r - 3)$

28. $(2y + 3)(4y^2 - 6y + 9)$

29. $(5p^2 + 3p)(p^3 - p^2 + 5)$

30. $(3k - 6)(2k + 1)$

31. $(6p - 3q)(2p - 7q)$

32. $(m^2 + m - 9)(2m^2 + 3m - 1)$

[5.4] *Find each product.*

33. $(a + 4)^2$

34. $(3p - 2)^2$

35. $(2r + 5s)^2$

36. $(r + 2)^3$

37. $(2x - 1)^3$

38. $(6m - 5)(6m + 5)$

39. $(2z + 7)(2z - 7)$

40. $(5a + 6b)(5a - 6b)$

41. $(2x^2 + 5)(2x^2 - 5)$

42. Explain why $(a + b)^2$ is not equal to $a^2 + b^2$.

[5.5] *Evaluate each expression.*

43. $5^0 + 8^0$

44. 2^{-5}

45. $\left(\dfrac{6}{5}\right)^{-2}$

46. $4^{-2} - 4^{-1}$

Simplify. Write each answer in exponential form, using only positive exponents. Assume all variables represent nonzero numbers.

47. $\dfrac{6^{-3}}{6^{-5}}$

48. $\dfrac{x^{-7}}{x^{-9}}$

49. $\dfrac{p^{-8}}{p^4}$

50. $\dfrac{r^{-2}}{r^{-6}}$

51. $(2^4)^2$

52. $(9^3)^{-2}$

53. $(5^{-2})^{-4}$

54. $(8^{-3})^4$

55. $\dfrac{(m^2)^3}{(m^4)^2}$

56. $\dfrac{y^4 \cdot y^{-2}}{y^{-5}}$

57. $\dfrac{r^9 \cdot r^{-5}}{r^{-2} \cdot r^{-7}}$

58. $(-5m^3)^2$

59. $(2y^{-4})^{-3}$

60. $\dfrac{ab^{-3}}{a^4b^2}$

61. $\dfrac{(6r^{-1})^2 \cdot (2r^{-4})}{r^{-5}(r^2)^{-3}}$

62. $\dfrac{(2m^{-5}n^2)^3(3m^2)^{-1}}{m^{-2}n^{-4}(m^{-1})^2}$

[5.6] *Perform each division.*

63. $\dfrac{-15y^4}{-9y^2}$

64. $\dfrac{-12x^3y^2}{6xy}$

65. $\dfrac{6y^4 - 12y^2 + 18y}{-6y}$

66. $\dfrac{2p^3 - 6p^2 + 5p}{2p^2}$

67. $(5x^{13} - 10x^{12} + 20x^7 - 35x^5) \div (-5x^4)$

68. $(-10m^4n^2 + 5m^3n^3 + 6m^2n^4) \div (5m^2n)$

[5.7] *Perform each division.*

69. $(2r^2 + 3r - 14) \div (r - 2)$

70. $\dfrac{12m^2 - 11m - 10}{3m - 5}$

71. $\dfrac{10a^3 + 5a^2 - 14a + 9}{5a^2 - 3}$

72. $\dfrac{2k^4 + 4k^3 + 9k^2 - 8}{2k^2 + 1}$

[5.8] *Write each number in scientific notation.*

73. 48,000,000

74. 28,988,000,000

75. .000065

76. .0000000824

Write each number without exponents.

77. 2.4×10^4

78. 7.83×10^7

79. 8.97×10^{-7}

80. 9.95×10^{-12}

Perform the indicated operations and write the answers without exponents.

81. $(2 \times 10^{-3}) \times (4 \times 10^5)$

82. $\dfrac{8 \times 10^4}{2 \times 10^{-2}}$

83. $\dfrac{12 \times 10^{-5} \times 5 \times 10^4}{4 \times 10^3 \times 6 \times 10^{-2}}$

84. $\dfrac{2.5 \times 10^5 \times 4.8 \times 10^{-4}}{7.5 \times 10^8 \times 1.6 \times 10^{-5}}$

85. There are 13 red balls and 39 black balls in a box. Mix them up and draw 13 out one at a time without returning any ball. The probability that the 13 drawings each will produce a red ball is 1.6×10^{-12}. Write the number given in scientific notation without exponents. (*Source:* Warren Weaver, *Lady Luck*, Doubleday & Company, 1963.)

86. According to Campbell, Mitchell, and Reece in *Biology Concepts and Connections* (Benjamin Cummings, 1994, p. 230), "The amount of DNA in a human cell is about 1000 times greater than the DNA in *E. coli*. Does this mean humans have 1000 times as many genes as the 2000 in *E. coli*? The answer is probably no; the human genome is thought to carry between 50,000 and 100,000 genes, which code for various proteins (as well as for tRNA and rRNA)."

Write each number from this quote using scientific notation.

(a) 1000

(b) 2000

(c) 50,000

(d) 100,000

MIXED REVIEW EXERCISES

Perform the indicated operations. Write answers with positive exponents. Assume that no denominators are equal to 0.

87. $19^0 - 3^0$

88. $(3p)^4(3p^{-7})$

89. 7^{-2}

90. $(-7 + 2k)^2$

91. $\dfrac{2y^3 + 17y^2 + 37y + 7}{2y + 7}$

92. $\left(\dfrac{6r^2 s}{5}\right)^4$

93. $-m^5(8m^2 + 10m + 6)$

94. $\left(\dfrac{1}{2}\right)^{-5}$

95. $(25x^2 y^3 - 8xy^2 + 15x^3 y) \div (5x)$

96. $(6r^{-2})^{-1}$

97. $(2x + y)^3$

98. $2^{-1} + 4^{-1}$

99. $(a + 2)(a^2 - 4a + 1)$

100. $(5y^3 - 8y^2 + 7) - (-3y^3 + y^2 + 2)$

101. $(2r + 5)(5r - 2)$

102. $(12a + 1)(12a - 1)$

103. Find a polynomial that represents the area of the rectangle shown.

2x – 3

x + 2

104. If the side of a square has a measure represented by $5x^4 + 2x^2$, what polynomial represents its area?

$5x^4 + 2x^2$

Chapter **5**

TEST

Perform the indicated operations.

1. $(5t^4 - 3t^2 + 7t + 3) - (t^4 - t^3 + 3t^2 + 8t + 3)$

1. _____

2. $(2y^2 - 8y + 8) + (-3y^2 + 2y + 3) - (y^2 + 3y - 6)$

2. _____

3. Subtract.

$9t^3 - 4t^2 + 2t + 2$
$\underline{9t^3 + 8t^2 - 3t - 6}$

3. _____

Simplify, and write each answer with only positive exponents.

4. $(-2)^3(-2)^2$

4. _____

5. $\left(\dfrac{6}{m^2}\right)^3, \quad m \neq 0$

5. _____

6. $3x^2(-9x^3 + 6x^2 - 2x + 1)$

6. _____

7. $(2r - 3)(r^2 + 2r - 5)$

7. _____

8. $(t - 8)(t + 3)$

8. _____

9. $(4x + 3y)(2x - y)$

9. _____

10. $(5x - 2y)^2$

10. _____

11. $(10v + 3w)(10v - 3w)$

11. _____

12. $(x + 1)^3$

12. _____

Evaluate each expression.

13. 5^{-4}

13. _____

14. $(-3)^0 + 4^0$

14. _____

15. $4^{-1} + 3^{-1}$

15. _____

Perform the indicated operations. In Exercises 16 and 17, write each answer using only positive exponents. Assume that variables represent nonzero numbers.

16. _____

16. $\dfrac{8^{-1} \cdot 8^4}{8^{-2}}$

17. _____

17. $\dfrac{(x^{-3})^{-2}(x^{-1}y)^2}{(xy^{-2})^2}$

18. _____

18. $\dfrac{8y^3 - 6y^2 + 4y + 10}{2y}$

19. _____

19. $(-9x^2y^3 + 6x^4y^3 + 12xy^3) \div (3xy)$

20. _____

20. $\dfrac{2x^2 + x - 36}{x - 4}$

21. _____

21. $(3x^3 - x + 4) \div (x - 2)$

Write each number in scientific notation.

22. (a) _____

(b) _____

22. (a) 344,000,000,000

(b) .00000557

Write each number without exponents.

23. (a) _____

(b) _____

23. (a) 2.96×10^7

(b) 6.07×10^{-8}

24. _____

24. What polynomial expression represents the area of this square?

$3x + 9$

25. _____

25. Give an example of this situation: the sum of two fourth-degree polynomials in x is a third-degree polynomial in x.

Cumulative Review Exercises

CHAPTERS R–5

Work each problem.

1. $\dfrac{2}{3} + \dfrac{1}{8}$

2. $\dfrac{7}{4} - \dfrac{9}{5}$

3. $8.32 - 4.6$

4. 7.21×8.6

5. A retailer has \$34,000 invested in her business. She finds that last year she earned 5.4% on this investment. How much did she earn?

Find the value of each expression if $x = -2$ and $y = 4$.

6. $\dfrac{4x - 2y}{x + y}$

7. $x^3 - 4xy$

Perform the indicated operations.

8. $\dfrac{(-13 + 15) - (3 + 2)}{6 - 12}$

9. $-7 - 3[2 + (5 - 8)]$

Decide what property justifies each statement.

10. $(9 + 2) + 3 = 9 + (2 + 3)$

11. $-7 + 7 = 0$

12. $6(4 + 2) = 6(4) + 6(2)$

Solve each equation.

13. $2x - 7x + 8x = 30$

14. $2 - 3(t - 5) = 4 + t$

15. $2(5h + 1) = 10h + 4$

16. $d = rt$ for r

17. $\dfrac{x}{5} = \dfrac{x - 2}{7}$

18. $\dfrac{1}{3}p - \dfrac{1}{6}p = -2$

19. $.05x + .15(50 - x) = 5.50$

20. $4 - (3x + 12) = (2x - 9) - (5x - 1)$

Solve each problem.

21. A 1-oz mouse takes about 16 times as many breaths as does a 3-ton elephant. (*Source: Dinosaurs, Spitfires, and Sea Dragons,* McGowan, C., Harvard University Press, 1991.) If the two animals take a combined total of 170 breaths per minute, how many breaths does each take during that time period?

22. If a number is subtracted from 8 and this difference is tripled, the result is three times the number. Find this number, and you will learn how many times a dolphin rests during a 24-hr period.

Solve each inequality.

23. $-8x \le -80$

24. $-2(x + 4) > 3x + 6$

25. $-3 \le 2x + 5 < 9$

Given $2x - 3y = -6$, find the following.

26. The intercepts of the graph

27. The graph

28. The slope of the line

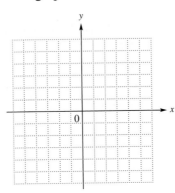

Solve the system using the method indicated.

29. $y = 2x + 5$
$\quad x + y = -4$ (Substitution)

30. $3x + 2y = 2$
$\quad 2x + 3y = -7$ (Elimination)

Evaluate each expression.

31. $4^{-1} + 3^0$

32. $2^{-4} \cdot 2^5$

33. $\dfrac{8^{-5} \cdot 8^7}{8^2}$

34. Write with positive exponents only: $\dfrac{(a^{-3}b^2)^2}{(2a^{-4}b^{-3})^{-1}}$.

35. Write in scientific notation: 34,500.

Perform the indicated operations.

36. $(7x^3 - 12x^2 - 3x + 8) + (6x^2 + 4) - (-4x^3 + 8x^2 - 2x - 2)$

37. $6x^5(3x^2 - 9x + 10)$

38. $(7x + 4)(9x + 3)$

39. $(5x + 8)^2$

40. $\dfrac{y^3 - 3y^2 + 8y - 6}{y - 1}$

Factoring and Applications

6

Wireless communication uses radio waves to carry signals and messages across distances. Cellular phones, one of the most popular forms of wireless communication, have become an invaluable tool for people to stay connected to family, friends, and work while on the go. In 2002 alone, U.S. sales of cellular phones totaled some $8835 million as 66% of all U.S. households used cell phones. (*Source: Microsoft Encarta Encyclopedia 2002;* Consumer Electronics Association.)

In Exercise 31 of Section 6.7, we use a *quadratic equation* to model the number of cell phones owned by Americans in recent years.

6.1 Factors; The Greatest Common Factor

OBJECTIVES

1 Find the greatest common factor of a list of numbers.

2 Find the greatest common factor of a list of variable terms.

3 Factor out the greatest common factor.

4 Factor by grouping.

Recall from **Section R.1** that to **factor** a number means to write it as the product of two or more numbers. The product is called the **factored form** of the number. For example,

$$12 = \underbrace{\overset{\text{Factors}}{6 \cdot 2}}_{\text{Factored form}}.$$

Factoring is a process that "undoes" multiplying. We multiply $6 \cdot 2$ to get 12, but we factor 12 by writing it as $6 \cdot 2$.

OBJECTIVE 1 Find the greatest common factor of a list of numbers. An integer that is a factor of two or more integers is a **common factor** of those integers. For example, 6 is a common factor of 18 and 24 because 6 is a factor of both 18 and 24. Other common factors of 18 and 24 are 1, 2, and 3. The **greatest common factor (GCF)** of a list of integers is the largest common factor of those integers. This means 6 is the greatest common factor of 18 and 24, since it is the largest of their common factors.

> **NOTE**
> Factors of a number are also divisors of the number. The greatest common factor is the same as the greatest common divisor.

EXAMPLE 1 Finding the Greatest Common Factor for Numbers

Find the greatest common factor for each list of numbers.

(a) 30, 45

First write each number in prime factored form.

$$30 = 2 \cdot 3 \cdot 5$$
$$45 = 3 \cdot 3 \cdot 5$$

Use each prime the *least* number of times it appears in *all* the factored forms. There is no 2 in the prime factored form of 45, so there will be no 2 in the greatest common factor. The least number of times 3 appears in all the factored forms is 1; the least number of times 5 appears is also 1. From this, the

$$\text{GCF} = 3^1 \cdot 5^1 = 3 \cdot 5 = 15.$$

(b) 72, 120, 432

Find the prime factored form of each number.

$$72 = 2 \cdot 2 \cdot 2 \cdot 3 \cdot 3$$
$$120 = 2 \cdot 2 \cdot 2 \cdot 3 \cdot 5$$
$$432 = 2 \cdot 2 \cdot 2 \cdot 2 \cdot 3 \cdot 3 \cdot 3$$

The least number of times 2 appears in all the factored forms is 3, and the least number of times 3 appears is 1. There is no 5 in the prime factored form of either 72 or 432, so the

$$\text{GCF} = 2^3 \cdot 3^1 = 24.$$

Continued on Next Page

(c) 10, 11, 14

Write the prime factored form of each number.

$$10 = 2 \cdot 5$$
$$11 = 11$$
$$14 = 2 \cdot 7$$

There are no primes common to all three numbers, so the GCF is 1.

> **Work Problem 1 at the Side.** ▶▶▶

OBJECTIVE 2 Find the greatest common factor of a list of variable terms. The terms x^4, x^5, x^6, and x^7 have x^4 as the greatest common factor because the least exponent on the variable x is 4.

$$x^4 = 1 \cdot x^4, \quad x^5 = x \cdot x^4, \quad x^6 = x^2 \cdot x^4, \quad x^7 = x^3 \cdot x^4$$

NOTE
The exponent on a variable in the GCF is the *least* exponent that appears on that variable in *all* the terms.

EXAMPLE 2 Finding the Greatest Common Factor for Variable Terms

Find the greatest common factor for each list of terms.

(a) $21m^7, -18m^6, 45m^8$

$$21m^7 = 3 \cdot 7 \cdot m^7$$
$$-18m^6 = -1 \cdot 2 \cdot 3 \cdot 3 \cdot m^6$$
$$45m^8 = 3 \cdot 3 \cdot 5 \cdot m^8$$

First, 3 is the greatest common factor of the coefficients 21, -18, and 45. The least exponent on m is 6, so the

$$GCF = 3m^6.$$

(b) $x^4y^2, x^7y^5, x^3y^7, y^{15}$

$$x^4y^2, \quad x^7y^5, \quad x^3y^7, \quad y^{15}$$

There is no x in the last term, y^{15}, so x will not appear in the greatest common factor. There is a y in each term, however, and 2 is the least exponent on y. The GCF is y^2.

(c) $-a^2b, -ab^2$

$$-a^2b = -1a^2b = -1 \cdot 1 \cdot a^2b$$
$$-ab^2 = -1ab^2 = -1 \cdot 1 \cdot ab^2$$

The factors of -1 are -1 and 1. Since $1 > -1$, the GCF is $1ab$ or ab.

NOTE
In a list of negative terms, sometimes a negative common factor is preferable (even though it is not the greatest common factor). In Example 2(c), for instance, we might prefer $-ab$ as the common factor. In factoring exercises, either answer will be acceptable.

---

1 Find the greatest common factor for each list of numbers.

(a) 30, 20, 15

$$30 = 2 \cdot 3 \cdot 5$$
$$20 = 2 \cdot \underline{\quad} \cdot \underline{\quad}$$
$$15 = 3 \cdot \underline{\quad}$$
$$GCF = \underline{\quad}$$

(b) 42, 28, 35

(c) 12, 18, 26, 32

(d) 10, 15, 21

② Find the greatest common factor for each list of terms.

(a) $6m^4, 9m^2, 12m^5$

$6m^4 = 2 \cdot \underline{\hspace{1cm}} \cdot m^4$

$9m^2 = 3 \cdot \underline{\hspace{1cm}} \cdot \underline{\hspace{1cm}}$

$12m^5 = 2 \cdot 2 \cdot \underline{\hspace{1cm}} \cdot \underline{\hspace{1cm}}$

$\text{GCF} = \underline{\hspace{1cm}}$

We find the greatest common factor of a list of terms as follows.

Finding the Greatest Common Factor (GCF)

Step 1 **Factor.** Write each number in prime factored form.

Step 2 **List common factors.** List each prime number or each variable that is a factor of every term in the list. (If a prime does not appear in one of the prime factored forms, it cannot appear in the greatest common factor.)

Step 3 **Choose least exponents.** Use as exponents on the common prime factors the *least* exponents from the prime factored forms.

Step 4 **Multiply.** Multiply the primes from Step 3. If there are no primes left after Step 3, the greatest common factor is 1.

◀◀◀ **Work Problem 2 at the Side.**

OBJECTIVE 3 **Factor out the greatest common factor.** The polynomial

$$3m + 12$$

has two terms, $3m$ and 12. The greatest common factor of these two terms is 3. We can write $3m + 12$ so that each term is a product with 3 as one factor.

(b) $-12p^5, -18q^4$

$$3m + 12 = 3 \cdot m + 3 \cdot 4$$
$$= 3(m + 4) \qquad \text{Distributive property}$$

The factored form of $3m + 12$ is $3(m + 4)$. This process is called **factoring out the greatest common factor.**

CAUTION
The polynomial $3m + 12$ is *not* in factored form when written as the *sum*

$$3 \cdot m + 3 \cdot 4. \qquad \text{Not in factored form}$$

(c) y^4z^2, y^6z^8, z^9

The *terms* are factored, but the polynomial is not. The factored form of $3m + 12$ is the *product*

$$3(m + 4). \qquad \text{In factored form}$$

Writing a polynomial as a product, that is, in factored form, is called **factoring** the polynomial.

(d) $12p^{11}, 17q^5$

EXAMPLE 3 **Factoring Out the Greatest Common Factor**

Factor out the greatest common factor.

(a) $5y^2 + 10y = 5y(y) + 5y(2) \qquad \text{GCF} = 5y$
$$= 5y(y + 2) \qquad \text{Distributive property}$$

Check by multiplying: $5y(y + 2) = 5y(y) + 5y(2)$
$$= 5y^2 + 10y. \qquad \text{Original polynomial}$$

Continued on Next Page

(b) $20m^5 + 10m^4 - 15m^3$

$$= 5m^3(4m^2) + 5m^3(2m) - 5m^3(3) \quad \text{GCF} = 5m^3$$

$$= 5m^3(4m^2 + 2m - 3) \quad \text{Factor out } 5m^3.$$

Check: $5m^3(4m^2 + 2m - 3) = 20m^5 + 10m^4 - 15m^3$ \quad Original polynomial

(c) $x^5 + x^3 = x^3(x^2) + x^3(1) = x^3(x^2 + 1)$ \quad Don't forget the 1.

(d) $20m^7p^2 - 36m^3p^4 = 4m^3p^2(5m^4) - 4m^3p^2(9p^2)$ \quad GCF $= 4m^3p^2$

$$= 4m^3p^2(5m^4 - 9p^2)$$

(e) $\dfrac{1}{6}n^2 + \dfrac{5}{6}n = \dfrac{1}{6}n(n) + \dfrac{1}{6}n(5)$ \quad GCF $= \frac{1}{6}n$

$$= \dfrac{1}{6}n(n + 5)$$

CAUTION
Be sure to include the **1** in a problem like Example 3(c). *Always check that the factored form can be multiplied out to give the original polynomial.*

> **Work Problem 3 at the Side.** ▶▶▶

EXAMPLE 4 **Factoring Out the Greatest Common Factor**

Factor out the greatest common factor.

(a) $a(a + 3) + 4(a + 3)$
The binomial $a + 3$ is the greatest common factor here.

Same

$$a(a + 3) + 4(a + 3) = (a + 3)(a + 4)$$

(b) $x^2(x + 1) - 5(x + 1) = (x + 1)(x^2 - 5)$ \quad Factor out $x + 1$.

> **Work Problem 4 at the Side.** ▶▶▶

OBJECTIVE **4** **Factor by grouping.** When a polynomial has four terms, common factors can sometimes be used to **factor by grouping.**

EXAMPLE 5 **Factoring by Grouping**

Factor by grouping.

(a) $2x + 6 + ax + 3a$
Group the first two terms and the last two terms, since the first two terms have a common factor of 2 and the last two terms have a common factor of a.

$$2x + 6 + ax + 3a = (2x + 6) + (ax + 3a)$$

$$= 2(x + 3) + a(x + 3)$$

The expression is still not in factored form because it is the *sum* of two terms. Now, however, $x + 3$ is a common factor and can be factored out.

--- **Continued on Next Page**

---

3 Factor out the greatest common factor.

(a) $4x^2 + 6x$

(b) $10y^5 - 8y^4 + 6y^2$

(c) $m^7 + m^9$

(d) $8p^5q^2 + 16p^6q^3 - 12p^4q^7$

(e) $\dfrac{1}{3}b^2 - \dfrac{2}{3}b$

(f) $13x^2 - 27$

4 Factor out the greatest common factor.

(a) $r(t - 4) + 5(t - 4)$

(b) $y^2(y + 2) - 3(y + 2)$

(c) $x(x - 1) - 5(x - 1)$

ANSWERS
3. (a) $2x(2x + 3)$
(b) $2y^2(5y^3 - 4y^2 + 3)$
(c) $m^7(1 + m^2)$
(d) $4p^4q^2(2p + 4p^2q - 3q^5)$
(e) $\dfrac{1}{3}b(b - 2)$
(f) no common factor (except 1)
4. (a) $(t - 4)(r + 5)$
(b) $(y + 2)(y^2 - 3)$
(c) $(x - 1)(x - 5)$

⑤ Factor by grouping.

(a) $pq + 5q + 2p + 10$

$$2x + 6 + ax + 3a = (2x + 6) + (ax + 3a) \qquad \text{Group terms.}$$
$$= 2(x + 3) + a(x + 3) \qquad \text{Factor each group.}$$
$$= (x + 3)(2 + a) \qquad \text{Factor out } x + 3.$$

The final result is in factored form because it is a *product*. Note that the goal in factoring by grouping is to get a common factor, $x + 3$ here, so that the last step is possible. Check by multiplying the binomials using the FOIL method from **Section 5.3.**

Check: $(x + 3)(2 + a) = 2x + ax + 6 + 3a \qquad$ FOIL
$$= 2x + 6 + ax + 3a, \qquad \text{Rearrange terms.}$$

which is the original polynomial.

(b) $2xy + 3y + 2x + 3$

(b) $6ax + 24x + a + 4 = (6ax + 24x) + (a + 4) \qquad$ Group terms.
$$= 6x(a + 4) + 1(a + 4) \qquad \begin{array}{l}\text{Factor each group;}\\\text{remember the 1.}\end{array}$$
$$= (a + 4)(6x + 1) \qquad \text{Factor out } a + 4.$$

Check: $(a + 4)(6x + 1) = 6ax + a + 24x + 4 \qquad$ FOIL
$$= 6ax + 24x + a + 4, \qquad \text{Rearrange terms.}$$

which is the original polynomial.

(c) $2a^2 - 4a + 3ab - 6b$

(c) $2x^2 - 10x + 3xy - 15y = (2x^2 - 10x) + (3xy - 15y) \qquad$ Group terms.
$$= 2x(x - 5) + 3y(x - 5) \qquad \begin{array}{l}\text{Factor each}\\\text{group.}\end{array}$$
$$= (x - 5)(2x + 3y) \qquad \begin{array}{l}\text{Factor out the common}\\\text{factor, } x - 5.\end{array}$$

Check: $(x - 5)(2x + 3y) = 2x^2 + 3xy - 10x - 15y \qquad$ FOIL
$$= 2x^2 - 10x + 3xy - 15y \qquad \text{Original polynomial}$$

(d) $x^3 + 3x^2 - 5x - 15$

(d) $t^3 + 2t^2 - 3t - 6 = (t^3 + 2t^2) + (-3t - 6) \qquad$ Group terms.
$$= t^2(t + 2) - 3(t + 2) \qquad \begin{array}{l}\text{Factor out } -3 \text{ so there is}\\\text{a common factor, } t + 2;\\-3(t + 2) = -3t - 6.\end{array}$$
$$= (t + 2)(t^2 - 3) \qquad \text{Factor out } t + 2.$$

Check: $(t + 2)(t^2 - 3) = t^3 - 3t + 2t^2 - 6 \qquad$ FOIL
$$= t^3 + 2t^2 - 3t - 6 \qquad \text{Original polynomial}$$

> **CAUTION**
> *Be careful with signs when grouping* in a problem like Example 5(d). It is wise to check the factoring in the second step, as shown in the example side comment, before continuing.

◄◄◄ Work Problem 5 at the Side.

Use these steps to factor a polynomial with four terms by grouping.

> **Factoring by Grouping**
>
> *Step 1*   **Group terms.** Collect the terms into two groups so that each group has a common factor.
>
> *Step 2*   **Factor within groups.** Factor out the greatest common factor from each group.
>
> *Step 3*   **Factor the entire polynomial.** Factor a common binomial factor from the results of Step 2.
>
> *Step 4*   **If necessary, rearrange terms.** If Step 2 does not result in a common binomial factor, try a different grouping.

EXAMPLE 6   **Rearranging Terms Before Factoring by Grouping**

Factor by grouping.

(a) $10x^2 - 12y + 15x - 8xy$

Factoring out the common factor of 2 from the first two terms and the common factor of x from the last two terms gives

$$10x^2 - 12y + 15x - 8xy = 2(5x^2 - 6y) + x(15 - 8y).$$

This does not lead to a common factor, so we try rearranging the terms. There is usually more than one way to do this. We try

$$10x^2 - 8xy - 12y + 15x,$$

and group the first two terms and the last two terms as follows.

$$\begin{aligned} 10x^2 - 8xy - 12y + 15x &= 2x(5x - 4y) + 3(-4y + 5x) \\ &= 2x(5x - 4y) + 3(5x - 4y) \\ &= (5x - 4y)(2x + 3) \end{aligned}$$

Check: $\begin{aligned}(5x - 4y)(2x + 3) &= 10x^2 + 15x - 8xy - 12y &&\text{FOIL} \\ &= 10x^2 - 12y + 15x - 8xy &&\text{Original} \\ &&&\text{polynomial}\end{aligned}$

(b) $2xy + 12 - 3y - 8x$

We need to rearrange these terms to get two groups that each have a common factor. Trial and error suggests the following grouping.

$$\begin{aligned} 2xy + 12 - 3y - 8x &= (2xy - 3y) + (-8x + 12) &&\text{Group terms.} \\ &= y(2x - 3) - 4(2x - 3) &&\text{Factor each group;} \\ &&&\text{be careful with signs.} \\ &= (2x - 3)(y - 4) &&\text{Factor out } 2x - 3.\end{aligned}$$

Since the quantities in parentheses in the second step must be the same, we factored out -4 rather than 4. *Check* by multiplying.

> **CAUTION**
> Use negative signs carefully when grouping, as in Example 6(b), or a sign error will occur. ***Always check by multiplying.***

Work Problem 6 at the Side. ▶▶▶

6 Factor by grouping.

(a) $6y^2 - 20w + 15y - 8yw$

(b) $9mn - 4 + 12m - 3n$

Real-Data Applications

Idle Prime Time

A positive integer greater than 1 is a **prime number** if its only factors are 1 and itself. Every positive integer can be written as a product of prime numbers in a unique way, except for the order of the factors. Finding new primes has intrigued people from ancient Greece to modern times. The *Great Internet Mersenne Prime Search* is a consortium headed by George Woltman and Scott Kurowski that has discovered seven world record primes. On May 15, 2004, Josh Findley discovered the prime number, $2^{24,036,583} - 1$. His calculation took over two weeks on his 2.4 GHz Pentium 4 computer. This prime number is nearly a million digits larger than the last prime found and has 7,235,733 decimal digits when written out. (*Source:* http://www.mersenne.org/prime.htm)

Prime numbers are essential in the development of unbreakable codes that, in an era of Internet commerce, ensure security in transmitting and storing computer data.

The oldest known method for finding prime numbers is the Sieve of Eratosthenes, similar to the version shown below. Numbers that are not prime (composite numbers) are eliminated and only the prime numbers are left. Begin with 2. Two is prime but multiples of 2 are not, so delete the remaining numbers in Column 2 and all of Columns 4 and 6. Three is prime, but multiples of 3 are not, so delete the remaining numbers in Column 3. Examine the remaining numbers and eliminate any that are composite (such as 25 or 91). The prime numbers are highlighted.

For Group Discussion

1. **Twin primes** occur in pairs that differ by 2. List all the twin primes from the table.

2. Observe that all prime numbers larger than 3 are in Columns 1 and 5. Each number in Column 5 is 1 less than a multiple of 6, and therefore has the form $6n - 1$. Each number in Column 1 has a similar structure, $6n + 1$. Show that the larger of each of these twin primes, found in the year 2000, has the form $6n + 1$:

   $$1{,}693{,}965 \times 2^{66{,}443} \pm 1$$
   and
   $$4{,}648{,}619{,}711{,}505 \times 2^{60{,}000} \pm 1.$$
   (*Hint:* Show that the leading term is divisible by both 2 and 3.)

SIEVE OF ERATOSTHENES

Col 1	Col 2	Col 3	Col 4	Col 5	Col 6
1	2	3	4	5	6
7	8	9	10	11	12
13	14	15	16	17	18
19	20	21	22	23	24
25	26	27	28	29	30
31	32	33	34	35	36
37	38	39	40	41	42
43	44	45	46	47	48
49	50	51	52	53	54
55	56	57	58	59	60
61	62	63	64	65	66
67	68	69	70	71	72
73	74	75	76	77	78
79	80	81	82	83	84
85	86	87	88	89	90
91	92	93	94	95	96
97	98	99	100	101	102

3. **Mersenne primes,** named for the 17th-century French monk Marin Mersenne, have the form $2^p - 1$, where p is a prime number. Not all such numbers are prime. Show that $2^{11} - 1$ is composite and $2^5 - 1$ is prime.

4. A **Sophie Germain prime,** named for an 18th-century French mathematician, is an odd prime p for which $2p + 1$ is also prime. For example, 5 is a Sophie Germain prime since 11 ($2 \cdot 5 + 1$) is prime, but 13 is not since 27 ($2 \cdot 13 + 1$) is composite. List the Sophie Germain primes from the table.

6.1 Exercises

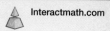

Find the greatest common factor for each list of numbers. See Example 1.

1. 12, 16   **2.** 18, 24   **3.** 40, 20, 4   **4.** 50, 30, 5

5. 18, 24, 36, 48   **6.** 15, 30, 45, 75   **7.** 4, 9, 12   **8.** 9, 16, 24

Find the greatest common factor for each list of terms. See Example 2.

9. $16y$, 24   **10.** $18w$, 27   **11.** $30x^3, 40x^6, 50x^7$

12. $60z^4, 70z^8, 90z^9$ **13.** $-x^4y^3, -xy^2$ **14.** $-a^4b^5, -a^3b$

15. $42ab^3, -36a, 90b, -48ab$ **16.** $45c^3d, 75c, 90d, -105cd$

Complete each factoring.

17. $9m^4 = 3m^2(\quad)$ **18.** $12p^5 = 6p^3(\quad)$ **19.** $-8z^9 = -4z^5(\quad)$

20. $-15k^{11} = -5k^8(\quad)$ **21.** $6m^4n^5 = 3m^3n(\quad)$ **22.** $27a^3b^2 = 9a^2b(\quad)$

23. $12y + 24 = 12(\qquad)$ **24.** $18p + 36 = 18(\qquad)$

25. $10a^2 - 20a = 10a(\qquad)$ **26.** $15x^2 - 30x = 15x(\qquad)$

27. $8x^2y + 12x^3y^2 = 4x^2y(\qquad)$ **28.** $18s^3t^2 + 10st = 2st(\qquad)$

Factor out the greatest common factor. See Examples 3 and 4.

29. $x^2 - 4x$ **30.** $m^2 - 7m$ **31.** $6t^2 + 15t$ **32.** $8x^2 + 6x$

33. $\dfrac{1}{4}d^2 - \dfrac{3}{4}d$ **34.** $\dfrac{1}{5}z^2 + \dfrac{3}{5}z$ **35.** $12x^3 + 6x^2$ **36.** $21b^3 - 7b^2$

37. $65y^{10} + 35y^6$ **38.** $100a^5 + 16a^3$ **39.** $11w^3 - 100$

40. $13z^5 - 80$ **41.** $8m^2n^3 + 24m^2n^2$ **42.** $19p^2y - 38p^2y^3$

43. $4x^3 - 10x^2 + 6x$ **44.** $9z^3 - 6z^2 + 12z$ **45.** $13y^8 + 26y^4 - 39y^2$

46. $5x^5 + 25x^4 - 20x^3$

47. $45q^4p^5 + 36qp^6 + 81q^2p^3$

48. $125a^3z^5 + 60a^4z^4 - 85a^5z^2$

49. $c(x + 2) + d(x + 2)$

50. $r(5 - x) + t(5 - x)$

51. $a^2(2a + b) - b(2a + b)$

52. $3x(x^2 + 5) - y(x^2 + 5)$

53. $q(p + 4) - 1(p + 4)$

54. $y^2(x - 4) + 1(x - 4)$

Factor by grouping. See Examples 5 and 6.

55. $5m + mn + 20 + 4n$

56. $ts + 5t + 2s + 10$

57. $6xy - 21x + 8y - 28$

58. $2mn - 8n + 3m - 12$

59. $3xy + 9x + y + 3$

60. $6n + 4mn + 3 + 2m$

61. $7z^2 + 14z - az - 2a$

62. $2b^2 + 3b - 8ab - 12a$

63. $18r^2 + 12ry - 3xr - 2xy$

64. $5m^2 + 15mp - 2mr - 6pr$

65. $w^3 + w^2 + 9w + 9$

66. $y^3 + y^2 + 6y + 6$

67. $3a^3 + 6a^2 - 2a - 4$

68. $10x^3 + 15x^2 - 8x - 12$

69. $16m^3 - 4m^2p^2 - 4mp + p^3$

70. $10t^3 - 2t^2s^2 - 5ts + s^3$

71. $y^2 + 3x + 3y + xy$

72. $m^2 + 14p + 7m + 2mp$

73. $2z^2 + 6w - 4z - 3wz$

74. $2a^2 + 20b - 8a - 5ab$

RELATING CONCEPTS (EXERCISES 75–78) For Individual or Group Work

In many cases, the choice of which pairs of terms to group when factoring by grouping can be made in different ways. To see this for Example 6(b), **work Exercises 75–78 in order.**

75. Start with the polynomial from Example 6(b), $2xy + 12 - 3y - 8x$, and rearrange the terms as follows: $2xy - 8x - 3y + 12$. What property from **Section 1.7** allows this?

76. Group the first two terms and the last two terms of the rearranged polynomial in Exercise 75. Then factor each group.

77. Is your result from Exercise 76 in factored form? Explain your answer.

78. If your answer to Exercise 77 is *no,* factor the polynomial. Is the result the same as the one shown for Example 6(b)?

6.2 Factoring Trinomials

Using FOIL, the product of the binomials $k - 3$ and $k + 1$ is

$$(k - 3)(k + 1) = k^2 - 2k - 3. \quad \text{Multiplying}$$

Suppose instead that we are given the polynomial $k^2 - 2k - 3$ and want to rewrite it as the product $(k - 3)(k + 1)$. That is,

$$k^2 - 2k - 3 = (k - 3)(k + 1). \quad \text{Factoring}$$

Recall from **Section 6.1** that this process is called factoring the polynomial. Factoring reverses or "undoes" multiplying.

OBJECTIVE **1** **Factor trinomials with a coefficient of 1 for the squared term.** When factoring polynomials with integer coefficients, we use only integers in the factors. For example, we can factor $x^2 + 5x + 6$ by finding integers m and n such that

$$x^2 + 5x + 6 = (x + m)(x + n).$$

To find these integers m and n, we first use FOIL to multiply the two binomials on the right side of the equation:

$$(x + m)(x + n) = x^2 + nx + mx + mn.$$

By the distributive property,

$$x^2 + nx + mx + mn = x^2 + (n + m)x + mn.$$

Comparing this result with $x^2 + 5x + 6$ shows that we must find integers m and n having a sum of 5 and a product of 6.

Product of m and n is 6.

$$x^2 + 5x + 6 = x^2 + (n + m)x + mn$$

Sum of m and n is 5.

Because many pairs of integers have a sum of 5, it is best to begin by listing those pairs of integers whose product is 6. Both 5 and 6 are positive, so we consider only pairs in which both integers are positive.

Work Problem 1 at the Side.

From Problem 1 at the side, we see that the numbers 1 and 6 and the numbers 2 and 3 both have a product of 6, but only the pair 2 and 3 has a sum of 5. So 2 and 3 are the required integers, and

$$x^2 + 5x + 6 = (x + 2)(x + 3).$$

Check by multiplying the binomials using FOIL. *Make sure that the sum of the outer and inner products produces the correct middle term.*

Check: $(x + 2)(x + 3) = x^2 + 5x + 6$

$$\begin{array}{c} 2x \\ 3x \\ \hline 5x \quad \text{Add.} \end{array}$$

This method of factoring can be used only for trinomials that have 1 as the coefficient of the squared term. Methods for factoring other trinomials will be given in the next two sections.

OBJECTIVES

1 Factor trinomials with a coefficient of 1 for the squared term.

2 Factor trinomials after factoring out the greatest common factor.

1 **(a)** List all pairs of positive integers whose product is 6.

(b) Find the pair from part (a) whose sum is 5.

ANSWERS
1. **(a)** 1, 6; 2, 3 **(b)** 2, 3

2 Factor each trinomial.

(a) $y^2 + 12y + 20$

First complete the given list of numbers.

Factors of 20	Sums of Factors
20, 1	20 + 1 = 21
10, ___	10 + ___ = ___
5, ___	5 + ___ = ___

(b) $x^2 + 9x + 18$

3 Factor each trinomial.

(a) $t^2 - 12t + 32$

First complete the given list of numbers.

Factors of 32	Sums of Factors
−32, −1	−32 + (−1) = −33
−16, ___	−16 + (___) = ___
−8, ___	−8 + (___) = ___

(b) $y^2 - 10y + 24$

EXAMPLE 1 Factoring a Trinomial with All Positive Terms

Factor $m^2 + 9m + 14$.

Look for two integers whose product is **14** and whose sum is **9**. List the pairs of integers whose products are 14. Then examine the sums. Only positive integers are needed since all signs in $m^2 + 9m + 14$ are positive.

Factors of 14	Sums of Factors	
14, 1	14 + 1 = 15	
7, 2	7 + 2 = 9	Sum is 9.

From the list, 7 and 2 are the required integers, since $7 \cdot 2 = 14$ and $7 + 2 = 9$. Thus,

$$m^2 + 9m + 14 = (m + 2)(m + 7).$$

Check: $(m + 2)(m + 7) = m^2 + 7m + 2m + 14$ FOIL

$$= m^2 + 9m + 14$$ Original polynomial

NOTE
In Example 1, the answer $(m + 2)(m + 7)$ also could have been written

$$(m + 7)(m + 2).$$

Because of the commutative property of multiplication, the order of the factors does not matter. ***Always check by multiplying.***

Work Problem 2 at the Side.

EXAMPLE 2 Factoring a Trinomial with a Negative Middle Term

Factor $x^2 - 9x + 20$.

Find two integers whose product is 20 and whose sum is −9. Since the numbers we are looking for have a *positive product* and a *negative sum*, we consider only pairs of negative integers.

Factors of 20	Sums of Factors	
−20, −1	−20 + (−1) = −21	
−10, −2	−10 + (−2) = −12	
−5, −4	−5 + (−4) = −9	Sum is −9.

The required integers are −5 and −4, so

$$x^2 - 9x + 20 = (x - 5)(x - 4).$$

Check: $(x - 5)(x - 4) = x^2 - 4x - 5x + 20$

$$= x^2 - 9x + 20$$

Work Problem 3 at the Side.

EXAMPLE 3 Factoring a Trinomial with Two Negative Terms

Factor $p^2 - 2p - 15$.

Find two integers whose product is -15 and whose sum is -2. If these numbers do not come to mind right away, find them (if they exist) by listing all the pairs of integers whose product is -15. Because the last term, -15, is negative, we need pairs of integers with different signs.

Factors of -15	Sums of Factors
$15, -1$	$15 + (-1) = 14$
$-15, 1$	$-15 + 1 = -14$
$5, -3$	$5 + (-3) = 2$
$-5, 3$	$-5 + 3 = -2$ Sum is -2.

The required integers are -5 and 3, so

$$p^2 - 2p - 15 = (p - 5)(p + 3).$$

Check: Multiply $(p - 5)(p + 3)$.

NOTE

In Examples 1–3, notice that we listed factors in descending order (disregarding sign) when we were looking for the required pair of integers. This helps avoid skipping the correct combination.

Work Problem 4 at the Side. ▶▶▶

As shown in the next example, some trinomials cannot be factored using only integers. We call such trinomials **prime polynomials.**

EXAMPLE 4 Deciding whether Polynomials Are Prime

Factor each trinomial.

(a) $x^2 - 5x + 12$

As in Example 2, both factors must be negative to give a positive product and a negative sum. First, list all pairs of negative integers whose product is 12. Then examine the sums.

Factors of 12	Sums of Factors
$-12, -1$	$-12 + (-1) = -13$
$-6, -2$	$-6 + (-2) = -8$
$-4, -3$	$-4 + (-3) = -7$

None of the pairs of integers has a sum of -5. Therefore, the trinomial $x^2 - 5x + 12$ *cannot be factored using only integers; it is a prime polynomial.*

(b) $k^2 - 8k + 11$

There is no pair of integers whose product is 11 and whose sum is -8, so $k^2 - 8k + 11$ is a prime polynomial.

Work Problem 5 at the Side. ▶▶▶

4 Factor each trinomial.

(a) $a^2 - 9a - 22$

(b) $r^2 - 6r - 16$

5 Factor each trinomial, if possible.

(a) $r^2 - 3r - 4$

(b) $m^2 - 2m + 5$

6 Factor each trinomial.

(a) $b^2 - 3ab - 4a^2$

(b) $r^2 - 6rs + 8s^2$

The procedure for factoring a trinomial of the form $x^2 + bx + c$ follows.

> **Factoring $x^2 + bx + c$**
> Find two integers whose product is c and whose sum is b.
>
> 1. Both integers must be positive if b and c are positive.
> 2. Both integers must be negative if c is positive and b is negative.
> 3. One integer must be positive and one must be negative if c is negative.

EXAMPLE 5 Factoring a Trinomial with Two Variables

Factor $z^2 - 2bz - 3b^2$.

Here, the coefficient of z in the middle term is $-2b$, so we need to find two expressions whose product is $-3b^2$ and whose sum is $-2b$. The expressions are $-3b$ and b, so

$$z^2 - 2bz - 3b^2 = (z - 3b)(z + b).$$

Check: $(z - 3b)(z + b) = z^2 + zb - 3bz - 3b^2$
$$= z^2 + 1bz - 3bz - 3b^2$$
$$= z^2 - 2bz - 3b^2$$

◀◀◀ **Work Problem 6 at the Side.**

7 Factor each trinomial completely.

(a) $2p^3 + 6p^2 - 8p$

OBJECTIVE 2 Factor trinomials after factoring out the greatest common factor. The trinomial in the next example does not have a coefficient of 1 for the squared term. (In fact, there is no squared term.) However, there may be a common factor.

EXAMPLE 6 Factoring a Trinomial with a Common Factor

Factor $4x^5 - 28x^4 + 40x^3$.

First, factor out the greatest common factor, $4x^3$.

$$4x^5 - 28x^4 + 40x^3 = 4x^3(x^2 - 7x + 10)$$

Now factor $x^2 - 7x + 10$. The integers -5 and -2 have a product of 10 and a sum of -7. The complete factored form is

$$4x^5 - 28x^4 + 40x^3 = 4x^3(x - 5)(x - 2). \quad \text{Include } 4x^3.$$

(b) $3x^4 - 15x^3 + 18x^2$

Check: $4x^3(x - 5)(x - 2) = 4x^3(x^2 - 7x + 10)$
$$= 4x^5 - 28x^4 + 40x^3$$

> **CAUTION**
> When factoring, *always look for a common factor first.* Remember to include the common factor as part of the answer. As a check, multiplying out the complete factored form should give the original polynomial.

ANSWERS
6. (a) $(b - 4a)(b + a)$
   (b) $(r - 4s)(r - 2s)$
7. (a) $2p(p + 4)(p - 1)$
   (b) $3x^2(x - 3)(x - 2)$

◀◀◀ **Work Problem 7 at the Side.**

6.2 Exercises

| FOR EXTRA HELP | Addison-Wesley Math Tutor Center | Math XL MathXL | Digital Video Tutor CD 5 Videotape 6 | Student's Solutions Manual | MyMathLab MyMathLab | Interactmath.com |

1. When factoring a trinomial in x as $(x + a)(x + b)$, what must be true of a and b, if the last term of the trinomial is negative?

2. In Exercise 1, what must be true of a and b if the last term is positive?

3. What is meant by a *prime polynomial*?

4. How can you check your work when factoring a trinomial? Does the check ensure that the trinomial is *completely* factored?

In Exercises 5–8, list all pairs of integers with the given product. Then find the pair whose sum is given. See the tables in Examples 1–4.

5. Product: 12; Sum: 7

6. Product: 18; Sum: 9

7. Product: -24; Sum: -5

8. Product: -36; Sum: -16

9. Which one of the following is the correct factored form of $x^2 - 12x + 32$?

   A. $(x - 8)(x + 4)$ **B.** $(x + 8)(x - 4)$
   C. $(x - 8)(x - 4)$ **D.** $(x + 8)(x + 4)$

10. What would be the first step in factoring $2x^3 + 8x^2 - 10x$?

Complete each factoring.

11. $x^2 + 15x + 44 = (x + 4)(\qquad)$

12. $r^2 + 15r + 56 = (r + 7)(\qquad)$

13. $x^2 - 9x + 8 = (x - 1)(\qquad)$

14. $t^2 - 14t + 24 = (t - 2)(\qquad)$

15. $y^2 - 2y - 15 = (y + 3)(\qquad)$

16. $t^2 - t - 42 = (t + 6)(\qquad)$

17. $x^2 + 9x - 22 = (x - 2)(\qquad)$

18. $x^2 + 6x - 27 = (x - 3)(\qquad)$

19. $y^2 - 7y - 18 = (y + 2)(\qquad)$

20. $y^2 - 2y - 24 = (y + 4)(\qquad)$

Factor completely. If a polynomial cannot be factored, write prime. *See Examples 1–4.*

21. $y^2 + 9y + 8$

22. $a^2 + 9a + 20$

23. $b^2 + 8b + 15$

24. $x^2 + 6x + 8$

25. $m^2 + m - 20$

26. $p^2 + 4p - 5$

27. $x^2 + 3x - 40$

28. $d^2 + 4d - 45$

29. $y^2 - 8y + 15$

30. $y^2 - 6y + 8$

31. $z^2 - 15z + 56$

32. $x^2 - 13x + 36$

33. $r^2 - r - 30$

34. $q^2 - q - 42$

35. $a^2 - 8a - 48$

36. $m^2 - 10m - 24$

37. $x^2 + 4x + 5$

38. $t^2 + 11t + 12$

Factor completely. See Examples 5 and 6.

39. $r^2 + 3ra + 2a^2$

40. $x^2 + 5xa + 4a^2$

41. $x^2 + 4xy + 3y^2$

42. $p^2 + 9pq + 8q^2$

43. $t^2 - tz - 6z^2$

44. $a^2 - ab - 12b^2$

45. $v^2 - 11vw + 30w^2$

46. $v^2 - 11vx + 24x^2$

47. $4x^2 + 12x - 40$

48. $5y^2 - 5y - 30$

49. $2t^3 + 8t^2 + 6t$

50. $3t^3 + 27t^2 + 24t$

51. $2x^6 + 8x^5 - 42x^4$

52. $4y^5 + 12y^4 - 40y^3$

53. $a^5 + 3a^4b - 4a^3b^2$

54. $z^{10} - 4z^9y - 21z^8y^2$

55. $m^3n - 10m^2n^2 + 24mn^3$

56. $y^3z + 3y^2z^2 - 54yz^3$

57. Use the FOIL method from **Section 5.3** to show that $(2x + 4)(x - 3) = 2x^2 - 2x - 12$. Why, then, is it incorrect to completely factor $2x^2 - 2x - 12$ as $(2x + 4)(x - 3)$?

58. Why is it incorrect to completely factor $3x^2 + 9x - 12$ as the product $(x - 1)(3x + 12)$?

6.3 Factoring Trinomials by Grouping

Trinomials like $2x^2 + 7x + 6$, in which the coefficient of the squared term is *not* 1, are factored with extensions of the methods from the previous sections. One such method uses factoring by grouping from **Section 6.1.**

OBJECTIVE **1** **Factor trinomials by grouping when the coefficient of the squared term is not 1.** Recall that a trinomial such as $m^2 + 3m + 2$ is factored by finding two integers whose product is 2 and whose sum is 3. To factor $2x^2 + 7x + 6$, we look for two integers whose product is $2 \cdot 6 = 12$ and whose sum is 7.

Sum is 7.

$$2x^2 + 7x + 6$$

Product is $2 \cdot 6 = 12$.

By considering pairs of positive integers whose product is 12, the necessary integers are found to be 3 and 4. We use these integers to write the middle term, $7x$, as $7x = 3x + 4x$. The trinomial $2x^2 + 7x + 6$ becomes

$$2x^2 + 7x + 6 = 2x^2 + \underbrace{3x + 4x}_{7x} + 6.$$

$$= (2x^2 + 3x) + (4x + 6) \qquad \text{Group terms.}$$
$$= x(2x + 3) + 2(2x + 3) \qquad \text{Factor each group.}$$

Must be the same

$$2x^2 + 7x + 6 = (2x + 3)(x + 2) \qquad \text{Factor out } 2x + 3.$$

Check: $(2x + 3)(x + 2) = 2x^2 + 7x + 6$

In the preceding example, we could have written $7x$ as $4x + 3x$. Factoring by grouping this way would give the same answer.

Work Problem 1 at the Side.

EXAMPLE 1 **Factoring Trinomials by Grouping**

Factor each trinomial.

(a) $6r^2 + r - 1$

We must find two integers with a product of $6(-1) = -6$ and a sum of 1.

Sum is 1.

$$6r^2 + r - 1 = 6r^2 + 1r - 1$$

Product is $6(-1) = -6$.

The integers are -2 and 3. We write the middle term, r, as $-2r + 3r$.

$$6r^2 + r - 1 = 6r^2 - 2r + 3r - 1 \qquad r = -2r + 3r$$
$$= (6r^2 - 2r) + (3r - 1) \qquad \text{Group terms.}$$
$$= 2r(3r - 1) + 1(3r - 1) \qquad \text{The binomials must be the same.}$$
$$= (3r - 1)(2r + 1) \qquad \text{Factor out } 3r - 1.$$

Check: $(3r - 1)(2r + 1) = 6r^2 + r - 1$

Continued on Next Page

OBJECTIVE

1 Factor trinomials by grouping when the coefficient of the squared term is not 1.

1 **(a)** Factor $2x^2 + 7x + 6$ by writing $7x$ as $4x + 3x$. Complete the following.

$2x^2 + 7x + 6$

$= 2x^2 + 4x + 3x + 6$

$= (2x^2 + \underline{}) + (3x + \underline{})$

$= 2x(x + \underline{}) + 3(x + \underline{})$

$= (\underline{})(2x + 3)$

(b) Is the answer in part (a) the same as in the example? (Remember that the order of the factors does not matter.)

ANSWERS
1. (a) $4x$; 6; 2; 2; $x + 2$ **(b)** yes

② Factor each trinomial by grouping.

(a) $2m^2 + 7m + 3$

(b) $5p^2 - 2p - 3$

(c) $15k^2 - km - 2m^2$

(b) $12z^2 - 5z - 2$

Look for two integers whose product is $12(-2) = -24$ and whose sum is -5. The required integers are 3 and -8, so

$$12z^2 - 5z - 2 = 12z^2 + 3z - 8z - 2 \qquad -5z = 3z - 8z$$

$$= (12z^2 + 3z) + (-8z - 2) \qquad \text{Group terms.}$$

$$= 3z(4z + 1) - 2(4z + 1) \qquad \begin{array}{l}\text{Factor each group;}\\\text{be careful with signs.}\end{array}$$

$$= (4z + 1)(3z - 2). \qquad \text{Factor out } 4z + 1.$$

Check: $(4z + 1)(3z - 2) = 12z^2 - 5z - 2$

(c) $10m^2 + mn - 3n^2$

Two integers whose product is $10(-3) = -30$ and whose sum is 1 are -5 and 6. Rewrite the trinomial with four terms.

$$10m^2 + mn - 3n^2 = 10m^2 - 5mn + 6mn - 3n^2 \qquad mn = -5mn + 6mn$$

$$= 5m(2m - n) + 3n(2m - n) \qquad \begin{array}{l}\text{Group terms;}\\\text{factor each group.}\end{array}$$

$$= (2m - n)(5m + 3n) \qquad \text{Factor out } 2m - n.$$

Check by multiplying.

◀◀◀ **Work Problem 2 at the Side.**

③ Factor each trinomial completely.

(a) $4x^2 - 2x - 30$

(b) $18p^4 + 63p^3 + 27p^2$

(c) $6a^2 + 3ab - 18b^2$

EXAMPLE 2 **Factoring a Trinomial with a Common Factor by Grouping**

Factor $28x^5 - 58x^4 - 30x^3$.

First factor out the greatest common factor, $2x^3$.

$$28x^5 - 58x^4 - 30x^3 = 2x^3(14x^2 - 29x - 15)$$

To factor $14x^2 - 29x - 15$, find two integers whose product is $14(-15) = -210$ and whose sum is -29. Factoring 210 into prime factors gives

$$210 = 2 \cdot 3 \cdot 5 \cdot 7.$$

Combine these prime factors in pairs in different ways, using one positive and one negative to get -210. The factors 6 and -35 have the correct sum, -29. Now rewrite the given trinomial and factor it.

$$28x^5 - 58x^4 - 30x^3 = 2x^3(14x^2 + 6x - 35x - 15)$$

$$= 2x^3[(14x^2 + 6x) + (-35x - 15)]$$

$$= 2x^3[2x(7x + 3) - 5(7x + 3)]$$

$$= 2x^3[(7x + 3)(2x - 5)]$$

$$= 2x^3(7x + 3)(2x - 5)$$

Check by multiplying.

CAUTION
Remember to include the common factor in the final result.

ANSWERS
2. (a) $(2m + 1)(m + 3)$
(b) $(5p + 3)(p - 1)$
(c) $(5k - 2m)(3k + m)$
3. (a) $2(2x + 5)(x - 3)$
(b) $9p^2(2p + 1)(p + 3)$
(c) $3(2a - 3b)(a + 2b)$

◀◀◀ **Work Problem 3 at the Side.**

6.3 Exercises

FOR EXTRA HELP

Tutor Center Addison-Wesley Math Tutor Center

Math*XL* MathXL

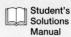 Digital Video Tutor CD 6 Videotape 6

Student's Solutions Manual

MyMathLab MyMathLab

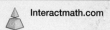 Interactmath.com

The middle term of each trinomial has been rewritten. Now factor by grouping. See Example 1.

1. $m^2 + 8m + 12$
$= m^2 + 6m + 2m + 12$

2. $x^2 + 9x + 14$
$= x^2 + 7x + 2x + 14$

3. $a^2 + 3a - 10$
$= a^2 + 5a - 2a - 10$

4. $y^2 - 2y - 24$
$= y^2 + 4y - 6y - 24$

5. $10t^2 + 9t + 2$
$= 10t^2 + 5t + 4t + 2$

6. $6x^2 + 13x + 6$
$= 6x^2 + 9x + 4x + 6$

7. $15z^2 - 19z + 6$
$= 15z^2 - 10z - 9z + 6$

8. $12p^2 - 17p + 6$
$= 12p^2 - 9p - 8p + 6$

9. $8s^2 + 2st - 3t^2$
$= 8s^2 - 4st + 6st - 3t^2$

10. $3x^2 - xy - 14y^2$
$= 3x^2 - 7xy + 6xy - 14y^2$

11. $15a^2 + 22ab + 8b^2$
$= 15a^2 + 10ab + 12ab + 8b^2$

12. $25m^2 + 25mn + 6n^2$
$= 25m^2 + 15mn + 10mn + 6n^2$

13. Which pair of integers would be used to rewrite the middle term when factoring $12y^2 + 5y - 2$ by grouping?

A. $-8, 3$ **B.** $8, -3$ **C.** $-6, 4$ **D.** $6, -4$

14. Which pair of integers would be used to rewrite the middle term when factoring $20b^2 - 13b + 2$ by grouping?

A. $10, 3$ **B.** $-10, -3$ **C.** $8, 5$ **D.** $-8, -5$

Complete the steps to factor each trinomial by grouping.

15. $2m^2 + 11m + 12$

(a) Find two integers whose product is

_____ · _____ = _____ and whose

sum is _____ .

(b) The required integers are _____ and

_____ .

(c) Write the middle term $11m$ as _____ +

_____ .

(d) Rewrite the given trinomial using four terms.

(e) Factor the polynomial in part (d) by grouping.

(f) Check by multiplying.

16. $6y^2 - 19y + 10$

(a) Find two integers whose product is

_____ · _____ = _____ and whose

sum is _____ .

(b) The required integers are _____ and

_____ .

(c) Write the middle term $-19y$ as _____ +

_____ .

(d) Rewrite the given trinomial using four terms.

(e) Factor the polynomial in part (d) by grouping.

(f) Check by multiplying.

Factor each trinomial by grouping. See Examples 1 and 2.

17. $2x^2 + 7x + 3$

18. $3y^2 + 13y + 4$

19. $4r^2 + r - 3$

20. $4r^2 + 3r - 10$

21. $8m^2 - 10m - 3$

22. $20x^2 - 28x - 3$

23. $21m^2 + 13m + 2$

24. $38x^2 + 23x + 2$

25. $6b^2 + 7b + 2$

26. $6w^2 + 19w + 10$

27. $12y^2 - 13y + 3$

28. $15a^2 - 16a + 4$

29. $24x^2 - 42x + 9$

30. $48b^2 - 74b - 10$

31. $2m^3 + 2m^2 - 40m$

32. $3x^3 + 12x^2 - 36x$

33. $32z^5 - 20z^4 - 12z^3$

34. $18x^5 + 15x^4 - 75x^3$

35. $12p^2 + 7pq - 12q^2$

36. $6m^2 - 5mn - 6n^2$

37. $6a^2 - 7ab - 5b^2$

38. $25g^2 - 5gh - 2h^2$

39. $5 - 6x + x^2$

40. $7 + 8x + x^2$

41. On a quiz, a student factored $16x^2 - 24x + 5$ by grouping as follows.

$$16x^2 - 24x + 5$$
$$= 16x^2 - 4x - 20x + 5$$
$$= 4x(4x - 1) - 5(4x - 1) \quad \text{His answer}$$

He thought his answer was correct since it checked by multiplying. Why was the answer marked wrong? What is the correct factored form?

42. On the same quiz, another student factored $3k^3 - 12k^2 - 15k$ by first factoring out the common factor $3k$ to get $3k(k^2 - 4k - 5)$. Then she wrote

$$k^2 - 4k - 5 = k^2 - 5k + k - 5$$
$$= k(k - 5) + 1(k - 5)$$
$$= (k - 5)(k + 1). \quad \text{Her answer}$$

Why was the answer marked wrong? What is the correct factored form?

6.4 Factoring Trinomials Using FOIL

OBJECTIVE **1** **Factor trinomials using FOIL.** This section shows an alternative method of factoring trinomials in which the coefficient of the squared term is not 1. This method uses trial and error.

To factor $2x^2 + 7x + 6$ (the same trinomial factored at the beginning of **Section 6.3**) by trial and error, we use FOIL backwards. We want to write $2x^2 + 7x + 6$ as the product of two binomials.

$$2x^2 + 7x + 6 = (\qquad)(\qquad)$$

The product of the two first terms of the binomials is $2x^2$. The possible factors of $2x^2$ are $2x$ and x or $-2x$ and $-x$. Since all terms of the trinomial are positive, we consider only positive factors. Thus, we have

$$2x^2 + 7x + 6 = (2x \qquad)(x \qquad).$$

The product of the two last terms, 6, can be factored as $1 \cdot 6, 6 \cdot 1,$ $2 \cdot 3,$ or $3 \cdot 2.$ Try each pair to find the pair that gives the correct middle term, $7x.$

> **Work Problem 1 at the Side.** ▶▶▶

In part (b) at the side, since $2x + 6 = 2(x + 3)$, the binomial $2x + 6$ has a common factor of 2, while $2x^2 + 7x + 6$ has no common factor other than 1. The product $(2x + 6)(x + 1)$ cannot be correct. (Part (c) also has one binomial factor with a common factor.)

> **NOTE**
> If the original polynomial has no common factor, then none of its binomial factors will either.

Now try the remaining numbers 3 and 2 as factors of 6.

$$(2x + 3)(x + 2) = 2x^2 + 7x + 6 \qquad \text{Correct}$$

$$\underline{\begin{array}{c} 3x \\ 4x \\ 7x \end{array}} \qquad \text{Add.}$$

Finally, we see that $2x^2 + 7x + 6$ factors as

$$2x^2 + 7x + 6 = (2x + 3)(x + 2).$$

Check by multiplying: $(2x + 3)(x + 2) = 2x^2 + 7x + 6.$

> **EXAMPLE 1** **Factoring a Trinomial with All Positive Terms Using FOIL**

Factor $8p^2 + 14p + 5.$

The number 8 has several possible pairs of factors, but 5 has only 1 and 5 or -1 and $-5.$ For this reason, it is easier to begin by considering the factors of 5. Ignore the negative factors since all coefficients in the trinomial are positive. If $8p^2 + 14p + 5$ can be factored, the factors will have the form

$$(\quad + 5)(\quad + 1).$$

Continued on Next Page

OBJECTIVE

1 **Factor trinomials using FOIL.**

Study Skills Workbook
Activity 5: Study Cards

1 Multiply to decide whether each factored form is correct or incorrect for

$$2x^2 + 7x + 6.$$

(a) $(2x + 1)(x + 6)$

(b) $(2x + 6)(x + 1)$

(c) $(2x + 2)(x + 3)$

ANSWERS
1. **(a)** incorrect **(b)** incorrect **(c)** incorrect

2 Factor each trinomial.

(a) $2p^2 + 9p + 9$

(b) $6p^2 + 19p + 10$

(c) $8x^2 + 14x + 3$

When factoring $8p^2 + 14p + 5$, the possible pairs of factors of $8p^2$ are $8p$ and p, or $4p$ and $2p$. Try various combinations, checking to see if the middle term is $14p$ in each case.

Since $14p$ is the correct middle term,

$$8p^2 + 14p + 5 = (4p + 5)(2p + 1).$$

Check: $(4p + 5)(2p + 1) = 8p^2 + 14p + 5$

$\blacktriangleleft\blacktriangleleft\blacktriangleleft$ **Work Problem 2 at the Side.**

EXAMPLE 2 **Factoring a Trinomial with a Negative Middle Term Using FOIL**

Factor $6x^2 - 11x + 3$.

Since 3 has only 1 and 3 or -1 and -3 as factors, it is better here to begin by factoring 3. The last term of the trinomial $6x^2 - 11x + 3$ is positive and the middle term has a negative coefficient, so we consider only negative factors. We need two negative factors because the *product* of two negative factors is positive and their *sum* is negative, as required.

Try -3 and -1 as factors of 3:

$$(\quad - 3)(\quad - 1).$$

The factors of $6x^2$ may be either $6x$ and x, or $2x$ and $3x$.

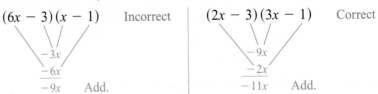

The factors $2x$ and $3x$ produce $-11x$, the correct middle term, so

$$6x^2 - 11x + 3 = (2x - 3)(3x - 1).$$

Check by multiplying.

3 Factor each trinomial.

(a) $4y^2 - 11y + 6$

(b) $9x^2 - 21x + 10$

NOTE
In Example 2, we might also realize that our initial attempt to factor $6x^2 - 11x + 3$ as $(6x - 3)(x - 1)$ *cannot* be correct since $6x - 3$ has a common factor of 3 and the original polynomial does not.

ANSWERS
2. (a) $(2p + 3)(p + 3)$
  (b) $(3p + 2)(2p + 5)$
  (c) $(4x + 1)(2x + 3)$
3. (a) $(4y - 3)(y - 2)$
  (b) $(3x - 5)(3x - 2)$

$\blacktriangleleft\blacktriangleleft\blacktriangleleft$ **Work Problem 3 at the Side.**

EXAMPLE 3 **Factoring a Trinomial with a Negative Last Term Using FOIL**

Factor $8x^2 + 6x - 9$.

The integer 8 has several possible pairs of factors, as does -9. Since the last term is negative, one positive factor and one negative factor of -9 are needed. Since the coefficient of the middle term is small, it is wise to avoid large factors such as 8 or 9. We try 4 and 2 as factors of 8, and 3 and -3 as factors of -9, and check the middle term.

$(4x + 3)(2x - 3)$ Incorrect

$6x$

$-12x$

$-6x$ Add.

Now we try interchanging 3 and -3, since only the sign of the middle term is incorrect.

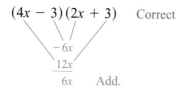

$(4x - 3)(2x + 3)$ Correct

$-6x$

$12x$

$6x$ Add.

This combination produces $6x$, the correct middle term, so

$$8x^2 + 6x - 9 = (4x - 3)(2x + 3).$$

Work Problem 4 at the Side. ▶▶▶

EXAMPLE 4 **Factoring a Trinomial with Two Variables**

Factor $12a^2 - ab - 20b^2$.

There are several pairs of factors of $12a^2$, including

$$12a \text{ and } a, \quad 6a \text{ and } 2a, \quad \text{and} \quad 4a \text{ and } 3a,$$

just as there are many possible pairs of factors of $-20b^2$, including

$$20b \text{ and } -b, \quad -20b \text{ and } b, \quad 10b \text{ and } -2b,$$
$$-10b \text{ and } 2b, \quad 4b \text{ and } -5b, \quad \text{and} \quad -4b \text{ and } 5b.$$

Once again, since the coefficient of the middle term is small, avoid the larger factors. Try the factors $6a$ and $2a$ and $4b$ and $-5b$.

$$(6a + 4b)(2a - 5b)$$

This cannot be correct, as mentioned before, since $6a + 4b$ has 2 as a common factor, while the given trinomial does not. Try $3a$ and $4a$ with $4b$ and $-5b$.

$$(3a + 4b)(4a - 5b) = 12a^2 + ab - 20b^2 \quad \text{Incorrect}$$

Here the middle term is ab, rather than $-ab$. Interchange the signs of the last two terms in the factors.

$$(3a - 4b)(4a + 5b) = 12a^2 - ab - 20b^2 \quad \text{Correct}$$

Work Problem 5 at the Side. ▶▶▶

---

4 Factor each trinomial, if possible.

(a) $6x^2 + 5x - 4$

(b) $6m^2 - 11m - 10$

(c) $4x^2 - 3x - 7$

(d) $3y^2 + 8y - 6$

5 Factor each trinomial.

(a) $2x^2 - 5xy - 3y^2$

(b) $8a^2 + 2ab - 3b^2$

ANSWERS

4. (a) $(3x + 4)(2x - 1)$
   (b) $(2m - 5)(3m + 2)$
   (c) $(4x - 7)(x + 1)$
   (d) prime
5. (a) $(2x + y)(x - 3y)$
   (b) $(4a + 3b)(2a - b)$

6 Factor each trinomial.

(a) $36z^3 - 6z^2 - 72z$

EXAMPLE 5 Factoring Trinomials with Common Factors

Factor each trinomial.

(a) $15y^3 + 55y^2 + 30y$

First factor out the greatest common factor, $5y$.

$$15y^3 + 55y^2 + 30y = 5y(3y^2 + 11y + 6)$$

Now factor $3y^2 + 11y + 6$. Try $3y$ and y as factors of $3y^2$ and 2 and 3 as factors of 6.

$$(3y + 2)(y + 3) = 3y^2 + 11y + 6 \qquad \text{Correct}$$

The complete factored form of $15y^3 + 55y^2 + 30y$ is

$$15y^3 + 55y^2 + 30y = 5y(3y + 2)(y + 3).$$

Check by multiplying.

(b) $-24a^3 - 42a^2 + 45a$

The common factor could be $3a$ or $-3a$. If we factor out $-3a$, the first term of the trinomial will be positive, which makes it easier to factor.

$$-24a^3 - 42a^2 + 45a = -3a(8a^2 + 14a - 15) \qquad \text{Factor out } -3a.$$
$$= -3a(4a - 3)(2a + 5) \qquad \text{Use trial and error.}$$

Check by multiplying.

CAUTION
This caution bears repeating: *Remember to include the common factor in the final factored form.*

(b) $-24x^3 + 32x^2y + 6xy^2$

◀◀◀ Work Problem 6 at the Side.

6.4 Exercises

Decide which is the correct factored form of the given polynomial.

1. $2x^2 - x - 1$

   A. $(2x - 1)(x + 1)$ **B.** $(2x + 1)(x - 1)$

2. $3a^2 - 5a - 2$

   A. $(3a + 1)(a - 2)$ **B.** $(3a - 1)(a + 2)$

3. $4y^2 + 17y - 15$

   A. $(y + 5)(4y - 3)$ **B.** $(2y - 5)(2y + 3)$

4. $12c^2 - 7c - 12$

   A. $(6c - 2)(2c + 6)$ **B.** $(4c + 3)(3c - 4)$

5. $4k^2 + 13mk + 3m^2$

   A. $(4k + m)(k + 3m)$ **B.** $(4k + 3m)(k + m)$

6. $2x^2 + 11x + 12$

   A. $(2x + 3)(x + 4)$ **B.** $(2x + 4)(x + 3)$

Complete each factoring.

7. $6a^2 + 7ab - 20b^2 = (3a - 4b)(\qquad)$

8. $9m^2 - 3mn - 2n^2 = (3m + n)(\qquad)$

9. $2x^2 + 6x - 8 = 2(\qquad)$
$$= 2(\quad)(\quad)$$

10. $3x^2 - 9x - 30 = 3(\qquad)$
$$= 3(\quad)(\quad)$$

11. $4z^3 - 10z^2 - 6z = 2z(\qquad)$
$$= 2z(\quad)(\quad)$$

12. $15r^3 - 39r^2 - 18r = 3r(\qquad)$
$$= 3r(\quad)(\quad)$$

13. For the polynomial $12x^2 + 7x - 12$, 2 is not a common factor. Explain why the binomial $2x - 6$, then, cannot be a factor of the polynomial.

14. Explain how the signs of the last terms of the two binomial factors of a trinomial are determined.

Factor each trinomial completely. See Examples 1–5.

15. $3a^2 + 10a + 7$

16. $7r^2 + 8r + 1$

17. $2y^2 + 7y + 6$

18. $5z^2 + 12z + 4$

19. $15m^2 + m - 2$

20. $6x^2 + x - 1$

21. $12s^2 + 11s - 5$

22. $20x^2 + 11x - 3$

23. $10m^2 - 23m + 12$

24. $6x^2 - 17x + 12$

25. $8w^2 - 14w + 3$

26. $9p^2 - 18p + 8$

27. $20y^2 - 39y - 11$

28. $10x^2 - 11x - 6$

29. $3x^2 - 15x + 16$

30. $2t^2 + 13t - 18$

31. $20x^2 + 22x + 6$

32. $36y^2 + 81y + 45$

33. $40m^2q + mq - 6q$

34. $15a^2b + 22ab + 8b$

35. $15n^4 - 39n^3 + 18n^2$

36. $24a^4 + 10a^3 - 4a^2$

37. $15x^2y^2 - 7xy^2 - 4y^2$

38. $14a^2b^3 + 15ab^3 - 9b^3$

39. $5a^2 - 7ab - 6b^2$

40. $6x^2 - 5xy - y^2$

41. $12s^2 + 11st - 5t^2$

42. $25a^2 + 25ab + 6b^2$

43. $6m^6n + 7m^5n^2 + 2m^4n^3$

44. $12k^3q^4 - 4k^2q^5 - kq^6$

If a trinomial has a negative coefficient for the squared term, such as $-2x^2 + 11x - 12$, it may be easier to factor by first factoring out the common factor -1:

$$-2x^2 + 11x - 12 = -1(2x^2 - 11x + 12)$$
$$= -1(2x - 3)(x - 4).$$

Use this method to factor the trinomials in Exercises 45–50.

45. $-x^2 - 4x + 21$

46. $-x^2 + x + 72$

47. $-3x^2 - x + 4$

48. $-5x^2 + 2x + 16$

49. $-2a^2 - 5ab - 2b^2$

50. $-3p^2 + 13pq - 4q^2$

RELATING CONCEPTS (EXERCISES 51–56) For Individual or Group Work

One of the most common problems that beginning algebra students face is this: If an answer obtained doesn't look exactly like the one given in the back of the book, is it necessarily incorrect? Often there are several different equivalent forms of an answer that are all correct. **Work Exercises 51–56 in order,** *to see how and why this is possible for factoring problems.*

51. Factor the integer 35 as the product of two prime numbers.

52. Factor the integer 35 as the product of the negatives of two prime numbers.

53. Verify the following factored form: $6x^2 - 11x + 4 = (3x - 4)(2x - 1)$.

54. Verify the following factored form: $6x^2 - 11x + 4 = (4 - 3x)(1 - 2x)$.

55. Compare the two valid factored forms in Exercises 53 and 54. How do the factors in each case compare?

56. Suppose you know that the correct factored form of a particular trinomial is $(7t - 3)(2t - 5)$. Based on your observations in Exercises 51–55, what is another valid factored form?

6.5 Special Factoring Techniques

By reversing the rules for multiplication of binomials from **Section 5.4,** we obtain rules for factoring polynomials in certain forms.

OBJECTIVES

1 Factor a difference of squares.

2 Factor a perfect square trinomial.

OBJECTIVE 1 Factor a difference of squares. The formula for the product of the sum and difference of the same two terms is

$$(a + b)(a - b) = a^2 - b^2.$$

Reversing this rule leads to the following special factoring rule.

> **Factoring a Difference of Squares**
> $$a^2 - b^2 = (a + b)(a - b)$$

For example,

$$m^2 - 16 = m^2 - 4^2 = (m + 4)(m - 4).$$

As the next examples show, the following conditions must be true for a binomial to be a difference of squares.

1. Both terms of the binomial must be squares, such as

$$x^2, \quad 9y^2, \quad 25, \quad 1, \quad m^4.$$

2. The terms of the binomial must have different signs (one positive and one negative).

EXAMPLE 1 Factoring Differences of Squares

Factor each binomial, if possible.

$$a^2 - b^2 = (a + b)(a - b)$$

(a) $x^2 - 49 = x^2 - 7^2 = (x + 7)(x - 7)$

(b) $y^2 - m^2 = (y + m)(y - m)$

(c) $z^2 - \dfrac{9}{16} = z^2 - \left(\dfrac{3}{4}\right)^2 = \left(z + \dfrac{3}{4}\right)\left(z - \dfrac{3}{4}\right)$

(d) $x^2 - 8$

Because 8 is not the square of an integer, this binomial is not a difference of squares. It is a prime polynomial.

(e) $p^2 + 16$

Since $p^2 + 16$ is a *sum* of squares, it is not equal to $(p + 4)(p - 4)$. Also, using FOIL,

$$(p - 4)(p - 4) = p^2 - 8p + 16 \neq p^2 + 16$$

and

$$(p + 4)(p + 4) = p^2 + 8p + 16 \neq p^2 + 16,$$

so $p^2 + 16$ is a prime polynomial.

430 Chapter 6 Factoring and Applications

1 Factor, if possible.

(a) $p^2 - 100$

(b) $x^2 - \dfrac{25}{36}$

(c) $x^2 + y^2$

(d) $9m^2 - 49$

(e) $64a^2 - 25$

2 Factor completely.

(a) $50r^2 - 32$

(b) $27y^2 - 75$

(c) $25a^2 - 64b^2$

(d) $k^4 - 49$

(e) $81r^4 - 16$

ANSWERS
1. (a) $(p + 10)(p - 10)$
   (b) $\left(x + \dfrac{5}{6}\right)\left(x - \dfrac{5}{6}\right)$
   (c) prime
   (d) $(3m + 7)(3m - 7)$
   (e) $(8a + 5)(8a - 5)$
2. (a) $2(5r + 4)(5r - 4)$
   (b) $3(3y + 5)(3y - 5)$
   (c) $(5a + 8b)(5a - 8b)$
   (d) $(k^2 + 7)(k^2 - 7)$
   (e) $(9r^2 + 4)(3r + 2)(3r - 2)$

> **CAUTION**
> As Example 1(e) suggests, *after any common factor is removed, a sum of squares cannot be factored.*

EXAMPLE 2 Factoring Differences of Squares

Factor each difference of squares.

$$a^2 \;-\; b^2 \;=\; (a \;+\; b)\,(a \;-\; b)$$

(a) $25m^2 - 16 = (5m)^2 - 4^2 = (5m + 4)(5m - 4)$

(b) $49z^2 - 64 = (7z)^2 - 8^2 = (7z + 8)(7z - 8)$

> **NOTE**
> As in previous sections, you should *always check a factored form by multiplying.*

Work Problem 1 at the Side.

EXAMPLE 3 Factoring More Complex Differences of Squares

Factor completely.

(a) $81y^2 - 36$
First factor out the common factor, 9.

$$81y^2 - 36 = 9(9y^2 - 4) \qquad \text{Factor out 9.}$$
$$= 9[(3y)^2 - 2^2]$$
$$= 9(3y + 2)(3y - 2) \qquad \text{Difference of squares}$$

(b) $9x^2 - 4z^2 = (3x)^2 - (2z)^2 = (3x + 2z)(3x - 2z)$

(c) $p^4 - 36 = (p^2)^2 - 6^2 = (p^2 + 6)(p^2 - 6)$
Neither $p^2 + 6$ nor $p^2 - 6$ can be factored further.

(d) $m^4 - 16 = (m^2)^2 - 4^2$
$$= (m^2 + 4)(m^2 - 4) \qquad \text{Difference of squares}$$
$$= (m^2 + 4)(m + 2)(m - 2) \qquad \text{Difference of squares again}$$

> **CAUTION**
> Remember to factor again when any of the factors is a difference of squares, as in Example 3(d). Check by multiplying.

Work Problem 2 at the Side.

OBJECTIVE **2** **Factor a perfect square trinomial.** The expressions 144, $4x^2$, and $81m^6$ are called *perfect squares* because

$$144 = 12^2, \quad 4x^2 = (2x)^2, \quad \text{and} \quad 81m^6 = (9m^3)^2.$$

A **perfect square trinomial** is a trinomial that is the square of a binomial. For example, $x^2 + 8x + 16$ is a perfect square trinomial because it is the square of the binomial $x + 4$:

$$x^2 + 8x + 16 = (x + 4)(x + 4)$$
$$= (x + 4)^2.$$

For a trinomial to be a perfect square, *two of its terms must be perfect squares*. For this reason, $16x^2 + 4x + 15$ is not a perfect square trinomial because only the term $16x^2$ is a perfect square.

On the other hand, even if two of the terms are perfect squares, the trinomial may not be a perfect square trinomial. For example, $x^2 + 6x + 36$ has two perfect square terms, but it is not a perfect square trinomial. (Try to find a binomial that can be squared to give $x^2 + 6x + 36$.)

We can multiply to see that the square of a binomial gives one of the following perfect square trinomials.

> ### Factoring Perfect Square Trinomials
> $$a^2 + 2ab + b^2 = (a + b)^2$$
> $$a^2 - 2ab + b^2 = (a - b)^2$$

The middle term of a perfect square trinomial is always twice the product of the two terms in the squared binomial. (This was shown in **Section 5.4.**) Use this to check any attempt to factor a trinomial that appears to be a perfect square.

EXAMPLE 4 Factoring a Perfect Square Trinomial

Factor $x^2 + 10x + 25$.
  The term x^2 is a perfect square, and so is 25. Try to factor the trinomial as

$$x^2 + 10x + 25 = (x + 5)^2.$$

To check, take twice the product of the two terms in the squared binomial.

$$2 \cdot x \cdot 5 = 10x$$

Twice First term — of binomial
Last term of binomial

Since $10x$ is the middle term of the trinomial, the trinomial is a perfect square and can be factored as $(x + 5)^2$. Thus,

$$x^2 + 10x + 25 = (x + 5)^2.$$

> **Work Problem 3 at the Side.** ⟩⟩⟩

EXAMPLE 5 Factoring Perfect Square Trinomials

Factor each trinomial.

(a) $x^2 - 22x + 121$
  The first and last terms are perfect squares ($121 = 11^2$ or $(-11)^2$). Check to see whether the middle term of $x^2 - 22x + 121$ is twice the product of the first and last terms of the binomial $x - 11$.

Continued on Next Page

---

3 Factor each trinomial.

(a) $p^2 + 14p + 49$

(b) $m^2 + 8m + 16$

(c) $x^2 + 2x + 1$

4 Factor each trinomial.

(a) $p^2 - 18p + 81$

(b) $16a^2 + 56a + 49$

(c) $121p^2 + 110p + 100$

(d) $64x^2 - 48x + 9$

(e) $27y^3 + 72y^2 + 48y$

$$2 \cdot x \cdot (-11) = -22x$$

Twice — First term — Last term

Since twice the product of the first and last terms of the binomial is the middle term, $x^2 - 22x + 121$ is a perfect square trinomial and

$$x^2 - 22x + 121 = (x - 11)^2.$$

Same sign

Notice that the sign of the second term in the squared binomial is the same as the sign of the middle term in the trinomial.

(b) $9m^2 - 24m + 16 = (3m)^2 + 2(3m)(-4) + (-4)^2 = (3m - 4)^2$

Twice — First term — Last Term

(c) $25y^2 + 20y + 16$

The first and last terms are perfect squares.

$$25y^2 = (5y)^2 \quad \text{and} \quad 16 = 4^2$$

Twice the product of the first and last terms of the binomial $5y + 4$ is

$$2 \cdot 5y \cdot 4 = 40y,$$

which is not the middle term of $25y^2 + 20y + 16$. This trinomial is not a perfect square. In fact, the trinomial cannot be factored even with the methods of the previous sections; it is a prime polynomial.

(d) $12z^3 + 60z^2 + 75z = 3z(4z^2 + 20z + 25)$ Factor out $3z$.

$$= 3z[(2z)^2 + 2(2z)(5) + 5^2]$$
$$= 3z(2z + 5)^2$$

> **NOTE**
> 1. The sign of the second term in the squared binomial is always the same as the sign of the middle term in the trinomial.
> 2. The first and last terms of a perfect square trinomial must be *positive,* because they are squares. For example, the polynomial $x^2 - 2x - 1$ cannot be a perfect square because the last term is negative.
> 3. Perfect square trinomials can also be factored using grouping or FOIL, although using the method of this section is often easier.

◄◄◄ Work Problem 4 at the Side.

The methods of factoring discussed in this section are summarized here.

Special Factoring Rules

Difference of squares	$a^2 - b^2 = (a + b)(a - b)$
Perfect square trinomials	$a^2 + 2ab + b^2 = (a + b)^2$
	$a^2 - 2ab + b^2 = (a - b)^2$

Answers
4. **(a)** $(p - 9)^2$ **(b)** $(4a + 7)^2$ **(c)** prime
(d) $(8x - 3)^2$ **(e)** $3y(3y + 4)^2$

6.5 Exercises

1. To help you factor a difference of squares, complete the following list of squares.

$1^2 =$ _____ $2^2 =$ _____ $3^2 =$ _____ $4^2 =$ _____ $5^2 =$ _____

$6^2 =$ _____ $7^2 =$ _____ $8^2 =$ _____ $9^2 =$ _____ $10^2 =$ _____

$11^2 =$ _____ $12^2 =$ _____ $13^2 =$ _____ $14^2 =$ _____ $15^2 =$ _____

$16^2 =$ _____ $17^2 =$ _____ $18^2 =$ _____ $19^2 =$ _____ $20^2 =$ _____

2. To use the factoring techniques described in this section, you will sometimes need to recognize fourth powers of integers. Complete the following list of fourth powers.

$1^4 =$ _____ $2^4 =$ _____ $3^4 =$ _____ $4^4 =$ _____ $5^4 =$ _____

3. The following powers of x are all perfect squares: $x^2, x^4, x^6, x^8, x^{10}$. Based on this observation, we may make a conjecture (an educated guess) that if the power of a variable is divisible by _____ (with 0 remainder), then it is a perfect square.

4. Which of the following are differences of squares?

A. $x^2 - 4$ **B.** $y^2 + 9$ **C.** $2a^2 - 25$ **D.** $9m^2 - 1$

Factor each binomial completely. Use your answers in Exercises 1 and 2 as necessary. See Examples 1–3.

5. $y^2 - 25$

6. $t^2 - 16$

7. $p^2 - \dfrac{1}{9}$

8. $q^2 - \dfrac{1}{4}$

9. $m^2 - 12$

10. $k^2 - 18$

11. $9r^2 - 4$

12. $4x^2 - 9$

13. $36m^2 - \dfrac{16}{25}$

14. $100b^2 - \dfrac{4}{49}$

15. $36x^2 - 16$

16. $32a^2 - 8$

17. $196p^2 - 225$

18. $361q^2 - 400$

19. $16r^2 - 25a^2$

20. $49m^2 - 100p^2$

21. $100x^2 + 49$

22. $81w^2 + 16$

23. $p^4 - 49$

24. $r^4 - 25$

25. $x^4 - 1$

26. $y^4 - 16$

27. $p^4 - 256$

28. $16k^4 - 1$

29. When a student was directed to factor $x^4 - 81$ completely, his teacher did not give him full credit when he answered $(x^2 + 9)(x^2 - 9)$. The student argued that because his answer does indeed give $x^4 - 81$ when multiplied out, he should be given full credit. Was the teacher justified in her grading of this item? Why or why not?

30. The binomial $4x^2 + 16$ is a sum of squares that *can* be factored. How is this binomial factored? When can a sum of squares be factored?

31. In the polynomial $9y^2 + 14y + 25$, the first and last terms are perfect squares. Can the polynomial be factored? If it can, factor it. If it cannot, explain why it is not a perfect square trinomial.

32. Which of the following are perfect square trinomials?

    A. $y^2 - 13y + 36$ **B.** $x^2 + 6x + 9$ **C.** $4z^2 - 4z + 1$ **D.** $16m^2 + 10m + 1$

Factor each trinomial completely. It may be necessary to factor out the greatest common factor first. See Examples 4 and 5.

33. $w^2 + 2w + 1$ **34.** $p^2 + 4p + 4$ **35.** $x^2 - 8x + 16$

36. $x^2 - 10x + 25$ **37.** $t^2 + t + \dfrac{1}{4}$ **38.** $m^2 + \dfrac{2}{3}m + \dfrac{1}{9}$

39. $x^2 - 1.0x + .25$ **40.** $y^2 - 1.4y + .49$ **41.** $2x^2 + 24x + 72$

42. $3y^2 - 48y + 192$ **43.** $16x^2 - 40x + 25$ **44.** $36y^2 - 60y + 25$

45. $49x^2 - 28xy + 4y^2$ **46.** $4z^2 - 12zw + 9w^2$ **47.** $64x^2 + 48xy + 9y^2$

48. $9t^2 + 24tr + 16r^2$ **49.** $50h^3 - 40h^2y + 8hy^2$ **50.** $18x^3 + 48x^2y + 32xy^2$

RELATING CONCEPTS (EXERCISES 51–54)   For Individual or Group Work

*We have seen that multiplication and factoring are reverse processes. We know that multiplication and division are also related. To check a division problem, we multiply the quotient by the divisor to get the dividend. To see how factoring and division are related, **work Exercises 51–54 in order.***

51. Factor $10x^2 + 11x - 6$.

52. Use long division from **Section 5.7** to divide $10x^2 + 11x - 6$ by $2x + 3$.

53. Could we have predicted the result in Exercise 52 from the result in Exercise 51? Explain.

54. Divide $x^3 - 1$ by $x - 1$. Use your answer to factor $x^3 - 1$.

Summary Exercises on Factoring

As you factor a polynomial, ask yourself these questions to decide on a suitable factoring technique.

Factoring a Polynomial

1. **Is there a common factor?** If so, factor it out.

2. **How many terms are in the polynomial?**

   Two terms: Check to see whether it is a difference of squares.

   Three terms: Is it a perfect square trinomial? If the trinomial is not a perfect square, check to see whether the coefficient of the second-degree term is 1. If so, use the method of **Section 6.2.** If the coefficient of the squared term of the trinomial is not 1, use the general factoring methods of **Sections 6.3** and **6.4.**

   Four terms: Try to factor the polynomial by grouping.

3. **Can any factors be factored further?** If so, factor them.

Factor each polynomial completely. Remember to check by multiplying.

1. $32m^9 + 16m^5 + 24m^3$

2. $2m^2 - 10m - 48$

3. $14k^3 + 7k^2 - 70k$

4. $9z^2 + 64$

5. $6z^2 + 31z + 5$

6. $m^2 - 3mn - 4n^2$

7. $49z^2 - 16y^2$

8. $100n^2r^2 + 30nr^3 - 50n^2r$

9. $16x^2 + 20x$

10. $20 + 5m + 12n + 3mn$

11. $10y^2 - 7yz - 6z^2$

12. $y^4 - 81$

13. $m^2 + 2m - 15$

14. $6y^2 - 5y - 4$

15. $32z^3 + 56z^2 - 16z$

16. $15y^2 + 5y$

17. $z^2 - 12z + 36$

18. $9m^2 - 64$

19. $y^2 - 4yk - 12k^2$

20. $16z^2 - 8z + 1$

21. $6y^2 - 6y - 12$

22. $x^2 + \dfrac{1}{2}x + \dfrac{1}{16}$

23. $p^2 - 17p + 66$

24. $a^2 + 17a + 72$

25. $k^2 + 9$

26. $108m^2 - 36m + 3$

27. $z^2 - 3za - 10a^2$

28. $2a^3 + a^2 - 14a - 7$

29. $4k^2 - 12k + 9$

30. $a^2 - 3ab - 28b^2$

31. $16r^2 + 24rm + 9m^2$

32. $3k^2 + 4k - 4$

33. $n^2 - 12n - 35$

34. $a^4 - 625$

35. $16k^2 - 48k + 36$

36. $8k^2 - 10k - 3$

37. $36y^6 - 42y^5 - 120y^4$

38. $5z^3 - 45z^2 + 70z$

39. $8p^2 + 23p - 3$

40. $8k^2 - 2kh - 3h^2$

41. $54m^2 - 24z^2$

42. $4k^2 - 20kz + 25z^2$

43. $6a^2 + 10a - 4$

44. $15h^2 + 11hg - 14g^2$

45. $m^2 - 81$

46. $10z^2 - 7z - 6$

47. $125m^4 - 400m^3n + 195m^2n^2$

48. $9y^2 + 12y - 5$

49. $m^2 - 4m + 4$

50. $36x^2 + 32x + 9$

51. $27p^{10} - 45p^9 - 252p^8$

52. $10m^2 + 25m - 60$

53. $4 - 2q - 6p + 3pq$

54. $k^2 - \dfrac{64}{121}$

55. $64p^2 - 100m^2$

56. $m^3 + 4m^2 - 6m - 24$

57. $100a^2 - 81y^2$

58. $8a^2 + 23ab - 3b^2$

59. $a^2 + 8a + 16$

60. $4y^2 - 25$

6.6 Solving Quadratic Equations by Factoring

Galileo Galilei (1564–1642) developed theories to explain physical phenomena and set up experiments to test his ideas. According to legend, Galileo dropped objects of different weights from the Leaning Tower of Pisa to disprove the belief that heavier objects fall faster than lighter objects. He developed a formula for freely falling objects described by $d = 16t^2$, where d is the distance in feet that an object falls (disregarding air resistance) in t seconds, regardless of weight.

The equation $d = 16t^2$ is a *quadratic equation.* A quadratic equation contains a squared term and no terms of higher degree.

> **Quadratic Equation**
>
> A **quadratic equation** is an equation that can be written in the form
> $$ax^2 + bx + c = 0,$$
> where a, b, and c are real numbers, with $a \neq 0$. The given form is called **standard form.**

$$x^2 + 5x + 6 = 0, \quad 2t^2 - 5t = 3, \quad y^2 = 4 \qquad \text{Quadratic equations}$$

In these examples, only $x^2 + 5x + 6 = 0$ is in standard form.

> **Work Problems 1 and 2 at the Side.** ▶▶▶

Up to now, we have factored *expressions,* including many quadratic expressions of the form $ax^2 + bx + c$. In this section, we use factored quadratic expressions to solve quadratic *equations.*

OBJECTIVE 1 Solve quadratic equations by factoring. We use the **zero-factor property** to solve a quadratic equation by factoring.

> **Zero-Factor Property**
>
> **If a and b are real numbers and $ab = 0$, then $a = 0$ or $b = 0$.**
>
> In words, if the product of two numbers is 0, then at least one of the numbers must be 0. One number *must* be 0, but both *may* be 0.

EXAMPLE 1 Using the Zero-Factor Property

Solve each equation.

(a) $(x + 3)(2x - 1) = 0$

The product $(x + 3)(2x - 1)$ is equal to 0. By the zero-factor property, the only way that the product of these two factors can be 0 is if at least one of the factors equals 0. Therefore, either $x + 3 = 0$ or $2x - 1 = 0$.

$$
\begin{array}{lll}
x + 3 = 0 & \text{or} \quad 2x - 1 = 0 & \text{Zero-factor property} \\
x = -3 & 2x = 1 & \text{Solve each equation.} \\
& x = \dfrac{1}{2} &
\end{array}
$$

Continued on Next Page

1 Which of the following equations are quadratic equations?

  A. $y^2 - 4y - 5 = 0$

  B. $x^3 - x^2 + 16 = 0$

  C. $2z^2 + 7z = -3$

  D. $x + 2y = -4$

2 Write each quadratic equation in standard form.

  (a) $x^2 - 3x = 4$

  (b) $y^2 = 9y - 8$

ANSWERS
1. A, C
2. (a) $x^2 - 3x - 4 = 0$
   (b) $y^2 - 9y + 8 = 0$

❸ Solve each equation. Check your solutions.

(a) $(x - 5)(x + 2) = 0$

(b) $(3x - 2)(x + 6) = 0$

(c) $z(2z + 5) = 0$

The given equation, $(x + 3)(2x - 1) = 0$, has two solutions, -3 and $\frac{1}{2}$. *Check* these solutions by substituting -3 for x in the original equation, $(x + 3)(2x - 1) = 0$. Then start over and substitute $\frac{1}{2}$ for x.

If $x = -3$, then

$$(x + 3)(2x - 1) = 0$$

$$(-3 + 3)[2(-3) - 1] = 0 \quad ?$$

$$0(-7) = 0. \quad \text{True}$$

If $x = \frac{1}{2}$, then

$$(x + 3)(2x - 1) = 0$$

$$\left(\frac{1}{2} + 3\right)\left(2 \cdot \frac{1}{2} - 1\right) = 0 \quad ?$$

$$\frac{7}{2}(1 - 1) = 0 \quad ?$$

$$\frac{7}{2} \cdot 0 = 0. \quad \text{True}$$

Both -3 and $\frac{1}{2}$ result in true equations, so they are solutions to the original equation.

(b)
$$y(3y - 4) = 0$$

$$y = 0 \quad \text{or} \quad 3y - 4 = 0 \quad \text{Zero-factor property}$$

$$3y = 4$$

$$y = \frac{4}{3}$$

Check these solutions by substituting each one in the original equation. The solutions are 0 and $\frac{4}{3}$.

◀◀◀ **Work Problem 3 at the Side.**

> **NOTE**
> The word *or* as used in Example 1 means "one or the other or both."

In Example 1, each equation to be solved was given with the polynomial in factored form. If the polynomial in an equation is not already factored, first make sure that the equation is in standard form. Then factor.

EXAMPLE 2 **Solving Quadratic Equations**

Solve each equation.

(a) $x^2 - 5x = -6$

First, write the equation in standard form by adding 6 to each side.

$$x^2 - 5x = -6$$

$$x^2 - 5x + 6 = 0 \quad \text{Add 6.}$$

Now factor $x^2 - 5x + 6$. Find two numbers whose product is 6 and whose sum is -5. These two numbers are -2 and -3, so the equation becomes

$$(x - 2)(x - 3) = 0. \quad \text{Factor.}$$

$$x - 2 = 0 \quad \text{or} \quad x - 3 = 0 \quad \text{Zero-factor property}$$

$$x = 2 \quad \text{or} \quad x = 3 \quad \text{Solve each equation.}$$

Continued on Next Page

Check: If $x = 2$, then

$$2^2 - 5(2) = -6 \quad ?$$
$$4 - 10 = -6 \quad ?$$
$$-6 = -6. \quad \text{True}$$

If $x = 3$, then

$$3^2 - 5(3) = -6 \quad ?$$
$$9 - 15 = -6 \quad ?$$
$$-6 = -6. \quad \text{True}$$

Both solutions check, so the solutions are 2 and 3.

(b)

$$y^2 = y + 20$$

$$y^2 - y - 20 = 0 \qquad \text{Write in standard form.}$$
$$(y - 5)(y + 4) = 0 \qquad \text{Factor.}$$
$$y - 5 = 0 \quad \text{or} \quad y + 4 = 0 \qquad \text{Zero-factor property}$$
$$y = 5 \quad \text{or} \qquad y = -4 \qquad \text{Solve each equation.}$$

Check the solutions 5 and -4 by substituting in the original equation.

Work Problem 4 at the Side. ▶▶▶

In summary, follow these steps to solve quadratic equations by factoring.

Solving a Quadratic Equation by Factoring

Step 1 **Write the equation in standard form,** that is, with all terms on one side of the equals sign in descending powers of the variable and 0 on the other side.

Step 2 **Factor** completely.

Step 3 **Use the zero-factor property** to set each factor with a variable equal to 0, and solve the resulting equations.

Step 4 **Check** each solution in the original equation.

EXAMPLE 3 **Solving a Quadratic Equation with a Common Factor**

Solve $4p^2 + 40 = 26p$.

$$4p^2 - 26p + 40 = 0 \qquad \text{Standard form}$$
$$2(2p^2 - 13p + 20) = 0 \qquad \text{Factor out 2.}$$
$$2p^2 - 13p + 20 = 0 \qquad \text{Divide each side by 2.}$$
$$(2p - 5)(p - 4) = 0 \qquad \text{Factor.}$$
$$2p - 5 = 0 \quad \text{or} \quad p - 4 = 0 \qquad \text{Zero-factor property}$$
$$2p = 5 \qquad\qquad p = 4 \qquad \text{Solve each equation.}$$
$$p = \frac{5}{2}$$

Check the solutions $\frac{5}{2}$ and 4 by substituting in the original equation.

CAUTION

A common error is to include the common factor 2 as a solution in Example 3. *Only factors containing **variables** lead to solutions.*

Work Problem 5 at the Side. ▶▶▶

④ Solve each equation. Check your solutions.

(a) $m^2 - 3m - 10 = 0$

(b) $r^2 + 2r = 8$

⑤ Solve each equation. Check your solutions.

(a) $10a^2 - 5a - 15 = 0$

(b) $4x^2 - 2x = 42$

ANSWERS

4. **(a)** $-2, 5$ **(b)** $-4, 2$

5. **(a)** $-1, \dfrac{3}{2}$ **(b)** $-3, \dfrac{7}{2}$

6 Solve each equation. Check your solutions.

(a) $49m^2 - 9 = 0$

(b) $p(4p + 7) = 2$

(c) $m^2 = 3m$

EXAMPLE 4 Solving Quadratic Equations

Solve each equation.

(a) $16m^2 - 25 = 0$

We can factor the left side of the equation as the difference of squares (**Section 6.5**).

$$16m^2 - 25 = 0$$

$$(4m + 5)(4m - 5) = 0 \qquad \text{Factor.}$$

$$4m + 5 = 0 \quad \text{or} \quad 4m - 5 = 0 \qquad \text{Zero-factor property}$$

$$4m = -5 \quad \text{or} \qquad 4m = 5 \qquad \text{Solve each equation.}$$

$$m = -\frac{5}{4} \quad \text{or} \qquad m = \frac{5}{4}$$

Check the solutions $-\frac{5}{4}$ and $\frac{5}{4}$ in the original equation.

(b) $k(2k + 5) = 3$

We need to write this equation in standard form.

$$k(2k + 5) = 3$$

$$2k^2 + 5k = 3 \qquad \text{Multiply.}$$

$$2k^2 + 5k - 3 = 0 \qquad \text{Subtract 3.}$$

$$(2k - 1)(k + 3) = 0 \qquad \text{Factor.}$$

$$2k - 1 = 0 \quad \text{or} \quad k + 3 = 0 \qquad \text{Zero-factor property}$$

$$2k = 1 \qquad \qquad k = -3$$

$$k = \frac{1}{2}$$

Check that the solutions are $\frac{1}{2}$ and -3.

(c) $y^2 = 2y$

$$y^2 - 2y = 0 \qquad \text{Standard form}$$

$$y(y - 2) = 0 \qquad \text{Factor.}$$

$$y = 0 \quad \text{or} \quad y - 2 = 0 \qquad \text{Zero-factor property}$$

$$y = 2$$

Check that the solutions are 0 and 2.

CAUTION

In Example 4(b), the zero-factor property could not be used to solve the equation $k(2k + 5) = 3$ in its given form because of the 3 on the right. *The zero-factor property applies only to a product that equals 0.*

In Example 4(c), it is tempting to begin by dividing each side of the equation $y^2 = 2y$ by y to get $y = 2$. Note that we do not get the other solution, 0, if we divide by a variable. (We *may* divide each side of an equation by a *nonzero* real number, however. For instance, in Example 3 we divided each side by 2.)

ANSWERS

6. (a) $-\frac{3}{7}, \frac{3}{7}$ **(b)** $-2, \frac{1}{4}$ **(c)** $0, 3$

Work Problem 6 at the Side.

NOTE
Not all quadratic equations can be solved by factoring. A more general method for solving such equations is given in **Chapter 9.**

OBJECTIVE **2** **Solve other equations by factoring.** We can also extend the zero-factor property to solve equations that involve more than two factors with variables, as shown in Examples 5 and 6. (These equations are *not* quadratic equations. Why not?)

EXAMPLE 5 **Solving an Equation with More Than Two Variable Factors**

Solve $6z^3 - 6z = 0$.

$$6z^3 - 6z = 0$$
$$6z(z^2 - 1) = 0 \qquad \text{Factor out } 6z.$$
$$6z(z + 1)(z - 1) = 0 \qquad \text{Factor } z^2 - 1.$$

By an extension of the zero-factor property, this product can equal 0 only if at least one of the factors equals 0. Write and solve three equations, one for each factor with a variable.

$$6z = 0 \quad \text{or} \quad z + 1 = 0 \quad \text{or} \quad z - 1 = 0$$
$$z = 0 \quad \text{or} \qquad z = -1 \quad \text{or} \qquad z = 1$$

Check by substituting, in turn, 0, -1, and 1 in the original equation. The solutions are 0, -1, and 1.

Work Problem 7 at the Side. ▶▶▶

EXAMPLE 6 **Solving an Equation with a Quadratic Factor**

Solve $(2x - 1)(x^2 - 9x + 20) = 0$.

$$(2x - 1)(x^2 - 9x + 20) = 0$$
$$(2x - 1)(x - 5)(x - 4) = 0 \qquad \text{Factor } x^2 - 9x + 20.$$
$$2x - 1 = 0 \quad \text{or} \quad x - 5 = 0 \quad \text{or} \quad x - 4 = 0 \qquad \text{Zero-factor property}$$
$$x = \frac{1}{2} \quad \text{or} \qquad x = 5 \quad \text{or} \qquad x = 4$$

Check. The solutions are $\frac{1}{2}$, 5, and 4.

Work Problem 8 at the Side. ▶▶▶

CAUTION
In Example 6, it would be unproductive to begin by multiplying the two factors together. Keep in mind that the zero-factor property and its extension requires the product of two or more factors to equal 0. Always consider first whether an equation is given in the appropriate form to apply the zero-factor property.

---

7 Solve each equation. Check your solutions.

(a) $r^3 - 16r = 0$

(b) $x^3 - 3x^2 - 18x = 0$

8 Solve each equation. Check your solutions.

(a) $(m + 3)(m^2 - 11m + 10) = 0$

(b) $(2x + 5)(4x^2 - 9) = 0$

ANSWERS
7. **(a)** $-4, 0, 4$ **(b)** $-3, 0, 6$
8. **(a)** $-3, 1, 10$ **(b)** $-\dfrac{5}{2}, -\dfrac{3}{2}, \dfrac{3}{2}$

Real-Data Applications

Factoring Trinomials Made Easy

To factor a trinomial using FOIL, we must find the *Outer* and *Inner* coefficients that sum to give the coefficient of the middle term. Our approach begins with a **key number,** found by multiplying the coefficients of the first and last terms of the trinomial. For the trinomial $6x^2 - x - 2$, for instance, the key number is -12 since $6(-2) = -12$.

Step 1 Display the factors of -12 by entering $Y_1 = -12/X$ in a graphing calculator (Screen 1), and using an automatic table (Screen 2). Factors of -12 are automatically displayed in pairs as $1, -12$; $2, -6$; $3, -4$; $4, -3$; and $6, -2$ (Screen 3). You could scroll up or down to find other factors. Note that $5, -2.4$ and $7, -1.714$ are not acceptable factor pairs since -2.4 and -1.714 are not integers.

| Screen 1 | Screen 2 | Screen 3 | Screen 4 | Screen 5 |

Step 2 Find the pair of factors that sum to the *middle* term coefficient, -1. We can let the calculator do this, too. Enter $Y_2 = X + -12/X$ (Screen 4). In this case, X is one of the factors, and $-12/X$ is the other, so Y_2 will give the sum. Look for -1 in the Y_2 column in Screen 5. (You may have to scroll up or down to find it.)

Step 3 Screen 5 shows that the coefficients of the outer and inner products are 3 and -4. Write $6x^2 - x - 2$ as $6x^2 + 3x - 4x - 2$. Using factoring by grouping,

$$(6x^2 + 3x) + (-4x - 2) = 3x(2x + 1) - 2(2x + 1)$$
$$= (2x + 1)(3x - 2).$$

For Group Discussion

Factor each trinomial given in the column heads of the table. First find the key number, and then use a calculator to find the coefficients of the outer and inner products of FOIL. Finally, factor by grouping.

Trinomial	$3x^2 - 2x - 8$	$2x^2 - 11x + 15$	$10x^2 + 11x - 6$	$4x^2 + 5x + 3$
Key Number	-24 (Why?)			
Outer, Inner Coefficients				
Factor by Grouping				(*Hint:* What does it mean if the middle term coefficient is *not* listed in the Y_2 column?)

6.6 Exercises

Solve each equation, and check your solutions. See Example 1.

1. $(x + 5)(x - 2) = 0$

2. $(x - 1)(x + 8) = 0$

3. $(2m - 7)(m - 3) = 0$

4. $(6k + 5)(k + 4) = 0$

5. $t(6t + 5) = 0$

6. $w(4w + 1) = 0$

7. $2x(3x - 4) = 0$

8. $6x(4x + 9) = 0$

9. $\left(x + \dfrac{1}{2}\right)\left(2x - \dfrac{1}{3}\right) = 0$

10. $\left(a + \dfrac{2}{3}\right)\left(5a - \dfrac{1}{2}\right) = 0$

11. $(.5z - 1)(2.5z + 2) = 0$

12. $(.25x + 1)(x - .5) = 0$

13. $(x - 9)(x - 9) = 0$

14. $(2x + 1)(2x + 1) = 0$

15. What is wrong with this "solution"?
$$2x(3x - 4) = 0$$
$$x = 2 \quad \text{or} \quad x = 0 \quad \text{or} \quad 3x - 4 = 0$$
$$x = \frac{4}{3}$$
The solutions are 2, 0, and $\frac{4}{3}$.

16. What is wrong with this "solution"?
$$x(7x - 1) = 0$$
$$7x - 1 = 0 \qquad \text{Zero-factor property}$$
$$x = \frac{1}{7}$$
The solution is $\frac{1}{7}$.

Solve each equation, and check your solutions. See Examples 2–6.

17. $y^2 + 3y + 2 = 0$

18. $p^2 + 8p + 7 = 0$

19. $y^2 - 3y + 2 = 0$

20. $r^2 - 4r + 3 = 0$

21. $x^2 = 24 - 5x$

22. $t^2 = 2t + 15$

23. $x^2 = 3 + 2x$

24. $m^2 = 4 + 3m$

25. $z^2 + 3z = -2$

26. $p^2 - 2p = 3$

27. $m^2 + 8m + 16 = 0$

28. $b^2 - 6b + 9 = 0$

29. $3x^2 + 5x - 2 = 0$

30. $6r^2 - r - 2 = 0$

31. $6p^2 = 4 - 5p$

32. $6x^2 = 4 + 5x$

33. $9s^2 + 12s = -4$

34. $36x^2 + 60x = -25$

35. $y^2 - 9 = 0$

36. $m^2 - 100 = 0$

37. $16k^2 - 49 = 0$

38. $4w^2 - 9 = 0$

39. $n^2 = 121$

40. $x^2 = 400$

41. $x^2 = 7x$

42. $t^2 = 9t$

43. $6r^2 = 3r$

44. $10y^2 = -5y$

45. $g(g - 7) = -10$

46. $r(r - 5) = -6$

47. $z(2z + 7) = 4$

48. $b(2b + 3) = 9$

49. $2(y^2 - 66) = -13y$

50. $3(t^2 + 4) = 20t$

51. $5x^3 - 20x = 0$

52. $3x^3 - 48x = 0$

53. $9y^3 - 49y = 0$

54. $16r^3 - 9r = 0$

55. $(2r + 5)(3r^2 - 16r + 5) = 0$

56. $(3m + 4)(6m^2 + m - 2) = 0$

57. $(2x + 7)(x^2 + 2x - 3) = 0$

58. $(x + 1)(6x^2 + x - 12) = 0$

59. Galileo's formula for freely falling objects, $d = 16t^2$, was given at the beginning of this section. The distance d in feet an object falls depends on the time elapsed t in seconds. (This is an example of an important mathematical concept, a *function*.)

   (a) Use Galileo's formula and complete the following table. (*Hint:* Substitute each given value into the formula and solve for the unknown value.)

t in seconds	0	1	2	3		
d in feet	0	16			256	576

   (b) When $t = 0$, $d = 0$. Explain this in the context of the problem.

   (c) When you substituted 256 for d and solved for t, you should have found two solutions, 4 and -4. Why doesn't -4 make sense as an answer?

6.7 Applications of Quadratic Equations

We can use factoring to solve quadratic equations that arise in applications. We follow the same six problem-solving steps given in **Section 2.4**.

OBJECTIVES

1 Solve problems about geometric figures.

2 Solve problems about consecutive integers.

3 Solve problems using the Pythagorean formula.

4 Solve problems using given quadratic models.

Solving an Applied Problem

Step 1 **Read** the problem, several times if necessary, until you *understand* what is given and what is to be found.

Step 2 **Assign a variable** to represent the unknown value, using diagrams or tables as needed. Write down what the variable represents. Express any other unknown values in terms of the variable.

Step 3 **Write an equation** using the variable expression(s).

Step 4 **Solve** the equation.

Step 5 **State the answer.** Does it seem reasonable?

Step 6 **Check** the answer in the words of the original problem.

OBJECTIVE 1 Solve problems about geometric figures. Some of the applied problems in this section require one of the formulas given on the inside covers of the text.

EXAMPLE 1 Solving an Area Problem

The Monroes want to plant a rectangular garden in their yard. The width of the garden will be 4 ft less than its length, and they want it to have an area of 96 ft^2. (ft^2 means square feet.) Find the length and width of the garden.

Step 1 **Read** the problem carefully. We need to find the dimensions of a garden with area 96 ft^2.

Step 2 **Assign a variable.**

Let x = the length of the garden.

Then $x - 4$ = the width. (The width is 4 ft less than the length.)

See Figure 1.

Figure 1

Step 3 **Write an equation.** The area of a rectangle is given by

$$Area = LW = Length \times Width. \quad \text{Area formula}$$

Substitute 96 for area, x for length, and $x - 4$ for width.

$$A = LW$$
$$96 = x(x - 4) \quad \text{Let } A = 96, L = x, W = x - 4.$$

Continued on Next Page

1 Solve each problem.

(a) The length of a rectangular room is 2 m more than the width. The area of the floor is 48 m^2. Find the length and width of the room.

x

$x + 2$

Step 4 **Solve.**

$$96 = x^2 - 4x \qquad \text{Distributive property}$$
$$0 = x^2 - 4x - 96 \qquad \text{Standard form}$$
$$0 = (x - 12)(x + 8) \qquad \text{Factor.}$$
$$x - 12 = 0 \quad \text{or} \quad x + 8 = 0 \qquad \text{Zero-factor property}$$
$$x = 12 \quad \text{or} \qquad x = -8$$

Step 5 **State the answer.** The solutions are 12 and -8. A rectangle cannot have a side of negative length, so discard -8. The length of the garden will be 12 ft. The width will be $12 - 4 = 8$ ft.

Step 6 **Check.** The width is 4 ft less than the length; the area is $12 \cdot 8 = 96 \text{ ft}^2$.

> **CAUTION**
> When solving applied problems, ***always check solutions*** against physical facts and discard any answers that are not appropriate.

◀◀◀ **Work Problem 1 at the Side.**

OBJECTIVE 2 Solve problems about consecutive integers. Recall from **Section 2.4** that **consecutive integers** are integers that are next to each other on a number line, such as 5 and 6, or -11 and -10. **Consecutive odd integers** are *odd* integers that are next to each other, such as 5 and 7, or -13 and -11. **Consecutive even integers** are defined similarly; for example, 4 and 6 are consecutive even integers, as are -10 and -8.

(b) The length of each side of a square is increased by 4 in. The sum of the areas of the original square and the larger square is 106 in^2. What is the length of a side of the original square?

> **PROBLEM-SOLVING HINT**
> In consecutive integer problems, if x represents the first integer, then for
> two consecutive integers, use $x, \quad x + 1;$
> three consecutive integers, use $x, \quad x + 1, \quad x + 2;$
> two consecutive even or odd integers, use $x, \quad x + 2;$
> three consecutive even or odd integers, use $x, \quad x + 2, \quad x + 4.$

EXAMPLE 2 Solving a Consecutive Integer Problem

The product of the numbers on two consecutive post-office boxes is 210. Find the box numbers.

Step 1 **Read** the problem. Note that the boxes are numbered consecutively.

Step 2 **Assign a variable.**

     Let $x =$ the first box number.

     Then $x + 1 =$ the next consecutive box number.

     See Figure 2.

x $x + 1$

Figure 2

Step 3 **Write an equation.** The product of the box numbers is 210, so

$$x(x + 1) = 210.$$

ANSWERS
1. **(a)** length: 8 m; width: 6 m   **(b)** 5 in.

— **Continued on Next Page**

Step 4   **Solve.**

$$x(x + 1) = 210$$

$$x^2 + x = 210 \qquad \text{Distributive property}$$

$$x^2 + x - 210 = 0 \qquad \text{Standard form}$$

$$(x + 15)(x - 14) = 0 \qquad \text{Factor.}$$

$$x + 15 = 0 \quad \text{or} \quad x - 14 = 0 \qquad \text{Zero-factor property}$$

$$x = -15 \quad \text{or} \qquad x = 14$$

Step 5   **State the answer.** The solutions are -15 and 14. Discard the solution -15 since a box number cannot be negative. When $x = 14$, then $x + 1 = 15$, so the post-office boxes have the numbers 14 and 15.

Step 6   **Check.** The numbers 14 and 15 are consecutive and their product is $14 \cdot 15 = 210$, as required.

> **Work Problem 2 at the Side.** ⟩⟩⟩

2 Solve the problem.
   The product of the numbers on two consecutive lockers at a health club is 132. Find the locker numbers.

EXAMPLE 3   **Solving a Consecutive Integer Problem**

The product of two consecutive odd integers is 1 less than five times their sum. Find the integers.

Step 1   **Read** carefully. This problem is a little more complicated.

Step 2   **Assign a variable.** We must find two consecutive *odd* integers.

> Let $x = $ the smaller integer.
>
> Then $x + 2 = $ the next larger odd integer.

Step 3   **Write an equation.** According to the problem, the product is 1 less than five times the sum.

The product	is	five times the sum	less 1.
↓	↓	↓	↓
$x(x + 2)$	$=$	$5(x + x + 2)$	$- \ 1$

Step 4   **Solve.**

$$x^2 + 2x = 5x + 5x + 10 - 1 \qquad \text{Distributive property}$$

$$x^2 + 2x = 10x + 9 \qquad \text{Combine like terms.}$$

$$x^2 - 8x - 9 = 0 \qquad \text{Standard form}$$

$$(x - 9)(x + 1) = 0 \qquad \text{Factor.}$$

$$x - 9 = 0 \quad \text{or} \quad x + 1 = 0 \qquad \text{Zero-factor property}$$

$$x = 9 \quad \text{or} \qquad x = -1$$

Step 5   **State the answer.** We need to find two consecutive odd integers.

If $x = 9$ is the smaller, then $x + 2 = 9 + 2 = 11$ is the larger.

If $x = -1$ is the smaller, then $x + 2 = -1 + 2 = 1$ is the larger.

There are two sets of answers here since integers can be positive or negative.

Step 6   **Check.** The product of the first pair of integers is $9 \cdot 11 = 99$. One less than five times their sum is $5(9 + 11) - 1 = 99$. Thus 9 and 11 satisfy the problem. Repeat the check with -1 and 1.

> **Work Problem 3 at the Side.** ⟩⟩⟩

3 Solve each problem.

   (a) The product of two consecutive even integers is 4 more than two times their sum. Find the integers.

   (b) Find three consecutive odd integers such that the product of the smallest and largest is 16 more than the middle integer.

CAUTION
Do *not* use $x, x + 1, x + 3$, and so on to represent consecutive odd integers. To see why, let $x = 3$. Then $x + 1 = 3 + 1 = 4$ and $x + 3 = 3 + 3 = 6$, and 3, 4, and 6 are not consecutive odd integers.

OBJECTIVE 3 Solve problems using the Pythagorean formula. The next example requires the Pythagorean formula from geometry.

Pythagorean Formula

If a right triangle (a triangle with a 90° angle) has longest side of length c and two other sides of lengths a and b, then

$$a^2 + b^2 = c^2.$$

The longest side, the **hypotenuse,** is opposite the right angle. The two shorter sides are the **legs** of the triangle.

EXAMPLE 4 Using the Pythagorean Formula

Ed and Mark leave their office, with Ed traveling north and Mark traveling east. When Mark is 1 mi farther than Ed from the office, the distance between them is 2 mi more than Ed's distance from the office. Find their distances from the office and the distance between them.

Step 1 **Read** the problem again. We must find three distances.

Step 2 **Assign a variable.** Let x represent Ed's distance from the office, $x + 1$ represent Mark's distance from the office, and $x + 2$ represent the distance between them. Place these on a right triangle, as in Figure 3.

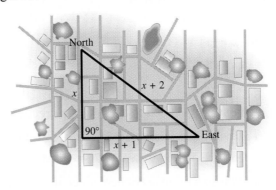

Figure 3

Step 3 **Write an equation.** Substitute into the Pythagorean formula.

$$a^2 + b^2 = c^2$$
$$x^2 + (x + 1)^2 = (x + 2)^2$$

Continued on Next Page

Step 4 **Solve.**
$$x^2 + x^2 + 2x + 1 = x^2 + 4x + 4$$
$$x^2 - 2x - 3 = 0 \qquad \text{Standard form}$$
$$(x - 3)(x + 1) = 0 \qquad \text{Factor.}$$
$$x - 3 = 0 \quad \text{or} \quad x + 1 = 0 \qquad \text{Zero-factor property}$$
$$x = 3 \quad \text{or} \qquad x = -1$$

Step 5 **State the answer.** Since -1 cannot represent a distance, 3 is the only possible answer. Ed's distance is 3 mi, Mark's distance is $3 + 1 = 4$ mi, and the distance between them is $3 + 2 = 5$ mi.

Step 6 **Check.** Since $3^2 + 4^2 = 5^2$, the answer is correct.

CAUTION

When solving a problem involving the Pythagorean formula, be sure that the expressions for the sides are properly placed.

$$\textbf{leg}^2 + \textbf{leg}^2 = \textbf{hypotenuse}^2$$

Work Problem 4 at the Side. ▶▶▶

OBJECTIVE 4 Solve problems using given quadratic models. In Examples 1–4, we wrote quadratic equations to model, or mathematically describe, various situations and then solved the equations. Now we are given the quadratic models and must use them to determine data.

EXAMPLE 5 Finding the Height of a Ball

A tennis player can hit a ball 180 ft per sec (125 mph). If she hits a ball directly upward, the height h of the ball in feet at time t in seconds is modeled by the quadratic equation

$$h = -16t^2 + 180t + 6.$$

How long will it take for the ball to reach a height of 206 ft?

A height of 206 ft means $h = 206$, so we substitute 206 for h in the equation and then solve for t.

$$206 = -16t^2 + 180t + 6 \qquad \text{Let } h = 206.$$
$$-16t^2 + 180t + 6 = 206 \qquad \text{Interchange sides.}$$
$$-16t^2 + 180t - 200 = 0 \qquad \text{Standard form}$$
$$4t^2 - 45t + 50 = 0 \qquad \text{Divide by } -4.$$
$$(4t - 5)(t - 10) = 0 \qquad \text{Factor.}$$
$$4t - 5 = 0 \quad \text{or} \quad t - 10 = 0 \qquad \text{Zero-factor property}$$
$$t = \frac{5}{4} \quad \text{or} \qquad t = 10$$

Since we found two acceptable answers, the ball will be 206 ft above the ground twice (once on its way up and once on its way down)—at $\frac{5}{4}$ sec and at 10 sec. See Figure 4.

206 ft

Figure 4

Work Problem 5 at the Side. ▶▶▶

4 Solve the problem.

The hypotenuse of a right triangle is 3 in. longer than the longer leg. The shorter leg is 3 in. shorter than the longer leg. Find the lengths of the sides of the triangle.

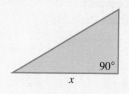

5 Solve the problem.

The number of impulses fired after a nerve has been stimulated is modeled by

$$I = -x^2 + 2x + 60,$$

where x is in milliseconds (ms) after the stimulation. When will 45 impulses occur? Do you get two solutions? Why is only one answer given?

ANSWERS
4. 9 in., 12 in., 15 in.
5. After 5 ms; There are two solutions, -3 and 5; Only one answer makes sense here because a negative answer is not appropriate.

6 Solve the problem.

Use the model in Example 6 to find the annual percent increase in spending on hospital services in 1995. Give your answer to the nearest tenth. How does it compare to the actual data from the table?

EXAMPLE 6 Modeling Increases in Hospital Costs

The annual percent increase y in spending on hospital services in the years 1994–2001 can be modeled by the quadratic equation

$$y = .37x^2 - 4.1x + 12,$$

where $x = 4$ represents 1994, $x = 5$ represents 1995, and so on. (*Source:* Center for Studying Health System Change.)

(a) Use the model to find the annual percent increase to the nearest tenth in 1997.

Since $x = 4$ represents 1994, $x = 7$ represents 1997. Substitute 7 for x in the equation.

$$y = .37(7)^2 - 4.1(7) + 12 \quad \text{Let } x = 7.$$

$$y = 1.4 \qquad\qquad\qquad \text{Round to the nearest tenth.}$$

Spending on hospital services increased about 1.4% in 1997.

(b) Repeat part (a) for 2001.

$$y = .37(11)^2 - 4.1(11) + 12 \quad \text{For 2001, let } x = 11.$$

$$y = 11.7$$

In 2001, spending on hospital services increased about 11.7%.

(c) The model used in parts (a) and (b) was developed using the data in the table below. How do the results in parts (a) and (b) compare to the actual data from the table?

Year	Percent Increase
1994	1.8
1995	.8
1996	.5
1997	1.3
1998	3.4
1999	5.8
2000	7.1
2001	12.0

From the table, the actual data for 1997 is 1.3%. Our answer, 1.4%, is slightly high. For 2001, the actual data is 12.0%, so our answer of 11.7% in part (b) is a little low.

◀◀◀ **Work Problem 6 at the Side.**

NOTE

A graph of the quadratic equation from Example 6 is shown in Figure 5. Notice the basic shape of this graph, which follows the general pattern of the data in the table—it decreases from 1994 to 1996 and then increases from 1997 to 2001. We consider such graphs of quadratic equations, called *parabolas,* in **Chapter 9.**

Our data is for $x = 4$ to $x = 11$.

Figure 5

6.7 Exercises

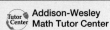
1. To review the six problem-solving steps first introduced in **Section 2.4,** complete each statement.

   Step 1: _____ the problem, several times if necessary, until you understand what is given and what must be found.

   Step 2: Assign a _____ to represent the unknown value.

   Step 3: Write a(n) _____ using the variable expression(s).

   Step 4: _____ the equation.

   Step 5: State the _____.

   Step 6: _____ the answer in the words of the _____ problem.

2. A student solves an applied problem and gets 6 or -3 for the length of the side of a square. Which of these answers is reasonable? Explain.

In Exercises 3–6, a figure and a corresponding geometric formula are given. Using x as the variable, complete Steps 3–6 for each problem. (Refer to the steps in Exercise 1 as needed.)

3.

$x + 1$

$2x + 1$

Area of a parallelogram: $A = bh$

The area of this parallelogram is 45 sq. units. Find its base and height.

4.
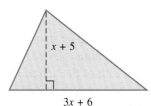
$x + 5$

$3x + 6$

Area of a triangle: $A = \frac{1}{2}bh$

The area of this triangle is 60 sq. units. Find its base and height.

5.

$x - 8$

$x + 8$

Area of a rectangular rug: $A = LW$

The area of this rug is 80 sq. units. Find its length and width.

6.

4

x $x + 2$

Volume of a rectangular Chinese box: $V = LWH$

The volume of this box is 192 cu. units. Find its length and width.

Solve each problem. Check your answers to be sure they are reasonable. Refer to the formulas on the inside covers. See Example 1.

7. The length of a VHS videocassette shell is 3 in. more than its width. The area of the rectangular top side of the shell is 28 in.^{2}. Find the length and width of the videocassette shell.

8. A plastic box that holds a standard audiocassette has length 4 cm longer than its width. The area of the rectangular top of the box is 77 cm^2. Find the length and width of the box.

9. The dimensions of a Gateway EV700 computer monitor screen are such that its length is 3 in. more than its width. If the length is increased by 1 in. while the width remains the same, the area is increased by 10 in.^{2}. What are the dimensions of the screen? (*Source:* Author's computer.)

10. The keyboard of the computer in Exercise 9 is 11 in. longer than it is wide. If both its length and width are increased by 2 in., the area of the top of the keyboard is increased by 54 in.^{2}. Find the length and width of the keyboard. (*Source:* Author's computer.)

11. A ten-gallon aquarium is 3 in. higher than it is wide. Its length is 21 in., and its volume is 2730 in.^{3}. What are the height and width of the aquarium?

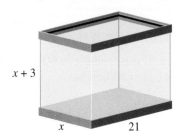

12. A toolbox is 2 ft high, and its width is 3 ft less than its length. If its volume is 80 ft^3, find the length and width of the box.

13. A square mirror has sides measuring 2 ft less than the sides of a square painting. If the difference between their areas is 32 ft^2, find the lengths of the sides of the mirror and the painting.

14. The sides of one square have length 3 m more than the sides of a second square. If the area of the larger square is subtracted from 4 times the area of the smaller square, the result is 36 m^2. What are the lengths of the sides of each square?

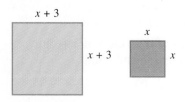

Solve each problem about consecutive integers. See Examples 2 and 3.

15. The product of the numbers on two consecutive volumes of research data is 420. Find the volume numbers.

16. The product of the page numbers on two facing pages of a book is 600. Find the page numbers.

17. The product of two consecutive integers is 11 more than their sum. Find the integers.

18. The product of two consecutive integers is 4 less than four times their sum. Find the integers.

19. Find two consecutive odd integers such that their product is 15 more than three times their sum.

20. Find two consecutive odd integers such that five times their sum is 23 less than their product.

21. Find three consecutive even integers such that the sum of the squares of the smaller two is equal to the square of the largest.

22. Find three consecutive even integers such that the square of the sum of the smaller two is equal to twice the largest.

Use the Pythagorean formula to solve each problem. See Example 4.

23. The hypotenuse of a right triangle is 1 cm longer than the longer leg. The shorter leg is 7 cm shorter than the longer leg. Find the length of the longer leg of the triangle.

24. The longer leg of a right triangle is 1 m longer than the shorter leg. The hypotenuse is 1 m shorter than twice the shorter leg. Find the length of the shorter leg of the triangle.

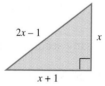

25. Terri works due north of home. Her husband Denny works due east. They leave for work at the same time. By the time Terri is 5 mi from home, the distance between them is 1 mi more than Denny's distance from home. How far from home is Denny?

26. Two cars left an intersection at the same time. One traveled north. The other traveled 14 mi farther, but to the east. How far apart were they then, if the distance between them was 4 mi more than the distance traveled east?

27. A ladder is leaning against a building. The distance from the bottom of the ladder to the building is 4 ft less than the length of the ladder. How high up the side of the building is the top of the ladder if that distance is 2 ft less than the length of the ladder?

28. A lot has the shape of a right triangle with one leg 2 m longer than the other. The hypotenuse is 2 m less than twice the length of the shorter leg. Find the length of the shorter leg.

Solve each problem. See Examples 5 and 6.

29. An object propelled from a height of 48 ft with an initial velocity of 32 ft per sec after t seconds has height

$$h = -16t^2 + 32t + 48.$$

48 ft

(a) After how many seconds is the height 64 ft? (*Hint:* Let $h = 64$ and solve.)

(b) After how many seconds is the height 60 ft?

(c) After how many seconds does the object hit the ground? (*Hint:* When the object hits the ground, $h = 0$.)

(d) The quadratic equation from part (c) has two solutions, yet only one of them is appropriate for answering the question. Why is this so?

30. If an object is propelled upward from ground level with an initial velocity of 64 ft per sec, its height h in feet t seconds later is

$$h = -16t^2 + 64t.$$

(a) After how many seconds is the height 48 ft?

(b) The object reaches its maximum height 2 sec after it is propelled. What is this maximum height?

(c) After how many seconds does the object hit the ground?

(d) The quadratic equation from part (c) has two solutions, yet only one of them is appropriate for answering the question. Why is this so?

31. The table shows the number of cellular phones (in millions) owned by Americans.

Year	Cellular Phones (in millions)
1990	5
1992	11
1994	24
1996	44
1998	62
2000	109
2002	140

Source: Cellular Telecommunications
Industry Association.

We used the data to develop the quadratic equation

$$y = .866x^2 + 1.02x + 5.29,$$

which models the number of cellular phones y (in millions) in the year x, where $x = 0$ represents 1990, $x = 2$ represents 1992, and so on.

(a) Use the model to find the number of cellular phones in 1996 to the nearest tenth. How does the result compare to the actual data in the table?

(b) What value of x corresponds to 2002?

(c) Use the model to find the number of cellular phones in 2002 to the nearest tenth. How does the result compare to the actual data in the table?

(d) Assuming that the trend in the data continues, use the quadratic equation to predict the number of cellular phones in 2005 to the nearest tenth.

RELATING CONCEPTS (EXERCISES 32–40)   For Individual or Group Work

The U.S. trade deficit represents the amount by which exports are less than imports. It provides not only a sign of economic prosperity but also a warning of potential decline. The data in the table shows the U.S. trade deficit for 1995 through 2000.

Year	Deficit (in billions of dollars)
1995	97.5
1996	104.3
1997	104.7
1998	164.3
1999	271.3
2000	378.7

Source: U.S. Department of Commerce.

*Use the data to **work Exercises 32–40 in order.***

32. How much did the trade deficit increase from 1999 to 2000? What percent increase is this (to the nearest percent)?

33. The U.S. trade deficit might be approximated by the linear equation

$$y = 40.8x + 66.9,$$

where y is the deficit in billions of dollars. Here $x = 0$ represents 1995, $x = 1$ represents 1996, and so on. Use this equation to approximate the trade deficits in 1997, 1999, and 2000.

34. How do your answers from Exercise 33 compare to the actual data in the table?

35. The trade deficit y (in billions of dollars) might also be approximated by the quadratic equation

$$y = 18.5x^2 - 33.4x + 104,$$

where $x = 0$ again represents 1995, $x = 1$ represents 1996, and so on. Use this equation to approximate the trade deficits in 1997, 1999, and 2000.

36. Compare your answers from Exercise 35 to the actual data in the table. Which equation, the linear one in Exercise 33 or the quadratic one in Exercise 35, models the data better?

37. We can also see graphically why the linear equation is not a very good model for the data. To do so, write the data from the table as a set of ordered pairs (x, y), where x represents the years since 1995 and y represents the trade deficit in billions of dollars.

38. Plot the ordered pairs from Exercise 37 on the graph.

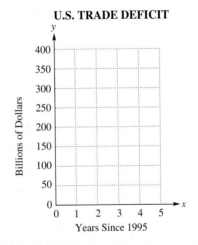

U.S. TRADE DEFICIT

Recall from **Chapter 3** that a linear equation has a straight line for its graph. Do the ordered pairs you plotted lie in a linear pattern?

39. Assuming that the trend in the data continues and since the quadratic equation modeled that data fairly well, use the quadratic equation to predict the trade deficit for the year 2002.

40. The actual trade deficit for 2002 was 417.9 billion dollars.

   (a) How does the actual deficit for 2002 compare to your prediction from Exercise 39?

   (b) Should the quadratic equation be used to predict the U.S. trade deficit for years after 2000? Explain.

Chapter 6

SUMMARY

KEY TERMS

6.1

factor An expression A is a factor of an expression B if B can be divided by A with 0 remainder.

factored form An expression is in factored form when it is written as a product.

greatest common factor (GCF) The greatest common factor is the largest quantity that is a factor of each of a group of quantities.

factoring The process of writing a polynomial as a product is called factoring.

6.2 prime polynomial A prime polynomial is a polynomial that cannot be factored using only integers.

6.5 perfect square trinomial A perfect square trinomial is a trinomial that can be factored as the square of a binomial.

6.6 quadratic equation A quadratic equation is an equation that can be written in the form $ax^2 + bx + c = 0$, with $a \neq 0$.

standard form The form $ax^2 + bx + c = 0$ is the standard form of a quadratic equation.

6.7 hypotenuse The longest side of a right triangle, opposite the right angle, is the hypotenuse.

legs The two shorter sides of a right triangle are the legs.

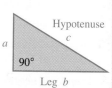

TEST YOUR WORD POWER

See how well you have learned the vocabulary in this chapter. Answers, with examples, follow the Quick Review.

1. **Factoring** is
   A. a method of multiplying polynomials
   B. the process of writing a polynomial as a product
   C. the answer in a multiplication problem
   D. a way to add the terms of a polynomial.

2. A polynomial is in **factored form** when
   A. it is prime
   B. it is written as a sum
   C. the squared term has a coefficient of 1
   D. it is written as a product.

3. The **greatest common factor** of a polynomial is
   A. the least integer that divides evenly into all the terms of the polynomial
   B. the least term that is a factor of all the terms in the polynomial
   C. the greatest term that is a factor of all the terms in the polynomial
   D. the variable that is common to all the terms in the polynomial.

4. A **perfect square trinomial** is a trinomial
   A. that can be factored as the square of a binomial
   B. that cannot be factored
   C. that is multiplied by a binomial
   D. where all terms are perfect squares.

5. A **quadratic equation** is an equation that can be written in the form
   A. $y = mx + b$
   B. $ax^2 + bx + c = 0 \ (a \neq 0)$
   C. $Ax + By = C$
   D. $x = k$.

6. A **hypotenuse** is
   A. either of the two shorter sides of a triangle
   B. the shortest side of a right triangle
   C. the side opposite the right angle in a right triangle
   D. the longest side in any triangle.

QUICK REVIEW

Concepts	Examples

6.1 *Factors; The Greatest Common Factor*
Finding the Greatest Common Factor (GCF)

Step 1 Write each number in prime factored form.

Step 2 List each prime number or each variable that is a factor of every term in the list.

Step 3 Use as exponents on the common prime factors the least exponents from the prime factored forms.

Step 4 Multiply the primes from Step 3.

Find the greatest common factor of $4x^2y$, $-6x^2y^3$, and $2xy^2$.

$$4x^2y = 2 \cdot 2 \cdot x^2 \cdot y$$
$$-6x^2y^3 = -1 \cdot 2 \cdot 3 \cdot x^2 \cdot y^3$$
$$2xy^2 = 2 \cdot x \cdot y^2$$

The greatest common factor is $2xy$.

Factoring by Grouping

Step 1 Group the terms.

Step 2 Factor out the greatest common factor from each group.

Step 3 Factor a common binomial factor from the results of Step 2.

Step 4 If necessary, rearrange terms and try a different grouping.

Factor by grouping.

$$2a^2 + 2ab + a + b = (2a^2 + 2ab) + (a + b)$$
$$= 2a(a + b) + 1(a + b)$$
$$= (a + b)(2a + 1)$$

6.2 *Factoring Trinomials*
To factor $x^2 + bx + c$, find m and n such that $mn = c$ and $m + n = b$.

$$x^2 + bx + c$$

with $mn = c$ and $m + n = b$

Then $x^2 + bx + c = (x + m)(x + n)$.

Check by multiplying.

Factor $x^2 + 6x + 8$.

$$x^2 + 6x + 8$$

with $mn = 8$ and $m + n = 6$

$m = 2$ and $n = 4$

$x^2 + 6x + 8 = (x + 2)(x + 4)$

Check: $(x + 2)(x + 4) = x^2 + 4x + 2x + 8$
$$= x^2 + 6x + 8$$

6.3 *Factoring Trinomials by Grouping*
To factor $ax^2 + bx + c$ by grouping, first find m and n.

$$ax^2 + bx + c$$

with $m + n = b$ and $mn = ac$

Then factor $ax^2 + mx + nx + b$ by grouping.

Factor $3x^2 + 14x - 5$.

-15

Find two integers with a product of $3(-5) = -15$ and a sum of 14. The integers are -1 and 15.

$$3x^2 + 14x - 5 = 3x^2 - x + 15x - 5$$
$$= (3x^2 - x) + (15x - 5)$$
$$= x(3x - 1) + 5(3x - 1)$$
$$= (3x - 1)(x + 5)$$

Concepts	*Examples*
6.4 *Factoring Trinomials Using FOIL* To factor $ax^2 + bx + c$ by trial and error, use FOIL backwards.	By trial and error, $$3x^2 + 14x - 5 = (3x - 1)(x + 5).$$
6.5 *Special Factoring Techniques* **Difference of Squares** $$a^2 - b^2 = (a + b)(a - b)$$ **Perfect Square Trinomials** $$a^2 + 2ab + b^2 = (a + b)^2$$ $$a^2 - 2ab + b^2 = (a - b)^2$$	Factor. $$4x^2 - 9 = (2x + 3)(2x - 3)$$ $$9x^2 + 6x + 1 = (3x + 1)^2$$ $$4x^2 - 20x + 25 = (2x - 5)^2$$
6.6 *Solving Quadratic Equations by Factoring* **Zero-Factor Property** If a and b are real numbers and $ab = 0$, then $a = 0$ or $b = 0$. **Solving a Quadratic Equation by Factoring** *Step 1* Write the equation in standard form. *Step 2* Factor. *Step 3* Use the zero-factor property. *Step 4* Check.	If $(x - 2)(x + 3) = 0$, then $x - 2 = 0$ or $x + 3 = 0$. Solve $2x^2 = 7x + 15$. $$2x^2 - 7x - 15 = 0$$ $$(2x + 3)(x - 5) = 0$$ $$2x + 3 = 0 \quad \text{or} \quad x - 5 = 0$$ $$2x = -3 \qquad\qquad x = 5$$ $$x = -\frac{3}{2}$$ The solutions $-\frac{3}{2}$ and 5 satisfy the original equation.
6.7 *Applications of Quadratic Equations* **Pythagorean Formula** In a right triangle, the square of the hypotenuse equals the sum of the squares of the legs. $$a^2 + b^2 = c^2$$ 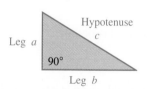	In a right triangle, one leg measures 2 ft longer than the other. The hypotenuse measures 4 ft longer than the shorter leg. Find the lengths of the three sides of the triangle. Let x = the length of the shorter leg. Then $$x^2 + (x + 2)^2 = (x + 4)^2.$$ Solve this equation to get $x = 6$ or $x = -2$. Discard -2 as a solution. Check that the sides measure 6 ft, $6 + 2 = 8$ ft, and $6 + 4 = 10$ ft.

ANSWERS TO TEST YOUR WORD POWER

1. B; *Example:* $x^2 - 5x - 14 = (x - 7)(x + 2)$
2. D; *Example:* The factored form of $x^2 - 5x - 14$ is $(x - 7)(x + 2)$.
3. C; *Example:* The greatest common factor of $8x^2$, $22xy$, and $16x^3y^2$ is $2x$.
4. A; *Example:* $a^2 + 2a + 1$ is a perfect square trinomial; its factored form is $(a + 1)^2$.
5. B; *Examples:* $y^2 - 3y + 2 = 0$, $x^2 - 9 = 0$, $2m^2 = 6m + 8$
6. C; *Example:* See the triangle included in the Quick Review above for **Section 6.7.**

Real-Data Applications

Stopping Distance

The overall *stopping distance* is the sum of the *thinking distance* (how far the car travels once you realize you have to brake) and the *braking distance* (how far the car travels after you apply the brakes).

The data in the table represents three distinct relationships. The *input* is speed in miles per hour for all three relationships. The *output* is thinking distance in feet for the first relationship, braking distance in feet for the second relationship, and overall stopping distance in feet for the third relationship.

Speed	Thinking Distance	Braking Distance	Overall Stopping Distance
20 mph	20 ft	20 ft	40 ft
30 mph	30 ft	45 ft	75 ft
40 mph	40 ft	80 ft	120 ft
50 mph	50 ft	125 ft	175 ft
60 mph	60 ft	180 ft	240 ft
70 mph	70 ft	245 ft	315 ft

Source: Pass Your Driving Theory Test, British School of Motoring (1996).

For Group Discussion

1. In the relationship between thinking distance and speed, the *output* (y) is numerically the same as the *input* (x).

   (a) Write the equation that expresses this relationship.

   (b) When the speed is doubled from 20 mph to 40 mph, how does the thinking distance change?

   (c) Does the same pattern hold true if a 30 mph speed is doubled?

   (d) Is the equation linear or quadratic? Explain.

2. The relationship between braking distance and speed is given by the equation $y = \frac{1}{20}x^2$.

   (a) Show that this equation corresponds to the table values for speeds of 20 mph and 40 mph.

   (b) When the speed is doubled from 20 mph to 40 mph, how does the braking distance change?

   (c) Does the same pattern hold true if a 30 mph speed is doubled?

   (d) Is the equation linear or quadratic? Explain.

3. The relationship between overall stopping distance and speed is based on the equations in Problems 1 and 2.

   (a) Use those results to write the equation that expresses the relationship between overall stopping distance and speed.

   (b) Is the equation linear or quadratic? Explain.

   (c) A *rule of thumb* for calculating overall stopping distance is to take speed in *tens* of miles per hour, divide by 2, add 1, and multiply the result by the speed in miles per hour. For example, at 40 mph, the rule says: $4 \div 2 + 1 = 3$; $3 \times 40 = 120$ ft. Show why this rule of thumb works. [*Hint:* Factor the right side of the equation in part (a).]

Chapter **6**

REVIEW EXERCISES

[6.1] *Factor out the greatest common factor or factor by grouping.*

1. $7t + 14$

2. $60z^3 + 30z$

3. $35x^3 + 70x^2$

4. $100m^2n^3 - 50m^3n^4 + 150m^2n^2$

5. $2xy - 8y + 3x - 12$

6. $6y^2 + 9y + 4xy + 6x$

[6.2] *Factor completely.*

7. $x^2 + 5x + 6$

8. $y^2 - 13y + 40$

9. $q^2 + 6q - 27$

10. $r^2 - r - 56$

11. $r^2 - 4rs - 96s^2$

12. $p^2 + 2pq - 120q^2$

13. $8p^3 - 24p^2 - 80p$

14. $3x^4 + 30x^3 + 48x^2$

15. $m^2 - 3mn - 18n^2$

16. $y^2 - 8yz + 15z^2$

17. $p^7 - p^6q - 2p^5q^2$

18. $3r^5 - 6r^4s - 45r^3s^2$

19. $x^2 + x + 1$

20. $3x^2 + 6x + 6$

[6.3–6.4]

21. To begin factoring $6r^2 - 5r - 6$, what are the possible first terms of the two binomial factors, if we consider only positive integer coefficients?

22. What is the first step you would use to factor $2z^3 + 9z^2 - 5z$?

Factor completely.

23. $2k^2 - 5k + 2$

24. $3r^2 + 11r - 4$

25. $6r^2 - 5r - 6$

26. $10z^2 - 3z - 1$

27. $5t^2 - 11t + 12$

28. $24x^5 - 20x^4 + 4x^3$

29. $-6x^2 + 3x + 30$

30. $10r^3s + 17r^2s^2 + 6rs^3$

[6.5]

31. Which one of the following is a difference of squares?
  A. $32x^2 - 1$ **B.** $4x^2y^2 - 25z^2$
  C. $x^2 + 36$ **D.** $25y^3 - 1$

32. Which one of the following is a perfect square trinomial?
  A. $x^2 + x + 1$ **B.** $y^2 - 4y + 9$
  C. $4x^2 + 10x + 25$ **D.** $x^2 - 20x + 100$

Factor completely.

33. $n^2 - 64$

34. $25b^2 - 121$

35. $49y^2 - 25w^2$

36. $144p^2 - 36q^2$

37. $x^2 + 100$

38. $x^2 - \dfrac{49}{100}$

39. $z^2 + 10z + 25$

40. $r^2 - 12r + 36$

41. $9t^2 - 42t + 49$

42. $16m^2 + 40mn + 25n^2$

43. $54x^3 - 72x^2 + 24x$

44. $x^2 + \dfrac{2}{3}x + \dfrac{1}{9}$

[6.6]   *Solve each equation, and check the solutions.*

45. $(4t + 3)(t - 1) = 0$

46. $(x + 7)(x - 4)(x + 3) = 0$

47. $x(2x - 5) = 0$

48. $z^2 + 4z + 3 = 0$

49. $m^2 - 5m + 4 = 0$

50. $x^2 = -15 + 8x$

51. $3z^2 - 11z - 20 = 0$

52. $81t^2 - 64 = 0$

53. $y^2 = 8y$

54. $n(n - 5) = 6$

55. $t^2 - 14t + 49 = 0$

56. $t^2 = 12(t - 3)$

57. $(5z + 2)(z^2 + 3z + 2) = 0$

58. $x^2 = 9$

[6.7]   *Solve each problem.*

59. The length of a rug is 6 ft more than the width. The area is 40 ft². Find the length and width of the rug.

60. The surface area S of a box is given by

$$S = 2WH + 2WL + 2LH.$$

A treasure chest from a sunken galleon has dimensions as shown in the figure. Its surface area is 650 ft². Find its width.

61. The length of a rectangle is three times the width. If the width were increased by 3 m while the length remained the same, the new rectangle would have an area of 30 m². Find the length and width of the original rectangle.

62. The volume of a rectangular box is 120 m³. The width of the box is 4 m, and the height is 1 m less than the length. Find the length and height of the box.

63. The product of two consecutive integers is 29 more than their sum. What are the integers?

64. Two cars left an intersection at the same time. One traveled west, and the other traveled 14 mi less, but to the south. How far apart were they then, if the distance between them was 16 mi more than the distance traveled south?

West

x

$x - 14$

South

If an object is propelled upward with an initial velocity of 128 ft per sec, its height h in feet after t seconds is

$$h = 128t - 16t^2.$$

Find the height of the object after each period of time.

65. 1 sec

66. 2 sec

67. 4 sec

68. For the object described above, when does it return to the ground?

69. Annual revenue in millions of dollars for eBay is shown in the table.

Year	Annual Revenue (in millions of dollars)
1997	5.1
1998	47.4
1999	224.7
2000	431.4
2001	748.8
2002	1214.1

Source: eBay.

Using the data, we developed the quadratic equation

$$y = 47.8x^2 - .135x + 7.65$$

to model eBay revenues y in year x, where $x = 0$ represents 1997, $x = 1$ represents 1998, and so on.

(a) Use the model to find eBay revenue (to the nearest tenth) in 2001. How does your answer compare to the actual data from the table?

(b) Use the model to predict annual revenue (to the nearest tenth) for eBay in 2003.

(c) Revenue for eBay through the third quarter of 2003 was $1516.7 million. Given this information, do you think your prediction in part (b) is reliable? Explain.

MIXED REVIEW EXERCISES

70. Which of the following is *not* factored completely?

    A. $3(7t)$ **B.** $3x(7t + 4)$ **C.** $(3 + x)(7t + 4)$ **D.** $3(7t + 4) + x(7t + 4)$

71. Although $(2x + 8)(3x - 4) = 6x^2 + 16x - 32$ is a true statement, the polynomial is not factored completely. Explain why and give the complete factored form.

Factor completely.

72. $z^2 - 11zx + 10x^2$

73. $3k^2 + 11k + 10$

74. $15m^2 + 20mp - 12m - 16p$

75. $y^4 - 625$

76. $6m^3 - 21m^2 - 45m$

77. $24ab^3c^2 - 56a^2bc^3 + 72a^2b^2c$

78. $25a^2 + 15ab + 9b^2$

79. $12x^2yz^3 + 12xy^2z - 30x^3y^2z^4$

80. $2a^5 - 8a^4 - 24a^3$

81. $12r^2 + 8rq - 15q^2$

82. $100a^2 - 9$

83. $49t^2 + 56t + 16$

Solve.

84. $t(t - 7) = 0$

85. $x^2 + 3x = 10$

86. $25x^2 + 20x + 4 = 0$

Solve each problem.

87. A lot is shaped like a right triangle. The hypotenuse is 3 m longer than the longer leg. The longer leg is 6 m longer than twice the length of the shorter leg. Find the lengths of the sides of the lot.

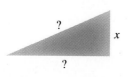

88. A pyramid has a rectangular base with a length that is 2 m more than the width. The height of the pyramid is 6 m, and its volume is 48 m³. Find the length and width of the base.

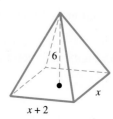

89. The product of the smaller two of three consecutive integers is equal to 23 plus the largest. Find the integers.

90. If an object is dropped, the distance d in feet it falls in t seconds (disregarding air resistance) is given by the quadratic equation

$$d = 16t^2.$$

Find the distance an object would fall in the following times.

(a) 4 sec   **(b)** 8 sec

91. The floor plan for a house is a rectangle with length 7 m more than its width. The area is 170 m². Find the width and length of the house.

92. The triangular sail of a schooner has an area of 30 m². The height of the sail is 4 m more than the base. Find the base of the sail.

93. The numbers of alternative-fueled vehicles, in thousands, in use for the years 1998–2001 are given in the table.

Year	Number (in thousands)
1998	384
1999	407
2000	432
2001	456

Source: Energy Information Administration, Alternatives to Traditional Fuels, 2001.

Using the data, we developed the quadratic equation

$$y = .25x^2 - 25.65x + 496.6$$

to model the number of vehicles y in year x. Here we used $x = 98$ for 1998, $x = 99$ for 1999, and so on.

(a) What prediction for 2002 is given by the equation?

(b) Why might the prediction for 2002 be unreliable?

Chapter 6

TEST

Study Skills Workbook
Activity 12: Final Exams

1. Which one of the following is the correct, completely factored form of $2x^2 - 2x - 24$?

   A. $(2x + 6)(x - 4)$ **B.** $(x + 3)(2x - 8)$

   C. $2(x + 4)(x - 3)$ **D.** $2(x + 3)(x - 4)$

   1. _____

Factor each polynomial completely.

2. $12x^2 - 30x$

   2. _____

3. $2m^3n^2 + 3m^3n - 5m^2n^2$

   3. _____

4. $2ax - 2bx + ay - by$

   4. _____

5. $x^2 - 9x + 14$

   5. _____

6. $2x^2 + x - 3$

   6. _____

7. $6x^2 - 19x - 7$

   7. _____

8. $3x^2 - 12x - 15$

   8. _____

9. $10z^2 - 17z + 3$

   9. _____

10. $t^2 + 2t + 3$

    10. _____

11. $x^2 + \dfrac{1}{36}$

    11. _____

12. $y^2 - 49$

    12. _____

13. $9y^2 - 64$

    13. _____

14. $x^2 + 16x + 64$

    14. _____

15. $4x^2 - 28xy + 49y^2$

    15. _____

16. $-2x^2 - 4x - 2$

    16. _____

17. $6t^4 + 3t^3 - 108t^2$

    17. _____

18. $4r^2 + 10rt + 25t^2$

    18. _____

19. _____

20. _____

21. _____

22. _____

23. _____

24. _____

25. _____

26. _____

27. _____

28. _____

29. _____

30. _____

19. $4t^3 + 32t^2 + 64t$

20. $x^4 - 81$

21. Why is $(p + 3)(p + 3)$ *not* the correct factored form of $p^2 + 9$?

Solve each equation.

22. $(x + 3)(x - 9) = 0$

23. $2r^2 - 13r + 6 = 0$

24. $25x^2 - 4 = 0$

25. $x(x - 20) = -100$

26. $t^2 = 3t$

Solve each problem.

27. The length of a rectangular flower bed is 3 ft less than twice its width. The area of the bed is 54 ft². Find the dimensions of the flower bed.

28. Find two consecutive integers such that the square of the sum of the two integers is 11 more than the smaller integer.

29. A carpenter needs to cut a brace to support a wall stud, as shown in the figure. The brace should be 7 ft less than three times the length of the stud. If the brace will be anchored on the floor 15 ft away from the stud, how long should the brace be?

Brace

Wall stud

15 ft

30. The number of U.S. cable TV networks y from 1984 through 2003 can be approximated by the quadratic equation

$$y = 1.06x^2 - 4.77x + 47.9,$$

where $x = 0$ represents 1984, $x = 1$ represents 1985, and so on. (*Source:* National Cable Television Association; FCC annual report.) Use the model to estimate the number of cable TV channels in 2000. Round your answer to the nearest whole number.

Cumulative Review Exercises

CHAPTERS R–6

Solve each equation.

1. $3x + 2(x - 4) = 4(x - 2)$

2. $.3x + .9x = .06$

3. $\dfrac{2}{3}n - \dfrac{1}{2}(n - 4) = 3$

4. Solve for P: $A = P + Prt$

5. From a list of "everyday items" often taken for granted, adults were recently surveyed as to those items they wouldn't want to live without. Complete the results shown in the table if 500 adults were surveyed.

Item	Percent That Wouldn't Want to Live Without	Number That Wouldn't Want to Live Without
Toilet paper	69%	
Zipper	42%	
Frozen foods		190
Self-stick note pads		75

(Other items included tape, hairspray, pantyhose, paper clips, and Velcro.)

Source: Market Facts for Kleenex Cottonelle.

Solve each problem.

6. At the 2002 Winter Olympics in Salt Lake City, the top medal winner was Germany with 35. Germany won 9 more silver medals than bronze and 4 fewer gold medals than silver. Find the number of each type of medal won. (*Source: World Almanac and Book of Facts*, 2004.)

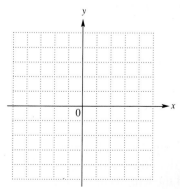

7. Although the gender wage gap is narrowing, in 2002 women working full time earned, on average, 77.5 cents for every dollar earned by their male counterparts. How much would a female office worker have earned for a comparable job that paid a male colleague $45,000? (*Source:* Bureau of Labor Statistics.)

8. Find the measures of the marked angles.

$(2x + 16)°$ $(x + 23)°$

9. Fill in each blank with *positive* or *negative*. The point with coordinates (a, b) is in

(a) quadrant II if a is _____ and b is _____.

(b) quadrant III if a is _____ and b is _____.

Consider the equation $y = 12x + 3$. Find the following.

10. The x- and y-intercepts

11. The slope

12. The graph

13. The points on the graph show the number of U.S. radio stations in the years 1995–2002, along with the graph of a linear equation that models the data.

    (a) Use the ordered pairs shown on the graph to find the slope of the line to the nearest whole number. Interpret the slope.

    (b) Use the graph to estimate the number of radio stations in the year 2000. Write your answer as an ordered pair of the form (year, number of radio stations).

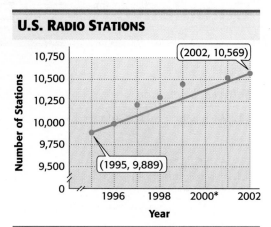

U.S. RADIO STATIONS

(2002, 10,569)

(1995, 9,889)

Source: M Street Corporation.
* Data for 2000 unavailable.

Solve each system of equations.

14. $4x - y = -6$
    $2x + 3y = 4$

15. $5x + 3y = 10$
    $2x + \dfrac{6}{5}y = 5$

Evaluate each expression.

16. $2^{-3} \cdot 2^5$

17. $\left(\dfrac{3}{4}\right)^{-2}$

18. $\dfrac{6^5 \cdot 6^{-2}}{6^3}$

19. $\left(\dfrac{4^{-3} \cdot 4^4}{4^5}\right)^{-1}$

Simplify each expression and write the answer using only positive exponents. Assume no denominators are 0.

20. $\dfrac{(p^2)^3 p^{-4}}{(p^{-3})^{-1} p}$

21. $\dfrac{(m^{-2})^3 m}{m^5 m^{-4}}$

Perform the indicated operations.

22. $(2k^2 + 4k) - (5k^2 - 2) - (k^2 + 8k - 6)$

23. $(9x + 6)(5x - 3)$

24. $(3p + 2)^2$

25. $\dfrac{8x^4 + 12x^3 - 6x^2 + 20x}{2x}$

Factor completely.

26. $2a^2 + 7a - 4$

27. $10m^2 + 19m + 6$

28. $8t^2 + 10tv + 3v^2$

29. $4p^2 - 12p + 9$

30. $25r^2 - 81t^2$

31. $2pq + 6p^3q + 8p^2q$

Solve each equation.

32. $6m^2 + m - 2 = 0$

33. $8x^2 = 64x$

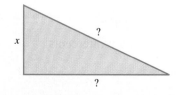

34. The length of the hypotenuse of a right triangle is 3 m more than twice the length of the shorter leg. The longer leg is 7 m longer than the shorter leg. Find the lengths of the sides.

Answers to Selected Exercises

In this section we provide the answers that we think most students will obtain when they work the exercises using the methods explained in the text. If your answer does not look exactly like the one given here, it is not necessarily wrong. In many cases there are equivalent forms of the answer that are correct. For example, if the answer section shows $\frac{3}{4}$ and your answer is .75, you have obtained the right answer but written it in a different (yet equivalent) form. Unless the directions specify otherwise, .75 is just as valid an answer as $\frac{3}{4}$.

In general, if your answer does not agree with the one given in the text, see whether it can be transformed into the other form. If it can, then it is the correct answer. If you still have doubts, talk with your instructor.

DIAGNOSTIC PRETEST

(page xxix)

1. 18 **2.** $\frac{253}{24}$ or $10\frac{13}{24}$ **3.** 28.322 **4. (a)** .0099 **(b)** 472%

5. $-|35|$ **6.** 56 **7.** 0 **8.** 4 **9.** -2 **10.** New York: 8,084,316; Los Angeles: 3,798,981 **11.** 58°, 122°

12. $x \le 5$

13. x-intercept: (5, 0); y-intercept: (0, -2)

14. -4 **15.** $y = -x + 1$
16.

17. (2, 3) **18.** no solution **19.** Marla: 61 mph; Rick: 53 mph
20.

21. $-2m^3 - 9m - 5$ **22.** $49z^2 + 42zw + 9w^2$ **23.** $-\frac{3}{10}$

24. (a) 4.45×10^8 **(b)** .000234 **25.** $(3x - 4)(x + 2)$

26. $(4n + 7)(4n - 7)$ **27.** $-3, 5$ **28.** 15 in. by 11 in.

29. $\frac{x + 5}{x + 4}$ **30.** $-\frac{1}{3r}$ **31.** $\frac{z^3 + 2z^2 + 3z}{(z - 3)(z + 3)}$ **32.** $y + 1$ **33.** 0

34. $12 - 2\sqrt{35}$ **35.** $2\sqrt{10}$ **36.** 27 **37.** $3 + 2\sqrt{5}, 3 - 2\sqrt{5}$

38. $\frac{-3 + \sqrt{17}}{4}, \frac{-3 - \sqrt{17}}{4}$

39. vertex: (0, 5)

40. function; domain: $\{-2, -1, 0, 1, 2\}$; range: $\{0, 1, 4\}$

CHAPTER R PREALGEBRA REVIEW

Section R.1 (page 9)

1. true **3.** false; The fraction $\frac{17}{51}$ can be simplified to $\frac{1}{3}$.

5. false; *Product* indicates multiplication, so the product of 8 and 2 is 16. **7.** prime **9.** composite **11.** composite **13.** neither
15. $2 \cdot 3 \cdot 5$ **17.** $2 \cdot 2 \cdot 3 \cdot 3 \cdot 7$ **19.** $2 \cdot 2 \cdot 31$ **21.** 29

23. $\frac{1}{2}$ **25.** $\frac{5}{6}$ **27.** $\frac{1}{5}$ **29.** $\frac{6}{5}$ **31.** A **33.** $\frac{24}{35}$ **35.** $\frac{6}{25}$

37. $\frac{6}{5}$ or $1\frac{1}{5}$ **39.** $\frac{232}{15}$ or $15\frac{7}{15}$ **41.** $\frac{10}{3}$ or $3\frac{1}{3}$ **43.** 12 **45.** $\frac{1}{16}$

47. $\frac{84}{47}$ or $1\frac{37}{47}$ **49.** Multiply the first fraction (the dividend) by the reciprocal of the second fraction (the divisor) to divide two fractions.

51. $\frac{2}{3}$ **53.** $\frac{8}{9}$ **55.** $\frac{27}{8}$ or $3\frac{3}{8}$ **57.** $\frac{17}{36}$ **59.** $\frac{11}{12}$ **61.** $\frac{4}{3}$ or $1\frac{1}{3}$

63. 6 cups **65.** $618\frac{3}{4}$ ft **67.** $\frac{9}{16}$ in. **69.** $\frac{5}{16}$ in. **71.** $16\frac{5}{8}$ yd

73. $\frac{1}{20}$ **75.** more than $1\frac{1}{25}$ million

Section R.2 (page 21)

1. (a) 6 **(b)** 9 **(c)** 1 **(d)** 7 **(e)** 4 **3. (a)** 46.25 **(b)** 46.2 **(c)** 46
(d) 50 **5.** C **7.** B **9.** $\frac{4}{10}$ **11.** $\frac{64}{100}$ **13.** $\frac{138}{1000}$ **15.** $\frac{3805}{1000}$

17. 139; 143.094 **19.** 27; 25.61 **21.** 10; 15.33 **23.** 82; 81.716
25. 17; 15.211 **27.** .006; .006 **29.** 90; 116.48 **31.** 7; 7.15
33. 2; 2.05 **35.** 6000; 5711.6 **37.** .2; .162 **39.** To add or subtract decimals, line up the decimal points in a column, add or subtract as usual, and move the decimal point straight down in the sum or difference. **41.** .125 **43.** .25 **45.** $.\overline{5}$; .556 **47.** $.1\overline{6}$; .167 **49.** To convert a decimal to a percent, move the decimal point two places to the right and attach a percent symbol (%). **51.** .54 **53.** 1.17
55. .024 **57.** .0625 **59.** .008 **61.** 75% **63.** .4% **65.** 128%
67. 30% **69.** 75% **71.** $83.\overline{3}$% **73. (a)** $\frac{2}{32}$ **(b)** $\frac{2}{32}$

CHAPTER 1 THE REAL NUMBER SYSTEM

Section 1.1 (page 29)

1. true **3.** false; Using the guidelines for order of operations gives $4 + 3(8 - 2) = 4 + 3(6) = 4 + 18 = 22$. **5.** false; The correct translation is $4 = 16 - 12$. **7.** 49 **9.** 144 **11.** 64

13. 1000 **15.** 81 **17.** 1024 **19.** $\frac{16}{81}$ **21.** .000064

23. The 4 would be applied last because we work first inside the parentheses. **25.** 58 **27.** 13 **29.** 32 **31.** 19 **33.** $\frac{49}{30}$ **35.** 12

37. 36.14 **39.** 26 **41.** 4 **43.** 95 **45.** 12 **47.** 14 **49.** $\frac{19}{2}$

51. false **53.** true **55.** true **57.** false **59.** false **61.** true
63. $15 = 5 + 10$ **65.** $9 > 5 - 4$ **67.** $16 \neq 19$ **69.** $2 \leq 3$
71. Seven is less than nineteen. True **73.** One-third is not equal to three-tenths. True **75.** Eight is greater than or equal to eleven. False
77. $30 > 5$ **79.** $3 \leq 12$ **81.** Alaska, Texas, California, Idaho
83. Alaska, Texas, California, Idaho, Missouri

Section 1.2 (page 35)

1. 11 **3.** $13 + x$; 16 **5.** expression; equation **7.** The equation would be $5x - 9 = 49$. **9.** Answers will vary. Two such pairs are $x = 0, y = 6$ and $x = 1, y = 4$. To find a pair, choose one number, substitute it for a variable, then calculate the value for the other variable. **11. (a)** 64 **(b)** 144 **13. (a)** $\frac{7}{8}$ **(b)** $\frac{13}{12}$ **15. (a)** 9.569

(b) 14.353 **17. (a)** 52 **(b)** 114 **19. (a)** 12 **(b)** 33

21. (a) 6 **(b)** $\frac{9}{5}$ **23. (a)** $\frac{4}{3}$ **(b)** $\frac{13}{6}$ **25. (a)** $\frac{2}{7}$

(b) $\frac{16}{27}$ **27. (a)** 12 **(b)** 55 **29. (a)** 1 **(b)** $\frac{28}{17}$

31. (a) 3.684 **(b)** 8.841 **33.** $12x$ **35.** $x - 2$ **37.** $7 - \frac{1}{3}x$

39. $2x - 6$ **41.** $\frac{12}{x + 3}$ **43.** $6(x - 4)$ **45.** The word *and* does not signify addition here. In the phrase "the product of a number and 6," *and* connects two quantities to be multiplied. **47.** no
49. yes **51.** yes **53.** no **55.** yes **57.** yes **59.** $x + 8 = 18$

61. $2x + 5 = 5$ **63.** $16 - \frac{3}{4}x = 13$ **65.** $3x = 2x + 8$

67. expression **69.** equation **71.** $12.52; more by $.03
72. $14.00; same **73.** $14.49; less by $.04 **74.** $14.99; more by $.04

Section 1.3 (page 45)

1. 4 **3.** 0 **5.** One example is $\sqrt{13}$. There are others.

7. (a) $3, 7$ **(b)** $0, 3, 7$ **(c)** $-9, 0, 3, 7$ **(d)** $-9, -1\frac{1}{4}, -\frac{3}{5},$

$0, 3, 5.9, 7$ **(e)** $-\sqrt{7}, \sqrt{5}$ **(f)** All are real numbers.

9. 40,000 **11.** -9000 **13.**

15.

17.

19. -11 **21.** -21 **23.** -100 **25.** $-\frac{2}{3}$ **27.** false **29.** true

31. (a) 2 **(b)** 2 **33. (a)** -6 **(b)** 6 **35. (a)** $\frac{3}{4}$ **(b)** $\frac{3}{4}$ **37.** 7

39. -12 **41.** $-\frac{2}{3}$ **43.** 9 **45.** false **47.** true **49.** No; the statement is false for one number, 0. **51.** fuel/other utilities from 2001 to 2002 **53.** 2000 to 2001

Section 1.4 (page 51)

1. Add -2 and 5. **3.** Add -1 and -3. **5.** 2 **7.** -3 **9.** -10

11. -13 **13.** -15.9 **15.** 5 **17.** 13 **19.** 0 **21.** -8 **23.** $\frac{3}{10}$

25. $\frac{1}{2}$ **27.** $-\frac{3}{4}$ **29.** -1.6 **31.** -8.7 **33.** -25 **35.** $-\frac{1}{4}$

37. true **39.** false **41.** true **43.** false **45.** true **47.** false
49. It must be negative and have the larger absolute value.
50. The sum of a positive number and 5 cannot be -7.
51. It must be positive and have the larger absolute value.
52. The sum of a negative number and -8 cannot be 2.
53. Add the absolute values of the numbers. The sum will be negative. **55.** $-5 + 12 + 6$; 13 **57.** $[-19 + (-4)] + 14$; -9

59. $[-4 + (-10)] + 12$; -2 **61.** $\left[\frac{5}{7} + \left(-\frac{9}{7}\right)\right] + \frac{2}{7}$; $-\frac{2}{7}$

63. $-$80 **65.** -184 m **67.** 37 yd **69.** 120°F **71.** $-$107
73. -12

Section 1.5 (page 59)

1. -8; -6 **3.** $7 - 12$; $12 - 7$ **5.** -4 **7.** -10 **9.** -16

11. 11 **13.** 19 **15.** -4 **17.** 5 **19.** 0 **21.** $\frac{3}{4}$ **23.** $-\frac{11}{8}$

25. $\frac{15}{8}$ **27.** 13.6 **29.** -11.9 **31.** -2.8 **33.** -6.3 **35.** -28

37. -18 **39.** $\frac{37}{12}$ **41.** -42.04 **43.** For example, let $a = 1, b = 1$

or let $a = 2, b = 2$. In general, choose $a = b$. **45.** 8
47. For example, $-8 - (-2) = -6$. **49.** $4 - (-8)$; 12
51. $-2 - 8$; -10 **53.** $[9 + (-4)] - 7$; -2
55. $[8 - (-5)] - 12$; 1 **57.** $-58°$F **59.** 14,776 ft
61. $-$80 **63.** $105,000 **65.** 17 **67.** $1045.55 **69.** 469 B.C.
71. $323.83 **73.** 14 ft **75.** 40,776 ft **77.** -1.6% **79.** $4900
81. $8800 **83.** positive **85.** positive

Section 1.6 (page 73)

1. greater than 0 **3.** less than 0 **5.** greater than 0 **7.** -28

9. 30 **11.** 0 **13.** $\frac{5}{6}$ **15.** -2.38 **17.** $\frac{3}{2}$ **19.** -3 **21.** -2

23. 16 **25.** 0 **27.** undefined **29.** $\frac{3}{2}$ **31.** C **33.** 3 **35.** 7

37. 4 **39.** -3 **41.** -1 **43.** negative; impossible to tell
45. 68 **47.** -228 **49.** 1 **51.** 0 **53.** -6 **55.** undefined
57. $-12 + 4(-7)$; -40 **59.** $-1 - 2(-8)(2)$; 31

61. $-3[3 - (-7)]$; -30 **63.** $\frac{3}{10}[-2 + (-28)]$; -9

65. $\frac{-20}{-8 + (-2)}$; 2 **67.** $\frac{-18 + (-6)}{2(-4)}$; 3 **69.** $\frac{-\frac{2}{3}\left(-\frac{1}{5}\right)}{\frac{1}{7}}$; $\frac{14}{15}$

71. $9x = -36$ **73.** $\frac{x}{4} = -1$ **75.** $x - \frac{9}{11} = 5$ **77.** $\frac{6}{x} = -3$

78. 42 **79.** 5 **80.** $8\frac{2}{5}$ **81.** $8\frac{2}{5}$ **82.** 2 **83.** $-12\frac{1}{2}$

Summary Exercises on Operations with Real Numbers (page 77)

1. -16 **2.** 4 **3.** 0 **4.** -24 **5.** -17 **6.** 76 **7.** -18

8. 90 **9.** 38 **10.** 4 **11.** -5 **12.** 5 **13.** $-\frac{7}{2}$ or $-3\frac{1}{2}$ **14.** 4

15. 13 **16.** $\frac{5}{4}$ or $1\frac{1}{4}$ **17.** 9 **18.** $\frac{37}{10}$ or $3\frac{7}{10}$ **19.** 0 **20.** 25

21. 14 **22.** 0 **23.** -4 **24.** $\frac{6}{5}$ or $1\frac{1}{5}$ **25.** -1 **26.** $\frac{52}{37}$ or $1\frac{15}{37}$

27. $\frac{17}{16}$ or $1\frac{1}{16}$ **28.** $-\frac{2}{3}$ **29.** 3.33 **30.** 1.02 **31.** -13 **32.** 0

33. 24 **34.** -7 **35.** 37 **36.** -3 **37.** -1 **38.** $\frac{1}{2}$ **39.** $-\frac{5}{13}$

40. 5 **41.** undefined **42.** 0

Section 1.7 (page 85)

1. B **3.** C **5.** B **7.** G **9.** commutative property
11. associative property **13.** inverse property **15.** inverse
property **17.** identity property **19.** commutative property
21. distributive property **23.** identity property **25.** distributive
property **27. (a)** 0 **(b)** 1, -1 **29.** $25 - (6 - 2) = 25 - 4 = 21$
and $(25 - 6) - 2 = 19 - 2 = 17$. Since these results are different,
subtraction is not associative. **31.** $7 + r$ **33.** s
35. $-6x + (-6)7; -6x - 42$ **37.** $w + [5 + (-3)]; w + 2$
39. We must multiply $\frac{3}{4}$ by 1 in the form $\frac{3}{3}$: $\frac{3}{4} \cdot \frac{3}{3} = \frac{9}{12}$. **41.** 2
43. $5(3 + 17); 100$ **45.** $4t + 12$ **47.** $-8r - 24$ **49.** $-5y + 20$
51. $-16y - 20z$ **53.** $8(z + w)$ **55.** $7(2v + 5r)$
57. $24r + 32s - 40y$ **59.** $-24x - 9y - 12z$ **61.** $-4t - 5m$
63. $5c + 4d$ **65.** $3q - 5r + 8s$ **67.** Answers will vary. For
example, "putting on your socks" and "putting on your shoes"
69. false **71.** (foreign sales) clerk; foreign (sales clerk) **73.** 0
74. $-3(5) + (-3)(-5)$ **75.** -15 **76.** The product $-3(-5)$
must equal 15, since it is the additive inverse of -15.

Section 1.8 (page 93)

1. C **3.** A **5.** $15x$ **7.** $5t$ **9.** $4r + 11$ **11.** $5 + 2x - 6y$
13. $-7 + 3p$ **15.** -12 **17.** 5 **19.** 1 **21.** -1 **23.** 74
25. Answer will vary. For example, $-3x$ and $4x$ **27.** like
29. unlike **31.** like **33.** unlike **35.** We cannot "add" two
unlike terms to obtain a single term, so we must be able to identify
like terms in order to combine them. **37.** $1 - 2x$
39. $-\frac{1}{3}t - \frac{28}{3}$ **41.** $-4.1r + 4.2$ **43.** $-2y^2 + 3y^3$
45. $-19p + 16$ **47.** $-\frac{3}{2}y + 16$ **49.** $-16y + 63$
51. $(x + 3) + 5x; 6x + 3$ **53.** $(13 + 6x) - (-7x); 13 + 13x$
55. $2(3x + 4) - (-4 + 6x); 12$ **57.** Wording may vary. One
example is "the difference between 9 times a number and the sum
of the number and 2." **59.** $1000 + 5x$ (dollars)
60. $750 + 3y$ (dollars) **61.** $1000 + 5x + 750 + 3y$ (dollars)
62. $1750 + 5x + 3y$ (dollars)

Chapter 1 Review Exercises (page 99)

1. 625 **2.** .00000081 **3.** .009261 **4.** $\frac{125}{8}$ **5.** 27 **6.** 200

7. 7 **8.** $\frac{20}{3}$ **9.** $13 < 17$ **10.** $5 + 2 \neq 10$ **11.** Six is less than

fifteen. **12.** Answers will vary. One example is $2 + 5 \geq \frac{16}{2}$.

13. 30 **14.** 60 **15.** 14 **16.** 13 **17.** $x + 6$ **18.** $8 - x$

19. $6x - 9$ **20.** $12 + \frac{3}{5}x$ **21.** yes **22.** no **23.** $2x - 6 = 10$

24. $4x = 8$ **25.** equation **26.** expression

27.

28.

29.

30.

31. -10 **32.** -9 **33.** $-\frac{3}{4}$ **34.** $-|23|$ **35.** true **36.** true

37. true **38.** false **39.** -3 **40.** -19 **41.** -7 **42.** 9

43. -6 **44.** -4 **45.** -17 **46.** $-\frac{29}{36}$ **47.** -10 **48.** -19

49. $(-31 + 12) + 19; 0$ **50.** $[-4 + (-8)] + 13; 1$ **51.** $-\$8$

52. 87°F **53.** -11 **54.** -1 **55.** 7 **56.** $-\frac{43}{35}$ **57.** 10.31

58. -12 **59.** 2 **60.** 1 **61.** $-4 - (-6); 2$
62. $[4 + (-8)] - 5; -9$ **63.** \$713.4 billion
64. 1 min, 28.89 sec **65.** The first step is to change subtracting
-6 to adding its opposite, 6. So the problem becomes $-8 + 6$.
This sum is -2. **66.** Yes; for example,
$-2 - (-6) = -2 + 6 = 4$, a positive number.
67. \$13.5 billion **68.** $-\$11.3$ billion **69.** $-\$2.2$ billion

70. \$5.0 billion **71.** 36 **72.** -105 **73.** $\frac{1}{2}$ **74.** 10.08

75. -20 **76.** -10 **77.** -24 **78.** -35 **79.** 4 **80.** -20

81. $-\frac{3}{4}$ **82.** 11.3 **83.** -1 **84.** undefined **85.** 1 **86.** 0

87. -18 **88.** -18 **89.** 125 **90.** -423

91. $-4(5) - 9; -29$ **92.** $\frac{5}{6}[12 + (-6)]; 5$ **93.** $\frac{12}{8 + (-4)}; 3$

94. $\frac{-20(12)}{15 - (-15)}; -8$ **95.** $\frac{x}{x + 5} = -2$ **96.** $8x - 3 = -7$

97. identity property **98.** identity property **99.** inverse property
100. inverse property **101.** associative property **102.** associative
property **103.** distributive property **104.** commutative property
105. $(7 + 1)y; 8y$ **106.** $-12 \cdot 4 - 12(-t); -48 + 12t$
107. $3(2s + 4y); 6s + 12y$ **108.** $-1(-4r) + (-1)(5s);$
$4r - 5s$ **109.** $17p^2$ **110.** $16r^2 + 7r$ **111.** $-19k + 54$
112. $5s - 6$ **113.** $-45t - 23$ **114.** $-45t^2 - 23.4t$

115. $-2(3x) - 7x; -13x$ **116.** $\frac{x + 9}{x - 6}$ **117.** No. The use of

and there indicates the two quantities that are to be multiplied.
118. Answers may vary. For example, "3 times the difference

between 4 times a number and 6" **119.** 16 **120.** $\frac{25}{36}$ **121.** -26

122. $\frac{8}{3}$ **123.** $-\frac{1}{24}$ **124.** $\frac{7}{2}$ **125.** 2 **126.** 77.6 **127.** $-1\frac{1}{2}$

128. 11 **129.** $-\frac{28}{15}$ **130.** 24 **131.** -11 **132.** -6

133. $2x - 1400 = 25,800$; x represents the amount spent in 2002.

134. $\frac{x}{3x - 14}$; x represents the number.

Chapter 1 Test (page 105)

1. true **2.** false **3.**

4. $-|-8|$ (or -8) **5.** -1.277 **6.** $\frac{-6}{2 + (-8)}; 1$ **7.** negative

8. 4 **9.** $-2\frac{5}{6}$ **10.** 2 **11.** 6 **12.** 108 **13.** 11 **14.** $\frac{30}{7}$

15. -70 **16.** 3 **17.** 178°F **18.** D **19.** A **20.** E **21.** B **22.** C **23.** $-9x^2 - 6x - 8$ **24.** identity and distributive properties **25. (a)** -18 **(b)** -18 **(c)** The distributive property tells us that the two methods produce equal results.

CHAPTER 2 EQUATIONS, INEQUALITIES, AND APPLICATIONS

Section 2.1 (page 113)

1. A and C **3.** A and B **5.** 12 **7.** -3 **9.** 4 **11.** -9 **13.** 6.3 **15.** -16.9 **17.** -10 **19.** -13 **21.** 10 **23.** 7 **25.** -4 **27.** 3 **29.** -2 **31.** 4 **33.** 2 **35.** -4 **37.** 4 **39.** 0 **41.** $\frac{7}{15}$ **43.** 7 **45.** -4 **47.** 13 **49.** 29 **51.** 18 **53.** Answers will vary. One example is $x - 6 = -8$.

Section 2.2 (page 119)

1. $\frac{3}{2}$ **3.** 10 **5.** $-\frac{2}{9}$ **7.** -1 **9.** 6 **11.** -4 **13.** .12 **15.** -1 **17.** To get x alone on the left side, divide each side by 4, the coefficient of x. **19.** 6 **21.** $\frac{15}{2}$ **23.** -5 **25.** $-\frac{18}{5}$ **27.** 12 **29.** 0 **31.** -12 **33.** 40 **35.** -12.2 **37.** -48 **39.** -35 **41.** 72 **43.** 14 **45.** $-\frac{27}{35}$ **47.** 3 **49.** -5 **51.** 7 **53.** 0 **55.** -6 **57.** Answers will vary. One example is $\frac{3}{2}x = -6$. **59.** $-4x = 10; -\frac{5}{2}$

Section 2.3 (page 127)

1. -1 **3.** 5 **5.** 1 **7.** $-\frac{5}{3}$ **9.** -1 **11.** no solution **13.** all real numbers **15.** D **17.** Simplify each side separately. Use the addition property to get all variable terms on one side of the equation and all numbers on the other, and then combine terms. Use the multiplication property to get the equation in the form $x = $ a number. Check the solution. **19.** 7 **21.** 0 **23.** $\frac{3}{25}$ **25.** 60 **27.** 4 **29.** 5000 **31.** 800 **32.** Yes, you will get $(100 \cdot 2) \cdot 4 = 800$. This is a result of the associative property of multiplication. **33.** No, because $(100a)(100b) = 10,000ab \neq 100ab$. **34.** The distributive property involves the operation of addition as well. **35.** Yes; the associative property of multiplication is used. **36.** no **37.** $-\frac{72}{11}$ **39.** 0 **41.** -6 **43.** 15 **45.** all real numbers **47.** no solution **49.** $12 - q$ **51.** $a + 12; a - 5$ **53.** $\frac{t}{10}$

Summary Exercises on Solving Linear Equations (page 131)

1. -5 **2.** 4 **3.** -5.1 **4.** 25 **5.** -25 **6.** -6 **7.** -3 **8.** -16 **9.** 7 **10.** $-\frac{96}{5}$ **11.** 5 **12.** 23.7 **13.** all real numbers **14.** 1 **15.** -16 **16.** no solution **17.** 6 **18.** 3 **19.** no solution **20.** $\frac{7}{3}$ **21.** 25 **22.** -10.8 **23.** 3 **24.** 7 **25.** 2 **26.** all real numbers **27.** $-\frac{2}{7}$ **28.** 10 **29.** $\frac{14}{17}$ **30.** $-\frac{5}{2}$ **31.** all real numbers **32.** 64

Section 2.4 (page 141)

1. The procedure should include the following steps: read the problem carefully; assign a variable to represent the unknown to be found; write down variable expressions for any other unknown quantities; translate into an equation; solve the equation; state the answer; check your solution. **3.** D; there cannot be a fractional number of cars. **5.** A; distance cannot be negative. **7.** 7 **9.** -8 **11.** 6 **13.** -3 **15.** California: 59 screens; New York: 48 screens **17.** Democrats: 48; Republicans: 51 **19.** Bruce Springsteen and the E Street Band: $115.9 million; Céline Dion: $80.5 million **21.** wins: 59; losses: 23 **23.** 1950 Denver nickel: $8.00; 1945 Philadelphia nickel: $7.00 **25.** ice cream: 44,687.9 lb; topping: 537.1 lb **27.** 35 lb **29.** Airborne Express: 3; Federal Express: 9; United Parcel Service: 1 **31.** gold: 35; silver: 39; bronze: 29 **33.** 36 million mi **35.** A and B: 40°; C: 100° **37.** no **39.** $x - 1$ **41.** 18° **43.** 39° **45.** 50° **47.** 68, 69 **49.** 146, 147 **51.** 10, 12 **53.** 10, 11 **55.** $4.66 billion, $5.27 billion, $6.20 billion

Section 2.5 (page 153)

1. (a) The perimeter of a plane geometric figure is the distance around the figure. **(b)** The area of a plane geometric figure is the measure of the surface covered or enclosed by the figure. **3.** four **5.** area **7.** perimeter **9.** area **11.** area **13.** $P = 26$ **15.** $A = 64$ **17.** $b = 4$ **19.** $t = 5.6$ **21.** $I = 1575$ **23.** $r = 2.6$ **25.** $A = 50.24$ **27.** $V = 150$ **29.** $V = 52$ **31.** $V = 7234.56$ **33.** about 154,000 ft^2 **35.** perimeter: 13 in.; area: 10.5 in.^{2} **37.** 194.48 ft^2 **39.** 23,800.10 ft^2 **41.** length: 36 in.; volume: 11,664 in.^{3} **43.** 48°, 132° **45.** 51°, 51° **47.** 105°, 105° **49.** $t = \frac{d}{r}$ **51.** $H = \frac{V}{LW}$ **53.** $b = P - a - c$ **55.** $r = \frac{I}{pt}$ **57.** $h = \frac{2A}{b}$ **59.** $W = \frac{P - 2L}{2}$ or $W = \frac{P}{2} - L$ **61.** $h = \frac{3V}{\pi r^2}$ **63.** $m = \frac{y - b}{x}$ **65.** $r = \frac{M - C}{C}$ or $r = \frac{M}{C} - 1$

Section 2.6 (page 163)

1. (a) C **(b)** D **(c)** B **(d)** A **3.** $\frac{6}{7}$ **5.** $\frac{18}{55}$ **7.** $\frac{5}{16}$ **9.** $\frac{4}{15}$ **11.** 10-lb size; $.439 **13.** 32-oz size; $.093 **15.** 128-oz size; $.044 **17.** 36-oz size; $.049 **19.** A percent is a ratio where the basis of comparison is 100. For example, 27% represents the ratio of 27 to 100. **21.** 35 **23.** 7 **25.** 2 **27.** -1 **29.** 5 **31.** $-\frac{31}{5}$ **33.** $28.35 **35.** 4 ft **37.** 203.3 million vehicles **39.** 6.875 fluid oz **41.** $733.16 **43.** 9.234 **45.** 200% **47.** 30,000 **49.** 27% **51.** C **53.** 5.8% **55.** 79.0% **57.** $304 **59.** 284% **61.** $252 **63.** $293 **65.** 30 **66. (a)** $5x = 12$ **(b)** $\frac{12}{5}$ **67.** $\frac{12}{5}$ **68.** Both methods give the same solution.

Summary Exercises on Solving Applied Problems (page 167)

1. 243 votes **2.** 48 **3.** 9 tanks **4.** 9 lb **5.** 4 **6.** 2 cm **7.** 80° **8.** 100° **9.** 3 **10.** -3 **11.** 15 **12.** 28 **13.** 36 quart cartons **14.** length: 9 ft; width: 3 ft **15.** 104°, 104° **16.** 140°, 40° **17.** 24.34 in. **18.** 727.28 in.^{2} **19.** 2.5 cm **20.** 12.42 cm **21.** Mr. Silvester: 25 yr old; Mrs. Silvester: 20 yr old **22.** Chris: 19 yr old; Josh: 9 yr old **23.** $16\frac{2}{3}$% **24.** $2.99

25. 4000 calories   **26.** 420 mi   **27.** cherry: 1200 lb; spoon: 5800 lb   **28.** Mike Weir: 281; Tiger Woods: 290   **29.** 510 calories

30. $16\frac{1}{2}$ oz   **31.** \$36.29   **32.** 38.3%   **33.** approximately 2593 mi   **34.** 32 gold medals   **35.** 32-oz size; \$.053   **36.** 50-oz size; \$.094

Section 2.7 (page 177)

1. $x > -4$ **3.** $x \le 4$ **5.** $-1 < x < 2$ **7.** $-1 < x \le 2$
9. Use an open circle if the symbol is $>$ or $<$. Use a closed circle if the symbol is $\ge$ or $\le$.

11. ——— 4   **13.** ——— -3
15. ——— 8 10   **17.** ——— 0 10

19. It would imply that $3 < -2$, which is false.

21. $z \ge 1$ ——— 1
23. $k \ge 5$ ——— 5
25. $n < -11$ ——— -11

27. It must be reversed when multiplying or dividing by a negative number.

29. $x < 6$ ——— 6
31. $x \ge -10$ ——— -10
33. $t < -3$ ——— -3
35. $x \le 0$ ——— 0
37. $r > 20$ ——— 20
39. $x \ge -3$ ——— -3
41. $r \ge -5$ ——— -5
43. $x < 1$ ——— 1
45. $x \le 0$ ——— 0
47. $x \ge 4$ ——— 4
49. $p < 32$ ——— 32
51. $x \ge \frac{5}{12}$ ——— $\frac{5}{12}$ 0
53. $k > -21$ ——— -21

55. 88 or more   **57.** all numbers greater than 16   **59.** It has never exceeded 40°C.   **61.** 32 or greater   **63.** 15 min

65. ——— 0 4
66. ——— 0 4

67. ——— 0 4
68. It is the set of all real numbers.
——— 0 4
69. The graph would be the set of all real numbers.

Chapter 2 Review Exercises (page 185)

1. 9   **2.** 4   **3.** -6 **4.** $\frac{3}{2}$ **5.** 20   **6.** $-\frac{61}{2}$ **7.** 15   **8.** 0

9. no solution   **10.** all real numbers   **11.** $-\frac{7}{2}$ **12.** 20

13. Hawaii: 6425 mi²; Rhode Island: 1212 mi²   **14.** Seven Falls: 300 ft; Twin Falls: 120 ft   **15.** 80°   **16.** 11, 13   **17.** $h = 11$

18. $A = 28$ **19.** $r = 4.75$ **20.** $V = 3052.08$ **21.** $W = \frac{A}{L}$

22. $h = \frac{2A}{b + B}$ **23.** 135°, 45°   **24.** 100°, 100°

25. perimeter: 326.5 ft; area: 6538.875 ft²   **26.** diameter: 46.78 ft; radius: 23.39 ft   **27.** $\frac{3}{2}$ **28.** $\frac{5}{14}$ **29.** $\frac{3}{4}$ **30.** $\frac{1}{12}$ **31.** $\frac{7}{2}$

32. $-\frac{8}{3}$ **33.** $\frac{25}{19}$ **34.** 40% means $\frac{40}{100}$ or $\frac{2}{5}$. It is the same as the ratio of 2 to 5.   **35.** $6\frac{2}{3}$ lb   **36.** 36 oz   **37.** 50,000 fish

38. 375 km   **39.** 17.48   **40.** 175%   **41.** $33\frac{1}{3}$%   **42.** 2500

43. \$17,800   **44.** \$350.46

45. ——— -4 **46.** ——— 7
47. ——— -5 6   **48.** ——— $\frac{1}{2}$ 0
49. $x \ge -3$ ——— -3
50. $t < 2$ ——— 2
51. $x \ge 3$ ——— 3
52. $k \ge 46$ ——— 46
53. $x < -5$ ——— -5
54. $w < -37$ ——— -37

55. 88 or more   **56.** all numbers less than or equal to $-\frac{1}{3}$

57. 7   **58.** $d = \frac{C}{\pi}$ **59.** $x < 2$ **60.** -9 **61.** 70

62. $\frac{13}{4}$ **63.** no solution   **64.** all real numbers   **65.** 46,700 fish

66. 6   **67.** United States: 34; Canada: 17   **68.** gold: 16; silver: 25; bronze: 17   **69.** 44 m   **70.** 70 ft   **71.** 263-oz size; \$.076
72. \$67.50   **73.** 92 or more   **74.** 51°, 51°

Chapter 2 Test (page 189)

1. 6   **2.** -6 **3.** $\frac{13}{4}$ **4.** -10.8 **5.** no solution   **6.** 21   **7.** 30

8. all real numbers   **9. (a)** Spurs: 88; Nets: 77   **(b)** 44 field goals   **10.** Hawaii: 4021 mi²; Maui: 728 mi²; Kauai: 551 mi²

11. 50° **12. (a)** $W = \dfrac{P - 2L}{2}$ or $W = \dfrac{P}{2} - L$ **(b)** 18
13. 100°, 80° **14.** 75°, 75° **15.** 6 **16.** -29 **17.** 24-oz size;
$.145 **18.** 2300 mi **19.** 37.7% **20. (a)** $x < 0$
(b) $-2 < x \le 3$
21. $x < 11$
22. $x \ge -3$
23. $x \le 4$

24. 83 or more **25.** When an inequality is multiplied or divided
by a negative number, the direction of the symbol must be reversed.

Cumulative Review Exercises: Chapters R–2
(page 191)

1. $\dfrac{3}{8}$ **2.** $\dfrac{3}{4}$ **3.** $\dfrac{31}{20}$ **4.** $\dfrac{551}{40}$ or $13\dfrac{31}{40}$ **5.** 6 **6.** $\dfrac{6}{5}$ **7.** 34.03

8. 27.31 **9.** 30.51 **10.** 56.3 **11.** 35 yd **12.** $7\dfrac{1}{2}$ cups

13. $67\dfrac{1}{8}$ lb **14.** $1899.94 **15.** true **16.** true **17.** 7 **18.** 1

19. 13 **20.** -40 **21.** -12 **22.** undefined **23.** -6 **24.** 28

25. 1 **26.** 0 **27.** $\dfrac{73}{18}$ **28.** -64 **29.** -134 **30.** $-\dfrac{29}{6}$

31. distributive property **32.** commutative property **33.** inverse
property **34.** identity property **35.** $7p - 14$ **36.** $2k - 11$

37. 7 **38.** -4 **39.** -1 **40.** $-\dfrac{3}{5}$ **41.** 2 **42.** -13 **43.** 26

44. -12 **45.** $c = P - a - b$ **46.** $s = \dfrac{P}{4}$

47. $z \le 2$
48. $r < 1$

49. $2018.69 **50.** $3750 **51.** $230.50 **52.** $98.45
53. 30 cm **54.** 16 in.

CHAPTER 3 GRAPHS OF LINEAR EQUATIONS AND INEQUALITIES IN TWO VARIABLES

Section 3.1 (page 203)
1. Snoopy; 31% **3.** Since 26% is twice as much as 13%, we can
expect twice as many adults to favor Charlie Brown.
5. Ohio (OH): about 8000 million eggs; Iowa (IA): about 10,000
million eggs **7.** North Carolina (NC); about 2500 million eggs
9. from 1975 to 1980; about $.75 **11.** The price of a gallon of gas
was decreasing. **13.** does; do not **15.** y **17.** 6 **19.** yes
21. yes **23.** no **25.** yes **27.** no **29.** No. For two ordered
pairs (x, y) to be equal, the x-values must be equal and the y-values
must be equal. Here we have $4 \ne -1$ and $-1 \ne 4$. **31.** 11
33. $-\dfrac{7}{2}$ **35.** -4 **37.** -5 **39.** 4; 6; -6; $(0, 4)$; $(6, 0)$; $(-6, 8)$
41. 3; -5; -15; $(0, 3)$; $(-5, 0)$; $(-15, -6)$ **43.** -9; -9; -9
45. -6; -6; -6 **47.** 8; 8; 8 **49.** $(2, 4)$ **51.** $(-5, 4)$
53. $(3, 0)$ **55.** negative; negative **57.** positive; negative

59. If $xy < 0$, then either $x < 0$ and $y > 0$ or $x > 0$ and $y < 0$.
If $x < 0$ and $y > 0$, then the point lies in quadrant II. If $x > 0$ and
$y < 0$, then the point lies in quadrant IV.

61.–70.

71. -3; 6; -2; 4

73. -3; 4; -6; $-\dfrac{4}{3}$

75. -4; -4; -4; -4
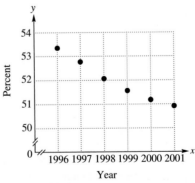

77. The points in each graph appear to lie on a straight line.
79. (a) (1996, 53.3), (1997, 52.8), (1998, 52.1), (1999, 51.6),
(2000, 51.2), (2001, 50.9) **(b)** (2002, 51.0) indicates that 51.0 percent of college students in 2002 graduated within 5 years.

(c) 4-YEAR COLLEGE STUDENTS
GRADUATING WITHIN 5 YEARS

(d) The points appear to be approximated by a straight line. Graduation rates for 4-year college students within 5 years are decreasing.

81. (a) 157, 141, 125, 109 **(b)** (20, 157), (40, 141), (60, 125), (80, 109)

(c)

TARGET HEART RATE ZONE
(Upper Limit)

The points lie in a linear pattern.

Section 3.2 (page 217)

1. 5; 5; 3

3. 1; 3; −1

5. −6; −2; −5

7. A **9.** D **11.** (12, 0); (0, −8) **13.** (0, 0); (0, 0)
15. Choose a value *other than* 0 for either x or y. For example, if $x = -5, y = 4$.

17.

19.

21.

23.

25.

27.

29.

31.

33. (a) 151.5 cm, 174.9 cm, 159.3 cm

(b)

HEIGHTS OF WOMEN

(c) 24 cm; 24 cm **35. (a)** 93 **(b)** 93 **(c)** They are the same.
37. between 93 and 149 **39. (a)** 1995: 20.7; 1996: 21.8;
1998: 24.1 (all in gallons) **(b)** 1995: 20.3; 1996: 22.1; 1998: 23.9
(all in gallons) **(c)** They differ by .4, .3, and .2 gallon, respectively.
41. (a) $30,000 **(b)** $15,000 **(c)** $5000 **(d)** After 5 yr, the SUV
has a value of $5000. **43. (a)** The equation is a fairly good model.
(b) The actual debt for 1996 is about 500 billion dollars; this is
about 30 billion dollars more than the amount given by the equation. **(c)** No. Data for future years might not follow the same pattern, so the linear equation would not be a reliable model.

Section 3.3 (page 231)

1. $\frac{3}{2}$ **3.** $-\frac{7}{4}$ **5.** 0 **7.** Rise is the vertical change between two
different points on a line. Run is the horizontal change between two
different points on a line. **9.** Yes, the answer would be the same. It
doesn't matter which point you start with. The slope would be
expressed as the quotient of −6 and −4, which simplifies to $\frac{3}{2}$.
10.–13. Answers will vary.

15. His answer is incorrect. Because he found the difference
$3 - 5 = -2$ in the numerator, he should have subtracted in the
same order in the denominator to get $-1 - 2 = -3$. The correct
slope is $\frac{-2}{-3} = \frac{2}{3}$.

17. $\dfrac{5}{4}$ **19.** $\dfrac{3}{2}$ **21.** -3 **23.** 0 **25.** undefined **27.** $-\dfrac{1}{2}$

29. 5 **31.** $\dfrac{1}{4}$ **33.** $\dfrac{3}{2}$ **35.** 0 **37.** undefined **39.** 1

41. (a) negative **(b)** 0 **43. (a)** positive **(b)** negative

45. (a) 0 **(b)** negative **47.** $\dfrac{4}{3}$; $\dfrac{4}{3}$; parallel **49.** $\dfrac{5}{3}$; $\dfrac{3}{5}$; neither

51. $\dfrac{3}{5}$; $-\dfrac{5}{3}$; perpendicular **53.** $\dfrac{8}{27}$ **54.** 232 thousand or 232,000

55. positive; increased **56.** 232,000 students **57.** -1.66
58. negative; decreased **59.** 1.66 students per computer

Section 3.4 (page 241)
1. D **3.** B **5.** $y = 3x - 3$ **7.** $y = -x + 3$ **9.** $y = 4x - 3$
11. $y = 3$ **13.** A vertical line has undefined slope, so there is no value for m. Also, there is no y-intercept, so there can be no value for b.

15.

17.

19.

21. $y = \dfrac{1}{2}x + 4$

23. $y = -\dfrac{2}{5}x - \dfrac{23}{5}$

25. $y = 2$

27. $x = 3$ (no slope-intercept form) **29.** $y = \dfrac{2}{3}x$

31. $y = 2x - 7$ **33.** $y = -2x - 4$ **35.** $y = \dfrac{2}{3}x + \dfrac{19}{3}$

37. $y = x - 3$ **39.** $y = -\dfrac{5}{7}x - \dfrac{54}{7}$ **41.** $y = -\dfrac{2}{3}x - 2$

43. $x = 3$ (no slope-intercept form) **45.** $y = \dfrac{1}{3}x + \dfrac{4}{3}$

47. $y = \dfrac{3}{4}x - \dfrac{9}{2}$ **49.** $y = -2x - 3$ **51.** $(0, 32)$; $(100, 212)$

52. $\dfrac{9}{5}$ **53.** $F - 32 = \dfrac{9}{5}(C - 0)$ **54.** $F = \dfrac{9}{5}C + 32$

55. $C = \dfrac{5}{9}(F - 32)$ **56.** $86°$ **57.** $10°$ **58.** $-40°$

59. (a) \$400 **(b)** \$.25 **(c)** $y = .25x + 400$ **(d)** \$425 **(e)** 1500

61. (a) $(1, 1125)$, $(3, 1239)$, $(5, 1314)$, $(7, 1338)$, $(9, 1379)$

(b) yes

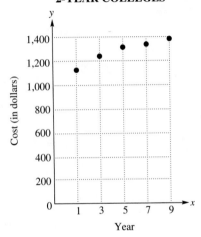

AVERAGE ANNUAL COSTS AT 2-YEAR COLLEGES

(c) $y = 23.33x + 1169$ **(d)** \$1426

Summary Exercises on Graphing Linear Equations (page 247)
1. -3; $(0, -6)$ **2.** -2; $(0, -4)$ **3.** -4; $(0, -3)$
4. -5; $(0, -8)$ **5.** $\dfrac{3}{2}$; $(0, 6)$ **6.** $\dfrac{5}{3}$, $(0, 5)$

7.

8.

9.

10.

11.

12.

13. (a) 1 **(b)** $(0, -3)$ **(c)**

14. (a) 1 **(b)** $(0, -5)$ **(c)**

15. (a) $-\dfrac{1}{2}$ **(b)** $(0, 2)$ **(c)**

16. (a) $-\dfrac{1}{3}$ **(b)** $(0, -2)$ **(c)**

17. (a) $\dfrac{4}{5}$ **(b)** $(0, -4)$ **(c)**

18. (a) $\dfrac{6}{5}$ **(b)** $(0, -6)$ **(c)**

19. (a) $-\dfrac{2}{3}$ **(b)** $(0, 4)$ **(c)**

20. (a) $-\dfrac{5}{2}$ **(b)** $(0, 5)$ **(c)**

21. (a) $\dfrac{1}{3}$ **(b)** $(0, -2)$ **(c)**

22. (a) $\dfrac{1}{2}$ **(b)** $(0, 2)$ **(c)**

23. (a) $\dfrac{1}{4}$ **(b)** $(0, 0)$ **(c)**

24. (a) $-\dfrac{1}{5}$ **(b)** $(0, 0)$ **(c)**

Section 3.5 (page 253)

1. false **3.** true **5.** $>$ **7.** $\leq$

9.

$x + y \geq 4$

11.

$x + 2y \geq 7$

13.

$-3x + 4y > 12$

15.

$x > 4$

17. Use a dashed line if the symbol is $<$ or $>$. Use a solid line if the symbol is $\leq$ or $\geq$.

19.

$x + y \le 5$

21.

$x + 2y < 4$

23.

$2x + 6 > -3y$

25.

$y \ge 2x + 1$

27.

$x \le -2$

29.

$y < 5$

31.

$y \ge 4x$

33. Every point in quadrant IV has a positive x-value and a negative y-value. Substituting into $y > x$ would imply that a negative number is greater than a positive number, which is always false. Thus, the graph of $y > x$ cannot lie in quadrant IV.

35. (a)

$x + y \ge 500$

(b) (500, 0) and (200, 400); Other answers are possible.

Chapter 3 Review Exercises (page 261)

1. 2.0% **2.** (1996, 57.1), (1997, 56.6), (1998, 56.2), (1999, 55.8), (2000, 55.5), (2001, 55.1) **3.** 1997; .5% decrease **4.** There is a general trend of decreasing percents of private school students earning a degree within five years. **5.** $-1; 2; 1$ **6.** $2; \dfrac{3}{2}; \dfrac{14}{3}$

7. $0; \dfrac{8}{3}; -9$ **8.** 7; 7; 7 **9.** yes **10.** no **11.** yes

12.–15.

16. x is positive in quadrants I and IV; y is negative in quadrants III and IV. Thus, if x is positive and y is negative, (x, y) must lie in quadrant IV. **17.** In the ordered pair $(k, 0)$, the y-value is 0, so the point lies on the x-axis. In the ordered pair $(0, k)$, the x-value is 0, so the point lies on the y-axis. **18.** II **19.** III **20.** no quadrant

21. $\left(-\dfrac{5}{2}, 0\right)$; (0, 5) **22.** $\left(-\dfrac{7}{2}, 0\right)$; (0, −7) **23.** $\left(\dfrac{8}{3}, 0\right)$; (0, 4)

24.

$2x - y = 3$

25.

$x + 2y = -4$

26.

$x + y = 0$

27. $-\dfrac{1}{2}$ **28.** $-\dfrac{2}{3}$ **29.** 0 **30.** undefined **31.** 3 **32.** $\dfrac{2}{3}$

33. $\dfrac{3}{2}$ **34.** $-\dfrac{1}{3}$ **35.** undefined **36.** 0 **37.** $\dfrac{3}{2}$ **38. (a)** 2

(b) $\dfrac{1}{3}$ **39.** parallel **40.** perpendicular **41.** neither **42.** 0

43. $y = -x + \dfrac{2}{3}$ **44.** $y = -\dfrac{1}{3}x + 1$ **45.** $y = x - 7$

46. $y = \dfrac{2}{3}x + \dfrac{14}{3}$ **47.** $y = -\dfrac{3}{4}x - \dfrac{1}{4}$ **48.** $y = -\dfrac{1}{4}x + \dfrac{3}{2}$

49. $y = 1$ **50.** $x = \dfrac{1}{3}$ **51. (a)** $y = -\dfrac{1}{3}x + 5$ **(b)** slope: $-\dfrac{1}{3}$;

y-intercept: (0, 5) **(c)**

(0, 5) (3, 4)
$x + 3y = 15$

52.

$3x + 5y > 9$

53.

$2x - 3y > -6$

54.

55. A   **56.** C, D   **57.** A, B, D   **58.** D   **59.** C   **60.** B

61. $\left(-\dfrac{5}{2}, 0\right)$; $(0, -5)$; -2

62. $(0, 0)$; $(0, 0)$; $-\dfrac{1}{3}$

63. no x-intercept; $(0, 5)$; 0

64. $y = -\dfrac{1}{4}x - \dfrac{5}{4}$ **65.** $y = -3x + 30$ **66.** $y = -\dfrac{4}{7}x - \dfrac{23}{7}$

67.

68.

69. 3.0%   **70.** Since the graph falls from left to right, the slope is negative.   **71.** (1997, 44.2), (2002, 41.2)
72. $y = -.6x + 1242.4$ **73.** $-.6$; yes   **74.** 43.6, 43.0, 42.4, 41.8
75. 40.6%; No. The equation is based on data only for 1997 through 2002.

Chapter 3 Test (page 267)
1. \$1.06   **2.** \$.45   **3.** from 2000 to 2002
4. x-intercept: $(2, 0)$; y-intercept: $(0, 6)$

5. x-intercept: $(0, 0)$; y-intercept: $(0, 0)$

6. x-intercept: $(-3, 0)$; y-intercept: none

7. x-intercept: none; y-intercept: $(0, 1)$

8. x-intercept: $(4, 0)$; y-intercept: $(0, -4)$

9. $-\dfrac{8}{3}$ **10.** -2 **11.** undefined   **12.** $\dfrac{5}{2}$ **13.** 0   **14.** $y = 2x + 6$

15. $y = \dfrac{5}{2}x - 4$ **16.** $y = -9x + 12$ **17.** $y = -\dfrac{3}{2}x + \dfrac{9}{2}$

18.

19.

20. The slope is positive since food and drink sales are increasing.
21. (0, 43), (30, 376); 11.1   **22. (a)** 1990: \$265 billion;
1995: \$320.5 billion   **(b)** In 2000, food and drink sales were \$376 billion.

Cumulative Review Exercises: Chapters R–3 (page 271)

1. $\dfrac{301}{40}$ or $7\dfrac{21}{40}$ **2.** 6   **3.** 7   **4.** $\dfrac{73}{18}$ or $4\dfrac{1}{18}$ **5.** true   **6.** -43

7. distributive property   **8.** $-p + 2$ **9.** $h = \dfrac{3V}{\pi r^2}$ **10.** -1

11. 2   **12.** -13 **13.** $x > -2.6$

14. $x > 0$

15. $t \leq -4$

16. high school diploma: \$36,722; bachelor's degree: \$65,922
17. 13 mi **18. (a)** 89.33, 81.21, 78.16 **(b)** In 1980, the winning time was approximately 85.27 sec. **19. (a)** \$7000 **(b)** \$10,000
(c) about \$30,000 **20.** $(-4, 0); (0, 3)$ **21.** $\dfrac{3}{4}$

22.

$-3x + 4y = 12$

23. 6 **24.** perpendicular **25.** $y = 3x - 11$ **26.** $y = 4$

CHAPTER 4 SYSTEMS OF LINEAR EQUATIONS AND INEQUALITIES

Section 4.1 (page 279)
1. B, because the ordered pair must be in quadrant II. **3.** There is no way that the sum of two numbers can be both 2 and 4 at the same time. **5.** no **7.** yes **9.** yes **11.** no
We show the graphs here only for Exercises 13–17.
13. $(4, 2)$ **15.** $(0, 4)$

17. $(4, -1)$

19. $(1, 3)$ **21.** $(0, 2)$ **23.** no solution **25.** infinite number of solutions **27.** $(4, -3)$ **29.** no solution
31. $y = -\dfrac{3}{2}x + 3; y = -\dfrac{3}{2}x + \dfrac{5}{2}$; The graphs are parallel lines.
32. $y = 2x - 4; y = 2x - 4$; The graphs are the same line.
33. $y = \dfrac{1}{3}x - \dfrac{5}{3}; y = -2x + 8$; The graphs are intersecting lines.
34. Exercise 31: no solution; Exercise 32: infinite number of solutions; Exercise 33: one solution **35.** 1989–1997 **37.** 1989: share 20%; 1998: share 16% **39.** If the coordinates of the point of intersection are not integers, the solution will be difficult to determine from a graph. **41.** Answers will vary, but the lines must intersect at $(-2, 3)$.

Section 4.2 (page 289)
1. No, it is not correct, because the solution is the ordered pair $(3, 0)$. The y-value must also be determined. **3.** $(3, 9)$ **5.** $(7, 3)$
7. $(-2, 4)$ **9.** $(-4, 8)$ **11.** $(3, -2)$ **13.** infinite number of solutions **15.** $\left(\dfrac{1}{3}, -\dfrac{1}{2}\right)$ **17.** no solution

19. infinite number of solutions **21.** $(36, -35)$ **23.** no solution
25. $(2, -3)$ **27.** $(10, -12)$ **29.** $(-4, 2)$ **30.** To find the total cost, multiply the number of bicycles (x) by the cost per bicycle (400 dollars) and add the fixed cost (5000 dollars). Thus, $y_1 = 400x + 5000$ gives this total cost (in dollars).
31. $y_2 = 600x$ **32.** $y_1 = 400x + 5000, y_2 = 600x$, solution: $(25, 15,000)$ **33.** 25; 15,000; 15,000

Section 4.3 (page 295)
1. true **3.** true **5.** $(-1, 3)$ **7.** $(-1, -3)$ **9.** $(-2, 3)$
11. $\left(\dfrac{1}{2}, 4\right)$ **13.** $(3, -6)$ **15.** $(7, 4)$ **17.** $(0, 4)$ **19.** $(-4, 0)$
21. $(0, 0)$ **23.** no solution **25.** infinite number of solutions
27. $(2, 9)$ **29.** $(-6, 5)$ **31.** $\left(-\dfrac{6}{5}, \dfrac{4}{5}\right)$ **33.** $\left(\dfrac{1}{8}, -\dfrac{5}{6}\right)$
35. $(11, 15)$ **37.** no solution **39.** infinite number of solutions
41. $1141 = 1991a + b$ **42.** $1465 = 1999a + b$
43. $1991a + b = 1141, 1999a + b = 1465$; solution: $(40.5, -79,494.5)$ **44.** $y = 40.5x - 79,494.5$ **45.** 1424.5 (million); This is slightly less than the actual figure. **46.** Since the data do not lie in a perfectly straight line, the quantity obtained from an equation determined in this way will probably be "off" a bit. We cannot put too much faith in models such as this one, because not all sets of data points are linear in nature.

Summary Exercises on Solving Systems of Linear Equations (page 299)
1. (a) Use substitution since the second equation is solved for y.
(b) Use elimination since the coefficients of the y-terms are opposites. **(c)** Use elimination since the equations are in standard form with no coefficients of 1 or -1. Solving by substitution would involve fractions. **2.** The system on the right is easier to solve by substitution because the second equation is already solved for y.
3. (a) $(1, 4)$ **(b)** $(1, 4)$ **(c)** Answers will vary. **4. (a)** $(-5, 2)$
(b) $(-5, 2)$ **(c)** Answers will vary. **5.** $(2, 6)$ **6.** $(-3, 2)$
7. $\left(\dfrac{1}{3}, \dfrac{1}{2}\right)$ **8.** no solution **9.** $(3, 0)$ **10.** $\left(\dfrac{3}{2}, -\dfrac{3}{2}\right)$
11. infinite number of solutions **12.** $(9, 4)$ **13.** $\left(-\dfrac{5}{7}, -\dfrac{2}{7}\right)$
14. $(4, -5)$ **15.** no solution **16.** $(-4, 6)$ **17.** $\left(\dfrac{19}{3}, -5\right)$
18. $\left(\dfrac{22}{13}, -\dfrac{23}{13}\right)$ **19.** $(-12, -60)$ **20.** $(2, -4)$ **21.** $(18, -12)$
22. $(-2, 1)$ **23.** $\left(13, -\dfrac{7}{5}\right)$ **24.** infinite number of solutions

Section 4.4 (page 307)
1. D **3.** B **5.** D **7.** C **9.** the second number; $x - y = 48$; The two numbers are 73 and 25. **11.** Cher: 84; Rolling Stones: 33
13. *The Lord of the Rings: The Return of the King*: \$361.1 million; *Finding Nemo*: \$339.7 million **15.** Terminal Tower: 708 ft; Key Tower: 950 ft **17. (a)** 45 units **(b)** Do not produce; the product will lead to a loss. **19.** 46 ones; 28 tens **21.** 2 DVDs of *Miracle*; 5 Linkin Park CDs **23.** \$2500 at 4%; \$5000 at 5% **25.** Japan: \$17.19; Switzerland: \$13.15 **27.** 80 L of 40% solution; 40 L of 70% solution **29.** 30 lb at \$6 per lb; 60 lb at \$3 per lb
31. 30 barrels at \$40 per barrel; 20 barrels at \$60 per barrel
33. bicycle: 15 mph; car: 55 mph **35.** car leaving Cincinnati: 55 mph; car leaving Toledo: 70 mph **37.** Roberto: 17.5 mph; Juana: 12.5 mph **39.** boat: 10 mph; current: 2 mph
41. plane: 470 mph; wind: 30 mph

Section 4.5 (page 317)

1. C   **3.** B

5.

7.

9.

11.

13.

15.

17.

19.

31.
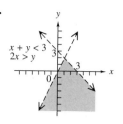

32. B   **33.** B   **34.** $(2, 0)$ **35.** $(-4, 15)$ **36.** no solution

37.

38.

39.

40. 8 in., 8 in., and 13 in.   **41.** New England 24, Indianapolis 14
42. **(a)** years 0–6   **(b)** year 6; about \$650

Chapter 4 Review Exercises (page 323)

1. yes   **2.** no   **3.** $(3, 1)$ **4.** $(0, -2)$ **5.** infinite number of
solutions   **6.** no solution   **7.** It is not a solution of the system
because it is not a solution of the second equation, $2x + y = 4$.
8. $(2, 1)$ **9.** $(3, 5)$ **10.** $(6, 4)$ **11.** no solution   **12.** $(7, 1)$
13. $(-5, -2)$ **14.** $(-4, 3)$ **15.** infinite number of solutions
16. **(a)** 2   **(b)** 9   **17.** $(9, 2)$ **18.** $\left(\dfrac{10}{7}, -\dfrac{9}{7}\right)$ **19.** $(8, 9)$

20. $(2, 1)$ **21.** Subway: 13,247 restaurants; McDonald's: 13,099
restaurants   **22.** *Modern Maturity:* 20.5 million; *Reader's Digest:*
15.1 million   **23.** length: 27 m; width: 18 m   **24.** 13 twenties;
7 tens   **25.** 25 lb of \$1.30 candy; 75 lb of \$.90 candy
26. plane: 250 mph; wind: 20 mph   **27.** \$7000 at 3%; \$11,000 at
4%   **28.** 60 L of 40% solution; 30 L of 70% solution

29.

30.

Chapter 4 Test (page 327)

1. $(2, -3)$ **2.** It has no solution.   **3.** $(1, -6)$ **4.** $(-35, 35)$
5. $(5, 6)$ **6.** $(-1, 3)$ **7.** $(0, 0)$ **8.** no solution   **9.** infinite
number of solutions   **10.** $(12, -4)$ **11.** Memphis and Atlanta:
394 mi; Minneapolis and Houston: 1176 mi   **12.** Disneyland:
12.7 million; Magic Kingdom: 14.0 million   **13.** $33\dfrac{1}{3}$ L of 25%
solution; $16\dfrac{2}{3}$ L of 40% solution   **14.** slower car: 45 mph; faster
car: 60 mph

15.

16.

Cumulative Review Exercises: Chapters R–4 (page 329)

1. $-1, 1, -2, 2, -4, 4, -5, 5, -8, 8, -10, 10, -20, 20, -40, 40$
2. 1   **3.** commutative property   **4.** distributive property
5. inverse property   **6.** 46   **7.** $-\dfrac{13}{11}$ **8.** $\dfrac{9}{11}$ **9.** $x > -18$

10. $x > -\dfrac{11}{2}$ **11.** width: 8.16 in.; length: 10.74 in.

12.

13.

14. $-\dfrac{4}{3}$ **15.** $-\dfrac{1}{4}$ **16.** $y = \dfrac{1}{2}x + 3$ **17.** $y = 2x + 1$

18. (a) $x = 9$ **(b)** $y = -1$ **19.** $(-1, 6)$ **20.** $(3, -4)$

21. no solution **22.** 405 adults and 49 children

23. 19 in., 19 in., 15 in. **24.**

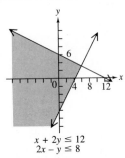

$x + 2y \le 12$
$2x - y \le 8$

CHAPTER 5 EXPONENTS AND POLYNOMIALS

Section 5.1 (page 337)

1. 7; 5 **3.** 8 **5.** 26 **7.** 1; 6 **9.** 1; 1 **11.** 2; $-19, -1$
13. 2; 1, 8 **15.** $2m^5$ **17.** $-r^5$ **19.** cannot be simplified;
$.2m^5 - .5m^2$ **21.** $-5x^5$ **23.** $5p^9 + 4p^7$ **25.** $-2y^2$
27. already simplified; 4; binomial **29.** already simplified;
$6m^5 + 5m^4 - 7m^3 - 3m^2$; 5; none of these **31.** $x^4 + \dfrac{1}{3}x^2 - 4$; 4;
trinomial **33.** 7; 0; monomial **35. (a)** -1 **(b)** 5 **37. (a)** 19
(b) -2 **39. (a)** 36 **(b)** -12 **41. (a)** -124 **(b)** 5
43. 175 ft **44.** 87 ft; $(1, 87)$ **45.** \$7.20 **46.** \$27
47. $5m^2 + 3m$ **49.** $4x^4 - 4x^2$ **51.** $\dfrac{7}{6}x^2 - \dfrac{2}{15}x + \dfrac{5}{6}$
53. $12m^3 - 13m^2 + 6m + 11$ **55.** $8r^2 + 5r - 12$
57. $5m^2 - 14m + 6$ **59.** $4x^3 + 2x^2 + 5x$
61. $-18y^5 + 7y^4 + 5y^3 + 3y^2 + y$ **63.** $-2m^3 + 7m^2 + 8m - 9$
65. $8x^2 + 8x + 6$ **67.** $8t^2 + 8t + 13$ **69.** $-11x^2 - 3x - 3$
71. The degree of a term is determined by the exponents on the
variables, but 3 is not a variable. The degree of $3^4 = 3^4x^0$ is 0.
73. $13a^2b - 7a^2 - b$ **75.** $c^4d - 5c^2d^2 + d^2$
77. $12m^3n - 11m^2n^2 - 4mn^2$

Section 5.2 (page 347)

1. 1 **3.** false **5.** false **7.** $(-2)^5$ **9.** $\left(\dfrac{1}{2}\right)^6$ **11.** $(-8p)^2$
13. The expression $(-3)^4$ means $(-3)(-3)(-3)(-3) = 81$,
while -3^4 means $-(3 \cdot 3 \cdot 3 \cdot 3) = -81$. **15.** base: 3; exponent: 5; 243 **17.** base: -3; exponent: 5; -243 **19.** base: $-6x$;
exponent: 4 **21.** base: x; exponent: 4 **23.** The product rule does
not apply to $5^2 + 5^3$ because it is a *sum*, not a product.
$5^2 + 5^3 = 25 + 125 = 150$ **25.** 5^8 **27.** 4^{12} **29.** $(-7)^9$
31. t^{24} **33.** $-56r^7$ **35.** $42p^{10}$ **37.** 4^6 **39.** t^{20} **41.** 7^3r^3
43. $5^5x^5y^5$ **45.** $8q^3r^3$ **47.** $\dfrac{1}{2^3}$ **49.** $\dfrac{a^3}{b^3}$ **51.** $\dfrac{9^8}{5^8}$ **53.** $(-2)^3x^6y^3$
55. $3^2a^6b^4$ **57.** $\dfrac{5^5}{2^5}$ **59.** $\dfrac{9^5}{8^3}$ **61.** $2^{12}x^{12}$ **63.** $(-6)^5p^5$
65. $6^5x^{10}y^{15}$ **67.** x^{21} **69.** $2^2w^4x^{26}y^7$ or $4w^4x^{26}y^7$ **71.** $-r^{18}s^{17}$

73. $\dfrac{5^3a^6b^{15}}{c^{18}}$ or $\dfrac{125a^6b^{15}}{c^{18}}$ **75.** $25m^6p^{14}q^5$ **77.** $16x^{10}y^{16}z^{10}$
79. $30x^7$

Section 5.3 (page 355)

1. $x^2 + 7x + 12$ **3.** $2x^3 + 7x^2 + 7x + 2$ **5.** distributive
7. $-6m^2 - 4m$ **9.** $6p - \dfrac{9}{2}p^2 + 9p^4$ **11.** $6y^5 + 4y^6 + 10y^9$
13. $12x^3 + 26x^2 + 10x + 1$ **15.** $20m^4 - m^3 - 8m^2 - 17m - 15$
17. $6x^6 - 3x^5 - 4x^4 + 4x^3 - 5x^2 + 8x - 3$
19. $5x^4 - 13x^3 + 20x^2 + 7x + 5$ **21.** $n^2 + n - 6$
23. $8r^2 - 10r - 3$ **25.** $9x^2 - 4$ **27.** $9q^2 + 6q + 1$
29. $6t^2 + 23st + 20s^2$ **31.** $-.3t^2 + .22t + .24$
33. $x^2 - \dfrac{5}{12}x - \dfrac{1}{6}$ **35.** $\dfrac{15}{16} - \dfrac{1}{4}r - 2r^2$ **37.** $6y^5 - 21y^4 - 45y^3$
39. $30x + 60$ yd^2 **40.** $30x + 60 = 600$; 18 **41.** 10 yd by 60 yd
42. \$2100 **43.** 140 yd **44.** \$1260 **45.** The answers are
$x^2 - 16$, $y^2 - 4$, and $r^2 - 49$. Each product is the difference of
the square of the first term and the square of the last term of the
binomials.

Section 5.4 (page 361)

1. (a) $4x^2$ **(b)** $12x$ **(c)** 9 **(d)** $4x^2 + 12x + 9$ **3.** $a^2 - 2ac + c^2$
5. $p^2 + 4p + 4$ **7.** $16x^2 - 24x + 9$ **9.** $.64t^2 + 1.12ts + .49s^2$
11. $25x^2 + 4xy + \dfrac{4}{25}y^2$ **13.** $16a^2 - 12ab + \dfrac{9}{4}b^2$
15. $-16r^2 + 16r - 4$ **17. (a)** $49x^2$ **(b)** 0 **(c)** $-9y^2$
(d) $49x^2 - 9y^2$; Because 0 is the identity element for addition,
it is not necessary to write "+ 0." **19.** $q^2 - 4$ **21.** $4w^2 - 25$
23. $100x^2 - 9y^2$ **25.** $4x^4 - 25$ **27.** $49x^2 - \dfrac{9}{49}$ **29.** $9p^3 - 49p$
31. $(a + b)^2$ **32.** a^2 **33.** $2ab$ **34.** b^2 **35.** $a^2 + 2ab + b^2$
36. They both represent the area of the entire large square.
37. 1225 **38.** $30^2 + 2(30)(5) + 5^2$ **39.** 1225 **40.** They are
equal. **41.** $m^3 - 15m^2 + 75m - 125$ **43.** $8a^3 + 12a^2 + 6a + 1$
45. $81r^4 - 216r^3t + 216r^2t^2 - 96rt^3 + 16t^4$
47. $3x^5 - 27x^4 + 81x^3 - 81x^2$
49. $-8x^6y - 32x^5y^2 - 48x^4y^3 - 32x^3y^4 - 8x^2y^5$
51. 512 cu. units

Section 5.5 (page 371)

1. negative **3.** negative **5.** positive **7.** 0 **9.** 1 **11.** -1
13. 0 **15.** 0 **17.** 2 **19.** $\dfrac{1}{64}$ **21.** 16 **23.** $\dfrac{49}{36}$ **25.** $\dfrac{8}{15}$
27. $-\dfrac{7}{18}$ **29.** 1 **30.** $\dfrac{5^2}{5^2}$ **31.** 5^0 **32.** $5^0 = 1$; This supports the
definition of a 0 exponent. **33.** $\dfrac{1}{9}$ **35.** $\dfrac{1}{6^5}$ **37.** 6^3 **39.** $2r^4$
41. $\dfrac{5^2}{4^3}$ **43.** $\dfrac{p^5}{q^8}$ **45.** r^9 **47.** $\dfrac{x^5}{6}$ **49.** $3y^2$ **51.** x^3 **53.** 7^3
55. $\dfrac{1}{x^2}$ **57.** $\dfrac{4^3x}{3^2}$ or $\dfrac{64x}{9}$ **59.** $\dfrac{x^2z^4}{y^2}$ **61.** $6x$ **63.** $\dfrac{1}{m^{10}n^5}$
65. $\dfrac{5}{16x^5}$ **67.** $\dfrac{36q^2}{m^4p^2}$

Summary Exercises on the Rules for Exponents (page 373)

1. $\dfrac{6^{12}x^{24}}{5^{12}}$ **2.** $\dfrac{r^6s^{12}}{729t^6}$ **3.** $10^5x^7y^{14}$ **4.** $-128a^{10}b^{15}c^4$ **5.** $\dfrac{729w^3x^9}{y^{12}}$
6. $\dfrac{x^4y^6}{16}$ **7.** c^{22} **8.** $\dfrac{1}{k^4t^{12}}$ **9.** $\dfrac{11}{30}$ **10.** $y^{12}z^3$ **11.** $\dfrac{x^6}{y^5}$ **12.** 0

13. $\frac{1}{z^2}$ 14. $\frac{9}{r^2s^2t^{10}}$ 15. $\frac{300x^3}{y^3}$ 16. $\frac{3}{5x^6}$ 17. x^8 18. $\frac{y^{11}}{x^{11}}$

19. $\frac{a^6}{b^4}$ 20. $6ab$ 21. $\frac{61}{900}$ 22. 1 23. $\frac{343a^6b^9}{8}$ 24. 1

25. -1 26. 0 27. $\frac{27y^{18}}{4x^8}$ 28. $\frac{1}{a^8b^{12}c^{16}}$ 29. $\frac{x^{15}}{216z^9}$ 30. $\frac{q}{8p^6r^3}$

31. x^6y^6 32. 0 33. $\frac{343}{x^{15}}$ 34. $\frac{9}{x^6}$ 35. $5p^{10}q^9$ 36. $\frac{7}{24}$

37. $\frac{r^{14}t}{2s^2}$ 38. 1 39. $8p^{10}q$ 40. $\frac{1}{mn^3p^3}$ 41. -1 42. $\frac{3}{40}$

Section 5.6 (page 377)

1. $6x^2+8$; 2; $3x^2+4$ 3. $3x^2+4$; 2 (These may be reversed.); $6x^2+8$ 5. To use the method of this section, the divisor must be just one term. This is true of the first problem, but not the second.
7. $30x^3-10x+5$ 9. $-4m^3+2m^2-1$ 11. $4t^4-2t^2+2t$
13. $a^4-a+\frac{2}{a}$ 15. $-2x^3+\frac{2x^2}{3}-x$ 17. $1+5x-9x^2$
19. $\frac{4x^2}{3}+x+\frac{2}{3x}$ 21. $9r^3-12r^2-2r+1-\frac{2}{3r}$
23. $-m^2+3m-\frac{4}{m}$ 25. $-4b^2+3ab-\frac{5}{a}$
27. $\frac{12}{x}-\frac{6}{x^2}+\frac{14}{x^3}-\frac{10}{x^4}$ 29. No, $\frac{2}{3}x$ means $\frac{2x}{3}$, which is not the

same as $\frac{2}{3x}$. In the first case we multiply by x; in the second case we

divide by x. Yes, $\frac{4}{3}x^2=\frac{4x^2}{3}$. In both cases we are multiplying by x^2.

31. $15x^5-35x^4+35x^3$ 33. 1423
34. $(1\times10^3)+(4\times10^2)+(2\times10^1)+(3\times10^0)$
35. x^3+4x^2+2x+3 36. They are similar in that the coefficients of the powers of ten are equal to the coefficients of the powers of x. They are different in that one is a number while the other is a polynomial. They are equal if $x=10$.

Section 5.7 (page 383)

1. The divisor is $2x+5$; the quotient is $2x^3-4x^2+3x+2$.
3. Divide $12m^2$ by $2m$ to get $6m$. 5. $x+2$ 7. $2y-5$
9. $p-4+\frac{44}{p+6}$ 11. $r-5$ 13. $2a-14+\frac{74}{2a+3}$
15. $4x^2-7x+3$ 17. $3y^2-2y+2$ 19. $3k-4+\frac{2}{k^2-2}$
21. x^2+1 23. $2p^2-5p+4+\frac{6}{3p^2+1}$ 25. x^3+6x-7
27. x^2+1 29. $2x^2+\frac{3}{5}x+\frac{1}{5}$ 31. x^2+x-3 units 33. 33
34. 33 35. They are the same. 36. The answers should agree.

Section 5.8 (page 389)

1. 6.1309×10^9; 5.8689×10^9 3. 6.9627×10^{10}; 1.8104×10^{11}
5. in scientific notation 7. not in scientific notation; 5.6×10^6
9. not in scientific notation; 4×10^{-3} 11. not in scientific notation; 8×10^1 13. A number is written in scientific notation if it is the product of a number whose absolute value is between 1 and 10 (inclusive of 1) and a power of 10. 15. 5.876×10^9
17. 8.235×10^4 19. 7×10^{-6} 21. -2.03×10^{-3}
23. 750,000 25. 5,677,000,000,000 27. -6.21 29. .00078
31. .000000005134 33. 6×10^{11}; 600,000,000,000
35. 1.5×10^7; 15,000,000 37. 6.426×10^4; 64,260
39. 3×10^{-4} 41. 4×10^1 43. 2.6×10^{-3} 45. about 3.3
47. about $63,000,000,000 49. about .276 lb

Chapter 5 Review Exercises (page 395)

1. $22m^2$; degree 2; monomial 2. p^3-p^2+4p+2; degree 3; none of these 3. already in descending powers; degree 5; none of these 4. $-8y^5-7y^4+9y$; degree 5; trinomial
5. $-5a^3+4a^2$ 6. $2r^3-3r^2+9r$ 7. $11y^2-10y+9$
8. $-13k^4-15k^2-4k-6$ 9. $10m^3-6m^2-3$
10. $-y^2-4y+26$ 11. $10p^2-3p-11$ 12. $7r^4-4r^3-1$
13. 4^{11} 14. $(-5)^{11}$ 15. $-72x^7$ 16. $10x^{14}$ 17. 19^5x^5
18. $(-4)^7y^7$ 19. $5p^4t^4$ 20. $\frac{7^6}{5^6}$ 21. $3^3x^6y^9$ 22. t^{42}
23. $6^2x^{16}y^4z^{16}$ 24. The product rule for exponents does not apply here because we want the sum of 7^2 and 7^4, not their product.
25. $10x^2+70x$ 26. $-6p^5+15p^4$ 27. $6r^3+8r^2-17r+6$
28. $8y^3+27$ 29. $5p^5-2p^4-3p^3+25p^2+15p$
30. $6k^2-9k-6$ 31. $12p^2-48pq+21q^2$
32. $2m^4+5m^3-16m^2-28m+9$ 33. $a^2+8a+16$
34. $9p^2-12p+4$ 35. $4r^2+20rs+25s^2$
36. $r^3+6r^2+12r+8$ 37. $8x^3-12x^2+6x-1$
38. $36m^2-25$ 39. $4z^2-49$ 40. $25a^2-36b^2$ 41. $4x^4-25$
42. $(a+b)^2=(a+b)(a+b)=a^2+2ab+b^2$. The term $2ab$
is not in a^2+b^2. 43. 2 44. $\frac{1}{32}$ 45. $\frac{5^2}{6^2}$ or $\frac{25}{36}$ 46. $-\frac{3}{16}$
47. 6^2 48. x^2 49. $\frac{1}{p^{12}}$ 50. r^4 51. 2^8 52. $\frac{1}{9^6}$ 53. 5^8
54. $\frac{1}{8^{12}}$ 55. $\frac{1}{m^2}$ 56. y^7 57. r^{13} 58. $(-5)^2m^6$ 59. $\frac{y^{12}}{2^3}$
60. $\frac{1}{a^3b^5}$ 61. $2\cdot6^2\cdot r^5$ 62. $\frac{2^3n^{10}}{3m^{13}}$ 63. $\frac{5y^2}{3}$ 64. $-2x^2y$
65. $-y^3+2y-3$ 66. $p-3+\frac{5}{2p}$
67. $-x^9+2x^8-4x^3+7x$ 68. $-2m^2n+mn^2+\frac{6n^3}{5}$
69. $2r+7$ 70. $4m+3+\frac{5}{3m-5}$ 71. $2a+1+\frac{-8a+12}{5a^2-3}$
72. $k^2+2k+4+\frac{-2k-12}{2k^2+1}$ 73. 4.8×10^7
74. 2.8988×10^{10} 75. 6.5×10^{-5} 76. 8.24×10^{-8}
77. 24,000 78. 78,300,000 79. .000000897
80. .00000000000995 81. 800 82. 4,000,000 83. .025
84. .01 85. .0000000000016 86. (a) 1×10^3 (b) 2×10^3
(c) 5×10^4 (d) 1×10^5 87. 0 88. $\frac{3^5}{p^3}$ 89. $\frac{1}{7^2}$
90. $49-28k+4k^2$ 91. y^2+5y+1 92. $\frac{6^4r^8s^4}{5^4}$
93. $-8m^7-10m^6-6m^5$ 94. 2^5 95. $5xy^3-\frac{8y^2}{5}+3x^2y$
96. $\frac{r^2}{6}$ 97. $8x^3+12x^2y+6xy^2+y^3$ 98. $\frac{3}{4}$
99. a^3-2a^2-7a+2 100. $8y^3-9y^2+5$
101. $10r^2+21r-10$ 102. $144a^2-1$ 103. $2x^2+x-6$
104. $25x^8+20x^6+4x^4$

Chapter 5 Test (page 399)

1. $4t^4+t^3-6t^2-t$ 2. $-2y^2-9y+17$ 3. $-12t^2+5t+8$
4. $(-2)^5$ or -2^5 5. $\frac{6^3}{m^6}$ 6. $-27x^5+18x^4-6x^3+3x^2$
7. $2r^3+r^2-16r+15$ 8. $t^2-5t-24$ 9. $8x^2+2xy-3y^2$
10. $25x^2-20xy+4y^2$ 11. $100v^2-9w^2$
12. x^3+3x^2+3x+1 13. $\frac{1}{625}$ 14. 2 15. $\frac{7}{12}$ 16. 8^5

17. x^2y^6 **18.** $4y^2 - 3y + 2 + \dfrac{5}{y}$ **19.** $-3xy^2 + 2x^3y^2 + 4y^2$

20. $2x + 9$ **21.** $3x^2 + 6x + 11 + \dfrac{26}{x-2}$ **22. (a)** 3.44×10^{11}

(b) 5.57×10^{-6} **23. (a)** 29,600,000 **(b)** .0000000607
24. $9x^2 + 54x + 81$ **25.** Answers will vary. One example is
$(-4x^4 + 3x^3 + 2x + 1) + (4x^4 - 8x^3 + 2x + 7)$
$= -5x^3 + 4x + 8.$

Cumulative Review Exercises: Chapters R–5 (page 401)

1. $\dfrac{19}{24}$ **2.** $-\dfrac{1}{20}$ **3.** 3.72   **4.** 62.006   **5.** \$1836   **6.** -8 **7.** 24

8. $\dfrac{1}{2}$ **9.** -4 **10.** associative property   **11.** inverse property

12. distributive property   **13.** 10   **14.** $\dfrac{13}{4}$ **15.** no solution

16. $r = \dfrac{d}{t}$ **17.** -5 **18.** -12 **19.** 20   **20.** all real numbers

21. mouse: 160; elephant: 10   **22.** 4   **23.** $x \geq 10$

24. $x < -\dfrac{14}{5}$ **25.** $-4 \leq x < 2$ **26.** $(0, 2)$ and $(-3, 0)$

27.   **28.** $\dfrac{2}{3}$ **29.** $(-3, -1)$ **30.** $(4, -5)$

31. $\dfrac{5}{4}$ or $1\dfrac{1}{4}$ **32.** 2   **33.** 1   **34.** $\dfrac{2b}{a^{10}}$ **35.** 3.45×10^4

36. $11x^3 - 14x^2 - x + 14$ **37.** $18x^7 - 54x^6 + 60x^5$
38. $63x^2 + 57x + 12$ **39.** $25x^2 + 80x + 64$ **40.** $y^2 - 2y + 6$

CHAPTER 6   FACTORING AND APPLICATIONS

Section 6.1 (page 411)
1. 4   **3.** 4   **5.** 6   **7.** 1   **9.** 8   **11.** $10x^3$ **13.** xy^2 **15.** 6
17. $3m^2$ **19.** $2z^4$ **21.** $2mn^4$ **23.** $y + 2$ **25.** $a - 2$

27. $2 + 3xy$ **29.** $x(x - 4)$ **31.** $3t(2t + 5)$ **33.** $\dfrac{1}{4}d(d - 3)$

35. $6x^2(2x + 1)$ **37.** $5y^6(13y^4 + 7)$
39. no common factor (except 1)   **41.** $8m^2n^2(n + 3)$
43. $2x(2x^2 - 5x + 3)$ **45.** $13y^2(y^6 + 2y^2 - 3)$
47. $9qp^3(5q^3p^2 + 4p^3 + 9q)$ **49.** $(x + 2)(c + d)$
51. $(2a + b)(a^2 - b)$ **53.** $(p + 4)(q - 1)$
55. $(5 + n)(m + 4)$ **57.** $(2y - 7)(3x + 4)$
59. $(y + 3)(3x + 1)$ **61.** $(z + 2)(7z - a)$
63. $(3r + 2y)(6r - x)$ **65.** $(w + 1)(w^2 + 9)$
67. $(a + 2)(3a^2 - 2)$ **69.** $(4m - p^2)(4m^2 - p)$
71. $(y + 3)(y + x)$ **73.** $(z - 2)(2z - 3w)$
75. commutative property   **76.** $2x(y - 4) - 3(y - 4)$
77. No, because it is not a product. It is the difference between
$2x(y - 4)$ and $3(y - 4)$.   **78.** $(2x - 3)(y - 4)$; yes

Section 6.2 (page 417)
1. a and b must have different signs.   **3.** A prime polynomial is
one that cannot be factored using only integers in the factors.
5. 1 and 12, -1 and -12, 2 and 6, -2 and -6, 3 and 4, -3 and
-4; the pair with a sum of 7 is 3 and 4.   **7.** 1 and -24, -1 and
24, 2 and -12, -2 and 12, 3 and -8, -3 and 8, 4 and -6, -4 and
6; the pair with a sum of -5 is 3 and -8.   **9.** C   **11.** $x + 11$

13. $x - 8$ **15.** $y - 5$ **17.** $x + 11$ **19.** $y - 9$
21. $(y + 8)(y + 1)$ **23.** $(b + 3)(b + 5)$
25. $(m + 5)(m - 4)$ **27.** $(x + 8)(x - 5)$
29. $(y - 5)(y - 3)$ **31.** $(z - 8)(z - 7)$ **33.** $(r - 6)(r + 5)$
35. $(a - 12)(a + 4)$ **37.** prime   **39.** $(r + 2a)(r + a)$
41. $(x + y)(x + 3y)$ **43.** $(t + 2z)(t - 3z)$
45. $(v - 5w)(v - 6w)$ **47.** $4(x + 5)(x - 2)$
49. $2t(t + 1)(t + 3)$ **51.** $2x^4(x - 3)(x + 7)$
53. $a^3(a + 4b)(a - b)$ **55.** $mn(m - 6n)(m - 4n)$
57. The factored form $(2x + 4)(x - 3)$ is incorrect because
$2x + 4$ has a common factor of 2, which must be factored out for
the trinomial to be *completely* factored.

Section 6.3 (page 421)
1. $(m + 6)(m + 2)$ **3.** $(a + 5)(a - 2)$ **5.** $(2t + 1)(5t + 2)$
7. $(3z - 2)(5z - 3)$ **9.** $(2s - t)(4s + 3t)$
11. $(3a + 2b)(5a + 4b)$ **13.** B   **15. (a)** 2; 12; 24; 11
(b) 3; 8 (Order is irrelevant.)   **(c)** $3m$; $8m$
(d) $2m^2 + 3m + 8m + 12$ **(e)** $(2m + 3)(m + 4)$
(f) $(2m + 3)(m + 4) = 2m^2 + 11m + 12$
17. $(2x + 1)(x + 3)$ **19.** $(4r - 3)(r + 1)$
21. $(4m + 1)(2m - 3)$ **23.** $(3m + 1)(7m + 2)$
25. $(2b + 1)(3b + 2)$ **27.** $(4y - 3)(3y - 1)$
29. $3(4x - 1)(2x - 3)$ **31.** $2m(m - 4)(m + 5)$
33. $4z^3(8z + 3)(z - 1)$ **35.** $(3p + 4q)(4p - 3q)$
37. $(3a - 5b)(2a + b)$ **39.** $(5 - x)(1 - x)$ **41.** The student
stopped too soon. He needs to factor out the common factor $4x - 1$
to get $(4x - 1)(4x - 5)$ as the correct answer.

Section 6.4 (page 427)
1. B   **3.** A   **5.** A   **7.** $2a + 5b$ **9.** $x^2 + 3x - 4$; $x + 4, x - 1$,
or $x - 1, x + 4$ **11.** $2z^2 - 5z - 3$; $2z + 1, z - 3$, or
$z - 3, 2z + 1$ **13.** The binomial $2x - 6$ cannot be a factor because it has a common factor of 2, but the polynomial does not.
15. $(3a + 7)(a + 1)$ **17.** $(2y + 3)(y + 2)$
19. $(3m - 1)(5m + 2)$ **21.** $(3s - 1)(4s + 5)$
23. $(5m - 4)(2m - 3)$ **25.** $(4w - 1)(2w - 3)$
27. $(4y + 1)(5y - 11)$ **29.** prime   **31.** $2(5x + 3)(2x + 1)$
33. $q(5m + 2)(8m - 3)$ **35.** $3n^2(5n - 3)(n - 2)$
37. $y^2(5x - 4)(3x + 1)$ **39.** $(5a + 3b)(a - 2b)$
41. $(4s + 5t)(3s - t)$ **43.** $m^4n(3m + 2n)(2m + n)$
45. $-1(x + 7)(x - 3)$ **47.** $-1(3x + 4)(x - 1)$
49. $-1(a + 2b)(2a + b)$ **51.** $5 \cdot 7$ **52.** $(-5)(-7)$
53. The product of $3x - 4$ and $2x - 1$ is $6x^2 - 11x + 4$.
54. The product of $4 - 3x$ and $1 - 2x$ is $6x^2 - 11x + 4$.
55. The factors in Exercise 53 are the opposites of the factors in
Exercise 54.   **56.** $(3 - 7t)(5 - 2t)$

Section 6.5 (page 433)
1. 1; 4; 9; 16; 25; 36; 49; 64; 81; 100; 121; 144; 169; 196; 225;
256; 289; 324; 361; 400   **3.** 2   **5.** $(y + 5)(y - 5)$

7. $\left(p + \dfrac{1}{3}\right)\left(p - \dfrac{1}{3}\right)$ **9.** prime   **11.** $(3r + 2)(3r - 2)$

13. $\left(6m + \dfrac{4}{5}\right)\left(6m - \dfrac{4}{5}\right)$ **15.** $4(3x + 2)(3x - 2)$

17. $(14p + 15)(14p - 15)$ **19.** $(4r + 5a)(4r - 5a)$
21. prime   **23.** $(p^2 + 7)(p^2 - 7)$ **25.** $(x^2 + 1)(x + 1)(x - 1)$
27. $(p^2 + 16)(p + 4)(p - 4)$ **29.** The teacher was justified,
because it was not factored *completely*; $x^2 - 9$ can be factored as
$(x + 3)(x - 3)$. The complete factored form is
$(x^2 + 9)(x + 3)(x - 3)$.   **31.** No, it is not a perfect square since
the middle term would have to be $30y$.   **33.** $(w + 1)^2$

35. $(x - 4)^2$ **37.** $\left(t + \dfrac{1}{2}\right)^2$ **39.** $(x - .5)^2$

41. $2(x + 6)^2$ **43.** $(4x - 5)^2$ **45.** $(7x - 2y)^2$
47. $(8x + 3y)^2$ **49.** $2h(5h - 2y)^2$ **51.** $(2x + 3)(5x - 2)$
52. $5x - 2$ **53.** Yes. We saw in Exercise 51 that
$(2x + 3)(5x - 2) = 10x^2 + 11x - 6.$ **54.** The quotient is
$x^2 + x + 1$, so $x^3 - 1 = (x - 1)(x^2 + x + 1)$.

Summary Exercises on Factoring (page 435)

1. $8m^3(4m^6 + 2m^2 + 3)$ **2.** $2(m + 3)(m - 8)$
3. $7k(2k + 5)(k - 2)$ **4.** prime **5.** $(6z + 1)(z + 5)$
6. $(m + n)(m - 4n)$ **7.** $(7z + 4y)(7z - 4y)$
8. $10nr(10nr + 3r^2 - 5n)$ **9.** $4x(4x + 5)$
10. $(4 + m)(5 + 3n)$ **11.** $(5y - 6z)(2y + z)$
12. $(y^2 + 9)(y + 3)(y - 3)$ **13.** $(m - 3)(m + 5)$
14. $(2y + 1)(3y - 4)$ **15.** $8z(4z - 1)(z + 2)$
16. $5y(3y + 1)$ **17.** $(z - 6)^2$ **18.** $(3m + 8)(3m - 8)$
19. $(y - 6k)(y + 2k)$ **20.** $(4z - 1)^2$ **21.** $6(y - 2)(y + 1)$
22. $\left(x + \dfrac{1}{4}\right)^2$ **23.** $(p - 6)(p - 11)$ **24.** $(a + 8)(a + 9)$
25. prime **26.** $3(6m - 1)^2$ **27.** $(z + 2a)(z - 5a)$
28. $(2a + 1)(a^2 - 7)$ **29.** $(2k - 3)^2$ **30.** $(a - 7b)(a + 4b)$
31. $(4r + 3m)^2$ **32.** $(3k - 2)(k + 2)$ **33.** prime
34. $(a^2 + 25)(a + 5)(a - 5)$ **35.** $4(2k - 3)^2$
36. $(4k + 1)(2k - 3)$ **37.** $6y^4(3y + 4)(2y - 5)$
38. $5z(z - 2)(z - 7)$ **39.** $(8p - 1)(p + 3)$
40. $(4k - 3h)(2k + h)$ **41.** $6(3m + 2z)(3m - 2z)$
42. $(2k - 5z)^2$ **43.** $2(3a - 1)(a + 2)$
44. $(3h - 2g)(5h + 7g)$ **45.** $(m + 9)(m - 9)$
46. $(5z - 6)(2z + 1)$ **47.** $5m^2(5m - 13n)(5m - 3n)$
48. $(3y - 1)(3y + 5)$ **49.** $(m - 2)^2$ **50.** prime
51. $9p^8(3p + 7)(p - 4)$ **52.** $5(2m - 3)(m + 4)$
53. $(2 - q)(2 - 3p)$ **54.** $\left(k + \dfrac{8}{11}\right)\left(k - \dfrac{8}{11}\right)$
55. $4(4p + 5m)(4p - 5m)$ **56.** $(m + 4)(m^2 - 6)$
57. $(10a + 9y)(10a - 9y)$ **58.** $(8a - b)(a + 3b)$
59. $(a + 4)^2$ **60.** $(2y + 5)(2y - 5)$

Section 6.6 (page 443)

1. $-5, 2$ **3.** $3, \dfrac{7}{2}$ **5.** $-\dfrac{5}{6}, 0$ **7.** $0, \dfrac{4}{3}$ **9.** $-\dfrac{1}{2}, \dfrac{1}{6}$ **11.** $-.8, 2$
13. 9 **15.** Set each *variable* factor equal to 0, to get $2x = 0$ or
$3x - 4 = 0$. The solutions are 0 and $\dfrac{4}{3}$. **17.** $-2, -1$ **19.** $1, 2$
21. $-8, 3$ **23.** $-1, 3$ **25.** $-2, -1$ **27.** -4 **29.** $-2, \dfrac{1}{3}$
31. $-\dfrac{4}{3}, \dfrac{1}{2}$ **33.** $-\dfrac{2}{3}$ **35.** $-3, 3$ **37.** $-\dfrac{7}{4}, \dfrac{7}{4}$ **39.** $-11, 11$
41. $0, 7$ **43.** $0, \dfrac{1}{2}$ **45.** $2, 5$ **47.** $-4, \dfrac{1}{2}$ **49.** $-12, \dfrac{11}{2}$
51. $-2, 0, 2$ **53.** $-\dfrac{7}{3}, 0, \dfrac{7}{3}$ **55.** $-\dfrac{5}{2}, \dfrac{1}{3}, 5$ **57.** $-\dfrac{7}{2}, -3, 1$
59. (a) $64; 144; 4; 6$ **(b)** No time has elapsed, so the object
hasn't fallen (been released) yet. **(c)** Time cannot be negative.

Section 6.7 (page 451)

1. Read; variable; equation; Solve; answer; Check; original
3. *Step 3:* $45 = (2x + 1)(x + 1)$; *Step 4:* $x = 4$ or $x = -\dfrac{11}{2}$;
Step 5: base: 9 units; height: 5 units; *Step 6:* $9 \cdot 5 = 45$
5. *Step 3:* $80 = (x + 8)(x - 8)$; *Step 4:* $x = 12$ or $x = -12$;
Step 5: length: 20 units; width: 4 units; *Step 6:* $20 \cdot 4 = 80$
7. length: 7 in.; width: 4 in. **9.** length: 13 in.; width: 10 in.
11. height: 13 in.; width: 10 in. **13.** mirror: 7 ft; painting: 9 ft
15. $20, 21$ **17.** $-3, -2$ or $4, 5$ **19.** $-3, -1$ or $7, 9$
21. $-2, 0, 2$ or $6, 8, 10$ **23.** 12 cm **25.** 12 mi **27.** 8 ft

29. (a) 1 sec **(b)** $\dfrac{1}{2}$ sec and $1\dfrac{1}{2}$ sec **(c)** 3 sec **(d)** The
negative solution, -1, does not make sense since t represents time,
which cannot be negative. **31. (a)** 42.6 million; The result using
the model is a little less than 44 million, the actual number for
1996. **(b)** 12 **(c)** 142.2 million; The result is a little more than
140 million, the actual number for 2002. **(d)** 215.4 million
32. 107.4 billion dollars; 40% **33.** 1997: 148.5 billion dollars;
1999: 230.1 billion dollars; 2000: 270.9 billion dollars. **34.** The
answers using the linear equation are not at all close to the actual
data. **35.** 1997: 111.2 billion dollars; 1999: 266.4 billion dollars;
2000: 399.5 billion dollars **36.** The answers in Exercise 35 are
fairly close to the actual data. The quadratic equation models
the data better.
37. $(0, 97.5), (1, 104.3), (2, 104.7), (3, 164.3), (4, 271.3), (5, 378.7)$
38. no

U.S. TRADE DEFICIT

39. 776.7 billion dollars **40. (a)** The actual deficit is quite a bit
less than the prediction. **(b)** No, data for later years might not follow the same pattern.

Chapter 6 Review Exercises (page 461)

1. $7(t + 2)$ **2.** $30z(2z^2 + 1)$ **3.** $35x^2(x + 2)$
4. $50m^2n^2(2n - mn^2 + 3)$ **5.** $(x - 4)(2y + 3)$
6. $(2y + 3)(3y + 2x)$ **7.** $(x + 3)(x + 2)$ **8.** $(y - 5)(y - 8)$
9. $(q + 9)(q - 3)$ **10.** $(r - 8)(r + 7)$
11. $(r + 8s)(r - 12s)$ **12.** $(p + 12q)(p - 10q)$
13. $8p(p + 2)(p - 5)$ **14.** $3x^2(x + 2)(x + 8)$
15. $(m + 3n)(m - 6n)$ **16.** $(y - 3z)(y - 5z)$
17. $p^5(p - 2q)(p + q)$ **18.** $3r^3(r + 3s)(r - 5s)$ **19.** prime
20. $3(x^2 + 2x + 2)$ **21.** r and $6r, 2r$ and $3r$ **22.** Factor out z.
23. $(2k - 1)(k - 2)$ **24.** $(3r - 1)(r + 4)$
25. $(3r + 2)(2r - 3)$ **26.** $(5z + 1)(2z - 1)$ **27.** prime
28. $4x^3(3x - 1)(2x - 1)$ **29.** $-3(x + 2)(2x - 5)$
30. $rs(5r + 6s)(2r + s)$ **31.** B **32.** D **33.** $(n + 8)(n - 8)$
34. $(5b + 11)(5b - 11)$ **35.** $(7y + 5w)(7y - 5w)$
36. $36(2p + q)(2p - q)$ **37.** prime **38.** $\left(x + \dfrac{7}{10}\right)\left(x - \dfrac{7}{10}\right)$
39. $(z + 5)^2$ **40.** $(r - 6)^2$ **41.** $(3t - 7)^2$ **42.** $(4m + 5n)^2$
43. $6x(3x - 2)^2$ **44.** $\left(x + \dfrac{1}{3}\right)^2$ **45.** $-\dfrac{3}{4}, 1$ **46.** $-7, -3, 4$
47. $0, \dfrac{5}{2}$ **48.** $-3, -1$ **49.** $1, 4$ **50.** $3, 5$ **51.** $-\dfrac{4}{3}, 5$
52. $-\dfrac{8}{9}, \dfrac{8}{9}$ **53.** $0, 8$ **54.** $-1, 6$ **55.** 7 **56.** 6
57. $-\dfrac{2}{5}, -2, -1$ **58.** $-3, 3$ **59.** length: 10 ft; width: 4 ft
60. 5 ft **61.** length: 6 m; width: 2 m

62. length: 6 m; height: 5 m **63.** 6, 7 or $-5, -4$ **64.** 26 mi
65. 112 ft **66.** 192 ft **67.** 256 ft **68.** after 8 sec
69. (a) \$771.9 million; the answer using the model is a little high.
(b) \$1727.6 million **(c)** No, the prediction seems low. If eBay revenues were \$1516.7 million through three quarters, they were approximately \$500 million per quarter, which would lead to annual revenue in 2003 of about \$2000 million. **70.** D
71. The factor $2x + 8$ has a common factor of 2. The complete factored form is $2(x + 4)(3x - 4)$. **72.** $(z - x)(z - 10x)$
73. $(3k + 5)(k + 2)$ **74.** $(3m + 4p)(5m - 4)$
75. $(y^2 + 25)(y + 5)(y - 5)$ **76.** $3m(2m + 3)(m - 5)$
77. $8abc(3b^2c - 7ac^2 + 9ab)$ **78.** prime
79. $6xyz(2xz^2 + 2y - 5x^2yz^3)$ **80.** $2a^3(a + 2)(a - 6)$
81. $(2r + 3q)(6r - 5q)$ **82.** $(10a + 3)(10a - 3)$
83. $(7t + 4)^2$ **84.** 0, 7 **85.** $-5, 2$ **86.** $-\dfrac{2}{5}$
87. 15 m, 36 m, 39 m **88.** length: 6 m; width: 4 m
89. $-5, -4, -3$ or 5, 6, 7 **90. (a)** 256 ft **(b)** 1024 ft
91. width: 10 m; length: 17 m **92.** 6 m
93. (a) 481 thousand vehicles **(b)** The estimate may be unreliable because the conditions that prevailed in the years 1998–2001 may have changed, causing either a greater increase or a greater decrease in the numbers of alternative-fueled vehicles.

Chapter 6 Test (page 467)
1. D **2.** $6x(2x - 5)$ **3.** $m^2n(2mn + 3m - 5n)$
4. $(2x + y)(a - b)$ **5.** $(x - 7)(x - 2)$ **6.** $(2x + 3)(x - 1)$
7. $(3x + 1)(2x - 7)$ **8.** $3(x + 1)(x - 5)$
9. $(5z - 1)(2z - 3)$ **10.** prime **11.** prime
12. $(y + 7)(y - 7)$ **13.** $(3y + 8)(3y - 8)$ **14.** $(x + 8)^2$
15. $(2x - 7y)^2$ **16.** $-2(x + 1)^2$ **17.** $3t^2(2t + 9)(t - 4)$
18. prime **19.** $4t(t + 4)^2$ **20.** $(x^2 + 9)(x + 3)(x - 3)$
21. $(p + 3)(p + 3) = p^2 + 6p + 9 \neq p^2 + 9$ **22.** $-3, 9$
23. $\dfrac{1}{2}, 6$ **24.** $-\dfrac{2}{5}, \dfrac{2}{5}$ **25.** 10 **26.** 0, 3 **27.** 6 ft by 9 ft
28. $-2, -1$ **29.** 17 ft **30.** 243

Cumulative Review Exercises: Chapters R–6 (page 469)
1. 0 **2.** .05 **3.** 6 **4.** $P = \dfrac{A}{1 + rt}$ **5.** 345; 210; 38%; 15%
6. gold: 12; silver: 16; bronze: 7 **7.** \$34,875 **8.** 110° and 70°
9. (a) negative; positive **(b)** negative; negative

10. $\left(-\dfrac{1}{4}, 0\right)$, $(0, 3)$ **11.** 12 **12.**

13. (a) 97; A slope of 97 means that the number of radio stations increased by about 97 stations per year. **(b)** (2000, 10,375)
14. $(-1, 2)$ **15.** no solution **16.** 4 **17.** $\dfrac{16}{9}$ **18.** 1 **19.** 256
20. $\dfrac{1}{p^2}$ **21.** $\dfrac{1}{m^6}$ **22.** $-4k^2 - 4k + 8$ **23.** $45x^2 + 3x - 18$
24. $9p^2 + 12p + 4$ **25.** $4x^3 + 6x^2 - 3x + 10$
26. $(2a - 1)(a + 4)$ **27.** $(2m + 3)(5m + 2)$
28. $(4t + 3v)(2t + v)$ **29.** $(2p - 3)^2$ **30.** $(5r + 9t)(5r - 9t)$
31. $2pq(3p + 1)(p + 1)$ **32.** $-\dfrac{2}{3}, \dfrac{1}{2}$ **33.** 0, 8
34. 5 m, 12 m, 13 m

CHAPTER 7 RATIONAL EXPRESSIONS AND APPLICATIONS

Section 7.1 (page 479)
1. (a) $3; -5$ **(b)** $q; -1$ **3.** A rational expression is a quotient of polynomials, such as $\dfrac{x + 3}{x^2 - 4}$. **5.** 0 **7.** $\dfrac{5}{3}$ **9.** $-3, 2$
11. never undefined **13. (a)** 1 **(b)** $\dfrac{17}{12}$ **15. (a)** 0 **(b)** $-\dfrac{10}{3}$
17. (a) $\dfrac{9}{5}$ **(b)** undefined **19. (a)** $\dfrac{2}{7}$ **(b)** $\dfrac{13}{3}$ **21.** No, not if the number is 0. Division by 0 is undefined. **23.** $3r^2$ **25.** $\dfrac{2}{5}$
27. $\dfrac{x - 1}{x + 1}$ **29.** $\dfrac{7}{5}$ **31.** $m - n$ **33.** $\dfrac{3(2m + 1)}{4}$ **35.** $\dfrac{3m}{5}$
37. $\dfrac{3r - 2s}{3}$ **39.** $\dfrac{x + 1}{x - 1}$ **41.** $\dfrac{z - 3}{z + 5}$ **43.** -1 **45.** $-(m + 1)$
47. -1

Answers may vary in Exercises 49–53.
49. $\dfrac{-(x + 4)}{x - 3}, \dfrac{-x - 4}{x - 3}, \dfrac{x + 4}{-(x - 3)}, \dfrac{x + 4}{-x + 3}$
51. $\dfrac{-(2x - 3)}{x + 3}, \dfrac{-2x + 3}{x + 3}, \dfrac{2x - 3}{-(x + 3)}, \dfrac{2x - 3}{-x - 3}$
53. $-\dfrac{3x - 1}{5x - 6}, \dfrac{-(3x - 1)}{5x - 6}, -\dfrac{-3x + 1}{-5x + 6}, \dfrac{3x - 1}{-5x + 6}$
55. $x^2 + 3$

Section 7.2 (page 487)
1. (a) B **(b)** D **(c)** C **(d)** A **3.** $\dfrac{4m}{3}$ **5.** $\dfrac{40y^2}{3}$ **7.** $\dfrac{2}{c + d}$
9. $\dfrac{16q}{3p^3}$ **11.** $\dfrac{7}{r^2 + rp}$ **13.** $\dfrac{z^2 - 9}{z^2 + 7z + 12}$ **15.** 5 **17.** $-\dfrac{3}{2t^4}$
19. $\dfrac{1}{4}$ **21.** To multiply two rational expressions, multiply the numerators and multiply the denominators. Write the answer in lowest terms. **23.** $\dfrac{10}{9}$ **25.** $-\dfrac{3}{4}$ **27.** -1 **29.** $\dfrac{-9(m - 2)}{m + 4}$
31. $\dfrac{p + 4}{p + 2}$ **33.** $\dfrac{(k - 1)^2}{(k + 1)(2k - 1)}$ **35.** $\dfrac{4k - 1}{3k - 2}$ **37.** $\dfrac{m + 4p}{m + p}$
39. $\dfrac{10}{x + 10}$ **41.** Division requires multiplying by the reciprocal of the second rational expression. In the reciprocal, $x + 7$ is in the denominator, so $x \neq -7$.

Section 7.3 (page 493)
1. C **3.** C **5.** 30 **7.** x^7 **9.** $72q$ **11.** $84r^5$ **13.** $2^3 \cdot 3 \cdot 5$
15. The least common denominator is their product.
17. $28m^2(3m - 5)$ **19.** $30(b - 2)$ **21.** $c - d$ or $d - c$
23. $k(k + 5)(k - 2)$ **25.** $(p + 3)(p + 5)(p - 6)$ **27.** $\dfrac{20}{55}$
29. $\dfrac{-45}{9k}$ **31.** $\dfrac{26y^2}{80y^3}$ **33.** $\dfrac{35t^2r^3}{42r^4}$ **35.** $\dfrac{20}{8(m + 3)}$ **37.** $\dfrac{8t}{12 - 6t}$
39. $\dfrac{14(z - 2)}{z(z - 3)(z - 2)}$ **41.** $\dfrac{2(b - 1)(b + 2)}{b^3 + 3b^2 + 2b}$

Section 7.4 (page 501)
1. E **3.** C **5.** B **7.** G **9.** $\dfrac{11}{m}$ **11.** b **13.** x **15.** $y - 6$
17. To add or subtract rational expressions with the same denominator, combine the numerators and keep the same

Index